IRELAND SINCE 1939

Henry Patterson

OXFORD
UNIVERSITY PRESS

OXFORD
UNIVERSITY PRESS

Great Clarendon Street, Oxford OX2 6DP

Oxford University Press is a department of the University of Oxford.
It furthers the University's objective of excellence in research, scholarship,
and education by publishing worldwide in

Oxford New York

Auckland Bangkok Buenos Aires Cape Town Chennai
Dar es Salaam Delhi Hong Kong Istanbul Karachi Kolkata
Kuala Lumpur Madrid Melbourne Mexico City Mumbai Nairobi
São Paulo Shanghai Singapore Taipei Tokyo Toronto

with an associated company in Berlin

Oxford is a registered trade mark of Oxford University Press
in the UK and in certain other countries

Published in the United States
by Oxford University Press Inc., New York

British Library Cataloguing in Publication Data

Data available

Library of Congress Cataloging in Publication Data

Data available

ISBN 0–19–289313–0

1 3 5 7 9 10 8 6 4 2

Typeset in Minion
by RefineCatch Limited, Bungay, Suffolk
Printed in Great Britain by
T.J. International Ltd, Padstow, Cornwall

For Ann Browne 1949–2000

ACKNOWLEDGEMENTS

This book could not have been written without the support, intellectual and otherwise, provided by fellow researchers, colleagues and friends. The project itself was suggested by my friend Paul Bew who has continued to be a major source of ideas and stimulation, as has my colleague Arthur Aughey. Particular parts of the text have benefited from the work and helpful suggestions of Rogelio Alonso, George Boyce, Paul Dixon, David Fitzpatrick, Tom Garvin, Paddy Gillan, Gordon Gillespie, Arthur Green, Graham Gudgin, Ellen Hazelkorn, Greta Jones, Dennis Kennedy, Steven King, Martin Knox, Anthony McIntyre, Deirdre McMahon, Peter Mair, Patrick Maume, and Paul Teague. The University of Ulster has been generous in its provision of study leave and support for visits to archives. I am grateful for the assistance of the staff in the Public Record Office of Northern Ireland, the Public Record Office at Kew, the National Archives, Dublin, the Library at the University of Ulster, Jordanstown, the Linenhall Library, Belfast, the National Library and the House of Orange, and to the Party Officers of the Ulster Unionist Council for granting me access to the UUC papers in the PRONI. Linda Moore was a major source of support throughout. The book is dedicated to Ann Browne who died in 2000 and who embodied the best anti-sectarian impulses of Northern Ireland's '1968' generation. She recognised very early that the language of civil and human rights could easily be captured for more traditional agendas.

CONTENTS

LIST OF MAPS

1. Modern Ireland: Towns, Counties, and Provinces

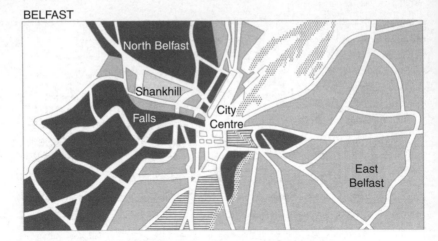

BELFAST

North Belfast

Shankhill

Falls

City Centre

East Belfast

PREDOMINANTLY CATHOLIC

PREDOMINANTLY PROTESTANT

MIXED AREAS

COMMERCIAL/ INDUSTRIAL AREAS

RIVER

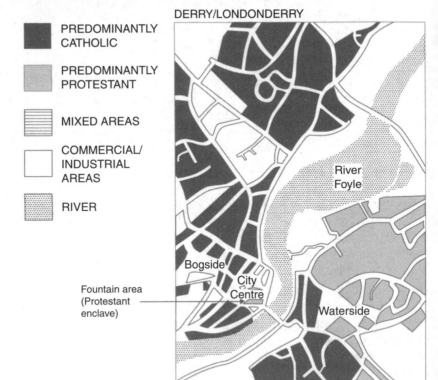

DERRY/LONDONDERRY

River Foyle

Bogside

City Centre

Fountain area (Protestant enclave)

Waterside

2. Maps of Belfast and Derry

1

The Legacy of Partition

The Dynamics of Unionist Rule

Two decades after the end of one world war and as another loomed, the two states that had emerged out of the conflicts between Irish nationalism and the British state and between nationalism and Ulster Unionism appeared even more deeply antagonistic to each other than at the time of their formation. The Ulster Unionist Party had come quickly to embrace the devolved institutions of government created by the Government of Ireland Act (1920). These institutions had been established not in response to a movement for self-government in the north of Ireland but rather as a part of the British government's attempt at a general settlement of the Irish question. The provisions in the Act for a separate parliament and administration in Northern Ireland had been accepted reluctantly by Unionists whose struggle against Irish nationalism was motivated by a desire to maintain the status quo of British governance from Westminster, not by any positive vision of regional self-government. However, even before the Northern Ireland parliament had shifted from temporary accommodation in a Presbyterian theological college to the overblown grandeur of a new building with a classical-Greek-style façade in the Stormont estate in East Belfast in 1932,[1] the attractions of devolution for the Unionist Party had become compelling.

In part, the change in attitude was a product of their experience during the negotiation of the Anglo-Irish Treaty (1921). The Treaty, which provided for a twenty-six county state with the status of a dominion within the British Empire, split Sinn Féin, the revolutionary nationalist movement that had led the political and military campaign against British rule in the War of Independence (1919–21). Lloyd George had for a time attempted to persuade the Unionists to accept Irish unity in order to ensure that what was perceived to be the less anglophobic section of Sinn Féin would triumph over the more militant section of the nationalist movement.[2] Fears of 'betrayal' by British politicians increased the attractiveness of an institutional buffer between Belfast and London. A related but distinct concern was to be as untrammelled as possible in dealing with what was perceived to be a hostile Catholic minority.

Although the Government of Ireland Act asserted, in section 75, the ultimate sovereignty of the Westminster parliament, which also retained all the crucial fiscal powers, it extended to the devolved parliament 'power to make laws for the peace, order and good government'. Law and order issues would be at the centre of the Unionist government's concerns from the inception of the state for reasons that stemmed from the nature of Unionism as an organized movement and also from the specific conditions in which the new state was created.

From the emergence of the Home Rule threat in the 1880s Ulster Unionists had reserved the right to resist rule from Dublin, seen as both economically and socially regressive and hostile to their Protestant and British identities, by force if necessary. The formation of the Ulster Volunteer Force (UVF) in 1913 as part of the Ulster Unionist Council's strategy of opposition to the Liberal government's Home Rule Bill was the most substantial manifestation of Unionism's conviction that pro-posals that would alter radically their citizenship of the United Kingdom dissolved normal conditions of loyalty to the constitution.[3] The UVF's drilling and subsequent importation of arms had the unintended consequence of assisting radical nationalists in their challenge to the still-dominant constitutionalist tradition of John Redmond and the Irish Parliamentary Party. Although Redmond had maintained control of the nationalist paramilitary formation, the Irish Volunteers, which had been formed in response to the creation of the UVF, his support for the British war effort led to a radical nationalist scission, which was to provide the nucleus for the armed insurrection in Dublin at Easter, 1916. The insurrection and the subsequent execution of its leaders did much to strengthen the forces making for the militarization of Irish politics, which, by the time the Government of Ireland Act was passed, had produced in Sinn Féin and the IRA much more implacable opponents for Unionists.

The post-Rising upsurge of revolutionary nationalism had powerful reverberations for the Catholic and nationalist minority in the new state in the North. They had opposed partition as much and perhaps more because it would put them under a Protestant regime as for its violation of the unity of the 'historic Irish nation'. Catholics comprised a third of the population of the new state, although with a majority in two of the six counties—Tyrone and Fermanagh—and in the second city, London-derry. Their political affiliations were divided between the Nationalist

Party led by Joe Devlin, a Belfast politician who had been one of Redmond's chief lieutenants before 1914, and Sinn Féin, the party that had displaced it in the rest of Ireland in the 1918 Westminster election. The survival of Redmondism in Northern Ireland reflected the distinctive history of the region's Catholics, which has been well described by Enda Staunton: 'The hemmed in situation of northern Catholics, the weakness of their middle class and the consequently disproportionate clerical influence left them strongly insulated from trends in the rest of Ireland.'[4] From the inception of the state an important basis for the strength of constitutional nationalism lay in the fear amongst a sizeable sector of Catholics that Sinn Féin's political militancy and the IRA's activities would contribute to sectarian violence from which the Catholic community, particularly in Belfast, would be the main losers.

In 1918 Sinn Féin had not asked for a mandate for the use of force against British rule, but its clear identification with the 1916 insurrection allowed its military wing, the IRA, to initiate its armed struggle in 1919 with a substantial degree of popular acquiescence, if not active support. However, in Ulster the IRA's armed campaign, based on the simplistic assumption that the only substantial obstacle to Irish self-determination was British rule, ignited a sectarian conflagration, which, beginning with the mass expulsion of Catholics from the shipyards and engineering plants in Belfast in July 1920, would over the next two years result in 453 deaths, 7,500 expulsions from workplaces, and 5,000 evictions from homes.[5] The majority of victims were Catholics.

The shipyard expulsions and much of the subsequent Protestant violence was the work of unofficial vigilante groups and armed gangs. However, the decision of the fledgling government to control and discipline Protestant reaction to the IRA through the integration of unofficial 'vigilance' groups and the recently reconstituted UVF into a Special Constabulary would colour Catholic attitudes to the security apparatus of the state for decades to come. Although Unionist leaders would at times accept that there was no necessary connection between being a Catholic and being 'disloyal', and hence there was provision for the state's police force, the Royal Ulster Constabulary, to have a Catholic complement of one-third, the three-tier Special Constabulary was from formation to dissolution an almost totally Protestant force. At its high point of mobilization against the IRA in 1922–3, its three sections had a total of 14,200 Specials mobilized while the RUC was only 1,200 strong.[6] But even when any substantial IRA threat had disappeared in the later 1920s the part-time 'B Specials' had a membership of 12,000. This dwarfed the RUC, which when it reached its full complement had 3,000 members.[7]

The 1922 Constabulary Act provided for a third of the RUC to be Catholic, recruited directly from the former members of the Royal Irish Constabulary, and this led to almost a third of the force's NCO/junior-officer level being Catholic. However, Catholic representation at rank-and-file level was considerably less at 13.7 per cent. Overall, the Catholic share of the police would stagnate in the inter-war period and begin to decline from the 1950s when the RIC generation began to retire.[8] This, in part, reflected the partisan flavour given to the state's security apparatus by the Specials and the sanctioning by the government of a request by some members of the RUC to be allowed to form an Orange lodge.

The populist and sectarian dimensions of the new regime must be related to the violent and threatening conditions of its early years. A British government official sent to Belfast in 1922 described the dominant Unionist mentality:

The Protestant community of the North feels that it is an outpost of civilisation set precariously on the frontiers of Bolshevism. It believes that the British government has betrayed it and at best that its cause is misunderstood in England.[9]

Sir James Craig, the Ulster Unionist Prime Minister, had met Michael Collins, the IRA leader and head of the new provisional government in Dublin in January 1922, in an attempt to establish a *modus vivendi* between the two states. The first Craig/Collins pact exchanged Collins' calling off of a southern economic boycott of Belfast for Craig's commitment to have expelled Catholic workers reinstated in the shipyards. However, Collins continued to support Catholic school teachers and nationalist-controlled local authorities who refused to recognize the new state. He also secretly approved a series of IRA raids across the border into Fermanagh and Tyrone, which led to the kidnapping of forty-two prominent loyalists who were to be used as bargaining counters to secure the release of IRA prisoners. IRA killings of B Specials and violent loyalist reprisals in Belfast, including a bomb attack that killed six children, were part of a deteriorating situation in the North, which in March claimed the lives of thirty-five Catholics and eighteen Protestants.[10]

In a desperate effort to stop this downward spiral of violence, the two leaders met at the end of March and agreed a second and more far-reaching pact. At its core was a proposal that in Belfast police patrols in religiously mixed areas would be composed of equal numbers of Protestants and Catholics and that all Specials not needed for this force should be stood down. There was also provision for an Advisory Committee of Catholics to assist in the recruitment of their co-religionists for the Specials. The British government was to provide £500,000 for relief works to employ expelled workers. Here there was the outline of a non-sectarian Northern Ireland as far as security and employment policy was concerned. It was in line with a declaration by Craig in February 1921 that 'The rights of the minority must be sacred to the majority . . . it will only be by broad views, tolerant ideas and real desire for liberty of conscience that we here can make an ideal of the parliament and executive.'[11] As Professor Joe Lee has pointed out, Craig 'could at times show physical and even moral courage well above the ordinary'.[12] He had chosen the liberal Unionist, Lord Londonderry, as his first Minister of Education and the Londonderry Education Act of 1923 had attempted to provide for a secular, integrated system of primary education. Although it failed, largely because of the united and bitter opposition of Catholic and Protestant churches, it had reflected a genuine desire on the Prime Minister's part for reconciliation of the two religious traditions.

The non-fulfilment of both Craig/Collins pacts and Craig's failure to deliver on his early non-sectarian rhetoric were largely a product of two factors. One was the regime's fear of divisions in the Protestant community and a resultant propensity to indulge grass-roots loyalism. As the British official sent to investigate nationalist allegations of police involvement in murderous reprisals for IRA attacks noted, 'Ministers are too close to their community and cannot treat their ministries as from a distance.' The other factor was reflected in his conclusion that the basic reason for the collapse of the second pact was the failure of the IRA to abide by clause 6, which provided for a cessation of armed activity in the North.[13] Instead the IRA had killed one Unionist MP, burnt the houses of others, and the Irish army had added its contribution by an 'invasion' of Fermanagh in May 1922.

The period of state formation established a negative and long-lasting dialectic between the sectarian and populist aspects of the northern regime and an aggressive and threatening approach from Dublin, both of which undermined conciliatory tendencies within northern nationalism. Key Ulster Catholic leaders, particularly in Belfast, had initially favoured some form of recognition of Craig's regime but support for such a strategy was weakened by IRA attacks and unofficial Protestant reprisals. The tone of nationalist politics was increasingly set by the more militant and rejectionist voices from the border areas where Catholics were in a majority. The result was disastrous for the Catholic community. They did not contest the gerrymandering of the local government election boundaries by the electoral commission set up in 1922 under the control of the Minister of Home Affairs' nominee, Sir John Leech. The 1924 election revealed the vital importance of the commission's work. As Michael Farrell notes, 'Some of the results were bizarre. In the Omagh Rural Council area with a 61.5 per cent Catholic majority, the nationalists had won the council in 1920 with 26 seats to 13. After Leech's endeavours the Unionists held it with 21 seats to 18.'[14] The nationalist boycott of the Leech commission gave the Unionists a ready-made excuse. Thus when the British Council of Jews asked the British Home Secretary how it was that 59,000 Protestants in Tyrone elected sixteen representatives to the county council while 74,000 Catholics elected only eleven, a senior official in the Ministry of Home Affairs explained:

When electoral areas were being fixed the Nationalists absolutely refused to take any part in the inquiries or to come and state their case and it was completely impossible for the persons who were holding the inquiry to look after their interests in these areas.[15]

The gerrymandering naturally increased opportunities for discrimination in local government employment. As one official admitted, 'There can be little doubt that in those areas where there was a Protestant majority in the councils, in practice posts do not often go to Catholics.'[16] The Unionist leadership was not totally united on this issue. The head of the Northern Ireland Civil Service (NICS), Sir Wilfred Spender, hoped (and claimed that Craig did too) that it would be possible to induce some of the councils to use their powers of co-option to secure a better representation of minorities. He also opposed discrimination against Catholics by local government agencies.[17] Such doubts and reservations within the Unionist leadership were to prove of little significance in the absence of Catholic attempts to exploit them.

While discriminatory practices were most developed in Unionist-controlled local authorities in the west of the province, central government was also affected. Although a number of Catholics were appointed to senior posts in the NICS, there were clear instances of discrimination from the beginning and over sixty appointments were made without normal selection procedures being observed at all. At the Ministry of Home Affairs, the Minister, Robert Dawson Bates, refused to allow Catholic appointments. In 1926 the Minister of Labour and future Prime Minister, John Andrews, found two 'Free Staters' in his ministry when he

returned from holiday and immediately initiated a tightening of regulations to disqualify such candidates. In 1927 the Minister of Agriculture
boasted that there were only four Catholics in his ministry.[18] Spender
and successive Ministers of Finance, perhaps because of their annual
negotiations with the Treasury, were concerned that such excesses could
produce a destabilizing intervention from London. They were also
strongly pre-Keynesian and critical of the regime's propensity to make
'extravagant' public expenditure commitments to solidify communal
solidarity.

But Craig's populist policy of 'distributing bones' to Ulster Unionism's supporters, while it was the despair of the officials at the Ministry
of Finance,[19] reflected the fact that his political life, particularly in his
later and least impressive years, had been dominated by the fear of
Protestant schism. From its inception his government was attacked for
not being sufficiently 'Protestant' and for its failure to shield its working-
class supporters from the depressed economic conditions of the inter-
war years. Divisions along class and intra-sectarian fissures were most
threatening in the heartlands of proletarian Unionism in Belfast.

The city, with a population of 437,000 in 1937[20]—nearly one-third of
the total for the province—had from the beginning of the previous
century suffered periodic outbursts of sectarian violence. While these
were often sparked by political developments in the broader conflict
between Unionism and Irish nationalism, they also reflected competition over employment and housing among Protestant and Catholic
workers. The development from the mid nineteenth century of shipbuilding and engineering industries with a workforce dominated by
skilled Protestant artisans contributed strongly to a less open labour
market than the older linen industry where Catholics had been represented more equally. Together with the city's increasingly unenviable
record for sectarian violence, which acted as a deterrent for Catholic
migrants from the Ulster countryside, Belfast's emergence as a major
centre of heavy industry helped to explain the decline of the Catholic
proportion of Belfast's population from 34 per cent in 1861 to 23 per cent
in 1911.

The history of the shipyards showed much evidence of a strong class
consciousness manifest in industrial militancy but also of the most brutal sectarianism. In 1919 shipyard and engineering workers had brought
the city's economic activity to a halt by a general strike for shorter hours.
But a Unionist Party leadership, aghast at the possibilities of a divided
Protestant community, was soon able to use the intensifying IRA

campaign as an object lesson in the need for communal solidarity. More extreme loyalist voices alleged that the shipyards and engineering plants had suffered a process of 'peaceful penetration' by Sinn Féiners and extreme socialists when 'loyal' workers had been serving king and country.

The Unionist Party's linkage with the Orange Order provided it with ready access to the fears and grievances of working-class Protestants. The Order had been founded in 1795 in county Armagh as a sort of primitive trade union of Protestant weavers concerned to exclude Catholic competitors from the developing linen industry. It had won the patronage of the landlord class who saw it as a major resource against a feared Catholic *jacquerie*. Organized in county and district lodges, its annual parades on 12 July to commemorate the victory of William of Orange at the battle of the Boyne (1690) were seen by its critics as a prime cause of sectarian conflict. Down to the 1880s it had been based on an alliance between the landlords and clergy of the established Church of Ireland and farmers, labourers, and weavers: an institution within which lower-class Protestants could mix with their 'betters' in the defence of the Protestant interest in Ireland and ultimately of the Union itself. Politically it acted as an electoral machine for the Conservatives. The province's Presbyterian, Liberal tradition, strongly represented amongst the bourgeoisie of Belfast and the tenant farmer class, had been cool or hostile to the Order because of its links with the Tories and the Church of Ireland. However, the common threat of Home Rule had led to the fusion of Tories and Liberals and a Presbyterian influx to the Order seen as the best grass-roots defender of the constitutional status quo. When the directing body of Unionism, the Ulster Unionist Council, was set up in 1905, the Orange Order was provided with a substantial representation and its membership expanded rapidly during the mobilization against Home Rule. Its political importance resided not simply in the fact that it had representation as of right in the party at all levels, or that the overwhelming bulk of Unionist MPs and cabinet members were members, but also in its ability to criticize the party and the government if they were seen to deviate from the defence of Protestant interests.

During the mobilizations against Home Rule, liberal Unionists had been careful to emphasize that the Unionist case should be put in secular terms, fearing that too much emphasis on Orange and Protestant themes would undermine support in the rest of the United Kingdom.[21] At the core of the secular Unionist argument had been the economic success of the north-east of Ireland under the Union, symbolized above all by the shipyards, engineering factories, and linen mills of Belfast. After 1921 secular Unionism went into recession as depressed economic conditions challenged the Unionist Party's ability to contain the force of plebeian Protestant discontent within its ranks and this was a major factor in encouraging the stridently anti-Catholic rhetoric which disfigured the speeches of leading Unionist politicians in the 1930s.

The industries that had been at the core of Ulster Unionists' self-confidence before 1914 were to experience major problems in the inter-war period. Although the shipyards had performed creditably in the 1920s given a situation of world-wide overcapacity, the slump in world trade after 1929 hit the two firms hard, with employment in the winter of 1932–3 at only a tenth of its 1929–30 level and an unemployment rate of over 80 per cent. The smaller of the two yards, Workman Clark, closed down in 1935 and although the Harland and Wolff enterprise absorbed some of its plant and labour force and made serious efforts to diversify production, shipbuilding employment at the outbreak of war was 10,000—an improvement on the mere 2,000 at the depth of the depression but just half of the figure for 1929.[22] The engineering sector was given an injection of energy with the establishment of the Short and Harland aircraft factory in 1937, an enterprise which employed over 6,000 by May 1939. But although shipbuilding and engineering had begun to pull out of recession by 1939, the region's largest employer of manufacturing labour, the linen industry, faced the bleaker prospect of changes in fashion and lifestyle that consigned linen to the status of a luxury product. There was a contraction in employment in the industry from 75,000 in 1924 to 57,000 in 1939 and at that time 20 per cent of its workers were unemployed.

Agriculture, which in 1926 employed a third of the male and a quarter of the total labour force, suffered like shipbuilding and linen production from adverse international trends: overcapacity and a sluggish growth in demand. Dominated by small farms (70 per cent were under 30 acres and 86 per cent under 50), its concentration on dairying and livestock, where prices declined less than cereals, was the main reason for a slight improvement in its position in the inter-war period relative to the industry in the rest of the UK. Per capita output, which was 46 per cent of the British level in 1924–5, had reached 53 per cent by 1939. Nevertheless, rural Ulster remained miserably poor. In 1930 Keynes had described the living standards of the region's small farmers as 'almost unbelievable' and the wages of farm labourers in the 1930s were less than the unemployment benefit paid to an unemployed married man.[23] Despite migration to the towns, the level of unemployment in agriculture was over 20 per cent in 1939. The economy as a whole experienced persistently high unemployment rates, with on average 19 per cent of the insured labour force unemployed between 1923 and 1930 and 27 per cent between 1931 and 1939. In 1939 the figure was 23 per cent, compared with 10 per cent in Britain.[24]

The increasingly sectarian tone of the northern state in the 1930s reflected the internal tensions that unemployment and poverty created for a governing party that was committed to the notion of 'parity' in a range of social services with the rest of the UK. As unemployed Protestant and Catholic workers rioted together against Belfast's niggardly system of outdoor relief in 1932, the Unionist élite worried that the capacity of the Orange Order to bind together the classes in the Protestant community was weakening. The Order found its membership in decline as the new state firmly established itself and unemployment sapped the commitment of its working-class members.[25] This thinning of the ranks in the heartland of working-class loyalism was a major concern to the Unionist leadership, although they still looked to the Ulster Unionist Labour Association, created in 1918 to counter socialistic influence on the Protestant working class, to win over the 'cream' of the working class.[26]

The gravity of the economic situation meant that the appeasement of sectarianism was not sufficient to deal with the threat of working-class disaffection. The 'anti-populists' such as Spender and Hugh Pollock, the Minister of Finance, had used the Loans Guarantee Act, by which the government guaranteed loans made to business concerns, as a means of preserving employment in the shipyards. The government also continued to fund public works as a method of relieving unemployment after the Treasury had ceased to do so in the rest of the UK.[27] But despite these economic responses, there was no escaping the sour sectarian edge of Unionist politics in the 1930s.

A weakening of Orange influence was accompanied by the development of the more rabid, and less controllable, form of sectarian demands associated with the Ulster Protestant League (UPL) founded in 1931 to 'keep Ulster Protestant' by ensuring that Protestant employers only took on 'loyalists'. A loose alliance of lower-middle-class evangelicals and the poorest sections of the Protestant working class, it was allowed the use of the Unionist Party headquarters to hold its meeting and was patronized by leading members, most notably the Minister of Agriculture and future Prime Minister, Basil Brooke.[28] The UPL had thrived in the more febrile environment created by the victory of Eamon de Valera and Fianna Fáil in the 1932 elections in the South. De Valera's indulgence in the political theatre of intervention in the Stormont elections in 1933 when he was returned on an abstentionist ticket for South Down (another Fianna Fáiler won West Tyrone) contributed to a Unionist obsession with the supposed threat of a large-scale inflow of 'disloyalists' across the border.

Basil Brooke, in the 1930s the only rising star in the Unionist firmament, identified himself intimately with these concerns. Educated at Winchester and Sandhurst, he was a scion of the 'fighting Brookes', a county Fermanagh landowning family with a record of military service and, since the 1880s, of providing militant leadership against the advances of nationalism. Although his own service in India and the Boer War had confirmed his imperialism, while action during the First World War had led him to consider the possibility of Irish unity as a price for wholehearted Irish support against Germany, his return to the role of local landlord and Unionist and Orange leadership in Fermanagh led to an increasingly parochial and sectarian tone in his politics. The organizational and leadership capacity that he had displayed in the establishment of the Special Constabulary in his area had brought him to Craig's attention and, combined with his relative youth, personal charm, and strong family connections with the English military and landed elite, marked him out in a party whose leadership was ageing and suffering from a severe lack of ability. Entering parliament in 1929, he became Minister of Agriculture in 1933, providing the government with one of its few examples of policy activism and earning the reluctant admiration of Spender as one of the two competent members of the cabinet.

However, Brooke did not allow the regular visits to the cabinet room at Stormont to dilute his public commitment to the more fevered expressions of Unionism in Fermanagh. The county was typical of those parts of Northern Ireland where Protestants were in a minority but still dominated local government through the creative drawing of constituency boundaries. In Fermanagh 25,000 Unionists had seventeen seats on the county council while 35,000 nationalists had only seven. Like other leading figures in border-county Unionism, Brooke was fixated on the twin threats of 'infiltration' from the South and any potential weakening of Protestant unity by those who put economic grievances before communal solidarity. These included Protestant farmers encouraged by speculation that de Valera's government would abolish land annuity payments to demand that Stormont do likewise. Fear of possible independent farmers' candidates splitting the Unionist vote led Brooke to denounce 'semi-Protestants and semi-loyalists'.[29] His subsequent political career would be dogged by the reputation for pugnacious sectarianism he acquired in the 1930s. Speaking to Fermanagh Orangemen in 1933, he urged Protestant employers to employ 'Protestant lads and lassies' and boasted of his own Catholic-free estate. He gave dire warnings of a plot to overturn the Unionist majority in the North through 'infiltration' and 'peaceful penetration' from the South and of Catholics 'getting in everywhere' because of laxity and complacency amongst Protestant employers.[30]

This exclusivist tone was reflected at the centre of provincial government where Sir James Craig declared in a parliamentary debate in 1934 that Northern Ireland was a 'Protestant Parliament and a Protestant State'. Perhaps conscious of giving a potent propaganda weapon to critics of his government, he counter-posed his statement to the increasingly clear alignment of church and state in the South and claimed that he was opposed to the employment of 'disloyalists' but not of Catholics as long as they were loyal to the state. However, the distinction between Catholic and 'disloyalist' was subverted by his own communal definition of the state and by the public pronouncements of senior ministers like J. M. Andrews, Minister of Labour, who assured ultra-Protestants, kept awake at night by the allegation that twenty-eight of the thirty-one porters at Stormont were Catholics, that he had investigated and found there to be only one Catholic, there on a temporary basis.[31]

The increasingly Catholic and nationalist tone of the Free State intensified sectarian animosities in the North. Events like the state-sponsored celebration of the centenary of Catholic Emancipation in 1929, the appointment of a minister at the Vatican in the same year, and the holding of the international Eucharistic Congress in 1932 in Dublin were given heavy coverage in Unionist newspapers and Orange platforms, as was the declaration by the Bishop of Down and Connor, Joseph MacRory, in December 1931 that it was doubtful if the Protestant churches were part of the Church of Christ.[32] There was no shortage of Protestant clerics to respond in kind and 1931 had already seen anti-Catholic riots in Portadown, Armagh, and Lisburn.[33]

The intensifying sectarian tone was accompanied by concern at de Valera's continuing links with those who still insisted they had the right to wage war against the northern state. The IRA's support for Fianna Fáil during the 1932 election, the mass release of IRA prisoners as soon as de Valera took power, the organization's open drilling and recruiting, and the expression of violently anti-partitionist sentiments by some of his senior colleagues[34] all contributed to the perception of the South as having entered into a new and aggressive posture.

But while such factors may help explain the responsiveness of Craig's government to ultra pressures throughout the 1930s, they do little to excuse it. After attacks on pilgrims travelling South to the Eucharistic Congress, Dawson Bates arranged with the Attorney General that the Protestant offenders should be treated leniently.[35] In Belfast, where discontent on issues of unemployment and housing could be exploited by both loyalist and labour critics, the attractions of assuaging such discontent through the patronage of ethnic militancy were obvious, but so were the dangers. The first sectarian killing of a Catholic since the 1920–2 period occurred in Belfast in 1933 and there was sectarian rioting in 1934 and during the celebrations of George V's Silver Jubilee in the spring of 1935, which had led to the imposition of a curfew in May. The clearly febrile atmosphere had produced an unprecedented decision by Dawson Bates to ban all processions in the city but after the threat of open defiance from the Orange Order and the intervention of the Prime Minister, the ban was rescinded in time for the July processions. The parades sparked off the only prolonged and serious outbreak of violence in the city between 1922 and 1969: ten days of riots in which seven Protestants and three Catholics were killed. Apart from the deaths the Catholic community was clearly at the receiving end of the violence, with 430 Catholic families being evicted compared to 64 Protestant families.[36] The result was the sort of press coverage in the Free State and the UK that the few critics of Craig's populism within the regime feared would spur Westminster to investigate the way devolved power was being exercised in the North. When it did in fact produce precisely this result, defenders of the government would turn the focus of discussion southward to ensure that the blemishes of Unionist rule were explained away by the providing of a lurid depiction of developments in the other Irish state.

Conservatism in Power: The Irish Free State 1922–32

The 'Irish Revolution', as a number of scholars have pointed out, was a solely political one. Ireland's chance of a social revolution had been undermined by the land reforms sponsored by the British state, which created an increasingly conservative peasant proprietorship in the four decades before independence. An estimated two-thirds to three-quarters of Irish farmers had become owners of their land by the outbreak of the First World War. A leading member of the pro-Treaty section of Sinn Féin described the dynamics of this conservative revolution: 'Getting rid of foreign control rather than vast social and economic changes was our aim.'[37] The result is summed up by John M. Regan:

The revolutionary and civil wars were fought over constitutional forms and symbols, fundamentally the republic versus the Crown, and ultimately on the source of sovereignty. Though there was undoubtedly a class component to both conflicts it did not come to dominate the issue of national sovereignty.[38]

The fundamental priority that Sinn Féin attached to social consensus, with its conservative implications, goes far to explaining the speed with which a stable society, complete with the structures of a democratic political system, was achieved after a decade of revolution and civil war. The new Irish state was governed, like its northern counterpart, by a bicameral parliament whose procedures were loosely modelled on those of Westminster. The constitution of the Irish Free State, negotiated with Britain after the Treaty in 1922, had created a form of parliamentary democracy. The lower house, named Dáil Eireann in order to maintain continuity with the revolutionary first Dáil composed of the Sinn Féiners victorious in the 1918 general election, was elected by proportional representation. The constitution provided for a system of cabinet government: an executive council bound by collective responsibility and headed by a president.

The constitution was only able to come into effect after the Civil War (1922–3), in which there were between 4,000 and 5,000 deaths (compared with 1,200 in the War of Independence).[39] The pro-Treaty victors had to create a new party from the top down from elements of existing political and politico-military organizations. From its inception Cumann na nGaedhael (from 1933 Fine Gael) defined itself as the party of the Treaty, law and order, and Commonwealth status. Its focus on the defence and consolidation of the state was understandable: the prosecution of the war had cost the state £17 million and material destruction was estimated at about £30 million. Demilitarization was essential both to consolidate the fledgling democracy and to cut the large defence budget. A key decision had already been made during the Civil War: the new police force, the Garda Siochana, was to be unarmed. The decision to create a new army, breaking with ambiguities that had characterized civil–military relations between the Dáil and the IRA during the War of Independence, was a source of considerable resentment amongst sections of the pro-Treaty military, and the rapid demobilization and reduction in the army's size announced in 1923 produced a failed 'Army Mutiny' in 1924.

The government's economic and social philosophy was conservative, reflecting in large part the straitened circumstances of the early years of state building, but also its ties with the Catholic professional and business class and in the countryside with the larger farmers who had a strong vested interest in the maintenance of the existing relationship with the British market. Its dominant personality was not its leader, William T. Cosgrave, but Kevin O'Higgins, the Minister of Home Affairs. Élitist, authoritarian, an enthusiast for the Commonwealth, and an ardent believer in the moral virtues of balanced budgets, O'Higgins did not rouse surprise when one of the early decisions of the government was to cut the old age pension by a shilling a week. He was a strong supporter of the Department of Finance's imposition of best British Treasury practice. The government's hard-nosed image was encapsulated in the icy declaration by the Minister of Industry and Commerce, Patrick McGilligan, in 1924 that 'People may have to die in this country and die of starvation.'[40]

The Treatyites had been excoriated for their acceptance of British insistence that all members of the Dáil had to take an oath of allegiance to the British monarch and the new government was condemned for other manifestations of its 'pro-Imperialist' mentality. These included its use of the upper house, the Seanad, to make overtures to the South's rapidly dwindling Protestant population: Cosgrave had used his powers of nomination to the body to appoint sixteen former Unionists. This, along with the existence of proportional representation, allowed the minority a degree of representation but needs to be set against the radical shrinkage in the Protestant population, which occurred during the national revolution, and the increasingly Catholic ethos of public policy.

The census of 1926 showed that almost a third of Protestants in the twenty-six counties had gone since 1911. The Catholic population of the new state was 2,751,269 while there were just 220,723 non-Catholics.[41] Although the withdrawal of the British garrison after 1921 was in part responsible for the decline, the distinct sectarian edge of the national revolution was another. Thus in Cork, the most violent of all Irish counties involved in the War of Independence, Protestants made up 7 per cent of the population but 36 per cent of the 200 civilians shot by the IRA, and 85 of the 113 houses burned belonged to Protestants. In just one night in April 1922 ten Cork Protestants were killed by the IRA allegedly as 'spies' or 'informers' but in reality as a sectarian reprisal for attacks on Catholics in Belfast. They included businessmen, farmers, a lawyer, a curate, a post-office clerk, and a farm labourer. Hundreds of Protestants went into hiding or fled their homes, abandoning farms and shops. Many did not stop until they arrived in England or Belfast.[42]

Cosgrave's desire to reach out to the minority was commendable but its positive effects were undermined by his and his colleagues' eagerness to reflect Catholic morality in legislation. In 1925 divorce was outlawed, leading W. B. Yeats to warn the government, 'You will create an impassable barrier between South and North.'[43] Protestants, North and South, subsequently saw the creation of the Censorship Board in 1930 as further evidence of the Catholicization of the public sphere in the Free State. This and the state's commitment to the creation of a 'Gaelic Civilization', through making the Irish language compulsory for the Intermediate and Leaving Certificate and for jobs in the civil service, would do little to help the realization of the first objective of its party programme: 'To secure the unity of Ireland and to unify the diverse elements of the Nation in a common bond of citizenship.'[44]

For all its contradictions, the desire of Cosgrave's government to work out a more harmonious relationship with the North was sincere and reflected in its acceptance of the demise of the Boundary Commission in 1925. Under Article 12 of the Treaty the Commission was given the task, if Northern Ireland exercised its right to secede from the Free State, of determining the boundaries between the two states as specified by the ambiguous formula 'in accordance with the wishes of the inhabitants, so far as it may be compatible with economic and geographic conditions'.[45] Held out by Lloyd George as a major tactical inducement to the Sinn Féin negotiators, it had encouraged them to hope for such substantial transfers of territory to the Free State that the North would be made unviable. However, when the Commission was eventually constituted in 1924, Lloyd George had departed the scene and Collins' death removed the Irish leader who would have been most able to press a maximalist position. With Craig firmly ensconced in power, refusing to nominate the North's representative but sure of the sympathy of the British government's substitute (the former editor of liberal Unionist *Northern Whig*), the eventual report, which left the northern state virtually intact and even proposed some minor transfers from the Free State, was unsurprising, although still acutely embarrassing for Cosgrave.

Rather than implement the report, the three governments signed a tripartite boundary agreement on 3 December 1925. It confirmed the existing boundary and released the Free State from the significant financial liabilities it had incurred under the Treaty. Cosgrave's attempt to obtain concessions from Craig in the agreement on the treatment of Catholics in the North failed, although Craig did offer a 'fair deal' for the minority.[46] The Council of Ireland, that provision for North–South co-operation under the Government of Ireland Act, had its powers transferred to the government of Northern Ireland but the agreement did provide for representatives of the two governments to meet to consider matters of mutual concern. The benign possibilities that might have flowed from Dublin's recognition of the northern state were not to be realized. In part this reflected the northern regime's too-easy indulgence of sectarianism. South of the border it was a product of the growing political strength of those who had been defeated in the Civil War.

Fianna Fáil and the Republicanization of the South

There is no doubt that Fianna Fáil has been the dominant political force in modern Ireland. In the fifty-year period (1922–72) following the establishment of the Free State, the party held governmental office for no fewer than thirty-four years. For most of this period the party's success was intimately linked with its enigmatic and machiavellian leader, Eamon de Valera. Born in New York in 1882, his Irish mother had sent him back to Ireland at the age of two when his Spanish father died. Brought up by relatives on a small farm in county Limerick, he was educated by the Christian Brothers and the Holy Ghost Fathers at Blackrock College, which produced many of the new state's religious and political élite. His early formation encouraged some of his key characteristics: industry, asceticism, and self-discipline, accompanied by emotional distance and cold calculation. His rural petty bourgeois background, education, and white-collar position made him typical of that generation of earnest young men and women, the development of whose nationalism was deeply influenced by the movement to revive the Irish language. He joined the Gaelic League in 1908 and the Irish Volunteers in 1913. He was the oldest leader of the 1916 insurrection to survive, his death sentence being commuted because of his American birth.

After the Rising he became the President of the ascendant Sinn Féin party and titular head of the Irish Volunteers, later the Irish Republican Army. He was the main political opponent of the Treaty and after the

Civil War of the anti-Treatyite Sinn Féin, which in the first election to the Dáil after the conflict in 1923 won 27.4 per cent of the vote and forty-four seats to Cumann na nGaedheal's 39 per cent and sixty-three seats.[47] De Valera and his allies in the leadership of the anti-Treatyites were soon convinced that the new dispensation had enough popular legitimacy to make any attempt at its physical overthrow unthinkable and this forced them into a parting of the ways with their more fundamentalist colleagues in Sinn Féin and the IRA, who wanted to maintain the twin policies of abstention from the Dáil and the underground preparation of the IRA for the overthrow of the states North and South.

The Gaelic name meaning 'Warriors of Destiny' and its subtitle 'The Republican Party' demonstrated de Valera's determination to monopolize the legacy of 1916 and the national revolution. The first two aims set out in the party's constitution were the ending of partition and the restoration of the Irish language as the spoken language of the people.[48] The nationalist and Gaelic dimensions of the party's project were crucial in de Valera's determination to bring as many of the anti-Treatyites as possible with the new formation. Although the two aims might have appeared contradictory given northern Protestants' generally disdainful attitude to the Irish language, they were essential in defining Fianna Fáil as more than a mere political party but rather, as de Valera portrayed it, a movement for national redemption.

However, for all this lofty nationalist idealism the leaders of the new party demonstrated a ruthless pragmatism, a sure grasp of the material dimension of party appeal and a Leninist approach to organization and propaganda.The party was still committed not to take its seats in the Dáil until the oath of allegiance was removed. However, the assassination of Kevin O'Higgins, the government's strong man, by IRA dissidents in July 1927 forced de Valera's hand. Emergency legislation enforced the oath as a *sine qua non* of participation in constitutional politics and Fianna Fáil complied, telling their supporters that 'hard-headed common sense is not incompatible with true nationalist idealism.'[49]

Once it began to participate fully in constitutional politics, Fianna Fáil adopted a left-of-centre social and economic programme, attacking the government for its conservatism and not simply its alleged pro-British orientation. In its first electoral contest in June 1927, Fianna Fáil had been attacked by the leader of the Labour Party for allegedly drawing twelve of its fifteen manifesto pledges from earlier Labour programmes.[50] Its electoral success was based on more than stealing

Labour's clothes, for from its inception the party's leadership had poured all their energies into building a formidable political machine. At the core of the party-building process were the numerous old IRA companies that were transformed into local *cumainn* (branches). The famed discipline of the party, together with its lack of serious debate and the authoritarian tinge to internal culture, derived from this militarist component in its formation. Founded in March 1926, by November the party had 460 *cumainn* and by the summer of 1927 it had 1,000.[51] By contrast, Cumann na nGaedheal never grasped the possibilities inherent in mass organization and many of its leaders maintained a patrician contempt for party branches, which were seen as a hindrance to the work of government. This élitist disdain for the demands of a competitive party system combined with the government's reactionary economic and social policies to ease Fianna Fáil's road to power.

Although de Valera would periodically claim that he had been deeply influenced by the ideas of the socialist leader and 1916 martyr James Connolly and the party's progressive image, Fianna Fáil cultivated business support from its earliest days promising a more radical regime of tariff protection and proclaiming its concern to govern in the national interest. It was with the support of those whom the party's national organizer referred to as its two hundred or so 'wealthy friends',[52] together with their rich American friends, that the party was able to launch a daily paper, the *Irish Press*, in 1931.

Although Seán Lemass, architect of the party's electoral hegemony in urban areas, boasted of the 'slightly constitutional' nature of Fianna Fáil, de Valera demonstrated that there were strict limits to his willingness to accommodate those republicans who refused to accept the new constitutional order he set out to create when the party took office for the first time in 1932. Many members of the IRA had deserted the organization to join Fianna Fáil as it emerged as a radical nationalist challenger to what it depicted as the reactionary pro-British policies of Cumann na nGaedheal. The leadership of the IRA had instructed its members to work and vote for the party in the elections of 1932 and 1933, and the first two years of the new government saw a significant increase in IRA militancy and in the bitterness of political and ideological conflicts.

The new government was faced with an economy already suffering from the shock to the country's exports delivered by the Great Depression. The all-important cattle trade was experiencing major problems and these economic concerns were overlain by the widespread fear amongst the larger farmers of de Valera's 'communistic' agrarian policies.

It was from this class that most of the support for the short-lived Blueshirt movement derived: an unstable mixture of civil war animosities, economic self-interest, and fascist sympathies.

Unionist newspapers would make much of the street clashes between Blueshirts and the IRA in the 1932–4 period, depicting the South as in a state of burgeoning chaos. In fact de Valera showed a clear willingness to use repressive measures in the form of military tribunals against what were depicted as opposing sets of extremists. After offering the IRA a number of carrots, from mass releases of prisoners in 1932 to employment in the state's security apparatus, and failing to extinguish its élitist vision of itself as the 'real' government of Ireland, he did not hesitate to outlaw the organization in 1936.

Like Craigavon, de Valera proved much more successful in marginalizing political challengers from the extremes than he did in delivering on the economic and social dimensions of his political project. Like his northern counterpart, constitutional questions would prove important means of compensating for economic and social failures. His relentless war of attrition against the imperial vestiges in the Treaty settlement which had seen the abolition of the oath of allegiance, the position of Governor-General, and the scrapping of the Seanad, and which was replaced with a new body more in line with Catholic vocational theory, culminated in the promulgation of a new constitution, adopted by referendum on 1 July 1937. With its Articles 2 and 3, which laid territorial and jurisdictional claim to Northern Ireland, its indebtedness to Catholic social theory, a ban on divorce, and, in Article 44, its recognition of the 'special position' of the Catholic Church, it deepened the North–South divide. Despite this, de Valera continued to pressurize the British government to reopen the partition issue and attempted to use the resolution of other unfinished business from the Treaty settlement to achieve this.

The refusal of de Valera in July 1932 to continue to transfer to the British Exchequer the annuity payments due from Irish farmers under the various British Land Acts provoked retaliatory British duties on Irish exports. The subsequent economic war, together with the already significant effects of the slump in international demand, saw the value of the most important single item in exports, live cattle, decline from £19.7 million in 1929 to £6.1 million in 1934.[53] The economic war and the adverse international conditions served to accelerate and at the same time to justify Fianna Fáil's own economic and social project, which it liked to portray, at least in the early 1930s, as broadly 'progressive'. In the countryside it stood for a generalized agrarian radicalism. In order to break Irish dependence on the British market, it was argued that tillage production should be favoured over a strong emphasis on livestock. Tillage was to be encouraged to meet domestic grain demand and help make the country self-sufficient in food. The party's rhetoric depicted the small farmer rather than the large rancher as the stable basis of the Irish nation. The Land Commission was to be used to redistribute land on a large scale to small farmers and landless men. As many families as possible were to be settled on the land. Radical agrarianism was complemented by a strong commitment to industrialize through the vigorous use of import tariffs and quotas. The protected home market was to be saved as much as possible for native capitalists by the Control of Manufactures legislation to limit the power of foreign businessmen. The programme was given a left-of-centre tone by a commitment to welfarist policies in areas including pensions, unemployment insurance, and housing. De Valera, who was not adverse to summoning up the ghost of James Connolly, the socialist martyr of the 1916 insurrection, had gone as far as declaring that his government's objective was to end the conditions that had forced hundreds of thousands of Irishmen to emigrate since the Great Famine of the 1840s.[54] By the end of the decade, if some of the undoubted achievements of the Fianna Fáil project were visible, so too were its limitations.

This was particularly clear in rural Ireland, where the government's agrarian radicalism sharply diminished as fear of a decline in living standards led to a growing emphasis on the need to trade with the nearest large market. In 1935 a Coal–Cattle pact was agreed with Britain and from 1936 onwards there was a steady reintegration of Irish agriculture into the British market. The impact of Fianna Fáil efforts to alter radically Irish agriculture was slight. By 1939 the tillage acreage was a mere 2 per cent above its 1930 level and cattle raising remained the dominant enterprise despite a severe price decline. The flight from the land continued and the decline of the small farmer class was not arrested. After the initial spurt the pace of land redistribution had slowed considerably by the late 1930s. Delegates to Fianna Fáil's annual conference in 1938 complained about the government's desertion of its small farmer constituency and a new political party, Clann na Talmhan (Children of the Land), was created that year as an expression of small-farmer discontent,[55] which was strong along the western seaboard and in the south-west where there was a concentration of small farmers working poorer land in districts that were particularly hard hit by emigration.

By 1938 Fianna Fáil, which had come to power with a disproportionate reliance on the votes of small farmers and with a regional support base that was stronger in the west than in the centre and east of the state, had begun to acquire the status of a majority 'catch-all' party with an extremely wide and diverse electoral constituency. Its loss of some electoral support from disappointed farmers and landless men had been diminished by the 1933 Unemployment Assistance Act, which for the first time provided support to small farmers and farm labourers. These groups together with the urban working class were also beneficiaries of the most significant of the government's social improvements: a crash slum-clearance and house-building programme that led to the construction or renovation of 132,000 houses between 1932 and 1942. An average of 12,000 houses a year were built with state aid between those years, compared with fewer than 2,000 a year between 1923 and 1931. Housing was one area of social expenditure in which de Valera's government clearly outperformed Craigavon's.[56]

Central to Fianna Fáil's electoral success were those economic and welfare policies that allowed it to appeal to both the working class and an expanding manufacturing bourgeoisie. Although there is some dispute about whether official figures that show industrial employment rising from 162,000 in 1931 to 217,000 in 1938 may in part be a product of improved enumeration procedures,[57] even the sceptics agree that a substantial increase did occur.[58] This was complemented by the government's more frequent use of publicly owned corporations than its predecessor, when private enterprise was unwilling or unable to develop national resources. These included an Irish Sugar Company, a Turf Development Board, an Industrial Credit Company, the Irish Tourist Board, and a national airline, Aer Lingus. As more and more of the actual or aspirant manufacturing class shifted their political loyalties to a party once perceived as practically 'Bolshevist', the urban working class saw in the Fiánna Fail government a welcome break with the conservatism and pro-rural bias of its predecessor. Although some of the more radical impulses of Seán Lemass as Minister of Industry and Commerce were countered by the formidable conservatism of the officials in the Department of Finance supported by the Minister Seán MacEntee, Lemass did much in the decade to successfully establish his claim that the existence of Fianna Fáil made the Irish Labour Party unnecessary. For all Irish Labour's resentment at having its policy clothes stolen by Lemass, some of the leaders of the Irish trade union movement increasingly saw Fianna Fáil as an ally. As the membership of trade unions affiliated to the Irish Trade Union Congress grew from 95,000 in 1933 to 161,000 in 1938, this was unsurprising.[59] The pro-labour bias of the government was also perceived in measures designed to improve working conditions through the introduction of Joint Industrial Councils, Trade Boards, and the Conditions of Employment Act (1936).

But the gains of this activism were almost exhausted by 1938. The limits of import-substitution industrialization on the basis of a small home market had been reached by the end of the 1930s. Consumers often paid for the undoubted employment gains with higher prices and inferior products. Small-scale and inefficient production meant much of the new industry would be incapable of selling abroad. What extra jobs were created were insufficient to absorb rural depopulation and unemployment had reached 145,000 in January 1936.[60] The problem was in part a reflection of the fact that emigration, the traditional solution to the Irish economy's inability to employ its people, had been blocked by the Great Depression. Despite de Valera's claim in a speech to Irish emigrants in London in 1933 that 'We shall not rest until we have lifted the doom of exile which for so long lain upon hundreds of thousands of Irishmen in every generation',[61] there was a major resumption of emigration to the United Kingdom from 1935 once that country's economy began to show signs of recovery.[62]

The Irish Labour Party hoped to benefit from the dissatisfaction of those who had looked to Fianna Fáil for a more radical set of policies on both the economy and the national question. Created in 1912 by the Irish trade unions, it had faced the daunting task of development in a political system where the predominant fault line in the 1920s and 1930s reflected a national and not a class issue. During the Civil War, Labour had deplored the excesses of both sides while trying to emphasize the primacy of socio-economic issues. In the 1920s the party continued to decry the concentration on constitutional issues left by the Treaty and the Civil War. Before Fianna Fáil clearly committed itself to constitutional politics and entered the Dáil, Labour was able to establish itself as a moderate, reformist alternative to Cumann na nGaedheal. In the election of 1923 it won 10.9 per cent of the vote and fourteen seats. In the next election in June 1927 its support had risen to 12.6 per cent and twenty-two seats out of 153. However, once Fianna Fáil entered the Dáil the party was faced with an even more formidable competitor for the working-class vote. For although the small size of the South's working class (14.6 per cent of the workforce in 1936)[63] militated against the development of the party, it was also the case that even within this restricted constituency Labour was not the hegemonic force.

Most noticeable was its stark weakness in the two main urban centres, Cork and Dublin. From the 1920s until the 1960s, Labour's strongholds were in a number of largely agricultural counties in the east and south-east where the state's agrarian proletariat was concentrated. Neglected by Fianna Fáil, whose agrarian policies were fixated on the needs of the small farmers, these labourers constituted a third of the agricultural workforce in twelve counties and it was in these counties, including Wexford, Waterford, and Tipperary, that Labour's most reliable support existed. Elsewhere the party's structure and plodding concentration on material issues narrowed its appeal.

Until 1930 it maintained its organic link with the trade union movement: of its forty-four candidates in the June 1927 election, twenty-seven were trade union officials. The trade union movement, which had expanded significantly during the 1916–21 period, was badly hit by the depressed economic conditions of the 1920s and its urban heartland in Dublin was seriously damaged by a bitter conflict within the country's largest union, the Irish Transport and General Workers' Union. At the heart of the dispute was the role of James Larkin, who had founded the union in 1908 and incarnated the spirit of intransigent revolutionary syndicalism that had manifested itself in his partnership with the Marxist founder of the Irish Labour Party, James Connolly, and in his charismatic leadership of the workers during the Dublin Lock-Out of 1913. Out of Ireland from 1914 to 1923, he returned to a radically different situation but showed no inclination to scale down what William O'Brien and the other moderate organization men who ran the ITGWU considered his unrealistically maximalist vision of trade union struggle. Bitter internal wranglings, a court case, and finally Larkin's expulsion from the ITGWU in 1924, led to his formation of a rival union, the Workers' Union of Ireland.

Larkin's mythic status amongst the Dublin working class meant that the dispute had severe implications for Labour in the city. The ITGWU leadership's involvement in the party led to a bitter Larkinite assault on Labour's timidity and its moderation on constitutional issues. Larkin had been a strong opponent of the Treaty and he echoed IRA taunts about the party's English leader, Thomas Johnson, being an imperialist who could not understand Irish nationalism.[64] In fact Labour did move closer to Fianna Fáil from 1927 onwards, making it clear that it would be prepared to consider a coalition agreement with Fianna Fáil if that party entered the Dáil.[65] This strategy simply confused some of its supporters, while others who had been attracted by its pro-Treaty stance now deserted it. In the September 1927 election, the first after de Valera led his supporters into the Dáil, Labour's support dropped to 9 per cent and thirteen seats as the electorate polarized between the two major parties. It did particularly badly in Dublin, where a Larkinite assault resulted in Johnston losing his seat.

As long as Fianna Fáil's promises of a progressive, republican project were untested by office or, as in the early 1930s, in the first flush of realization, Labour faced a real danger of obliteration as a distinctive political force, as was evident in its electoral performance in 1932 when it won a mere 7.7 per cent.[66] Supporting de Valera's minority government in 1932 brought further decline as Fianna Fáil appealed for a secure majority with which to implement its programme, and in the snap 1933 election Fianna Fáil's support rose from 44.5 per cent to 49.7 per cent, while Labour was reduced to its worst-ever performance with a mere 5.5 per cent. Its new leader was a prominent trade unionist, William Norton, General Secretary of the Post Office Workers' Union. Norton's leadership was a sharp break with the past. He had played a central role in the severing of the link with the unions in 1930 to enable the party to appeal beyond such a sectional constituency. A convinced nationalist, he was friendly with de Valera and ditched Labour's neutrality on constitutional issues in favour of a straightforward acceptance of mainstream republicanism.[67] There were signs that as the limits of Fianna Fáil's social radicalism became clear, Norton's left republicanism might bring gains. In the 1937 election Labour's support rose to 10.3 per cent and thirteen seats. However, de Valera's capacity to exploit the unfinished business of Anglo-Irish relations to marginalize any Labour challenge was far from exhausted and together with anti-communism would have little problem in pushing the party back to the political margins.

Here de Valera's triumph in the Anglo-Irish Agreement on 25 April 1938 was decisive. The British Prime Minister, Neville Chamberlain, was determined to do as much as possible, short of the coercion of the North, to put relations with de Valera on a new and amicable basis. In part this reflected a concern to end the bitterness of centuries but he also saw success as a means of providing an example of appeasement in action.[68] The centrepiece of the Agreement was the return of those ports that Britain had retained control of under the Treaty: Cobh, Berehaven, and Lough Swilly. Chamberlain's hope that de Valera might consider a defence treaty to allow Britain access to them in times of war proved illusory. The economic war was ended on terms extremely favourable to Ireland: the British agreed to drop their demand for a settlement of the financial dispute over the land annuities from £26 million to £10 million. Ireland was granted the same trade terms as other dominions, with the result that while UK exports to Ireland were still subject to restrictions, Irish exports gained free entry to the British market.[69] British attempts to press Belfast's demand for lower duties on Ulster exports to the South were rebuffed with the claim that such a concession was impossible, given the oppression of Catholics in the North. For the first time since 1922, inquiries into the activities of the Stormont regime were carried out by the Home Office and the Dominions Office.[70]

Capitalizing on his triumph, de Valera called an election for June 1938 focusing on how the Agreement would make Irish neutrality possible in world conflict and claiming that he was much more optimistic about an end to partition than he had been in 1932.[71] The result was a major victory for Fianna Fáil, which won over 50 per cent of the vote, its share rising from 45.2 per cent to 51.9 per cent. However, as Professor Joe Lee has pointed out, de Valera was wise to seize the opportunity offered by the Agreement to snatch his election triumph. A deteriorating economic and financial situation was reflected in a harsh budget in May 1939.[72] Nothing had come of the investigations into the North and while neutrality would be a massively popular policy in the South, it would deepen the division on the island at the same time as world war rescued a moribund Unionist regime.

2

War and the Welfare State

Nationalists and the Second World War

The attitudes of northern nationalists to the war were heavily influenced by their fraught relation with the state. However, there were significant differences of approach that reflected the longer-term division between the Nationalist Party and Sinn Féin. In the early years of the new regime nationalists in Belfast and the east of the province had been more inclined to support participation in parliament as a means of high-lighting injustices and pressuring for redress, particularly in the area of education. Living in areas where Catholics were in a minority, and with the bitter experience of the inter-communal violence of the 1920–2 period, they were less likely to be supporters of republican militancy. The influence of Joe Devlin's constitutional and reformist populism had been decisive here. Support for abstentionism and Sinn Féin was much stronger in the west and south of Northern Ireland where nearness to the border and the existence of local Catholic majorities had initially encouraged hopes of a strategy of exit from the state through reparti-tion. Most northern republicans had been pro-Treaty and after the col-lapse of the Boundary Commission in 1925 had moved towards an uneasy coalition with the Devlinites and the Catholic Church to adopt a policy of qualified and fitful participation in the northern parliament. A new organization, the National League of the North, was set up in 1928 with Devlin as President and Cahir Healy, a Fermanagh insurance agent who had been a founding member of Sinn Féin, as Secretary.[1] Commit-ted to the 'national reunification of Ireland', the new organization's initial tendency to support Devlin's policy of participation was from the start unpopular with a sizeable section of those from the pro-Treaty Sinn Féin tradition, and as the 1930s progressed the support for abstentionism grew.

Devlin's own participation in parliament had only ever been a partial and qualified one, the main purpose of which was to campaign for the defence of Catholic education in the North. On this question at least he had the support of the bitterly anti-Unionist Archbishop of Armagh,

Cardinal Joseph MacRory, and the other northern bishops. The universal concern of the Catholic Church that it control all aspects of the education of Catholic children was in Northern Ireland complicated by the distrust and antagonism felt by the hierarchy towards the new state. The liberal Minister of Education, Lord Londonderry, had, in the Education Act of 1923, tried to refashion the North's education system along more integrated lines by excluding religious instruction while at the same time creating three classes of elementary school, each enjoying a different level of financial assistance. Only those that were fully controlled by local authority education committees were fully funded by the Ministry of Education for salaries, running costs, and capital expenditure. Those that accepted a management committee with four members chosen by the school trustees and two representatives of the education committee received all the cost of salaries, half the running costs, and a discretionary amount towards capital costs. The 'four and two' committees were rejected as the thin end of the wedge of total control by a Protestant state and thus Catholic schools became part of the 'voluntary' sector where the Ministry paid the salaries but there was no contribution to running and capital costs. Lord Londonderry's genuine but abstract liberalism—he had naïvely considered the 'four and two' committees as a compromise attractive to both the Protestant and Catholic Churches—actually disadvantaged the Catholic Church, which lost the grants it had received under the pre-partition provisions amounting to two-thirds of its building and equipment costs. Pressure from the Protestant churches and the Orange Order forced the government to modify the 1923 Act to ensure that schools controlled by the local authorities were 'safe for Protestant children' by providing for representation of Protestant clergy on appointments committees and by installing religious education. As compensation the 1930 Education Act provided Catholic schools with capital grants of 50 per cent.[2]

The 1930 Act had come as a result of a threat by the Catholic bishops to take legal action against the 1923 Act, which they claimed violated the provision of the Government of Ireland Act forbidding the endowment of any church. This victory, compared to the futile manoeuvrings of nationalist politicians, encouraged a process by which the Catholic population of Northern Ireland increasingly focused its practical horizons on building a distinct civil society within a Protestant-dominated state. The inter-war period had seen a proliferation of Catholic organizations: the Catholic Arts Guild, the Catholic Young Men's Society, the Legion of Mary, the Catholic Boy Scouts, and even a Catholic Billiards

League. At a time when the openly proclaimed policy of the government
was that the state was a Protestant one, the seeming dead-end of constitutional or semi-constitutional opposition, together with the flourish-
ing Catholic 'state within a state', tended to increase the influence of
abstentionist sentiment within nationalist politics.

The victory of Fianna Fáil in the 1932 election had strengthened
republican optimism. IRA membership in the North rose significantly
while northern supporters of Fianna Fáil such as Eamon Donnelly, a
former republican/abstentionist MP for Armagh, and pockets of 'anti-
Treaty republicans' such as the National Defence Association in the
Newry and South Armagh area, began to campaign vigorously against
any recognition of the northern parliament. In the 1933 Stormont election the National League's candidate in South Armagh was defeated by a
republican abstentionist and Eamon de Valera was nominated and
returned unopposed by nationalists in South Down.[3] Devlin himself saw
his majority in Belfast Central cut into by a republican prisoner and
after his death in 1934 northern nationalism lacked any substantial figure
who could have attempted to bring its fractious elements together.

The 1935 riots in Belfast inevitably strengthened northern Catholics'
sense of themselves as a besieged minority within a hostile society and
with a government that was, at best, indifferent to their fate.[4] Those such
as Devlin's successor as MP for Belfast Central, the Catholic barrister
T. J. Campbell, who continued to favour attendance at Stormont, were
increasingly overshadowed by supporters of abstentionism either as a
tactic or a fundamental matter of principle. The government had
responded to de Valera's success in the 1933 election by introducing
legislation that required all candidates in Stormont elections to make
a declaration that they would take their seat if elected. Republicans
were still able to pressurize Healy and the other nationalist MP for
Fermanagh-Tyrone to step down in favour of abstentionist candidates in
the 1935 Westminster election but Healy was strongly opposed to any
attempt to adopt a similar strategy for Stormont. However, northern
sympathizers of Fianna Fáil led by Eamon Donnelly, now a Fianna Fáil
TD, favoured a radical strategy of boycotting Stormont combined with
northern nationalists being allowed to take seats in the Dáil. In the 1938
Stormont election the result of these divisions was that in three nationalist constituencies the local organizations refused to nominate candidates
and the seats were lost, reducing nationalist representation to eight MPs.

By the time of the 1938 Anglo-Irish negotiations, the dominant political tendency in northern nationalism was to look expectantly to de

Valera to sort out partition as part of his negotiations with Chamberlain. Healy and other nationalist MPs had travelled to London during the negotiations to meet de Valera and press him to ensure that partition was put at the centre of the negotiations. De Valera was told that it would be a betrayal if he settled the trade and defence disputes and ignored partition. But as he had already demonstrated in his opposition to the proposal to allow northern MPs to sit in the Dáil, de Valera's primary concern was with the consolidation and defence of his twenty-six-county state and he was not prepared to allow a settlement that so clearly favoured the Irish to be delayed or even prevented by pressure from the North.

Northern nationalist frustration and anger with the Fianna Fáil leader over the 1938 agreements with London were intense. However, despite this de Valera was still able to get Healy to launch a series of anti-partition rallies in the autumn of 1938. He wanted to use these as part of his anti-partition campaign in Britain and the US.[5] However, for de Valera the central purpose of the campaign was to establish internationally a clear sense of Irish grievance that would allow him to justify Irish neutrality in the coming conflict. Neutrality was the goal, not unity, and de Valera was hostile to any attempt whether it came from Downing Street or nationalists in the six counties to raise the unity issue.

Alienation from Fianna Fáil produced a fusion of its supporters in the North with the group of parliamentarians under the direction of Healy in the formation of a new organization, the Six Counties Men's Association. It was supported in the South by republican critics of de Valera, including the former chief of staff of the IRA, Seán MacBride, and the former Blueshirt leader and Nazi supporter, General Eoin O'Duffy. Three of its leading members in the North welcomed the possibility of a German victory, telling the German minister in Dublin that they were prepared to 'place the Catholic minority in the north under the protection of the Axis powers'.[6] Healy was interned in Brixton prison between July 1941 and September 1942 under an order signed by the Home Secretary Herbert Morrison because of suspicions of pro-German activities. Although Healy protested that he was neither anti-British nor pro-Nazi,[7] intercepted correspondence with a Fermanagh priest suggested a policy of collaboration in the event of a German invasion.[8]

Such pro-German sentiment was strongly developed in the ranks of the northern IRA. While support for the IRA dwindled in the South during the 1930s due to the attractive power of the initial period of Fianna Fáil radicalism, the organization grew in strength in Northern

Ireland through a mixture of the misplaced hopes generated by de Valera's victory and the attendant intensification of sectarian passions in the North. Although most of the Belfast IRA was outside the city at a training camp in the South when the sectarian violence of 1935 began,[9] the organization's role as a communal defence force received a boost, much to the despair of some of the more left-wing republicans in the South who wanted the IRA to bridge the gap with the Protestant working class. The IRA's newspaper had complained that Belfast republicans were 'on the whole possessed of a bigotry that is dangerous to the cause they have at heart' and the left-republican Peader O'Donnell bluntly proclaimed 'we haven't a battalion of IRA men in Belfast; we just have a battalion of armed Catholics'.[10] These rather pious criticisms simply missed the point that for many northern republicans the main enemy was not the abstractions of 'British rule' or 'imperialist imperialism' but the six-county Protestant state and what were seen as its repressive and discriminatory manifestations.

Northern republicanism was able to exploit the state's increasingly repressive response to republican marches and commemorations. Conflicts over the right to march had been a recurrent feature of the social and political history of the North for well over a century. Orangeism's determination to mark out as much as possible of northern territory as Protestant and Unionist public space was periodically contested by both Catholic and nationalist organizations. The Ancient Order of Hibernians, which developed in the late nineteenth century as a defender of Catholic interests and a counter to Orangeism, had been closely linked to Devlin's party. Its acceptance of partition, coupled with the resurgence of republicanism after 1916, had seen it go into slow decline.[11] Its annual parades on St Patrick's Day and on Lady's Day in August were largely limited to predominantly Catholic villages and small towns. Although these parades could at times be the occasion of conflicts with local loyalists, they were generally not interfered with by the police. It was very different with public manifestations of republicanism, which were frequently prohibited under regulations of the Special Powers Act even when they took place in areas like the Falls Road district of Belfast, which were predominantly nationalist.[12] Throughout the inter-war period, but particularly in the 1930s, the main manifestation of northern republicanism was the annual commemoration of the 1916 Easter insurrection. These, particularly the largest ones in Belfast and Derry, were regularly banned and as a result the RUC found itself in conflict, not simply with a few hundred republicans, but with much larger numbers of Catholics who had gathered to watch the parades. In 1937 there were serious disturbances on the Falls Road when, in enforcing a ban, the RUC baton-charged the crowds of spectators.[13]

The rise in northern nationalist expectations during 1938, first during the Anglo-Irish negotiation and subsequently because of the de Valera-inspired anti-partition rallies in the autumn, produced a predictable increase in conflict with the state and sections of the Unionist population. Grass-roots Unionist annoyance at anti-partitionist demonstrations where the Irish national anthem, *The Soldier's Song*, was sung led to the government introducing a new regulation under the Special Powers Act banning it, despite the advice of the Inspector General of the RUC that such a ban could not be enforced except by exacerbating communal conflict and disorder.[14] As war approached, this pattern of nationalist and republican assertiveness, Protestant reaction, and state repression established itself. The IRA's bombing campaign in England inevitably encouraged a Unionist identification of nationalist politics and subversion. When the British government refused to extend conscription to the province in May 1939, Sir Basil Brooke blamed 'the minority in our midst . . . either afraid or too despicable to take a hand in the defence of the country . . . prepared to go to any lengths to prevent the loyal and brave men of this country from doing their duty'.[15] The IRA responded by a demonstration on the Falls Road where there was a burning of thousands of recently distributed gas masks.[16] When war was declared, Catholic workers at Harland and Wolff were evicted by gangs of fellow employees and Catholic mill girls were forced to quit, while police escorts accompanied Protestant workers leaving Mackies Foundry on the Springfield Road in West Belfast.[17]

Anti-state sentiment was not a simple response to repression and discrimination. It was also an expression of an autonomous sense of Irish national identity produced through church and school and reinforced in the institutions of Catholic civil society from newspapers to sporting and cultural organizations. At its core was a vision of Catholics, whatever their social class, as belonging to a victimized community. A report by the Irish National Council of the YMCA into the experience of young unemployed Catholics attending a work camp near Belfast in 1940 gave clear evidence of the potentially explosive mixture of economic exclusion, anti-police sentiment, and nationalism. The report claimed that 'quite good boys' who had been looking for jobs failed to get them in workplaces where the majority of workers were Protestant and where Protestant boys from the camp were being constantly taken on. Talking to the Catholic boys, they came across strong anti-RUC sentiment: 'To them the police were all prejudiced against the Catholic areas of the city, all laws were bad laws because they were English laws and every moral argument was propaganda.' One of the best boys in the camp, 'tidy, clean, above the average in intelligence, a good worker', was an ardent supporter of the IRA: 'he firmly believed that we would be better off under Nazi rule'.[18]

Cardinal MacRory might not have gone quite as far, although the Nazis believed that he was in favour of German action to end partition.[19] But he did nothing to encourage any softening of anti-state feeling, declaring that Catholics in Northern Ireland had neither freedom nor justice.[20] However, it is important to register the complexity of Catholic attitudes. It was not true, as F. H. Boland of the Department of External Affairs claimed in April 1941, that 'the vast majority of Nationalists in the six-county area are absolutely pro-German on account of their unjustified treatment by the British government and its Belfast puppet'.[21] A delegation of northern nationalists who met de Valera in October 1940 provided him with a detailed analysis of three strands of opinion within the Catholic community: some supported the IRA, others wanted to assist the northern government in its defensive measures against a possible German invasion and the third group was content to trust Fianna Fáil and support his policy by not co-operating with Stormont.[22]

Pro-Germanism tended to be secondary to anti-British and anti-Stormont feelings, which were the dominant sentiments. The support for limited assistance to the government was strongest in Belfast where the city's two nationalist MPs were willing to sit on a defence committee created by Craig in the summer of 1940.[23] Although the Catholic community had been united in opposition to Craig's call for conscription, there is some evidence, particularly for Belfast, that a tradition of service in the British forces, a product more of economic necessity and the desire for action and adventure than loyalty to the state, asserted itself during the war.[24] Northern Ireland's only Victoria Cross in the Second World War was won by a Catholic. The *Irish News*, Belfast's Catholic daily, maintained the Redmonite tradition and referred to IRA men who raided banks and post offices as 'bandits'.[25] Its coverage of the progress of the war was pro-Allied. Thus although it was in Belfast that the IRA concentrated its efforts to disrupt the war effort and that it obtained its main martyr when Tom Williams was executed for the killing of a Catholic RUC man in west Belfast on Easter Sunday 1942, its Catholic community was not unified in hostility to the war effort.

The strong republican current that had been manifested in the early years of the war went into recession as the war progressed. In part this reflected the vigorous repression North and South and the disorientating effect of the 'Hayes Affair' in June 1941, when the Chief of Staff of the IRA was arrested and interrogated by his own comrades who believed he was a police informer.[26] The devastation of large parts of Belfast in four German air raids in April and May 1941, which killed 1,100 people and damaged over half the city's housing stock,[27] may have weakened the pro-German convictions of some northern Catholics. Brian Moore, whose novel *The Emperor of Ice Cream* portrays that grim and chaotic time in the city's history, has described how the Blitz destroyed his surgeon father's Axis sympathies: 'My father, who was pro-German, when he saw what the Germans were able to do, when he saw what modern warfare was really like, when they blow up your home, that was all, things were over.'[28] Cardinal MacRory, concerned that anti-British sentiment had been undermined by the Blitz, warned the German minister in Dublin that more attacks would stir up anti-German feeling.[29]

Although Craigavon's government had ensured that any possible Catholic participation in the Home Guard was minimized by basing it on the B Specials, there was some shared wartime experience in civil defence activities as air-raid wardens, fire-fighters, and rescue workers.[30] The halting of Orange marches during the war—its critics claimed it was to avoid the embarrassment of the large numbers of loyalists of fighting age who had not joined up—substantially reduced possible occasions of sectarian conflict. The effective ending of unemployment by 1943, as a result of the massive expansion of the North's traditional industries brought about by wartime demand, softened the material edge of Catholic grievance. The Nationalist Party in Belfast had, since Devlin's death, become increasingly identified with the interests of the Catholic middle class of solicitors, teachers, doctors, and publicans. Its conservatism at a time when even Northern Ireland was being affected by the UK-wide swing to the left lost it two of its councillors, who joined the Northern Ireland Labour Party in January 1942.[31] However, the interpenetration of class and sectarianism in the life of the city meant that the nationalists' appeal to a predominantly working-class constituency could also be outflanked by more militant forms of anti-partitionism. When the sitting nationalist MP for the Stormont constituency of Falls died in 1942, his proposed successor was defeated by Eamon Donnelly running on an abstentionist ticket. This reflected Catholic anger at the execution of Tom Williams, who was a native of the constituency. When a few months later the Catholics of West Belfast had a choice between an NILP candidate and an abstentionist for the Westminster constituency, they voted massively in favour of Jack Beattie of the NILP, who won the seat. Beattie was a strongly anti-partitionist socialist and he was seen as the candidate most likely to defeat the Unionist Party, which held the seat. Nevertheless, his victory indicated that the city's Catholic working class was inclined to express its nationalism in a pragmatic and left-of-centre way.

In Derry, despite the bitter Catholic resentment at the gerrymandered system of the city's government, the war years saw a lessening of local antagonisms. As in Belfast this had a clear material basis in the unprecedented wartime prosperity of the local shirt and shipbuilding industries and the substantial amount of work associated with the creation of the US naval station, which became the Allies' most westerly base for repair and refuelling.[32] Local asperities were temporarily displaced with the influx of tens of thousands of American servicemen whose superior resources and novelty value made them attractive to local women and earned them the resentment of Derry men irrespective of religious denomination. The city's Catholic bishop encouraged his flock to participate in the war effort by involving themselves in civil defence activities[33] and, as in the Great War, Derry men of both traditions enlisted in the British forces.[34] Unlike Belfast where the war years saw the emergence of a Labour and republican-Labour challenge to the Nationalist Party, which was maintained after 1945, in Derry traditional forms of nationalism went into temporary decline to be reinvigorated in the post-war period. The local injustice was such a glaring one that although the world-wide cataclysm could temporarily diminish its significance, its continued existence ensured that by the end of the war, Derry nationalists would be in the forefront of attempts to relaunch a coherent northern nationalist party.

What little we know of nationalism outside Belfast and Derry in the war years seems to indicate a sense of disorientation and a lack of energy or direction. When the nationalist MP for Mid-Derry died in 1941, such was the apathy and enervation in party ranks that the writ for a by-election was not moved until 1945.[35] With only one nationalist MP at Stormont for most of the war, it was unsurprising that Seán MacEntee, a prominent member of de Valera's government, could publicly criticize the Nationalist Party for condemning its supporters to 'political futility for 22 years'.[36]

Stormont and the Challenge of War

The lacklustre response of Lord Craigavon's government to the outbreak of war confirmed the opinion of the head of the Northern Ireland civil service, Sir Wilfred Spender, that the devolved regime had become a threat to the cause of the Union.[37] Reduced by age (he was 69) and recurring illnesses to one hour of work a day, Craig's frequent long vacations outside the province did nothing to discourage his paternalist indulgence of the most sectarian and parochial strands of loyalist opinion. The increasingly rigid sectarian tone of Unionism in the 1930s had reflected, the liberal Minister of Education Lord Charlemont was convinced, 'the gradual increase of pressure from independent organisations, leagues, Socialism; all the political expressions of Ulster individualism'.[38] When Craig called a general election in February 1938, ostensibly as a response to de Valera's raising of the partition issue in the Anglo-Irish negotiations, his main domestic concern was the challenge of a new Progressive Unionist organization. This had been founded in 1937 by a Westminster Unionist MP W. J. Stewart, who had broken from the party to challenge the government's record on employment, housing conditions, and agriculture. Not for the first or last time did southern irredentism powerfully contribute to the marginalization of significant challenges to Unionist Party hegemony. Support for the Unionist Party rose from 72,000 in the previous general election to 186,000, while the Progressive Unionists got 47,888 votes and won no seats.[39]

The despair of Spender at Craig's style of government could only have been deepened by the administration's inability to adjust to the demands of war. In part this reflected the deadening effects of two decades of unchallenged power. By the outbreak of war the average age of his cabinet was 62 and four of its seven members had been in government since 1921. John Andrews, Minister of Finance, was born in the same year as Craig and, despite clear signs of physical debility, was to be the Prime Minister's successor. From a family with major interests in flax spinning and railways, Andrews was President of the Ulster Unionist Labour Association and a strong supporter of running the state on communal lines. John Milne Barbour, whose undistinguished record as Minister of Commerce made him the butt of much Labour and Independent Unionist criticism, was 71. Barbour, who had combined his Commerce position with that of Parliamentary Secretary to the Ministry of Finance, had been one of the few figures in the government (the

Minister of Finance from 1921–37, Hugh Pollock, was another) who were unhappy with Craig's Protestant populism. Robert Dawson Bates, one of the younger members of the cabinet at 62, was a rigid and strident proponent of the view that the state's first priority should be to guard against the internal and external nationalist threat. Despite his exaggerated sense of the precarious position of his government, he persisted in living in the northern seaside town of Portrush, 70 miles from his department. The result, as Spender bitterly noted, was, despite fuel rationing, a yearly distance of over 30,000 miles for his large official car and frequent and prolonged absences from his department.[40]

Although persuaded by Chamberlain not to press the issue in the broader interest of the war effort,[41] Craig and his ministers resented the exclusion of Northern Ireland from conscription, particularly as they saw in the decision an indication of British desire to conciliate de Valera in the interests of possible Irish participation in the war. They were also concerned that, without conscription, the Unionist community's commitment to the war effort might be shown to be less than enthusiastic. In the opening phase of the war recruits came forward at a rate of 2,500 per month but this had fallen to less than 1,000 by the spring of 1940. There was a brief upsurge in the aftermath of Dunkirk, but by December 1940 monthly recruitment levels had fallen to 600 and the long-term trend was downward.[42]

Memories of the terrible losses of the Ulster Division at the Somme in 1916 may have kept recruitment figures down. The local sectarian dynamics of the northern state also played a part. Basil Brooke had appealed early in the war for people to 'set aside the Orange and Green dispute and co-operate fully with the government. If this war goes against us the only flag that will fly over Belfast or Dublin will be the swastika.'[43] But just as for many nationalists the ending of partition ranked higher than resisting fascism, for a large number of Unionists the world conflict could not distract their attention from the possible threat to the local balance of power that wartime mobilization could bring. The sectarian violence that had devastated Belfast between 1920 and 1922 had in part been fuelled by loyalist resentment at what was perceived to be the 'peaceful penetration' of Ulster by Catholics, who took the jobs of Protestants who had volunteered for military service. The bitter legacy of economic competition in the 1930s helped to encourage a recrudescence of such fears during the early years of the war when unemployment remained a problem. A direct appeal by the government to those northern Catholics who were sympathetic to the Allied cause might well have served to lessen Protestant reluctance to volunteer. Tommy Henderson, the Independent Unionist MP for Shankill, an often strident voice for the interests of this heartland of the Protestant working class, became so frustrated with the low recruitment figures that he demanded that Craig actively campaign in nationalist areas: 'tell them what the Roman Catholic countries had suffered at the hands of Hitler . . . he would be surprised at the good response'.[44] The government's response was to put Basil Brooke in charge of a recruiting campaign. The Unionist politician most associated with the demand that Protestant employers only take on co-religionists was a less than inspired choice and this was compounded by Brooke's decision to use the Unionist Party machine to organize the campaign.

With the end of the 'phoney war' and the formation of a new and more dynamic government in Britain, the contrast with what the official historian of the North's war effort called 'a sense of inertia . . . of fumbling uncertainty'[45] was stark. In May 1940 Edmond Warnock, a junior minister at Home Affairs, resigned from the government, denouncing its failure to mobilize the province for any of the demands of the war and accusing it of being 'in a state of lethargy, almost a coma'.[46] In June he was followed by another junior minister who echoed the views of those Unionists who were sympathetic to the idea of an understanding with de Valera to ensure access to southern ports and airfields. Up until Dunkirk, support for the idea of North and South uniting within the Empire as the only way of guaranteeing Britain's survival had only been articulated at the liberal fringe of the Unionist Party. Now it got the support of junior members of the government and at least one Westminster Unionist MP, Dr James Little, who declared he was prepared to stand by the side of 'any man, however much in other matters he might differ from me, who was willing to unite with me in defending the land of my birth against Nazi domination . . . we are all proud to be Irishmen and no land on the face of the earth do we love so well as this land.'[47]

Even that stalwart of the interests of border Unionists, Basil Brooke, was wracked by the conflicting pulls of parochial dominance and the call of an empire in peril. He had carried on his family's long tradition of military service, and of his three sons who enlisted, two were killed. A nephew of Sir Alan Brooke, Chief of the Imperial General Staff, he was an enthusiastic proponent of the North's total mobilization and of the priority of the world conflict over local considerations. Sounded out by an Independent member of the Dáil on his opinion of the sort of deal being broached with Dublin—to join the war in return for post-war unification—he claimed that such a proposal would split the cabinet but that he would vote in favour.[48]

Brooke, recognized even by the government's critics to be an energetic and effective Minister of Agriculture,[49] might have hoped to succeed Craig. However, when the Prime Minister died in November 1940, the province's semi-detached relation to the war effort was apparent in Andrews' unchallenged succession. Sir Wilfred Spender saw Andrews as totally incapable of rising to the challenge of war, mired as he was in the worst aspects of Craig's legacy: the obsessive concern to placate every parochial loyalist and Orange pressure group. His new cabinet showed little sign of growing back-bench pressure for radical change. Brooke was moved to Commerce, which he struggled to turn from a small and ineffective ministry, the butt of much criticism from those who held it responsible for the continuing high levels of unemployment, to the central directing core of wartime economic policy. The rest of the changes were an ineffective interchange of patently superannuated figures. The epitome of Andrews' leadership style was the promotion of Milne Barbour, the much criticized former Commerce minister, to Finance—the first example Spender could think of where a minister was promoted for incompetence. Brooke was replaced at Agriculture by Herbert Dixon, Lord Glentoran, the Chief Whip whose hold on Andrews stemmed from his reputation as a fixer or, as one critic uncharitably put it, 'a notorious "twister" '.[50]

The first major indication that the change of leadership had done nothing to quell a rising tide of criticism of the regime's lack of energy and direction was the by-election caused by Craig's death. The Unionist Party lost North Down by a wide margin in a high poll to an Independent. A month later, in April 1941, the Belfast blitz provided devastating evidence for its critics of the complacency and incompetence of the government. In the worst of the attacks, on the night of 15–16 April, over 800 were killed, the highest casualty rate in one night's bombing of any city in the UK. The total number of deaths was 1,100 while over 56,000 of the city's houses, about half of its stock, were damaged, leaving 100,000 people temporarily homeless. Although the origins of Belfast being the British city least physically and psychologically prepared for the blitz lay in part in the advice from London in the early months of the war that Northern Ireland was unlikely to be attacked,[51] subsequent more pessimistic analysis had not produced any substantial improvement in the city's defences.

The government shared responsibility for the protection of the city with its Corporation, which demonstrated on a smaller scale the deadening and corrupting effects of untrammelled one-party rule, in this case extending back before partition. The abolition of proportional representation for local government elections, although its main objective was to reduce the number of councils controlled by nationalists, severely damaged the electoral prospects of the NILP in Belfast. Here Labour's widely spread but thin support was under-represented in a simple majority system, unlike the nationalists, whose support was heavily concentrated in a few largely Catholic wards.[52] In the last election for the Corporation before the war, eighteen of the Unionist Party's nineteen seats were obtained without a contest, as were the Nationalist Party's three, while the NILP, which had not contested any seats since 1937, had no councillors. The local Unionist political machine, the 'City Hall party', was largely oblivious to the possible effects of its conservative and complacent stewardship on an increasingly embattled government. Belfast's citizens had virtually no air-raid shelters and a fire brigade of only 230 full-time men, which the Corporation refused to expand even after the Luftwaffe had attacked cities in the north of England and Scotland. The indifference and neglect of the Corporation, particularly to the poor and vulnerable, was further highlighted in June 1940 when a Home Affairs inquiry revealed extensive corruption and incompetence in the management of Whiteabbey Sanatorium and another inquiry concluded that 'In respect of personal medical services, Belfast falls far short of what might be expected in a city of its size and importance.'[53]

The government's fear of conflict with the Belfast Unionist machine made it resist demands for the dissolution of the Corporation but it did bring in commissioners to run the city for the duration of the war. Harry Midgley of the NILP had been prominent in the campaign that forced an inquiry into Whiteabbey and he shook Andrews' government when he won a by-election in Willowfield, a largely Protestant constituency in East Belfast, in December 1941. Regarded as a safe Unionist seat, which the NILP had not contested before, Midgley's large margin of victory showed that Northern Ireland was not immune to the UK-wide shift to the left in public opinion that occurred during the early years of the war as a reaction to what was seen as the establishment's appeasement of fascism and consequent lack of an effective strategy for winning the war.[54] With the USSR an ally from June 1941, attacks on socialism disappeared from the speeches of Conservative and Unionist politicians, and as the state's role in economic and social life expanded massively, Andrews was warned by some of his brighter and frustrated junior ministers of the wide belief that 'the present socialistic policy of the (UK) government must continue if not be intensified when peace comes'.[55]

Much of the dissatisfaction with Andrews' government stemmed from the continuing existence of unemployment at a time when there was a situation of labour shortage in the rest of the UK. When the war started there were 63,112 unemployed in Northern Ireland, 19.3 per cent of the insured population. The British unemployment figure was 8.3 per cent. By November 1940, while the British rate was 5.2 per cent, unemployment in the North had risen to 71,633, a rate of 21.3 per cent. The most important single factor in explaining this situation was one outside the government's control: the collapse of the linen industry because of the loss of its major sources of flax in Russia, the Baltic states, and Belgium as a result of the war. Unemployment in the industry, which employed 57,000 workers, one sixth of the insured population, increased from 11,261 at the outbreak of the war to reach 20,450 in November 1940.[56]

It was also the case that the lack of war contracts, about which the Belfast government complained, reflected a perception in the main supply departments that Northern Ireland suffered from higher production costs as a result of shortages of some types of skilled labour and from the extra transport costs involved for raw materials and finished products. Devolution itself had created major institutional impediments to an effective mobilization of the North's capital and labour resources. These were reflected in the administrative problems caused by the necessity of integrating the North's devolved structures with the new UK-wide system of regional Area Boards created by the Ministry of Supply. There was no direct liaison between the Ministries of Labour in Belfast and London and, as Harold Wilson, a young Board of Trade civil servant, noted, 'So far as can be seen there is little or no economic co-ordination between Great Britain and Northern Ireland. Ulster is not represented on the Production Council, the Labour Supply Board, the Economic Policy Committee or Industrial Capacity Committee.' Although Wilson criticized the failure of Whitehall departments and the UK government to do more to integrate Northern Ireland into the war effort, his main strictures were aimed at the conservatism of local management, the uncooperative attitude of trade unions, and the ineffectiveness of the Stormont administration. The result was, as he noted dispiritedly, that 'At the end of 15 months of war Ulster, so far from becoming an important centre of munitions production, has become a depressed area.'[57]

However, within months of Wilson's reports there was evidence that the unemployment problem was well on the way to being resolved. By the time of the Belfast blitz the unemployed total was reduced to 43,600, with a drop of over 40 per cent in male unemployment in the two previous months. Harland and Wolff, which had received less than its fair share of Admiralty contracts in the late 1930s,[58] was to make a significant contribution to wartime output not only building naval and merchant ships but also landing craft, tanks, anti-aircraft guns, and searchlights. Employment in the yard, which stood at 10,500 at the outbreak of war, had risen to 23,500 by March 1941[59] and reached a wartime peak of 30,800 in December 1944.[60] Short and Harland's aircraft factories, whose workforce stood at 6,000 in 1939, employed 11,319 by 1941,[61] producing Stirling bombers and Sunderland flying boats. The engineering industry was increasingly employed on a range of work from aircraft fuselage production to shells, bombs, and radar equipment. Linen's problems were lessened by contracts for parachutes, tents, and uniforms. As the military authorities embarked on the building of army and navy bases and aerodromes across the province, much of the surplus labour in agriculture and the building trades was quickly absorbed. Added to this were the 23,000 men who enlisted and the 28,000 workers who went to Britain in the first two years of the war.[62]

The decease in the unemployment figures did little to increase the government's popularity. This was in part because much of the new employment was the product of the broader British mobilization and critics claimed that things would have been even better but for the incompetent response of the local administration. Added to this was the increasingly hopeful if fractious atmosphere encouraged by the UK-wide shift to the left. Robert Graecan, one of the editors of the *Northman*, a new literary journal based in Belfast's Queen's University, described the 'thorough-going shake-up' that the war gave to such a conservative and inward-looking region:

Go into our cafes and pubs, workshops and recreation centres and hear them speak of social conditions, of plans for post-war economic and physical reconstruction, talk knowingly of the Beveridge Report, of Britain's relations with the Soviet Union . . . and of the clean, decent world we are all hoping and working for.[63]

Long accustomed to see itself as a delicate flower wilting in a environment parched by the flames of bourgeois philistinism, sectarian division, and provincial narrow-mindedness, the North's small literary intelligentsia was temporarily buoyed up with new, contrasting, and ultimately chimerical visions of the future. These ranged from the poet John Hewitt's idea of Ulster regionalism as a common source of pride for Catholics and Protestants to socialisms with conflicting republican and Commonwealth loyalties.[64]

However, whatever the limitations of this intellectual revival, its energy and optimism derived from the temporary dulling of the sectarian passions of the 1930s brought about by the material improvements and widening of horizons associated with the war. Even the Prime Minister was affected. Andrews, as President of the Ulster Unionist Labour Association, was critical of what he saw as Treasury sabotage of Northern Ireland's right to parity of public services with the rest of the UK. Although social conditions in housing, health, and education had improved during the inter-war period, they still lagged behind those of Britain as a whole.[65] As Andrews pointed out to his cabinet, in areas such as mortality rates for expectant mothers and infants, the gap had widened, something the NILP was concentrating on in its criticism of the government. To the dismay of Spender and the Treasury, the Prime Minister committed his government to an ambitious programme of post-war reconstruction. Responding to Treasury criticism that such a commitment went beyond Stormont's limited financial powers, Andrews explained to the Chancellor of the Exchequer that Northern Ireland could not be insulated from the British debate about the nature of post-war economic and social policy:

In numerous public utterances of responsible people the minds of our people have been directed more than ever before towards what is called a 'new order' or a 'fair deal', the 'scandal that poverty should exist' and the 'horrors associated with the slums'.[66]

Despite the horror that Andrews' approach provoked among some of his colleagues and a substantial sector of the Protestant middle class, he was successful in extracting a grudging acceptance from the Chancellor of the Exchequer that the North could incur extra expenditure to make up 'leeway': its backwardness in infrastructure and social provision.[67] A Post-War Planning Committee was created in July 1942 and although it was chaired by Brooke, who shared Spender's scepticism about Andrews' public commitments, it did mark the first faltering step in the government's initially reluctant acceptance of the welfare state. However, although the embrace of welfarism would be a crucial long-term factor in the strengthening of Unionist Party hegemony, it did little to shore up

Andrews' decrepit administration. In January 1943 Jack Beattie of the
NILP won the West Belfast seat at Westminster in a by-election with a 30
per cent slump in the Unionist vote[68] and in April 1943, despite the fact
that almost half the Unionist MPs at Stormont had government posts,
a rebellion of back-benchers and junior ministers forced Andrews'
resignation.

Class Conflict and Sectarianism

A significant factor in Unionist Party dissatisfaction with Andrews was
his perceived weakness in dealing with the increasing industrial
militancy that had affected Belfast from 1941. During the war Northern
Ireland provided 10 per cent of the British total of working days lost
through strikes while accounting for only 2 per cent of the UK's workforce.[69] Although some Unionists were prepared to blame this on subversive immigrants from the South, who allegedly flooded North to get
jobs in the expanding war industries, there is more solid evidence that
roots it in the recent industrial history of the region. Andrews' willingness to adopt a conciliatory approach to the workers reflected clear
evidence of rigid, authoritarian, and obstructive managerial attitudes,
particularly in the shipyards and the aircraft factories. These stimulated
the resurgence of a tradition of militancy that had lain dormant for two
decades.

During the Great War a powerful unofficial shop stewards' movement
had developed in Belfast's shipbuilding and engineering industries and
in the immediate post-war period the city had been convulsed by industrial militancy, culminating in a three-week general strike that shut down
the city in January 1919. Deepening unemployment and the sectarian
tensions associated with the intensifying conflict between the IRA and
the British state had allowed loyalist militants to refocus Protestant
working-class anger from employers to 'disloyalists' who were claimed
to have 'infiltrated' the North's industries, taking the jobs of loyalists
who had enlisted. The result was the mass workplace expulsions of
Catholics and socialists in July 1920 which severely weakened trade union
organization in the city. Two subsequent decades of heavy unemployment had resulted in a situation of cowed workers and employers used
to the exercise of unchallenged power. By the end of 1941 the war had
produced a radical shift in the industrial balance of power. Employers
and the official trade union movement had to come to terms with a new

shop stewards' movement which used the alliance with the Soviet Union and the demands of industrial mobilization to carve out a role for itself in joint production committees, which the government encouraged as a way of maximizing production.[70]

For many workers, attitudes to the domestic war effort were coloured by memories of inter-war insecurity and hostility and distrust towards foremen and management. Ministers and officials in London complained of a lack of co-operation and goodwill, which seemed endemic in Northern Ireland's industrial relations. Harland and Wolff's productivity was lower than that of any British yard and absenteeism was twice as high as that in the worst yards in the UK. A British official who visited Short and Harland's plants in late 1942 estimated that the firm was working at a mere 65 per cent efficiency and complained that 'any amount of people are drawing pay for loafing about'. The firm had an unenviable record for strikes and it has been suggested that there and elsewhere industrial relations problems stemmed from the rapid recruitment 'from all and sundry', which allowed 'disloyal elements' to 'infiltrate' the workforce.[71] However, despite tight RUC surveillance of industrial militants it was difficult to find suitable subversives. As a senior Stormont official explained to London about one major strike at Short and Harland, 'It is led by agitators whose motivation is sometimes doubtful though we cannot obtain proof of their subversive intention.'[72]

Part of the government's problem in finding scapegoats for the strikes was that many of those who would traditionally have been seen as subversives were members of the Communist Party. After the invasion of the USSR it shifted from an anti-war position that had led to the jailing of some of its leading members and became the most vociferous champion of the subordination of sectional interests to the war effort. By 1943 the party had 1,000 members, the vast majority Protestant workers in key industries.[73] Andrews, who had helped found the Ulster Unionist Labour Association in 1918 to attack 'Bolshevist' influence in the Belfast labour movement, now publicly praised 'our gallant Russian allies who are fighting with such wonderful bravery in the common cause of freedom'.[74] Communists, who were active in the shop stewards' movement, did all they could in order to prevent strikes and denounced those that did take place.[75]

The government was also aware that workers had genuine grievances. Andrews explained to the Cabinet Committee on Manpower that the trade unions in Harland and Wolff had pointed out that the best way to deal with absenteeism at the shipyards was to do something about the primitive welfare facilities, particularly the lack of workers' canteens.[76] Management dismissal of any role for unions in schemes for improving productivity was common. The main cause of militancy was the use made by management of the wartime legal framework outlawing strikes. The Conditions of Employment and National Arbitration Order, introduced throughout the UK in August 1940, prohibited strikes and lockouts and created a National Arbitration Tribunal to deal with disputes. Workers and unions found the arbitration machinery excessively slow and the result was a temptation to unilateral action. However, in Northern Ireland, employers, the police, and the judiciary showed a markedly more repressive response to such action than their counterparts in the rest of the UK. Thus during the first two years the Order was in place 2,068 workers were prosecuted in Britain while in Northern Ireland the figure was 2,271.[77]

As the war increased the power of labour, with trade union membership rising from 114,000 in 1941 to 147,000 in 1945,[78] tensions developed within Unionism between the government and the party's need to maintain harmonious relations among the main social classes in the Protestant community and the complaints of an industrial bourgeoisie and provincial middle class that was increasingly obsessed with the government's alleged capitulation to 'socialistic' trends imported from the rest of the UK. It is these tensions that contributed powerfully to the dissatisfaction with Andrews. Brooke was dismayed at Andrews' approach to industrial unrest. The Prime Minister intervened to have fines imposed on workers for strike action reduced despite the opposition of Brooke and Dawson Bates.[79] When the management of Short and Harland provoked a mass strike in October 1942 by sacking two shop stewards, Brooke was in favour of a hardline response but Andrews chose a more emollient approach by setting up a court of inquiry, which, although it criticized the shop stewards, supported their reinstatement.[80] Churchill and Herbert Morrison, the Home Secretary, were critical of what they saw as a dangerous concession to an illegal strike[81] but Andrews continued to exasperate London and infuriate Ulster's business class by refusing to use troops to move goods and raw materials from the Belfast docks during a carters' strike in March 1943.[82] Within a month Andrews had gone but if the middle class hoped for a hardening of approach from his successor they were to be disappointed.

Brooke came to the premiership as a champion of industrial discipline but he was soon forced to take a broader and more politicized view of industrial relations. In March 1944 a strike of engineers at Harland

and Wolff for increased pay was supported by a sympathy action at Short and Harlands. Despite instructions from union leaders in London to return to work, over 14,000 workers remained out for three weeks, severely disrupting essential war work and eventually the government had five leading shop stewards arrested. When the stewards were sentenced to three months' imprisonment, the industrial action spread to include dockers, who closed the port of Belfast.[83] Brooke had tried to persuade Churchill to treat the dispute exceptionally by having the wage claim dealt with quickly but had received no support from London.[84] Only Brooke's direct intervention to persuade the shop stewards that if they accepted bail an appeal would be assured of a sympathetic hearing, together with employers' offer of a pay rise, succeeded in getting the men back to work.[85]

The strike had also seen evidence of the way in which the government attempted to dissipate class tensions within the Protestant community by blaming unrest on those who wanted to exploit grievances to advance anti-partitionism. During the strike the RUC had visited the homes of leading shop stewards to find out, according to William Lowry, the Minister of Home Affairs, whether the shop stewards' movement 'was made up almost exclusively of Roman Catholics who were natives of Eire'.[86] Here Brooke's administration carried on with one of the most inglorious aspects of Andrews' legacy of Protestant populism. Concern with 'Eirean infiltration' had been a major concern of Andrews' government since the beginning of 1942 when some of its loyalist critics accused it of importing southern workers when northerners were still unemployed. The expansion of the North's industries in 1941 had acted as a magnet for the 7,000 Irish citizens who crossed the border that year. Of these about 900 had been brought north by the Ministry of Labour to fill skilled jobs in engineering, shipbuilding, and the construction industry for which there were no suitable local workers. Accused by the Independent Unionist MP for the Shankill Road that his government was 'importing Fifth Columnists', Andrews immediately created a cabinet subcommittee to investigate the problem of 'infiltration' from Éire.[87]

The investigation concluded that there was no economic threat to northern workers as most of the imported workers did work for which there was no adequate supply of local labour and also that the temporary nature of their employment meant that they would be unable to qualify for unemployment benefit, which required residence for five years. It also dismissed any danger to security as 'greatly exaggerated' and concluded that no special measures were necessary.[88] Despite this, Andrews' desire to deflect ultra-loyalist criticisms and Dawson Bates' obsessive concerns with republican threats to the war effort ensured that this was not the last word on the matter.

Bates, with Andrews' support, approached Herbert Morrison in March 1942 asking for new powers to control movement from the South. He focused on recent police raids that had produced evidence of IRA preparations for a renewed campaign.[89] The IRA's various violent manifestations on Easter Sunday, including the killing of Constable Williams, may have lessened any doubts harboured at Westminster about the proposed legislation. Under the 'Residence in Northern Ireland Restriction Order' introduced at Westmister in October 1942, all British subjects (a category into which, despite de Valera's new constitution, the Irish still fitted) not normally resident in Northern Ireland on 1 January 1940 were required to obtain a permit from the Ministry of Home Affairs if they wished to stay in Northern Ireland for longer than six weeks. Permits were to be issued where the person was needed to fill a job vacancy for which there was no suitable local candidate.[90]

The existence of the new legislation simply intensified pressure on the government to be seen to defend the employment prospects of Protestants no matter how unsuitable or badly qualified they were for the needs of the wartime economy. Even Andrews' administration was prepared, on occasion, to withstand this pressure in the interests of the war effort. The cabinet supported the Minister of Labour when he permitted the importation of skilled quarry workers from the South who were urgently needed to produce the stone for building bases and air fields. But as he pointed out, 'there will be protests against bringing men from Eire while there are still unemployed men on our register, no matter how unfit or unsuitable such unemployed men might be.' The cabinet decided that in this case the needs of the war effort should come before the defence of Protestant interests, particularly when it was pointed out to them that the local representatives of the British and American armed forces might inform their superiors that the government was putting narrow political interests before the anti-fascist struggle.[91]

Brooke, for all his criticisms of Andrews' failure to respond effectively to the demands of total war, showed himself only too willing to bring the most parochial sectarian grievances to the cabinet table. A complaint to the Prime Minister from a county Fermanagh Unionist about a Ministry of Agriculture veterinary inspector who was a southerner was brought to cabinet despite the fact the Permanent Secretary of the Ministry of

Agriculture had defended the appointment, pointing out that the man was a distinguished graduate of University College Cork with exceptionally good qualifications in dairy science, which were much superior to those of northern candidates.[92]

However, although the permits legislation demonstrated the degree to which even the cataclysm of world war could not displace the primacy of parochial sectarian concerns for many Unionists, its actual application showed that the government was not always a simple creature of the demands of its supporters. Between the introduction of the legislation and September 1946, permits were granted to 36,447 Éire citizens and 21,881 to workers from the rest of the UK. Permits were refused to 18 per cent of Éire applicants compared to only 2 per cent of non-Éire applicants.[93] Brooke's strategy was to control grass-roots pressure by its controlled indulgence. Thus the champions of a loyalist labour policy were apparently indulged while the demand of Protestant employers and farmers for badly needed labour from the South were largely satisfied and the female members of the Protestant middle class were not denied access to their traditional source of maids and kitchen staff.

By 1944 the problem of unemployment had disappeared but the cabinet was increasingly concerned with the spectre of a post-war crisis brought about by economic readjustment, the return of Protestants from the forces, and an influx of southerners attracted by the new benefits of the welfare state. Ironically, the minister most perturbed by apocalyptic visions of a post-war invasion was Harry Midgley, the ex-NILP firebrand. He had resigned from the Labour Party in 1942 because he claimed it was increasingly dominated by anti-partitionists; he and his supporters set up a Commonwealth Labour Party. When Brooke formed his first government, he attempted to give it a more progressive tone by bringing in Midgley as Minister of Public Security. However, the deep reservations that many members of the Unionist Party had about the Beveridge Report were also reflected in substantial opposition to Midgley's role in government. His increasing fixation with the imminent deluge of southerners was an attempt to establish his loyalist credentials. However, by his exaggerated focus on the magnetic influence that the Beveridge proposals would have on citizens of Éire, he unintentionally stiffened the resistance of a substantial sector of the party to Stormont adopting the welfare state. The rejection of Beveridge on a class basis was amplified by fears of loss of ethnic dominance. The result was that the government fought the 1945 election on a strong anti-socialist platform, although it also stated that it would introduce whatever social reforms were brought in the rest of the UK. This contradictory message contributed to a substantial Protestant working-class vote for the NILP and other left-of-centre parties. Labour parties of various shades won 32 per cent of the total Northern Ireland vote and five seats, while in the Belfast constituencies the 'non-Nationalist left', which included the NILP, the Commonwealth Labour Party, and the Communist Party, won 40 per cent of the vote to the Unionists' 50 per cent.[94] While the electoral system ensured that the NILP won only two seats, the vote for the left helped to convince Brooke that his government had to embrace the welfare state no matter how much this enraged many of the region's middle class.

3

'Minding Our Own Business':
Éire during the Emergency

Defending Neutrality

De Valera, combining the positions of Taoiseach and Minister of External Affairs, proved skilled in exploiting the domestic political advantages of international developments. Dublin's relations with London and Belfast were inevitably affected by the deteriorating international situation during the 1930s. De Valera used Irish membership of the League of Nations to portray Ireland as the vanguard of small nations threatened by the rapacious designs of bigger states and to provide a moral justification for Irish neutrality in any future world conflict. Neutrality during a major conflict in which Great Britain was involved was also a resounding statement of Irish independence and sovereignty, albeit in a truncated twenty-six-county form. Even before the return of the Treaty ports de Valera made it clear that neutrality would be his government's policy and that this would be the case even in the event of an end of partition. He also tried to reassure the British by asserting that he would resist any attempt by Germany to use Irish territory as a base for attacking Britain.[1]

The favourable terms of the 1938 Agreement and, above all, the return of the ports, which made neutrality feasible, were major ingredients in Fianna Fáil's electoral victory in 1938 with 52 per cent of the vote and seventy-seven seats. Increasingly the party portrayed itself as the only effective guarantee of Éire's insulation from the horrors of war. Fine Gael was disorientated by de Valera's success in ending the economic war and in persuading the British to respect neutrality. Its support, which had picked up as the economic war began to bite, slumped seriously after the 1938 Agreement from 33 per cent and forty-five seats in that year's election to 20 per cent and thirty seats in 1944.[2]

De Valera was well aware of the formidable pressures that he would be under in the event of war and had been a strong supporter of Neville Chamberlain's appeasement policies, praising the Prime Minister's

Munich Agreement as 'the highest peak of human greatness'.[3] However, Hitler's occupation of Prague in March 1939 finally dispatched any lingering illusions that appeasement could contain Berlin's expansionist appetites and posed an unprecedented challenge to the very existence of the southern state. Although the return of the ports made neutrality possible, it by no means ensured that it could be successfully maintained. Dr Eduard Hempel, the German minister in Dublin, reported to Berlin in June 1939 that it was improbable that neutrality could survive an Anglo-German war and there was at least one cabinet minister who privately doubted the possibility of a continuing policy of neutrality.[4] De Valera had admitted the fragility of the policy when he had accepted that Ireland's role as an important supplier of food to the British market could lead, in the event of war between Britain and Germany, to attacks on Irish ports to destroy this trade and that 'if we were attacked our forces would be combined with the British forces for the defence of Ireland'.[5]

The decision to return the Treaty ports had reflected Chamberlain's belief that, whatever their strategic value to Britain in wartime, this would be negated by the southern state's lack of goodwill. Although the chiefs of staff supported the decision to return the ports, they did point out that in the event of a war with Germany, the non-availability of the Irish ports would seriously hamper naval operations.[6] They were also aware that the Irish state simply lacked the military capacity to defend its neutrality. When the war broke out the country was almost defenceless with an army of just 7,000 poorly equipped regulars, which, with reserves, provided a force of 20,000 upon mobilization.[7] The new Irish Marine Service, established in November 1939 to defend Irish territorial waters, consisted of two ex-fisheries patrol boats with six motor torpedo boats on order from Britain,[8] while the Air Corps was incapable of policing the skies over Dublin, let alone the country as a whole.[9]

The day after Germany invaded Poland on 2 September 1939, the Dáil met to amend the constitution to allow a State of Emergency to be declared for the duration of hostilities. De Valera made reference at this meeting to those who mistakenly thought that it would be sufficient for neutrality to be declared for it to become a reality, while in fact it would need national determination to protect it 'at every stage'.[10] Yet during the 'phoney war' the conservative priorities of the Department of Finance ensured that even the meagre forces available in September 1939 were reduced and it took the German invasion of the Low Countries on 10 May 1940 to force the government to approve plans for an expansion of the army to 40,000 and the launch of a national recruiting drive in June.[11] After an initial surge of recruitment, spurred by a widespread but temporary fear of invasion, the Irish army experienced great difficulty in reaching its target wartime strength. This reflected its low levels of pay, which compared unfavourably with those of the British armed forces and also with wages available for Irish labour in the factories, shipyards, and building sites of Northern Ireland and Great Britain. As a result desertion was common.[12] It was not until the spring of 1943 that the Chief of Staff could report that his troops had passed from the stage of barrack-square training to being an 'effective and mobile field force'.[13] Even then the army lacked the most basic forms of equipment to support its role: it had almost no anti-aircraft defences, no armour worth the name, and was desperately short of artillery, anti-aircraft weapons, transport, and munitions. Given this situation the British intelligence estimate, made during the period of maximum German threat between the fall of France in May 1940 and the German attack on Russia in June 1941, that the Irish army could have offered some form of organized resistance for between a week and ten days, was perhaps over-optimistic.[14]

The real defenders of Irish neutrality against a threat from Germany were the Royal Navy and the British forces in Northern Ireland, who would have been expected to cross the border to expel any invaders from the Third Reich. The officials of the Department of Finance had used this reality in their resistance to demands for increased defence spending in the late 1930s. What Professor Joe Lee refers to as the state's 'astonishing achievement' in reducing public expenditure as a proportion of gross domestic product between 1939 and 1945 indicates that the real burden of defending neutrality fell on the shoulders of the British.[15]

De Valera, the Nazis, and the IRA

De Valera displayed considerable political skill in responding to the conflicting pressures from London and Berlin and in presenting what was a British-biased neutrality as an even-handed assertion of Irish independence and self-respect. Part of his success in this was due to the covert nature of the arrangements on intelligence and military co-operation with the UK. The Irish government was acutely aware of the danger of German exploitation of IRA activity against Northern Ireland or of a possible campaign in Britain. It was also under pressure from London because of British fears that 'fifth column' activities would be unchecked by the Irish security services.[16] The activities of a small group of German expatriates who were active Nazis had begun to concern Irish military intelligence in the late 1930s. The new state's desire to develop its indigenous resources, economic and cultural, had created openings for a small but significant influx of Germans. In 1926 a contract for the construction of the hydroelectric scheme on the River Shannon was given to the German firm of Siemens-Schuckert, which brought in a number of engineers and technicians, some of whom married and settled in Ireland. In 1938 the director of Siemens-Schuckert was one of the main Nazis in Dublin. German prominence in the fields of the archaeology and language of Celtic Ireland had also provided a bridgehead between the two countries and the leading Nazi in Dublin, Dr Adolph Mahr, was the Director of the National Museum.[17] A German who acted as an adviser to the Turf Development Board also functioned as a Nazi intelligence agent, travelling the country and photographing railway stations, river bridges, and reservoirs.[18] The most bizarre case was the German who headed the Irish army's School of Music and who had sought permission from the Chief of Staff to set up a branch of the Nazi Party in Dublin.[19]

Shortly after the 1938 Agreement, and to give practical effect to his promises that Éire would not be a base for hostile activity against Britain, de Valera sent to London officers from the Irish army and Joe Walshe, Secretary of the Department of External Affairs, to discuss defence and intelligence co-operation with the British. One result was that MI5 was asked to assist in the formation of a new Irish counter-espionage service within the Irish army. By the outbreak of war the two intelligence services were in regular correspondence on the activities of German agents, Irish Nazi sympathizers, and IRA–German collaboration. Walshe was an admirer of Mussolini and when the war began he favoured an Axis victory.[20] For him co-operation with the British intelligence services served to quieten concern in London about the security threat of German intelligence operations in Ireland and lessen the possibility of a British invasion. However, the British, who had reservations about the capacity of the Irish counter-espionage service, were ultimately more impressed by the ruthlessness of de Valera's response to the IRA threat.

Although many IRA men had been won over to Fianna Fáil since 1932, through a mixture of patronage and de Valera's success in convincing them that he could achieve the destruction of the Treaty settlement non-violently, a sizeable rump remained. Under the leadership of the resolute militarist Seán Russell, the IRA declared war on Britain in January

1939 and launched a bombing campaign in British cities that was to claim seven dead and almost 200 wounded by the end of the year. The leadership of the IRA was eager to enlist German assistance, deluding themselves that a victorious Nazism would respect Ireland's independence. Using the novelist Francis Stuart as an emissary, the IRA had opened up contacts with the *Abwehr*, the military-controlled German foreign intelligence service.[21] Although the dominant German policy towards Ireland was to ensure that its neutrality was preserved, twelve *Abwehr* agents did land in Éire between 1939 and 1943 aiming to make contact with the IRA and develop plans for joint action in the North.[22]

De Valera's response to this direct threat to his pledge that the territory of his state would not be used as a base for attacks against Britain was swift. The Offences Against the State Act, introduced in June 1939, allowed for the creation of special courts and increasing police powers to search, arrest, and detain.[23] However, when a number of imprisoned IRA men went on hunger strike, de Valera was reluctant to allow them to die, especially as one was a veteran of the 1916 Rising. Six were released, despite the misgivings of his Minister of Justice, Gerry Boland, whom de Valera had appointed on the outbreak of war precisely because he was both tough and loyal.[24]

The IRA's response to this concession was an audacious raid on the Irish army's ammunition stores in the Magazine Fort in Dublin's Phoenix Park, which removed explosives and over one million rounds of ammunition. Although the bulk of the material was recovered, the raid marked the end of any tendency to concession. An amendment to the Emergency Powers Act in January 1940 allowed the introduction of internment without trial. Over 500 were interned and another 600 committed under the Offences Against the State Act during the war years.[25] With the IRA writing to newspapers, claiming grandiloquently that the 'Government of the Republic' would no longer tolerate censorship of its activities by de Valera's government, the public position of the government was expressed by Seán MacEntee, who warned the IRA that 'in a continental state such criminals would have a speedy court-martial and an equally expeditious execution'.[26] Service on the republican side during the revolutionary period would no longer be an insurance, as the government displayed a ruthlessness which it denounced when the British and Northern Ireland authorities executed IRA men.

One particularly stark example was George Plant, executed in March 1942 for the killing of an alleged IRA informer. He had fought during the War of Independence, then on the anti-Treaty side during the Civil War, and while on the run had emigrated to the United States. He did not return to Ireland until 1940 and, as his defence put it, 'His prolonged absence from the country did not enable him to appraise the change of circumstances.' Many in Fianna Fáil, remembering their own recent past, were profoundly uneasy about the action taken against men like Plant.[27] Seán Lemass, who was close to breaking with the government on the issue, was reminded by his mother that Plant and others were doing precisely what he and others had done a quarter of a century earlier.[28]

Nevertheless, despite such conscience wrestling and criticism from the grass-roots of the party, the government maintained unity. When the Special Criminal Court discharged Plant because the only evidence against him was that of retracted statements by the two other IRA men accused of the murder, he was re-arrested and tried by a military court, which sentenced him to death. Five other IRA men were executed during the war and another three were allowed to die on hunger strike. Despite the overt political conflict between the two Irish states, there was also covert co-operation against the IRA threat. A link between the RUC and the Garda was established soon after the outbreak of the war to exchange intelligence on IRA activities.[29] Little wonder that when the IRA took over a broadcasting station in Cork in April 1940, the core of its address to the populace was a denunciation of de Valera as 'Judas'.[30]

The good relations between the British and Irish intelligence services were an important element in a range of Irish activities that gave the operation of neutrality a degree of bias towards the Allies. These included the exchange of meteorological information; the relaying to the British of information gathered by the Irish coast-watching service on German planes, ships, and submarines in or near Irish territory and waters; permission for the over-flying of Irish airspace in northern Donegal by Allied aircraft for easier access to the Atlantic; and close co-operation between the military authorities North and South.[31]

These forms of covert co-operation led Maurice Moynihan, Secretary to de Valera's cabinet, to exclaim in May 1941, 'We could not do more if we were in the war.'[32] A British intelligence analysis of the impact of neutrality on the war effort tended to support Moynihan's view. Acknowledging the shipping losses incurred because of the lack of access to southern Irish ports, it argued that neutral Ireland was still of more value than a belligerent Ireland would have been. If Ireland had entered the war on the Allied side, the resultant conscription would have denied the British war effort the Irish servicemen and workers who did in fact cross the border or the Irish Sea. At the same time, given that a belligerent Ireland was judged not to be in a position to defend itself against a German attack, Britain would have had to supply its new ally with arms and men, both of which were scarce.[33]

Over 45,000 southern Irish men and women volunteered for the British forces during the war, compared to about 44,000 from the North. Even more important, however, were the 120,000 who went to work in Britain and Northern Ireland:

So great was the need for this Irish labour before and during the Battle of Britain in 1940 that without it the airdromes, so desperately needed, could not have been built, and great as the need for Irish labour was then, it increased throughout the war as the calls on our manpower became great.[34]

This relatively benign assessment of neutrality, written with the benefit of hindsight, should not be allowed to obscure the fact that in the period of maximum German threat, after the fall of Norway and Denmark and the attack on the Low Countries, there was deep concern in British government circles about Dublin's stance. It was reflected in Churchill's assertion in November 1940 that the denial of the ports was 'a most heavy and grievous burden . . . which should never have been placed on our shoulders'.[35] Denial of the ports to the Royal Navy, which reduced significantly its capacity to provide convoy protection, was reckoned by the Admiralty to have cost 368 ships and 5,070 lives during the war.[36]

Such calculations challenge what the Cork-based historian Geoffrey Roberts has called 'the pragmatic pro-neutrality narrative', which still dominates academic and popular approaches to the issue in the Republic. According to this narrative, neutrality was a necessary policy, which benefited Ireland and the Allies alike.[37] But as Roberts points out, during the early phase of the war, when it looked as if Germany might win, Irish co-operation with Britain was curtailed. Moreover, the secret contributions of the Irish state were far outweighed by the tens of thousands of Irish men and women who on their own initiative volunteered for service in the British forces or became war workers in Britain. The Irish state's role here was one of turning a blind eye to Irish military volunteers and actively facilitating the mass migration of Irish labour, which, if it had remained at home, might have presented major social and political problems.[38]

Neutrality and Partition

It has been argued that the continuing strength of anti-British feeling in the political culture of the South made the neutrality policy the only conceivable one.[39] At the time, even liberal Unionists in the North tended to see de Valera's options as strongly constrained by the effect of his party's strident anglophobia and irredentism in the period since 1932.[40] Sir John Maffey, the UK Representative in Dublin, noted 'It is remarkable how even the "pro-British" group, men who have fought for the Crown and are anxious to be called up again . . . agree generally in supporting the policy of neutrality for Eire.'[41] The main opposition parties found it difficult to avoid tail-ending Fianna Fáil views of neutrality and security issues. De Valera created a consultative Conference on Defence in May 1940 in which Fine Gael and Labour had representatives. Although in fact consultation was minimal, it very effectively neutered the opposition for the duration of the Emergency.[42]

On 16 June, for the first time since the Civil War, before an enormous crowd in the centre of Dublin, the leaders of all three parties stood together on a joint platform to launch a national recruiting campaign for the army and a new part-time Local Security Force. By 1941 this had 100,000 members and the Irish correspondent of the pro-Commonwealth *Round Table* noted the unifying effects of the campaign to defend neutrality: 'Men who fought on opposite sides in the Civil War are now drilling and working together. British veterans of 1914 are serving in the local security force side by side with men who fought against the British.'[43] The fact that James Dillon, the deputy leader of Fine Gael, was forced to resign from the party in February 1942 for arguing in the aftermath of the Japanese attack on Pearl Harbor that Ireland should, on moral grounds, ally itself with America,[44] has encouraged the view that there was no alternative.

Yet, in the summer of 1940 when the German threat to both Ireland and Britain was at its height and there was a real sense of fear and panic in official circles in Dublin, the leaders of Fine Gael urged de Valera to abandon neutrality in return for British action on partition. On 10 May Germany invaded the Low Countries and on 16 May de Valera had a meeting with Sir John Maffey, at which he asked for Britain's assistance in the event of a German invasion.[45] The arrest in Dublin of an Irishman of German extraction who had been one of the IRA's go-betweens with Germany and in whose house was found a large amount of money, maps, and other equipment belonging to a recently arrived German agent, increased Irish apprehension about Hitler's intentions. It encouraged an intensification of the process of constructing a covert set of intelligence and security arrangements with the British. De Valera's emissaries to London, whilst their offers of covert co-operation with the British war effort were positively received, had major problems persuading the British that arms and equipment should be provided to the Irish army but that there could be no question of British troops being invited into Ireland until the Irish themselves had begun to resist the invaders.[46]

London's doubts about the military capacity of the Irish state, which were probably not assuaged by de Valera's boast that they were 'very good hedge fighters',[47] were shared by leading members of the main opposition party. Soon after the withdrawal of Allied forces from Dunkirk, de Valera received a Fine Gael memorandum that argued that the only way of preventing a German invasion was to provide a unified defence command for the whole island and invite in French and British troops. Aware of the danger of a nationalist backlash against such a decision, it suggested that the 'logical consequence' of the cross-border defence arrangements would be the 'subsequent impossibility of survival for the anachronism of Northern Ireland'.[48]

The Fine Gael approach was to be echoed in the British proposals that Neville Chamberlain's emissary, Malcolm MacDonald, discussed with de Valera in Dublin in the third week of June. The offer envisaged the South immediately joining the Allies and the setting up of an all-Ireland Defence Council in return for an immediate British declaration of acceptance of the principle of a united Ireland and the creation of a North–South body to work out the practical details of such a union.[49] De Valera's rejection of the proposal, which centred on his scepticism about the ability of any British government to deliver Unionist acquiescence, has tended to be accepted as the only feasible response in the circumstances.[50] Certainly the vehemence of Craig's reaction when he was provided with the details of the British offer indicated a central difficulty with the British proposal.

Yet the Unionist position in June 1940 was more vulnerable than at any time since 1921. Craig's own leadership at such a time of crisis was itself increasingly subject to internal party criticism because of the regime's lack of preparedness for the challenge of wartime mobilization. The Unionist leadership was open to the charge of putting a narrow sectarian 'little Ulsterism' before the interests of not just the British Empire but also 'Christian civilization' threatened by Nazi barbarism.

Basil Brooke's subsequent recollection of the period highlighted the fear that they would be faced with an agonizing choice: 'I had an awful feeling that had we refused we would have been blamed for whatever disasters ensued.' Brooke's son claimed that at the time his father had told him that faced with the choice between 'western civilization' and Irish unification, he would have to accept the latter.[51]

There is also some evidence that public opinion in the South was less of a potential obstacle to an alliance with Britain than has been asserted. The British intelligence evaluation was that the return of the ports had increased good will towards Britain but that the attitude of the average Irishman was 'of indifference to either side, except in so far as the acts of either belligerent might affect his own or Irish interests generally'.[52] In a context in which a move to end neutrality was linked to a British commitment to unity, it might not have been beyond de Valera's considerable political skills to carry a majority of the southern electorate with him. Even the semi-official biography of de Valera notes that in those circumstances 'the whole atmosphere would have been so completely transformed that one can only speculate as to what path Ireland would or would not have chosen.'[53] However, although there is some evidence to suggest that in the summer of 1940 the country would have split two-thirds to one-third in favour of participation on Britain's side, anti-British sentiment would have been much stronger within the ruling party. James Dillon, the lone figure in the Dáil who would by the end of 1941 openly reject neutrality, did not think that de Valera had a choice in June 1940, given that he would have split his party if he had jettisoned neutrality.[54]

The Unionist leadership was saved from having to consider such an excruciating choice by de Valera's clear preference for defending the integrity of the existing twenty-six-county state and the unity of Fianna Fáil over what might have been a historic opportunity to undermine partition. W. T. Cosgrave, the leader of Fine Gael, was wasting his time when, after de Valera's rejection of the British proposals, he continued to press privately for entry to the war on Britain's side using the prize of unity to attract the Fianna Fáil leader.[55] In fact, de Valera's own pronouncements on the issue had made it clear that the territorial completion of the national revolution would always take second place to the imperative of maintaining as broad a coalition of 'national' forces and sentiment behind Fianna Fáil. Just as any trade concessions to northern manufacturers in 1938 had been ruled out by a combination of southern economic interests and Fianna Fáil fundamentalists, de Valera had, in a memorable speech in the Senate in February 1939, made it clear that he would not accept unity at the price of the project of restoring the Irish language.[56] Those in London or among the Opposition in the Dáil who saw in the offer of unity, even if it had been more of a realistic possibility, a chance of ending neutrality, misunderstood the deeply partitionist dynamics of Fianna Fáil rule.

Another important factor behind support for neutrality in 1940 was the widespread belief that Britain was going to lose the war, something that was not an unwelcome prospect to some. Hempel, the German minister in Dublin, reported to Berlin that his discussions with Joseph Walshe and Frederick Boland of the Department of External Affairs showed an Irish government concerned to ensure that in the event of Britain's defeat, Germany would support 'an entirely independent united Irish state', displaying a wilful blindness to the record of Nazi treatment of small neutral countries on the continent.[57] Walshe's pro-German position—he declared to David Gray, the US envoy in Dublin, that 'no-one outside of Great Britain believed that Great Britain was fighting for something worthwhile'[58]—was shared by the leader of Ireland's Catholics, Cardinal MacRory, Archbishop of Armagh. A north-erner who saw partition as placing Britain on the same moral level as Nazism, he was believed by the Germans to favour an invasion to end partition.[59] In October 1941 he publicly supported the idea of a negoti-ated peace.[60] Such opinion was probably more extreme than that of most cabinet ministers and senior civil servants. However, although de Valera's own inclinations were in favour of an Allied victory,[61] the rigor-ous censorship regime did little to challenge the world-view of those who dismissed the war as a manifestation of inter-imperialist rivalry in which partition made Britain morally equivalent to the Nazis.

Such views were widespread at both élite and mass level. The *Round Table*'s pro-Allied Irish correspondent described public opinion as not pro-German 'but by no means enthusiastically pro-British . . . the popu-lar view may perhaps be best summed up in the words of one old farmer, who on being asked to express his views on the war said "I hope England will be nearly beat".'[62] Arrland Usher, a southern Protestant who favoured neutrality, claimed that most southerners either took no inter-est in the war or had a 'detached and comfortable interest which one might take in a serial "thriller"'. His description of the views of 'most educated Irishmen' indicated an attitude of insular superiority: 'England they would tell you was a "liberal" or secularist state, Germany was a "pagan" state and there was no great difference between them.'[63]

Frank Aiken, as Minister for the Co-ordination of Defensive Measures, had responsibility for censorship. From Armagh, Commander of the Fourth Northern Division of the IRA at the time of the Treaty and Chief of Staff of the anti-Treaty IRA at the end of the Civil War, he was considered, even by some of his own colleagues, to be a bigot as well as deeply anti-British.[64] His rigidity had led to his being shifted from the Ministry of Defence in 1939. In his new ministry he did all within his considerable powers to ensure that the coverage of the war excluded any hint of a moral preference or any news of the nature of the Nazi regime that would trouble those who treated it as little worse than the 'Stormont dictatorship'. At times it appeared that Aiken was prepared to allow pro-Nazi propaganda. Thus the *Dundalk Examiner*, of which he was a shareholder, was permitted to publish an editorial praising the Nazi organization as 'the natural protector of the Catholic Church', while statements critical of the Nazis for the persecution of Catholics in Germany and Poland made by the Bishop of Münster and the Irish Bishop of Achonry were censored.[65] Aiken ensured that the sufferings of Stalingrad's population were kept from the pages of Ireland's newspapers for fear of eliciting pro-Soviet sentiment. Reports of atrocities from German-occupied Europe, starting with the first stories of Gestapo executions of 'mental defectives' and mass executions of Polish Jews in early 1941, were stopped. This was justified by Aiken on the grounds of the use of atrocity stories by Allied propaganda in the First World War and by his contention that the Soviet record was as bad as that of the Nazis.[66]

The leaders of Fine Gael and Irish Labour shared such sentiments. When Dillon spoke in the Dáil in favour of the unity of 'all Christian men' to repel the Nazi threat, his leader William Cosgrave repudiated his views, claiming that 'the British were not thinking of the Ten Commandments'.[67] Labour's William Norton berated Dillon for his pro-Allied line: 'when the propaganda machines of the belligerents were working overtime to mislead the people of the world it was good Irish policy to mind our own business.'[68] They thus contributed to the high moral tone of neutrality and unintentionally to de Valera's political dominance as the policy's champion. To forsake neutrality risked a major domestic convulsion that would have damaged Fianna Fáil more than Fine Gael. This may help explain the fact that even after the US entered the war, and the chances of a German invasion receded with other neutral states adopting pro-Allied shifts in policy, Ireland maintained the policy unaltered.[69] A sense of Irish superiority to two sets of morally equivalent belligerents, while it might have provided a source of psychological support for de Valera's neutrality policy, would contribute powerfully to the state's international isolation at the end of the war as well as deepening the sense of embittered alienation from the South amongst northern Unionists. The moral myopia associated with the state's promotion of neutrality was most flagrantly exposed in de Valera's infamous visit to the German Ambassador in Dublin to present his condolences on the death of Hitler.

Much of the recent discussion on neutrality has tended to reject the harsh judgement of Professor Leland Lyons, who used the metaphor of Plato's cave to suggest that during the Emergency the Irish relegated themselves to a shadow world.[70] A recent account of Irish culture during the period has dismissed the allegation that the South remained 'insularly indifferent to the war and uninformed or incurious about its course'.[71] Yet the author, who was a schoolboy in Wexford during the war, relates that he was only able to follow the North African campaign and the battle of Stalingrad by listening to the BBC.

A similar defence of neutrality was made during the war by Sean O'Faolain, the novelist and commentator who in the 1940s provided an outlet for dissent and social criticism as editor of *The Bell*. Responding to charges from, amongst others, the American historian Henry Steele Commager that de Valera and the Irish people were ignorant of the war and blind to the moral issue at stake, he defended the Irish against the charge of ignorance by referring to 'British and American radio, news services, newspapers, periodicals and books', which were all available in Ireland.[72] The problem with this argument was that the critics were focusing, not on the reality of everyday life in Ireland, where it was indeed possible to find out about the war from external sources, but on the official policies of the Irish state, where censorship led to such absurdities as the banning of the import of a book on the persecution of the Catholic Church under the Third Reich.[73]

O'Faolain, who would not tolerate British or American critics of neutrality, did on other occasions lament the effects: 'Our people, are, it would seem, self-absorbed to an amazing degree, so self-absorbed as to be cut off, in a way that one would hardly have thought possible in this modern world of constant inter-communication, from all detachment, critical sense, a sense of proportion and even a sense of humour.'[74] Neutrality from this perspective encouraged the most self-satisfied and parochial elements of Irish society and would pose a major problem of adjustment when the state wished to reintegrate itself into a wider world when the war ended. It also deepened the division on the island and made the ending of partition even more unlikely than it appeared in 1939. As O'Faolain put it, the different relation to the war North and South 'must increase the gap beyond bridging by creating two completely discordant modes of life'.[75] MI5's assessment of neutrality was stark: 'he [de Valera] provided the British people with an overwhelming reason for the maintenance of partition'.[76]

Social Conflict during the Emergency

Despite the strong national consensus in favour of neutrality and the government's rigorous use of censorship to marginalize dissenting opinions, the period was characterized by the emergence of considerable social and economic discontent, which for a time seemed to portend a radical shift in the nature of political opposition in the state with the Irish Labour Party displacing Fine Gael as the major anti-Fianna Fáil force.

Within the government there was acute concern that Britain's wartime priorities, not to mention resentment over neutrality, could have severely disruptive effects on the economy, which was dependent on the British market to take the vast bulk of its exports, and which imported much of the fuel, machinery, and raw materials for its manufacturing industries from Britain. In the month of Dunkirk, de Valera met with Irish bankers to solicit assistance, pointing to the possibly subversive potential of the large pool of urban unemployed,[77] while in July 1940, Seán Lemass, who had been moved into a new Ministry of Supplies, tried to persuade the cabinet of the need for a strongly interventionist and progressive set of economic and social policies. These would be necessary, he argued, to deal with the inevitably very high level of unemployment in the event of the state's total economic isolation.[78] Luckily for the economic conservatives in the cabinet, for instance Seán MacEntee and the officials of the Department of Finance, who saw the Emergency as a golden opportunity for a national exercise in belt-tightening, British resentment at neutrality was not allowed to obstruct the important contribution of Irish farmers, economic migrants, and recruits to the anti-fascist struggle.

The revival of the British economy after 1935 helped to ease the government's problems in delivering on promises of job creation. The changed international conditions threatened this convenient, if potentially politically embarrassing way of disposing of the state's surplus labour force. It forced the Irish state into an unprecedented degree of co-operation with Britain, which clearly challenged de Valera's ability to present neutrality as a policy that did not tilt to one or other of the belligerents. At the outbreak of the war the British had introduced the requirement of an identity card for all persons travelling to the UK. The Department of External Affairs co-operated in the running of the scheme, but in the aftermath of the evacuation of Dunkirk, controls were tightened and the government was faced with the choice of allowing such restrictions to disrupt seriously the flow of Irish workers to Britain or, for the first time, negotiating a framework by which the state would facilitate workers who wished to go to Britain. The resultant agreement of July 1941 ensured that well over 100,000 Irish migrants travelled to Britain during the war.[79]

The potentially disruptive effect of this exodus on the government's attempt to build a national consensus around neutrality was noted by the state's chief censor: 'stories picturing thousands of starving Irish workers flocking across to the bombed areas of England or to join the British forces . . . have simply got to be stopped if public morale is not to be hopelessly compromised.'[80] The small group of left-wing activists, largely from the Communist Party of Ireland, who had been struggling to organize the Dublin unemployed since 1939, did their utmost to point out the contradiction between neutrality and the government's covert migration policy. Prior to Hitler's invasion of the Soviet Union in June 1941, the CPI had denounced the war as an 'inter-imperialist' conflict rather than an anti-fascist one, and had been supportive of neutrality while criticizing de Valera for his repression of the 'anti-imperialist' IRA. Even before the Irish–British agreement to facilitate migration, these leftists were publicly denouncing official notices in the central Dublin Labour Exchange, asking the unemployed to volunteer for work in England.[81] Strict censorship of the press, police surveillance of meetings, and the internment and imprisonment of leading activists all helped to minimize public debate on the true nature of neutrality.

Police concern over leftist exploitation of the unemployed had disappeared by early 1942. In part this reflected the effectiveness of British construction sites and munitions factories in helping to drain the pool of unemployed, although there were still 70,000 in 1943.[82] It was also a result of the Communist Party's shift to an anti-neutrality policy after the Soviet Union entered the war on the Allied side. This resulted in the liquidation of the party in the South where its members entered the Irish

Labour Party. Although the vigorous pro-war policies of the Communist Party in Northern Ireland could not be openly espoused in neutral Ireland, the former communists who had dominated the leadership of the unemployed agitation lost any interest in pointing out the contradictions between neutrality and the facilitation of economic migration to Britain.

Without the safety-valve of emigration neutral Ireland could well have faced a social revolution. Despite the best efforts of Aiken's censorship regime Éire could not be totally insulated from what was happening across the Irish Sea or in Northern Ireland. This was reflected in the amount of real social conflict that existed during the Emergency. British newspapers and magazines continued to circulate, though in reduced numbers. More importantly, many of the 52 per cent of households in large towns and cities and of the 13 per cent in rural areas that had radio sets listened in to the BBC.[83] The long history of emigration to Britain and the tens of thousands of men and women who went to work or enlist during the war meant that there was a cross-channel network of personal and familial links, which provided a constant flow of information about conditions on the other island. Closer to home there were no restrictions on North–South movement and there was awareness of the rapidly improving economic conditions in Northern Ireland.[84]

Fianna Fáil's ability to present itself as a national movement that paid special attention to the needs of the working class, an image particularly cultivated by Seán Lemass, was severely challenged during the war. Lemass himself was replaced at Industry and Commerce by the acerbic and economically right-wing Seán MacEntee. Prior to the shift of positions, MacEntee had been Minister of Finance and had shared the view of its senior officials that the government's commitments to job creation and increased spending on social welfare were 'economically unsound'.[85] His last pre-war budget in May 1939 had increased direct and indirect taxation and his successor, Seán T. O'Kelly, introduced an emergency budget in November 1939 that further turned the screw and sparked a rash of strikes as workers attempted to get wage increases to compensate for the rise in the cost of living.[86] The government rallied behind MacEntee's advocacy of a repressive response. A strike by Dublin Corporation workers caused MacEntee to warn the workers that they were posing a revolutionary threat and the government and the local bishop exerted themselves to help the Corporation resist the strikers.[87] Using the argument that exceptional circumstances demanded a move away from peacetime forms of industrial relations, MacEntee imposed a Standstill Order on Wages in May 1940 and outlawed strikes. Although the Order was relaxed somewhat in 1942, restrictions on union rights remained and real wages dropped by 30 per cent between 1939 and 1943. While the cost of living rose by two-thirds during the Emergency, wages increased by a third and pre-war real wage levels were not achieved again until 1949.[88]

Although supplies of some foodstuffs, such as potatoes, eggs, and meat, were adequate, other staples, such as tea, butter, and margarine, were scarce.[89] A combination of moral persuasion and compulsory tillage orders more than doubled wheat output between 1939 and 1944, leading to a darkening of the colour of bread and prompting one historian to comment sardonically, 'The furore over wheat revealed the Irish concept of hardship—how white would the bread be.'[90] From this perspective Ireland had a relatively cosy war. Compared to most of Europe this was certainly the case but Irish perspectives were more narrowly focused on the North and Britain, where there was much to excite the feeling that the burdens of the Emergency were far from being equally shared. Although rationing of some commodities had existed from early in the war, a general rationing scheme was not introduced until June 1942 and profiteering and black marketeering were rife. Coal imports, for which the country was totally dependent on Britain, fell to one-third of the 1938–9 level by 1944–5. Rationing of coal was introduced in January 1941 but by September there was only one week's supply of domestic coal left in Dublin.[91] The government had launched a campaign to increase the tonnage of turf drawn from peat bogs as a substitute. Although this was organized through the state's Turf Development Board, the turf produced was sold through private fuel merchants, some of whom had close relations with Fianna Fáil, leading to charges of both nepotism and profiteering.[92]

That the Emergency years were far from cosy for the poorest sections of Irish society was clear from the statistics of tuberculosis mortality. Between 1939 and 1941 mortality rates rose in both Irish states. However, while in Northern Ireland tuberculosis mortality in 1945 had fallen below its 1939 level, it was still higher in the southern state in 1947 than it had been in 1939. While other indices of health sensitive to poverty fell rapidly from the middle of the war in Northern Ireland, in the South infant mortality, a sure guide to trends in living standards, rose during the Emergency. Greta Jones has argued that in the 1940s tuberculosis in Ireland became symbolic of the failure of the government to tackle social deprivation and injustice. Dublin, with its concentration of the poorest working-class families often living in overcrowded housing conditions, was at the core of the state's tuberculosis problem. In 1936–41 Dublin's population accounted for one-fifth of the total population of the state but one-third of all deaths from tuberculosis.[93]

It was not simply the brutal realities of deteriorating conditions that produced increasing dissent, but the perception of a government that had forgotten its only very recent protestations of social radicalism and concern for the worst-off sectors of Irish society. For some of its former supporters Fianna Fáil had gone over to the class enemy. Disillusion with the party was obviously most worrying when it manifested itself in the capital but it was much more widespread. In 1941, the dole in rural areas, the most important indicator of Fianna Fáil's social concern in the 1930s, was stopped. In response one of those very rare creatures in rural Ireland, a female communist, addressing a large audience of unemployed labourers in Foynes, county Limerick, voiced an increasingly common anti-Fianna Fáil sentiment: 'They started off by passing acts helpful to the workers . . . but they had given way to the farmers and industrialists, the people who had the money.'[94]

The government had made some attempts to retrieve its 1930s image of social concern through a number of welfare reforms: free food and fuel for the poorest were introduced in 1941 and 1942 and un-employment benefits were increased in 1942. However, these did little to decrease dissatisfaction amongst the majority of workers, who faced a substantial increase in the cost of living at a time when the state not only froze wages but appeared to want to intervene decisively in a radical restructuring of the trade union movement.

Splitting the Labour Movement

Irish trade unionism had been divided for some time over the desire of the leadership of the largest union, the Irish Transport and General Workers' Union (ITGWU), for a 'rationalization' of the movement into far fewer industrial organizations, which would eliminate smaller unions and also diminish the influence of the British-based amalgamated unions which continued to organize in the South after independence. Lemass, as Minister of Industry and Commerce, had been strongly in favour of the ITGWU's ideas, in part because of his desire to give a streamlined union movement a role in a more corporatist form of economic policy-making, and also because he was opposed on nationalist grounds to so many Irish workers still being members of British-based unions.[95]

The General Secretary of the ITGWU, William O'Brien, was Lemass's main ally in the trade union movement. He instigated the decision of the Irish Trade Union Congress to set up a Commission of Inquiry into union structures in 1936. At that time the ITUC, which had unions affiliated from both sides of the border, represented 134,000 workers in forty-nine unions. While two of these had over 10,000 members each, seventeen had memberships of less than 500. Inter-union conflicts between craft and general unions and Irish and British unions certainly weakened the movement and meant there was a serious argument for radical reform.[96] O'Brien's objective in seeking agreement on a rationalization into ten industrial unions may well have had the objective of strengthening weakly organized workers in rural areas and smaller towns to resist government and employer demands that they accept low wages as the price of a job.[97] However, many of his critics saw his proposals as being aimed at eliminating the British unions, and absorbing the small unions into a much enlarged ITGWU. The Commission of Inquiry failed to agree, split as it was between Irish and British unions, and in 1939 a Council of Irish Unions was set up to promote O'Brienite ideas. It provided the union base of support for Seán MacEntee's Trade Union Bill, which was published in April 1941 and contributed powerfully to the subsequent disastrous split in the political and industrial wings of the labour movement.

The bill proposed that all unions had to obtain a licence to allow them to negotiate and lodge a financial deposit with the High Court. There was to be a tribunal with the power to grant one or more unions the sole right to negotiate for a category of workers where these represented a majority of the workers. Although officials from the Department of Industry and Commerce had consulted the ITUC executive and the Congress of Irish Unions and had received tacit support, the publication of the bill sparked off a substantial movement of opposition spearheaded by the Dublin Trades Council and by the Irish Labour Party, which saw in the bill a powerful issue with which to amplify existing working-class dissatisfaction with the government's performance. On 22 June 1941, the day that Hitler launched *Operation Barbarossa* against the Soviet Union, the Trades Council organized the largest demonstration of working-class anti-government resolve since the formation of the state. The crowd cheered the ageing union firebrand, Jim Larkin, when he set alight a copy of the bill.[98]

Speakers at the meeting had bemoaned the fact that a city with such a substantial working class should not return one Labour Party representative to the Irish parliament. However, the combination of falling living standards and resentment over the wages freeze and the Trade Union Bill appeared to be set to change this. There was a large increase in Labour Party membership, with the number of branches rising from 174 in 1941 to 750 in 1943.[99] In the municipal elections in August 1942, the party became the largest group on the Dublin Corporation and in the general election in 1943 the Labour vote was 15.7 per cent, a 10 per cent improvement on the previous election, and it gained eight new seats, winning a total of seventeen.[100] Its vote in Dublin exceeded its national average for the first time, seeming to indicate that it could become more than a party of rural and small-town protest and actually challenge Fianna Fáil for the support of the capital's working class.[101]

However, Fianna Fáil, which had been at the receiving end of anti-communist allegations from the incumbent government in 1931 and 1932, was by 1943 not averse to using similar tactics against a growing Labour Party threat. It was helped by the bitter legacy of an intra-ITGWU dispute between William O'Brien and Jim Larkin.[102]

Larkin, who had won a North Dublin seat as an Independent Labour candidate in the 1937 election, had subsequently joined the Labour Party and attempted to get an official Labour nomination but this was resisted by O'Brien and the ITGWU, who had provided financial support for a number of TDs (*Teachta Dála*: Deputy or Member of the Dáil) who were union members. Larkin's political radicalism had diminished substantially by the end of the 1930s and he had severed any connection with communism.[103] The division in the union movement over the question of rationalization and the suspicion of many that O'Brien had given tacit support and encouragement to the MacEntee Trade Union Bill resulted in Larkin assuming a central role in opposition to the bill and an increasingly bitter response from O'Brien and the ITGWU. In 1943 the Dublin Labour Party nominated Larkin as a Dáil candidate and he was returned in the election of that year.

During the election campaign, which Fianna Fáil had fought under the conservative slogan 'Don't change horses when crossing the stream',[104] MacEntee had waged a lurid anti-communist campaign against Labour, alleging that the party had been infiltrated by a middle-class intelligentsia and, if that was not damning enough, adding that they were taking their orders from Moscow.[105] The decision of the Communist Party of Ireland to dissolve its small organization in the

South in 1941 was accompanied by a direction to its former members to enter the Dublin Labour Party and work for an end to Irish neutrality. Former communists and other radicals, along with Larkin and his son, formed a new Central Branch of the Labour Party, which was soon closely monitored by the Special Branch, whose reports were the basis for MacEntee's campaign.[106] Lemass, who still hankered after an image as the leader of the left wing of Fianna Fáil, was less than happy with MacEntee's claims that the Labour Party was 'honeycombed with agents of the Comintern'.[107] He asked him to keep out of Labour strongholds during the campaign, fearing that a backlash against these lurid claims would damage transfers from Labour to Fianna Fáil.

The 1943 election result was a severe setback for Fianna Fáil, whose share of the vote dropped from 51.9 per cent in 1938 to 41.9 per cent and who lost ten seats.[108] The blow was softened by the fact that Fine Gael also experienced a severe rebuff, with a drop of support from 33.3 per cent to 23.1 and a loss of 13 seats. Its losses were in large part attributable to the party's support for neutrality, which eroded its difference with Fianna Fáil and encouraged some of its supporters to vote for Independents and Clann na Talmhan. Nevertheless, the discomfiture of Fianna Fáil's main rival could not hide the significant rise in support for Labour, particularly in Dublin where it doubled its first preference vote. Whatever contribution MacEntee's exaggerated rhetoric may have made to the loss of Fianna Fáil support was insubstantial compared to working-class dissatisfaction on issues like the wage freeze and the erosion of living standards. Anti-communism, although it embarrassed Lemass, was still a formidable resource, especially given that the much more radical departures in economic policy that he considered necessary to stem working-class discontent would be rejected by the rest of the cabinet.

The sort of denunciations of communist infiltration that MacEntee had specialized in during the election campaign would appear in a new and more pervasive form when O'Brien's ITGWU disaffiliated from the Labour Party in January 1944 and five of its eight TDs split from the party to form a new National Labour Party. The ITGWU attacked the 'Larkinite and Communist Party elements' who, it was claimed, had taken over the Labour Party.[109] The split and the anti-communist assault put the leadership of the Labour Party on the defensive. It launched its own inquiry into communist involvement, which, although it resulted in the expulsion of a mere six members,[110] had allowed the terms of debate in the labour movement to be clearly defined by the Catholic nationalist right. The report of the inquiry proclaimed that the party's programme 'is based on a set of principles in keeping with Christian doctrine and wholly at variance with the principles of atheistic communism'.[111] Labour's leader, William Norton, faced with a snap general election in May 1944, declared that the Labour Party 'proudly acknowledges the authority of the Catholic Church in all matters relating to public policy and public welfare'.[112] But, weakened and demoralized by the split, the Labour vote sank to 9 per cent and eight seats, with the National Labour Party winning 3 per cent and four seats.[113]

The trade union movement subsequently succumbed to the long-standing tension between Irish and British unions. This was now further inflamed by the nationalist assault on the pro-Allied position adopted, not just by Irish communists, but by those unions with British head-quarters and a strong base in Northern Ireland. Symptomatic of the assault was the publication by the National Labour Party of a pamphlet by Alfred O'Rahilly, President of University College Cork and a frequent contributor to the right-wing Catholic weekly *The Standard*, which had run a series of exposés of alleged communist infiltration of the Labour Party. O'Rahilly's *The Communist Front and the Attack on Irish Labour* widened the assault to include the influence of British-based unions and communists in the ITUC. In January 1944 the ITUC executive had declined an invitation to attend a world trade union conference on the war economy and reconstruction, which was to be hosted in London by the British TUC. When this decision was reversed, after a campaign by British-based unions, fifteen unions disaffiliated and created a Congress of Irish Unions with the ITGWU at its core in April 1945. This split, although the exact membership figures of each organization are dis-puted,[114] was a disastrous blow to the Irish left's hope that the South would experience the increasing shift to the left that was becoming manifest in public opinion in Britain and even in Northern Ireland.

The Cold War started in Ireland before the defeat of fascism. The outpourings of *The Standard*, recycled in the pronouncements of the NLP and CIU, encouraged a strong public sentiment that there was only one global enemy of Irish faith and fatherland: the USSR. The theme of a communist conspiracy to destroy Irish neutrality through the manipula-tion of the labour movement had split that movement and removed a significant threat to Fianna Fáil. In the longer term it ensured that when the continuing social and economic dissatisfaction with the government manifested itself, it would not be in secular-class terms but through a new left-republican formation, which would deepen the political and ideological division on the island that neutrality had done so much to consolidate.

Éire and Beveridge

The Second World War was, for many of those on the Allied side, not simply a struggle for military victory, but for a better society. In Britain it meant a commitment to a comprehensive welfare state and full employment. The initial reaction of de Valera's cabinet to the Churchill government's acceptance of the Beveridge Report in 1942 was one of vulgar political fear. It was felt that the Irish labour movement had been given a tremendous propaganda weapon by the British decision. Hugo Flinn, a parliamentary secretary to the Minister of Finance, set out the prospect in a letter to de Valera:

The publication of this report, its adoption by public opinion in England and the promise of the Six County Government to implement it if adopted at Westminster is a 'god send' for the Labour party and, properly worked worth quite a few seats.

Every wildest claim made by them may be made to seem possible of accomplishment: 'if this can be done by England after a horribly costly war, what could not be done by a country that has remained at peace?'[115]

Flinn, a Cork man who had spent much of his life running the family fish business in England and who had no involvement in the independence struggle,[116] personified what Fianna Fáil's critics saw as its growing conservatism.[117]

Lemass was the only member of the government who favoured a radical response to the challenge of Beveridge. Authorized by the cabinet to prepare an analysis of the report, he was prepared to endorse publicly Beveridge's objective of overcoming the 'giants of want, disease, ignorance, squalor and idleness'.[118] By this time he had reclaimed his former Department of Industry and Commerce, which he combined with Supply, providing him with the institutional and policy-making clout with which he attempted to push government planning for the postwar period in a more social democratic direction. He bombarded his colleagues with quotations from 'modern economic research', which usually meant Beveridge, Keynes, or Nicholas Kaldor. His argument was that post-war Ireland should maintain many of the controls, particularly on labour, that had been introduced during the Emergency. These should be developed into a new set of relations between the state, employers, and unions that aimed to achieve trade-offs between full employment, improvements in productivity, and wage restraint.[119] Aware of the limited capacity of Irish capitalism to generate new jobs, he also proposed an ambitious set of post-war state spending schemes in areas such as afforestation, drainage, fisheries, hospitals, and housing.[120] The objective was full employment and he argued that such arrangements would need the state to adopt a 'new kind of budget policy' that transcended the narrow accounting priorities of balancing the books.

Unsurprisingly, such notions were anathema to the Department of Finance, which saw them as 'bureaucratic control of the most oppressive and objectionable kind'. Lemass' economic theorists were dismissed as the 'Escapist school of economics'. The Finance view was that the Beveridge proposals were unaffordable for a country like Ireland and the government needed to avoid any further commitments to social welfare improvements. The only sure way to deal with unemployment was through measures to improve the efficiency and productivity of Irish agriculture and to cut taxes.

De Valera, while not totally sharing this perspective, was not comfortable with Lemass's radicalism. His inclination was to try to persuade the Irish people of the attractiveness of his own folksy vision of an Ireland which put spiritual values above vulgar material concerns and which should put up with economic problems as the price of being saved from the horrors of war. In a Dáil debate on unemployment in August 1940, he declared that a small community like Ireland should be content with 'frugal comfort' and that unemployment was a problem that defied solution.[121] His famous St Patrick's Day radio address in 1943 has, as Charles Townshend has noted, been frequently quoted 'more often in mockery than in admiration':[122]

The Ireland which we dreamed of would be the home of a people who valued material wealth only as the basis of right living, of a people who were satisfied with frugal comfort and devoted their leisure to things of the spirit—a land whose countryside would be bright with cosy homesteads, whose fields and villages would be joyous with the joy of industry, with the romping of sturdy children, the contests of athletic youths and the laughter of comely maidens, whose firesides would be the forums for serene old age.

This Rousseauesque vision of a land dominated by family farms and industry dispersed to small towns and villages avoiding the extreme inequalities of fully-fledged capitalism, and the 'servile state' associated with socialism and communism, remained a powerful influence on Irish political life. As critics at the time and since have pointed out, de Valera failed to provide any realistic ideas about how this vision was to be realized at a time when many of the policies of his government actually undermined it.[123] However, whatever its lack of economic realism, the speech reflected a keen awareness of the threat to his party's support in the west of Ireland because of small-farmer discontent. This focused on what was seen as the government's failure to deliver on the constitution's commitment to 'settle as many families as possible on the land'. The threat from Clann na Talmhan was a real one as the 1943 election demonstrated: it won 11 per cent of the vote and fourteen seats but in some of Fianna Fáil's western heartland, where its support had been highest in the 1930s, the vote for the Clann was almost double its national average while there were big drops in support for de Valera's party.[124]

It was to this threat that the core sentiments of the St Patrick's Day speech were directed. So also was de Valera's resistance to pressure from Lemass, on this issue at least in alliance with the Department of Finance, that there be a fundamental re-examination of the commitment to further land redistribution and of the large number of smallholdings that would never be able adequately to support their owners, let alone the need to improve significantly the productivity of Irish agriculture.[125] In this sense the sentimental ruralism of the speech had very real effects as part of the successful traditionalist resistance to those in favour of full-blooded capitalist development of Irish agriculture.

It also reflected de Valera's problem, verging on incapacity, of integrating the realities of urban life and poverty into his vision of Ireland. During the 1943 election campaign he had declared that 'there is nobody in this country who is not getting proper food' and that 'every section of the community has had the careful regard of the government.'[126] The sizeable support for Labour in Dublin was a resounding response to this myopia, as was the increasingly active role played by individual Catholic bishops in dealing with or highlighting urban poverty.

The Catholic hierarchy and clergy, drawn in large part from the rural bourgeoisie, had traditionally been uncomprehending and unsympathetic to the conditions of the urban working class. However, since the publication in 1931 of Pope Pius XI's encyclical *Quadragesimo Anno* with its promotion of corporatist ideas of social organization, there had been a belated development of a Catholic social movement in

Ireland. At times combining corporatist ideas with open worship of Franco and Mussolini, it had provided what little intellectual backbone the Blueshirt movement possessed. But corporatist ideas also influenced some in Fianna Fáil and clerics close to the party. The provisions for the second chamber in the 1937 constitution were heavily influenced by corporatist thought.

John Charles McQuaid, who was appointed Archbishop of Dublin in 1940, played a central role in developing the Church's social involvement. A long-standing friend of de Valera, who had pressed his candidacy on the Vatican, McQuaid was a former headmaster of Blackrock College, an élite Catholic school run by the Holy Ghost Fathers. De Valera had taught there and his son was a pupil. McQuaid rapidly developed a high-profile role for the Church's charitable role in Dublin and made it clear that he was aware of the reality of those excluded from de Valera's vision. His first lenten pastoral in 1941, at a time when government ministers were taking a hard line against strikes, declared that 'The very widespread yearning for social peace is itself proof of the grave need for social reform.'[127] In April 1941 he created the Catholic Social Service Conference, which set out to co-ordinate and expand Catholic welfare work in the diocese and transformed the quality of social work in Dublin, providing up to 250,000 free meals a month.

It was this substructure of Church-organized and privately financed charity that de Valera was prepared to bank on as the practical alternative to Beveridge. For although the work done by the Church could on one level be seen as a criticism of the inadequacies of the state, the Church itself was in the forefront of the ideological assault on the principles underlying the Beveridge Report. McQuaid was an opponent of the expansion of state welfare services[128] and within the cabinet he could rely on Seán MacEntee to scour British and Irish newspapers and journals for Catholic criticisms of Beveridge, particularly those that echoed the section of the Irish constitution that guaranteed the family as bearing the primary responsibility for the education and welfare of its members. Beveridge threatened to make the state 'omnicompetent', according to one cleric who had recently been made the first Professor of Sociology at Maynooth, the national seminary.[129] Thus even when clerics criticized the inadequacies of existing welfare services, they were careful to ensure that any proposed alternative relied on the development of their existing role and did not involve any expansion of the role of the state. Such criticism could be acutely embarrassing to the government, as when in 1944 Dr Dignan, Bishop of Clonfert, produced a pamphlet on the existing health service in which he described the medical assistance service, on which a large section of the population depended for medical care, as tainted by 'destitution, pauperism and degradation'.[130] Yet it was the very Catholic social teaching underlying Dignan's critique that was used ideologically to bury Lemass's radical proposals and which greatly assisted in the political offensive against the upsurge of support for the Labour Party in 1943.

It was of course true that only the massive expansion in the functions and size of the state in wartime Britain made the post-war welfarism and Keynesian economic management possible. A radical such as Lemass faced an Irish situation in which, despite the large increase in state regulation of private economic activity, there was an actual shrinkage in the proportion of national income taken by the state during the Emergency.[131] The implementation of his policies would have brought the government into conflict not only with the traditionally conservative mercantile, financial, and large-farmer interests, some of whom had begun to soften their anti de Valera positions in the late 1930s, but also with the new bourgeoisie that had grown up under protectionism. They would have solidified and expanded Fianna Fáil's support in what remained a large but minority constituency, the urban and rural working class. They might have won back support lost to Clann na Talmhan but they would have unleashed the sort of distributional class warfare that de Valera had set up Fianna Fáil precisely to avoid. Neutrality and its ideological buttressing by anti-communism and Catholic social thought made a conservative response politically sustainable but left the state seriously unprepared for the challenges of the post-war world.

4

Stagnation: Ireland 1945–59

Ireland's post-war history contrasts with that of most Western European states, where the war proved to be a watershed in social, economic, and political terms. Neutrality was seen as a temporary interruption of policies that had produced economic growth and the consolidation of the state in the 1930s and consequently there was little sense of a need for change. The major political challenge to de Valera's government would come from those who charged it with forsaking the radical social republicanism of the 1930s and were thus demanding a reinvigoration of the autarkic and irredentist themes of classic de Valeraism rather than a change of course. It would take the shock of economic crisis and accelerated population loss in the mid-1950s to force a radical rethinking of isolationist economics and the adoption of a more realistic tone in the state's approach to the North.

Protectionism under Pressure

The main motivation for those in government prepared to consider the need for new policy directions was the fear of a destabilizing influx of workers who had gone to the UK during the war. This was a major concern for Lemass when he produced a substantial document on full employment for the cabinet's Economic Policy Committee in January 1945. In fact the main challenge to the southern state in the next decade would not be the high levels of unemployment exacerbated by returned emigrants but an intensification of the wartime exodus to Britain. Data on net emigration indicate that over 30,000 people left Ireland annually in the immediate post-war period and this figure rose to over 50,000 in the 1950s.[1] Irish nationalists had, since the Great Famine in the 1840s, defined emigration as the gravest symptom of British misrule. Political independence, land reform, and state-sponsored economic development were supposed to lead to an end of the problem. In the year before Fianna Fáil first won power de Valera had claimed that the implementation of his party's development proposals could provide the means of

existence for a population of 20 million.² A mixture of land redistribution, a shift from pasture to tillage, and the development of indigenous
industry, together with the closure or severe restriction of emigration
opportunities in the 1930s, did see a lessening of the rate of population
decline. But as Kevin O'Shiel, a member of the Land Commission
that was charged with land redistribution, put it in a memorandum on
agrarian strategy for the cabinet in 1942, the 'dry rot' might be ceasing
but there was little sign of a rural resurgence:

In 1847 there were 6,700,000 of us in Eire's Twenty-Six Counties with 4,000,000
sheep and cattle and 3,129,000 acres of tillage. Today we are about 2,968,000 with
7,000,000 cattle and sheep and 1,845,000 acres of tillage.³

O'Shiel, like de Valera, was a firm believer in what he termed the
'national school', which viewed the land question as more than a simple
matter of economics, in contrast to the 'big business' view that prioritized efficiency and productivity, which inevitably led to larger holdings
and a diminishing demand for labour. Land and the rural communities
it supported formed the basis for the preservation of the nation's essential character expressed in history, legends, folklore, customs, and
language. The objective of agrarian policy was not to maximize productivity but 'to make the land maintain as large a number of tradition-
preserving cells as possible . . . as many families as possible on holdings
large enough to assure them a fair measure of frugal comfort'. While
these ideas were clearly reflected in government policy and in de Valera's
St Patrick's Day address in 1943, they were under increasing pressure
from elements in the political and administrative élite.

The problem was clear, even to O'Shiel, who pointed out that of the
344,500 holdings in the state, at least 200,000 could be regarded
'uneconomic' as the farmer could not support himself and his family as
at even a level of a 'frugal livelihood'. A high percentage of these
uneconomic holdings were in the 'congested districts' along the western
seaboard from Donegal to Kerry. The west of Ireland, with its high
concentration of native Irish speakers, had been at the core of the cultural definition of Irishness for de Valera and his party, and their agrarian policy had had real effects in maintaining the small-farm economy in
the west. Part of O'Shiel's critique of existing policy was that the activities of the Land Commission had been largely concentrated in these
areas, where vast tracts of land were bog, moor, and mountainside and
much of the remainder was land of very poor quality. Almost half of the
land redistributed since the process began under the British had been in

the western province of Connaught. However, if the government had acceded to his desire to extend land redistribution to the richer areas, it would have risked disrupting the all-important cattle trade with Britain, which depended on the large cattle farms long denounced by Fianna Fáil radicals as 'ranches' and their owners as parasitic 'graziers'.

The attempt to alter radically the balance between tillage and pasture had been silently given up by the middle of the 1930s when the centrality of the cattle trade in earning the surplus necessary for the importation of machinery and raw materials for the industrialization drive had been recognized in the Coal–Cattle Pact negotiated with Britain in 1935. De Valera admitted before the war that 'the flight from the land was a fact'[4] but this was the extent of his concessions to economic realism. The land redistribution programme was slowed down and there would be no indulgence of O'Shiel's demand for something just short of 'a whole-sale obliteration of the big graziers'. But de Valera still wanted agrarian policy to pursue two objectives: the maximization of food production and the retention of as many families on the land as possible, which were essentially incompatible.[5]

Lemass, who had asked his leader in vain for an indication of which objective he prioritized, went on to produce his own radical proposals for post-war agriculture in a long memorandum on full employment in 1945. He suggested the 'displacement' of the worst farmers, if necessary through state powers of compulsory purchase:

It is necessary to ensure that the Nation's resources of agricultural land are fully utilised. The rights of owners should not include the right to allow land to go derelict or to be utilised below its reasonable productive capacity. Only a limited number of families can be settled on the land, on economic holdings, and policy must be directed to ensuring that ownership will be confined to persons willing and capable of working them adequately.[6]

The radicalism of his approach to agriculture was anathema to most of his colleagues, combined as it was with a far-reaching set of proposals for Keynesian budgetary policy, a substantial expansion of the state's role in industrial development, a new system of economic planning involving the trade unions, and a critical review of the workings of protectionism. It was predicated on the assumption of an economic and political crisis detonated by the return of the tens of thousands of men and women who had migrated to Britain during the war. Pressure for this sort of change was reduced radically as it became clear that wartime migrants were not returning. It was also the case that despite wartime emigration, the 1946 census showed a decline of only 0.4 per cent and that the bulk of this was accounted for by a sharp drop in the Protestant population while there was a small increase in the number of Catholics.[7] A new census in 1951 was the first since 1841 to register an increase in population.[8] These apparently favourable demographic trends were accompanied by a post-war consumption boom as people tried to make up for the dearth of goods during the Emergency. Personal expenditure rose by almost a quarter between 1945 and 1950 and industrial output rose by two-thirds.[9]

But beneath these short-term improvements the problems that had motivated Lemass's radicalism remained. The increased output of Irish industry was destined mainly for the domestic market and even by the end of the 1950s exports of manufactured goods represented only a small percentage of total exports. Over 80 per cent of industrial firms in the Republic employed fewer than 50 persons and lacked the resources for research, improved production methods, and the development of export markets.[10] At the same time the Republic's dependence on imports for machinery and raw materials contributed, along with the demands of Irish consumers for a range of imported consumer goods, to recurrent balance of payments crises. A protected domestic market did provide the basis for some continued expansion but the small size of the market put an inherent limitation on the capacity of Irish industry to absorb what became the largest rural exodus since the worst periods of population loss under British rule.

The 1940s saw a decisive shift in the attitude of many rural dwellers to life in the countryside. A commission appointed in 1948 to examine emigration and other population problems noted the unanimity of view expressed to them by those with direct experience of rural life: 'the relative loneliness, dullness and generally unattractive nature of life in many parts of rural Ireland, compared with the pattern of life in urban centres and with that in easily accessible places outside the country'.[11] The limited amount of industrial development since the 1930s, together with the much greater employment opportunities in Britain, broke whatever limited attraction subsistence living on the family farm had for tens of thousands of young men and women. The post-Famine domin-ance of the 'stem family' system of inheritance, where the land was passed intact to the eldest son, had produced a society with an extremely low marriage rate and a high age at marriage.[12] The social and sexual casualties of this system, particularly the younger sons and daughters without dowries to make them an attractive match and thus condemned to celibacy, now voted with their feet for the building sites, hospitals, and hotels of post-war Britain. Agriculture had a total workforce of 580,000 in 1946; by 1951 this had dropped to 504,000, and by 1961 to 376,000.[13]

Fianna Fáil's post-war agrarian and industrial policies did little to address this exodus. The government's main priority in agricultural policy was to restore the relatively favourable terms for exports to Britain provided in the 1938 Trade Agreement. There had been a decrease of 35 per cent in agricultural exports to the UK from 1939 to 1946, which the Irish blamed on inadequate UK prices. After the war the scope for increased agricultural exports at satisfactory prices was further adversely affected by food rationing in Britain and increasing competition from cheap Commonwealth food.[14] Irish industry was also continuing to suffer from British reluctance to allow scarce supplies of coal and industrial raw materials to cross the Irish Sea. When de Valera opened negotiations with the British in September 1947, his priorities were the revival of the cattle trade to its pre-war level and countering resistance from the British to further industrialization in the South. The latter stemmed from Britain's economic weakness, which had led to the suspension of sterling convertibility against the dollar in August 1947. Ireland's external assets, which were held in sterling, had increased from £163 million in 1939 to £450 million in 1945 and the British Treasury was concerned lest too rapid a process of Irish industrialization ran these down as they were used to buy dollars to import machinery and raw materials. In response de Valera was insistent that 'it was the fixed policy of the Eire government to develop their own industries insofar as they were capable of doing so. Eire did not wish to remain a predominantly agricultural country whose economy would be based on the export of manufactured goods.'[15]

The Irish were successful in persuading the British to respect their right to pursue independent economic policies but the price of a substantial coal allocation was the acceptance that, in the words of Patrick Smith, the Irish Minister of Agriculture, Éire's agricultural production had 'to fit in with the British programme'.[16] De Valera, who had boasted in the 1930s that Irish agriculture could do without the English market, was quoted in a British Treasury document as calling for the 'dovetailing of the two economies'.[17] The limit of his agrarian radicalism was a demand, conceded by the British, for the removal of differential between Irish fat cattle and animals fattened in Britain. Although the negotiations were interrupted by the 1948 general election, the Trade Agreement signed by the inter-party government in June 1948 was based on the elements largely agreed on by de Valera. While this meant that fewer cattle were exported to be fattened in England, thus increasing the value of cattle exports, it added little to the employment-generating capacity of Irish agriculture at the same time as the agreement intensified dependence on the British market, which in the mid-1950s was taking 86 per cent of Irish agricultural exports.[18]

If the more diversified and labour-intensive agriculture that had been the aspiration of Fianna Fáil agrarian radicalism was now clearly chimerical, it only served to underline the limitations of the party's industrial strategy. Lemass had, in 1945, hinted at the possibility of breaking with a key tenet of economic nationalism when he informed the cabinet that 'While it is desirable that all industries should be owned and controlled by Irish nationals, there is less reason for insistence on national ownership of export industries than of industries supplying only the home market.'[19] It would be another twelve years before he was able to implement this idea with the amendment of the Control of Manufacturers Acts of the 1930s to make substantial foreign investment possible. Already being sharply attacked by even sympathetic observers for being too accommodating to foreign interests,[20] the immediate post-war political conjuncture with its temporary surge of a radical social-republican threat to Fianna Fáil was inimical to such iconoclasm. Yet, without a new source of employment generation based on foreign capital developing the export capacity that indigenous industry lacked, the other arm of potential industrial strategy was doomed by the overwhelming resistance from the party's powerful allies amongst the manufacturing bourgeoisie that had developed behind tariff walls.

Lemass, the main sponsor of protectionism in the 1930s, was well aware by the end of the war of the inefficiencies and restrictive practices that protectionism had permitted. Speaking to a group of businessmen in 1947, he explained that protective tariffs and other import restrictions were going to be much less important in the future.[21] He was attempting to prepare the ground for his controversial Industrial Efficiency Bill, which proposed to establish a new and powerful Prices Commission to enquire into prices, prevent cartels, and promote efficiency. Manufacturers would be required to participate in 'development councils' which included workers and third parties to promote efficiency, and recalcitrant industrialists were to have their directors' fees stopped. Together with the establishment of a Labour Court in 1946 as an instrument of industrial conciliation, the bill was an attempt to promote the modernization of Irish industry in a semi-corporatist fashion. Visionary in the bleak conditions of post-war Ireland, apart from the fierce resistance of some of Lemass's former business allies, the major practical problem was that successful modernization would often have meant more rather than less unemployment. Until the nettle of foreign capital was grasped, Lemass's modernizing project provided no way out of the impasse created by a shrinking agriculture and a stagnant industrial sector. The bill fell victim to Fianna Fáil's ejection from office after sixteen years in power. A large role in the defeat was played by the surge in support for a new party, Clann na Poblachta, whose main themes were an embarrassing reprise of the more radical republican sentiments expressed by de Valera and Lemass two decades previously.

The First Inter-party Government

Alvin Jackson has provocatively described the decade after 1948 as 'the heyday of Irish Butskellism . . . an era characterised by unrelenting party warfare but also by minimal ideological and policy distinctions'.[22] But the post-war consensus in Britain was constructed around the welfare state and a commitment to full employment achieved through Keynesian techniques of economic management. In stark contrast, what consensus emerged in Ireland was in this period centred on resistance to British welfarism on the basis of the social teachings of the Catholic Church and the prioritizing of the balance of payments over economic growth and employment creation.

In the immediate post-war period it became apparent that Fianna Fáil could not count for long on the gratitude of voters for being saved from the hazards of war. This was clear in 1945 from the results of the first election for the office of President, a post created under the 1937 constitution and originally held with all-party agreement by the Protestant Gaelic revivalist Douglas Hyde. The independent candidate Patrick McCartan polled an impressive 20 per cent of the vote. McCartan, who had a solid republican pedigree, was supported by disaffected IRA men, Labour, and Clann na Talmhan. This quickly improvised coalition was to encourage the emergence of a more serious challenge to Fianna Fáil with the creation of Clann na Poblachta in July 1946.

The new party was yet another attempt to meld republicanism with left-of-centre politics, a project that could be traced back to the writings of James Connolly and which had its previous most significant manifestation in the Republican Congress in the 1930s. However, the leftism of the Clann owed much more to papal encyclicals than to the sort of Marxism that had influenced the republican radicals of the 1930s. Its leader, Seán MacBride, had briefly been Chief of Staff of the IRA in the 1930s. MacBride had been born into the republican aristocracy. His mother, Maud Gonne, was a lifelong activist in the nationalist cause and his father, Major John MacBride, was executed for his part in the Easter Rising. He had left the IRA arguing that de Valera's new constitution showed that full sovereignty and an end to partition could be achieved constitutionally. De Valera's robust response to the IRA during the war had been the prime cause of his disillusion with Fianna Fáil. A barrister, he had spent the war years defending IRA men and came to public notice when he represented the family at the inquest of the former Chief of Staff of the IRA Seán McCaughey, who died on hunger strike in 1946.[23] Twenty-two of the twenty-seven members of the provisional executive of the Clann had been active members of the IRA at some stage in their lives and for them the priority was to press on for the full republican objectives that de Valera was seen to have betrayed.

Yet MacBride's own experience of republican politics in the two decades after the Civil War had taught him that Fianna Fáil's rise to a hegemonic position in Irish politics depended on an ability to provide a left-of-centre social and economic programme as well as a radical nationalist agenda. It was therefore the Clann that did much to ensure that emigration was a major issue in electoral politics, using it to highlight the winners and losers in de Valera's Ireland:

The nation is being weakened by the forced emigration of its youth. A small section has been enabled to accumulate enormous wealth while unemployment and low wages, coupled with an increasing cost of living, are the lot of the workers.[24]

The party also proposed that the state assume responsibility for full employment based on a minimum wage related to the cost of living. Underlying such demands was MacBride's commitment to the economic ideas set out in the iconoclastic Minority Report to the Commission of Inquiry into Banking, Currency and Credit written by P. J. O'Loghlen. This had attacked the direction of economic policy followed by all governments since 1923. It doubted the ability of the private sector to generate sufficient employment and supported comprehensive government intervention in areas including industrial development, afforestation, land reclamation, and a public housing drive. All this would be financed by severing the link with sterling and repatriating the sterling assets held by Irish nationals. O'Loghlen had cited papal encyclicals to support his arguments and MacBride was careful to establish the Catholic credentials of his party's economic and social programme. He vigorously espoused the social welfare plan devised by Bishop Dignan of Clonfert, which was rejected out of hand by MacEntee in 1944, and the Clann made it clear, in a manner that would return to haunt it, that the family was the basic unit of society and that the state could not encroach on the fundamental responsibilities of the heads of families in the social and moral spheres.[25]

The radical tone of Clann's economic and social programme made it attractive to a younger generation who had grown up after the Civil War and were less influenced by the party loyalties the conflict had generated in their parents. It was partly to appeal to this group that MacBride chose Noel Browne, a young doctor with a passionate commitment to the eradication of tuberculosis, as his Minister of Health. Noel Hartnett, the man responsible for recruiting Browne to the party, was typical of another important source of recruits and voters: disillusioned Fianna Fáil activists. The feeling that de Valera's government had turned its back on the central agrarian and cultural goals of the revolutionary generation had begun to be articulated in the party itself. Michael Joe Kennedy, a prominent Fianna Fáil TD, wrote to Frank Gallagher, Director of the government information services, in December 1946 complaining that the agrarian and language policies of the party had been jettisoned:

The Land Commission has ceased to function . . . and two ministers [Land and Agriculture] are proclaiming . . . that there are too many people on the land. Our language policy is as dead as a dodo . . . We'll have English holiday camps in Gormanstown and beautiful international airports as your name is Frank Gallagher but the Irish Ireland programme will be watered down before Fianna Fáil leaves office.[26]

Hartnett had been a member of Fianna Fáil's national executive but had resigned in 1937 in protest at the decision to accept a £1,000 donation from a businessman.[27] Like that of the teachers, small businessmen, and lawyers who dominated the executive of the Clann,[28] Hartnett's social philosophy was for a nostalgic return to what Richard Dunphy has described as the 'essentially petty-bourgeois ideology' of 1920s republicanism.[29] Fianna Fáil was accused of selling out to big business, bankers, and graziers and betraying its working-class and small-farmer supporters. The Ireland that de Valera still admitted to dreaming about was the one that the Clann claimed could still be created if the will was there: an Ireland of small farms and small and medium-sized factories run by patriotic Irish capitalists with contented and healthy workers. Although the state was assigned a large role in the Clann's economic and social vision, charges of communism were deflated by the party's proclamation that it would put a priority on rehabilitating the moral fibre of the nation from the attacks of 'modern materialism' and other 'alien, artificial and unchristian concepts of life'.[30]

Conditions could hardly have been better for a challenge to Fianna Fáil. An excessively wet summer in 1946 followed by one of the coldest winters on record hit agriculture and domestic consumers badly. Things were made even worse by a serious energy crisis brought about by a major cutback in coal supplies from Britain. In consequence, transportation became chaotic and the already marked shortage of raw materials was exacerbated, forcing many industries to close. The country ran a serious balance of payments deficit of over £25 million in 1947. Bread rationing was reintroduced in January 1947 as was soap rationing and, critically, beer and porter supplies were drastically reduced. There was a widespread popular anger sparked by high prices (these had more than doubled during the war), a scarcity of goods, and black-marketeering. A Lower Prices Council set up by Dublin Trades Council was able to bring out crowds of up to 100,000 and, in an unprecedented movement for such a patriarchal society, the Irish Housewives' Association set up a Women's Parliament where 300 delegates representing over 300,000 women made a range of demands, from that for the provision of hot dinners for all school children to the dottily xenophobic one for restrictions on the 'influx of tourists'.[31]

Lemass and the government appeared to turn their backs on earlier pro-trade union stances in the face of widespread pressure from workers wanting to recuperate the decline in their living standards associated with the wartime wage standstill. A wave of strikes or threatened strikes hit the docks, buses, banks, insurance offices, and the crucial flour milling industry. But it was the government's victory over striking teachers that harmed it most politically and provided the Clann with a powerful new source of support. A pre-war wage demand, revived after the end of the wage freeze, was brusquely dismissed by Tom Derrig, the Minister of Education, and the government showed no inclination to use Lemass's recently established Labour Court as a possible means of arbitration. The strike by the teachers' union (the Irish National Teachers' Organization; INTO) focused on Dublin, with teachers in the rest of the country being levied to support their striking colleagues. It lasted from March to October, when the teachers, defeated, returned to work. The government took a hard and uncompromising line. It spurned an offer by the Archbishop of Dublin, John Charles McQuaid, to mediate, and striking teachers who invaded the pitch during the All-Ireland football final were brutally dispersed by the police. The policy backfired and left a legacy of bitterness. National teachers were traditionally regarded as the backbone of Fianna Fáil, the organic intellectuals of the national revolution, essential for the realization of de Valera's commitment to the Irish language and culture. Many teachers left Fianna Fáil and teachers became the organizational bedrock of the new party.

Three scandals involving allegation of corrupt practices by ministers, two of them implicating Lemass, contributed to the pervasive sense of malaise. Although only one junior minister was forced to resign and Lemass was cleared of all the charges, the Clann made effective use of the issue of 'political decadence' and won two by-elections in Dublin County and Tipperary in the autumn of 1947. Worryingly for Fianna Fáil, not only had MacBride defeated Tommy Mullins, the high-profile National Secretary of the party in Dublin, but both the Clann victories had been helped by substantial vote transfers from Labour and Fine Gael candidates. De Valera attempted to pre-empt the new party's development by calling an early general election, in the knowledge that his Minister of Local Government, Seán MacEntee, had just carried out a quite radical revision of constituency boundaries designed to advantage the larger parties. His strategy nearly succeeded. Dizzy with its by-election successes and with the totally unrealistic hope of challenging Fianna Fáil's dominance, the Clann put up candidates in every constituency, ninety-three in all, which was more than Fine Gael. With only rudimentary organization in most constituencies and many candidates new to electoral politics, if not to underground activity, the result was a major disappointment.

Despite nine extra Dáil seats being available, Fianna Fáil lost eight, giving it a total of sixty-eight and its share of the poll dropped 7 per cent to 41.8 per cent, the same as in the bad year of 1943. Fine Gael's share of the vote dropped slightly to 19.8 per cent although it gained one seat, giving it a total of thirty-one. The two Labour parties' overall share of the vote was more or less unchanged with 8.7 per cent for Labour and 2.6 per cent for National Labour. However, the number of Labour seats rose significantly with it winning an extra six, while National Labour gained one, giving it a total of five. Labour had benefited from the Clann's overambitious decision to put up candidates in every constituency. While many of these candidates were defeated, their vote transfers went disproportionately to Labour candidates. This helps to explain why the Clann got 2 per cent more of the national vote than the two Labour parties: 13.2 per cent, while winning nine fewer seats—a total of ten seats. Clann na Talmhan, which lost support to MacBride's party, saw its vote halved to 5.6 per cent and won seven seats.[32]

Peter Mair has argued that Labour and the Clann faced a crucial choice: they could either allow Fianna Fáil to remain in office as a minority administration and allow themselves time to mobilize a radical alternative to the two main Civil War parties; or they could subordinate their differences in the interests of forming a broad anti-Fianna Fáil alliance, which would inevitably involve and be dominated by Fine Gael as the largest of the potential coalition partners.[33] Although some in the Labour Party and the Clann had favoured a 'Republican–Labour–Farmer' alliance against Fianna Fáil and Fine Gael, the failure of the Clann to make a major breakthrough ruled this out. Ironically, it was MacBride's own mistaken belief that the international situation was favourable to radical action on partition that made him eager to contemplate coalition with a party led by a man, General Richard Mulcahy, whose role in the Civil War led the strongly republican element in the Clann to regard him as a 'bloody murderer'.[34] Mulcahy had suggested a possible Fine Gael–Labour–Clann na Talmhan coalition during the 1944 election.[35] At the time Lemass had denounced this on the basis that Labour would end up as the tail end of a Fine Gael coalition implementing 'anti-national policies'. While the first inter-party government would put an end to a decade of electoral decline for Fine Gael, it would do so partly on the basis of that party repudiating the less anglophobic and pro-Commonwealth themes of its discourse that Mulcahy had articulated in 1944.[36]

Many people expected the inter-party government to break up almost immediately. It was, after all, based on an uneasy and purely expedient alliance between the conservative Fine Gael, the sectional Clann na Talmhan, two antagonistic Labour groups, and the untried Clann na Poblachta. How would, for example, the desire of William Norton, the Labour Tánaiste, for a generous social security scheme, and the determination of Patrick McGilligan, Fine Gael's Finance Minister, to keep a close eye on government expenditure, be reconciled? Nevertheless, the government lasted from February 1948 to May 1951 and had some considerable achievements, particularly in the area of social policy.

Mulcahy's easy acceptance of a Clann veto on his becoming Taoiseach and the filling of that position by John A. Costello, a barrister and former Attorney General in his late fifties, eased the process of government formation. Costello had few of the resources for strong leadership. His personal style was more suited to the court room than the political platform. He was not party leader, had no choice in who became a minister, and had none of the patronage normally enjoyed by a Taoiseach. He therefore had in part to rely on his acknowledged skills as chairman of government meetings to deal with the numerous areas of potential inter-party conflict. He was helped by his good relations with MacBride, whom he had helped to persuade to take up constitutional politics through their common membership of the Law Library,[37] and was also on friendly terms with leaders of the Labour Party through family connections and common involvement on hospital boards. But most significant in limiting the scope for conflict was his government's willingness to borrow to finance capital expenditure and a shared set of Catholic and nationalist values.

Fine Gael's Patrick McGilligan was seen by the economic conservatives in Finance and the Central Bank as a safe Minister of Finance. His first budget took an axe to estimates prepared by Fianna Fáil, which had planned an increase in spending on food subsidies, rural electrification, and the treatment of tuberculosis. His views on Norton's proposals to overhaul and extend the state's social welfare system were clear in some of his notes for the 1948 budget: 'Social services—levelling down— . . . servile state . . . all taken by state to pay out pocket money.'[38] Despite this, some commentators have seen the introduction of a capital budget in 1950 as a triumph of Keynesianism.[39] But, as Brian Girvin has noted, the capital budget was not part of an overall strategy to facilitate growth in the economy and there continued to be a commitment to a balanced budget.[40] McGilligan's central purpose remained the traditional Fine Gael one of lowering the rate of income tax.

The idea for the capital budget came from Patrick Lynch, a young Finance official who was seconded to the Department of the Taoiseach to act as Costello's personal economic adviser. He had discussed it with Alexis FitzGerald, an adviser to the Taoiseach who was also Costello's son-in-law.[41] It attracted Costello because it represented a *via media* between the conflicting economic and social views of McGilligan and MacBride. Although MacBride's ministerial domain was a non-economic one, his strongly developed economic views and his desire to promote the socially radical image of the Clann led him into direct conflict with Finance. He remained a strong proponent of the need for more state investment in areas such as land reclamation, afforestation, housing, and health to be financed through the repatriation of sterling assets. MacBride's department was also responsible for Ireland's participation in the European Recovery Programme: the Marshall Plan. Between May 1948 and May 1951 the country received £6 million in grants and £46 million in loans. This did something to ease intra-government conflicts over public expenditure issues and its emollient effects were amplified by an unprecedented willingness to resort to borrowing: £65 million was borrowed through national loans between 1948 and 1950.[42] It was in this way that some of the major social achievements of the government were financed. There was a remarkable improvement in house building, particularly in the countryside. In 1945 it was estimated that 110,000 new houses were required to deal with the immediate need.[43] In 1947, 744 local authority houses had been completed. By 1950, through the effort of the National Labour Minister for Local Government, T. J. Murphy, the annual figure had risen to over 8,000. In the countryside the Minister of Agriculture, James Dillon, had used a large amount of the Marshall Aid to launch the Land Project, which aimed to reclaim four million acres through drainage and fertilization and, by providing new holdings and extra employment, did much to launch Fine Gael's electoral recovery in the 1950s.[44]

The Mother and Child Crisis

But the main social achievement of the government was in public health, where the Clann's Minister of Health, Dr Noel Browne, gave a clear political lead and urgency to the anti-tuberculosis campaign. There had been a sharp increase in the tuberculosis death rate during the war years, in contrast to that in Northern Ireland, which, after an initial rise, had declined by 1945. The southern Irish death rate from tuberculosis in 1945 was 124 per 100,000 compared to 80 in the north, 79 in Scotland and 62 in England and Wales.[45] The government's response had been constrained by the dominant feeling that Ireland could not afford the sort of welfare state envisaged in the Beveridge Report and also by the Catholic Church's resolute opposition to government intervention in these areas. They believed that the provision of social and medical benefits by the state undermined the integrity of the family. When the initiative for a more activist policy had been taken by non-governmental organizations and private individuals who set up an Anti-Tuberculosis League in 1942, this was sabotaged by the Catholic Archbishop of Dublin, John McQuaid, who saw it as a Trojan horse for the expansion of the powers of the state. A Red Cross investigation in 1943 pointed out that there were only 2,110 beds for tuberculosis patients, the majority in small voluntary and local authority institutions. This left a shortfall of 4,500 beds by current international standards of treatment. Growing dissatisfaction with sanatorium conditions and the treatment of patients had led to the Tuberculosis (Establishment of Sanatoria) Act in 1945 and the Public Health Act of 1947. Despite this, the number of beds for tuberculosis patients had only increased to 3,701 in 1948, and only a third of these were in institutions that had access to the latest clinical and diagnostic facilities.

Browne had been recruited to the Clann by Noel Hartnett when he was working at Newcastle Sanatorium. Browne's passion for the fight against tuberculosis came from bitter personal experience: his parents and three sisters had all been killed by the disease. He was educated in England where he and his siblings had been forced to move after the death of his parents. He later studied medicine at Trinity College, Dublin. Browne had succumbed to tuberculosis himself in 1940[46] and been treated in England, subsequently working in English hospitals before returning to Ireland in 1945. Having been treated and having worked in English sanatoria, he was scornful of the services available to tuberculosis sufferers in Ireland. He had played a central role in making the disease a major issue during the election campaign and was, to the chagrin of some of the older and more ideologically driven members of the party, chosen by MacBride to be the other Clann member of the government. In government he secured a remarkable expansion in anti-tuberculosis services. By the time he left office in 1951 the total number of beds had risen to 6,857. Expenditure on the disease increased almost fourfold between 1948 and 1953, the largest increase in any area of health and social services.[47] Just as the Clann had modernized political campaigning by the use of the cinema with its effective propaganda film *Our Country*, Browne's department ran a national tuberculosis-awareness campaign using posters, radio, and film. He achieved all this by liquidating the assets of the Hospital Sweepstake Fund, which until then had been used stintingly to cover the working deficits of hospitals. Now Browne, despite the unease of McGilligan, used not just the fund's interest but also its capital to finance the department's ambitious programme.[48]

Browne's single-mindedness, his crusading zeal, impatience with his more conservative colleagues, and an inevitable amount of political naïvety given his relative youth and lack of political or administrative experience, led him to bear a disproportionate amount of the blame for the Mother and Child affair that pitted the young minister against the leaders of the Catholic Church and rocked the government in Ireland to its foundations. The origins of the crisis lay in Fianna Fáil's 1947 Health Act, which included provisions for a free health-care scheme for mothers and for children up to the age of 16. The hierarchy had written to de Valera expressing their disapproval of parts of the Act but the response of the government was not tested as it was soon out of office. As was the 'normal' practice for communications between the political and clerical élites, this was carried on behind the scenes, concealed from the public at large and the incoming government.

When Browne decided, in 1950, to reactivate the provisions in the 1947 Act he was already out of favour with the hierarchy. They were unhappy with the trend towards greater state control of and investment in the health service, of which the anti-tuberculosis campaign was one clear manifestation.[49] Browne's medical training at Trinity College made him inevitably an object of suspicion. Trinity was regarded as a bastion of the Protestant Ascendancy and any Catholic who attended it was at risk of contamination. The bishops had long made clear their disapproval of attendance by Catholics, who were urged to go to one of the three constituent colleges of the National University, which were thought 'sufficiently safe in regard to faith and morals'.[50] McQuaid had tightened the screw in 1944 with a ban on attendance unless he granted permission, which would only be given 'for grave and valid reasons'. Failure to heed the ban was a mortal sin and meant a refusal of the Sacraments.

The hierarchy's objections to the scheme were set out in a letter to Costello that denounced the measure as 'a ready-made instrument for future totalitarian aggression'. The right to provide for the health of children belonged to parents and the state's role was purely subsidiary: to help the 'indigent or neglectful' 10 per cent through some sort of means-tested benefit. Along with the threat to parental responsibility, the scheme's provisions for health education in regard to motherhood were seen as the thin end of the wedge that could lead to Trinity-educated doctors advising 'Catholic girls and women' on sex, chastity, and marriage, which could include advice on birth-control and abortion.[51]

Browne, who was summoned to McQuaid's residence to be informed of the contents of the letter, appears to have accepted that the provision for education might have to be reconsidered but he was not prepared to move on the question of a means test. What remains unclear is whether his subsequent quixotic attempt to persuade the hierarchy that the scheme was compatible with Catholic moral law if not with the Church's social teachings was a reflection of naïvety or a disingenuous cover for a desire to provoke a crisis in the Clann and government because of his dissatisfaction with MacBride's leadership.[52] However, there is little doubt about his passionate commitment on the issue. In speeches in 1948 he revealed that the deaths of Irish infants in their first year of life during the previous five-year period had been 55 per cent higher than in England and Wales, and he was convinced that one of the reasons for the differential was the absence of a national system of maternity education and care for all mothers.[53] McQuaid offered him no comfort with a peremptory declaration that Catholic social teaching meant 'Catholic moral teaching in regard to things social'.[54] Browne published the details of the scheme on 6 March 1951 and a month later McQuaid told Costello that the hierarchy had rejected the scheme. The cabinet met the next day and, with the exception of Browne, voted to drop the scheme and prepare another one in conformity with Catholic social teaching. When Browne did not resign immediately MacBride demanded that he do so, hastening the decomposition of the Clann as its urban radical element departed in disgust. The loss of Browne and another TD, Jack McQuillan, over the affair accelerated the process by which the government's majority had already begun to be whittled away and when there were defections from Clann na Talmhan over the price paid to farmers for milk, the government was brought down in April.

What did the affair reveal about the relationship between Church and state? According to Joe Lee, 'Browne was probably his own worst enemy, despite the competition from Costello, MacBride and McQuaid'.[55] The most substantial history of the inter-party government agrees: 'much of the blame for the crisis must rest on Browne himself'.[56] It is true that the hierarchy was only one of the forces ranged against Browne. The Irish Medical Association, which feared that the Mother and Child scheme would undermine doctors' earnings from private practice, denounced it as a form of socialized medicine and state control. Other members of the government found Browne a very difficult colleague and it has been suggested that without the antagonism of these other forces, the hierarchy's intervention might not have been so decisive.[57] Yet the evidence of the unalloyed and enthusiastic loyalty of Costello and his colleagues to the Church is compelling. The message of 'respectful homage' sent by the new government to Pope Pius XII spoke of their 'desire to repose at the feet of Your Holiness the assurance of our filial loyalty and devotion as well as our firm resolve to be guided in all our work by the teachings of Christ and to strive for the attainment of social order in Ireland based on Christian principles'. This out-deferred de Valera and prompted an unprecedented protest from Maurice Moynihan, the secretary to the cabinet.[58]

MacBride, later an icon of the Irish republican left and a Lenin Peace Prize winner, was a particularly depressing example of what Professor Ronan Fanning has termed 'the near feudal deference' of the government to the hierarchy in general and the Archbishop of Dublin in particular.[59] As soon as he was first elected to the Dáil, he hand-delivered a letter to the Archbishop's house paying his 'humble respects' and, like his future government, putting himself 'at your Grace's disposal . . . . Both as a Catholic and a public representative I shall always welcome any advice which Your Grace may be good enough to give me.'[60] Later he would urge McQuaid to appoint an ecclesiastical adviser to the Irish delegation of the Council of Europe to advise on Catholic teaching on social, political, and diplomatic questions. This invitation for the Church to be publicly involved in the formation of Irish foreign policy was ignored by the astute cleric, who preferred more opaque channels of influence.

The fact that MacBride had been, however briefly, Chief of Staff of the IRA may have encouraged these abject overtures to prove his reliability. In the same way, a government including a party full of unrepentant republicans and some social radicals may have seen its profuse Catholicism as an insurance policy against Fianna Fáil's tendency to resort to 'red peril' scares when it suited. Yet there could be no doubting the deep, obedient Catholicism of Costello who, like at least four other members of his government, was a member of the Catholic society the Knights of St Columbanus. Founded in 1922 to counter anti-Catholic discrimination by Freemasons and others, it was soon accused of organizing discrimination itself.[61]

Costello's willingness to sacrifice a colleague and put the future of his government at serious risk reflected not just personal religiosity and inter-party manoeuvring but a church that was in a particularly peremptory mode. The post-war development of Irish Catholicism was divergent from that of most other European countries, where the Church's support for inter-war authoritarianism produced a reaction in the form of a less authoritarian Catholicism. Instead, Ireland experienced a mood of increasing 'integralism': the desire to make it an even more totally Catholic state than it had yet become.[62] One factor in explaining this divergence was the neutrality which insulated the South from the social and moral upheaval produced by direct involvement in the war. Another was the fear of 'contamination' from across the Irish Sea as Britain embarked on a post-war embrace of the welfare state and 'socialistic' planning. One of the reasons that the hierarchy was so concerned about emigration was the high level of female emigrants attracted by the demand for nurses and domestic help in post-war Britain. The threat to the moral purity of these young women from life in 'heathen' England prompted some bishops, supported by Seán Mac-Bride, to propose a ban on the emigration of women under 21.[63] Other more realistic voices in the Church recognized that emigration continued to act as a safety valve by siphoning off many of the most thoughtful and energetic voices of potential criticism in Irish society, and the proposal was rejected.

For those who remained, the Church still maintained a strident and ever-watchful cordon sanitaire against the threat of communist ideological penetration. The Church's anti-socialism was nothing new, as both Connolly and Larkin had had bruising encounters with it before partition. However, the development of the Cold War gave the struggle against the 'reds' a fresh intensity. It mattered little that the Irish Communist Party, revived in 1948 as the Irish Workers' League, was tiny. The Irish bishops were determined to demonstrate that Ireland's Catholics were in the vanguard of the struggle against the communist threat.[64] During the Italian general election of 1948, Archbishop McQuaid appealed over *Radio Eireann* for funds to fight the communists and within a month £20,000 had been collected.[65] The arrests and show trials of Catholic prelates in Eastern Europe produced a display of intense and affronted solidarity. A rally in Dublin in protest against the imprisonment of Cardinal Mindszenty of Hungary attracted 150,000— considerably more than the same year's all-party anti-partition protest against the Ireland Act.

It would be wrong to assume that the Church's pretensions were uncritically accepted by all elements in Catholic Ireland. The failure of the CIU to hegemonize southern trade unionism was in itself an indication of one important group that resisted the integralist agenda. When Archbishop D'Alton of Armagh suggested that the trade union movement affiliate to the International Federation of Christian Trade Unions, a body consisting mainly of Catholic trade unions, his advice was heeded by the CIU but rejected almost unanimously by the ITUC. [66] The strong support given to Browne and the small number of TDs who supported him in the 1951 general election showed that, in Dublin at least, there was a significant amount of disquiet with the Church's opposition to the health proposals, leading Dr D'Alton to complain that 'we are more deeply infected than we think with the virus of secularism and materialism'.[67] Yet the fact remained that there was little inclination within the political élite to risk a conflict with the hierarchy. As the Fine Gael Minister of Justice, Seán MacEoin, put it, 'I don't want to get a belt of a crozier.'[68] At a time when electoral outcomes had a new element of unpredictability, neither the leaders of any potential coalition government nor those of Fianna Fáil had an interest in handing their opponents the role of the most demonstrably loyal sons of the Church.

De Valera had imposed a discipline of total silence on his party during the Dáil debate on Browne's resignation, saving for himself the sole dismissive line: 'I think we have heard enough.' When Fianna Fáil returned to power, its new Health Bill was not the ambitious scheme of Noel Browne. Mothers and infants were to be given free treatment but infants were covered only up to the age of six weeks rather than 16 years, and a means test of £600 was a central part of the scheme.[69] Initial clerical opposition was assuaged by de Valera's instruction to Lemass to ask McQuaid to suggest amendments to those sections of the draft legislation that the Church found obnoxious.[70] The implications of the Mother and Child affair for the anti-partitionist project were severe as the secretary of the Manchester branch of the Anti-Partition League pointed out in a letter to the *Irish Times*:

Let us look for a moment at the situation through 'Ulster' eyes, and we will see people enjoying the benefits of Britain's progressive National Health scheme, without the indignity of a means test. It does not strengthen their desire to unite with the South if by doing so these things would be taken from them because they conflicted with some 'Christian principle'.[71]

The Contradictions of Anti-partitionism

Fianna Fáil's failure to make progress on ending partition had been high on the agenda of those who formed Clann na Poblachta. Seán MacBride was convinced that the strategic needs of the USA and Britain in the struggle with the USSR would make both powers more amenable to Irish demands. At the same time he was also aware of the economic, social, and cultural divisions on the island that made the achievement of unity problematic and something that could not be brought about simply by producing a change of policy in London. During the general election campaign, while supporting the idea of opening up the Irish parliament to elected representatives from Northern Ireland, he also admitted that until social and economic standards in the South were at least as good as those in Northern Ireland, it would be impossible to expect even nationalists in the North to be interested in unity.[72] In government he supported the development of closer economic and cultural relations with the North, and although his more grandiose scheme for a customs union along the lines of the proposed Benelux scheme came to nothing, a number of limited but significant forms of co-operation with Stormont were agreed: a buyout of the bankrupt Great Northern Railway, drainage of Lough Erne, and a joint fisheries commission for Lough Foyle. However, the potentialities for improving North–South relations inherent in such forms of functional co-operation were undermined by the decisions to declare a Republic and to reject an invitation to join NATO.

Costello's coalition displayed a depressing continuity with de Valera's penchant for combining rhetorical anti-partitonism with a *realpolitik* which prioritized electoral competition in the South. Fine Gael had traditionally been the party that favoured close co-operation with Britain and the Commonwealth; indeed, during the war Mulcahy had made a strongly pro-Commonwealth speech advocating that Éire resume active membership when the hostilities were over.[73] During the election campaign it was clear that Fine Gael was divided on the question of continuing Commonwealth links, for while Mulcahy defended the legislative basis for Commonwealth membership, the External Relations Act, other prominent members supported its repeal. The External Relations Act of 1936 was one of two pieces of legislation rushed through the Dáil in response to the abdication of the King Edward VIII. The Constitution Amendment Act had abolished the residual functions of the British monarch in the internal affairs of the Irish Free State but the External Relations Act had confirmed a continuing role for the King in external affairs. For as long as the Free State remained a part of the Commonwealth the King, as head of that association, had a role in diplomatic and consular appointments and international agreements. Although a purely symbolic role, it sat uneasily with the fact that under de Valera's constitution of 1937 Ireland now had its own head of state. Britain's representative in Dublin, Lord Rugby, was convinced that de Valera wanted to maintain the Act as a bridge to the North, but feared that the emergence of Clann na Poblachta might force him to propose repeal it in order to cover Fianna Fáil's flank from more extreme nationalist attacks.[74] In fact the repeal of the Act had not featured as a significant issue during the campaign and MacBride publicly accepted that the new government could not claim a mandate for repeal. That Costello would announce a decision to get rid of the Act within six months of the formation of his government said more about inter-party competition in the Free State than it did about his government's possession of a coherent set of policies on Anglo-Irish relations and Northern Ireland.

Costello took the initiative on the issue and his main motivation seems to have been to pre-empt a Dáil private member's motion to repeal the Act from Peadar Cowan, a fractious former member of Clann na Poblachta who had been expelled from the party in June 1948 for opposing acceptance of Marshall Aid. Costello also feared a Fianna Fáil assault on the coalition's republican and anti-partitionist credentials as de Valera, on losing office, embarked on a tour of America, Australia, and Britain to denounce the 'artificial division' of his country. More positively, there was the possibility that by taking the initiative in removing the last symbolic links with the Crown and the Commonwealth, Fine Gael would, once and for all, make it impossible for Fianna Fáil to question its 'national' credentials and break out of the downward spiral of election performances that had led Rugby to refer to the possible 'elimination of Fine Gale [*sic*]'.[75] Yet the relatively narrow range of considerations that led the Taoiseach unexpectedly to announce the end of the Act on a visit to Canada in September 1948 was evident not just from the annoyed surprise of his colleagues, who had not formally approved the decision, but from the government's outrage at what might have been considered a likely British response—the Ireland Act of 1949. The implications of the decision to leave the Commonwealth for the government's strongly pronounced policy on ending partition does not appear to have been seriously considered by either Costello or MacBride.

The only original thinking on partition in the government came from the Minister of Finance. Patrick McGilligan saw in the tensions of the Cold War a way in which the new republic could join NATO and also approach the Commonwealth about a mutual defence treaty. This, he argued, would help shift attitudes in the North and make a 'healthy reunion' a possibility. But as Troy Davis has pointed out, the Finance

Minister's radical memorandum, prepared for his Fine Gael cabinet colleagues, was at fundamental variance with Costello and MacBride's policy of making Irish defence co-operation with the Western powers contingent on unification.[76]

McGilligan's blueprint, which fully justified Patrick Lynch's description of his having the 'finest and most original mind',[77] could have done much to bridge the ideological divide on the island through a shared stake in the defence of 'Western civilization'. His colleagues' lack of interest reflected the fear of a break with MacBride and a premature end to a coalition that was clearly serving to restore Fine Gael's credibility as a party of government. The result was a foreign policy that only served to convince those European and American politicians that paid any notice to MacBride's frequent foreign trips of Ireland's irredeemable parochialism.

MacBride was encouraged in his misreading of American attitudes to the strategic significance of Ireland's participation in the proposed NATO alliance by his friendship with George Garrett, who had been appointed American Minister Plenipotentiary to Ireland in 1947.[78] Unlike his predecessor, David Gray, who had become a fervent supporter of Ulster Unionism and was cordially detested by de Valera, Garrett, 'a typical Hibernophile Irish American',[79] pushed for a radical change in established American policy on the Ulster question. Arguing that a united Ireland would contribute strategically to Western defence measures, he suggested that Washington pressure London for the application to Northern Ireland of its 'enlightened policy' in India and other parts of the Empire. The response of officials in the State Department to Garrett's proposals was critical and dismissive. The State Department's Director of European Affairs, John Hickerson, pointed out that the claim that a majority of Irishmen on both sides of the border wanted unity simply ignored the desires of a majority in Northern Ireland. He also disputed, on the basis of Ireland's wartime neutrality, Garrett's strategic argument:

If the Dublin Government were to gain control of Northern Ireland, facilities in that area might be denied us in the future, just as they have been denied . . . in the past. With the United Kingdom in control of Northern Ireland we have . . . every reason to count on the use of its bases . . . I am sure you will agree that this is a powerful argument for this Government's favouring the continued control of Northern Ireland by the United Kingdom.[80]

Despite this analysis, delivered in May 1948, which continued to be the basis of American policy throughout MacBride's tenure at External Affairs, he maintained what Seán MacEntee termed the 'sore thumb' approach to Ireland's foreign policy. While making it clear that Ireland was in solidarity with the West in its struggle to contain communism, he then added that the Irish desire to play a useful role on the international stage was nullified by the 'injustice' of the 'artificial division' of the country. When, in January 1949, the American government asked what the Irish reaction to an invitation to become a member of NATO would be, MacBride's rejection of membership justified itself in terms of the danger of a nationalist uprising against his government for 'selling out' the North. This approach caused severe disquiet not simply in Fine Gael but even in Fianna Fáil, where the appeal of an international crusade against 'atheistic materialism' to some extent counteracted the more solipsistic forms of anti-partitionism. It was on this issue, where the Church's virulent anti-communism made it sympathize with the NATO project, that MacBride chose to display an autonomy distinct from his usual eagerness to please Archbishop McQuaid. This of course fitted easily into a long-established pattern of intransigent republicanism's willingness to risk clerical condemnation in the interests of a nationalist agenda.

Yet there remained the suspicion that for all the emphasis he and Costello placed on the partition issue, the real focus of their attention was not the 'occupied six counties' but the brooding presence of de Valera. For surely, as some critics at the time pointed out, echoing McGilligan's internal memorandum for Fine Gael, NATO membership with the UK would have increased the pressure on Ulster Unionism to at least co-operate more closely with Dublin. Instead, as R. P. Mortished, an ex-Irish Labour Party politician and now Chairman of the Labour Court, put it, the government's attitude 'on the problem of the defence of Christian Civilisation against Soviet Communism was completely negative and futilely isolationist'.[81] While it is possible that MacBride's passionate nationalism blinded him to these realities, it seems more likely that his major motivation was the urge to cede no ground that de Valera could have used electorally. It was also the case that he faced an intransigent republican rump in his own party that could not stomach collaboration with Britain even if it was aimed at Stalin.

As part of his determination that Fianna Fáil would not exploit the freedom of opposition to embarrass the government on its northern policy, MacBride had proposed an all-party committee on partition. This became a reality during the heated exchanges between Belfast and

Dublin provoked by the repeal of the External Relations Act. Responding to Brooke's calling of a Stormont election to register loyalist unity in the face of this challenge, Costello invited the leaders of all parties in the Dáil to a meeting in Dublin's Mansion House to consider ways of helping anti-partition candidates in the northern elections. The meeting's main result, a collection to be held outside Catholic churches throughout the South on 30 January 1949, was hailed by MacBride as 'the first real sign of unity in the national sense since 1921'.[82] Unionists were predictably delighted with this manifestation of southern Catholic-nationalist intent to 'interfere' and used it to great effect in wiping out the NILP.

The effect of official anti-partitionism in solidifying Unionist resistance to change might have been of lesser import if there had been any indication that the campaign was having an effect in London, which was, after all, supposedly the real source of the division of the island. Instead Costello and MacBride were faced with the Ireland Act and in response cranked up the ideological assault on the North. The Mansion House Committee was kept in existence to produce a stream of anti-partitionist propaganda under the direction of Frank Gallagher, who had been for many years de Valera's principal assistant in press and propaganda affairs. Part of MacBride's motivation for transferring responsibility for anti-partition propaganda from his ministry to an all-party committee heavily influenced by a Fianna Fáil traditionalist may have stemmed from his strong suspicion of the allegedly pro-British sympathies of some officials in Iveagh House. Frederick Boland, who was Secretary of the Department of External Affairs when MacBride was appointed, later claimed that his minister's first words to him were a request for a list of all the British agents working in the department.[83] Boland, a pragmatic nationalist, found working for MacBride an uncongenial experience and moved to the position of Irish Ambassador in London in 1950. His subsequent memoranda and those of Conor Cruise O'Brien, whom MacBride had promoted to a new post of Information Officer, provide some early evidence of a growing awareness of the futility of the Irish state's official policy on the North.

O'Brien, who claims that he was already weary of 'the usual anti-partition rubbish',[84] had an opportunity to dissect its shortcomings when he had to respond to a full-frontal assault on the Mansion House Committee by the ex-Free State cabinet minister Ernest Blythe. A member of that rare breed of northern Protestants who supported Gaelic and separatist ideals and was imprisoned during the 1916 Rising, Blythe had

produced a devastatingly critical analysis of the anti-partition campaign.
O'Brien summarized his arguments in a memorandum for Boland:

1 The British will not coerce the North to join us. The maximum which we can
   achieve by our propaganda would be to get British troops to leave Northern
   Ireland.
2 If the British do leave, the North will fight. Mr Blythe believes that because of
   their industry and probable British aid they would be likely to win.
3 Guerrilla activity in the North would be a pretext for pogroms and the mass
   expulsion of the Nationalist population.
4 In these conditions our propaganda campaign abroad, however well conducted, cannot lead to effective action and serves only to increase contention
   between ourselves and the Unionists.
5 There is therefore no prospect of bringing in the North except by peaceful
   persuasion. This would be a long-term jób of 20 to 50 years.[85]

Blythe's own proposals centred on a pledge from the Irish government
that they would not coerce the North, coupled with support for initiatives to increase co-operation in the social and cultural sphere as a
means of lessening Unionist suspicions. He also urged northern nationalists to end policies of non-recognition and to participate actively in the
public life of the state. O'Brien criticized the 'unreality' of some of these
proposals but accepted that there was a good deal of strength in Blythe's
basic contention: 'that the hard core of the Ulster Unionists will only be
made harder by direct attacks, threats and propaganda campaigns'.

O'Brien added one concern that had not featured in Blythe's critique
by suggesting that Unionists should be assured that in a united Ireland
there would be no question of Irish laws on divorce and censorship
being extended to them. This reference to what he called 'their very real
fears of Catholic coercion and domination' would soon be reflected in a
revived emphasis on the religious dimension in Unionist arguments
even before the Mother and Child débâcle. It was sparked by the statistics on religious denominations in the Interim Report of the Irish
Census of 1946, which showed a sharp decline of 13 per cent in the state's
Protestant population during the previous decade. Speeches by Unionist
politicians increasingly focused on what one referred to as an inexorable
tendency to 'the complete and utter extinction of the Protestant
population south of the border'.[86]

There could be no doubting the embarrassment caused to the
anti-partition cause by such figures. The government's response was to
prepare statistics on the position of Protestants in the economic and

public life of the state. Thus Protestants who represented 5.7 per cent of the total population of the state were 26 per cent of those who owned farms of over 2,000 acres, 25 per cent of male professionals, 45 per cent of bank officials, and 32 per cent of all industrial employees. Given that this reflected a pre-partition Protestant pre-eminence in such fields, the statistics were not particularly reassuring, since they demonstrated little about how the minority felt about the direction of public policy since 1922. It seemed to echo the loyalist argument in the North that if things were as bad as nationalists claimed, why had the Catholic population of the state increased since partition? That more middle-class Protestants had not chosen to leave Ireland was not much of a response to Unionist attacks. For as a leading government statistician pointed out, the figures for the decline reflected the fact that non-Catholics had emigrated at a markedly higher rate than Catholics in the decade. This was due to 'pull' factors: 'this class, relatively well-educated . . . could make a living here but they could do much better for themselves abroad in an environment that suits them'.[87]

While the pull of higher wages and salaries in Britain was one dimension of the problem, the fact remained that many had gone to serve in the Forces and an 'environment that suits them' was an oblique reference to the reality of low-intensity unhappiness with what many southern Protestants saw as the anti-British and confessional nature of the Irish state. In 1950 Protestant concerns were reinforced by the Tilson judgement, in which the High Court in Dublin ruled that a Protestant husband who had signed the declaration required by the Catholic Church in mixed marriages that the children would be brought up as Catholics had to cede custody of his children to his estranged wife.[88] The strict censorship of publications, particularly the banning of anything that dealt with artificial methods of contraception, was a long-standing grievance, while compulsory Irish in schools aroused much Protestant resentment.[89] It was also noticeable that in the official response to Unionist criticisms, the bulk of statistical material on employment related to the private sector. The claim was made that in government service and the judiciary Protestants were well represented, although the only example given was that they were two of the eleven members of the Supreme and High Courts. There was no response to the Unionists who pointed out that in three border counties of Donegal, Cavan, and Monaghan with a Protestant population of nearly 15 per cent there were virtually no Protestants on the public payroll.[90]

Unionist concerns were obviously exacerbated by the Mother and

Child affair. More significantly for the anti-partition campaign were the reverberations of the affair in Britain. The Unionist Party's publicity department produced 10,000 copies of a pamphlet, 'Southern Ireland: Church or State?', which was largely a reproduction of the correspondence between Browne, Costello, and the hierarchy together with extracts from the Dáil debate on the affair. Copies were sent to every member of the British Houses of Parliament, to US Senators and members of the House of Representatives, and to legislators in Canada, Australia, and New Zealand.[91] The pamphlet had been preceded by one on the Tilson case and the propaganda offensive appears to have had some effects in Britain, where it undermined support for the anti-partitionist cause in the Labour Party. Boland, who was now Irish Ambassador in London, reported on one significant Labour figure affected by it when he recorded a visit of Aneurin Bevan, the former Minister of Health in Attlee's government, to the Irish Embassy. Bevan was a member of the 'Friends of Ireland' group of Labour MPs and was accompanied by Hugh Delargy, the group's secretary. Bevan's criticism of the Stormont regime, Boland noted, was based not on the 'moral aspects' of the argument for Irish unity but on his anti-Toryism and 'the rage he feels that partition gives the Tories nine seats in the House to which they are not entitled'. His attitude to Ireland was, the ambassador complained, those of a 'typical Britisher', particularly on the legitimacy of Unionists' religious and economic concerns:

He is almost fanatically anti-Catholic. He has the idea that the Church exercises a constant and irresistible pressure on the government of the 26 Counties and he quotes the Dr Browne episode freely as proof of his belief, adding that he was on the point of sending a public message of support to Dr Browne at the height of the crisis when Hugh Delargy dissuaded him from the idea. He is also given to arguing with some vehemence that we ourselves have made the task of ending partition infinitely more difficult by our neutrality in the war and our subsequent repeal of the External Relations Act . . . he constantly harps on the comparison between the social services in the 6 Counties and in the rest of Ireland, asking how we expect, with our standards of welfare benefits, to attract a people already enjoying the best social services in the world.[92]

Concern about the allegedly persecuting nature of the Catholic Church where it was in a position to influence state policy did become an issue for more than the Protestant fundamentalist fringe in early 1950s Britain. Boland attached a perhaps inflated role to the publication of a book on the Catholic Church in America by the anti-Catholic writer Paul Blanshard. Blanshard subsequently visited Ireland and his book *The*

Irish and Catholic Power was published in 1954 with a foreword by the Ulster Unionist MP H. Montgomery Hyde. Boland was also concerned by British newspapers' coverage of the intolerant treatment of Protestant churches in Spain and Latin America. Suspicion of the Catholic Church was, he claimed, 'the only point upon which the Tory outlook of the Church of England and the theoretical socialism of the *New Statesman* and the *Tribune* agree'.[93] If the dormant embers of anti-Catholicism in British national identity were being rekindled, it could only damage the Irish state's ideological assault on the North.

When some of those frustrated by the evident failure of the official anti-partition campaign resorted to traditional physical force methods, the result was the virtual collapse of the campaign in Britain. Delargy, whose loyalty to the Bevanite left was greater than his commitment to Irish nationalism, became increasingly alienated from his former allies. The nadir of traditional forms of anti-partitionism appeared to have been reached with the launch of the IRA campaign in 1956. A few months later Delargy confessed to Lord Brookeborough that 'He had always attacked me on all occasions . . . but now he was satisfied that we were right and he had told Eire that he would have nothing to do with them.'[94] But before any shift in policy toward the North could take place, a fundamental reassessment of the economic direction of the Irish state would have to be forced on a reluctant political élite.

The Economics of National Survival

The 1950s have been described by the economic historian Cormac O'Gráda as 'a miserable decade for the Irish economy'.[95] Real national income virtually stagnated between 1950 and 1958. Agriculture, which still employed 40 per cent of the workforce in 1951,[96] experienced a decline of almost a quarter in the numbers employed during the decade.[97] This reflected a sharp drop in the small-farm sector, which was drained by the opening up of employment opportunities in Britain and was not associated with any significant improvement in productivity. Net agricultural output rose by only 7 per cent in the periods 1950–2 and 1958–60, reflecting the continuing dominance of Irish agriculture by the demands of the British market.[98] Britain was still taking almost 90 per cent of Irish agricultural exports at the end of the 1950s[99] but the advantages that Irish ministers believed the 1948 Trade Agreement would bring had not been realized. The dependence on Britain tied the Irish economy into what, at a time of unprecedented economic growth in the international economy, was the tortoise of Western Europe. The position was worsened by the British system of farm deficiency payments, which depressed prices on the British market.

The record of Irish industry in the period has been the subject of some academic dispute. The dominant critical view has been ably articulated by Liam Kennedy, who points out that industrial output expanded at a 'miserable' 1.3 per cent per annum.[100] A large part of the blame for this is attributed to an outdated protectionist regime. However, in a defence of the protectionist strategy, Brian Girvin argues that it can be counted a limited success, even in the 1950s. Manufacturing industry, the development of which was at the core of protectionism, did expand from 119,000 in 1950 to 134,000 in 1960.[101] In fact, for all that Unionists would boast of the patent economic superiority of Northern Ireland, growth in the manufacturing sector in Northern Ireland during the 1950s was inferior to that in the South.[102]

The problem of unemployment was concentrated on agriculture and the construction industry, which were hit by two highly deflationary budgets in 1952 and 1956 and by the conservative policies followed by successive Ministers of Finance throughout the decade. The 15,000 job increase in manufacturing did little to compensate for the haemorrhage from agriculture, which employed 504,000 in 1951 and 376,000 in 1961, or for the loss of 25,000 construction jobs in the same period.[103] Therefore, although the protected industrial sector did more than hold its own, it remains the case, as Girvin admits, that the Irish state lacked a 'domestic engine of growth' that would have allowed it to take advantage of the general buoyancy of the international economy. Stormont was able to ease the pain associated with the decline of traditional industries by policies geared to the attraction of foreign capital and by substantial increases in public expenditure, courtesy of assistance from the British Treasury. However, south of the border the issue of foreign capital raised the ideological hackles of many in Fianna Fáil, while the strong influence of pre-Keynesian thinking in the Department of Finance acted as a major deflationary influence for most of the decade.

Lemass's willingness to press for radical revisions of policy on protectionism and the possible use of foreign capital in the late 1940s vanished for most of the next decade as he concentrated on the immediate political task of attacking those who had replaced Fianna Fáil in government. When his successor as Minister of Industry and Commerce, the Fine Gael politician Daniel Morrisey, established the

Industrial Development Association in 1948, it seemed a posthumous victory for the Lemass approach to industrial policy. The IDA was given authority to encourage new industry and expand and modernize that already existing. It was also empowered to examine the effects of protection and applications for tariffs. However, Lemass was bitterly critical of the IDA and promised to abolish it when he returned to power. Although there were potential structural problems involved in the relationship between the IDA and the Department of Industry and Commerce, which had lost most industrial policy functions to the new body, his opposition to it stemmed primarily from a desire to mend his fences with Fianna Fáil's allies in the industrial bourgeoisie following their hostile reaction to his earlier Industrial Efficiency Bill.[104] It also reflected the broader Fianna Fáil concern to undermine the nationalist credentials of the inter-party government in the economic field as on the partition question.

Not only did Lemass have to forget his earlier critical approach to Irish industry, but his strong expansionist and Keynesian instincts were clearly subordinated to Seán MacEntee's electioneering attacks on the profligacy of the inter-party government. Back in government as Minister of Finance in 1951, MacEntee was confronted by a major balance of payments crisis caused by the rapid increase in imported consumer goods after years of austerity, the deterioration in the terms of trade caused by the devaluation of sterling in 1949, and the general post-Korean War economic crisis. MacEntee, who later used the term 'monetarist' to describe his approach, responded with the harshest budget in the history of the state. He announced another shilling in the pound on income tax; increases in the price of petrol, tobacco, spirits, and beer; as well as impending increases in the price of the working-class staples of butter, bread, tea, and sugar.

The reaction was sharp. A Labour Party rally in Dublin, to protest against the severity of the budget, was followed by disturbances in which a number of people were injured. Unemployment, which had stood at 36,000 when the inter-party government left office in July 1951, had risen to 57,000 two years later.[105] In the spring of that year a Dublin Unemployed Association was created and it embarrassed the government with sit-down protests in the city centre. Lemass, who had explained the increase in the Fianna Fáil vote in the 1951 election by the party's winning over of a larger slice of the working-class vote,[106] was dismayed by such developments. The fervid anti-communism of the period still weakened opposition to the government. The collapse of the

Unemployed Association was in part brought about by a sustained campaign in the press emphasizing the alleged role of communists within it.[107] But anti-communism was not a sufficient basis to compensate for MacEntee's slap in the face to Fianna Fáil's working-class supporters. Even de Valera's normal tendency to acquiesce in the conservative prescriptions of the Department of Finance went temporarily into abeyance and he asked his cabinet for proposals to stimulate employment.[108] This provided Lemass with the backing he needed to counter-attack and get support for some increase in state investment to stimulate the economy. A National Development Fund was created to finance road improvements and other infrastructural works and an Undeveloped Areas Act aimed at decentralizing industrial development away from the eastern seaboard towards the west in general and the Gaeltacht areas in particular.[109]

Yet the amount of resources involved was small and the attempt to get industries to establish in the west was futile, given the major obstacles that the Control of Manufacturers legislation placed in the way of foreign investment anywhere in Ireland. Lemass's radicalism had not deserted him but he still faced formidable resistance from fiscal conservatives in government and from a large sector of Irish industry that was opposed to any reconsideration of protectionism and to any hint that the state would adopt a more positive view of foreign capital. Yet the impasse of the Irish economy was starkly evident. A report by American experts in 1952 had confirmed that Irish industry was largely lethargic, inefficient, and unready for competition in the world market. Lemass showed a willingness to discourage the more outrageous forms of protectionist feather-bedding in a Restrictive Practices Act of 1953 designed to eliminate price-fixing and in January 1954 announced that he had asked the IDA to review the whole policy of protection. He also returned to a potentially explosive issue: the possibility of a break with the central tenet of Sinn Féin economic philosophy, namely Irish ownership of Irish resources.

On 1 May 1953 Lemass declared 'We welcome foreign capital coming into Irish industrial development when it brings with it new opportunities for expansion and new industrial techniques.'[110] He attempted to counter the inevitable misgivings of party activists by emphasizing that foreign capital did not mean *British* capital. However, the fact remained that for republican ideologues foreign capital was a far more explosive issue than protectionism. Protectionism was only a means to an end: the building up of a native Irish industry. In theory at least it would be possible to abandon protectionism and maintain Irish control of Irish industry. The introduction of foreign capital on a large scale ended the dream once and for all. It was one thing to grumble about the inefficiency and low profit margins of protected industry; it was quite another to reject a fundamental thesis of Irish republicanism. At this time Lemass's embrace of foreign capital was only a very partial and, as it turned out, temporary one. It would take another election defeat and a subsequent economic and demographic crisis to force through an acceptance of foreign capital along with state investment as the twin growth engines that would lift the economy out of its mid-1950s slough.

Lemass's former good relations with the trade union movement had been damaged by MacEntee's deflationary policies and as moves got under way in October 1953 to overcome the eight-year split in the trade union movement, the importance of reconstructing his 'special relationship' with trade union leaders was emphasized. Yet rather than confront the forces of conservatism within his government de Valera decided to mobilize the traditional rural and small-town support, particularly in the west and south-west. After by-election defeats in Cork City and Louth in March 1954 he dissolved the Dáil and the campaign that followed was notable for the degree to which economic issues dominated the agenda. Costello succeeded in putting Fianna Fáil on the defensive by committing a Fine Gael-led government to a mildly inflationary programme of tax cuts, increased food subsidies, and higher social benefits. Lemass's own expansionary instincts were submerged by MacEntee's traditionalist broadside against Fine Gael's 'irresponsibility' and he was reduced to lame attacks on Fine Gael's alleged lack of commitment to protecting Irish industry. The result was de Valera's second electoral defeat. Fianna Fáil dropped from seventy-two to sixty-five seats while Fine Gael continued its post-1948 rise, from forty-five to fifty seats. A clear beneficiary of MacEntee's economic dominance was the reunited Irish Labour Party which moved from sixteen to nineteen seats. The lesson was clear: on the two occasions, 1948 and 1954, when Fianna Fáil approached the electorate with an essentially orthodox economic record, it had been rejected. The failure of strategy in electoral terms would give Lemass a golden opportunity to identify Fianna Fáil with economic expansionism.

The second inter-party government was made up of Fine Gael, Labour, and Clann na Talmhan, with Clann na Poblachta's three TDs supporting it but not participating in government. Its first budget in May 1955 increased old age pensions and other welfare benefits.

However, the mildly ameliorative effects of the budget were soon obliterated by increasing evidence that the economy was moving rapidly out of control. A balance of payments deficit of £5.5 million in 1954 had rocketed to £35.6 million by the end of 1955. This was in part fuelled by a consumer boom arising from a successful union campaign for a national wage increase but also by a drop in cattle and processed-food exports to the UK, where demand had been hit by a credit squeeze and a deflationary budget.[111]

Gerard Sweetman, McGilligan's replacement as Minister of Finance, reacted with a series of vigorous measures. In March 1956 he imposed special import levies on sixty-eight classes of commodities and introduced new taxes on a wide range of consumer goods. The screw was tightened further in July with a widening of the range of import levies and further increases in indirect taxation. Costello, aware of the stress that these measures were putting on Labour's participation in government, tried to lighten the gloom by important new departures in the area of foreign investment. In October 1956 he announced a plan for national development that had at its core a special incentive to encourage exports by a 50 per cent remission of tax on profits derived from increased exports. Already his government had incurred traditionalist criticism by accepting the proposal of an Anglo-American oil combine to build an oil refinery in Cork Harbour. And when the Labour leader and Minister of Industry and Commerce, William Norton, toured Europe and the US to seek foreign capital, Lemass rediscovered the virtues of Sinn Féin economics and de Valera denounced the government for not 'keeping Ireland for the Irish'.[112]

Given Lemass's own shifting views on protectionism and foreign capital, such criticisms were not in themselves particularly damaging. What destroyed the coalition was the increasing sense of national crisis generated by the publication of the preliminary report of the census of 1956. This disclosed that the population, at 2,894,822, was the lowest ever recorded for the state and there had been a decline of 65,771 since 1951. Although the natural increase between 1951 and 1956 was greater than during any period since 1881, the net emigration was higher, at 200,394, than at any period since 1881, a time of intense nationalist criticism of the iniquities of British rule. The year of the fortieth anniversary of the foundational event of the Irish state, the Easter Rising, was one in which the *Irish Times* could editorialize, in response to the census figures, 'If the trend disclosed . . . continues unchecked, Ireland will die—not in the remote unpredictable future, but quite soon.'

Fine Gael and the government as a whole were severely divided over how to respond to the crisis. Costello and Norton had not favoured Sweetman's strategy and Norton was placed under particular pressure by the growing discontent in his party and in the trade union movement. But it was the withdrawal of support by Seán MacBride and the other two Clann na Poblachta representatives that brought the government down in January 1957. The motion of no confidence, although it was in part motivated by anger at the arrest of IRA men by the Irish police, focused on the government's failure to devise an effective long-term economic policy. There was some basis for the Fianna Fáil jibe that a multi-party government could not provide the coherence of principle and strategy necessary to respond to such a profound economic challenge. It was also the case that out of power it would have mercilessly harried the government if it had taken radical measures. Only Fianna Fáil, with its skill in portraying itself as the true inheritor of 1916, was in a position to revise fundamentally the economic nostrums of the national revolution.

It was the aggressively Keynesian themes of Lemass that dominated the Fianna Fáil election campaign. Its main press appeal was headed 'This is the issue: how to put our men and machines to work'.[113] The resultant triumph for the party—a gain of thirteen seats from sixty-five to seventy-eight and its highest ever share of the poll at 53 per cent—[114] meant that Lemass's position as Tánaiste and heir apparent to de Valera had been made impregnable. He was able to insist that MacEntee be moved from Finance to Health and be replaced by one of his closest political allies, Jim Ryan.[115] However, the main immediate beneficiaries of the expansionary ethos that Lemass had given to the election campaign were the party old guard. The result was a sharp contrast to the North, where a *Times* special correspondent noted that while Brookeborough's cabinet was filled with 'vigorous and youngish men', de Valera's government was 'remarkable' for the continuing representation of the revolutionary generation:

Four of his twelve colleagues served, as he did, in the Easter Rising. This is almost exactly in time and approximately in spirit, as though about half Mr. Macmillan's government wore the Mons Star. Three others of the thirteen took part in the 'War of Independence'. The hold on the republic of this ageing group of men is far stronger than that of the coalition which preceded it.[116]

De Valera, 74 and almost blind when he became Taoiseach for the last time, would not hand over to Lemass for another two years, much to his deputy's increasing frustration. But although the changes in economic policy came more slowly than Lemass wanted, there was no doubting that new directions were being set down.

One indication was the important role played by the dynamic and intellectually formidable Secretary of the Department of Finance, T. K. Whitaker. Whitaker had been recommended for the top position in Finance in 1956 by the economically traditionalist Gerard Sweetman. Sweetman may have been impressed by Whitaker's analysis of the unsatisfactory performance of the Irish economy, which he explained by a low level of investment for which he blamed a too rapid expansion of personal and state expenditure in the post-war period. He was particularly critical of high levels of state expenditure in areas of 'social' investment such as housing. He was also dismissive of the application of Keynesian ideas to Ireland.[117] There was an implicit target in this section of the analysis—the 'Clery's Ballroom speech', a strongly Keynesian manifesto delivered by Lemass to the Fianna Fáil organization in Dublin on 1 October 1955. This manifesto was an adaptation of the 1954 Vanoni Plan for post-war reconstruction in Italy.[118] In it Lemass attacked the view, still dear to the hearts of Finance officials, 'that the sole object of government policy should be to keep public expenditure at the lowest possible level'.[119] Its centrepiece was a proposal to create 100,000 jobs in five years through a major programme of public expenditure

However, for the first two years of the new government Jim Ryan's budgets reflected the traditional Finance view. There were cuts in the public capital programme with severe deflationary effects. Whitaker was aware that Lemass's imminent shift to the Taoiseach's position would demand more from his department than the assertion of traditional arguments. The previous government's decision to set up a Capital Investment Advisory Committee without reference to Finance had come as a shock and there was a fear that Lemass's growing ascendancy would result in either Industry and Commerce or the Department of the Taoiseach seizing the initiative in economic policy.[120] Therefore, when Whitaker asked Ryan for authorization to work out an integrated programme of national development for the next five or ten years, he was aiming as much at maintaining Finance's hegemony in the policy process as at addressing what he admitted was a mood of national despondency.

What has subsequently been recognized as the Lemass–Whitaker partnership in forging a new course out of the 1950s stagnation needs to be seen as a much more ambiguous and tension-filled relationship.

Whitaker's report, subsequently published as *Economic Development*, was delivered to the government in May 1958. As Brian Girvin has noted, the report's influence on subsequent economic success may have been exaggerated.[121] There was much in it that reflected the traditional policy style and approach of the Department of Finance and some at least would have made painful reading for Lemass, particularly the jibe at 'setting up fanciful employment targets'. There was an emphasis on the primacy of export-oriented agriculture, something that Lemass rejected as an approach because it failed to comprehend that industry was the only possible engine of future growth. A major aim of the report was to restrict demand and here it resulted in a continuation of the deflationary impact of budgetary policy. Only in its recommendations for an easing of the restrictions on foreign investment in Ireland, for a move towards freer trade, and in favour, at least formally, of the need for a development perspective to be at the centre of state policy, was there a compatibility with Lemass's views.

There were some clear differences between *Economic Development* and the White Paper *Programme for Economic Expansion*, published in November 1958. The *Programme* set out a clear growth target of 2 per cent a year in the 1959–63 period and specified a five-year investment programme. There was also more emphasis on industry and some of Whitaker's suggested cuts in areas such as farm price subsidies and the rural electrification programme were not implemented.[122] Whatever positive psychological impact the very notion of a plan for economic expansion may have had on actual economic performance was insufficient to counteract the rather minimalist nature of the proposed government expenditure. Despite the government's projection of it as a £220 million Five Year Plan, there was only £53 million in actual new expenditure, the rest being composed of pre-Whitaker commitments.

The crucial event for the inauguration of the expansion of the 1960s was not the publication of either document but Lemass's election as Taoiseach by the Dáil on 23 June 1959. After this it became clear that Lemass would dominate economic policy formation and give the *Programme* a much more expansionary significance than Whitaker was happy with. No longer would the balance of payments be fetishized as the OEEC was informed that the next balance of payments crisis would be met through the depletion of reserves rather than by deflationary measures. At the same time the proposals for government expenditure in the *Programme* were substantially exceeded after 1959 to the chagrin of such champions of financial orthodoxy as the Central Bank.

The relationship between the adoption of economic programming and the economic success of the 1960s is still a matter of debate for scholars but the dominant tendency is one of scepticism.[123] Certainly the public expenditure and budgetary components of *Economic Development* and the *Programme* would not in themselves have caused the turn-round from an average annual growth rate of 1 per cent between 1950 and 1958 to a 4 per cent annual average between 1959 and 1973.[124] It was the broader political dimension of the 'watershed' documents that was crucial. The notion of a critical moment in the life of the nation demanding radical new measures made it easier for Lemass to justify the reversal of policy involved in legislation in 1958 that made the first serious breach in the Control of Manufactures Acts. This, together with the existing provision for tax relief on profits from exports, laid the basis for the transformation in Ireland's external trade that would occur in the next decade as manufactured goods replaced cattle and other agricultural products as the largest category in Irish exports. But Lemass was aware that further liberalization of the Irish economy would be demanded in the context of the broader European tendency to free trade. In particular, protectionism would have to be phased out. This, he realized, could be politically difficult given the strong threat to the jobs of many workers, often Fianna Fáil supporters, in the protected industries. To make change more acceptable, the strongly Keynesian perspectives he had first set out in 1945 needed to be maintained. As a result, public policy and the political climate in Ireland was to move more significantly to the left than at any time since the formation of the state.

5

Modernization and Resistance: Northern Ireland 1945–63

Ulster Unionism and British Socialism

Despite the British Labour Party's traditional sympathy with Irish nationalism, the strategic importance of Northern Ireland during the war had impressed itself upon leading members of the Attlee government. Although Chuter-Ede, the Home Secretary, surprised and annoyed some of his officials by referring to Brooke's administration as 'remnants of the old ascendancy class . . . very frightened of the catholics and of the world trend to the left',[1] he soon became a strong defender of Stormont against the interventionist demands of the substantial backbench 'Friends of Ireland' group. The key pro-Stormont minister in London was Herbert Morrison. Like many in the Labour Party, Morrison had been unsympathetic to Unionism but the war transformed his attitude. As Home Secretary he had regularly visited Belfast and in a speech in 1943 praised the loyalty of the North contrasting this with Irish neutrality and declared that it was bound to have a permanent effect on the attitude of the British people to the two Irish states.[2] Although he had no direct involvement in Irish policy after the war, as Lord President and Leader of the House of Commons his views were influential on other senior members of the government, particularly Attlee and Lord Addison, the Dominions Secretary. In 1946, after a private visit to Ireland during which he had met de Valera and Lemass, he wrote a memorandum for the cabinet in which he advocated total support for partition whatever the consequences for Britain's relationship with Éire. He had also come North, where he was privately dismissive of de Valera's regime: 'Éire was in a bad way . . . the Government had no real human sympathy for the people.' He impressed on his Unionist hosts the need to cultivate Chuter-Ede and emphasized that the Attlee government did not intend to continue with nationalization beyond electricity, gas, and transport, praising Brooke's government for 'behaving like moderate socialists'.[3]

However, the pragmatic approach adopted by Brooke in his dealings with Labour had been assailed from the start by those who, like one senior Stormont official, denounced the direction of Brooke's government between 1945 and 1950 as 'the path of the fellow-travellers to the Socialist State'.[4]

For some in the government and party, the division of powers set out in the Government of Ireland Act, which had assumed a *laissez faire* world, had been superseded by the pro-Keynesian policy consensus at Westminster. This meant, according to Sir Roland Nugent, the Minister of Commerce, that Britain, even when the Conservatives returned to power, would accept a large amount of government planning and direction. While this was perhaps appropriate for a largely urban and industrial society, such policies were alien to Northern Ireland where the importance of small-scale agriculture and medium-sized family firms produced a strongly individualist culture. The only way to avoid a major constitutional crisis that would play into the hands of anti-partitionists was to negotiate a much larger degree of independence in the form of the dominion status enjoyed by Australia and Canada.[5]

Nugent's vision of a largely independent Ulster liberating local agriculture and industry from 'socialistic bureaucracy' and with lower rates of direct taxation had at least one major problem. As the only working-class member of the cabinet, William Grant, the Minister of Health and Local Government, pointed out: 'Any suggestion that our party had deserted its Unionist principles for Conservatism, or as our enemies would say, reactionary Toryism, would almost certainly result in the loss of a substantial portion of our Unionist-Labour support.'[6] The fact that support for dominion status had by 1947 become significant within the party reflected the dominance within it of the urban and rural middle class. This group was prone to complain that the North, rather than being a net beneficiary of the post-war welfare settlement, was being over-taxed to support a range of benefits that would only serve to undermine the 'sturdy individualism' of the province's workers. The war years had seen a large increase in the taxation generated in Northern Ireland, a combination of increased income produced by economic expansion and increases in tax rates. In 1939–40 income tax raised in Northern Ireland amounted to £4,485 million, and by 1944–5 it had risen to £18,711 million, while customs and excise revenue had quadrupled. As a result of these buoyant revenues the Imperial Contribution, Northern Ireland's share of the cost of the UK's defence and foreign policy, had soared from £1.3 million in 1939 to £36 million in

1945.[7] At the core of the support for dominion status was the longing of the province's bourgeoisie and farming class for a reactionary utopia, an effectively independent state with low taxes and minimal social services.

Brooke's increasingly hard and dismissive tone towards dominion status reflected economic, political, and constitutional considerations. He was influenced by the major financial benefits that flowed to the Northern Ireland Exchequer through a series of agreements negotiated with the Treasury from 1946. These ensured that the key principles of 'parity' and 'step-by-step' were maintained at a time when the range of services and benefits was being extended radically. The agreements covered national insurance (including unemployment, sickness, maternity, and retirement benefits) and Social Services (which dealt with non-contributory entitlements including national assistance, family allowances, old age pensions, and health). Essentially they allowed for the transfer of resources to Northern Ireland when it could not pay for the cost of these services out of its own tax revenues. There was also provision for the Ministry of Finance to divert revenue from the Imperial Contribution to a new capital-purposes fund to support industrial development and other projects. It was made clear to Brooke and his ministers that the price of these favourable financial arrangements was closer Treasury control of the North's budgetary process.

The economics of the dominion status case simply disregarded the fact that Northern Ireland could not maintain her post-war standards of social services on her own income, even ignoring the questions of the cost of defence and law and order. Farmers might whinge about having to pay national insurance contributions for their labourers, yet if the province became a dominion they would also lose the benefits of price guarantees for their produce, which represented a payment from the British Exchequer of £13 million in 1948. Brooke pointed this out to a Tyrone landowner who had written to him demanding that the premier 'cease to follow England along her socialist road to ruin'.[8]

Brooke had to take the possibility of defections of Protestant workers seriously. Even some of the leading proponents of dominion status in the cabinet accepted that it was not an option if it involved any deterioration in working-class living standards, a fairly damning concession to political realism. Brooke spelled out the danger to a party rally in Larne:

The government is strongly supported by the votes of the working class who cherish their heritage in the Union and to whom any tendency towards separation from Britain is anathema . . . The backbone of Unionism is the Unionist Labour Party. Are those men going to be satisfied if we reject the social services and other benefits we have by going step by step with Britain?[9]

Brooke was convinced that any move to change radically the frame-work of the Government of Ireland Act would reopen the Irish ques-tion at Westminster and 'once that Act is open for fundamental amendment, Westminster would, some would say gladly, seek to merge Northern Ireland with Éire rather than grant greater independence to Northern Ireland'.[10] This greatly exaggerated the amount of anti-partitionist sentiment in the higher reaches of the British state. More typical would have been the reflections of a senior Home Office official on the danger that 'if Éire workers continue to flood North there will in some future election be a Nationalist majority and a Government that wants to break with the United Kingdom and join with Éire'. The experience of the war, which showed the vital importance of British control of the coast and ports of Northern Ireland, meant that such a prospect 'may raise grave strategic problems'.[11] This sort of thinking determined the civil service advice to the Attlee cabinet after the Free State's withdrawal from the Commonwealth in 1948 that 'it will never be to Great Britain's advantage that Northern Ireland should form a territory outside his Majesty's jurisdiction. Indeed it would seem unlikely that Great Britain would ever be able to agree to this even if the people of Northern Ireland desired it.'[12] The government did not go as far as this but in the Ireland Act of 1949 there was a significant strengthening of the Unionist position by the assurance that Northern Ireland would not cease to be part of the UK without the consent of the provincial parliament.

By 1948, the Prime Minister had won the economic and political arguments within the cabinet and the parliamentary party where the leading proponent of dominion status, the MP for South Tyrone, W. F. McCoy, had the support of just two other MPs. There remained much unease at the general direction of government policy in the party at constituency level, particularly in rural areas and in the border counties. Here the conservatism of farmers was allied with a broader fear of the disruptive effects of welfarism on the local class and sectarian balance of power. A prominent Unionist in Londonderry supported dominion status as a means by which the government could ensure that the only immigrants from the South were members of its Protestant minority. In this way the extra labour needed if the city was to expand would not undermine Protestant control of its government.[13] The welfare state and the associated drive by Stormont to build up alternative sources of employment to the traditional staples created much internal turbulence within Unionism and it implicitly raised major questions about the future direction of the state. McCoy's supporters were aghast not simply at the possibility of a deluge from the South but also at clear evidence of less deferential working-class Unionists. As one female party activist complained to the MP, 'things had come to a pretty pass' when McCoy's services were declined at the opening of an Orange fete in Dungannon because of his support for policies that were perceived to threaten a recently opened factory. The local Orangemen were apparently all pro-Labour.[14] For many rural and border Unionists, Brooke's support for the welfare state and new industrial development policies was a slap in the face for 'loyal farmers' who, as one wife of a Tyrone landowner put it, 'are more valuable voters than the factory workers, whose politics may be inclined to be Red or Green!'[15]

Although Brooke gave no strategic ground to the government's critics, he did make a number of significant tactical concessions. British schemes were modified for local conditions. The legislation to create a new public housing body, the Northern Ireland Housing Trust, bitterly attacked at the Ulster Unionist Council in 1946, departed from the British pattern by providing subsidies for private builders.[16] A Statistics of Trade Bill similar to one introduced in the rest of the UK to provide government with a range of information from the private sector, including value and ownership of fixed capital, created waves of apoplexy in chambers of commerce and Unionist associations and was watered down.[17] Fears of 'Eirean infiltration' and attendant shifts in the sectarian balance of power were assuaged by persuading the British government to accept the replacement of the wartime system of residence permits with a new Safeguarding of Employment Act in 1947. This demanded that anyone who was not born in Northern Ireland or could not fulfil stringent residence requirements had to obtain a work permit from the Ministry of Labour. There was also a residence requirement of five years for eligibility for welfare benefits, something not required in the rest of the UK. The central concerns of the Unionists in border areas had been addressed in Stormont's rejection of the British Local Government Franchise Act, which extended the franchise to all citizens over 21. Disenfranchisement of many working-class Protestants was considered a small price to be paid if ruling 'loyal' minorities were to be defended against the nationalist majorities. The pressures from sections of Unionism most prone to see the post-war world as more full of threat than promise damaged Brooke's limited attempts to improve relations with the minority community.

Brookeborough's Regime and Catholics

The conventional wisdom about Sir Basil Brooke's two decades in power is that a major opportunity for change was missed. Sabine Wichert expresses it well: 'For the first time Unionism was in a position to use the chances of post-war changes to improve life in the province substantially and thereby, however indirectly, make a positive case for Stormont rule.'[18] Instead, under the leadership of a rigid and sectarian Prime Minister, it was a period of social and economic change but political stagnation. More recently released archival material shows a more complex picture. It is reflected in a subtle analysis of a major conflict within Unionism in the early 1950s made by an Irish government official:

There is a definite cleavage of opinion between those like Lord Brookeborough and Mr Brian Maginess who believe that the best way of preserving partition . . . is to pursue 'moderate' policies designed to pacify the minority and impress opinion abroad, and those Unionists like Mr Minford, Mr Norman Porter and Mr Harry Midgley who consider that the only sure course lies in an uncompromising adherence to Orange and Protestant principles.[19]

The analysis had been prompted by the poor performance of the Unionist Party in the 1953 Stormont election when it had lost two seats and was attacked by Independent Unionists who accused the Prime Minister, who had become Viscount Brookeborough in 1952, of appeasing Catholics and nationalists. This backlash was a response to an attempt by the Prime Minister, supported by the more liberal elements in his cabinet, to tone down the more stridently sectarian aspects that the Stormont regime had acquired in the 1930s and make a direct appeal to the minority to accept partition for the economic and social benefits it delivered.

The motivation behind this shift was a dual one. The Prime Minister believed that changed national and international circumstances demanded a more emollient public face from Ulster Unionism. As his nationalist critics were aware, not only would future British governments have more leverage with Stormont because of the increased financial dependence attendant on integration into the welfare state, the new US-dominated 'Free World' was ideologically committed to principles of democracy and freedom from discrimination that could be easily integrated into the traditional anti-partitionist repertoire. After 1945 Brooke's diaries reflect his concern to educate an often recalcitrant party in the new realities: 'I told them that the Convention on Human Rights compelled us to be fair and I insisted that I was not going to be responsible for discrimination.'[20] Clearly much had changed from the days when he had boasted of not having a Catholic about the place.

There was more to this than concern with the province's image in the rest of the UK. Like his few liberal colleagues, he appears to have accepted that a combination of circumstances made a more inclusive form of Unionism a possibility. The modernizers believed that the benefits of the welfare state had encouraged a pragmatic acceptance within the Catholic community that partition, now a quarter of a century old, was the inescapable framework within which they must work out their future. Such pragmatism was increasingly encouraged by the travails of the southern economy. Brian Maginess, the Minister of Home Affairs and the most optimistic interpreter of post-war trends, told the Prime Minister that 'the number of Roman Catholics who are gradually coming to have faith in us, our permanent constitutional position and our fair administration, would appear to be increasing considerably.'[21] Brooke publicly echoed the analysis, proclaiming during the 1951 general election campaign that 'even in Nationalist areas electors are beginning to realise that life in British Ulster is to be preferred to existence in a Gaelic republic'.[22]

The sharp disparity between social conditions North and South created by Northern Ireland's integration into the British welfare state was undeniable and while Unionists made much of it in their propaganda war with Dublin, there was a genuine, if myopic hope that such clear material advantages would lessen Catholic alienation from the state. At the first post-war Orange Order celebrations Brooke referred to the new system of family allowances as one indication of the government's 'progressive policy', which he claimed was aimed at benefiting 'all sections of the community'.[23] From family allowances, where 5 shillings a week was provided for each child after the first, in comparison to two shillings and sixpence for each child after the first two in the South, to unemployment benefit, where a single man got 24 shillings in the North and 15 shillings in the South and a married couple 40 shillings in the North and 22 shillings in the South, and with equally significant differences in sickness benefits and pensions, the welfare advantages of northern citizenship were clear.[24] Within three years of the end of the war the North was also enjoying a comprehensive health service, free at the point of delivery, which, as Professor Lyons pointed out, was so much better than what existed in the South that little comparison was possible.[25] The

Education Act of 1947 began the process of developing mass secondary education in the province, which resulted in the number of secondary school students increasing from under 20,000 in 1945 to 104,000 by the time Brookeborough resigned.[26] It increased the capital grants for voluntary (i.e. Catholic) schools from 50 per cent to 65 per cent. It was complemented by the provision of grants for university students, which contributed to a more than doubling of the number of students at Queen's University in the twenty years after 1945.[27]

Housing was another area where there was substantial progress. According to a government survey carried out in 1943, 100,000 of the province's houses, almost a third, needed to be replaced rapidly and, in order to deal fully with substandard and overcrowded dwellings, another 100,000 new houses would be necessary.[28] The Housing Act of 1945 provided for the first time for a large expansion of subsidized local authority housing, breaking with the pre-war policies that had relied on private enterprise for the bulk of new housing. Aware of the obstacles that a combination of sectarianism and a concern for minimizing rate bills might have on a housing drive based solely on local authorities, the government had created the Northern Ireland Housing Trust with powers to clear slums and build and let houses throughout Northern Ireland. There was a substantial increase in the provision of housing after 1945: by 1961, 95,326 new houses had been built compared with 50,000 in the whole inter-war period.[29] More than half, 56,000, were provided by either local authorities or the Housing Trust. From the outset, to the chagrin of many Unionist councillors, Housing Trust allocations were based on a points system and the system was free of allegations of discriminatory intent. Even in the much more contentious area of local authority housing, the record of a small number of Unionist-controlled authorities west of the river Bann has, because of their role in sparking the civil rights movement in the 1960s, been allowed to convey an overly black picture of the housing situation in the post-war period. Councils such as those of Dungannon, Omagh, and Armagh, which built few houses for Catholics, were not typical—even west of the river Bann where fear of giving houses, and thus local author-ity votes to potential nationalist or Sinn Féin voters, was strong. Even in those districts that became the focus for civil rights agitation, the com-plaint was often not that Catholics were refused houses but that they were confined to wards where they were already a majority in order not to disturb the electoral balance. Recent academic studies of the question have tended to emphasize that there were no complaints against the majority of local authorities and the veteran nationalist MP, Cahir Healy, actually praised local authorities in Belfast, Antrim, and Down for their fairness in allocating houses.[30] On the eve of the dissolution of the Stormont parliament, Catholics, who comprised 26 per cent of households in Northern Ireland, occupied 31 per cent of local authority households.[31]

Even in the most contentious area of policing and public order there were signs of an attempt to soften the harder edges of the regime. Brian Maginess began to withdraw many of the regulations made under the Special Powers Act and in 1950 came to cabinet with a proposal to repeal the Act in its entirety.[32] Both he and Brooke supported the policy of the Inspector General of the RUC that, unless there was a substantial threat to public order, nationalist parades should not be interfered with. Worse from the point of view of more traditionalist Unionists, Maginess supported the police when they put limits on Orange parades, most dramatically in his ban of an Orange march along the predominantly nationalist Longstone Road in county Down in 1952.[33]

The universalistic implications of British welfarism and the more liberal and inclusive type of Unionism associated with it brought an inevitable reaction. For many Unionists, particularly in the border areas, they flew in the face of the post-war resurgence of anti-partitionist politics within the North, supported as it was by a much more aggressive international campaign by the inter-party government in the South after 1948. Despite the province's less than sterling contribution on the volunteering and industrial fronts during the war, nationalist resistance to conscription and the South's neutrality fed a strong current of resentful indignation that the minority should receive any benefits from the post-war settlement. The sentiments expressed by the Unionist MP Dehra Parker to county Derry Orangemen were commonplace: 'These people who are protected under our laws are turning around and biting the hand that feeds them and are trying to blacken Ulster's good name at home and abroad.'[34]

The Orange Order, whose membership had declined during the depressed conditions of the inter-war period and which had forgone its traditional parades during the war, reasserted itself as a major force within Unionism after 1945. The post-war expansion in state services and expenditures provided the Order with a whole range of new opportunities to pressurize party and government to ensure the proper defence of Orange and Protestant interests. The 1947 Education Act was seen by many Orangemen as a major concession to the Catholic Church and the Order waged a rearguard action against the implementation of the Act and for the replacement of the Minister of Education, Colonel Hall-Thompson. When the Minister further enraged the Unionist right and the Order by proposing in 1949 that the state should pay the employer's portion of Catholic teachers' national insurance contributions, Orange pressure was so great that the Prime Minister had to attend a meeting of its supreme authority, the Grand Lodge of Ireland, to explain the government's position. He attempted to convince the leaders of the Order that the government had to be fair to all sections of the people and that 'they would still have a large minority in Northern Ireland and if they were treated unfairly as an "oppressed people" it would create a bad impression in England'. His listeners were clearly reluctant to accept such conciliatory ideas for, as one reverend gentleman from county Antrim put it, 'Not a single Roman Catholic was dissatisfied with the bill. They were getting butter on their bread and they wanted more butter.'[35] Brooke was only able to save the bill by sacrificing Hall-Thompson, whom he persuaded to resign and be replaced by the Labour renegade Harry Midgley, who had joined the Unionist Party in 1947. Midgley, embittered by the role the Catholic Church had played in his election defeat in the 1930s when he had been a champion of the Spanish Republic against the Church's hero Francisco Franco, had become evangelical in his opposition to 'concessions' to the Catholic school system.

The resignation of Hall-Thompson is illustrative of the need for a more nuanced reading of the relationship between the Order and the Unionist regime. The conventional view is of an 'Orange state' determined by the facts that the Order had direct representation at the party's ruling Ulster Unionist Council and the vast bulk of Unionist activists and almost all MPs and cabinet members were members. This, it is assumed, had a determining effect on a range of government policies. In fact, while Orange pressure almost always evoked a government response, it was often not one that satisfied Orange militants.

The Prime Minister expected the leadership of the Order to take heed of the imperative of maintaining Unionist unity and of not giving nationalists easy propaganda material. Thus although he lost his Minister of Education, the legislation was unaffected and Midgley's desire to claw back the increase in grants to Catholic schools in the 1947 Act was frustrated. It has been argued that Midgley's prejudices did have significant effects in ensuring that the Catholic sector got fewer resources than it might have from the large increase in government expenditure on education in the 1950s.[36] His ministry's estimates rose from less than £4 million in 1946 to more than £12 million in 1957. In the new sector of secondary intermediate schools, by 1957–8 there were 28,000 places in state (Protestant) schools and only 5,000 places in the voluntary (Catholic) sector. There were places for more than half the Protestant primary-school leavers but for less than a fifth of the potential demand from Catholic primary schools, although these contained 44 per cent of the primary-school population.[37] This was, in part at least, the price that Catholics paid for their Church's determination to maintain untrammelled control of its schools. Yet, as Unionists pointed out, the 65 per cent capital grant was higher than what was available in England, and a recent history of Ulster Catholics by a Jesuit referred to the provisions as generous.[38] Nevertheless, a yet more generous policy might have paid political dividends.

Where Midgley's views did seriously affect policy and provide the Catholic Church with justifiable cause for complaint was in the concession to the governing committees of schools within the wholly funded sector of the right to supervise denominational religious instruction and to assess teachers on 'faith and morals'. This substantially increased the influence of the Protestant clergy in the state sector. It was also the case that the often protracted process of getting planning approval for the building of new Catholic schools at times reflected strong grass-roots Orange pressure against what one Belfast lodge referred to as 'this subsidy of Popery and Nationalism which are the enemies of our Ulster heritage'.[39]

The strongest pressure against any 'appeasement' policies came, not from the Orange Order, which was internally divided on the issue, but from an upsurge of Protestant fundamentalism in the late 1940s and early 1950s. This was the period when a young evangelical preacher, Ian Paisley, first emerged as a scourge of those in government and the leadership of the Orange Order, who were allegedly making concessions to 'Popery' and Irish nationalism. The initial focus of attack was the 1947 Education Act denounced for 'subsidising Romanism'.[40] This was linked to claims that Brooke's government was acquiescing in an invasion of southerner Catholics getting jobs and buying up land in border areas. Sectarian animosities were intensified by developments in the South, where the influence of the Catholic Church on public policy was highlighted by the Mother and Child crisis in 1951, and by the preliminary report of the Irish census of 1946, which showed a decline of 13 per cent in the Protestant population in the 1936–46 period.[41] In Northern Ireland the Bishop of Derry, Dr Farren, made his own contribution to community relations when he referred to Catholics being 'contaminated' by going into non-Catholic halls for dances.[42]

Protestant and Orange dissatisfaction with the government's education policy was surpassed in intensity by an increasingly hysterical chorus of complaint about 'soft' public-order policy. Maginess's attempts to implement a more balanced approach, which culminated in the banning of the Orange march on the Longstone Road in 1952, produced a fierce reaction from the Order and from within the party at all levels. Reaction had intensified as a result of sectarian confrontations over the enthusiastic displays of the Union flag occasioned by the coronation of Queen Elizabeth II in June 1953. Some loyalists had insisted on the display of the flag on houses and businesses in the heart of predominantly Catholic and nationalist areas like the Falls Road, and the RUC had only been able to prevent riots by persuading the loyalists to remove the flags.[43] For the government's loyalist critics this amounted to a cowardly ceding of public space to nationalism. Their disquiet was magnified when nationalists in the predominantly Catholic village of Dungiven, in county Londonderry, prevented a coronation day march by an Orange band.[44]

The government's alleged 'appeasement' policy was the main element in the campaign of the group of Independent Unionists who made substantial inroads into the Unionist Party vote in the 1953 election. Paisley's brand of Protestant fundamentalism was influential during the election that saw Hall-Thompson defeated by Norman Porter, an ally of Paisley who was the editor of the *Ulster Protestant*, a monthly paper fixated on the government's 'subsidies to Popery'. Brookeborough's response was a substantial tack to the right. Brian Maginess was shifted from Home Affairs and was never again a substantial figure in the government. In deference to loyalist fundamentalists, and against the advice of the Inspector General of the RUC, a Flags and Emblems Act was passed in 1954. This obliged the police to protect the display of the Union flag anywhere in Northern Ireland and empowered them to remove any other flag or emblem whose display threatened a breach of the peace. The latter provision would be used by loyalist ultras to demand that the RUC remove the Irish Tricolour even when it was being displayed in a predominantly nationalist area.[45]

There was increasing evidence of a reluctance on the Prime Minister's part to challenge the demands and prejudices of his more extreme supporters. He was prepared to support a Family Allowances Bill in 1956, which, while increasing allowances in line with Britain, proposed to abolish payments for the fourth and subsequent children. It was clearly aimed at penalizing Catholics but Brookeborough only reconsidered when some of the Unionist MPs at Westminster pointed out that even their Tory allies would criticize what would be seen as a blatant piece of discriminatory legislation.[46] Behind the scenes he exerted himself in the interests of those Derry Unionists who were afraid that if the government's industrial development policies were successful, the new industries would employ too many 'disloyalists'.[47] The Prime Minister's intervention appears to have been decisive in ensuring that the US multinational Dupont, which was planning a major investment in the city, appointed the secretary of Derry Unionist Association as its personnel officer.[48] Although the appointment did not prevent Dupont becoming a large employer of Catholics, it was an indication of Brookeborough's firm belief that he had to show a continuing responsiveness to the most reactionary voices in the party. These depressing concessions to sectarian pressures were not uninfluenced by increasing signs of a resurgence of republican militarism, which culminated in the launching of a full-scale campaign against the northern state in December 1956.

Even without pressure from Protestant fundamentalists and the IRA, there were strict limits to the more inclusive form of Unionism proposed by Brookeborough and Maginess. It did little to address nationalist grievances about discrimination in the employment practices of central and local government. The charge of 'vicious sectarian discrimination'[49] ignored important dimensions of the problem: lower levels of educational attainment and the attitude of suspicious hostility adopted by some Catholics to those of their co-religionists who joined the civil service or the police.[50] It also ignored the fact that at manual labour and clerical level Catholics generally received their proportionate share of public employment. Yet there could be no denying the stark under-representation of the minority in the higher ranks of the civil service, local government, and the judiciary. At the end of the 1950s Catholics comprised only 6 per cent of the higher ranks of the Northern Ireland civil service defined to include the hardly exalted grade of staff officer.

While discrimination was not solely responsible, it undoubtedly played a role. Brookeborough's conception of fairness seems to have entailed a belief that Catholics should have a proportionate share of the total number of public service jobs while leaving Protestant dominance of key positions unchallenged. In 1956, after Orange concern about

Catholics employed in Belfast law courts, he asked Brian Maginess, the Attorney General, to get figures that he hoped would soothe his critics: 'Brian showed that in the higher grades the proportion of Unionists was very high indeed and in the lower grades not worse than three to one. I said we had to be fair in giving employment but we need not go further than that.'[51] While he accepted that Catholics had a right to their share of the positions as law clerks, he was determined that there should be no more than one Catholic among the senior judiciary. A Catholic had been appointed to the Supreme Court in 1949, giving the minority one out of forty senior positions in the higher courts. When the Lord Chief Justice nominated a Catholic QC for a High Court judgeship in 1956, Brookeborough told him he would oppose it: 'I did not like the idea of another Nationalist on the bench.'[52] The man concerned, Cyril Nicholson, was a prominent opponent of republican violence and a proponent of a more positive engagement by Catholics with the state.

While the undoubted material improvements of the post-war period—real income per head rose by one-third during the 1950s—did not have as strong an effect in lessening the minority's alienation from the state as liberal Unionists had hoped, they also reflected resentments over actual or alleged discrimination in private employment. Although a largely political explanation of the Catholic economic disadvantage emphasizing the role of the 'Orange state' is increasingly seen as inadequate by scholars,[53] the facts of Catholic disadvantage are undisputed. There was clear Protestant over-representation in skilled, supervisory, and managerial positions and massive predominance in industries like shipbuilding, engineering, and aircraft production, which provided well-paid and relatively secure employment. Catholics were over-represented in the unskilled and the unemployed and crowded into industries such as construction and transport where wages were lower and employment more insecure.[54] In workplaces such as the shipyard there were strong Orange and loyalist influences on hiring, although they were countered to some degree by trade union organization. Perhaps even more important than overt pressure was the pervasive influence of kin and neighbourhood in a society with high levels of residential segregation on what was a largely informal recruiting mechanism.

If longer-term structural factors disadvantaged Catholics in the industrial heartland, they also produced a clear east–west gradient in unemployment and living standards. The core of the industrial economy of the province remained the greater Belfast area. The government was accused of favouring majority Protestant areas like Belfast and the east of the province in its industrial development policies and neglecting the western periphery where Catholics were in a majority.[55] In fact the Stormont regime did show some concern for high levels of unemployment in Londonderry, Strabane, and other largely nationalist towns, particularly after a visiting British Labour Party delegation in 1954 warned of its potential for civil unrest and potential subversion.[56] However, the Ministry of Commerce officials involved in the government's programme of advanced factory building had major problems interesting potential investors in what were perceived to be remote areas which, although they had high percentage rates of unemployment, lacked large pools of the skilled and experienced labour that incoming industrialists often demanded. Although Belfast had the lowest rate of unemployment in the North, it also possessed the largest pool of unemployed skilled labour and this, together with its port, meant that many new industries simply refused to look beyond its boundaries. As the Minister of Commerce explained to the cabinet in 1956, 'we are not in as strong a position as to be able to turn away industry that is prepared to come to Belfast or not at all.'[57]

Although the charge of malign neglect of the west will not hold up, there was undoubtedly a tendency to pay more attention to the large concentrations of unemployed Protestants in the east, whose dissatisfaction could mean a loss of significant electoral support. There was also the complacent assumption that unemployed Catholics would remain acquiescent because they had a realistic grasp of conditions in the South. When, in 1954, R. A. Butler, the Tory Chancellor of the Exchequer, questioned Stormont about the British Labour Party claim that high unemployment could lead to 'serious political trouble' in places like Derry and Newry, Brian Maginess dismissed the idea as 'complete nonsense . . . so long as these people continue to enjoy Northern Ireland rates of unemployment benefit or national assistance . . . we have no fear of any kind of trouble.'[58]

The fear of senior Derry Unionists that new industries would undermine their control of the city by bringing in an unmanageable influx of Catholic workers had an inhibiting effect on attracting new industries. Teddy Jones, the Unionist MP for the City of Londonderry constituency, was the main messenger boy for the city's Unionist hierarchy. Indeed, his lobbying ensured that these fears were discussed at the highest level of the state, where a cabinet sub-committee was set up to try and ensure that industrial development was made compatible with continuing Unionist control of the city. Lord Brookeborough exerted himself to ensure that government departments and the Housing Trust did all they could to address the problem.[59]

Apart from its effect on employment, the local Unionist power structure also impacted on the city's housing. To maintain the situation, where in 1961 Derry was 67 per cent Catholic but still under Unionist control, it was necessary that as far as possible all new housing for Catholics was in the south ward, where two-thirds of the city's Catholics were concentrated.[60] The need to maintain the gerrymandered system meant, not simply a reluctance to house Catholics in the other two wards on the part of Derry corporation, but also severe restraints on where the Northern Ireland Housing Trust could build. The result was a substantial amount of overcrowding and a long waiting list, largely Catholic, for public housing.[61]

The Derry situation epitomized the dynamics of the regime's sectarianism, which was more about the central government's complicity in a limited number of flagrantly unjust situations than Stormont being an activist 'Orange state'. There were limits to Brookeborough's willingness to indulge Jones and his friends in the north-west. When he received a letter from the MP opposing any further industrial development in Derry, the perversity of this caused the Prime Minister to exclaim, 'No government can stand idly by and allow possible industries not to develop.'[62] Derry Unionists did not prevent Dupont's government supporting investment in the city in the late 1950s or Brookeborough's vigorous lobbying of London to prevent the closure of the Navy's anti-submarine training base at Eglinton, near Derry, in 1958.[63] But the existence of a local authority with such deep hostility to development had serious effects on the government's industrial development policy. By the beginning of the 1960s Derry had a potentially explosive combination of unemployment and housing shortage, both of which could be given a plausible political explanation in terms of a hard-faced Unionist élite.

'An Invertebrate Collectivity': The Dilemmas of Northern Nationalism

The reaction of the leaders of nationalism to Labour's victory in 1945 was the predictable obverse of loyalist apprehension. Attaching an exaggerated importance to Labour's already frayed tradition of pro-Unity sentiment and to the formation of the back-bench pressure group 'The

Friends of Ireland' at Westminster, the ten nationalist MPs elected to Stormont in 1945 promoted a new organization, the Anti-Partition League (APL), whose purpose was to energize and unify nationalism within Northern Ireland and press London to re-open the partition question. The role of the US as the dominant power in the non-communist world and Britain's economic and strategic dependence on America were seen as giving a new opportunity for Irish-American lobbying of Washington. Expectations of progress from London were soon dashed as the Attlee government's pro-Union sentiment became obvious. By 1947 the APL was denouncing Labour as the enemy and beginning to consider the possibility of attempting to organize the Irish vote in Britain to punish Attlee at the next election.

The nationalist MPs returned to Stormont in 1945 were largely drawn from the Catholic rural and small-town middle class: farmers, lawyers, journalists, auctioneers, and publicans drawn predominantly from the west and south of the province.[64] Belfast nationalism had never recovered from the death of Devlin and his combination of pragmatic nationalism and pro-Labour views. The city returned one nationalist MP in 1945, the barrister T. J. Campbell, who soon shocked the party by accepting a county court judgeship. The nationalists were subsequently never to hold a Belfast seat and their local government base in the city had almost vanished by the early 1950s. They were pushed aside, not by the more militant nationalism of Sinn Féin, but by organizations labelling themselves Socialist Republican and, after a split in the NILP in 1949, Irish Labour. The nationalists' lack of appeal to the Catholic working class in Belfast was not unrelated to their strong denunciation of the welfare state, which it was proclaimed might be suitable to an industrial nation like Britain but was 'wholly unsuitable to an area such as the Six Counties which is predominantly agrarian and under-populated'. Echoing the Unionist right's arguments, it was alleged that the 'extravagant scale' of benefits provided by the welfare state and the national health service would reduce the 'people' to bankruptcy.[65]

The nationalists' conservatism was a northern manifestation of the Catholic Church's opposition to the welfare state for its allegedly 'totali-tarian' dangers. It reflected the strong Catholic faith of nationalist MPs and the central role that the clergy played in their primitive electoral machine. Despite the formation of the APL the nationalists failed to develop a modern party organization. They concentrated on those areas where Catholics were in a majority. Six of their ten MPs were returned without a contest in 1945. The only real activity was carried on by registration committees dedicated to ensuring that all eligible Catholics were registered to vote and as many as possible of the 'other side' had their eligibility challenged. Candidates were chosen at conventions often presided over by a priest and composed of delegates selected at after-mass meetings. As Dr Conor Cruise O'Brien, then an official of the Department of External Affairs, noted, 'The nature of the structure at parish level plays into the hands of those who regard the nationalists in the Six Counties as a purely sectarian organization.'[66]

O'Brien acerbically commented that the APL 'can hardly be called an organization at all; it is an invertebrate collectivity. It has an allegiance but no policy.' Although nationalist hopes in radical action from the Labour government were quickly disappointed, they were replaced by what would prove to be an equally empty faith in the new inter-party government in Dublin. Seán MacBride, as Minister of External Affairs, had promised to provide a right of audience in the Dáil for northern nationalist MPs and to nominate leading northerners to the Senate.[67] This seemed to offer nationalists a form of institutional involvement in the southern state after more than two decades of much resented neglect. However, the proposal was too much for MacBride's colleagues and it was vetoed by Costello. Nevertheless, before disillusion could set in, the torpid waters of northern nationalism were churned up by the decision to repeal the External Relations Act and declare a republic.

The president of the APL and the leader of the nationalist MPs at Stormont, James McSparran, a barrister who was MP for Mourne, saw the purpose of attending Stormont and Westminster as highlighting the iniquities of Unionist rule, not to elicit reform but rather to embarrass the British government sufficiently to make it willing to re-open the partition issue. Rather predictably, the adoption of a much more rhet-orically republican tone by the Irish government produced a shattering blow to such hopes. The Ireland Act, by strengthening the Unionists' constitutional guarantee, produced a strong emotional reaction in the South that only served to underline the futility of constitutional anti-partitionism. The creation of the all-party Anti-Partition Campaign and its raising of funds for nationalist candidates in the 1949 Stormont elec-tion by a collection outside Catholic churches throughout the island helped to ensure that the election was fought in the most viciously sectarian environment since the 1930s.

The inter-party government's rhetorical breach in the wall of north-ern nationalist isolation had an energizing effect, particularly in border areas like Derry where Eddie McAteer, the leading APL politician in the city, attempted to give a new activist edge to anti-partitionist politics. In a pamphlet, *Irish Action*, he suggested a nationalist campaign of obstruction against Stormont involving a refusal to deal with such bodies as the Inland Revenue and the Post Office.[68] More realistic was his determination to exploit Derry Catholics' still raw resentment over the gerrymander of the city's government. Nationalist resentment at the gerrymander was amplified by the determination of Unionists to define the centre of the city, enclosed within its plantation walls, as a loyalist public space. The upsurge of nationalist self-confidence in 1948 led to a proposal for a large anti-partition demonstration in Derry, which was banned under the Special Powers Act. McAteer became active in challenging future bans on nationalist parades within the city centre. The local Catholic bishop, Dr Neil Farren, was opposed to what he regarded as 'anti-partitionist stunts' but McAteer saw in the inevitable conflicts with the police a means of maintaining a sharp sense of Catholic grievance and counteracting the integrative effects of the welfare state.[69]

When the return of de Valera to power in 1951 brought a shift towards a softer line on the North and an attempt to build up practical links in areas such as cross-border co-operation on transport and electricity production, the response from the APL was hostile. McAteer denounced the 'fraternization' policy as shoring up partition, and when officials of the South's Electricity Supply Board were invited to meet their northern counterparts at a lunch in Derry the event was boycotted by the APL. A frustrated Conor Cruise O'Brien, charged with liaising with the APL, noted the criticisms but added 'they did not have any alternative policy to propose . . . their main interest was in the local situation in Derry and in how it could be exploited for the discomfiture of Unionists rather than in any general strategy on partition.'[70]

The IRA's 1956 Campaign

McAteer's interest in more militant tactics reflected an awareness that as the sound and fury of southern-sponsored anti-partitionism dissipated in failure, it would leave the APL dangerously vulnerable to republican exploitation of the disenchantment with constitutionalism amongst a younger generation of nationalists. MacBride's presence in government had contributed to a decline in police activity against the IRA in the Republic and enabled it to regroup and be in a better position to benefit from the rise and decline of official anti-partitionist fervour. Calculating that as long as violence was directed at the northern state, popular sympathy for 'the boys' would weaken the southern state's capacity to act against them, a military council was created in 1951 to plan a full-scale campaign.[71] Although the Ebrington Territorial Army base in Derry was raided for arms in 1951, the return of de Valera to power appears to have weakened IRA capacity to operate in the North. The next, and much more spectacular, raid, on Gough Army Barracks in Armagh, did not take place until June 1954, when a new inter-party government was in power.

Out of office, MacBride had done his best to encourage republican militancy by coming North to speak in favour of the IRA dissident Liam Kelly, who won the Mid Tyrone seat in the 1953 Stormont election. Kelly, who was expelled from the IRA for unauthorized 'operations', went on to establish a party, Fianna Uladh (Soldiers of Ulster), and a military organization, Saor Uladh (Free Ulster). He followed MacBride in arguing that republicans should accept the legitimacy of the Republic and direct their energies solely against Stormont. This made him popular beyond the republican hard-core. Cahir Healy, whose Westminster seat for Fermanagh and South Tyrone was vulnerable to republican challenge, bewailed the support given to Kelly in the South, particularly by the Fianna Fáil supporting *Irish Press*, whose editor believed, despite the policy of de Valera, that only force would get rid of the border.[72]

MacBride, who was supporting the new coalition from the back benches, managed to get Kelly nominated for the Senate. At a time when the Senator was serving a year's imprisonment for seditious statements during the election, MacBride's action helped to strengthen republican self-confidence, already boosted by the Armagh raid. Although McAteer had been enthusiastic about the effects of the raid in 'keeping up morale amongst a population which had been cowed and defeated',[73] many of his colleagues in the APL were dismayed by the signs that disillusion with constitutional politics was feeding into increasing sympathy for those prepared to use methods of physical force. Brookeborough's concession to the right on the Flags and Emblems Act gave the republicans a major propaganda victory when, on Kelly's release in August 1954, the RUC's attempt to prevent the flying of the Irish flag by a crowd of 10,000 that had gathered to welcome him in his home village of Pomeroy caused a major riot.[74]

In an evaluation of opinion in the wake of the Armagh raid, Conor

Cruise O'Brien noted that while the event was 'greeted with universal approbation and even glee by all Nationalists in the Six Counties', many of those who applauded did so 'in a more or less "sporting" spirit without reflecting on the consequences of the actions or the logical conclusion of the policy behind them'. Bloodshed would alienate support for the IRA.[75] There was bloodshed during the next IRA arms raid, a botched attack on Omagh Army Barracks in October 1955. Five soldiers were wounded, two of them seriously. However, the absence of deaths amongst what even the Taoiseach referred to as 'forces of occupation', and the fact that the eight young men arrested, all southerners, were sentenced to long prison terms, ensured that moral and prudential qualms were submerged by waves of sympathy for what was widely perceived to be a group of brave young idealists.[76]

Sinn Féin was quick to exploit this popular mood and the APL's divided and demoralized state by putting up candidates, some of them serving time for the Omagh raid, for all the North's Westminster constituencies in the general election of May 1955. The result was a clear propaganda coup. It won Fermanagh and South Tyrone and Mid Ulster, where two of the imprisoned Omagh raiders were elected, and was able to boast of amassing the largest anti-partitionist vote ever: a total of 152,310 votes. Yet, as its APL critics bitterly but justly pointed out, this was a hollow victory. The size of the vote reflected the fact that the majority of seats had previously not been contested. As a result of Sinn Féin's intervention, Jack Beattie of the Irish Labour Party lost West Belfast to a Unionist and the other two nationalist seats at Westminster were lost to Unionists after the disqualification of the two Sinn Féin MPs. Nor could Sinn Féin use their vote as a popular sanction for future IRA violence, as their candidates had insisted that they were not asking people to vote for the use of force.[77]

Nevertheless, the apparent surge in republican political fortunes did quicken the pace of IRA preparations for a northern offensive. The IRA leadership was also anxious to pre-empt a rival campaign by Kelly after Saor Uladh attacked a police barracks in Roslea in Fermanagh in November 1955. 'Operation Harvest' was launched in December 1956. From the start its focus was on the border counties where, it was hoped, local IRA units assisted by 'flying columns' from the South would destroy communications links with the rest of the province, destroy RUC barracks, and, with the at least tacit support of local nationalists, create 'liberated zones' free of Stormont control. Whether this was seen as a prelude to a general nationalist uprising, perhaps provoked by a heavy-handed government response, or simply as a dramatic event that would force Britain to re-open the partition question is not clear.

The largely southern leadership of the IRA had a weak grasp of northern realities. Seán Cronin, the ex-Irish soldier who was IRA Chief of Staff and the strategist behind 'Operation Harvest', had some awareness of the dangers of IRA actions triggering the sort of sectarian violence that had occurred in the 1920s and in 1935. For this reason, and despite the complaints of northern IRA men, there were to be no attacks on the part-time and locally based B Specials.[78] Although the RUC were defined as legitimate targets, initially IRA attacks took the form of frontal assaults on police barracks by IRA members wearing surplus US and British army uniforms. The most famous attack of the campaign, on Brookeborough RUC station in January 1957, in which the IRA's main martyrs of the campaign, Sean South and Feargal O'Hanlon, were killed, typified this approach. Whatever the military futility and political obtuseness of this type of attack, its capacity to ignite sectarian animosities was less than the more classically terrorist attacks on police personnel by booby traps and ambushes carried out by local IRA men in civilian dress. Although the RUC death toll was comparatively light at six deaths, as the campaign failed to maintain its initial momentum and relied increasingly on local resources, it shifted to tactics more likely to provoke a violent loyalist response.[79]

That such attacks did not provoke a loyalist backlash was in large part due to the fact that the campaign was clearly a failure and had not affected Belfast. Although Cronin has claimed that Belfast was excluded from his plan to avoid sectarian confrontation,[80] it does not appear that this was known by the Belfast IRA, who had drawn up plans for attacks on targets ranging from RUC stations and the homes of policemen to contractors who did work for the security forces.[81] RUC intelligence on the Belfast IRA was good and the arrest, just before the campaign started, of one of their leading members who was in possession of important Belfast battalion documents was followed by a series of arrests that put the city's organization out of business for the rest of the campaign.[82]

Although the campaign was not called off until February 1962, its failure had been clear much earlier. Republicans had overestimated the degree of nationalist alienation from the Stormont regime and failed to understand that initial sympathy for what were often seen as brave but misguided idealists would not extend to the killing of policemen along with the attendant risks of loyalist retaliation. Condemnations of the campaign by Cardinal Dalton, the head of the Catholic Church in Ireland, and by the Taoiseach did not impress the RUC Special Branch, who thought they would not have the slightest effect on the IRA.[83] It was also the case that some of the local clergy in Fermanagh and Tyrone had strong republican sympathies. The defeated APL MP for Mid-Ulster was bitterly critical of the clergy of the constituency, some of whom had openly supported Sinn Féin, while others had instructed local convents not to vote and refused the APL the use of parochial halls during the 1955 campaign.[84] Liam Kelly's closest advisers were two local priests.[85] However, as the campaign continued, denunciations of IRA membership or support made by the local bishop and the clergy in Tyrone and Fermanagh were seen as having more effect.[86] Much more significant in determining the attitude of the vast bulk of nationalists to the campaign was the clear evidence from its earliest days that it was little more than a series of pinpricks against the formidable security apparatus of the northern state. The RUC, with the aid of 13,000 Specials, the assistance of the British army, and the introduction of internment, had little problem in ensuring that the idea of 'liberated zones' proved as illusory as the IRA appeal to the Protestants of Ulster to support Irish unity.[87] MacBride's support for the inter-party government did not prevent the coalition taking immediate action against the IRA, and when de Valera returned to power he did not hesitate to introduce internment. The result was clear from the RUC's figures for major incidents, which fell from 138 in 1957 to 80 in 1958 and 19 in 1959.[88]

Sinn Féin's vote in the 1959 Westminster election slumped by over a half compared with 1955, but there was little sign that the setback to militant republicanism would do anything to lift the APL out of its organizational and intellectual torpor. The success of the NILP in the 1958 elections served to underline the ineffectuality of the nationalist MPs at Stormont. An attempt by some of the less inert MPs together with Irish Labour and Republican MPs to dissolve the party and replace it with a new formation was only narrowly defeated.[89] The apparent collapse of the physical force tradition and the growing dissatisfaction of a section of the Catholic middle class with the ineffectual negativism of the APL opened up the possibility of a new more engaged and participationist type of nationalism. Unfortunately for the future of the North, the Unionist Party's increasing problems with its core support group, the Protestant working class, prevented a more positive engagement with these changes.

Economic Change and Unionist Politics

Despite the Brookeborough government's aggressively optimistic view of the economy in public, it had a much darker private assessment. For most of the period from 1945 to the early 1960s the major political foe of the regime was seen to be Irish nationalism. In its response to the anti-partitionist campaign it was easy for the government to point out the economic and social advantages that the Union brought to all the citizens of Northern Ireland. The British and American journalists who had arrived in Ireland to cover the IRA campaign were given the following riposte to nationalist tales of a northern minority thirsting for unity: 'In agriculture, in the social services, in education, in industrial development and in our standard of living, we are streets ahead of Éire and are strengthening our lead every day.'[90] The government's problem was that precisely because the majority of the electorate did not expect or desire to be part of an all-Ireland state, their frame of reference was British not Irish. Wages and unemployment levels in the rest of the UK were the standards against which Stormont's economic record would be judged.

This was not a record of unadulterated failure. The government had to deal with an economy that suffered from remoteness, higher transport costs, and a lack of domestic supplies of raw materials and fuel for industry. Its narrow range of staple industries had overcome these disadvantages but all of them faced major problems in the post-war period. In 1950 the province's economic structure was dominated by three staple industries: shipbuilding and engineering, linen, and agriculture. By the beginning of the 1960s agriculture still employed 14 per cent of the province's labour force compared to 4 per cent in the rest of the UK. It was the area's largest employer of labour although its workforce had declined from 101,000 in 1945 to 73,000 in 1960. This was the inevitable result of mechanization (there were 850 tractors in 1939 and 30,000 in 1960) and the elimination of smaller, uneconomic holdings, which the government encouraged. The result was an 80 per cent increase in output by 1960.[91] There were also improvements in productivity in linen as it faced competition from low-cost, ex-colonial producers and the expansion of the synthetic fibre industry. Substantial amounts of state support for modernization were given through a Re-equipment of Industry Act introduced in 1950. Such modernization entailed a substantial amount of rationalization and concentration of production and the inevitable closing of plants and shedding of labour. Between 1954 and 1964 the number of jobs in plants employing twenty-five workers or more (the bulk of the industry) fell from 56,414 to 33,957.[92]

Unlike linen, shipbuilding had maintained its role as the region's pre-eminent employer of skilled male labour up to the end of the 1950s. In 1950 more than one-tenth of the North's manufacturing jobs and one-fifth of those in Belfast were in Harland and Wolff. Employing 21,000 in four yards on the Queen's Island, it was the largest single shipbuilding complex in the world. Until 1955 its major problem was a steel shortage due to the rearmament programme. Subsequently, as with the rest of British shipbuilding, it came under increasing pressure from more productive continental and Japanese yards. By 1960 the yard was still employing over 22,000 workers and the unemployment rate among shipyard workers was just 2.5 per cent, a third of what it was in main British centres such as Tyneside and the Clyde. But at a time when world shipbuilding capacity was double what was required, the cabinet's employment committee was anticipating between 5,000 and 8,000 redundancies.[93] The crisis in shipbuilding turned out to be much worse than anticipated: employment was slashed by 40 per cent: 11,500 jobs between 1961 and 1964. It would coincide with fears of job losses in aircraft production at Short and Harland, whose workforce had fluctuated significantly in the post-war period and stood at 6,900 in 1962.[94] It was not part of either of the two main groups into which the British government planned to rationalize aircraft production, and its future appeared increasingly precarious. The problems created for Brookeborough's government by the decline of the staples were intensified by the province's demography. A birth-rate significantly higher than anywhere else in the UK fed through into a natural increase of 15,000 per annum throughout the 1950s.[95]

Pressure on the job-creating capacity of the economy created by the decline of the staples and new entrants to the labour market was to an extent relieved by the direct and indirect effects of government policy. Although its contemporary critics and some later commentators have criticized Brookeborough's administration for passivity, there is considerable evidence of a long-standing concern to counter the anticipated decline of traditional industries by a strategy of diversification based on the attraction of external investment. In 1944 the government had decided that inter-war legislation aimed at attracting new industry was inadequate and replaced it with the Industries Development Act, which aimed to attract British, American, and European firms by providing desirable packages, including newly built factory premises at low rents, the necessary infrastructure, and grants of up to one-third of capital cost, which could be exceeded for 'desirable' projects.[96] This legislation put the North in a favourable position compared to British regions suffering similar problems, which, under the 1945 Distribution of Industry Act, were subject to rigorous Treasury control. No advance factories were built in Britain between 1947 and 1959.[97]

By 1961 almost 48,000 new jobs had been created, an average of 2,500 per annum for the 1950s. New employment was also created by the substantial expansion of the public sector, particularly in the areas of health and education. Higher incomes were reflected in an expansion in the distributive trades. The total number of insured employees in the province increased from 438,000 in 1950 to 449,000 in 1960, broadly in line with the trend in the rest of the UK.[98] However, despite these positive developments, unemployment in the province never fell below 5 per cent and averaged 7.4 per cent for the decade, four times the national average and, more significantly, higher than the figures for other regional black spots such as Merseyside and Scotland.[99] The position would have been even worse had it not been for the fact that net migration was running at 9,000 per annum.[100]

Brookeborough, although already 62 in 1950 and subject to recurrent bouts of illness after an operation for a stomach ulcer in 1955, was initially quite effective in extracting extra resources from Westminster to mitigate the problem. He mercilessly exploited metropolitan gratitude for the North's wartime role and the more fundamental consideration that it was still of strategic value to the UK, given Irish neutrality. British annoyance at Dublin's anti-partition campaign also helped. In 1949, when unemployment in Northern Ireland was at 6.5 per cent, Attlee had written to his Home Secretary noting how much worse the situation was there in comparison with the rest of the UK and adding, 'It is, of course, of considerable political importance that we should do all we can to ensure full employment in Northern Ireland.'[101]

When the unemployment figure rose to a peak of 11 per cent in 1952 as a result of an international slump in textiles that hit linen badly, Brookeborough descended on Churchill and his ministers demanding a range of special measures. Although the Treasury and Board of Trade resisted, the Home Office stressed the political and strategic importance of helping 'Sir Basil':

The problem of unemployment in Northern Ireland was fundamentally different from that in this country because political considerations were involved which did not arise here. The adjacent Republic was politically hostile and there was in Northern Ireland a large dissident minority. Large numbers of unemployed constituted a potential source of serious civil disturbance, which might even lead in the long run to civil war.[102]

Brookeborough went home with extra Admiralty orders for ships, sub-contract work for Short and Harland, and new textile orders from the Ministry of Defence. He also extracted the setting up of a joint committee of British and Stormont officials to investigate possible long-term solutions to the problem. There was strong resistance from the Treasury and other Westminster departments to many of the proposals that the Stormont officials put forward, particularly the remittance of employers' national insurance contributions, but eventually a subsidy for the industrial use of coal and support for the creation, in 1955, of a Northern Ireland Development Council chaired by Lord Chandos were conceded.[103]

However, more important than these essentially palliative measures was the clear acceptance by the Treasury of the principle of 'parity plus'. It could be argued that this principle was implicit in the post-war agreements that underlay the extension of welfarism to the province. However, the formal statement of the new principles underlying the financial relationship between Belfast and London did strengthen Brookeborough's hand. In 1954 the Treasury representatives on the Joint Exchequer Board accepted not simply parity of social services and standards, but the necessity to incur special expenditure to make up a substantial leeway on such services and amenities as housing, schools, and hospitals. Crucially, it accepted the need for special expenditure to offset the economic disadvantage suffered by Northern Ireland by reason of geographical remoteness.[104] The result was clear by the end of the decade. In 1960 capital expenditure on hospitals in Northern Ireland over the previous five years was 12 per cent of the UK total at a time when the North's share of the population was 2.5 per cent. The share of the university building programme was 4.6 per cent; of roads, 5.3 per cent; and of housing, 3.6 per cent.[105] The success of Brookeborough and his officials in pushing the North's case for special treatment was reflected in the decline of the Imperial Contribution, which hovered between £17 and £20 million at the beginning of the 1950s but by 1961 had fallen to £8.7 million at a time when the annual subvention from Westminster had reached £44.8 million.[106]

If, despite this, the Prime Minister was under increasing political pressure on the unemployment question, it was in part because of rising popular expectations. The government's constant emphasis on how much better economic and social conditions were in the North compared to the Republic cut little ice with many of its trade union supporters who were, like 80 per cent of northern trade unionists, in British-based unions and whose fundamental economic, social, and cultural frames of reference were set by developments in the rest of the UK. The regime was the victim of its own propaganda, which, in response to the dominion status lobby, had emphasized Stormont's distinct powers and its relative autonomy from Westminster. This played into the hands of the NILP, whose solution to the unemployment problem was a more activist government.

The fundamental problem was that Stormont's demands for special treatment were regarded in London as having been quite substantially indulged by the mid-1950s and not even the onset of the IRA assault softened this attitude. To add to Brookeborough's problems, the UK investment boom of 1954–5 and what the Treasury perceived as inflationary pressures and a threat to the balance of payments led to a credit squeeze and interest rate rise. This had a severe impact on the linen industry in Belfast at the same time as UK firms were reluctant to consider new investments in the province. Unemployment, which stood at 6 per cent in June 1956, rose to 10 per cent in the same month in 1958.

The NILP had positioned itself skilfully to benefit from the government's problems. It had been devastated in the 1949 Stormont elections because of its internal divisions on the border and the resultant ambiguity, which allowed Unionists to depict it as a crypto-republican party. Its response was to take a clear pro-Union position, which led to the loss of its anti-partitionist elements who went on to set up branches of the Irish Labour Party in West Belfast, Derry, and Newry.[107] Its leading members lost few opportunities to denounce the 'Franco state' in the South and support the government in the use of internment and the Special Powers Act against the IRA. It also benefited from a critique of government economic policy in *The Economic Survey of Northern Ireland*, by two Queen's University economists, published in 1957. This had been commissioned by the Minister of Commerce in 1947 and delivered to his successor in 1955. Its publication had been delayed by the government for fear that it would buttress the NILP's attack, although the Minister of Commerce, Lord Glentoran, was able to quote an *Economist* review that described the *Survey* as giving 'a picture of the remarkable adaptation of the Northern Irish economy to the pace set by British economic progress—the adaptation of a hardy plant to an unpromising soil'.[108]

What the NILP extracted from the *Survey* was the idea that the various aids given to industry had not had a sufficient pay-off in terms of jobs created. This was linked to the accusation of a nepotistic link between the government, the Unionist Parliamentary Party, and local industrialists, in particular those involved in linen production. In the 1950s twelve of the fourteen Unionist MPs for Belfast constituencies had links with traditional industry as proprietors or managing directors.[109] It was certainly the case that pressure from local manufacturers, who feared that the Industries Development Act would bring in new firms that would compete for labour and force them to pay higher wages, had led to the introduction of a Re-equipment of Industry Bill in 1950, which compensated local firms by providing grants for new equipment and modernization. When the uptake on this was judged insufficient, a new and even more generous scheme, the Capital Grants to Industry Act, was introduced in 1954. Although modernization almost inevitably implied job losses, there was a widespread belief, shared by Terence O'Neill, who was Minister of Finance at the end of the 1950s, that the 'linen lords' were only interested in using government aid to buy up rivals and shut them down.[110]

Class-based tensions within the Unionist electoral bloc were nothing new but they were given increased potency by a relaxation of communal tension in Belfast, where the collapse of the Nationalist Party and the absence of any significant IRA activity did make it easier for Protestant workers to consider voting Labour. As early as the 1953 Stormont election, the Unionist Party headquarters at Glengall Street was bemoaning the fact that 'Our Party is losing the support of the lower paid income group and the artisans to the NILP.' The lack of any working-class Unionist MPs and the domination of Belfast Unionist representation by the local bourgeoisie were seen as important in encouraging defections. Whatever reserve of working-class deference still existed was weakened by social change as the heartlands of proletarian Unionism began to lose population to new housing estates in which the party had failed to establish a presence. Most significantly, Glengall Street noted that 'the "Big Drum" which has heretofore dominated Unionist politics' had lost its energizing power for at least a section of the working class.[111] In the 1958 election the NILP won four new seats in Belfast. Although two of these seats, in Oldpark and Pottinger, had a significant Catholic working-class population, the other two, Victoria and Woodvale, were solidly Protestant. The lesson was spelled out clearly in a ministerial discussion of unemployment:

The maintenance of a Unionist government at Stormont depends to a increasing degree on the success or otherwise of its economic policy. Particularly in the city of Belfast voters are considering such matters as unemployment when deciding how to cast their vote and unless success is achieved in reducing the present total of unemployment . . . the Unionist Party cannot hope to retain the allegiance of the working class population.[112]

With the strong prospect of serious redundancies in shipbuilding and the aircraft industry, an air of desperation descended on Brookeborough's ministers. The normally cautious O'Neill was so exercised by the threat that these redundancies 'would kill us off' that he may have reduced his colleagues to stunned silence by a proposal to drain Lough Neagh, the largest expanse of inland water in the British Isles, to create a new 'county Neagh' that would be leased out in 100 acre farms and have a new town at its centre.[113] The redundancies when they came were almost as bad as feared and they exhausted Brookeborough's declining capacity to bring back good economic news from London. Early in 1961 Harland and Wolff announced that 8,000 men would be paid off in the summer and later in the year Short and Harland declared that due to lack of orders there was a real danger of closure, threatening another 7,000 jobs. The year also saw the closure of the largest linen mill in Belfast, which employed 1,700 and had received a substantial amount of government assistance.[114]

Although the NILP did not win any new seats in the 1962 election, its share of the vote rose to 26 per cent from 16 per cent in 1958. It had fielded more candidates but there was clear evidence, accepted by Unionist headquarters, that it had consolidated its position in Belfast, where its total vote in the sixteen constituencies it contested was 58,811 while the Unionist vote in the same constituencies was 69,069.[115] The inroads made by the NILP into the core working-class constituency of Unionism was recognized by Sir George Clarke, Imperial Grand Master of the Orange Order, in a post-election speech in which he accepted that the election showed that the government needed a greater sense of urgency in dealing with unemployment. He also admitted that the Order contained ' a great many Labour men who, while wearing a sash, nevertheless had a different political outlook', adding that he had no quarrel with such members.[116] Clarke and some other leading Unionists recognized that the NILP had to be fought on its chosen terrain and that 'banging the drum' would be insufficient.

The problem was that Brookeborough, who was 72 when the 1960s began, increasingly appeared to have hung on to power too long, particularly when de Valera stepped down in 1959. Although Lemass was already 60 when he became Taoiseach, his promotion of a radical shift in the state's economic policies and the launch of the first economic development programme undermined the more complacent Unionist assumption about southern 'backwardness' and strengthened the critics of Brookeborough's lack of a long-term strategy for the northern economy. His semi-detached style of government, which had allowed him plenty of time for running his estate in Fermanagh, the indulgence of his beloved fishing and shooting, and occasional long winter cruises in sunnier climates, was increasingly seen as dangerously anachronistic. He became the butt of an effective NILP campaign against a 'part-time' and 'amateur' government. The death of the talented and moderate Maynard Sinclair in the *Princess Victoria* ferry disaster in 1953 had removed his most likely successor, while the marginalization of Brian Maginess, who left the cabinet to become Attorney General in 1956, meant that the government had no member who would have been a substantial enough figure to suggest an earlier exit to the Prime Minister. Four decades of power had inevitably bred complacency. The large number of uncontested seats produced many back-benchers whose only imperative was to satisfy the parochial and often sectarian pressures from their constituencies. The sectarian tone of Unionist politics had deterred a substantial section of the Protestant middle class from political involvement and drained the already shallow pool of ability from which Unionism could draw.[117]

Brookeborough had successfully weathered the arrival in power of Labour and the onset of the welfare state. Unionism now faced new threats on both the economic and political front that were beyond him. His success in extracting resources in the 1950s had reflected his ability to argue that the security interests of the UK as a whole would be threatened by economic decline in Northern Ireland and the possible political unrest it would stimulate. His charm and strong familial links with the metropolitan élite had helped Ulster's case at Westminster. By the end of the decade, with clear signs of the IRA's defeat and a new and apparently more pragmatic nationalism in the South, British governments had less reason to be concerned about the political and security implications of the North's unemployment figures. At the same time, Brookeborough's old allies were passing from the scene and he was increasingly perceived in London as a conservative obstacle to the modernization of the province's politics and better relations with Dublin.

In 1961 he had been able to extract a joint-study group of Stormont and Westminster officials chaired by Sir Robert Hall to look once again at unemployment. The Northern Ireland members suggested that the Treasury provide an employment subsidy to all manufacturing concerns in Northern Ireland but the idea was summarily dismissed.[118] When the Hall Report was published in October 1962, making it clear that there was a marked reluctance to grant more special assistance to bail Stormont out of a local political crisis, Brookeborough was finished. His successor, by transforming the discourse within which London was petitioned for more resources from short-term palliatives to one of regional planning and modernization, would succeed where Brookeborough had failed. Unfortunately, the energy and ingenuity that were used to transform thinking on economic policy were not extended to the area of community relations.

6

Expansion: the Republic 1959–73

Free Trade and Programming

An analysis of Anglo-Irish economic relations prepared by British officials in 1960 depicted Lemass's succession to de Valera as a political watershed:

With the ending of Mr. De Valera's lengthy dominance of the Irish political scene and the emergence of Mr. Lemass, himself a businessman, at the head of a more business-like administration, the political atmosphere in the South is changing. The spirit of 1916 and 1922 is on the wane. While it is too much to expect that any political leader in the Republic would ever abandon the hope that Partition will one day cease, Mr. Lemass has been realistic enough to admit that this must be a long term objective.

It was much less optimistic about the Republic's economic prospects:

Their efforts to diversify their economy by the development of secondary industry have had only limited success. They depend, and are likely to continue to depend for as far ahead as can be seen, on selling their agricultural goods to the United Kingdom, but their prospects of expanding their market here are very poor . . . it is impossible to be optimistic about the Republic's economic future.[1]

What has subsequently become seen as the 'Lemass/Whitaker watershed' in the economic history of the Republic was also less than obvious to most of the state's citizens at the time. During a symposium on Whitaker's *Economic Development*, one economist pointed out that, outside of a small circle in Dublin, the impact of the document's publication had been extremely limited. It had done little to lift the mood of despondency and loss of confidence that had settled on the nation.[2] Trade unionists criticized Whitaker for his refusal to put job creation as the primary objective of the development programme. Certainly there was little to spark popular enthusiasm in *Economic Development*. It was no selling point to inform the public that the implementation of the programme would lead to a doubling of national income after thirty-five years.[3] Although it was soon clear to informed observers that the repeal of restrictions on foreign investment was bringing a rapid influx of capital from the US and Europe, there was little sign that the new mood of optimism among sections of the political, industrial, and financial élite was percolating down to the broader population.

Lemass's reconsideration of the economic nationalist regime was threatening for employers and workers in those many sections of Irish industry that would find it difficult to compete with imports if there was a substantial reduction in the protective tariffs they enjoyed. Yet Lemass was aware that the creation of the European Economic Community and Britain's attitude to it would have profound implications for the Republic. Britain initially attempted to organize a rival group of countries to the EEC within a European Free Trade Area (EFTA). This threatened the privileged access of Irish agricultural exports to the British market and in response in 1959 Lemass had opened negotiations with Harold Macmillan's government to try to achieve a radical revision of the framework governing Anglo-Irish trade. In return for the extension of the British system of price support to Irish farmers, he offered the reintegration of the Republic's economy into that of the UK. Pressure from British farmers and the Northern Ireland government frustrated his proposals and very soon afterwards the EFTA project foundered.

However, this did nothing to blunt the drive to liberalize the Irish economy, for it was soon clear that Britain was reconsidering its attitude to the EEC and this meant Ireland had no option but to follow. As Lemass had explained to British officials in 1960, he 'did not believe that small countries could stand alone and the Republic had no alternative but to link her economy with that of the United Kingdom'.[4] With 90 per cent of its agricultural exports and 70 per cent of its exports of manufactured goods going to the UK, it would have been impossible for the Republic to consider joining the EEC if Britain had maintained its original sceptical position. In July 1961 Lemass announced that if Britain applied to join, Ireland would apply too. Thus whether it was going to be within a bilateral arrangement with London or within a European framework, it was being made clear to Irish industry that the days of a protected home market were numbered.

Resistance came from both the Federation of Irish Industry (FII) and Lemass's old department. Officials at Industry and Commerce argued that many of the 65,000 workers in the main protected industries would be vulnerable and that tariffs would have to be maintained for at least another decade.[5] However, some industrialists accepted that a phasing out of tariffs was inevitable. In 1960 Lemass had told the FII that they should study the problems that different sections of industry would face with freer trade. The organization had employed Garret FitzGerald, a young economics lecturer and financial journalist, to carry out a pilot study of the highly protected woollen and worsted industry. His report concluded that unless there were drastic improvements in efficiency and marketing, the industry would face serious difficulties under free trade conditions and many firms would disappear.[6] This survey encouraged the government to create a Committee on Industrial Organization (CIO) in 1961. Composed initially of representatives of industry, officials, and independent experts, it was extended to include workers' representatives and became the first of a number of tripartite institutions that Lemass was to use very successfully to build a national consensus around themes of economic modernization, growth, and planning.

The CIO surveyed twenty-two industries employing about half of the total workforce in manufacturing in the Republic. Its report painted a depressing picture. While there were some sectors that hoped to hold their own in a free trade situation, many more (including footwear, knitwear, wool, shirts, paper, steel, and electrical equipment) expected considerable losses and the possibility of going out of business.[7] Lemass's response was that only systematic tariff reduction would provide the necessary drive and discipline to ensure improvements in efficiency and an expansion of exports. Although this harsh message was somewhat softened by the fact that the government committed itself to a phased reduction, starting with across-the-board cuts of 10 per cent in 1963 and 1964, there was no concealing the fact that by end of the decade, or soon after, Irish industry would have to sink or swim in a free trade environment. But fundamental to pacifying industry and possible doubters in his own party was the clear commitment that liberalization did not mean *laissez faire*. An Industrial Reorganization Branch was created in Industry and Commerce and substantial amounts of financial and technical assistance were to be provided for those industries that demonstrated a commitment and a capacity to change.

De Gaulle's veto on Britain's application in 1963 did not lead to any let-up in pressure for change. Lemass returned to his earlier objective of a free trade agreement with Britain as a transitional measure towards eventual EEC membership. Although the Conservative government remained unsympathetic, the return of Labour in October 1964 was seen in Dublin as propitious. This initial optimism suffered a blow when, owing to a balance of payments crisis, the British imposed a 15 per cent levy on all imports with the exception of food and raw materials. However, Lemass skilfully used Wilson's desire for a breakthrough in Anglo-Irish relations to reopen the question of a free trade agreement and on 14 December 1965 the Anglo-Irish Free Trade Agreement was signed in London.

The Agreement seemed to some traditional nationalists a gross betrayal of Fianna Fáil's founding principles. In the Dáil Seán Treacy, a Labour Party TD from the republican heartland of county Kerry, attacked Fianna Fáil for reneging on their principles: '[they] have perpetrated an act of union with Britain more final, binding and irrevocable than the Charter of Henry II or the Act of Union'.[8] There was also opposition within the Department of External Affairs, which had produced a paper on the political implications of the Agreement arguing that that 'the resulting concentration of our trade "eggs" in one basket would inevitably have an inhibiting effect on our freedom of action in the political field and would expose us to greater political pressure by Britain'.[9]

Lemass displayed both his underlying radical purpose and his finely honed political skills in jettisoning economic nationalism. He contributed powerfully to a recasting of Irish nationalist discourse, which has been well summed up by Peter Mair:

Whereas in the earlier period the national interest had been seen to demand political, cultural and economic isolation, in the later period it came to imply the achievement of material prosperity. Independence *per se* was no longer sufficient, rather economic and social self-respect were necessary. . . . Nationalism remained a key motif, but by the 1960s the success of the nationalist endeavour was to be measured in wealth and economic growth rather in cultural or territorial integrity.[10]

Soon after becoming Taoiseach, Lemass had defined the supreme national task as 'to consolidate the economic foundation of our political independence . . . it should be no exaggeration to say that our survival as an independent state depended on our success'.[11] Economic success became the supreme national value because only through it could national unity be restored. While his approach to Ulster Unionism and the northern state could be refreshingly revisionist, he did not hesitate to use anti-partitionism as a means of giving a nationalist veneer to policies that could have appeared heretical to traditional Fianna Fáil supporters. Economic success in the Republic would remove one of the main Unionist objections to unification:

There are people today in the north-east of the country who say that we are here paying an uneconomic price for our freedom. We have got to prove them wrong. We have got to demonstrate that we can bring about a higher level of achievement and greater progress with freedom than without it.[12]

By 1961, with the first clear evidence of the success of the new policies, Lemass was publicly contrasting the 'dynamism' of the South with the North's growing unemployment problem and Brookeborough's resort to begging missions to London:

We are proving that there are better ways of dealing with the country's problems than by sending deputations to plead for help from others. The bread of charity is never very filling. I am convinced that the success of our economic programme can be a decisive factor in bringing about the change of outlook which the North requires and the discarding of all the old fallacies and prejudices on which partition has rested.[13]

Traditional territorial nationalism was also used to disarm the criticisms of tariff reductions that came from large sections of Irish industry. In advance of any free trade agreement with Britain, Lemass offered tariff reductions to northern manufactures to the chagrin of their counterparts in the Republic. When delegations of angry southern industrialists met Jack Lynch, the Minister of Industry and Commerce, they were rebuffed and told that the reductions 'would be a considerable help in reducing suspicion and advancing national unity'.[14]

The shift in nationalist discourse was impelled by harsh economic realities but it was soon rooted in economic success. By December 1962 a delighted Lemass could boast in the Dáil that 'in many industrial occupations [there was] a scarcity of workers and in many areas full employment had been realised'.[15] The performance of the Republic's economy for the next decade would continue to justify his early optimism. During the period 1959–72 manufacturing output increased by 5.9 per cent per annum as compared with an overall growth rate of just under 4 per cent. Employment in manufacturing rose from 169,000 to 212,000. The pattern of the export trade showed a marked change: in 1960 industrial goods represented only one-third of total exports, by 1972 this share had risen to 55 per cent. An important source of change was the influx of foreign capital attracted by the government's relaxation of controls, its commitment to join the EEC, its generous tax allowances, and other inducements and wages that were low by American and west European levels. By 1973 new foreign-owned firms employed some 40,000 workers, or one-fifth of the manufacturing workforce in the Republic.[16]

Economic historians sceptical of the role played by *Economic Development* and the *First Programme* have pointed out that during the 1960s international trade was buoyant, the terms of trade moved in Ireland's favour, and the doubling of the British rate of growth between 1959 and 1963 had a locomotive effect on the Irish economy.[17] It is also true that moves to open up the economy and attract foreign capital had been initiated by the two inter-party governments. Yet, it is difficult to deny the elements of decisiveness and coherence that Lemass gave to the process of reintegrating the Republic into the international economy. Perhaps even more important was his determination that Ireland's development strategy would not be based on a liberal model but would take a semi-corporatist form involving partnership between the state, trade unions, and employers.

The reunification of the trade union movement in the Irish Congress of Trade Unions in 1959 encouraged Lemass to return to some of the themes of social partnership that he had first raised during the Emergency. Some of his own close associates were critical of his allegedly benign and uncritical attitude towards the trade union movement. In fact, his approach towards the Irish trade union movement was, whatever its limitations as an economic strategy, not his Achilles' heel, but very much a vital political resource. It enabled him to re-establish Fianna Fáil's image as a broadly progressive force, something that had been severely damaged by its uninspiring performance in government and opposition during the 1950s. Gone was de Valera's emphasis on the virtue of frugality: as Lemass told delegates to the 1959 árd fheis, 'We used to say that we preferred freedom in a hair shirt to the fleshpots of serfdom, but that is not a choice we have to make. I believe in the beneficial force of disciplined nationalism.'[18]

Although there had been no trade union involvement in the formulation of the *First Programme*, the leader of the largest union in the country, the Irish Transport and General Workers' Union, praised the government for 'its imagination, initiative, enthusiasm and tendency to long term planning which has attracted many new industries to the country'.[19] The executive of ICTU was pleased to be wooed by Lemass through involvement in the CIO, in trade union advisory councils set up to consider problems of industrial adaptation to free trade, and, from 1963, in the new tripartite forum, the National Industrial Economic Council (NIEC) chaired by T. K. Whitaker.[20]

A central purpose of Irish corporatism, as of its European counterparts, was to control wage demands that could threaten Irish industry's competitiveness. In the period 1960–4 unit wage costs rose by 17 per cent in the Republic compared to 7 per cent in Britain.[21] Trade union leaders were expected, in return for a consultative role in economic policy-making and the promise of real economic and social gains for their members, to deliver wage discipline. From this perspective Irish corporatism failed. The removal of the fear of unemployment led to a new confidence amongst rank and file trade unionists who were determined to press for higher wages and shorter hours. There was a sharp upturn in industrial conflict: in 1964 Ireland topped the world league in man-hours lost through strikes.[22] Lemass's frustration with what he complained was the 'lack of cohesion and authority in the trade union movement'[23] had initially encouraged an attempt to impose discipline. A White Paper, *Closing the Gap*, published in February 1963, proposed that the Employer–Labour conference produce binding guidelines for wage increases and a pay freeze in the public sector. The sharp response from ICTU, which withdrew its representatives from all government-sponsored bodies including the CIO and the Employer–Labour conference, produced a rapid retreat and the rest of Lemass's premiership would see little application of the stick but much of the carrot in the government's approach to the unions. He was soon to declare that national policy should take a 'shift to the left' and promised more government measures to ensure the translation of economic progress into improved social conditions in areas such as education, health, and state benefits. This was more than rhetoric: social spending by government, which had declined from 14.8 per cent of GNP in 1952 to 13.7 per cent in 1962, rose to 16.6 per cent in 1966.[24] Lemass was also involved in the negotiations that led to the first national wage agreement in 1964, which some of his critics in the party regarded as too generous.

The political pay-off for Lemass's identification with economic programming and his positive relationship with the leadership of the trade union movement was clear in the 1965 general election. In his first election as Taoiseach in 1961 it had been too early for the gains of the new policies to be registered and, with a low turnout reflecting what Lee calls 'uncertain public morale', Fianna Fáil's vote dropped from 48.3 to 43.8 per cent and its number of seats from seventy-eight to seventy, leaving Lemass to lead a minority government.[25] However, in the 1965 election its share of the vote rose to 47.4 per cent and its number of seats to seventy-two, at a time when it faced the most significant challenge from the Labour Party since 1943. It was the first time in the party's history that it gained votes as an incumbent government after a full term of office.

But if the political achievement of Lemass was clear by the time of his retirement in 1966, his economic legacy was more ambiguous. Those who, like Whitaker, had doubts about his nudging of public policy to the left seemed to draw increasing support from the evidence that economic growth was accompanied by strikes, wage inflation, and increasingly large balance of payments deficits. Economic programming itself was being thrown into question by the widening gap between forecasts and results. While the *First Programme* had avoided setting specific targets, the *Second Programme*, launched in 1963, did commit itself to more precise objectives, including a net increase in employment of 81,000 by 1970 and a reduction of net emigration to 10,000 a year by the same date. While the forecasts for industrial growth were fulfilled, the continuing problems of agriculture meant unemployment remained higher than expected and emigration, which had fallen in the early 1960s, rose again in 1965 to over 20,000 and did not fall below 15,000 for any year between 1963 and 1967.[26] Government expenditure also rose faster than planned. As a result of these major discrepancies the *Second Programme* was brought to a premature conclusion and replaced by a (supposedly more realistic) *Third Programme* to cover the period 1969–72. Given the rapid economic transformations that the Republic was undergoing in the 1960s and its more open relation to the international economy, the whole programming project had an air of unreality about it. Yet, at its heart was Lemass's search for a development project based on class collaboration rather than conflict. This would leave a lasting imprint on public policy in the South.

Lemass and Northern Ireland

Lemass's reputation as a supreme iconoclast, as a corrosive radical force making an often reluctant party substitute reality for fantasy, has been seen as strongly vindicated in his policy towards Northern Ireland. Indeed Professor Lee has argued that he was the first Irish Taoiseach actually to have a northern policy.[27] The core of this policy was constructive engagement with Stormont and its symbolic highpoint was his meeting with Terence O'Neill at Stormont on 12 January 1965, the first such meeting since 1922. However, a close reading of his statements and action on the North reveals a more ambiguous record.

It is true that, as Jonathan Bardon states, Lemass abandoned the overt irredentism of previous governments.[28] However, some of what have been seen as his innovations—for example, the idea that northerners could only be attracted by a higher standard of living in the Republic—had already been articulated by de Valera, who had many other subtle and even heretical views on the subject. Despite the traditional nationalist fixation on Britain's primary responsibility for ending partition, de Valera as he approached retirement had shifted the focus, telling a group of American journalists in 1957, 'The solution of the partition question was strictly an Irish problem, one that must be worked out between Irish people in the north and south. It must be achieved on a satisfactory basis for both sides.'[29] This directly anticipated one of the central themes in Lemass's discourse on Northern Ireland. In his árd fheis speech in 1957 de Valera also raised the notion of functional co-operation that would dominate Lemass's approach: 'the proper way to try to solve the problem of partition was to endeavour to have as close relations as possible with the people of the Six Counties and get them to combine with us in matters of common concern.'[30]

If Lemass produced little that was new in the way of ideas on Northern Ireland, his premiership was notable for a serious attempt to implement ideas that de Valera had articulated but had done little about for fear of annoying the more republican section of the party and his veteran Minister of External Affairs, Frank Aiken. His more active approach to Northern Ireland was in part a reflection of his long immersion in economic and industrial policy, which made him prone to see the radical policy reversals of the late 1950s as creating the material basis for political accommodation. It has been already noted how he used the supreme importance attached to Irish unity in Fianna Fáil's traditional ideology to sell EEC membership to the party. However, there can be no doubting the genuineness of his belief that the dismantling of customs barriers associated with the European project would have major political spillover effects: 'In the long term economic considerations influence and determine political arrangements, the identity of economic interest in the two areas into which Ireland is now divided will, in time, bring about political unity.'[31] Although he was also prepared to recognize that the division on the island was more than a tariff barrier—'it represents a spiritual cleavage which has its origins deep in our history'—there could be no doubting his belief that religious and cultural divisions were increasingly anachronistic survivals that would be displaced by economic modernization. His own private religious agnosticism and his renowned lack of interest in the Irish language and the other cultural accoutrements of Irish identity,[32] so important to de Valera, caused him to underestimate the power of more primordial voices in both nationalism and loyalism.

His optimism was partly based on the positive response that some northern manufacturers had given to his proposal for a North–South free trade agreement. Despite the rejection of the proposal by Lord Brookeborough,[33] a number of northern businesses ignored Stormont and approached the Ministry of Industry and Commerce in Dublin directly to negotiate reductions. Eventually Brookeborough was forced to modify his line and declare publicly that he would not stand in the way of manufacturers who sought better treatment from Dublin.[34] Lemass was impressed with this Ulster bourgeois pragmatism and tried to encourage it as much as possible, asking the state airline, Aer Lingus, to consider ordering aircraft from Short Brothers and Harland and Irish Shipping to encourage Harland and Wolff to tender for vessels it needed.[35] Much of the optimism that pervaded his approach to the North was based on the apparent contrast between the difficult conditions facing the province's staple industries in the early 1960s and the first signs of economic expansion in the South. The publication of the Hall Report and its rejection of what he referred to as 'begging missions seeking British subsidies' were seen as prompting 'enlightened opinion' in Northern Ireland to reconsider the value of the continued division of the island. [36]

But, as some contemporary critics pointed out, there was a fundamental contradiction in Lemass' approach to the North. This was evident in the first major statement he made on Northern Ireland when he participated on an Oxford Union debate on partition on 15 October 1959. The speech certainly impressed some in the British political élite with its support for 'the growth of a practical system of co-operation between the two areas even in advance of any political arrangement' and the argument that 'quite apart from any views one may hold about the eventual reunification of Ireland, is it not commonsense that the two existing communities in our small island should seek every opportunity of working together in practical matters for their mutual and common good?' He had also warned that 'we cannot expect speedy results: the barriers of fear and suspicion in the minds of partitionists are too strong to be demolished quickly.'[37] But he also made clear that, although he believed the fundamental barriers to unity were internal ones, the British government could and should undo its historic responsibility for partition by declaring that it would like to see partition ended 'by agreement among the Irish'. Pressure on the British to declare in favour of the Irish nationalist project could only undermine the real efforts that were made to foster practical schemes of co-operation with Stormont.

While Brookeborough was in power and insisting on the Republic's full constitutional recognition of Northern Ireland as a condition of any North–South co-operation, there could be little progress. O'Neill initially maintained the same position but was under some pressure from the Conservative government to respond to Lemass's overtures.[38] With even the former Secretary to the Northern Ireland cabinet, Sir Robert Gransden, making it clear in private that he thought the demand for constitutional recognition 'completely unrealistic',[39] Lemass went some way to accommodate O'Neill. He used a Fianna Fáil dinner in Tralee in the republican heartland of county Kerry to make his most important speech on partition. In it he declared that he recognized that 'the government and parliament there exist with the support of a majority in the Six County area' and insisted that 'the solution of the problem of partition is one to be found in Ireland by Irishmen'.[40] Although he also referred to Northern Ireland as an 'artificial area', the speech represented a significant shift. As Robert Savage has noted, 'Mentioning the words "recognise" and the "Government and Parliament of Northern Ireland" in the same sentence was a significant gesture to Unionists and an extraordinary statement for a Fianna Fáil leader to make.'[41]

O'Neill gave a guarded welcome describing the speech as 'not without courage' but cautioned that

As long as every gesture of friendship and every possible co-operation was subordinate to a long-term undermining of the constitutional position, so long would they have to moderate with a good deal of caution their wish for co-operation with their neighbours.[42]

Lemass's response was to ask his ministers for proposals for an Irish agenda at civil service level on cross-border co-operation, thus putting aside the demand for a summit with all the difficulties that that could create for O'Neill.[43] The implication of all this was what the Secretary to the Department of the Taoiseach called a 'new departure' in the policy on partition, which would have at its core two elements: 'to disregard London as a factor in maintaining partition' and 'to concentrate on the Parliament and people in the Six Counties'.[44] However, the likelihood of a positive response from O'Neill was undermined by a number of speeches Lemass made on a visit to the USA less than a month later. In an address to the National Press Club in Washington, he called on the

British government to issue a statement that it would welcome an opportunity to end partition 'when Irishmen wanted to get rid of it'.[45] Later, at the United Nations, he repeated the request and added that 'he believed that the circumstances of partition were also under review in Britain'.[46]

So on the one hand Lemass pursued North–South co-operation, while on the other he challenged the legitimacy and permanence of the state with which he was proposing to co-operate. These conflicting strands of his position reflected the substantial resistance from the more national-istic elements within Fianna Fáil to 'concessions' to the Stormont regime. His Minister of External Affairs, Frank Aiken, was a bastion of traditional anti-partitionism and given his closeness to de Valera, a possible focus of resistance to any new direction on northern policy. It was Aiken who insisted on seeing the North as an imperialist vestige that Britain should look at in the context of its post-war decolonization process.[47] Lemass's policy of discouraging the civil service and Republic's radio and television services from referring to Northern Ireland as 'The Six Counties' was not popular with some of his colleagues[48] and his officials reported some political resistance from ministers to his pro-posals for North–South discussions at a civil service level.[49] Leading a minority government at a time when he was proposing a radical reversal of economic nationalism, too radical a shift on Northern Ireland policy could have had severe political repercussions within Fianna Fáil. The result was that when O'Neill decided to meet Lemass it was more in response to pressure from Harold Wilson than to any positive inducement from Dublin.

But if Lemass's northern policy only partially accommodated Unionist concerns, it did even less for Stormont's minority. The Taoiseach regarded northern nationalism as being as conservative and sectarian as the regime it opposed. In a speech to students at Queen's University after he retired, Lemass attributed a part of the responsibility for the North's problems to the 'narrow attitudes' of the Nationalist Party[50] and in a subsequent interview commented of northern nationalists that 'for them the day partition ended would be the day they would get their foot on the throat of the Orangemen'.[51] The sort of trips made by Conor Cruise O'Brien in the early 1950s to meet northern nationalists had been discontinued as the official anti-partition campaign had waned. By 1960 there had not been a visit to Northern Ireland by an official from External Affairs for over four years. Eddie McAteer complained that Dáil deputies had more contact with parliamentarians abroad than with nationalists in Stormont.[52] The attempt to develop functional co-operation with Stormont discouraged visits that Unionists might see as an attempt to destabilize the regime and a request from External Affairs for a resumption of visits 'if only to show the Six-County people that we are still with them' seems to have been ignored.[53]

What little interest Lemass had in northern nationalism seems to have focused on any signs of new thinking, particularly those associated with the formation of National Unity in 1959. He used Erskine Childers, a Protestant and the son of one of the first republicans executed during the Civil War, as his main link with developments in the North. This in itself was revealing, as he regarded Childers as a lightweight and after inheriting him as Minister of Lands demoted him twice within the space of two years.[54] Nevertheless, Childers' advice could only have encouraged the Taoiseach to continue with his focus on improving relations with Stormont while largely ignoring the concerns of the minority. After a visit to Belfast in March 1961 Childers wrote to Lemass of the 'utter breakdown of the Nationalist Party' and went on to give an analysis of the discrimination issue at stark variance with the traditional nationalist perspective:

Discrimination is decreasing, although it still exists. We hear of the local author-ities who show discrimination in the allocation of houses, but there are quite a number who are not guilty of this practice, about whom we hear nothing. Discrimination in industry varies enormously. Some of the new English and American industries permit no discrimination whatsoever; in some cases they have been suborned by local pressure. In the case of the older industries, a few are absolutely fair and square in their attitude. Others employ numbers accord-ing to the population in the district to make sure that no Catholic men ever become foremen. In fairness to managements in some industries, it would be the men themselves who would create the trouble and who exercise pressure through the shop stewards regardless of what the managers think.[55]

Within the Department of External Affairs there was little stomach for attempts by northern nationalists to raise the discrimination issue. Much of the material that had been used during the anti-partition cam-paign was out of date but when McAteer approached the Department with material for a new pamphlet the response was dismissive. A senior official was scathing:

I must assume that the facts and figures it mentions are correct. But I ask myself what is the purpose of the pamphlet? There is no need to tell Irish Nationalists. They have been given the facts over and over again in previous anti-partition propaganda. If the pamphlet is directed at a non-Irish audience I very much doubt if it will get farther than their waste-paper baskets. I am afraid it is regrettable but true that very little, if any, interest in the problems of the Northern Ireland minority is taken outside Ireland.[56]

Clearly, as the first stirrings of the civil rights movement emerged in Northern Ireland, Dublin was if anything even less concerned with the discrimination issue than was London. After the summit with O'Neill, Lemass's priorities were the consolidation of new links with the northern regime in areas such as trade and tourism. It was made clear to McAteer that he should not look to Dublin but lead his party into a more constructive relationship with the northern state and it was as a result of this pressure that the Nationalist Party at last agreed to become the Official Opposition at Stormont. The long-term significance of this approach was brutally spelled out by a Dublin official in response to demands from some in the Nationalist Party for support:

The alternative to taking any action at the present time must inevitably be that the gap between the Nationalists in the North and the people here will grow wider. This development will of course force the Nationalists to adopt policies which are fully in keeping with their status in the Six Counties.[57]

The next few years would see the frustration of this southern desire for the minority to sort out its relation with Stormont under its own steam, while those who had had deep reservations about the Lemass approach tried to use the northern crisis to overthrow the whole edifice of partition.

Politics and Social Change in the 1960s

John Horgan has described the 1960s as 'socially turbulent years'[58] and Kieran Allen has claimed that the Republic was significantly affected by the wave of political and cultural radicalization associated with the anti-Vietnam war movement and the student uprisings of 1968.[59] While in any international framework of comparison this might seem an exaggeration, there is no question that, after the stagnation of the previous decade, the state in the Republic faced an unprecedented range of traditional and new demands. Industrial militancy, while not a new phenomenon, did develop an intensity that led to the decade being labelled a period of 'unparalleled turbulence in Irish industrial relations'.[60] The multiplicity of trade unions made any national agreement negotiated between ICTU and employers difficult to enforce at a time when many groups of workers were keen to use improved economic conditions to extract the maximum that the market could bear. A sectional concern with the defence of pay relativities was an important source of militancy and there was also considerable tension between groups of rank-and-file trade unionists and national leaderships regarded as too inclined to compromise with employers and the state.

The authoritarian streak in Fianna Fáil's relation to the unions, first clearly evident during the Emergency, reappeared when in 1965 a breakaway union of telephonists began to picket telephone exchanges to support a demand for recognition. Lemass lambasted these 'anti-state activities' and strikers were jailed for breaching a government injunction against picketing. When their comrades attempted to protest outside the Dáil, the government did not hesitate to use the Offences against the State Act to ban such activities. In 1966 a strike by fitters in the state Electricity Supply Board (ESB) was met by legislation outlawing strike action in the industry and providing heavy fines against both unions and individual strikers. This produced a major confrontation in 1968 when the legislation was used to jail over fifty strikers in a dispute over pay.[61] The culmination of this period of unrestrained 'free-for-all' wage bargaining was the maintenance craftmen's strike in early 1969, which lasted for six weeks and was a source of unprecedented bitterness not simply between workers and employers but between the strikers and other unions and the leaders of ICTU.

Some on the Irish left interpreted this industrial militancy as a potential threat to capitalist rule.[62] This inflated its political significance. Just as in Northern Ireland militant trade union consciousness was quite compatible with traditional political affiliations, a Gallup survey found that only 37 per cent of trade unionists supported Labour.[63] However, it is unlikely that there was no spillover from industrial militancy into politics. There was a substantial increase in the size and self-confidence of the Irish Labour Party. William Norton resigned as leader in 1960. As Emmet O'Connor has noted, he had come to personify 'the achingly, conservative, clientilist style of Labour deputies'.[64] The dispiriting experience of the second inter-party government had left Labour, after the 1957 election, with 9 per cent of the vote and twelve Dáil deputies. Its only secure electoral base was amongst agricultural labourers and other rural workers in small towns and villages in Munster and Leinster. It had only one seat in Dublin.[65] Like Norton, most of its deputies were trade union officials whose main focus was on their union business and their constituencies. Conservative, Catholic, and fiercely anti-intellectual, they showed little interest in or concern about the national profile of the party or the need to seek new bases of support.

Norton's successor, Brendan Corish, had a background that was typical of the rural and personalistic basis of much of the Labour support at the time. He had won his Wexford constituency in a by-election caused by the death of his father and during the 1950s had shown little sign of a desire to swim against the stream, declaring in 1953 'I am an Irishman second; I am a Catholic first' and defending those involved in the Fethard-on-Sea boycott of Protestants in 1957.[66] However, as Labour leader he displayed some capacity to transcend his background. He encouraged the party to adopt a go-it-alone electoral strategy, rejecting future participation in a coalition government. The shift in Labour's ideological image was done in a gingerly fashion with Corish explaining that Labour's socialism was a 'Christian' variety and it would be towards the end of the decade before he dared to proclaim that 'the Seventies will be Socialist'. Yet there was clear evidence that, in the Dublin area in particular, Labour was trying hard to attract socially conscious sections of the middle class and a new generation of intellectuals and radicals through a more leftist profile.

Corish was heavily influenced by the new secretary of the party, Brendan Halligan.[67] Halligan's key strategic idea was that Labour should force the two larger parties to coalesce by itself adopting a distinctive left-wing identity. Arguing that the two main parties had lost their *raison d'être* as the generation formed by 1916 and the Civil War faded from the scene, he identified a historic opportunity for the Labour Party to realign the political system along a more 'normal' left/right cleavage. Although the strategy was flawed by its excessive voluntarism, it did force the party to modernize itself. There was a serious effort to expand the number of branches: Labour in 1964 had only 248 branches as compared with over 1,700 for Fianna Fáil and 600 for Fine Gael. By 1969 the party had 500 branches nationally, while in the same period the number in Dublin had risen from twenty-nine to eighty-three.[68] The party's traditional image as an appendage of the trade union movement was also undermined by the recruitment of a number of prominent intellectuals such as the Trinity academics Justin Keating and David Thornley and with the return to Ireland, after a high-profile diplomatic and academic career, of Dr Conor Cruise O'Brien. By the time of the 1969 election only a fifth of Labour candidates were trade union officials while the largest category was 'professionals'—in the 1961 election only one Labour candidate had been from this category.[69]

In the first two elections under Corish's leadership, Labour made steady progress with 11.6 per cent of the national vote and sixteen seats in 1961 and 15.4 per cent and twenty-two seats in 1965. Corish and his young advisers became convinced that the rapidity of economic and social change in the Republic made a major breakthrough a real possibility. The 1969 'New Republic' manifesto captured the mood of optimism:

The politics of the old Republic are over. The choice is no longer between two identical parties, divided only by the tragedy of history. The choice is now between the old Republic of bitterness, stagnation and failure, represented by the two Civil War parties, and the New Republic of opportunity, change and hope, represented by the Labour Party.[70]

Expectations were high and there was talk of a Labour government. Labour's share of the vote increased to 17 per cent but this reflected the fact that there had been a substantial increase in the number of candidates, from forty-four in 1965 to ninety-nine in 1969. The result was a shattering disappointment and marked the end of the go-it-alone policy. The party lost four seats nationally but this figure disguised a radical shift in the basis of support. The performance in the greater Dublin area was in fact very impressive: its number of seats increased from six to ten and its share of the vote from 18 per cent to 23 per cent, while in Dublin City it overtook Fine Gael for the first time in a general election and won eight seats in comparison with the single one it obtained in 1961. However, in its traditional rural bastions the results were disastrous, with a loss of six seats in Munster and two in Leinster.

Labour's optimism had clearly had some basis but its main defect lay in an overly unilinear view of the process of economic and social modernization in Ireland which ignored the continuing strength of rural and small-town Catholic traditionalism. Its activists blamed a 'red smear' campaign, carried on by Fianna Fáil. There had certainly been such a campaign with Labour being accused of wanting to introduce 'Cuban socialism' in Ireland. Visions of Labour imposing collective farms on the small farmers of Kerry and other areas may well have lost some Labour TDs crucial votes. More significant would have been the Catholic Church's long-standing identification of 'socialism' with atheism and its associated immoralities. One Fianna Fáil candidate in Mayo, not content with the totally unfounded claim that Labour in power would legislate for abortion and divorce, added, 'it would be great for the fellow who wanted a second wife every night'.[71] But the problem with the 'red smear' argument was that many of the party's own rural TDs were also dismayed at the radical noises coming from Dublin and did all they could to dissociate themselves from the party's national campaign, fighting the election on purely local issues and their record of constituency service. In a society in transition Labour's new-found radicalism would have disconcerted many of its traditional supporters no matter what Fianna Fáil chose to allege about it.

While a radicalized Labour Party was vulnerable in many constituencies—according to the 1971 census only 52 per cent of the Republic's population lived in towns with a population of 1,500 or above—it did have a substantial potential base of support in Dublin. Conor Cruise O'Brien, as a cosmopolitan intellectual, a divorcé who had remarried, and a supporter of the Republic establishing diplomatic links with Cuba, was the epitome of Labour's threat to traditional Catholic values. Yet, standing for the first time in Dublin North East he came second to Charles Haughey, the leading Fianna Fáil TD in the constituency.[72] The imperviousness of a sizeable section of Dublin's electorate to a traditionalist message can be explained by a number of factors. There was a tradition of working-class militancy in inner-city and North Dublin, and in the 1950s and 1960s this was amplified by the decanting of many working-class families to new corporation estates like Crumlin in the south of the city. Although government policy aimed at dispersing industrial development away from the east coast and the Dublin area in particular, in the early 1970s just under a half of the total manufacturing employment was still in the greater Dublin area.[73] Economic expansion encouraged the self-confidence associated with union militancy, which strained Fianna Fáil's relation with sections of the working class to the benefit of Labour, and this was given concentrated expression in Dublin. It was also the case that a substantial amount of the new public sector employment, which expanded significantly in the 1960s, was located in Dublin. The decade saw the beginning of a long-term process of expansion of white-collar unionization and militancy in the public sector.

Expansion also lessened the pressure to emigrate and, as this had affected younger workers disproportionately, it increased the size of that section of the working class less prone to accept clerical direction than their parents.[74] Although by international standards the Republic in the 1960s was still an intensely Catholic country, there was some evidence of change. A 1962 survey into the attitudes of Dublin Catholics towards religion and clerical authority carried out for the ultra-orthodox Archbishop of Dublin, John Charles McQuaid, revealed sharp differences between those who had completed secondary education and the rest. Whereas an extraordinary 88 per cent of the sample endorsed the proposition that the Church was the greatest source of good in the country, an almost equally massive 83 per cent of the educated group disagreed with it.[75] In the early 1960s less than one in five schoolchildren went on to complete secondary education. By the end of the 1970s this had risen to just under 50 per cent.[76] This rise in participation in secondary education and an associated expansion of higher education did much to produce what Tom Garvin has called the 'post-Catholic and à la carte Catholic' segment of the population.[77]

In the early 1960s Lemass and other members of the political élite displayed a continuing willingness to indulge clericalist pressure. A proposal from the Director of the National Library for a book-sharing arrangement with Trinity College, aimed at avoiding duplication and cutting costs, was submitted by Lemass to McQuaid for his opinion and dropped as soon as McQuaid opposed it. Similarly, an attempt by the Minister of Education to extend nationally an experiment in comprehensive schools begun in the western and border counties was threatened with opposition by McQuaid until he was reassured that they would be denominational, non-coeducational, and managed by the parish priest.[78] However, as the decade progressed there were some signs of a less deferential attitude. In part this reflected the more liberal environment encouraged by Pope John Paul XXIII and the Second Vatican Council, which had opened in Rome in October 1962. Vatican II, with its emphasis on improving relations with the Protestant churches and on a more demotic Catholicism, served to emphasize the conservative, not to say reactionary, position of the Irish hierarchy and of McQuaid in particular.

However, much of the change was an inevitable consequence of the radical turn in economic policy that was made at the end of the 1950s. The emphasis in *Economic Development* on the need for efficiency, competitiveness, and quality raised major questions over the sustainability of the state's continued acquiescence in an educational system whose whole ethos was so heavily influenced by the non-material values of the Catholic Church. As late as 1962 the annual report of the Council of Education, the official advisory body representing teachers and the Catholic school authorities, was arguing that the principal objective of education was the religious and moral development of the child and that the aim of science teaching in secondary school 'is cultural rather than practical'.[79] It also dismissed the idea of universal secondary education as utopian. With the exception of a separate system of vocational schools providing technical education, secondary schools charged fees until the late 1960s. The result of this approach was evident in the stark contrast with Northern Ireland. While secondary school enrolments had doubled in the South between 1945 and 1963, there had been a more than five-fold increase in the North.[80]

Lemass and his Minister of Education, Patrick Hillery, initiated reform with the appointment of a small expert body, chaired by the economist Patrick Lynch, which produced the seminal *Investment in Education* report in 1965. Its chosen focuses—on the relation between the education system and the country's manpower requirements and the participation rates of different socio-economic groups—were an implicit challenge to the status quo and the Church's heavy investment in it. The state's increasingly significant involvement in promoting change, which culminated in the introduction of free secondary education by Hillery's successor, Donogh O'Malley, in 1967, was one significant indication of the decline of the Church's hegemony in an area where its dominance had been hitherto uncontested.

Another was the area of censorship of books and films. Here the government's emphasis on Ireland's new openness to investment and trade and its desire to be a participant in the European project made it less willing to tolerate the image of the Republic as existing in a backward, priest-ridden time warp that was commonplace in the rest of the world. The strict censorship of films and books under legislation passed in the 1920s and concerned with anything 'subversive of public morality' and 'indecent or obscene' had been encountering increasing domestic criticism from the small Irish intelligentsia in the 1950s. The five-member Censorship of Publications Board had been reconstructed in 1957 in order to ensure a more liberal composition. However, the fact remained that previous decisions had resulted in almost all of the major literary works of the twentieth century being banned, including most of the best works of contemporary Irish writers.[81] Brian Lenihan, who became Minister of Justice in 1964, liberalized film censorship by the simple expedient of licensing films for viewing by persons above a certain age, and, in 1967, introduced legislation that provided for the unbanning of books after twelve years. The result was the release of over 5,000 titles. While the liberalism of the Irish censors still had very narrow limits, and novels that would be major literary successes in

Britain in the 1960s like *The Country Girls* by Edna O'Brien and *The Dark* by John McGahern continued to be banned, it was increasingly the censors and not the authors and publishers who were on the defensive.

A far more potent threat to traditional values than the appearance of Steinbeck or Sartre in bookshops in Dublin, Cork, and Galway was the arrival of television. From the early 1950s it had been possible to receive programmes from Britain and Northern Ireland in the border counties and along the east coast. A report prepared for the government in 1956 had estimated that 7,000 homes in the Republic had televisions. It warned about the dangers of cultural pollution, given that British programmes were 'governed by ideas that are wholly alien to the ordinary Irish home'. Particular exception was taken to the 'frank' treatment of sex and the emphasis on the royal family and the 'British way of life'.[82] A major motivation behind the setting up of an Irish Television Service, RTE, in 1961 was therefore a traditionally nationalist and Catholic one. However, the strong opposition of Whitaker and the Department of Finance to a publicly funded service meant that RTE, while run by a state-sponsored body, was financed by advertising and the dynamics of competition with BBC and Ulster Television soon exerted more influence on production values than did moral protectionism.

By the end of 1962 there were 93,000 television licences in the state and by 1970 the figure had soared to 438,000.[83] The relative inexperience of staff and the cost of making programmes meant that there was a substantial reliance on imports from Britain and the US. Combined with the influence of British television along the east coast and despite the aims of those who set it up, Irish television became a powerful force for the Anglo-Americanization of Irish popular culture. It also encouraged a more critical public discourse and a new openness to discussion of such issues as contraception and divorce on programmes including the phenomenally successful *Late Late Show*. Following trends in Britain there was a less cautious and deferential style in the handling of current affairs. In both countries the decade saw the emergence of political satire and a more daring and mocking mood that spread out from television to the staid preserve of radio and the print media. Lemass, who had seen in television a potent machine for propagating the gospel of modernizing nationalism, was soon disturbed by programmes that, as he saw it, focused too much on the defects and shortcomings of the Republic. He intervened privately and occasionally in public to try to curb unruly broadcasters but with little effect. Increasingly it became clear to all but the most obdurately reactionary politicians and clergy that the rules by which they exercised power and authority were being remade and that the mere invocation of the value of traditional forms of life and thought would be insufficient to defend them.

Factions in Fianna Fáil

Although television undoubtedly encouraged the long-term process of liberalization of Irish society, its capacity to bring almost instantaneous images of the flaring up of violence in Derry and Belfast in August 1969 into living rooms throughout the South provided a powerful impetus to a wave of territorial nationalism that seemed for a brief period to threaten the stability of the state. The northern eruption had all the more impact because of the effects it had on a governing party that was already showing signs of an unprecedented amount of internal division.

Lemass's approach to the leadership of party and government had differed starkly from that of de Valera. Whereas the latter had tended to deal with divisions through a process of avoidance or such extended discussion that unity was effected through boring dissidents into submission, Lemass's style was brusque and peremptory. The change of style was reflective of the much more radical and activist content of his government's programme of economic liberalization and modernization, which left less time to consider questions of party management at a time when some of Lemass's new departures were bound to cause internal conflict. The pursuit of a free trade agreement with Britain and the end of restrictions on foreign capital raised the hackles of the champions of protectionist economics in the party. The policy of *détente* with the Stormont regime was also deeply unsettling for those still loyal to the idea of it as an unjust 'Orange junta'. Lemass' engagement with the leaders of Irish trade unionism annoyed sections of the party suspicious of what was perceived as an anti-rural and anti-farmer bias and produced the first cabinet resignation on a policy question in the party's history when his Minister of Agriculture, Patrick Smith, left the government in protest at its alleged capitulation to 'trade union' tyranny.[84]

On top of radical policy reversals, Fianna Fáil had entered the process of transition to a leadership no longer sanctified by its participation in the Irish Revolution of 1916–23. Lemass had begun the process of organizational renewal following the defeat in the 1954 election. He had gradually brought in a potential replacement cadre for the 1916 generation. Some of these, including George Colley and Eoin Ryan, were the sons of the founding members of Fianna Fáil, while others, such as Brian Lenihan and Charles Haughey, were sons of republicans who had taken the Free State side during the Civil War. Together with Neil Blaney and Kevin Boland they had revitalized the Fianna Fáil electoral machine which had by the 1950s become tired and complacent. Haughey, Lenihan, and the brilliant but undisciplined and alcoholic Donogh O'Malley were fervent supporters of Lemassian economics. This was probably sufficient in itself to arouse the suspicion and hostility of those like Seán MacEntee and Frank Aiken who had long harboured doubts about the compatibility of the Lemass project with traditional republican values. However, it was the flamboyant lifestyle of the group labelled the *Camorra* by James Dillon, the Leader of Fine Gael, that caused most unease.[85] As the prosperity associated with economic expansion manifested itself in building and redevelopment programmes, property values rocketed, as did the fortunes of those whose insider knowledge allowed them to buy land that would be destined for development.

Haughey, who had entered the Dáil as TD for Dublin North East in 1957 and been appointed Minister of Justice at the age of 30 in 1961, was at the centre of rumours and allegations about what an opponent would later call 'low standards in high places'. Although the son-in-law of Lemass, his rapid promotion was a reflection of his undoubted abilities. Peter Berry, the formidable Secretary of the Department of Justice, declared him the best minister he had ever served.[86] But it was his connections with the worlds of business and property development through the accountancy firm that he and Harry Boland (the son of another leading member of Fianna Fáil) had founded and his increasingly ostentatious lifestyle that drew the most gossip. Haughey had bought his first racehorse in 1962 and by the end of the decade owned a number of them as well as a farm and one of the Blasket Islands off the coast of Kerry, which became his holiday retreat. In 1969 he bought Abbeyville in Kinsealy, county Dublin, an eighteenth-century mansion that had served as the summer home of several Lord Lieutenants of Ireland, and with it a 250 acre estate.[87] Some senior members of Fianna Fáil shared Gerry Boland's view that his son's partner 'would yet drag down the Party in the mire'.[88] Others such as Frank Aiken saw Haughey as the epitome of the 'materialistic' and 'de-nationalizing' effects of Lemass's leadership and wanted a successor who was truer to traditional republican values and not associated with what a survey of the decade referred to as 'an unsavoury get-rich-quick cabal ... [with] the sleek Mercedes and mohair suits'.[89]

Lemass was subsequently criticized by MacEntee and other Fianna Fáil veterans for failing to provide for a smooth succession.[90] This criticism tended to ignore the degree to which the post-1966 divisions in the party had their origins in inevitable tensions generated by the policy departures of the late 1950s. Fianna Fáil's traditional depiction of itself as a national movement rather than a mere political organization had as its corollary a strong emphasis on maintaining an outward show of disciplined unity and many in the party found the idea of a succession race deeply unsettling. But if there had to be a contest, there was at least a reassuring absence of any conflict of ideas. No candidate issued a statement of principles or publicly identified themselves with any policy positions. Of the two original front runners, Haughey and George Colley, the *Irish Times* commented that while Haughey was 'the modern man, essentially pragmatic and business-minded', Colley was a 'chip off the traditionalist block'.[91] The central attraction of Colley to the party elders who supported him was that he was seen as hostile to what was perceived as Haughey's ruthless materialism. In fact on central economic policy issues and on Northern Ireland there was no recorded difference of opinion between the two. Despite this, Lemass's original attempt to get either Dr Patrick Hilley or Jack Lynch interested in the succession may have reflected his fear that a Haughey/Colley contest would allow those traditionalists defeated in such key areas as free trade and Northern Ireland to stage a comeback.

Although Lynch had originally resisted Lemass's overtures, the decision of Neil Blaney to intervene in the contest brought further and this time successful pressure from the Taoiseach. A TD for the border constituency of Donegal, Blaney had little time for policies of *rapprochement* with Stormont and Lemass was aghast when he became a candidate. Jack Lynch had entered the Dáil as a TD for Cork in 1948 at the age of 31 and had been appointed Minister of Education by de Valera when Fianna Fáil returned to power in 1957. Under Lemass he had been centrally associated with the new directions in economic policy, first as Minister of Industry and Commerce and from 1965 as Minister of Finance, where he had developed a very good personal relationship with T. K. Whitaker. He was a strong supporter of Lemass's overtures to O'Neill but lacked the protective shield of a revolutionary pedigree, although this was compensated for to some degree by his record of prowess in Gaelic games, where he had the unique achievement of winning six senior All-Ireland hurling championships in succession.[92] Promoted by Lemass as a unity candidate, Lynch was accepted on those terms by both Blaney and

Haughey who withdrew from the contest and he easily defeated Colley by fifty-nine votes to nineteen in the election by the Fianna Fáil parliamentary party on 9 November 1966.

Lynch's initial reluctance to stand led to the other candidates for the leadership seeing his position as intrinsically short-term, a caretaker until the party got a leader more in tune with its traditions. Lynch's own low-key style, a strong desire for consensus, and his apparent lack of strong views on most issues led to the early years of his government being characterized by conservatism, lack of control over the cabinet, and the loss of the momentum of the Lemass years. Symptomatic was the Taca episode. Taca (Irish for 'support') was a party organization created in 1966 with the object of increasing financial support from the business community. Lemass had been involved in his own discreet fund-raising efforts in his later years, setting up a committee with John Reihill of the coal-importing family as chairman.[93] However, Taca, of which Haughey and Blaney were the foremost supporters, was an altogether cruder affair in its blatant exchange of potential political favours for donations. Supporters were invited to join by making an annual payment of £100 per year towards the party's electoral fund while the interest was used to fund dinners at which members of Taca could mix with cabinet ministers.[94]

Taca was seen by critics of Fianna Fáil as proof of the corruption of its founding principles, with Mairin de Burca of Sinn Féin claiming that 'the selfless idealism of Easter Week has become the self-seeking degeneracy of Taca'.[95] Within the party Colley, who had not given up his leadership ambitions, openly criticized Taca and demanded that the party return to its original tradition of seeking 'justice for all sections of the community but with special concern for the small man, the small farmer, the urban working man and the clerk'.[96] The Taca episode may well have contributed to the depth of the government's defeat in the referendum on a proposal to replace proportional representation with a simple majority system. The proposal was rejected by a decisive majority in October 1968 and the fact that this was the first time since 1932 that the party had failed to get more than 40 per cent in a national poll and that many TDs and senators had not campaigned for the change gave rise to much speculation about the future of Lynch's leadership.[97]

Fianna Fáil's victory in the 1969 election did much to shore up Lynch's leadership in the short term at least. He won in partnership with Haughey, whom he had made director of elections. Choosing to deal with his most formidable potential leadership opponent by a strategy of generous accommodation, he had made him Minister of Finance and tolerated Taca until internal criticism led to its being phased out in 1968. The 1969 campaign combined Haughey and Blaney's brutal anti-communist assault on Labour with Lynch's low-key but effective series of visits to convents to deliver the same message. The campaign was noteworthy as the first in which a leader's telegenic qualities had an effect. For whatever reservations some of his colleagues and the party grass-roots had about Lynch's lack of decisiveness, his soft-spoken, 'honest Jack' image on television was successful with the electorate.[98] The relations between Lynch and Haughey had been warm during the campaign but within months of victory, developments in Northern Ireland had opened up a chasm between them.

The Arms Crisis

Soon after the outbreak of major disorder in Derry and Belfast in August 1969, a senior Irish official recalled a journalist's caustic comment that 'our mass media and general public opinion only discovered the Six Counties on October 5 1968'.[99] In fact there is little evidence that the political and administrative class was much better prepared. In retirement Lemass had become a member of the Dáil Committee on the Constitution, which he had initiated when still Taoiseach. Its report in 1967 was characterized by a realism that some Fianna Fáil fundamentalists found disturbing. It argued that, so far from looking provisional, partition had 'hardened to a degree which only the vaguest of optimists can think of as temporary'[100] and suggested that Article 3 of the constitution, which laid legal claim to Northern Ireland, should be reformulated in less 'polemical' terms as an aspiration. Although Lynch sympathized with this approach, the strength of opposition within party and government dictated that nothing was done. When T. K. Whitaker, in his final year as Secretary to the Department of Finance, wrote to Charles Haughey, his minister, arguing the advantages of a recasting of Articles 2 and 3 in improving relations with Unionists, Haughey's response was vehemently republican, emphasizing that there was no moral objection to the use of force but only a practical one.[101]

For those like Lynch and Whitaker who wished to maintain Lemass's approach and for whom unity would come through North–South *rapprochement* assisted by some gentle prodding from London, the civil rights movement was a new, unpredictable, and not entirely welcome development. Lemass was initially dismissive, claiming that 'two or three wet days will finish things'.[102] While the British state, however reluctantly, was substantially increasing its involvement in Northern Ireland, the Irish government's approach was somnambulistic. As O'Neill's administration buckled in the spring of 1969, the Irish cabinet had its only discussion of Northern Ireland before the disastrous events of August. Frank Aiken was sent to New York to speak to the Secretary General of the United Nations but, as he explained to the British Ambassador in Dublin, the purpose of the UN initiative was a temperature-lowering exercise on both sides of the border.[103]

As northern temperatures stubbornly continued to rise, those who had favoured a moderate line could only watch with increasing dismay. Whitaker, who had moved from Finance to become Governor of the Central Bank, continued to impress on his former minister the need for moderation and responsibility. Echoing the views of those on the right of Unionism, he cautioned that Dublin should avoid playing into the hands of the 'extremists who are manipulating the civil rights movement and who wish to stir up trouble and disorder'. His hope that the Irish government could appeal to the civil rights movement for a period of restraint with an end to all street protests was ignored, as was his advice that it should 'do nothing to inflame the situation further, but aim to impress and encourage the moderates on both sides'.[104]

On 13 August, the day after the Apprentice Boys parade had ignited the 'Battle of the Bogside', Lynch attempted to get cabinet approval for an address to the nation which he proposed to make on RTE that evening. A substantial section of his government, led by Haughey, Blaney, and Kevin Boland, the Minister of Local Government, regarded the draft as too mild and forced a major revision. In his broadcast Lynch, while claiming that the Stormont government was no longer in control, opposed the introduction of British troops and called for the introduction of a UN peace-keeping force. With equal futility he requested the British government to enter into negotiations on the constitutional future of Northern Ireland. The Irish army was to open field hospitals for victims along the border and, in lines that would encourage nationalist hopes of more direct intervention and loyalist paranoia, he declared 'The Irish government can no longer stand by and see innocent people injured and perhaps worse.'[105] Both Blaney and Boland favoured Irish troops being sent across the border into Derry and Newry but the majority of their colleagues recoiled in horror from this lunatic counsel, precipitating Boland's unpublicized but temporary resignation from the government. But if the invasion option was rejected, Lynch appears to have been powerless to prevent some of his ministers from sponsoring what became a serious attempt to subvert partition by forming an alliance with those northern republicans who were to become the nucleus of the Provisional IRA.

Haughey was to play a central and, to many who had observed his previous political career, surprising role in what became known as the Arms Crisis. While Blaney and Boland's visceral anti-partitionism was not in question, many had doubts about Haughey's seeing in his involvement little more than an opportunistic use of the North in a bid to topple and replace Lynch. His public utterances had displayed no more than the conventional republicanism to be expected from any prominent member of Fianna Fáil. When he was appointed Minister of Justice in 1961 he had pinpointed the crushing of the IRA as his main objective and had reactivated the Special Criminal Court to achieve it.[106] He had, as Minister of Agriculture after the first O'Neill/Lemass summit, met with Harry West, his Unionist counterpart, and been a powerful advocate of the advantages of the Anglo-Irish Free Trade Agreement.[107] However, his private response to Whitaker's revisionist ideas on the North suggests there was more to his role than opportunism. The British Ambassador who met him in October 1969 came away convinced of his 'passion for unity' after Haughey told him that there was nothing he would not sacrifice for unity, including the position of the Catholic Church and Irish neutrality.[108] His father and mother came from Swatragh in county Tyrone and both had been active in the republican movement during the War of Independence.[109] Three decades after the crisis Haughey would refer to his family being 'deeply imbedded in the Northern Ireland situation' in one of his rare public comments on his involvement.[110] In fact his connections were with a part of Northern Ireland, Mid-Tyrone, which had a strongly republican tradition. It was for this area that the dissident IRA man Liam Kelly was returned to Stormont in the 1950s. In so far as his northern connections influenced Haughey, they were unlikely to have encouraged moderation. His father had fought on the pro-Treaty side during the Civil War—something for which Frank Aiken had never forgiven him—and this seems to have influenced Aiken's apparent detestation of his son.[111] This 'Free-Stater' stain on his pedigree may have encouraged a compensatory lurch into an alliance with Blaney and Boland. For Haughey, the events of August 1969 produced a powerful confluence of ideological affinity and political ambition.

Exploiting the febrile atmosphere of mid August, he and his allies seized temporary control of the government's response to northern events. As Minister of Finance he was given the responsibility by the cabinet for a relief fund of £100,000 for victims of the unrest in the North. He was, along with Blaney, part of a new cabinet sub-committee given the task of liaising with northern nationalists to promote 'a united cohesive force of anti-unionists and anti-partitionists'.[112] Over the next few months he and Blaney would both directly, and through a network of Irish military intelligence officers and other government employees seconded to work in Northern Ireland, establish links with some of the most militant elements of northern nationalism.

In response to the August events, a special section had been created in the Government Information Bureau aimed at improving liaison with nationalist opinion in Northern Ireland and putting the Irish case internationally. George Colley was given charge of this operation, which was largely staffed by public relations officers seconded from bodies such as *Bord Bainne*, the Irish Milk Marketing Board. Some of those employed would play key roles in linking Haughey and Blaney with those traditional republicans in Derry and Belfast who were most vociferous in their criticisms of Cathal Goulding, Chief of Staff of the IRA, for leaving Catholics undefended. Part of the £100,000 that Haughey assigned to the Northern Relief Fund thus found its way into the financing of a new virulently anti-partitionist and anti-Goulding newspaper, *The Voice of the North*, which began publication in October. It was edited by Seamus Brady, a former speech-writer for Blaney, who was until September 1969 an employee of the Government Information Bureau. His successor as editor was Hugh Kennedy, an employee of *Bord Bainne*, who had become Press Officer of the Central Citizens' Defence Committee in Belfast in the immediate aftermath of the August violence.[113] Both men and Captain James Kelly, an Irish Army intelligence officer, were active in promising northern republicans support as long as they cut their links with the 'communists' who controlled the IRA.

In August even constitutional politicians such as Paddy Devlin of the NILP and Gerry Fitt were arriving in Dublin demanding that if the government would not send in troops it should at least provide Catholics with weapons to defend themselves from further attacks. Although Lynch refused to meet them, Haughey and Blaney did and both were determined to obtain arms for the North. The purpose of these weapons was made clear in Captain Kelly's report to his superior, Colonel Michael Hefferon, the Director of Irish Army Intelligence, on 23 August:

It would seem to be now necessary to harness all opinion in the state in a concerted drive towards achieving the aim of reunification. Unfortunately, this would mean accepting the possibility of armed action of some sort as the ultimate solution.[114]

There were failed attempts to buy weapons in London, in which Haughey's brother Padraig was involved, and in the US. Eventually Captain Kelly was able to make an arrangement with a German arms dealer and the weapons were set to be flown from Vienna to Dublin on 21 April 1970. It was Haughey's failure to arrange clearance for the arms at Dublin airport, when his former Secretary at the Department of Justice, Peter Berry, made it clear the guns would be seized by the Irish Special Branch, that precipitated the Irish state's most serious crisis since its formation.

Although Lynch was informed of the plot by Berry, he attempted to contain its reverberations by accepting denials of involvement from both Blaney and Haughey. It was only when news about the failed importation was leaked to the Fine Gael leader, Liam Cosgrave, that Lynch was forced to act. On 5 May he demanded the resignation of the two ministers and, when they refused, he sacked them. He had already forced the resignation of his weak and incompetent Minister of Justice. Boland resigned in protest at the firings and so in one day Lynch had lost four senior ministers. Blaney and Haughey were subsequently arrested and charged with an attempt to import guns illegally into the state. The charges against Blaney were dismissed in a Dublin district court but Haughey along with Captain Kelly, a Belgian-born businessman, and a Belfast republican were brought to trial at the High Court where they were all eventually acquitted in October as the jury clearly found it difficult to accept that the arms importation did not have at least covert government sanction.

Although Lynch has been subject to criticism for not moving against the conspirators earlier, his defenders would suggest that he had played a subtle game, allowing Blaney and Haughey sufficient rope with which to hang themselves. His achievement, given the precariousness of his position, has been well summed up by Garret FitzGerald:

His handling of the Arms Crisis was very difficult for him: he was dealing with people who had deeper roots in the party than he had. His success in overcoming that difficulty and stabilising the Government and in marginalising those who had adventurous ideas about the North was of crucial importance to the stability of the state and of the island as a whole.[115]

On his acquittal Haughey demanded Lynch's resignation but the Taoiseach was able to use party members' overwhelming desire to maintain unity and stay in government against the much weaker mobilizing capacity of anti-partitionism. Such was the power of the imperative of party over 'national' unity that both Blaney and Haughey voted with the government against an Opposition motion of 'no confidence'.[116] Not since 1940 and de Valera's rejection of the British offer of unity in exchange for an end to neutrality had the primacy of twenty-six-county nationalism been so apparent. Public sympathy for the Catholic victims of northern violence was still strong but it clearly did not extend to support for those who appeared ready to contemplate direct involvement in arming one side in a potential sectarian civil war. A public opinion poll carried out just after Haughey's dismissal showed that 72 per cent of the electorate supported Lynch's decision while a staggering 89 per cent of those who had voted for Fianna Fáil in the last election still supported him as their preferred choice as Taoiseach.[117]

Haughey avoided any public confrontation with Lynch's stand on the North after August 1969, as the Taoiseach relied increasingly on the advice he was getting from T. K. Whitaker and also from senior officials in External Affairs. In a letter to Lynch, Whitaker referred disparagingly to the 'teenage hooliganism and anarchy' in Derry and Belfast during the worst of the August violence and warned against the 'terrible temptation to be opportunist—to cash in on political emotionalism—at a time like this'.[118] It was Whitaker who provided most of the text of a speech given by Lynch at Tralee on 20 September which firmly restated the most positive aspects of Lemass's conciliatory approach to Northern Ireland, emphasizing that the policy of seeking unity through agreement was of its nature a long-term one.[119]

This approach was also apparent in a major assessment of the Irish state's Northern Ireland policy produced by the Department of External Affairs in November 1969. It emphasized that the government's basic approach should remain that of seeking reunification 'by peaceful means through co-operation and consent between Irishmen. The use of force should be dismissed publicly as frequently as may appear necessary.' Unity itself was recognized to be made more difficult by the fact that the Republic was a 'confessional society' whereas a united Ireland would have to be pluralist. As a consequence, reforms to take account of the concerns of northern Protestants on such issues as divorce and birth control and also in education and the role of the Irish language should be considered. Lemass's legacy of functional co-operation with Stormont needed to be maintained and enhanced despite 'such temporary cooling of relations as have happened recently'. Most significant of all for the subsequent development of Anglo-Irish relations, it advocated the 'maximum discreet contact with Whitehall' at both official and ministerial level.[120]

By early 1970, as tensions in the North abated, Patrick Hillery, Minister of External Affairs, was being secretly briefed at the Foreign Office that 'a lot of steam had gone out of the situation' and that the only troublemakers were 'professional agitators' with little popular support.[121] Even when the Ballymurphy riots in April challenged this panglossian view, Eamonn Gallagher, the most senior Irish official liaising directly with northern nationalists, was unsympathetic to those involved, fearing that new disturbances in Ulster might help the Tories in the forthcoming British general election.[122] At a time when the British were impressing on Dublin the capacity of the army to ensure that Catholics anywhere in Northern Ireland were safe from the threat of another pogrom, and with the B Specials disbanded and the RUC disarmed, Blaney and Boland's open championing of the possible use of force to bring about unity appeared increasingly extremist. Lynch's moderation would remain unchallenged until the events of internment and Bloody Sunday unleashed another wave of irredentist emotion.

However, the pull of new interventionist urges was undermined by the emergence of the Provisionals and their offensive in the North that did much to tarnish the image of an 'oppressed people' awaiting salvation from the South. Fear of contagion from violence 'up there' became widespread. Lynch's new Minister of Justice, Desmond O'Malley, soon demonstrated a zeal to repress any subversive spillovers from the North. In December 1970 he announced that the government was considering the introduction of internment to deal with 'a secret armed conspiracy' that allegedly planned kidnappings, armed robberies, and murders—all activities in which the Provisional IRA was soon to be involved. In May 1971 the Offences Against the State Act was activated to create a 'special criminal court' of three judges sitting without a jury and in November a further amendment to the Act allowed the indictment of those suspected of membership of an illegal organization on the word of a senior police officer.[123] 'Honest Jack's' resort to repression appears to have done him no significant electoral damage, for although Fianna Fáil lost the 1973 election this was because a pre-election pact between Labour and Fine Gael meant that, despite Lynch's party increasing its share of the vote, the combined opposition returned more TDs.

In his address to Fainna Fáil's árd fheis in January 1970, Jack Lynch provided a convincing and passionate rebuttal of Blaney's claim in a famous tirade at Letterkenny in December 1969 that Fianna Fáil had never taken a decision to rule out the use of force to bring about unity. Echoing Lemass's Tralee speech of 1963, he informed the delegates that 'like it or not, we have to acknowledge that two-thirds of the one and a half million people who make up the population of the six counties wish to be associated with the United Kingdom'. The 'plain truth' was that they did not have the capacity to impose a solution by force and even if they had, 'would we want to adopt the role of an occupying conqueror over the million or so six county citizens who at present support partition?'[124]

Lynch had defeated the republican hawks within the party because their activities were perceived to threaten the security of the southern state. While Boland, who left Fianna Fáil to found a pure republican party, and Blaney, who was expelled, would remain marginalized as one-issue politicians, Haughey stayed in the party, sure in the support of its traditionalist wing, but by now well educated in the limited power of anti-partitionism in southern politics. The ending of partition would remain a largely unquestioned element of the national consensus and a powerful component of the internal political culture of Fianna Fáil. Yet throughout the 1970s opinion polls would not rank it high on the list of voters' priorities. The violence and intractability of the northern conflict ensured that unity remained a low-intensity aspiration. Haughey would be able to use the 'whiff of cordite' associated with the Arms Crisis as a significant resource in his ultimate displacement of Lynch but it was the failure of the latter's economic policies, not his Northern Ireland policy, that would prove decisive.

7

Terence O'Neill and the Crisis of the Unionist State

Liberal Unionism: Opportunities and Enemies

The problems facing those who wanted a more accommodating Unionism had been made clear in 1959 in a much publicized row over the question of whether Catholics could become members of the Unionist Party. The slump in Sinn Féin's vote in the 1959 general election—it dropped by almost 60 per cent, from 152,000 in 1955 to 63,000—was accompanied by an increase in the Unionist Party vote in the eight constituencies where there was a straight fight with Sinn Féin and there was evidence that this was a product of some Catholics voting Unionist.[1] The previous year at a Catholic social study conference at Garron Tower in north Antrim a number of the participants had argued that the way to obtain social justice for their community was to become more positively engaged in public life. The former Minister of Home Affairs and *bête noire* of loyalist militants, Brian Maginess, who was now Attorney General, saw in these developments a good reason to go public with a plea for a more inclusive Unionism. At a Young Unionist weekend school in Portstewart he spoke of the need to treat political opponents 'not as enemies but as fellow members of the community' and attacked those who made abusive references to the religious beliefs of others, a clear reference not simply to the increasing public profile of Ian Paisley but to the sectarian utterances of some members of his own party.[2]

However, it was the response of Sir Clarence Graham, Chairman of the Standing Committee of the Ulster Unionist Council, to a question about possible Catholic membership of the party which produced most reaction. His support for Catholics becoming parliamentary candidates enraged a substantial section of the government and party.[3] Brookeborough privately recognized that Catholic membership might indeed come about but was critical of Graham and Maginess for raising it in public as this 'will only delay matters'.[4] His bruising experience with Protestant populism in the early 1950s had left him determined to give no further hostages to the right. The result was a government immobilized by fear of schism and unable to respond to a real opportunity to develop a better relation with the minority community. Sir George Clarke, Grand Master of the Grand Orange Lodge of Ireland, proclaimed that the Order would never accept Catholics as members of the Unionist Party.[5] Privately he apologized to the Prime Minister for the hardline tone but explained it by the need to placate Orangemen annoyed not only by Graham's remarks but also by a government ban on a proposed Orange march through Dungiven. He was also concerned about the growing influence of Paisley in the Order.[6]

Paisley had been able to increase his support among loyalists worried by the IRA campaign and concerned about looming redundancies in the shipyards and the aircraft factories. An organization called Ulster Protestant Action had some limited success in recruiting in workplaces by demanding that any redundancies were not suffered by loyalists.[7] Such sectarian pressures had some echoes in mainstream Unionism. During the 1961 Belfast municipal elections the St George's ward Unionist Association produced a leaflet stating that its three candidates 'employ over 70 people, and have never employed a Roman Catholic'. In the same year a prominent Unionist, Robert Babington, told the Ulster Unionist Labour Association that the party should keep registers of unemployed loyalists from which employers would be invited to pick workers.[8]

Yet closet liberals in the cabinet might have taken some encouragement from a number of developments in the early 1960s. There was evidence of a more pragmatic and democratic nationalism taking root in sections of the Catholic middle class, particularly the expanding numbers of university graduates who had benefited from the 1947 Education Act. A new nationalist organization, National Unity, was set up in Belfast at the end of 1959 to give voice to those dissatisfied with the ineffectuality of traditional forms of nationalist and republican politics and to argue that any move towards unity had to have the consent of a majority in Northern Ireland.[9] The ecumenical movement and the pontificate of John XXIII helped to smoothe the edges of inter-church conflict. There was also some evidence that, in the greater Belfast area at least, there was a thawing in the communal cold war.

In their pioneering study of community relations published in 1962, Barritt and Carter noted that Catholics would now venture into the Protestant heartland of Sandy Row in search of work and had no fears about shopping on the Shankill Road, a judgement later confirmed in

Gerry Adams' autobiograpical account of growing up in Belfast in the early 1960s.[10] The Belfast correspondent of the *Irish Times* commented on the growing moderation of ordinary people: 'It is something composed of simple human feeling, a wish to live in peace, an unwillingness to hate irrationally, a recognition that Ireland's conflicts are small ones in today's world.'[11] This was evident in politics. Despite the advocacy of a sectarian approach to dealing with unemployment by Ulster Protestant Action and some Unionist politicians, even William Douglas, the crusty *apparatchik* who was Secretary of the Unionist Party, recognized that the challenge from the NILP in the 1962 election would have to be met on economic and social issues and that banging the tribal drum was no longer sufficient.[12]

Attitudinal change was in part a reflection of important social developments. The post-war improvement in living standards meant that the arrival of the 'consumer society', while not displacing traditional fixations, drained them of some of their emotional centrality. The move of significant numbers of Belfast's traditional working-class communities into new housing estates or to surrounding towns and villages such as Newtownabbey, Castlereagh, Dunmurry, and Lisburn, where many of the new industries were established on green-field sites, weakened traditional allegiances to the Unionist Party.[13] The arrival of television, while its impact was complex, helped to expand the horizons of a still intensely parochial society. The BBC had brought television to Northern Ireland in 1953, broadcasting from a small temporary transmitter in Belfast. A powerful new transmitter was built in Belfast in 1955 and the number of television sets in the North rose from 3,000 in 1953 to over 38,000 by 1956. The arrival of independent television provided a major stimulus to the market for sets.[14]

Traditionally the senior officials of the BBC in Belfast had been close to the viewpoint of the government but in the 1950s the Director General, Sir William Haley, had encouraged the local Controller to extend the areas for discussion and to bring differing viewpoints into civilized contention.[15] One result was *Your Questions*, a local version of the popular radio series *Any Questions*. First broadcast in 1954, it was produced by the Protestant socialist John Boyd and its regular contributers, who included Jack Sayers editor of the *Belfast Telegraph*, the liberal nationalist J. J. Campbell, the Oxford-educated NILP activist Charles Brett, and the Queen's University historian, J. C. Beckett, all of whom were proponents of the need for the political renovation of the North to be accomplished through a more constructive engagement between nationalism and Unionism.[16] However, the response of some leading members of the government to even such mild innovation was one of suspicious hostility. The up-and-coming Unionist politician, Brian Faulkner, was at the forefront with his condemnations of the BBC for its alleged anti-government bias. For Faulkner, as for a sizeable section of the cabinet and parliamentary party, someone like Sayers was too liberal to be an acceptable Unionist representative and Beckett's links with southern historians made his supposed neutrality suspect.[17]

When the *Tonight* programme sent Alan Whicker to Belfast in 1958 there was an outpouring of Unionist rage when Whicker informed viewers in the rest of the UK that in Northern Ireland policemen carried revolvers, pubs were open from morning to night, and betting shops had been legalized and carried on a brisk business. The Regional Controller apologized to the Northern Ireland public and *Tonight* did not show any of the remaining films.[18] Making allowance for some understandable annoyance at the programme's failure to deal with the ongoing, if declining, IRA campaign, there remained something disproportionate in the response. This brittle defensiveness that affected a substantial section of the Unionist community was a clear warning to those who would make too much of the first signs of the blunting of traditional antagonisms.

There was a geographical dimension to Unionist divisions. Barritt and Carter noted that while more tolerant feelings had become manifest in Belfast, the situation in rural areas, especially those near the border, was different. Here the IRA campaign had polarized the communities: 'the political and national issues have become more prominent and have brought a new hardness to attitudes.'[19] Unionists in border areas were also dealing with a nationalism that showed fewer signs of the questioning and flexibility that had begun to appear in the east of the province. The *Belfast Newsletter*, a traditionalist counterweight to Sayers' *Telegraph*, warned of the dangers of mellowing Unionist attitudes:

For Unionists in Belfast and its hinterland the border issue is at a discount, and many there think that they can forget about it altogether. But it is the one thing that matters in Nationalist held areas and is probably the big issue that matters among Nationalists of all persuasions throughout Ulster. Forgetting about the border is something that is expected of Unionists but not of Nationalists.[20]

It was to Brian Faulkner that those Unionists who were most unsettled by the vision of men like Maginess turned for leadership. Faulkner, who entered Stormont as MP for East Down in 1949, had become the dominant voice of the right in the government when Brookeborough promoted him from Chief Whip to Minister of Home Affairs in 1959. He had worked in his father's shirt manufacturing concern during the war and, worried that his lack of war service might hurt his progress in the Unionist Party, he cultivated an activist pro-Orange image as compensation.[21] He demanded an inquiry when Brian Maginess banned the Orange parade along the predominantly nationalist Longstone Road in 1952 and when the ban was lifted, in 1955 he led a march of 15,000 Orangemen along the road, guarded by hundreds of RUC men in full riot gear.[22] Faulkner had also criticized the government for not defending the right of an Orange band to march in the largely Catholic village of Dungiven in 1953. After the same band provoked a riot and a subsequent Catholic boycott of Protestant shops in July 1958, the following year's march was banned by Colonel Ken Topping, Maginess's successor at Home Affairs. Although previously identified as one of the cabinet's more reactionary figures,[23] Topping was now execrated by the Orange lodges and as soon as judgeship became available he was replaced by Faulkner, who allowed the band and 10,000 Orangemen to march through Dungiven in July 1960 sparking off two nights of rioting.[24]

Ambitious, energetic, and very able, Faulkner was clearly positioning himself for the succession to Brookeborough. His assault on liberalism in the party endeared him to many grass-roots Unionists, particularly outside Belfast. His industrial experience also led him to believe that the modernizers in the party were out of touch with working-class loyalists. As early as 1959 he warned those who saw the fall in support for Sinn Féin as indicative of a shift in the minority's attitude to the state that traditional nationalism was not a spent force but a 'volcano smoking harmlessly enough until the day when it flares up to engulf all those who live unsuspecting on its slopes'.[25] In the cabinet he was at the forefront of those who saw Lemass's proposals for practical co-operation between North and South as simply a more insidious form of anti-partitionism. Even the harmless Irish Association, composed of the great and the good and aimed at improved understanding between the citizens of the two states, was denounced by him as having an Irish nationalist agenda.[26] Connolly Gage, a former Unionist Party MP at Westminster, put the common liberal view of Faulkner when he argued that his succession to Brookeborough would be a 'disaster': 'it might put us in the South African category with knobs on'.[27]

In fact it was the Minister of Finance, Terence O'Neill, who succeeded Brookeborough as Prime Minister on 25 March 1963. Following the Conservative Party tradition, the new leader 'emerged' after consultations between the Governor, Lord Wakehurst, Brookeborough, and the Unionist Chief Whip, William Craig. A straw poll carried out by Craig amongst the Unionist MPs at Stormont gave O'Neill a comfortable lead over his two main rivals, Faulkner and J. L. O. Andrews, son of the former premier and a genial and affable Minister of Commerce.[28] However, it was widely believed in the party that O'Neill's 'superior' social standing weighed heavily in the Governor's decision.

He was the son of the Orange and Conservative MP Arthur Bruce O'Neill, the first Westminster MP to die at the front in the First World War. His mother was the daughter of Lord Crewe, a member of Asquith's cabinet, and he was brought up in London in his mother's liberal circle. Educated at Eton, he drifted through several stock-exchange jobs before military service in the Irish Guards during the Second World War. Although not a landowner himself, his family's secure membership of the social élite in county Antrim, where his uncle was a Westminster MP, had made it relatively easy to acquire the nomination for the Stormont constituency of Bannside in 1946. From his earliest days at Stormont he clearly felt that his social standing, military credentials, and metropolitan upbringing made him worthy of a place in Brookeborough's inner circle.[29] He first entered the government as a junior minister in 1948 and became Minister of Finance in 1956. Beneath the languid demeanour and the aristocratic drawl was what one of his closest civil service allies called a 'constructive ruthlessness'.[30] He made little attempt to disguise his low opinion of the quality of the average Unionist MP or of many of his cabinet colleagues. His aloof style, Brookeborough's failure to recommend him as his successor, and the lack of any direct role for members of the parliamentary party in his selection gave his critics a powerful argument about the new premier's lack of popular legitimacy.

O'Neillism Phase One: 'Stealing Labour's Thunder'

For the first two years of his premiership, O'Neill's priority was to respond to the NILP's charge that the regime was incapable of dealing with the problem of unemployment because of its reactionary ideology and its antiquated and amateurish style of government. Here he was able to make a distinctive break with the approach of his predecessor. As Minister of Finance, his difficult relation with his permanent secretary, Sir Douglas Harkness, stemmed in part from a belief that Harkness was too pliant to the demands of the Treasury and not robust enough in pressing the province's case for extra resources.[31] He had as a result got more directly involved in relations with Treasury officials than had been the case previously. Although part of his approach involved dining with them at the London St James Club, there was an increasingly clear O'Neillite approach to the financial relations with London to support his charm offensive. In essence it involved a shift away from Brookeborough's emphasis on the North's special circumstances and ad hoc responses to short-term crises of the local economy towards portraying Northern Ireland as a relatively backward region of the UK whose modernization would contribute the economic health of the kingdom as a whole.

Depression in many of Britain's heavy industries at the end of the 1950s had increased unemployment in the regions at the same time as there was evidence of 'over-heating' in the south-east, which was pushing up wages and threatening the balance of payments. The result was an increasing interest in developing a regional policy that would direct investment to those parts of Britain where resources were under-employed. Regional expansion could thus be seen as a contribution to a higher rate of national economic growth and became part of the 1960s vogue for national planning. Regional planning initiatives in Scotland and Wales were associated with new investments in 'growth centres', new towns and motorways.[32]

A long-standing conflict between the Stormont government and Belfast Corporation over the latter's desire to have the city's boundary extended provided the basis for a largely civil service-based initiative that allowed the province to plug profitably into these national initiatives. Brookeborough's cabinet had resisted the boundary extension because of a fear that it might increase the number of nationalist seats but eventually had to concede a request from the Corporation for a survey of the Belfast area by an independent consultant. Sir Robert Matthew, an eminent planner, was engaged and his report, published just before Brookeborough's resignation, was a much more ambitious document than its title implied. By dealing with the question of Belfast's boundary within the context of the future development of infrastructure in the province as a whole, it was a blueprint for a massive increase in public investment. It suggested the creation of a new city between Lurgan and Portadown, the development of a number of 'growth centres', and a major improvement in the transport system with a new motorway and road network.[33]

The Matthew Report would be the basis for O'Neill's subsequent success in extracting significantly more resources from the Treasury than his predecessor. However, at the time of Brookeborough's resignation the full implications of the Report were far from apparent and O'Neill's succession was not linked to any clear articulation of a distinctive philosophy on either the economy or community relations. At the same time there were some hints of what was to come. As Minister of Finance he had spoken of the need for the province to be more proactive in developing solutions to its economic problems and this might have been interpreted as an implicit criticism of Brookeborough's importuning London for more subsidies for local industry. Given that the challenge from the NILP had been in part based on the criticism of the government for being too ready to feather-bed local industrialists, O'Neill had a distinct advantage over Faulkner, who was a strident defender of the local bourgeoisie.

In his first speech to the Ulster Unionist Council, O'Neill defined his government's task as being 'to transform the face of Ulster'.[34] This transformation would be based, not on directly addressing Catholic demands for reform, but on a new approach to the economic and social modernization of the province. He referred to the Matthew Report as a way in which 'Northern Ireland could capture the imagination of the world'.[35] This would be as a region that had turned its back on its historic conflicts and united in the pursuit of full employment and higher living standards. His view of the modernization proposals in the Matthew Report and in the subsequent Wilson plan for economic development was that they would make such issues as discrimination and gerrymandering redundant:

As for the divisions in our society, I sometimes wonder whether we do much good by so frequently talking about them. There are so many things which should unite all Ulster people. If we emphasize these things, the divisions will seem less significant.[36]

Such an approach seemed dangerously superficial to liberal Unionists like Sayers, but they in their turn ignored the major political imperative under which any leader of the Unionist Party had to labour. This was to maximize support for the party in the Protestant electorate, given that very few Catholics would vote Unionist in the foreseeable future. Lord Brookeborough had lost support in the party because he appeared to be unable to stem losses to the NILP in the greater Belfast area. Winning back this support was the immediate priority for O'Neill. The consolidation of the Unionist bloc in the east of the province was a prerequisite for the pursuit of reforms in community relations as these, if they were to address some of the major complaints of the minority community, would inevitably lead to serious internal party conflict in Tyrone, Fermanagh, and Londonderry. The problem for O'Neill was that although this approach was successful in dealing with the NILP, it unintentionally sharpened community antagonisms.

Plans for economic expansion inevitably had sectarian implications, given the religious and political geography of the region. The fact that the Matthew Report's designated 'growth centres' were concentrated in the east of the region did little to discourage the traditional nationalist complaint about discrimination against Catholic majority areas in the west and south of Northern Ireland. When O'Neill announced the creation of an inter-departmental inquiry into the possible scope of economic planning in October 1963, the economic consultant chosen was the Oxford-trained Ulsterman Thomas Wilson, a committed Unionist who was Professor of Economics at Glasgow University. Wilson's report with an accompanying White Paper was published in February 1965. It set out an ambitious target of 65,000 new jobs and 64,000 new houses by 1970 and proved decisive in O'Neill's campaign against the NILP.[37] However, Wilson's view on where new industries should locate followed Matthew's suggestions and emphasized the difficulties of getting British and foreign industrialists interested in the peripheral parts of what seemed to them 'a discouragingly remote area on the very fringe of Europe'.[38] This was a bleak message for towns such as Derry, Strabane, and Enniskillen and intensified the perception among nationalists that the focus of O'Neill's development plans was on the Unionist communities in the east, symbolized above all by the location of the new city between the predominantly Protestant towns of Lurgan and Portadown.

Although there was no suggestion that Wilson was influenced by political or sectarian considerations, this was not to be the case with the report of the Lockwood Committee on Higher Education, which had been considering the case for a second university in the province. Although there was a potential base for this in Magee College in Derry, the report suggested that the best choice would be the largely Protestant town of Coleraine in county Londonderry. While many Derry Protestants participated in the protest campaign against the proposal, it was the fixation of the hierarchy of the city's Unionist Party on avoiding any significant economic and social development that would upset the sectarian balance which proved determinant.[39] Even the 'liberal' O'Neill was not immune to the corrosive influence of the sectarian myopia of some Derry Unionists, wondering how, if such a development took place, 'is it possible to insure against a radical increase in R.C. Papes?'[40] The triumph of parochial sectarianism did much to disillusion those Catholics and liberal nationalists who had looked to O'Neill for change. It came on top of the resignation of Geoffery Copcutt, the Englishman who had been appointed head of the design team for the new city that Matthew had recommended. Copcutt embarrassed the government with a public statement urging a special development plan for Derry and supporting its case for the new university. He also described the administration as a 'crisis-ridden regime, too busy looking over its shoulder to look outwards'.[41] The government's subsequent decision to name the city 'Craigavon' appeared to vindicate this judgement and seemed a world away from O'Neill's optimistic rhetoric about transforming the face of Ulster.

For O'Neill, these decisions were the price to be paid for the maintenance of party unity at a time when he was modernizing not only economic and social policies but also the style and structure of his government. Initially the demands of continuity and party unity demanded that his rivals for the leadership had key positions in his government with Jack Andrews at Finance and Faulkner at Commerce. However, he sought to bypass the cabinet and centralize the initiative in policy-making in a small group of senior and trusted official advisers centred on his Private Secretary, Jim Malley, and two key Northern Ireland civil service allies: the cabinet secretary, Cecil Bateman, and his private secretary, Ken Bloomfield.

His modernization project also resulted in a significant change in the structure of government with the creation of a new Ministry of Development. The creation of such a ministry had been recommended in the Matthew Report but the fact that it would involve the removal of planning powers from local authorities had ensured significant opposition from within party and cabinet. In response, O'Neill reshuffled his cabinet in July 1964 when most of his colleagues were on holiday. Although the shifts in personnel were not radical, the most significant being Jack Andrews' departure from the government, there was a realignment of cabinet responsibilities with the concentration of power over planning, transport, roads, local government and housing in the Ministry of Health and Local Government. William Craig, who as Chief Whip at the time of Brookeborough's resignation had been an important supporter of O'Neill, moved from Home Affairs to be the new Minister of Health and Local Government.[42] Finally, in January 1965, O'Neill was able to boast to Harold Wilson of the first major alteration to the structure of devolved government since its inception, with the creation of a Ministry of Development and the transformation of Health and Local Government into Health and Social Services.[43]

The new ministry, with its task of developing a 'master plan' for Northern Ireland, was the centrepiece of O'Neill's strategy for dealing with the challenge from the NILP. As such it would prove extremely effective. However, the disruptive effects of these reforms on local Unionist structures of power and patronage, together with his increasingly presidential style of government, produced a reaction within the party. This was manifest as early as the annual Ulster Unionist Council meeting in April 1965, where a resolution attacking the 'dictatorial manner' of recent government planning proposals was passed, as was one attacking encroachments of the powers of county councils. Worryingly for the Prime Minister, the fissure that had opened up between central government and local Unionist power structures was complemented by evidence of geographical and political contentions as well.

The debate on the Lockwood Report had produced unprecedented alliances at Stormont with only two Unionist MPs speaking in favour. The government was only able to ensure victory by making the vote on the report an issue of confidence.[44] Many Unionist MPs, and not only those in the west of the province, felt that O'Neill was prepared to allow the peripheral areas to stagnate and decline in pursuit of the defence of Unionism in the greater Belfast area. As Minister of Finance, O'Neill had set up a committee to investigate the loss-making railways run by the Ulster Transport Authority and when the Benson Report was published in July 1963 it recommended substantial line closures including Derry's two rail links to Belfast. Although one line was eventually reprieved, the Benson Report was a major factor in the formation of a 'Unionist Council of the West' by prominent Unionists in Derry, Tyrone, and Fermanagh to campaign against neglect by the centre.[45] There was also increasing evidence that those who attacked O'Neill's aloof presidential style, his centralizing of power, and his neglect of the outlying parts of the province saw him as too willing to accommodate the traditional enemies of Ulster.

O'Neill's decision to end decades of the cold war with Dublin by inviting Seán Lemass to meet him in Belfast in January 1965 was not revealed to his cabinet colleagues until the Taoiseach had arrived at

Stormont. Driven by a desire to placate pressure from London for improved relations with the South, O'Neill did not even bother to call a meeting of the Unionist MPs to explain his thinking on the issue.[46] The focus of the meeting was on low-key areas of possible common interest such as tourism and trade promotion, and the joint statement issued afterwards declared that the talks had not touched on 'constitutional or political questions'.[47] However, Lemass's inability to resist the temptation to portray it as a portent of more substantial constitutional changes[48] helped those, still in a minority in the parliamentary Unionist Party, who attacked him for weakening the union by talking to the Prime Minister of a hostile state.[49]

The increasing evidence of divisions in the party meant that O'Neill's success in what he termed 'stealing Labour's thunder'[50] paid fewer political dividends than he had hoped. The Unionist Party fought the 1965 Stormont election with a manifesto entitled 'Forward Ulster to Target 1970!' Labour's advance was firmly reversed with a 7 per cent swing to the Unionist Party in the contested constituencies and the loss of two Labour seats in Woodvale and Victoria. David Bleakley, the defeated Labour MP for Victoria, put his defeat down to the success of O'Neill's rhetoric of planning and job creation: 'for my voters Labour appeared to have lost its *raison d'être*'.[51] But if O'Neill's determination to defeat the NILP had been largely successful, the price was the opening up of divisions in his party that made it even more difficult to deal with reforms demanded by the minority.

O'Neillism and Discrimination

An unintended effect of O'Neill's commitment to the modernization of the North was a new mood of increasingly impatient expectation on the part of Catholics that the regime would address the issue of discrimination. Yet the dismal truth about O'Neill was that he displayed not the slightest hint that he wanted to do anything on this issue. Even his major ally in the press, Jack Sayers, was forced to deliver a critical review of O'Neill's first year in office:

It is indicative of government reluctance to admit that grievances exist and to forestall political attack that the National Assistance Board, the Housing Trust and the newly appointed Lockwood committee are without Catholic members.[52]

Already there were signs of disillusionment amongst those middle-class

Catholics who wanted a more positive relationship with the state. J. J. Campbell, a lecturer at St Joseph's teacher training college, and Brian McGuigan, a prominent Catholic lawyer, published private correspondence with O'Neill after he failed to reply to any of the three letters they sent him between August 1963 and March 1964. They had expressed some disappointment that he had not responded to increasing evidence of good-will from the Catholic community with appointments to bodies such as the Economic Council and the Lockwood Committee.[53] O'Neill's response was to blame the hierarchy of the Catholic Church for maintaining social divisions by insisting on segregated education and to allege that attempts to appoint Catholics had been turned down by those approached.[54] In fact there is little evidence of any serious effort to attract suitable Catholic candidates. Despite the post-war expansion in the size of the Catholic middle class, appointments to public bodies reflected the existence of what an NILP critic called 'the old boy network: since influential Protestants usually have never met their opposite numbers and indeed do not even know their names, the network to which ministers and senior officials belong fails to come up with the right answer.'[55]

But there was more to it than the complacent ignorance bred by decades of social and cultural segregation. While not reflecting an active discriminatory intent, it was in part a product of what Barritt and Carter described as a feeling of superiority amongst Protestants, which they explained in part as a relic of the former Protestant ascendancy but also as a result of 'the present day fact that a Catholic is more likely to be unskilled and poor than a Protestant'.[56] The result, as Charles Brett noted, was the usual excuse that 'it's hard to find a suitable person'. But when such feelings of social superiority were confronted with lists of suitable Catholics that had been submitted to the cabinet secretariat[57] and still no action was forthcoming, even such a stalwart of the regime as the *Belfast Newsletter* criticized the timidity and bad faith of O'Neill's government. When in March 1965 John Taylor, a leading Young Unionist and a member of the Executive of the Ulster Unionist Council, told a National Council of Civil Liberties conference on discrimination that it was confined to private firms, a *Newsletter* leader set him straight and challenged the Prime Minister to address Catholic complaints directly:

There are local authorities which cannot show clean hands and they are not in all cases Unionist . . . Discrimination breeds discrimination but in a community which is predominantly Protestant and which has such distasteful slogans as 'a

Protestant parliament for a Protestant people' to live down the lead must come from the majority party and the government it forms.

Captain O'Neill, by the initiative he has shown in his summit talks with Mr. Lemass, has created the proper atmosphere for a new approach to community problems inside Northern Ireland. The need now is for the government to follow up the signal success it has attained in external relations by similar conciliatory moves inside the province which will persuade Roman Catholics to play their full part in the affairs of the country.[58]

But the core of O'Neill's approach had been articulated by Taylor when he focused on the image of O'Neill's brave 'new Ulster': 'In the social and economic programmes now being outlined there is neither place nor time for discrimination.'[59] Even if the new city project and the Lockwood Report had not provided room for serious doubt on this claim, there remained the fact that O'Neillism offered economic growth in exchange for collective amnesia on the part of the Catholic community about past and present grievances. Behind this bland appeal to shared material interests there was a steely resolve to do nothing that would add to the strains that his anti-NILP strategy was placing on Unionist Party unity. The result was a failure to grasp a very brief historical moment when timely and rather minimalist concessions might have tied the Nationalist Party and the Catholic middle class into a more positive, if still subordinate, relationship to the Unionist state.

The Origins of the Civil Rights Movement

The origin of the most radical shift in nationalist strategy since partition was a local campaign against the housing policy of Dungannon Urban District Council by a group of young Catholic housewives who claimed they were living in cramped and unsanitary conditions because of the council's policy of discrimination in favour of Protestants. The Homeless Citizens' League, which they established with the help of two local doctors, Conn and Patricia McCluskey, in May 1963, adopted novel tactics such as protests at council meetings, lobbying of Stormont, and squatting.[60] As alleged discrimination in the allocation of public housing was to be the central precipitating factor in the civil rights movement, it is important to emphasize the very localized nature of this and other central civil rights issues. As the most systematic and judicious of the analyses of the issue puts it,

A group of local authorities in the west of the province provide a startlingly high proportion of the total number of complaints. All the accusations of gerrymandering, practically all the complaints about housing and regional policy, and a disproportionate amount of the charges about private and public employment come from this area.[61]

The overall record on housing in Northern Ireland after 1945 was not a discreditable one. Between June 1944 and December 1964, 45,920 council houses were built and the Northern Ireland Housing Trust erected 28,513 while 3,102 were built by other public bodies. This was a reasonable achievement when compared with the 100,000 new dwellings that 1943 Northern Ireland Housing Survey showed were needed.[62] Allegations of wholesale discrimination against Catholics in the allocation of housing simply do not stand up to serious scrutiny. This can be seen clearly in the 1971 census of population taken in the dying months of the Unionist regime. In that year there were 148,000 local authority dwellings in Northern Ireland, of which between 45,000 and 55,000 were occupied by Catholic families (depending on what is assumed about the religion of those who declined to answer the religion question in the census). Catholics had a disproportionately large share of local authority housing—even allowing for the on average lower incomes of the Catholic community—comprising 26.1 per cent of households but occupying 30.7 per cent of local authority households.[63]

However, misallocation where it did occur could be crude and blatant and was usually associated with situations where the two communities were closely balanced numerically or where an actual Protestant and Unionist minority controlled a local authority through the manipulation of electoral boundaries. In Dungannon there was a slight Catholic majority in the population but control of the council was firmly in Unionist hands through boundary manipulation.[64] Although much of the council's housing efforts went into slum clearance, from which Catholics benefited substantially since they were disproportionately affected by slum housing, there had been a marked reluctance to allocate houses to new Catholic families. The result was that in 1963 there were upwards of 300 families on the housing waiting list, some for as long as twelve years, and not one new Catholic family had been allocated a permanent house for thirty-four years while a few houses had been allocated to comfortably off Protestants.[65]

While such malpractices were confined to a small number of local authorities, their capacity to embarrass the regime was increased by its reluctance to respond to such indefensible behaviour. Instead there was a complacent tendency to dismiss complaints as part of the failed anti-partitionist agenda. This simply refused to recognize the radical shift in the tactics of protest associated with the Dungannon agitation, which from the beginning sought to increase its potency by drawing on media images of the ongoing struggle for black civil rights in the US. Just as blacks claimed equality and justice as part of their constitutional birth right and were prepared to use a range of tactics from 'sit-ins' at segregated lunch counters to mass marches to force action from the federal government, now Catholics were urged to turn to Westminster, to demand not British withdrawal but rather a new form of British involvement in Northern Ireland.

The McCluskeys along with other Catholic professionals signalled the new departure with the establishment of a Campaign for Social Justice (CSJ) on 17 January 1964. The campaign was a self-conscious break with the approach of the Nationalist Party. As Conn McCluskey explained to Eddie McAteer, the time had come to 'concentrate on getting our rights and trying to overcome gerrymandering . . . to mention the border just puts the Unionists' backs up and some other poor devils lose their chance of a house or a job'.[66] The CSJ now turned to British politicians, particularly within the Labour Party, with a captivatingly simple argument: 'we lived in a part of the UK where the British remit ran, we should seek the ordinary rights of British citizens which were so obviously denied us'.[67]

The leader of the Labour Party, Harold Wilson, had written to Patricia McCluskey in July 1964 'deploring' religious and other kinds of discrimination and supporting the NILP's proposals for new and impartial procedures for the allocation of public housing and a tribunal to deal with cases of alleged discrimination in public appointments.[68] In a second letter in September he pledged that a Labour government would do everything in its power to deal with infringements of justice in Northern Ireland. However, he also pointed out that this would be 'no easy task' and claimed that the most immediate way of getting progress would be to vote for NILP candidates in the forthcoming general election. As Bob Purdie has pointed out, 'Making the will-o'-the-wisp of an NILP electoral breakthrough a precondition for action by a Labour government was a safe way of putting off any action whatsoever.'[69]

Wilson's Huyton constituency had a large number of voters of Irish extraction and such grand gestures as his decision to have the remains of Roger Casement, executed for treason in 1916, returned to Ireland convinced many Unionists that he was sympathetic to Irish nationalism. Yet in his first years in power, Wilson did little to pressurize O'Neill on the discrimination issue. He and his Home Secretary, Frank Soskice, relied on the advice of senior Home Office officials traditionally sympathetic to the Stormont government:

Section 75 of the 1920 Act certainly provides technical authority for the United Kingdom parliament to impose legislation on Northern Ireland against the wishes of that government, but the consequences of such an act could only be a disastrous rupture between the two governments. Allegations of religious discrimination against Roman Catholics in Northern Ireland have a very long history. The commonest allegations are of gerrymandering in local government, favouritism in the making of appointments and bias in the allocation of houses by local authorities. There is no question that all these matters are squarely the area of 'peace, order and good government' for which the Northern Ireland government has full responsibility.[70]

Rather than give any public indication of concern about the Stormont regime, Soskice used the one and only visit by a Labour Home Secretary to the province between 1964 and August 1969 to declare of O'Neill's administration: 'From England we watch it, we admire it and we rejoice in it.'[71]

Part of the reason for Wilson's lack of action was O'Neill's own success in impressing on London that he was serious about change by his meeting with Lemass in January 1965. There was also the advice from the security services that, despite the end of the IRA campaign in 1962, the organization was preparing for a new assault. An alarmist report from the Special Branch in New Scotland Yard in November 1964, although discounting the likelihood of an imminent campaign, estimated that there were 3,000 men who had received some degree of training in the use of arms and explosives, of whom it was estimated that several hundred were sufficiently well trained to undertake active operations.[72] As O'Neill kept stressing to London the problems he faced in getting his cabinet and party colleagues to accept change, this report of an added threat by republicans may well have encouraged sympathy for an administration facing such conflicting challenges.

However, much more important factors were Labour's narrow parliamentary majority of three and the country's difficult economic situation, which dominated Wilson's concerns for the seventeen months of his first administration. Sir Oliver Wright, his Private Secretary at the time, subsequently commented, 'I cannot remember in my time in

Number 10 . . . that Ireland ever really rated very high in Wilson's pre-occupation.'[73] Other priorities and the tendency of the Home Office to defend the constitutional status quo encouraged Wilson to give the benefit of the doubt to O'Neill's modernizing intentions. However, his own clear sympathy for improved relations with Dublin,[74] and his increasing frustration with the support that Ulster Unionist MPs gave to the Conservative opposition in Westminster, alarmed O'Neill and was conducive to growing Labour back-bench interest in a more interventionist posture to Northern Ireland affairs.

The formation of the Campaign for Democracy in Ulster (CDU) in early 1965 by a group of Labour Party activists with strong left-wing republican influence provided an increasingly effective Westminster echo of the Campaign for Social Justice's anti-Stormont crusade. The CDU focused on section 75 of the Government of Ireland Act with its assertion of the ultimate supremacy of the Westminster parliament over 'all persons, matters and things' in Northern Ireland. This, it claimed, should allow for the appointment of a Royal Commission to investigate charges of discrimination and, if necessary, direct intervention by the British government to establish full civil rights for Catholics.[75]

The CDU soon had the support of around one hundred Labour MPs[76] and after the general election of March 1966 Wilson's attitude towards O'Neill showed some indication of a toughening. Labour now had a majority of 97 and CDU pressure was intensified by the return of Gerry Fitt as Republican Labour MP for West Belfast. This tough and shrewd former merchant seaman used his maiden speech to launch a passionate onslaught on the 'injustice' of the Stormont regime, ignoring the convention that domestic Northern Ireland affairs were not discussed at Westminster. At their first meeting after the election Wilson told O'Neill of the pressure he was under from the CDU and urged O'Neill to make 'a real effort . . . to meet some of the grievances which had been expressed; otherwise Westminster would be forced to act'.[77] O'Neill emphasized the fraught conditions in Northern Ireland that had followed the large republican celebrations of the fiftieth anniversary of the Easter Rising and the growing Paisleyite backlash and pleaded for breathing space before taking the reform process forward. The Home Secretary, Roy Jenkins, warned that any backsliding on reform would lead to direct rule but Wilson did make clear his continuing support for O'Neill and when he met the Irish Prime Minister in December, he asked Jack Lynch to understand O'Neill's 'problem': 'if he went ahead with reform too quickly he could face problems from within his own party'.[78]

When O'Neill returned to London in January 1967 he and his colleagues Bill Craig, Minister of Home Affairs, and Brian Faulkner got a rougher ride. Wilson again emphasized the pressure he was under from 150 Labour MPs, many of them from the 1966 intake: ' a new and irreverent generation who were challenging everything'. These MPs were already questioning the financial assistance given to Stormont by the British Exchequer and would ask why Northern Ireland should continue to be subsidized 'to operate a franchise system that no British government would consider for any independent Commonwealth state'. Jenkins claimed that pressure for reform in Derry was bound to grow. O'Neill's response was minimalist. He indicated his government's willingness to set up a statutory boundary commission to review all Stormont constituencies and to abolish the business vote in local elections. Craig used a forthcoming review of local government structures to procrastinate on the issue of universal suffrage in local government.[79]

But it was soon clear that while Wilson and Jenkins might be frustrated with Stormont's prevarication, they accepted O'Neill's argument that any attempt to push him too far would split his government and perhaps spark a Protestant uprising forcing direct rule. For all Wilson's and Jenkins' willingness to threaten intervention and direct rule, there could be little doubting their profound reluctance to be sucked into the 'Irish bog'. When Eddie McAteer wrote to Jenkins at the end of 1967 complaining of lack of progress on nationalist complaints, he got the standard brush-off: the matters in dispute were 'wholly within the constitutional ambit of the Parliament and Government of Northern Ireland'. He was advised to seek direct discussions with O'Neill.[80] The lack of movement by O'Neill combined with the increased debate on discrimination issues at Westminster encouraged those within the opposition who favoured more robust ways of making their grievances a public issue.

Civil Rights: A Republican/Communist Conspiracy?

The Northern Ireland Civil Rights Association (NICRA) was to play a central role in the intensifying crisis of the Unionist state from October 1968. Founded in February 1967, NICRA was subsequently alleged by William Craig to be a front for republicans and communists with a hidden anti-partitionist agenda. It was the case that republicans and some trade unionists with Communist Party affiliations dominated the executive committee of NICRA and that the leadership of the republican movement had decided to commit much of the energy of its northern members to the development of the civil rights movement. After the calling off of the 1956–62 campaign, the new Chief of Staff of the IRA, the republican socialist Cathal Goulding, had shifted the focus of the movement towards social agitation and left-wing politics. The Wolfe Tone Society, founded in 1963 and named after the Protestant leader of the United Irish insurrection of 1798, was created as part of Goulding's strategy of building a coalition of 'progressive and nationally-minded forces'. It was at a meeting of the Wolfe Tone Society in the house of a leading republican in Maghera, county Tyrone, in August 1966 that the decision to create NICRA was made.

Yet the view of NICRA and the subsequent development of the civil rights movement as a republican/leftist conspiracy is oversimplified. First, the priority of Goulding was to build the republican movement as a radical 'anti-imperialist' alternative to the Irish Labour Party: the focus of republican strategy was the South. Second, in Northern Ireland the priority was the reform of the Northern Ireland state, not its abolition. Pressure on Stormont from within Northern Ireland and from Westminster would, Goulding believed, force reforms on a reluctant Unionist Party that would split apart under the strain, thus freeing sections of the Protestant working class for 'progressive' politics and ultimately for republicanism. There was much that was naïve in the approach of Goulding and his leftist advisers on the North. In particular they consistently underestimated the strength of Paisleyism. However, for all their inadequacies, the Goulding group did realize that any armed assault on the northern state risked a major sectarian conflagration. Third, it was most unlikely that the mass mobilization of the Catholic community that developed after October 1968 could have been the work of such a small group, no matter how dedicated. The IRA in Belfast comprised a mere twenty-four members in 1962 and this number had grown to a less than formidable 120 by 1969.[81]

A less conspiratorial explanation of the growth of the civil rights movement was provided in the report of the Cameron Commission set up by O'Neill to investigate the violence that broke out in October 1968. The report argued that it was the emergence in the 1960s of a 'much larger Catholic middle class . . . which is less ready to acquiesce in the situation of assumed (or established) inferiority and discrimination than was the case in the past'[82] that was determinant. This stratum was created by the extension of secondary and higher education to working-class Catholics after 1945. Children of the British welfare state, they were less interested in the national question than in the fact that post-war expansion had disproportionately benefited Protestants.

There had indeed been a major expansion of the Catholic middle class under Stormont. The proportion of Catholics in professional and managerial occupations more than doubled between the censuses of 1911 and 1971 and this was clearly linked to the substantial expansion of the education, welfare, and health services after 1945. Yet this stratum remained a narrow one and the much broader appeal of the civil rights movement remains to be explained. Here Cameron undoubtedly ignored the more fundamental truth about the social structure of the Catholic community: that it seems to have been a case of that 'uneven and combined development' beloved of Trotskyists. For if the expansion of the Catholic middle class was one feature of the minority's experience under Stormont, the other was a substantial rise in the proportion of unskilled manual employees, mainly accounted for by a decline in the Catholic share of skilled manual workers.[83] While there was also a substantial decline in the proportion of Protestants in skilled manual occupations, this was compensated for by a rise in their relative share of lower-grade non-manual occupations while the Catholic share declined.

The deterioration of the position of working-class Catholics provided the economic and social basis for the explosion of support for the civil rights movement but this combustible material had been available for some time and it is necessary to develop the Cameron explanation to include a very specific political dimension. What provoked the mass support for the civil rights movement was a unique and very temporary fusion of 1960s ultra-leftism with a much more rooted sense of ethnic exclusion and oppression, which saw the civil rights movement, however inchoately, as an opportunity for striking a blow not simply at structures of discrimination but at the fundamentals of the northern state itself. Civil rights appealed precisely because it seemed to have the capacity to transcend the passivity that was a product of the failure of the two dominant traditions in Catholic politics: constitutional anti-partitionism and physical force republicanism.

Hemmed in by the rhetoric of O'Neill and Lemass and responding to the pressure of criticisms from such groups as National Unity and the Campaign for Social Justice, the Nationalist Party unenthusiastically shuffled towards modernity. In November 1964 it produced its first ever general policy statement with McAteer declaring that 'The Party is now anxious to step into the twentieth century.' However, this proved premature as many of the MPs resisted the idea of a modern party structure.[84] The first annual conference of the party did not occur until December 1965 and by then some of its younger members were pushing for a more radical realignment that would bring in the Republican Labour tradition in Belfast and for the adoption of 'left of centre' policies.[85] Fitt's return to Westminster and his high profile and good relations with many CDU MPs increasingly made him, rather than McAteer, seem the spokesman for Northern Ireland's nationalists. There was some irony here as Fitt's 'leadership' was almost entirely reliant on a capacity for media showmanship. His 'party' did not extend beyond two Belfast constituencies and, for all his talk of 'Connolly socialism', was based on very traditional forms of clientilism. His main publicity coup was the visit of three CDU MPs on a fact-finding tour of the province in April 1967. Yet while the visit may temporarily have raised the hopes of Labour intervention, there was little indication that this was even on the horizon when 1968 began. For all their activities, the CSJ, CDU, and NICRA had remarkably little to show in the way of results. The first year and a half of NICRA's existence was, according to the best scholarly account, 'a period of general ineffectuality'.[86]

But if there was little to show in the way of action by O'Neill or Wilson, there had been a noticeable loss of political and moral authority on the part of the nationalist political leadership. Increasingly attacked as ineffectual 'Green Tories' by a coalition of nationalist modernizers, republicans, and young leftist members of the NILP, Nationalist Party notables like McAteer were ignored even when their warnings about the dangers of street politics were to be proved prescient. McAteer's own experience of the polarizing effect of contested marches in Derry in the early 1950s may have contributed to his unease with the radical tactics suggested by Austen Currie, a young Queen's University graduate, who won the Stormont constituency of East Tyrone in 1964. Currie supported the squatting of homeless Catholic families in houses owned by Dungannon Rural District Council and told a student audience at Magee College in Derry that what was needed was 'more squatting, more acts of civil disobedience, more emphasis on "other means" and less on traditional political methods'.[87]

Nationalist leaders' reluctance to go down this road reflected social conservatism and the knowledge that their republican critics were better placed to exploit the housing issue at a local level. But there was also a deeper comprehension of the underlying sectarian geography of town and countryside in Ulster and of the danger that a more confrontational strategy would produce not reform, but major communal conflict. Younger nationalist modernizers, socialist republicans, and an increasingly influential group of leftist students all had a typically 1960s contempt for middle-aged politicians and what were seen as antiquated Orange and Green traditions. Yet the first civil rights march showed that, despite the non-sectarian language of the march organizers, many of the marchers and their opponents defined 'civil rights' in terms of traditional aspirations and antagonisms. The executive of NICRA had not initiated the march, from Coalisland to Dungannon, on 24 August 1968; the idea had come from Austen Currie, who had recently grabbed the headlines by squatting in a vacant house in Caledon, county Tyrone, to highlight a particularly obtuse decision by Dungannon Rural District Council to award a house to a young, single Protestant woman.[88]

The NICRA leaders were divided on the wisdom of taking their demand onto the streets. The veteran Belfast communist Betty Sinclair opposed the whole idea of marches and it was only local pressure from the leaders of the CSJ and republicans that ensured NICRA support for the march. Both the Inspector General of the RUC and Bernadette Devlin, the young Queen's University student from Cookstown, county Tyrone, who would have brief media fame as *la Pasionara* of the civil rights movement, agreed that, despite the marchers singing 'We shall overcome', the anthem of the black civil rights movement in the US, the march's dynamic was robustly nationalist and anti-state. The 2,000 or so marchers were accompanied by bands that played traditional nationalist and republican tunes and when the RUC prevented the march reaching the centre of Dungannon where local Unionists and Paisley supporters had organized a counter-demonstration, they were denounced as 'black bastards' by Gerry Fitt while Currie attacked O'Neill and 'the Orange bigots behind him'.[89]

The Inspector General of the RUC described the march as 'a republican parade rather than a civil rights march' and criticized NICRA for allowing its platforms to be used by 'extremists and trouble-makers'. In fact the leadership of the IRA was as keen as northern communists such as Betty Sinclair to prevent conflict with the RUC and loyalists, and the prominent role that republicans played in stewarding the march reflected this concern. However, as Bernadette Devlin subsequently pointed out, there was a naïvety in the NICRA executive's belief that their own non-sectarian reformist intent gave them the right to march where they wanted in Northern Ireland. Coalisland was 'ninety per cent republican'[90] and Protestant and Unionist perceptions of the civil rights movement were increasingly that it was just a new way for nationalists to undermine the state.

In fact the crisis of the Unionist regime was not the outworking of some 'republican-communist' conspiracy to destroy the state under the guise of civil rights. Like all significant historical events it was brought about by a combination of factors. Among the most crucial were O'Neill's reluctance to move quickly on reforms because of divisions within his cabinet and party, Wilson's desire to 'leave it to O'Neill' rather than risk a confrontation with Stormont, and the Nationalist Party's loss of direction. Nationalist disarray ushered in a period of fluidity and competition in Catholic politics which allowed relatively small groups of local militants to wield a significant influence on events.

This would have particularly momentous results in Derry. Here the Derry Housing Action Committee, a coalition of leftist republicans and the Trotskyist-influenced Derry Labour Party led by the charismatic ex-student Eamonn McCann, had already initiated a civil disobedience campaign against the Corporation's housing policies. In the aftermath of the Coalisland–Dungannon march, the DHAC asked NICRA to march in Derry. McCann and his comrades proposed a march that would enter the historic walled centre of the city, where previous attempts to organize nationalist parades had been banned. Although the leadership of NICRA went along with this plan on the basis that theirs was not a nationalist march but one for civil rights within the UK, there were severe misgivings about the potential for confrontation and violence. This was especially the case as the day chosen for the march was one on which the Protestant Apprentice Boys had an annual initiation ceremony attended by members from all over the North. William Craig banned the Apprentice Boys' parade and excluded the civil rights march from the predominantly Protestant Waterside, where it was supposed to start, and from the centre of the city. Although McAteer advised a post-ponement, as did Conn McCluskey of the Campaign for Social Justice, the leadership of NICRA was divided and a small but determined group of Derry radicals prevailed.

Although to the organizers' disappointment only 400 turned up for the start of the march in Duke Street,[91] the RUC's response and the presence of television cameras ensured that it would have an unprecedented effect in politically energizing the Catholic community throughout Northern Ireland. Gerry Fitt had brought three Labour MPs from England and local republicans ensured that the MPs and McAteer were pushed up against the RUC line blocking the march's route to the city centre. Although the Cameron Commission found that Fitt's conduct was 'reckless and wholly irresponsible in a person occupying his public positions',[92] the RUC response to relatively low-level verbal abuse and jostling was to baton both him and McAteer. Nationalist MPs had been batoned in the 1950s but, as one of the regime's most formidable opponents has noted, 'there had been no TV then and meanwhile expectations had changed'.[93] A group of student radicals from Belfast, who had arrived late, were able to complete the RUC's disgrace by throwing their placards and banners at the police, who responded with the baton charge that has become the foundational event for all subsequent media 'interpretations' of the causes of the subsequent decades of violence.

The television footage of RUC violence brought an abrupt end to Wilson's policy of 'leaving it to Terence'. The next civil rights march in Derry, on 16 October, saw over 15,000 marchers sweep into the city centre swamping RUC lines by force of numbers. The small group of activist students at Queen's University grouped around the Young Socialist Alliance exploited the RUC's over-reaction, and Craig's crude defence of it, to become the self-styled 'vanguard' of an unprecedented mobilization of what had hitherto been one of the most docile campuses in Western Europe. Its leading figure was Michael Farrell, a formidable debater influenced by both republican socialism and Trotskyism. Craig's ban on a student protest march about the Derry events led to the formation of People's Democracy (PD), a mass-based student organization with Farrell's militants styling themselves as its hard core.

Influenced by the upsurge of student radicalism in Europe and the US, and particularly by the 'May Events' in France, PD militants saw in the burgeoning civil rights marches the possibility of the North's own revolutionary situation. Although some were genuine, if naïve, in their belief that their commitment to a socialist project equally dismissive of Unionism and nationalism could appeal to the Protestant working class, others such as Farrell were prepared to settle for a solely Catholic insurgency dressed up in the Leninist notion that an uprising of Derry's Catholic proletariat would create a situation of 'dual power'.[94] With a sharp sense of the impact that Catholic mobilization and intensifying pressure from London was having in dividing and demoralizing the Unionist regime, the student radicals gave little thought to what would result if they succeeded in bringing down O'Neill. Adopting a crude Trotskyist approach that was contemptuous of 'mere' reforms aimed at 'buying off' the just rage of the masses, the radicals in the PD were to prove disastrously successful in undermining the real support for O'Neill's reformism that still existed despite the events of October.

Disintegration

In a memorandum for his cabinet colleagues, O'Neill set out the agonizing choices likely to face them in the aftermath of the Derry events:

> Can any of us truthfully say . . . that the minority has no grievance calling for a remedy? Believe me, I realise the appalling political difficulties we face. The first reaction of our own people to the antics of Fitt and Currie and the abuse of the world's Press is to retreat into old hard-line attitudes. But if this is all we can offer we face a period when we govern Ulster by police power alone . . . concessions . . . could well be the wisest course. We would have a very hard job to sell such concessions to our people, but in this critical moment may this not be our duty? We may even have to make a bitter choice between losing Londonderry and losing Ulster.[95]

Anticipating a demand for universal suffrage in local government elections from Wilson, O'Neill was faced with total inflexibility from his Minister of Home Affairs. Initially an ally of O'Neill who regarded him as bright and progressive when he made him one of the youngest-ever Unionist cabinet ministers, Craig's promotion to Home Affairs was disastrous. Blunt and outspoken, he had been used as O'Neill's 'battering ram' against local Unionist resistance to his original attempts to modernize government and party. However, as Minister of Home Affairs he made it clear that for him modernization did not extend to any indulgence of the civil rights agenda. Over-impressed by Special Branch reports on communist and republican involvement in NICRA, he publicly denounced its supposed ulterior agenda. He was also an early and strident voice against 'Westminster dictation'. O'Neill could have dealt with Craig's resistance—he did sack him in December—but Craig's obduracy was reinforced by the much more substantial figure of Brian Faulkner. Although Faulkner did not oppose franchise reform in principle,[96] he was at one with Craig in demanding that O'Neill stand up to pressure from Wilson.

At a Downing Street meeting on 4 November with Wilson and James Callaghan, who had replaced Roy Jenkins as Home Secretary, Craig refused to be moved by the Prime Minister's strongly expressed desire for the quick introduction of one-man-one-vote. He and Faulkner were also unsettled by Wilson's criticism of the police behaviour in Derry and his recommendation of an inquiry.[97] Although O'Neill tried to convince his government that Wilson would not be satisfied without franchise reform and that the UK government was not bluffing, the cabinet could not agree on the core issue, with Faulkner declaring that he was not prepared 'to yield to financial or economic duress'.[98] In the short term it was Craig and Faulkner who were vindicated in their assessment of the British Prime Minister as a paper tiger. For despite a direct threat from Wilson to impose universal adult suffrage if Stormont did not introduce it, when O'Neill informed him that it was not politically possible, he and Callaghan capitulated.[99]

A five-point reform package was announced on 21 November: the introduction of a points system for the allocation of public housing; the appointment of an ombudsman for Northern Ireland; the abolition of the business vote in local government elections; a review of the Special Powers Act; and the replacement of Londonderry Corporation by an appointed Development Commission. O'Neill's fear that without a commitment to one-man-one-vote it would be insufficient to satisfy the UK government or restrain the civil rights movement would soon be vindicated.[100] The longer franchise reform was delayed, the more debilitating were the effects on O'Neill's position. On the one hand it encouraged more civil rights marches, while on the other it strengthened the impression amongst the Unionist grass-roots that the government was reeling ineffectively before internal and external pressures. Even before the Londonderry events, the Unionist Party headquarters was receiving increasing numbers of letters complaining about the adverse media coverage of the situation in Northern Ireland and the government's failure to counter it effectively.[101] For a sizeable section of the party's grass-roots, if Catholics did have real grievances, then the extent of them was being grossly exaggerated by the civil rights movement, a movement that was perceived to be simply a more effective and dangerous reincarnation of the traditional nationalist enemy. O'Neill was seen as running a government that was more responsive to its opponents than to its supporters. A report on discussions with grass-roots members in September 1968 revealed the extent of the problem:

The ordinary loyalist no longer believes that the Unionist Party is an effective influence on the course of events . . . There is a feeling in many associations that those at the top of the Party are reaching out over the heads of the people who put them there. There was criticism that much of the legislation 'does not help Unionists and favours non-Unionists'.[102]

With William Craig publicly condemning the civil rights movement as 'bogus', blaming the Catholic Church's teaching on birth-control for any Catholic disadvantage in housing and employment, and warning Westminster that 'interference' would be resisted,[103] O'Neill made one last, desperate appeal in his 'Crossroads' broadcast on local television on 9 December. He appealed to the civil rights movement to 'take the heat out of the situation', claiming that his government was totally committed to a reforming process. To Unionists he emphasized the financial and economic support from Britain and attacked 'Protestant Sinn Feiners' who would not listen 'when they are told that Ulster's income is £200 million a year but that we can spend £300 million—only because Britain pays the balance'. He told them that Wilson's declared willingness to act over their heads if adequate reforms were not forthcoming would be fully within the terms of section 75 of the Government of Ireland Act. Most significantly, he tried to drain the local government franchise of the exaggerated importance it had assumed for many loyalists by pointing out that the adoption of the civil rights agenda would not lose the Unionist Party a single seat at Stormont.[104]

The response was encouraging. 'I Back O'Neill' coupons printed in the *Belfast Telegraph* were signed and returned by 150,000 supporters within days and NICRA announced that there would be a moratorium on marches until the middle of January. When Craig made another defiant speech vowing to resist any British interference, O'Neill sacked him. Then on 12 December the Unionist Parliamentary Party supported a vote of confidence in the Prime Minister by twenty-eight to four abstentions. Yet O'Neill had still to win the argument for one-man-one-vote in his own cabinet and he knew that the party in the three western counties of the province was solidly against any change. Some leading Unionists in the west were convinced that O'Neill had decided to sacrifice them in order to consolidate the Unionist cause in the greater Belfast area.[105] If O'Neill had decided to save unionist control of Northern Ireland by sacrificing unionist local domination in Derry and other peripheral areas, he needed a period of calm on the streets. While the leadership of NICRA was prepared to concede this, his ultra-left critics in the People's Democracy were not.

Concerned that the civil rights movement would come to a stop because its leadership was prepared to accept O'Neill's 'miserable reforms',[106] Michael Farrell and his couple of dozen supporters in the Young Socialist Alliance promoted the idea of a 'Long March' from Belfast to Derry. Modelled on the Selma–Montgomery march in Alabama in 1966, its aim was to force British intervention and reopen the Irish question. A mass meeting of the PD at Queen's had rejected the idea in early December, aware as many were of the strong possibilities of attacks on the march as it passed through strongly loyalist areas. However, using the New Left commitment to direct democracy for a more traditionally Leninist purpose, Farrell's supporters convened another meeting at the end of term when most students had gone home and got the decision reversed. Criticized by the mainstream leaders of the civil rights movement and with the support of only a few dozen students, the march set off on 1 January accompanied by eighty policemen. O'Neill had rejected loyalist demands to ban it but did remarkably little to ensure that it was adequately protected. The marchers were harried by loyalists at various places along the route while local republicans guarded them at night. On the final day of the march when its size had grown from forty people to several hundred it was attacked by 200 loyalists, some of whom were identified as off-duty B Specials, at Burntollet Bridge near Derry. Farrell had predicted that if the marchers were subject to a serious attack there would be an uprising in Derry and he was proved correct.[107] When the marchers arrived in the centre of the city, after another attack by loyalists in the Waterside, they unleashed a wave of anti-RUC rioting that transformed the situation and strengthened the hostility of many Catholics to the state. It marks the pivotal point at which the civil rights phase of the Troubles ended and the conflict began to focus on more ancient disputes over national and religious identities.

O'Neill saw the Derry violence as the end of his hopes of gradual reform from above and was only dissuaded from resigning by pressure from Wilson and Edward Heath, the Leader of the Opposition.[108] If the march had not taken place, he might at last have been forced to grasp the nettle of franchise reform. With Craig gone the only substantial voice of opposition would have been Faulkner. But Faulkner had made clear in cabinet that he had an open mind on the issue but was opposed to being seen to act under Westminster pressure. The strengthening of O'Neill's position after the 'Crossroads' speech and the favourable response of NICRA would have allowed him to present a change of policy as an expression of his government's own reformist intent. He might have lost some of his MPs but this was soon to happen in much more unfavourable circumstances. The 'Long March' destroyed this possibility. John Hume, who had emerged as the leader of more moderate opinion in Derry, now declared that the 'truce' on marching was over and that there would be a return to militant action.[109]

O'Neill pleaded with his cabinet to see that a simply repressive response would fail. Anticipating pressure from Wilson and Callaghan, he argued for an independent public inquiry into the disturbances and for acceptance of universal suffrage in local government: 'in resisting this molehill of reform we are allowing a mountain to fall upon us'.[110] Rebuffed on the central suffrage issue, he was able to extract support for the decision to set up a commission of inquiry into the recent disturbances to be headed by the Scottish judge Lord Cameron. A week later, on 23 January, Faulkner, who had opposed the idea of an inquiry in cabinet, resigned, declaring that the decision to set up the commission was an 'abdication of authority': the Prime Minister should have persuaded the party of the need for a change of policy on the franchise issue. Yet, as O'Neill pointed out at the last discussion of the franchise issue in the parliamentary party in November 1968, change had been opposed by the 'vast majority'.[111] Perhaps if Faulkner had come out earlier in support of reform this opposition could have been significantly reduced. O'Neill's anger at his colleague's late conversion was understandable. His decision to call a general election in February, a course of action that he had specifically rejected in the 'Crossroads' broadcast, reflected this anger as well as increasing desperation.

For the first time in its history the Unionist Party entered an election campaign divided. The existence of at least twelve MPs who were now openly calling for his resignation led O'Neill to impose a loyalty pledge on all candidates who had to support a reformist manifesto. The ultra-democratic structure of the Unionist Party, which left the choice of election candidates to individual constituency associations, resulted in the Prime Minister supporting 'unofficial' candidates against 'official' candidates from the right. Thirty-nine Unionists were returned: twenty-four 'official' Unionists and three 'unofficial' Unionists who supported O'Neill, ten 'official Unionists' who opposed the Prime Minister, and two undecided. Support for O'Neill was greatest in suburban constituencies in the greater Belfast area, while anti-O'Neillism was strongest in the border counties and in working-class Belfast constituencies.[112]

O'Neill had gambled on a comprehensive vote of confidence and a repudiation of his critics but the result, as a key aide has subsequently admitted, was 'muddied and inconclusive'.[113] All twelve of his Unionist critics were returned and in his own Bannside constituency he was returned on a minority vote of 7,745, with Ian Paisley polling 6,331 and the PD leader Michael Farrell 2,310. With the parliamentary party split and a narrow majority of support in the Ulster Unionist Council, O'Neill eventually delivered one-man-one-vote on 22 April, although only after a very narrow vote in favour. However, the resignation of the Minister of Agriculture, James Chichester-Clark, in protest at the timing of the decision was a final and stunning blow, the effect of which was amplified by bomb attacks on Belfast's water supply. Blamed on republicans, these were in fact an attempt by loyalist paramilitaries to create an atmosphere of crisis.

O'Neill resigned on 28 April and within a week a deeply divided parliamentary party chose Chichester-Clark over Brian Faulkner by a narrow majority of seventeen to sixteen. Although the government had finally conceded the core demand of the civil rights movement, developments since 1 January had shifted the conflict on to a different level, where what was at issue was the relationship between the police and an increasingly militant section of the Catholic working class. Derry would be the focus of this new and increasingly violent phase. The riots that had followed the arrival of the 'Long March' prefigured what was to come. Hours of rioting in the city centre were followed by the collapse of discipline among sections of the RUC, some of them drunk, who attacked people and property on the fringes of the Bogside, the city's oldest concentration of Catholic housing. Barricades were erected and traditionalist republicans, including Sean Keenan, began to carve out a role in 'citizens' defence' committees.[114] By the spring of 1969 confrontations between a hard core of unemployed Derry youth and the police had become regular events. Derry's violence had also an increasingly sectarian dimension as Catholic youths clashed with members of the small Protestant working class that lived on the predominantly Catholic west side of the River Foyle.

O'Neill's divided and pressurized government introduced a Public Order Bill in March 1969 outlawing many of the tactics used in the civil rights campaign. Protests against this culminated in a major confrontation between Catholic crowds, the RUC, and loyalists in the centre of Derry on 19 April, which developed into three days of rioting. RUC men pursuing a group of rioters entered a house in the Bogside and assaulted several members of the household, including the father, Samuel Devenny, who died from his injuries in July. The April riots completed the process by which in Derry the issue of 'civil rights' had given way entirely to that of 'defence', and that of 'discrimination' to complaints about the RUC.[115] The riots also had a clear demonstration effect across Northern Ireland where NICRA and the PD organized solidarity demonstrations. Many of these ended in rioting, which was particularly severe on the Falls Road. With a weak and divided government and an Opposition whose demands focused no longer on reforms but on the security apparatuses of the state, the Stormont regime had passed the point of no return.

8

Northern Ireland from Insurrection to the Anglo-Irish Agreement

The British State and the Birth of the Provisional IRA

By the spring of 1969 the violence in Londonderry was producing reverberations in Belfast. The city's IRA commander, Billy McMillen, a loyal supporter of Cathal Goulding's shift to the left, was under increasing criticism from a number of formidable traditionalist figures. These accused the leadership of neglecting the IRA's military role and leaving Catholics vulnerable to attack. McMillen had maintained a residual military role for the hundred or so volunteers who had to share twenty-four weapons between them.[1] Any major outbreak of communal violence was bound to overwhelm such paltry resources and McMillen was conscious of Goulding's determination that the IRA should not be drawn into sectarian warfare.

In April 1969 anti-RUC riots in the Ardoyne district of north Belfast had increased pressure on McMillen to prepare the IRA for 'defensive' action and in the marches of 12 July IRA members had been mobilized during clashes between Orange marchers and Catholics living in the inappropriately named 'Unity Walk' flats complex at the bottom of the Shankill Road. In the same month, during the reinterment of two IRA men executed in England in 1940, Jimmy Steele, a Belfast IRA veteran, launched a bitter attack on Goulding's leadership. Although he was suspended from the movement, the speech became a rallying point for those who were soon to emerge as the leaders of the Provisional IRA. The traditional march by the loyalist order, the Apprentice Boys, in Derry on 12 August was to give them their opportunity.

After the April clashes with the RUC the influence of the more moderate leaders of the civil rights movement in Derry had gone into precipitous decline. In July, soon after the death of Samuel Devenny, popularly believed to be a direct result of his beating by the RUC in April, the Derry Citizens' Action Committee, the 'middle-aged, middle class and middle of the road'[2] body, was superseded by the Derry

Citizens' Defence Association (DCDA). This was heavily dominated by local republicans and Seán Kennan was its chairman. But as Eamonn McCann, the Derry Trotskyist, noted, events were increasingly determined by 'the hooligans': the unemployed youth of the Bogside whose energy and aggression had done much to power the early civil rights movement but who were now set on a major confrontation with the police and loyalist marchers.[3] Although the DCDA had met with leaders of the Apprentice Boys and promised to provide effective stewarding on the day of the march, it put much more energy into preparing for the defence of the Bogside. Barricades were erected in anticipation of an RUC and loyalist 'invasion', heaps of stones were piled at strategic points, and over the four days that culminated in the march a local dairy lost 43,000 bottles as large numbers of petrol bombs were prepared.[4] The DCDA made little more than a token effort to prevent the march being stoned and for more than two hours a police cordon shielding marchers was subject to a constant hail of missiles before launching the series of baton charges that began 'the Battle of the Bogside'. An attempt by the RUC to follow the rioters into the Bogside was repulsed with barricades, bricks, and a rain of petrol bombs from the top of a block of high-rise flats and by 13 August 'Free Derry' had effectively seceded from the northern state.

With NICRA calling marches and demonstrations to relieve Derry nationalists by stretching the limited manpower of the 3,000-strong RUC, Chichester-Clark's government was told by Callaghan and his Home Office advisers that it must exhaust all the resources under its control, including the 8,500 B Specials, before a request for army assistance would be contemplated.[5] The result was disastrous. Robert Porter, the liberal Unionist whom O'Neill had appointed to Home Affairs shortly before his resignation, was told by the Home Office that he could allow the RUC to use a new weapon, CS gas, against rioters. Over two days, huge amounts were used and the Bogside became blanketed with gas.[6] This served simply to stiffen resistance, as did the television broadcast by the Taoiseach, Jack Lynch, on the evening of 13 August, in which he declared that his government could 'no longer stand by and see innocent people injured and perhaps worse'. By the next morning the RUC commander in Derry told Chichester-Clark that his men were exhausted and incapable even of holding the centre of the city.[7] Stormont then ordered a general mobilization of the B Specials. The Specials, who were conceived as a counter-terrorist force, had no training in crowd control or dealing with rioters. After forty-eight hours of rioting, with the RUC depleted by casualties and exhausted and with the prospect of a murderous confrontation between Derry Catholics and the Specials, Wilson and Callaghan agreed to the dispatch of troops.

In Belfast, where there had been attacks on RUC stations and some rioting on 13 August, the Lynch broadcast and the mobilization of the Specials contributed powerfully to the worst outbreak of communal violence since the 1920s. It centred on the streets that linked the Falls and Shankill Roads. While Catholics erected barricades on the Falls Road, crowds of Protestants, amongst whom were members of the recently mobilized Specials, gathered on the Shankill. A spring and summer of sectarian confrontations and minor riots had now culminated in the Derry conflagration that was the subject of two conflicting and destructive ethnic myths in Belfast. For Catholics it was a case of the Bogside residents being besieged by bloodthirsty RUC men and loyalists, while for Protestants, including many members of the RUC and Specials, the Bogside was in a state of IRA-sponsored insurrection. Both communities feared that their ethnic nightmare was about to become a reality in Belfast and acted accordingly.

Overreaction by the police led to the use of armoured cars mounted with machine-guns to disperse rioters. Protestant mobs pushing down towards the Falls Road petrol-bombed Catholic houses as they proceeded. In these confrontations and in similar ones in the Ardoyne area over 150 houses were destroyed. Seven people were killed including a 9-year-old Catholic boy, Patrick Rooney, who was asleep in his bedroom when he was struck by a stray RUC bullet. The small number of IRA members with a few handguns and a Thompson sub-machine-gun could do little to prevent the carnage. They were equally powerless the next day when, before British troops could be effectively deployed in the city's trouble spots, Protestants launched an attack on the Clonard district, a small Catholic enclave near the Shankill Road, after rumours that there were IRA snipers on the roof of Clonard Monastery. Gerald McAuley, a member of the Fianna, the IRA's youth wing, was shot dead and a whole Catholic street, Bombay Street, was razed. The burning of Bombay Street would become integrated into the founding mythology of the Provisional IRA, in which it was depicted as the inevitable consequence of the defenceless state of Belfast Catholics that resulted from the misguided policies of the 'Marxist' leadership in Dublin.[8]

British troops were on the streets of Belfast and Derry for the first time since 1935 but Wilson and Callaghan, who had both threatened to introduce direct rule if troops were sent in, now backtracked. For although direct rule had been on the British cabinet's agenda since the early months of 1969, there was an undercurrent of horror at the possibility of such a deepening of involvement. As early as February 1969 Callaghan had told the cabinet that direct rule was a 'serious option', although he added that independence for the North might be a 'preferable alternative'.[9] The truth was that although direct rule was held like a sword of Damocles over the heads of Chichester-Clark and his colleagues, neither Wilson nor Callaghan had the stomach for it. In part this reflected an understandable desire not to be drawn into what was seen as the bog of Irish politics, but it also reflected a fear of a Protestant backlash. Sir Harold Black, the Northern Ireland Cabinet Secretary, warned senior Whitehall figures that in the event of direct rule, 'there would be a frightening reaction by the Protestant community which would make anything that had happened up to now seem like child's play.'[10] The warning seemed to have the desired effect.

But if the British government recoiled from direct rule, it also made clear that Stormont could only continue to exist as a client regime under constant supervision at both ministerial and official levels. Called to Downing Street on 19 August, Chichester-Clark pre-emptively emasculated his government by proposing to give the Army's GOC in Northern Ireland supremacy over the RUC and Specials in security matters. Although the declaration issued after the meeting affirmed Northern Ireland's constitutional status, it had an implicitly critical tone, affirming that 'every citizen in Northern Ireland is entitled to the same equality of treatment and freedom from discrimination as obtains in the rest of the United Kingdom irrespective of political views or religion.'[11] Two senior civil servants were sent from Whitehall to work within the Stormont Cabinet Office and the Ministry of Home Affairs and Chichester-Clark accepted a British proposal for a committee of inquiry into policing, to be chaired by Sir John Hunt. The humiliation of the Stormont regime was complete when, in a subsequent television interview, Wilson indicated that the Specials were finished.

Callaghan's arrival for his first visit to the North deepened the impression of a new Westminster overlordship. Joint working groups of officials from Belfast and London were to examine how far Stormont's existing practices and commitments would ensure fair allocation of houses, avoidance of discrimination in public employment, and promote good community relations. Greeted as a conquering hero when he entered the Bogside, which like large sections of Catholic West Belfast was a 'no-go' area for the RUC and the British army, he had a much less positive reception on the Shankill Road.

This system of direct rule by proxy enraged the Unionist right and eventually unleashed a downward spiral of loyalist reaction and republican assertiveness. Lord Hunt's committee reported on 9 October, recommending that the RUC become an unarmed civilian force and the B Specials be disbanded to be replaced by the Ulster Defence Regiment, a locally recruited part-time military force under the control of the British army. In response, loyalists rioted for two nights on the Shankill Road and shot and killed the first RUC man to die since the IRA's 1950s campaign. Paisley's attacks on Chichester-Clark, whom he portrayed as Callaghan's submissive poodle, were increasingly influential in the Protestant community.

Although Callaghan had privately declared his desire 'to do down the Unionists',[12] he and his colleagues were soon convinced that there was no alternative but to support Chichester-Clark. Oliver Wright, a senior diplomat who had been Wilson's emissary to Rhodesia, was now sent to oversee the implementation of the reforms and 'put some stiffening into the administration'.[13] Although Unionist ministers feared that he would listen only to their critics,[14] his reports to Downing Street were surprisingly sympathetic to the good intentions of Chichester-Clark and his colleagues if not to their abilities: 'They were not evil men bent on maintaining power at all costs. They were decent, but bewildered men, out of their depth in the face of the magnitude of their problem.'[15] Wright was critical of the recently published Cameron Report into the 1968 disturbances because it displayed so little understanding of Protestant fears: 'not only the loss of political power within his own community, but his absorption into the larger society of Southern Ireland— alien in smell, backward in development and inferior in politics'. His central conclusion, one followed by Wilson's administration until it lost office, was that 'our central purpose should be to support the Northern Ireland government, both to keep the problem of Ulster at arm's length and because they alone can accomplish our joint aims by reasonably peaceful means.'[16]

By the beginning of 1970 there was a facile optimism in the British cabinet and Whitehall reflected in an *Irish Times* investigation into the new relationship between Stormont and Westminster: 'The British view is that the Northern Ireland problem "has been licked".'[17] At a meeting in the Foreign and Commonwealth Office in London in February, Wright informed Patrick Hillery, the Irish Minister of External Affairs, that 'a lot of steam had gone out of demonstrations' and that the only ones making trouble were 'professional anarchists'. Irish fears about the growing support for Paisley, whose Protestant Unionist Party had recently won two council seats in Belfast, were dismissed with the claim that Chichester-Clark had a 'moderate and united Unionist Party' behind him and that the prospect was one of 'steady improvement in the situation.'[18] This ignored the reverberations from the violence of the previous summer in which thousands of people, most of them Catholics, had lost their homes. This added a dangerous new sharpness to sectarian tensions in Belfast from which both Paisley's Protestant populism and the infant Provisional IRA were already benefiting.

Traditionalist republicans asserted themselves in the wake of the August violence. By September they had forced the Belfast IRA command to break its links with the national leadership and by the end of the year the nucleus of an alternative republican movement had emerged. When in December an IRA convention voted in favour of ending the policy of abstention from the Dáil, Goulding's critics seceded and created a Provisional Army Council. In January 1970 the political wing of the movement, Sinn Féin, also split. While the largely southern leadership of the Provisionals—men including the new Chief of Staff Seán MacStiofáin and Ruairí Ó Bradaigh—were driven by a fundamentalist commitment to the main tenets of republican ideology, many of their new supporters in the North were motivated by a mixture of ethnic rage against loyalists and the RUC and the increasingly fraught relation between the British army and sections of Belfast's Catholic working class.

Although the violence of August had created a reservoir of fear, resentment, and anger which the Provisionals could exploit, recent research has pointed to slow and limited growth of the organization until the spring of 1970. The first 'general army convention' of the Provisional IRA was attended by just thirty-four people.[19] Many of the young Catholics who approached veteran republicans to get trained in the use of arms saw the enemy not as British soldiers, who were enjoying a brief honeymoon period as the saviours of their communities, but as loyalists and the RUC. Republicans such as Cahill and the young Gerry Adams were aghast at the behaviour of Falls Road housewives giving cups of tea to soldiers while their daughters attended discos organized by the army. But as early as September 1969, Callaghan himself had admitted to his cabinet colleague Anthony Crosland that British troops were no longer popular: 'He had anticipated the honeymoon period wouldn't last very long and it hadn't.'[20] British soldiers soon found themselves in the unenviable position of policing major sectarian confrontations and acting as the first line of defence of a Unionist government under intense pressure from the loyalist right.

Republicans had long denounced Stormont as a 'police state'. However, the dominant characteristic of the RUC's response to the civil unrest after October 1968 had been its weakness and ineffectuality. In contrast the army, whose presence had grown from the pre-Troubles garrison of 2,000 to 7,500 by September 1969,[21] responded to rioting with often overwhelming force. The loyalists who rioted on the Shankill Road after the publication of the Hunt Report were the first to experience the difference. Two were shot dead and over sixty injured, with a police surgeon commenting that the injuries were the worst he had ever seen after a riot.[22] Given the atmosphere of intense sectarian animosity and potential confrontation which existed in the 'shatter-zones' of North and West Belfast, it was inevitable that the army's rough, brutal, and often indiscriminate response would be meted out to Catholics as well.

The first major conflict between Catholics and the army occurred in April 1970 after an Orange parade near the Ballymurphy estate in West Belfast, which was by then home to many of those displaced by the August violence.[23] It also saw the expulsion of Protestant families from the nearby New Barnsley estate. Further confrontations in West and East Belfast precipitated by Orange parades in June led to the first significant military actions by the Provisionals. IRA men defending the small Catholic enclave of the Short Strand in East Belfast shot dead two Protestants while republicans killed three Protestants in clashes on the Crumlin Road. The brutal sectarian headcount of five Protestants to one Catholic killed established the Provisionals' ghetto credibility over that of the more squeamish Official IRA, which had remained loyal to Goulding. The Provisionals experienced their first major influx of recruits since the previous August and accelerated their plans for moving from a largely defensive to an offensive posture.[24] A bombing campaign that had begun in Belfast in March 1970 was intensified in the autumn.

The growth of the Provisionals was encouraged by the combination of a Unionist government that was hostage to the right and by a new Conservative administration that was easy for republicans to portray as crudely pro-Unionist in sympathy. Ian Paisley and a supporter had been returned to Stormont in two by-elections held in April, Paisley taking particular relish from a victory in O'Neill's former constituency of

Bannside. Paisley went on to win the Westminster seat of North Antrim in the June general election. Callaghan was later to blame 'the far more relaxed and less focused regime' of Reginald Maudling, his successor as Home Secretary, for allowing the situation to deteriorate radically.[25] This too conveniently ignored the profoundly destabilizing effects of the policy of direct rule by proxy, which Wilson and he had bequeathed to Heath and Maudling. However, it is true that while Callaghan and Wilson were inclined to be cautious, Maudling and Heath were disposed to give the army its head. Maudling's own character has been described as 'brilliant if a little lazy'.[26] His strong aversion to the North's warring factions—'these bloody people'[27] as he referred to them—may have encouraged Sir Ian Freeland, the GOC in Northern Ireland, to a more aggressive approach than he would have adopted under Callaghan. It was Freeland who made the decision to impose a curfew on the Lower Falls area in July after a search for arms had provoked rioting. For two days, 3,000 troops supported by armour and helicopters conducted a massive house search whilst saturating the area in CS gas and taking on both the Official IRA, who controlled the Lower Falls, and the Provisionals in gun battles in which five people were killed.[28]

While Freeland had not consulted Chichester-Clark's government before imposing the curfew, a triumphalist tour of the area by the Stormont Minister of Information, who was a son of Lord Brookeborough, contributed to the politically disastrous results of this military operation, which marked the turning point in the relation between the army and the city's Catholic working class.[29] By the end of the summer the Provisionals had launched a bombing campaign against government buildings and commercial targets and were organizing the importation of weapons from the US. Their strategy aimed at provoking a more repressive response from Stormont including internment, which they correctly calculated would fail and lead to direct rule. Republican theology saw Britain as the enemy and the Provisionals did all in their power to reduce the conflict in Northern Ireland to one between the British state and the 'Irish people' without the complication of Stormont. They would be spectacularly successful in pushing the contradictions of direct rule by proxy to their limit and in bringing down Stormont but the price would be a low-intensity sectarian civil war.

The Belfast IRA killed their first unarmed RUC men in August 1970 but did not manage to kill a British soldier until February 1971. In March the particularly brutal murder of three young off-duty soldiers by Ardoyne Provisionals precipitated Chichester-Clark's resignation when

Heath refused his request for a toughening of security policy, including a military occupation of 'no-go' areas in Derry. Brian Faulkner, who easily defeated William Craig in the election to succeed Chichester-Clark, set out to restore the morale of his divided party by a determined reassertion of Stormont's role in security policy. Taking over the Home Affairs portfolio, he pressurized Heath and the new GOC General, Sir Harry Tuzo, to move from a containment policy to one of actively re-establishing the 'rule of law' in all parts of Northern Ireland.[30] He complemented this with an attempt to court moderate nationalists by offering a new system of powerful back-bench committees at Stormont, some of which would be chaired by the Opposition.

The IRA greeted Faulkner's accession with an intensification of its campaign. In Derry, where the Provisionals were still weak and where no shots had yet been fired, the RUC had been able to resume patrols in Bogside and Creggan.[31] With Seán MacStiofain complaining about lack of activity in Derry, the Provisional IRA in the city deliberately and abruptly escalated their activities against the army in early July.[32] They began to use the routine confrontations between the city's young unemployed rioters and the army as a cover for sniping and the throwing of gelignite bombs. Within days the army shot and killed two Catholic youths and all nationalist MPs withdrew from Stormont in protest.

In the year to July 1971, fifty-five people had died violently and there had been 300 explosions. Then the Provisionals launched their heaviest campaign of bombing in Belfast with ten explosions along the route of the 12 July Orange parades and some 'spectaculars', including the total destruction of a new printing plant for the *Daily Mirror*.[33] According to Faulkner, these summer bombings tipped the scales in favour of internment: 'I took the decision . . . no one objected.'[34] In fact, when he went to Downing Street on 5 August to get the approval of Heath and his colleagues, it was pointed out to him that neither the Chief of the General Staff nor the GOC believed internment was necessary from a strictly military point of view and the 'national and international implications' of such a serious step were stressed. Heath made the point that if internment was tried and failed, the only further option was direct rule.[35]

Launched at 04.15 in the morning of 9 August, 'Operation Demetrius' pulled in 337 of the 520 republicans on RUC Special Branch and Military Intelligence lists. These lists turned out to be grossly inadequate: they relied on outdated information about pre-1969 republicanism, which meant that while middle-aged veterans of earlier campaigns were arrested together with many Officials, many of the new recruits to the Provisionals were untouched.[36] Not one loyalist was interned, adding to the outrage in the Catholic community. Most damaging politically were the claims, later officially verified, that internees had been brutalized during arrest and interrogation and, in particular, that eleven men had been singled out for 'in-depth' interrogation. This involved being deprived of sleep, food, and drink and being forced to stand hooded and spread-eagled against a wall while being subject to high-pitched sound from a 'noise-machine'.[37]

Though the RUC and the army were satisfied that internment had damaged the Provisionals in Belfast, there was little evidence of this on the streets, where violence intensified dramatically. In 1971 prior to internment there had been thirty-four deaths, within two days of its introduction seventeen people had died, and by the end of the year 140 more.[38] By the beginning of October Heath was complaining that the crisis in Northern Ireland was threatening to jeopardize the success of the government's economic and defence policies and its approach to Europe. Despite this, he still gave priority to the defeat of the IRA by military means whatever this meant in terms of alienation of the minority and bad relations with Dublin.[39] However, other senior ministers and officials favoured an approach that kept the option of a United Ireland open. The consensus that emerged was that Faulkner should be pressed to consider a radical political initiative that would involve bringing 'non-militant republican Catholics' into the government, while the issue of internal reform would be separated from that of creeping reunification by holding a periodic referendum on the border. Faulkner rebuffed the pressure, telling Heath that he could not contemplate serving in government with republicans—amongst whom he included politicians such as John Hume and Gerry Fitt. He was too mindful of previous British failure to deliver on threats of direct rule and placed too much faith in ritualistic statements by British ministers ruling it out. In fact a belief that direct rule was likely had formed at the highest level of the British state by the autumn of 1971. The principal reason was the communal polarization generated by internment and an increasing inclination to reach out to the nationalist community by a radical break that would undermine support for the Provisionals. Suspension of Stormont had therefore become likely even before the tragedy of 'Bloody Sunday'.

In Derry the GOC had come to an agreement with leaders of

moderate Catholic opinion in August 1971 that the army would lower its profile in order to allow the 'extremists' to be marginalized. By the end of the year it was clear that the wager of moderation had failed: 'At present neither the RUC nor the military have control of the Bogside and Creggan areas, law and order are not being effectively maintained and the Security Forces now face an entirely hostile Catholic community numbering 33,000 in these two areas alone.'[40] This had allowed both sections of the IRA in the city large zones for rest and recuperation, from which they had emerged as the most formidable military challenge in the North. The large numbers of nationalist youth, 'Derry Young Hooligans' as the military commanders in the city referred to them, also used the 'no-go' areas as bases for sustained intrusions into the city centre, which was being decimated by the effects of rioting, arson, and Provisional bombs. By the end of the year, faced with an increasingly rampant level of 'Young Hooligan' activity, which the IRA often used as a means of luring soldiers into situations where they were vulnerable to snipers or nail-bombs, there was a feeling among some senior military commanders that a more aggressive posture was necessary. This was the background to the events of 'Bloody Sunday' on 30 January 1972 when, after rioting that had developed in the wake of a banned civil rights march, members of the Paratroop regiment, whose deployment in Derry had been questioned by local police and army commanders because of their reputation for gung-ho brutality, opened fire, killing thirteen civilians.

The material released to the Saville Inquiry into Bloody Sunday, set up in 1997 by the British Prime Minister, Tony Blair, provides no evidence that the killings were the result of a policy decision by either the Faulkner or Heath cabinets. Instead there was a clearly defined local dialectic leading to the disaster. Major-General Ford, the Commander of Land Forces who was responsible for day-to-day operational decisions in Northern Ireland, had come to the conclusion that a 'softly softly' approach to the Bogside and Creggan had placed an increasingly intolerable strain on his men as they faced strong and self-confident aggression from 'Derry Young Hooligans' and from the local IRA. He was contemptuous of the moderate advice coming from the local RUC commander, a Catholic. Afraid that the city centre itself was in danger of becoming a 'no-go' area, Ford had come to believe that only the shooting of identified 'ring leaders' would stop the rot.[41]

However, it needs to be emphasized that the Heath cabinet had no desire to push events in Derry to such a brutal conclusion:

As to Londonderry, a military operation to impose law and order would require seven battalions . . . It would be a major operation, necessarily involving civilian casualties, and thereby hardening even further the attitude of the Roman Catholic population.

Heath's own summing up of the situation on 11 January was that a military operation to 'reimpose law and order' in Derry might become inevitable but it should not be undertaken until there was a successful political initiative.[42] The British political and military establishment may have been prepared to contemplate civilian deaths in Derry during an operation against the IRA in the Bogside and Creggan, but only when they believed that the political conditions were right. This would entail a major political initiative and one was not yet on the horizon when 'Bloody Sunday' occurred. Less than a week before, the Chief of the General Staff, Sir Michael Carver, on a visit to the Province, had defined the 'IRA propaganda machine' as the main enemy.[43] The actions of the First Paratroop Regiment on 30 January provided that machine with sufficient fuel to guarantee years of effective work.

Direct Rule and the Fragmentation of Unionism

The Londonderry killings unleashed a wave of angry protest in the South that culminated in the burning of the British embassy in Dublin after it had been attacked by a crowd of more than 20,000. Amid a torrent of international criticism and with growing unease among his own colleagues and Tory back-benchers, Heath summoned Faulkner to Downing Street to discuss the possibility of a political initiative. Faulkner was confronted with a series of ideas, including repartition, a periodic border poll, supposedly to take the issue out of day-to-day politics, a broadening of his government to include members of the SDLP, and the transfer of all Stormont's security powers to Westminster.[44]

Unionism was driven towards a bitter and fevered fragmentation by the twin threats of Provisional violence and British intervention. Deaths from the security situation had risen from fourteen in 1969 to 174 in 1971. The first three months of 1972 produced eighty-seven more and that year would be the worst in three decades of violence with 470 deaths, 14 per cent of all those killed in Northern Ireland between 1969 and 1998. Other indices of sharply escalating violence were a rise in the number of shootings from seventy-three in 1969 to 1,756 in 1971 and of explosions from nine to 1,022 in the same period.[45] On 20 March the Provisionals made their most destructive and indiscriminate contribution to the tool-kit of terrorism with the first use of a car bomb in a devastating explosion in Belfast's Donegall Street. Claimed to be a blow at 'the colonial economic structure'[46] and the British ruling class, this Provisional bomb killed six people, most of them members of the crew of a bin-lorry.[47] With the IRA declaring that 1972 would be the 'Year of Victory' and Harold Wilson being prepared to meet leading Provisionals in Dublin and declare his support for their inclusion in all-party talks in the event of an IRA cease-fire, many Unionists scented betrayal, fearing that Wilson was a surrogate for Heath who would do anything to extricate his government from the Irish quagmire.[48]

This was the environment in which support for both radical constitutional change in the form of a possible independent loyalist state and the much more localistic and almost apolitical vigilantism of the emerging Protestant paramilitary groups developed. The politician who temporarily dominated the Protestant reaction was the ex-cabinet minister William Craig. He had played a leading role in all the anti-reformist movements that had developed since O'Neill had sacked him. He warned that if the British government abolished Stormont it would be met by massive resistance; a provisional government would be formed and, if necessary, Northern Ireland would go it alone.[49] As the IRA campaign intensified he criticized Faulkner's acquiescence in London's 'interference' in Stormont's security responsibilities and demanded the creation of a 'third force' of loyalists, essentially a return of the B Specials, to deal with the republican threat.[50] In the aftermath of 'Bloody Sunday', with rumours of imminent direct rule abounding, Craig launched Ulster Vanguard on 9 February. Although other leading members of Vanguard, such as the Presbyterian minister and leading Orangeman Martin Smyth, saw the organization as a means of reunifying the Unionist Party around more right-wing policies,[51] Craig's willingness to be closely and publicly associated with loyalist paramilitaries was an embarrassment to the staid and conservative figures who were the backbone of the right within the Party. Vanguard's initial role was to scare off any interventionist urges Heath might be planning to indulge by a theatrical politics of threat. Craig was borne in an ancient limousine, complete with motorcycle outriders, to mass rallies stiffened by the presence of paramilitaries in uniform, where he threatened violence: most graphically to a crowd of over 60,000 in Belfast's Ormeau Park on

18 March where he warned that 'if and when politicians fail us, it may be our job to liquidate the enemy'. He also threatened to form a provisional government if the British government attempted to impose a settlement that most Unionists rejected.[52]

However, when on 24 March Heath announced the suspension of the Stormont parliament after Faulkner and his cabinet refused a demand for the transfer of all security powers to London, Vanguard's response was a two-day general strike, which, although it was relatively successful, did little to obstruct the unfolding of British policy. The introduction of direct rule was hailed by the Provisional IRA as a victory, which they declared 'places us in a somewhat similar position to that prior to the setting up of partition and the two statelets. It puts the "Irish Question" in its true perspective—an alien power seeking to lay claim to a country for which it has no legal right.'[53] In fact the significance of direct rule was elsewhere: its introduction marked the definitive end of the 'Orange state' and it allowed the British government to introduce a strategy of reform 'from above'. Northern Protestants were inevitably divided in their reading of direct rule's significance and the conflicting inter-pretations of it put forward within a Unionist politics characterized by disarray and confusion.

Craig advocated an independent Ulster as the only defence against the IRA and a Conservative government that a Vanguard pamphlet portrayed as 'tired, even bored with Irish politics from which they wish to extricate themselves'.[54] But Vanguard's willingness to contemplate fundamental constitutional change and its association with Protestant paramilitary groups was unappealing to many Unionists. Distrust of the British governments was a much more widespread phenomenon amongst Unionists than a willingness to contemplate a radical loosening of the constitutional link with the British state.[55] There was also little evidence that the emergence of Protestant paramilitary groups as signifi-cant actors in inter-communal conflict had allowed them to develop the sort of political and ideological legitimacy that the Provisional IRA had achieved in the Catholic community.

The Ulster Volunteer Force (UVF) had been created in 1966 by ex-servicemen who worked in the shipyard and lived in the Shankill district of West Belfast. They had been involved with Ulster Protestant Action, founded in 1959 to ensure that Protestant employers looked after loyalists as redundancies threatened, and were influenced by the anti-ecumenical and anti-republican preaching of Ian Paisley. However, the UVF's murder of two Catholics in 1966 and the arrest of its leader Gusty

Spence and two of its associates dealt it a near-fatal blow and left little in the way of enduring organization or support.[56]

It was the communal violence in West and North Belfast in August 1969 and after internment that propelled Protestant paramilitarism from the lumpen fringes of loyalist activity to, at least temporarily, a more central role. Although the UVF would benefit from the violent and febrile conditions post-August 1969, the main organization to emerge was the Ulster Defence Association (UDA). The UDA was established in September 1971 out of the fusion of a number of vigilante groups that had emerged in North and West Belfast. At its peak in 1972 it had a membership of between 40,000 and 50,000 men.[57] The declared motivation of UDA was the defence of its communities from republican attacks. Most of the membership had full-time employment and so tended to play little part in the day-to-day running of the organization, coming out at night and weekends to man barricades or take part in marches and demonstrations, which were common in the centre of Belfast in 1972. However, a hard core of often unemployed members would work full time for the organization and, as in the smaller UVF, it was these who were also involved in offensive actions under the *nom de guerre* of the Ulster Freedom Fighters (UFF). Although the object of its attacks was defined as the republican movement, UFF targets extended well beyond known IRA men to include any Catholic unlucky enough to come into the path of one of its assassination squads. In the eighteen months after its first killing of a Catholic vigilante on the Crumlin Road in February 1972 it would kill over 200 more.[58] Although some of the more cerebral of its leaders would rationalize these sectarian killings as an attempt to dry up the reservoir of popular support and sympathy for the Provos in the Catholic community, many were ad hoc responses of small groups of UDA men enraged by an IRA attack and often inflamed by alcohol and sectarian hatred.

The gruesome nature of the tortures inflicted on some of the victims by the so-called 'Shankill Butcher' gang, a group of UVF men who operated in the mid and late 1970s, indicated a more nakedly sectarian agenda than that of the Provisionals.[59] However, the Provisionals were also tainted by sectarianism. Until the onset of the 'Ulsterization' of security policy in the mid 1970s, the Provisionals had a large and easily identifiable non-Protestant target in the British Army. Even then, however, their use of car bombs in Belfast and other town centres showed a cavalier disregard for the lives of civilians, the majority of them Protestants. Nor did the IRA hesitate in bombing pubs in Protestant areas: in

September 1971 a Provisional bomb at the *Four Step Inn* on the Shankill Road killed two people and injured twenty.[60]

Paisley was the most threatening challenge to Unionist Party in the decade after direct rule. There was nothing inevitable about this, for down to 1973 it was to William Craig that most disaffected Unionists looked to provide leadership against Faulkner's 'appeasement' policies. Although Paisley was by 1971 a member of both the Stormont and Westminster parliaments, his coarse and unsophisticated anti-Catholicism made him and his Protestant Unionist Party appear too extreme for the vast bulk of 'respectable' Unionists. His support was still largely confined to rural Ulster where he had, in such areas as North Antrim and Armagh, a following composed of a mixture of pietistic Protestants and members of the Orange Order.[61]

However, the hostility he had experienced from other MPs at Westminster led him to modify the more fanatical features of his public persona. He was also affected by his friendship with the Ulster Unionist MP for Shankill, Desmond Boal. Abrasive, intelligent, and one of the North's leading lawyers, Boal emphasized the importance of class issues if Paisleyism was to become an effective challenge to the Ulster Unionist Party (UUP). Both he and John McQuade, the ex-docker and ex-soldier who was MP for Woodvale in North Belfast, personified the dissident Unionist tradition which had produced previous independent Unionist MPs such as J. W. Nixon and Tommy Henderson, who combined ultra-loyalism and strong Orange credentials with a record of criticism of the Unionist Party on social and economic issues.[62]

At the formation of the Democratic Unionist Party (DUP) in September 1971, Boal defined it as being 'right wing in the sense of being strong on the constitution, but to the left on social issues'. But although some of its Belfast activists were from the NILP tradition, the bulk of the DUP's members were members of Paisley's Free Presbyterian Church. This provided the party with an infrastructure of dedicated and ultra-loyal activists who in time would emerge as a disciplined and monolithic threat to the defensive and divided Unionist Party. However, for most of the first two years of the DUP's existence the policy stances adopted by Paisley did much to confuse his supporters and limit his appeal. His opposition to internment, support for integration, and his remarks on the positive impact that changes in the Republic's constitution might have on Protestant attitudes to a united Ireland created confusion and incredulity amongst his supporters. It also evoked praise for his 'statesmanship' from leaders of the IRA, and a prediction from William

Whitelaw, first Secretary of State for Northern Ireland, that he would be 'the future leader of Northern Ireland'.[63]

In the short term his iconoclasm was little short of disastrous for the appeal of the party. When it was revealed that Whitelaw had had leading members of the IRA flown to London for secret talks in July 1972, calls for integration appeared both fatuous and positively dangerous. However, after 'Operation Motorman' had ended the 'no-go' status of the Bogside and the Creggan in July and it became clearer that the objective of British policy was a reformed Northern Ireland and not disengagement, the environment for a DUP take-off became more favourable. Paisley was assisted by Craig's political ineptitude.

Craig's verbal extremism intensified with a speech to the right-wing Monday Club in the House of Commons, in which he declared that he could mobilize 80,000 men to oppose the British government and added 'We are prepared to come out and shoot and kill.'[64] In February 1973 he told an audience in the Ulster Hall that an 'independent dominion of Ulster' would be viable economically. This vision might have enthused the largely middle-class activists of Vanguard, but it had little appeal to working-class loyalists, who wondered what would happen to the welfare state and many of their jobs in Craig's utopia. In the same month he identified Vanguard with a one-day general strike called by the UDA and the Loyalist Association of Workers (LAW) in protest at the internment of two loyalists, the first Protestants to be interned at a time when there were already hundreds of Catholics 'behind the wire'. LAW was composed of Protestant trade unionists in some of the North's key industries, including the main power stations in Belfast and Larne. The strike, which combined limited industrial muscle with significant paramilitary intimidation, shut down transport and the electricity supply in Belfast and was accompanied by widespread rioting and destruction of property. Five people died, including a fire-fighter shot by a loyalist sniper. The great majority of Unionists were appalled by these events and in their aftermath LAW fell apart and many on the Unionist right turned their backs on Craig.

Paisley exploited this weakening of Craig's position and was able to use the referendum on the Border held in March 1973 to bring the DUP back in from the periphery of loyalist politics.[65] The British government, relying on the poll to reassure Unionists that their constitutional position was secure, pressed ahead with plans for a return to devolved government in Northern Ireland. The White Paper *Northern Ireland Constitutional Proposals*, published in March, made it clear that any new administration must be based on some form of executive power-sharing between Unionists and nationalists and would also have an 'Irish Dimension': new institutional arrangements for consultation and co-operation between Dublin and Belfast. The new northern arrangements should be 'so far as is possible acceptable to and accepted by the Republic of Ireland'.[66]

At a time when violence, although somewhat lower in intensity than in the previous horrendous year, was claiming around thirty lives a month and with nationalists publicly committed to joint Dublin/London rule over the North as a 'transition' to unity, what is surprising is not the Protestant support for the right but rather the continued existence of a considerable constituency that was prepared to back Faulkner's qualified and ambiguous acceptance of the White Paper. A special meeting of the Ulster Unionist Council rejected an anti-White Paper motion, forcing Craig to lead his followers out of the Unionist Party to form a new organization, the Vanguard Unionist Progressive Party.[67] Former allies, including John Taylor, Harry West, and Martin Smyth, refused to follow him and resigned from Vanguard. The right was determined not to cede control of the Unionist Party to the Faulknerites and stayed inside to mobilize opinion against 'capitulation' to the British government's 'pro-republican' stratagems. Here they showed more political sense than those liberal Unionists who left the party to join the new non-sectarian Alliance Party. Established in April 1970, Alliance quickly gained support from middle-class Unionists in the greater Belfast area who had supported O'Neill. Their defection denuded the ranks of those within the Unionist Party who could more effectively have resisted the onward march of the right as well as splitting the pro-power-sharing constituency in the Protestant community.[68]

Paisley benefited from the confused and disorganized state of the Ulster Unionist Party. Direct rule had at one stroke removed the UUP's control of governmental and administrative power. No longer was the directing centre of Unionism located in the cabinet with its access to the substantial resources of the Northern Ireland civil service. Within months of the prorogation, Faulkner's old cabinet had collapsed as an effective political force and he was faced with an increasingly assertive set of officers from the party's ruling Ulster Unionist Council, within which the older and more traditional elements of the party were strongly ensconced.[69] Senior NICS officials such as Sir Harold Black and Kenneth Bloomfield, who had been at the core of the Stormont system, were now working within the new Northern Ireland Office, created to service William Whitelaw's ministerial team.[70] While Bloomfield was using his sharp political intelligence and considerable drafting skills in the preparation of the British government's constitutional proposals, Faulkner had to rely on the penny-farthing machine that was the Unionist Party's 'research and publicity' department, staffed by a few young graduates almost totally lacking in political experience. Given these exiguous resources, Faulkner's political achievements down to the end of 1973 were not inconsiderable.

After winning the support of the Ulster Unionist Council to participate in the constitutional experiment outlined in the White Paper, Faulkner applied all his undoubted resources of energy, courage, and verbal dexterity to selling a deal based on power-sharing with the SDLP and what he saw as 'merely' symbolic concession to nationalist sentiment in agreeing to the setting up of a Council of Ireland. The manifesto on which Faulkner proposed that the party's candidates contest the June 1973 elections for a new Northern Ireland Assembly contained the formula, soaked in ambiguity, 'we are not prepared to participate in government with those whose primary objective is to break the Union with Great Britain.'[71] Preparing to drop his previous opposition to sharing power with constitutional nationalists, he argued that any member of the proposed Executive had to take an oath under the Northern Ireland Constitution Act of 1973 'to uphold the laws of Northern Ireland', which would make them structurally, if not ideologically, Unionist.[72] This was a relatively subtle distinction for many Ulster Unionists to appreciate at a time when their predominant emotions were often ones of bewilderment and apprehension at the collapse of the Stormont regime, coupled with bitter resentment at those they considered responsible, amongst whom the leaders of the SDLP ranked almost as high as the Army Council of the Provisional IRA.

Resistance to this hint of compromise manifested itself in the refusal of a number of Unionist Party candidates for the Assembly elections to sign a pledge of support for the Manifesto. The Assembly of seventy-eight members was elected by proportional representation and the result showed fragmentation of the Unionist vote into four main segments: Faulkner's 'pledged' Unionists won 29 per cent of the first preference votes and twenty-four seats; 'unpledged' members of the Unionist Party, 8.8 per cent and eight seats; the DUP, 10.8 per cent and eight seats; and Vanguard, 10.5 per cent and seven seats. Together with three seats held by the anti-White Paper West Belfast Loyalist Coalition, the opponents of any compromise with constitutional nationalism had a slight majority of Unionist representation in the Assembly.[73] However, together with the SDLP, which had won 22 per cent of the vote and nineteen seats, and the Alliance's 9 per cent and eight seats, the parties supporting the proposed new dispensation had a commanding majority in the Assembly. Negotiations began between delegations of the three parties on the formation of an Executive. Faulkner, perhaps because of an exaggerated belief in the effect of the Border poll in generating a sense of constitutional security amongst Unionists, seriously overestimated his ability to sell the prospective deal to his party. He astounded the supportive but cautious Ken Bloomfield when, after a visit to his home in October by the Irish Foreign Minister, Garret FitzGerald, he agreed that the proposed Council of Ireland would not simply be a consultative body but would have executive powers.[74] Bloomfield's reaction—that it 'represented the crossing of a significant Rubicon ... I wondered if it would not have proved a bridge too far for the unionist community'[75]— accurately predicted the role that an overambitious 'Irish Dimension' would have in destroying reformist Unionism's prospects for two decades.

Social Democrats versus Provos: Nationalist Politics 1969–73

While the dynamic behind the Provisionals was found in the Catholic working class of North and West Belfast and Derry's Creggan and Bogside, the modernized constitutional nationalism of the Social Democratic and Labour Party had its social roots in the post-war educational revolution. Francis Mulhern, who as a teenager from a Catholic working-class background in county Fermanagh took part in the civil rights movement, provides an acute summation of the local effects of the Butler Education Act:

The local leaderships of the civil rights movement were to a striking degree highly educated, with teachers, present, past or future, most prominent in them. These people enjoyed a conventional authority, but unlike an earlier generation of their kind they were not a rarity and unlike the Nationalist notables they now displaced they wore their class differences lightly.[76]

The dominant intellectual influence in the SDLP came from the revisionist nationalist thinking associated first with the National Unity project in the early 1960s and then with the more politicized challenge to the Nationalist Party that emerged with the formation of the National Democratic Party (NDP) in 1965. The NDP's arguments for a participationist strategy that maintained a commitment to unity but only with the consent of a majority in the North, and for a modern democratic party structure, were central to the SDLP at its formation and of the almost 400 people who joined the new party, nearly 80 per cent had been NDP members.[77] The NDP made little progress because it had confined its activities to those areas where the Nationalist Party did not have seats and it was left to the civil rights movement to create that unprecedented mobilization of northern Catholics that made a frontal challenge to the party possible. In the February 1969 Stormont election the nationalists lost three of their nine seats to independents, all of whom had played a prominent part in the civil rights movement. Most shattering was the defeat of the nationalist leader, Eddie McAteer, by John Hume in the Foyle constituency. Over the next decade Hume would establish himself as the predominant strategic intelligence in non-violent Irish nationalism on the island. But this would also be a process in which constitutional nationalism adopted a harder and more implacable position.

In his early thirties when elected to Stormont, Hume had already established a reputation for incisive criticism of the negativity and conservatism of the Nationalist Party combined with a moderate and 'responsible' role in Derry's increasingly disturbed situation after 5 October 1968. From working-class origins, he had been empowered by the Education Act of 1947 to follow the traditional route of many middle-class Derry Catholics through the strict religious and nationalist environment of St Columb's Grammar School to the Catholic seminary at Maynooth. A loss of vocation led him into teaching in his home town and an increasingly prominent role in community politics through his active promotion of 'self-help' schemes such as the Credit Union movement and local housing associations. Hume's politics, while professedly left-of-centre, had little association with the city's labour tradition which by the end of the 1960s had become heavily influenced by Eamonn McCann's Trotskyism and leftist republicans. Derry's Catholic middle class of teachers, shopkeepers, and publicans looked to Hume and other members of the Citizens' Action Committee to curb the excesses and extremism of the leftists and republicans, who were seen as dangerously influential, particularly on the rioting activities of 'Derry Young Hooligans'.

During his campaign against McAteer, Hume had committed himself to working for a new political movement based on social democratic principles, which would be 'completely non-sectarian' and animated by the ideal that the future of Northern Ireland should be decided by its people.[78] However, the virtual insurrection in the Bogside in August 1969 and the impetus it gave to the rebirth of physical force republicanism would put increasing pressure on this initially moderate non-sectarian project. At Stormont, Hume attempted to unite the divergent elements of anti-Unionism into a coherent force. Nationalist Party hostility to this dangerous 'upstart' meant that the focus of his activities was a group of five MPs, comprising former civil rights leaders and two Belfast labourists, Gerry Fitt and Paddy Devlin.

Fitt and Devlin were essential to Hume's project of a serious political challenge to Unionism, for without them any new party would continue to replicate the largely rural and border-counties orientation of the Nationalist Party. Without a base in Belfast the party would also be absent from the cockpit of the struggle with resurgent republicanism. But both men, with their powerful personalities and strong Labour and socialist sentiments, fitted uneasily into the new formation. Fitt, an ex-merchant seaman who had done convoy duty to the USSR during the war, had built a political base in his native dock ward through a combination of republican socialist rhetoric and clientilism. A councillor from 1958, he had entered Stormont in 1962. But it was his victorious return as Republican Labour MP for West Belfast in the 1966 Westminster general election that allowed him to capture the attention of the British and Irish media as he gave powerful and eloquent expression to the merging civil rights critique of the Unionist regime. Fitt's seniority, his growing influence in the House of Commons, and his friendly relations, not only with members of Wilson's cabinet but also with leading Tories, helped to ensure that this arch-individualist who had little interest in questions of long-term strategy or party management became leader of the new party.[79]

From the start there were tensions. Fitt's predominant orientation towards Westminster-inspired reform of the North was at odds with Hume's increasingly close connections with the southern state. Fitt's almost instinctive class politics led him to be suspicious of Hume's social democratic philosophy. Here he shared a common suspicion of the 'f....g schoolteachers' who dominated the SDLP with Paddy Devlin, a more cerebral socialist but also a fiercely individualist and prickly individual. A republican internee during the war, Devlin had educated himself out of both nationalism and Catholicism to become a dogged and courageous exponent of socialism and secularism. He had won the Falls constituency for the NILP in the 1969 election. Fitt and Devlin insisted that any new organization should make clear its distance from traditional forms of Catholic nationalism by including in its name an identification with the North's Labour tradition, which both saw as the basis for a cross-sectarian appeal. Hume had to explain to an Irish official that the new formation would include the word 'Labour' in deference to Fitt and Devlin but asked him to assure Jack Lynch that there would be no connection between the new party and the British, Irish, or Northern Irish Labour Parties.[80] Fianna Fáil was not to be embarrassed by any outbreak of class politics in the North!

When the SDLP was launched in August 1970, Fitt emphasized its left-of-centre, non-sectarian philosophy. Its nationalism was expressed in a moderate and democratic form: 'To promote co-operation, friendship and understanding between North and South with a view to the eventual reunification of Ireland through the consent of the majority of the people in the North and South.'[81] One of the party's first policymakers has subsequently outlined the 'dream' of many members in 1970: 'to participate in a coalition government with the NILP and some liberal Unionists. Agreement within Northern Ireland might destroy many Unionists' fears [and] be a preliminary to agreement in Ireland.'[82]

However, just as the violence of August 1969 had pushed Devlin into rushing to Dublin to call for the defensive arming of northern Catholics, internment and Bloody Sunday forced a radicalization of the SDLP's attitudes to the state. In the immediate aftermath of Bloody Sunday, Hume gave an interview on Irish radio in which he said that for many people in the Bogside, 'it's a united Ireland or nothing. Alienation is pretty total.'[83] In a subsequent interview he claimed that reunification was 'a lot nearer than many people believed'.[84] Radicalization was obvious in the party's policy statement, *Towards a New Ireland*, published in September 1972, which called on Britain to make a formal declaration of intent in favour of a united Ireland and in the interim proposed that Northern Ireland be jointly ruled by Dublin and London. The document reflected the fear that the Provisionals could challenge the party for the leadership of the Catholic community.[85]

In fact, although the Provisionals had declared that 1972 would be their 'Year of Victory',[86] direct rule and the possibility of British-sponsored reforms created major problems for them. Many Catholics saw direct rule as a victory and an antechamber to more radical changes which made further republican violence unjustifiable. Even areas with strong support for the IRA, such as Andersonstown in West Belfast, developed local peace groups often linked to the Catholic Church. Such attitudes affected the IRA with reports that rank-and-file Provos in Belfast and Derry favoured a truce.[87] Pressure for a Provisional ceasefire was intensified when the Official IRA announced one in May. The Officials had been involved in a militarist competition with the Provisionals since internment. The results had been difficult to reconcile with their pretensions to non-sectarianism and the defence of working-class interests. The Derry Officials shot dead a prominent Unionist politician, Senator Barnhill, in December 1971. Then in retaliation for Bloody Sunday the Officials bombed the officers' mess of the Parachute Regiment in Aldershot killing seven people, including five female canteen workers and a Catholic chaplain. Finally, in April 1972, the Derry Officials 'executed' Ranger Best, a young Derry Catholic who had joined the British army and was home on leave. Convinced that such actions made political progress in the South impossible and could even allow the southern state to introduce internment, Goulding and a majority on the Army Council declared a cease-fire in May.[88]

Within the Provisionals there were clear signs of a North–South divide on a cease-fire. The cutting edge of the armed campaign was being provided by young working-class Catholics in Belfast, whose republicanism was more a product of the conflict with Protestants and the security forces since 1969 than any ideological commitment to a united Ireland or identification with the martyrs of 1916. Here suspicion that a cease-fire would allow the security forces to reassert their control of the IRA's base areas in North and West Belfast was strong and reflected in the scepticism of the IRA's Belfast commander, the former bookmaker Seamus Twomey, and the up-and-coming Provo strategist Gerry Adams. However, for leading members of the largely southern leadership of the Provos, including Daithi O'Connaill and Ruairi O'Bradaigh, the increasingly obvious sectarian effects of the bombing campaign, along with an exaggerated estimation of the British state's willingness to consider radical constitutional change, made a cease-fire attractive and an indefinite one was declared on 22 June.

The cease-fire was agreed in return for the granting of political status to their prisoners (some of whom were on hunger strike), the temporary release from detention of Gerry Adams, and the promise of direct talks at a high level. A six-man delegation led by Seán MacStiofain was secretly flown to London for talks with Whitelaw and senior officials. Its demands, which included a British declaration of intent to withdraw within three years, offered little to negotiate over. Whitelaw responded to MacStiofain's maximalist shopping list by pointing out that the British government was constrained by the consent provisions of the Ireland Act.[89] Within two weeks the Belfast IRA had brought the cease-fire to an end. The end of the cease-fire was followed by an intensification of the IRA's assault on Belfast, culminating on 21 July in 'Bloody Friday' when it placed twenty-six bombs in Belfast, killing eleven people and injuring 130. Seven people were killed in the city's main bus station and as the television cameras showed human remains being scooped up into black plastic bags, the Provisionals suffered a major blow to the moral credibility of their campaign. Whitelaw moved quickly to exploit popular revulsion and the 'no-go' areas in Belfast and Derry were reoccupied with a massive display of military might in 'Operation Motorman'. From this time on the Belfast IRA was increasingly subject to attrition and by the end of 1973 the organization increasingly had to centre its operations in rural areas such as South Armagh and mid-Ulster. In the South, Lynch's government adopted an increasingly tough stance with the closure of Sinn Féin's headquarters and the arrest of a number of senior republicans. In November the government dismissed the entire governing body of the Republic's television service after the showing of an interview with MacStiofain.[90]

The SDLP benefited significantly from the cease-fire and its violent aftermath. Republican willingness to halt their campaign and enter into discussions without an end to internment made it easier for the SDLP to get reinvolved in negotiations with the British and the Unionists. The utter inflexibility of the republican negotiators when they got their chance to put their demands to Whitelaw allowed them to be politically outflanked by the SDLP. The government's Green Paper, published in October, with its support for power-sharing and an 'Irish dimension' indicated that while a united Ireland might not be on the immediate agenda, northern Catholics were being offered the possibility of political gains that would have been virtually inconceivable even two years previously. That these possibilities would not be realized would be in large part the responsibility of the increasingly tough bargaining position that the SDLP adopted and whose main architect was John Hume.

In local government elections in May 1973 the SDLP showed that it had emerged as a significant political force with 13 per cent of the vote. For the first time since the death of Joe Devlin in the 1930s, a nationalist party could claim support in both the west and east of Northern Ireland as the influence of Fitt and Devlin ensured the party had a solid base in Belfast. Provisional Sinn Féin had urged a boycott of the elections and some of its strategists were concerned that the support for both the SDLP and the Republican Clubs, the political wing of the Officials, came from Provo sympathizers who rejected abstentionist tactics. The republican dilemma was even more obvious in the election for a new Assembly held in June. In these the SDLP emerged as the second-largest party with almost 160,000 votes, 22 per cent of the total, and nineteen seats.[91] Provisional unease over strategy was manifest in conflicting advice to their supporters, who were urged first to abstain and then to spoil ballot papers. A mere 1.2 per cent of ballots were spoiled and it was clear that the majority of northern nationalists had put their hopes in radical reform rather than armed struggle.

Hume, with the support of most of the SDLP Assembly members from constituencies outside Belfast, was convinced that the political fragmentation of Unionism and the British desire to build up the SDLP as a bulwark against the Provisionals meant that an 'interim' settlement combining power-sharing with a powerful Council of Ireland should be the only acceptable outcome of any negotiations. When Liam Cosgrave, the Taoiseach in the new Fine Gael–Labour coalition government, told a Conservative meeting in London that any pressure for movement on the partition issue 'would dangerously exacerbate tension and fears',[92] he provoked an angry response from the SDLP. Hume responded with a tough speech in which he advised Cosgrave's government not to underestimate its strength or to surrender its position to 'the false liberalism of placating the Unionists'.[93] SDLP delegations arrived in Dublin to make it clear that they saw Cosgrave's position as less robust than Fianna Fáil's[94] and as weakening their negotiating position with the British and the Unionists. Fearful of being portrayed as letting the 'separated brethren' down, the Irish government's official position soon shifted to one of uncritical support for Hume's analysis and prescriptions.

Sunningdale and the Ulster Workers' Council Strike

As the intense and exhausting process of inter-party talks at Stormont Castle under Whitelaw's chairmanship continued through October and November 1973, the Unionist negotiators were aware that opposition within the Protestant community was growing. On 20 November the Ulster Unionist Council narrowly turned down a proposal to reject power-sharing by 379 votes to 369. Despite the obviously precarious position of Faulkner, Hume, described by one of the most liberal of Faulkner's supporters as 'grim and unbending in negotiations',[95] remained implacable in his commitment to a Council of Ireland with substantial powers. It was SDLP insistence that 'nothing is agreed until everything is agreed' that prevented the immediate devolution of power following the successful conclusion of the talks. Instead Faulkner and his Unionist ministers in waiting had to participate in a conference with the SDLP, the Alliance Party, and the British and Irish governments to deal with the unresolved issue of the Council of Ireland.

The conference, held at the civil service college at Sunningdale in Berkshire between 6 and 9 December, was an unmitigated disaster for Faulkner's position in the Unionist community. Heath had viewed the deepening of his government's involvement in Northern Ireland affairs after direct rule as a necessary but unfortunate diversion of the time and abilities of some of his most important ministers. With the formation of the Executive his immediate inclination was to reduce the quality of his commitment. This meant the recalling of Whitelaw to Westminster to deal with the pressing problem of industrial militancy and his replacement by Francis Pym. If Whitelaw had been present at Sunningdale, his almost two years of experience in the North might have allowed him to make Heath more aware of the difficulties of Faulkner's position. As it was, the Unionist negotiators not only were confronted with the SDLP supported by a heavyweight Irish governmental team led by the Taoiseach, but also found themselves at loggerheads with Heath, who showed little patience with Unionist concerns that they were being asked to sign up to an agreement that would be unsellable at home.

Hume brushed aside the nagging concerns of his party leader that by pushing the role and powers of the Council of Ireland to the forefront of negotiations, the SDLP would make the position of Faulkner untenable. The only voice that was raised against Hume's maximalist agenda was that of Paddy Devlin, who, on seeing the full list of executive functions proposed for the Council of Ireland, exclaimed that it would result in his Unionist colleagues being hung from the lampposts when they got back to Belfast.[96] Heath's overwhelming desire for a deal and his impatience with Unionist concerns, which might have been checked by Whitelaw's knowledge of Ulster conditions, were unrestrained by Francis Pym. The result was disastrous for the new power-sharing government.

Although the extent of Unionist/SDLP differences on the functions and powers of the Council of Ireland meant that these areas were set aside for further discussion, the final communiqué, by agreeing that the Council would be created, provided Faulkner's enemies with a clear focus of attack, while the very lack of a clear definition of powers allowed the most extravagant claims to be made and believed. Faulkner had hoped for compensatory commitments from the Irish government on the removal of Articles 2 and 3 from the Irish constitution and the extradition of terrorist offenders. He got neither and even senior members of the Irish delegation feared that nationalism had been too successful at Sunningdale.[97]

On the day that the Sunningdale conference began, 600 delegates from Unionist Party constituency associations, Vanguard, the DUP, and the Orange Order agreed to form the United Ulster Unionist Council (UUUC) to oppose power-sharing. A special meeting of the UUUC on 4 January 1974, just four days after the Executive took office, passed a resolution opposing any Council of Ireland by 427 to 374 and Faulkner resigned as leader of the party. Despite this further blow to the Unionist pillar of the new devolved structures, the SDLP continued to inflame Protestant fears with claims such as that of one Assembly member, Hugh Logue, that the Council of Ireland was 'the vehicle that would trundle Unionists into a united Ireland'. Faulkner's earlier demands for constitutional recognition rebounded when on 16 January the High Court in Dublin ruled that the Irish government's recognition of the North in the agreement was 'no more than a statement of policy' with no constitutional significance.[98]

Faulkner hoped that the effective and mundane working of the new institutions would dissipate the fears of many ordinary Unionists but Heath's overriding concern with the challenge of industrial militancy in Britain impinged disastrously on Northern Ireland. Ignoring pleas from Faulkner, Gerry Fitt, and Pym that an election could be fatal for the Executive, Heath called a general election for 28 February. The UUUC, mobilizing with the slogan 'Dublin is only a Sunningdale away' and with one agreed candidate in each of the Westmister constituencies, annihilated the power-sharing parties, who compounded their problems by often putting up competing candidates in the same constituency.[99] The UUUC candidates won eleven of the North's twelve Westminster seats with 51 per cent of the total vote, while Faulkner's supporters achieved a miserable 13 per cent of the vote. The Executive had clearly lost all legitimacy with the bulk of the Unionist electorate and this is the key to understanding the British government's reaction to the unprecedented industrial action by the Ulster Workers' Council

(UWC), which was the occasion, but not the fundamental cause, of the Executive's collapse.

The UWC had been created in November 1973 by groups of loyalist trade unionists who had been involved in the discredited Loyalist Association of Workers. They were convinced that it would be easier to mobilize support against an unpopular Executive and the spectre of creeping unification associated with the Council of Ireland than it had been to protest about the internment of loyalist paramilitaries. Distrustful of most of the Unionist politicians who were opposed to Faulkner, they were determined to maintain their independence and take action with or without the politicians' blessing. Although the UWC maintained a notional separation from the main paramilitary organizations, its 'co-ordinating committee' (headed by the impressive Derry trade unionist and Vanguard activist Glen Barr) included UDA and UVF members. Its paramilitary links would be crucial in ensuring the withdrawal of labour in the first days of the strike that began on 15 May. The possible role of intimidation and violence had been one of the factors that had made the main leaders of Unionist opposition to the Executive reluctant to consider industrial action when the UWC issued its first public statement on 23 March. This threatened widespread civil disobedience unless fresh Assembly elections were held. The UUUC's response was to ignore the UWC and call for a boycott of southern goods by northern consumers instead.[100]

The motley crew of industrial militants and paramilitaries had read the popular mood better than the politicians, although even they did not expect the stunning victory that was to come. The SDLP and some leading Labour and Conservative politicians were to explain the success of the strike in terms of intimidation and the failure of the authorities to act decisively and early to keep roads open and remove the barricades erected by strike supporters. This simply ignored the extent of support for the strike in the Unionist community. Most Unionists perceived the course of events from 1968 to 1973 as one of continued political retreat, if not defeat. It was unlikely that they would accept in government those whom they considered as instrumental in bringing down the Stormont regime, especially when members of the SDLP still talked as if a united Ireland were an imminent possibility through the Council of Ireland. By the end of the first week of the strike the UWC had shut down the North's main industries and through its control of the Ballylumford power station at Larne had a stranglehold on electricity supply, which put it in a position to bring daily life to a standstill.

The new Labour administration showed no desire to confront the strikers for the sake of a terminally divided Executive; moreover the army's advice was that it would be disastrous to open up a second front against the Protestant paramilitaries at a time when its resources needed to be fully committed against the Provisionals. Harold Wilson's main contribution to the dénouement of power-sharing was a crassly mis-judged national television and radio broadcast in which he denounced the strikers as 'thugs and bullies' and their supporters as those who 'spend their lives sponging on Westminster'. Ken Bloomfield judged the broadcast 'catastrophically unhelpful' and in the days that followed even moderate Unionists sported pieces of sponge in their lapels.[101] A plan devised by John Hume, the Minister of Commerce, to use the army to take over a number of petrol stations to break the UWC's control of fuel supplies was leaked in advance by a sympathetic official—an indication of the defection *en masse* of the Protestant middle class—and the UWC announced a total shutdown of services. Faced with the possibility of the closure of hospitals and the probability of raw sewage flooding Belfast streets, the Executive resigned.[102]

Those commentators who saw in the victory of the UWC strike the emergence of a new proletarian leadership for Unionism had obviously never read Lenin's *What is to be done?*, with its powerful dissection of the limits of even the most militant forms of trade union consciousness. After the strike the UWC leadership, faced with decisions about the future, began to fragment. Sarah Nelson has described the various tendencies as follows: 'hardline Loyalists, more conciliatory, socially radical elements and people who had just not thought what constructive alternative they were aiming for'.[103] While Glen Barr, together with some leading members of the UVF, saw the UWC as the possible basis for the development of an independent working-class political grouping, the more influential groups were those dominated by support for Craig and Paisley.

Vanguard and the DUP appeared to be equal contenders in the competition to displace an Ulster Unionist Party which, although it was now firmly under the control of the right, remained enervated and demoralized after almost a decade of internecine conflict. Harry West, the bluff Fermanagh farmer whom O'Neill had sacked and Faulkner reinstated, had been elected leader of the party after Faulkner's resigna-tion. Personifying the rather inert and unimaginative conservatism of the old Unionist machine, he was no match for either Craig or Paisley. After October 1974, when he lost his Westminster seat for Fermanagh and

South Tyrone, his leadership was undermined by the increasingly important integrationist lobby led by the leader of the Ulster Unionist MPs at Westminster, the self-effacing but crafty MP for South Antrim, James Molyneaux, and his intellectual guru, the former Conservative MP for Wolverhampton, Enoch Powell, whose record of support for the Unionist cause while a Tory got him the UUUC nomination for South Down in the October 1974 Westminster general election.

Bereft of any ideas of its own for a way forward, the Wilson government arranged elections for a Constitutional Convention to consider what provision for the government of Northern Ireland was likely to command the most widespread support. The results, in May 1975, showed for the first time an Ulster Unionist Party which, although it remained the largest single party with 26 per cent of the vote and nineteen seats, had less support than the combined strength of Vanguard (13 per cent and fourteen seats) and the DUP (15 per cent and twelve seats).[104] An IRA truce and the attendant rumours of British plans for withdrawal led Craig to contemplate a radical policy shift to stabilize the situation. Through discussions with the SDLP he became convinced that post-UWC strike realism would make nationalists accept a deal confined to Northern Ireland. Even Paisley appears initially to have been receptive to Craig's idea of a voluntary coalition with the SDLP that would last for the duration of the 'national emergency' because of the intensified sectarian violence that was wracking the North at the time. However, when the proposal was made public in September it was disowned by a majority of Craig's own Vanguard colleagues, and Paisley, under the influence of Peter Robinson, then emerging as the dominant DUP figure in urban Ulster, reversed his position.[105] Craig and his supporters were suspended from the UUUC and Vanguard disappeared as a significant player in Unionist politics.

The decade after the demise of Vanguard was one in which Paisley seemed to dwarf all other contenders for the leadership of 'Protestant Ulster', and the DUP threatened to displace the Ulster Unionists as the hegemonic force within Unionism. Although Paisley made a number of miscalculations, the most significant being the abortive attempt to force the British government to return majority rule devolution through a general strike in 1977, West's party was in no condition to exploit them because of its own deep divisions on strategy between devolutionists and integrationists. The DUP's hard core of Free Presbyterian activists in its rural and small-town base areas was increasingly augmented by a group of youngish Belfast members, some of them graduates, who were extending the party's influence in the Protestant working class through involvement in community politics and local government. Lean and hungry for power, they took as their model Peter Robinson's expanding fiefdom in the Castlereagh area of East Belfast. Robinson, who was 29 when he won his first elected office for the DUP (as a councillor in Castlereagh in 1977) had been a Paisleyite activist since leaving grammar school in 1966 and his intellectual and organizational abilities had led Paisley to make him his secretary at Westminster in 1970. He became the DUP's general secretary in 1975 and played a central role in making it the most coherent and well-organized party in the North.[106] Robinson did not share the scruples of some of the Free Presbyterian members about associating with paramilitaries. While his cultivation of the UDA failed to force a change of British policy in 1977, it contributed significantly to the DUP's winning of its first Belfast constituencies in the Westminster general election of 1979, when Robinson defeated Bill Craig for East Belfast and his party colleague Johnny McQuade won North Belfast.[107] The tensions between the original hard core of Paisleyism, the conservative fundamentalists of areas such as North Antrim, and Robinson's more pragmatic, left-of-centre populism were easily enough contained through a combination of the integrating force of Paisley's personality and the healing balm of electoral success.

The success was certainly spectacular. Between the local government elections of 1973 and 1981 the DUP had expanded its number of councillors from twenty-one (4 per cent of the vote) to 142 (26.6 per cent), fractionally ahead of the UUP. From a narrow base, with representation in only seven of the North's twenty-six local authorities, the party was now represented on every council in Northern Ireland. Most spectacular was its advance in Belfast: from two seats to fifteen, making it the largest party on the council.[108] But it was the first direct election to the European Parliament in 1979 that came to symbolize Paisley's apparently hegemonic influence on Protestant Ulster. With Northern Ireland treated as one constituency, his own gargantuan appetite for electioneering—he claimed to have covered 122 miles on foot and 4,000 miles by car[109]—and the DUP's polished election machine, he delivered a devastating blow to the UUP, which had put up two candidates, John Taylor and Harry West. With 170,688 votes, 29.8 per cent of the total, Paisley topped the poll and claimed that he now spoke for a clear majority of the Unionist population. Between them the two UUP candidates obtained 125,169 votes, 22 per cent. West's particularly weak performance, which reflected his marked disinclination to pursue an active canvass, led to his resignation as leader of the UUP. A convinced devolutionist, his replacement by Molyneaux marked another stage in the increasingly integrationist tone of the party.

Padraig O'Malley, at this time of DUP ascendancy, wrote of Paisley:

he is the personification of the 'fearful Protestant', the embodiment of the Scots-Presbyterian tradition of uncompromising Calvinism that has always been the bedrock of militant Protestant opposition to a united Ireland. It is a tradition shaped by a siege mentality, and the almost obsessive compulsion to confirm the need for unyielding vigilance.[110]

This overplays the religious and irrational component in Paisleyism's success, important though it was, at the expense of those elements of the political conjuncture that were favourable to the DUP. The return of the Tories in 1979 had replaced a period of 'positive direct rule' under Roy Mason with another search for a devolutionary settlement under his successor Humphrey Atkins. Molyneaux's integrationist agenda—which his friendship with Mrs Thatcher's Northern Ireland spokesman, Airey Neave, had encouraged him to believe would be indulged when the Tories returned to power—had been pointedly ignored. When Atkins' initiative failed, in part because Molyneaux had cold-shouldered it, a resentful Thatcher turned towards an Anglo-Irish framework with a summit in Dublin with Charles Haughey in December 1980, in which she agreed to new institutional structures to reflect the 'unique relation ship' between the two islands and to further meetings to give 'special consideration to the totality of relations within these islands'. While Molyneaux continued to reassure his followers that he had the ear of the British Prime Minister, Paisley scented betrayal and launched the 'Carson Trail', a series of paramilitary-style rallies in which he vowed to go to any lengths to resist Thatcherite 'treachery'.

Fighting the Long War: British Policy 1974–85

Although by the time of direct rule a number of senior Conservative politicians such as Peter Carrington and William Whitelaw had come to agree with Harold Wilson that the only ultimate solution was unity, it was recognized that this would be a long-term process. Power-sharing devolution and an 'Irish Dimension' would, it was hoped, provide interim structures that, while providing stability, could be open to constitutional change. The collapse of the Sunningdale initiative had led

Wilson to set up a small, high-powered policy review group to take a radical look at Northern Ireland policy. Repartition, dominion status, and what Wilson called his 'nuclear option' of withdrawal were all considered. However, all were eventually rejected on the basis that they would most likely aggravate the problem.[111] Little hope had been vested in the possibility of northern politicians working out an agreement among themselves through the Convention, and as British policy-makers appeared to flounder rumours of a secret commitment to withdrawal gained currency.

The rumours had their origins in secret negotiations between British officials and the leadership of the Provisional IRA, which resulted in an IRA cease-fire that lasted for most of 1975. Ruairí Ó'Brádaigh and his allies in the leadership of the Provisionals had seen the UWC strike as a watershed that 'threw British policy totally into the melting pot . . . The word coming through was that every solution was up for consideration.'[112] The 'word' was conveyed by various officials from the Foreign Office and the security services, working out of Laneside, a nineteenth-century mansion on the shores of Belfast Lough where the Political Affairs section of the Northern Ireland Office preferred to have its meetings with paramilitaries away from possible media intrusion. The British officials did not discourage the Provisional belief that the Convention had been set up in the expectation that it would fail through loyalist intransigence, thus providing the British government with the justification for extrication. There is some evidence that the officials involved may have gone as far as talking about the 'structures of disengagement'.[113]

The British had hoped that a successful political initiative would enable the SDLP to politically marginalize the republicans and make their military defeat easier. Since Operation Motorman the Provisionals' campaign in Belfast and Derry had been curtailed radically and the political developments of 1973 put the IRA on the defensive. The level of violence had reduced considerably. With 470 deaths and over 10,000 recorded shootings, 1972 was by far the worst year in three decades of the 'Troubles'. By 1974 the number of deaths had fallen to 220 and shootings were down by two-thirds. In 1972, 105 British soldiers had been killed while by 1974 the figure was thirty.[114] However, the IRA compensated for setbacks in its urban strongholds by intensifying its campaign in rural areas such as mid-Ulster and south Armagh. It had also initiated a bombing campaign in England in 1973 to compensate for being forced on the defensive in the North and to attempt to galvanize the undoubtedly strong 'Troops Out' sentiment in British public opinion. The first deaths occurred when a bomb on a coach carrying British soldiers killed twelve people in February 1974. Bombings of pubs that were claimed to be 'military targets' because they were used by soldiers followed, with deaths and dozens of injured at Guildford and Woolwich. The culmination of this first mainland campaign was the bombing of the *Mulberry Bush* and the *Tavern in the Town* pubs in Birmingham on 21 November 1974 in which nineteen people were killed and 182 injured.[115]

Although the republicans were contained militarily, their continued capacity for violence, along with the weakening of the political arm of counter-insurgency strategy with the collapse of the power-sharing initiative, made the possibility of a cease-fire very attractive for the British. The cease-fire allowed the political embarrassment of internment to be ended. The murder and intimidation of witnesses and jurors had already resulted in the introduction of so-called Diplock Courts (named after Lord Diplock who, in 1973, had chaired a commission to investigate alternatives to internment), where persons accused of 'scheduled offences', that is those of a terrorist nature, could be tried in the absence of a jury. The Emergency Provisions Act of 1973, which introduced these courts, also repealed the Special Powers Act while re-enacting many of its provisions. Like the Prevention of Terrorism Act introduced after the Birmingham bombs, which allowed for detention for up to seven days and provided for the exclusion from the rest of the UK of 'undesirables' from the North, it was to apply for one year but was renewable annually. Both pieces of legislation became key components of the state's anti-terrorist strategy. Although they had a real effect in weakening paramilitary structures, they inevitably generated resentment in those Catholic working-class areas where they were often implemented in a heavy-handed and indiscriminate manner.[116]

The cease-fire also allowed the shift to a security strategy of 'Ulsterization' under which the primacy of the British army was replaced by the leading role of the RUC and the Ulster Defence Regiment. While this avoided the possibility of a 'Vietnam syndrome' in British politics, its effect in deepening sectarian divisions in Northern Ireland cannot be overemphasized. In the early 1970s there were over 23,000 British soldiers in Northern Ireland compared with 7,000 full-time and part-time police officers and 7,500 in the locally recruited Ulster Defence Regiment. By the end of the 1980s the number of British soldiers had declined to around 10,000 while the RUC had increased to 11,500 with the UDR maintaining its size at 7,500.[117] After 1976, while the IRA was still capable of dealing the British army occasional major blows—most spectacularly at Narrow Water near Warrenpoint in county Down in 1979 when its bombs killed eighteen soldiers—its most relentless campaign was aimed at local members of the security forces. These were largely Protestant and often, when part-timers, easy targets as they carried out their jobs as bus drivers, milkmen, and farm labourers. As the 'anti-imperialist struggle' increasingly killed Protestant members of the Irish working class, its effects on community relations began to concern even some members of the IRA's leadership, who were repulsed by the brutal and casual sectarianism of many of their northern comrades.[118]

Along with Ulsterization went a policy of criminalizing the IRA. The central development here was the ending of the system of political status, which, since 1972, had allowed paramilitary prisoners to organize their day-to-day existence in prison, including wearing their own clothes and running education classes instead of having to do the prison work doled out to 'ordinary decent criminals'. During the cease-fire Merlyn Rees announced that political status would be ended for all newly convicted paramilitary prisoners. With the IRA leadership confident that all its prisoners would soon be released as part of the process of British withdrawal, there was only the most formalistic of protests from republicans.[119]

Rees's successor as Secretary of State, the tough ex-miner Roy Mason, pursued the policies of criminalization and Ulsterization with a crude vigour. At his first press conference in September 1976 he announced that the IRA was 'reeling'.[120] A new Chief Constable, Kenneth Newman, who had come from the Metropolitan Police to implement the policy of police primacy, oversaw a process through which a major expansion of resources was focused on four new regional crime squads targeted at the IRA's most active units. Suspects were held under detention orders for up to seven days at RUC holding centres at Castlereagh in East Belfast and Gough Barracks, Armagh. Making use of Lord Diplock's permissive recommendation that confessions made under interrogation could be accepted unless it was proved that they had been extracted by torture, the RUC was able to deal such serious blows to the IRA that an IRA 'Staff Report' captured by the police in Dublin referred to it as 'contributing to our defeat'.[121] By the end of 1977 Mason was claiming that 'the tide had turned against the terrorists and the message for 1978 is one of real hope'.[122] In fact, 1978 was to see clear signs that the Provisionals had been able to regroup and reorganize.

The prime architect of the reorganization and strategic redirection of the Provisionals was Gerry Adams. A senior member of the Belfast IRA when he was re-arrested in July 1973, Adams spent the next four years in the IRA compounds at the Long Kesh prison. Here he took an increasingly critical line against the still largely southern leadership of the Provisionals. This in part reflected the hard sectarian edge of northern republicanism that detected in the southerners' *Eire Nua* document a deplorable tendency to accommodate Unionists. There was also a realistic assessment that the British state was not in the process of withdrawing from the North. But the main criticism that Adams and his supporters levelled against the leadership was their support for the cease-fire which had divided and demoralized the IRA. With their main targets temporarily out of reach, sections of the IRA became unofficially involved in violent conflict with the Official IRA who themselves had recently suffered a split with a more militaristic and ultra-leftist group who founded an Irish Republican Socialist Party with its own military wing, the Irish National Liberation Army. Even more politically damaging to the Provisionals was the sectarian settling of accounts with Protestant paramilitaries who had intensified their activities during the cease-fire. Acting under the flag of convenience of 'South Armagh Republican Action Force', Provisionals shot dead six Protestants in Tullyvallen Orange Hall in September 1975 and on 5 January 1976 stopped a minibus carrying workers, separated out the Protestants and machine-gunned them, killing ten. The eruption of support for a grass-roots anti-violence movement, the Peace People, after a car driven by an IRA man attempting to escape from soldiers ploughed into a Catholic mother and her four children in West Belfast, killing three of the children, was also a worrying sign of a potential drying up of toleration for the 'armed struggle' in Provisional heartlands.

The basis for Adams's rise to a dominant position in the republican movement was his role in ensuring that the IRA recovered from its near defeat in the mid 1970s. He promoted a reorganization of the IRA, replacing its old structure of geographically based brigades, battalions, and companies with small Active Service Units, whose members would be drawn from different areas for a specific task such as assassination or robbery. This cellular structure was designed to be less vulnerable to infiltration and disruption by the security forces. A new Northern Command was established, which ensured that Adams and his allies controlled the main area of IRA operations. The northerners made it clear that they did not expect an imminent British withdrawal but were prepared for a 'Long War' that could last for two decades or more. IRA activity would be refined and increasingly take the form of 'armed propaganda' aimed at a process of attrition of the British will to remain in the North.

The 'Long War' would be fought as much politically as militarily and Adams looked enviously at his rivals in the Officials who were enjoying increasing success as a left-wing political force in the South. He advocated that Sinn Féin become a campaigning political party rather than simply an IRA support organization. Adams and some of his lieutenants, for example Tom Hartley and Danny Morrison, adopted an increasingly left-wing language, which made them allies on the left wing of the British Labour Party. However, their major political breakthrough would come about, not because of this rather superficial radicalism, but through the unleashing of much more primordial passions in the North.

Mason had tried to buttress his robust security policies with a strong commitment to use the public sector and state investment to undermine the economic and social deprivation that he was convinced exacerbated communal conflict: 'The terrorists needed unhappiness and hopelessness'.[123] In the 1960s Northern Ireland had a thriving manufacturing sector, employing over 30 per cent of the workforce and returning the highest rates of productivity growth among the UK regions. The engine driving this impressive performance was the large number of multinationals that came to the region in this decade and the still sizeable indigenous industrial base in shipbuilding, aircraft production, and textiles. The twin pillars of this success were badly hit by the world-wide economic recession of the 1970s. The multinationals left the region as quickly as they had arrived and the international recession hit indigenous industry hard. As a result of this industrial collapse, employment in manufacturing fell to 18 per cent of the overall workforce and unemployment rose significantly.[124] In 1976 unemployment in the North, at 10 per cent, was double the national rate and in some areas in Catholic West Belfast the rate amongst adult males was over 50 per cent.[125]

Mason's response was to try to follow the recommendations of the Quigley Report, produced by four senior civil servants in 1976, which proposed a heavily subsidized economy with the state playing a much greater role until market conditions improved. Employment in the public sector increased by over 50 per cent during the 1970s compared to 22 per cent in the UK as a whole and Mason's period at the Northern Ireland Office accounted for a substantial part of this.[126] So strong was his economistic view of the causes of support for violence that he persuaded the cabinet to support an extremely high-risk venture in which an American entrepreneur proposed to build a futuristic sports car on a green-field site in West Belfast. The project eventually collapsed when Mrs Thatcher was in office in part because of a lack of demand for its cars but also because of the embezzling activities of its founder, John Delorean, who had siphoned off millions of pounds of public money for his private use.[127]

Mason's strong commitment to direct rule as an acceptable interim form of governing Northern Ireland together with his economic and social activism endeared him to many Unionists but did little to counter an increasingly militant tone in nationalist politics, reflected in John Hume's ascendancy in the SDLP. Hume, who as Minister of Commerce had denounced the UWC strike as a fascist takeover,[128] blamed the Wilson government for political cowardice in not standing firm and in using troops to break it. The year 1974 now entered the Irish nationalist chronology of shameful British capitulations to loyalist threats, along with 1912 and 1921. Although Fitt and Devlin had been prepared to respond to Craig's proposals for a voluntary coalition during the Convention, Hume was hostile. Even if Craig had been able to win the support of Unionists for voluntary coalition, the SDLP would probably have split over participation in what Hume and many of its members would have seen as a 'partitionist' administration.[129] The defeat of Craig's proposal ensured that the SDLP continued to shift in a more traditionally nationalist direction. At their conference in 1976 a motion calling for a British declaration of intent to withdraw was only narrowly defeated.[130]

Hume, who realized the dangers for the party of adopting a policy that would make it indistinguishable from the Provisionals, countered with a proposal for a 'third way' between the constitutional status quo and British withdrawal. This 'agreed Ireland' would be the result of a process beginning with a statement from the British government that 'its objective in Ireland was the bringing together of both Irish traditions in reconciliation and agreement'.[131] Subsequent talks amongst the northern parties should be jointly chaired by the British and Irish governments. By this time Hume had begun the process of constructing a coalition of important allies in Europe and the US which he hoped to mobilize to achieve sufficient pressure on Britain to bring a shift in policy. All this was too much for Paddy Devlin, who detected behind the language of 'agreement' and 'process' an iron determination to have the British state 'educate' the Protestants as to what their true interests were. For Devlin the essence of 'Hume-speak' was the desire to impose a settlement over the heads of the Unionist population. He resigned from the SDLP in 1977 and was soon followed by Fitt.

The 'greening' of the SDLP in 1978–9 was accelerated by increasing evidence that some RUC officers had brutalized suspects in Castlereagh and the fear that British policy was taking an integrationist direction. The Callaghan government's increasing vulnerability in the House of Commons led to negotiations with James Molyneaux to obtain Unionist votes and produced a commitment to deal with Northern Ireland's under-representation at Westminster. The promise of more seats enraged the SDLP and strengthened John Hume's argument that the conflict could only be resolved through a process of internationalization involving the US and the Irish government.

However, even with this alienation of mainstream nationalists, the Provisionals faced the new Tory government with little evidence that, despite a successful reorganization of their military machine, they had overcome their political weakness. This was in part a reflection of popular revulsion at some of their actions, particularly the fire-bombing of the La Mon House Hotel in county Down on 17 February 1978 when twelve people were incinerated. Gerry Adams recalls being 'depressed' at the carnage and fearing that his two years of work at reviving the Provisionals was in danger of going down the drain.[132] The victory of John Hume in the election for the European parliament in June 1979, in which he had come second to Paisley with almost a quarter of the votes cast, seemed to emphasize republicans' political irrelevance. Yet within two years, more by accident than by calculation, Adams would find himself in a position to launch an unprecedented political breakthrough for Sinn Féin.

A hint of what was to come was the 38,000 voters, 6 per cent of the total, in the European poll who had supported the former student revolutionary Bernadette McAliskey, née Devlin. She had stood as an independent supporting the demands of republican prisoners for political status. Since 1976 those convicted of terrorist offences had been placed in new cellular accommodation at what was now called the Maze prison, although republicans continued to refer to it as Long Kesh. In protest they had first refused to wear prison clothes, covering themselves with blankets, and subsequently radicalized their campaign by smearing the walls of their cells with excrement. By 1978 there were over 300 prisoners involved in the 'dirty protest'. Despite the fact that the squalor was self-inflicted and the Provisionals on the outside were carrying on a campaign of assassinating prison officers, in which eighteen were killed between 1976 and 1980,[33] the strongly nationalistic Archbishop of Armagh and Primate of All Ireland, Dr Tomas O Fiaich, denounced the H Blocks as 'unfit for animals' and compared them unfavourably with the sewers of Calcutta. Yet potent though the mixture of religion and nationalism that this traditionalist cleric embodied was, it did not acquire an overwhelming power until the IRA prisoners decided, against the advice of their leaders on the outside, to go on hunger strike. The strike, which began in October 1980, was called off after fifty-three days when it seemed that concessions were coming. When they did not materialize a second, more determined strike led by Bobby Sands, the Provisionals' Commanding Officer in the Maze, began in March 1981.

Marches in support of the prisoners, which prior to the hunger strikes had brought out a few hundred from the republican heartlands, now numbered tens of thousands motivated by what one commentator described as a 'tribal voice of martyrdom deeply embedded in the Gaelic, catholic nationalist tradition'.[134] By dying for their cause in this way, Sands and his comrades succeeded in overlaying the reality of the Provisionals' role as the main agency of violent death in the North with the cloak of victimhood. The death of Frank Maguire, the MP for Fermanagh and South Tyrone who was a republican sympathizer, provided an opportunity for a political breakthrough.

The normally cautious Adams was extremely nervous about putting forward a prisoners' candidate and only decided to do so after Bernadette McAliskey had expressed an interest in running as an independent. Bobby Sands was the choice. In a constituency evenly balanced between nationalists and Unionists, a decision by the SDLP to stand would have denied the hunger striker victory. Instead, responding to the emotional upsurge of support for the hunger strikers, the party decided not to enter the contest. With a turnout of 87 per cent Sands won by 30,492 votes to 29,046 for the Ulster Unionist Harry West.[135] Sands' victory was a propaganda coup of major proportions and it was soon followed by more gains as first Sands and then nine of his comrades died. By the time the hunger strikes were called off in October 1981, two hunger strikers had been elected to the Dáil and Sands' election agent, Owen Carron, had won the by-election caused by his death. Mrs Thatcher had kept an inflexible position throughout, maintaining 'Crime is crime is crime, it's not political.' In doing so she may have won the battle and lost the war. A more flexible position would have exposed the increasingly rigid position adopted by Gerry Adams and the republican leadership who sabotaged various attempts by clerics and the Irish government to broker a compromise.[136] Instead the 100,000 who turned out for Sands' funeral on 7 May demonstrated the political harvest that republicans would reap from this series of agonizing and drawn-out suicides. In the election for a new Assembly in Northern Ireland in 1982, Sinn Féin won 10 per cent of the vote to the SDLP's 18 per cent. In a politically even more significant result, they won 13 per cent in the 1983 Westminster election to the SDLP's 17 per cent and Gerry Adams defeated Gerry Fitt to become MP for West Belfast. The party of constitutional nationalism had paid a heavy price for its loss of nerve in Fermanagh and South Tyrone.

Fears of the imminent demise of constitutional nationalism propelled Mrs Thatcher towards the most radical British initiative on Ireland since partition. Ironically, although it was her mishandling of the hunger - strikes that had done so much to transform the political fortunes of republicanism, it would be the Unionist community, many of whom had applauded her hard line on the hunger strikers, who would be the main political losers from the political repercussions of the ten deaths.

The fact that Mrs Thatcher's close friend and former Northern Ireland spokesman Airey Neave had been a staunch ally of the Ulster Unionist Party and a supporter of integration had encouraged James Molyneaux in an uncritical faith in Thatcher's self-proclaimed 'Unionist instincts'.[137] But although she shared Neave's scepticism about a power-sharing deal between parties who had such conflicting national aspirations, she did not believe in the feasibility of any policy initiative that would, like integration, be rejected by the Dublin government. Concerned above all with the fact that Northern Ireland was the only place in the world where British soldiers were losing their lives, she looked to political leaders in the Republic for more co-operation in the intelligence, security, and judicial fields. It was this that had motivated her 1980 summit with Haughey and the subsequent agreement with Garret FitzGerald to establish an Anglo-Irish Inter-Governmental Council in November 1981. Although the refusal of Haughey's government to support European Union sanctions against Argentina during the Falklands War in 1982 had temporarily disrupted the emerging Anglo-Irish axis, FitzGerald's return to power, coinciding as it did with the eruption of Sinn Féin into Northern Irish politics, led to a renewed and more intensive engagement.

The negotiations that led to the signing of the Anglo-Irish Agreement by Thatcher and FitzGerald at Hillsborough Castle on 15 November

1985 had taken two years to complete and although the leader of the SDLP was kept in close touch with their contents by the Irish government throughout, the leaders of Unionism were excluded from the process. For Thatcher the prize was to be enhanced security co-operation from the Republic and the possibility that the majority of northern nationalists would support or acquiesce in the constitutional framework of the state in which they lived. The price she was willing to pay was a new role for the Republic in the governance of Northern Ireland.

Thatcher was adamant that formal British sovereignty over Northern Ireland was untouchable and ruled out FitzGerald's favoured option of joint authority. However, senior British officials, including the Cabinet Secretary, Sir Robert Armstrong, and the Foreign Secretary, Sir Geoffery Howe, were in favour of a radical initiative that would undermine the republican challenge even at the cost of Unionist outrage. They represented a section of opinion in Whitehall that saw the initiative as a first step in the process of decoupling Northern Ireland from the rest of the UK, precisely because the province was a drain on the political and economic resources of the British state.

At the time of her summit with FitzGerald in November 1984, when she publicly rejected all three constitutional options proposed by the New Ireland Forum, it appeared that Mrs Thatcher had turned her back on any notion of a new departure in Northern Ireland policy. It was certainly the case that her increasing conviction that the Republic would not be able to offer constitutional recognition of a new dispensation in Northern Ireland by removing Articles 2 and 3 from its constitution had made her more reluctant to innovate. The IRA's bombing of the Grand Hotel in Brighton during the Tory Party conference in October, which nearly killed her and did kill several leading Conservatives, had the same effect. It was Mrs Thatcher's ardent pursuit of the 'special relationship' with Washington that allowed the Anglo-Irish initiative to be resurrected.

Up until the 1960s the 'special relationship' had made US presidents reluctant to voice opinions on Northern Ireland and the State Department was regarded by Irish diplomats as having a pro-British bias on the issue of partition. However, during the 1970s the Department of Foreign Affairs under FitzGerald had made a concerted effort to increase Irish influence in Washington in order to marginalize support for the IRA and increase the influence of constitutional nationalism. Together with John Hume, FitzGerald and Seán Donlon, the Irish Ambassador, had built up a powerful support base on Capital Hill centred on four influential Irish-American politicians: Senators Edward Kennedy and Daniel Moynihan,

Governor Hugh Carey of New York, and Speaker of the House of Representatives, 'Tip' O'Neill. The 'Four Horsemen' had issued a joint statement on St Patrick's Day 1978 criticizing the lack of political progress under direct rule and alleging violations of civil rights by the security forces. They had been responsible for President Carter's unprecedented declaration that the US would support a deal in Northern Ireland involving the Irish government. Most worryingly for London, it was their pressure that was behind the decision of the State Department in 1979 to suspend the sale of handguns to the RUC.[138] It was US pressure that had led Thatcher, very much against her own instincts, to promote all-party devolution talks under her first Secretary of State for Northern Ireland, Humphrey Atkins. It was US intervention that proved decisive in getting stalled negotiations restarted after Thatcher's post-Forum fulminations. Speaker O'Neill wrote to Reagan shortly before a Thatcher–Reagan summit in December 1984 urging him not to tolerate British retrenchment. O'Neill had unprecedented leverage with Reagan because of his record of opposition to US funding of the 'Contras'—the counter-revolutionaries fighting against the Sandinista government in Nicaragua. The muting of O'Neill's criticism on Nicaragua was the price of the Irish state's most important political advance in relation to Northern Ireland since partition.[139]

At the core of the Agreement was the creation of an Anglo-Irish Inter-Governmental Council jointly chaired by the Secretary of State for Northern Ireland and the Irish Minister of Foreign Affairs. It was to be serviced by a joint secretariat of Irish and NIO officials, which the Irish government insisted be based in Maryfield in the suburbs of Belfast. The Conference was to deal on a regular basis with political, security, and legal matters, including the administration of justice and the promotion of cross-border co-operation. The British government committed itself, in what was an international treaty, to make 'determined efforts' to resolve any differences that arose within the Council. Although all this fell short of joint authority, the British claim that it was simply an 'institutionalization' of normal consultation with Dublin was not taken seriously in the Irish capital where the import of the Agreement was accurately summed up by an *Irish Times* political correspondent as 'a foothold in decisions governing Northern Ireland'.[140] Writing in August 1985, John Cole, the BBC's political editor and Ulster man, referred to the 'booby prize' that awaited Anglo-Irish strategy: 'The booby prize is when the Agreement is not good enough to attract the Nationalists and worrying enough to send the Unionists over the top.'[141]

It was soon clear that Mrs Thatcher had indeed won the booby prize. The Unionist community in Northern Ireland was united in angry rejection of the Agreement, or 'Diktat' as it was almost instantly christened. At the same time, although the expanding Catholic middle class greeted direct rule with a Dublin input as an ideal political framework, the core areas of working-class support for the IRA showed little sign of being impressed with the new dispensation. Although Sinn Féin support had peaked before the Agreement, there was no sign that it was now threatened by an electoral meltdown while IRA activity continued unabated and the actual level of violence increased. However, while the Agreement was initially denounced by republicans as part of a British counter-insurgency strategy, it would soon contribute to a major rethinking of republican strategy.

9

Ireland in Flux: the Republic 1973–2002

Industrialization by Invitation

In the thirty years after 1970 the economy and society of the Republic underwent a radical transformation that would have the unintended effect of making a historic compromise between the main political traditions on the island at last a real possibility. The prerequisite for this shift was the Lemass–Whitaker policy watershed in 1958–9 and the subsequent activist role of the state in the restructuring of the economy through its promotion of an export-orientated development strategy and the attraction of foreign direct investment. The structure of employment was transformed. The number at work in agriculture continued its long-term decline and the share of agricultural employment fell from 26 per cent in 1971 to just over 11 per cent in 1995. By 1996 the numbers at work in agriculture had fallen to 136,000, representing a decline of 50 per cent over the twenty-five years since 1971.

Persons at work by sector 1971–95 (%)[1]

	1971	1981	1991	1995
Agriculture	25.9	17.1	13.7	11.3
Manufacturing	23.1	22.9	21.7	21.2
Building	8.0	8.8	6.9	6.6
Transport	5.7	6.1	5.9	6.2
Distribution	13.6	14.6	15.1	15.0
Other market services	11.4	13.5	17.9	} 39.7
Non-market services	12.3	17.0	18.8	
TOTAL	100.0	100.0	100.0	100.0
Number (1,000)	1,049.4	1,145.9	1,134.0	1,233.6

The Republic was one of the few EU countries in which manufacturing employment did not shrink drastically in the 1970s and 1980s. This produced a major transition in the economic history of the island, where there was a shift in the primary locus of industrial activity from the North to the South. By 1977 the Republic had caught up with the North in terms of manufacturing output per head and by 1984 it was 60 per cent higher than in Northern Ireland. As Northern Ireland was labelled a stagnant 'workhouse economy' in the 1980s, when growth in manufacturing output averaged 0.1 per cent per annum, the Republic's rate of growth was 6 per cent per annum.[2] This impressive performance, together with a substantial expansion of the public sector, made the two decades after 1960 a period of unprecedented economic expansion and material improvements, particularly in comparison with the bleak and stagnant 1950s. GDP grew at 4 per cent per annum and real personable disposable income more than doubled by 1980.[3]

This improvement in economic performance was largely dependent on the growing number of branch plants of foreign companies attracted to the Republic by an extremely favourable tax regime and relatively low wages. By 1980 foreign-owned firms, predominantly from the USA but with strong representation from other European countries, accounted for one-third of employment in the manufacturing sector and 70 per cent of exports of manufactured goods.[4] Capital intensive and focused increasingly on high technology areas such as chemicals, office equipment, and instrument engineering, the experience of this sector was in stark contrast to that of traditional, indigenous industries such as textiles, clothing, and footwear. But integration into the world economy also increased the Republic's vulnerability to foreign competition and any significant shocks to the global system.

The Lynch government's White Paper of January 1972, which presented the case for membership of the EEC, had predicted that any jobs lost in the traditional sector would be more than compensated for by the additional employment created by foreign investment attracted to Ireland by the prospect of access to the wider EEC market.[5] This proved over-optimistic. The further dismantling of protection tended to snuff out rather than stimulate native Irish industry. By 1980 imports accounted for almost two-thirds of the sales of manufactured goods compared to about a third in 1960. The IDA could point to the development of the foreign-controlled electronics sector, which more than doubled its workforce in the decade after 1973. But in the same period employment in the traditional industries of clothing, textiles, and footwear declined by 40 per cent.[6]

Such problems were exacerbated by the more unstable international economic environment in the 1970s and 1980s. The five-fold increase in oil prices after the 1973 Yom Kippur War pushed up inflation and exercised a deflationary effect on demand in oil-importing countries. It had a particularly strong impact on the Republic, which was almost entirely dependent on imported energy sources. A fresh surge in oil prices in 1979 helped to precipitate a major international recession. This reduced the amount of internationally mobile investment at a time when Ireland was experiencing increased competition for a shrinking amount of funds. The development since the 1960s of a number of low-wage, newly industrializing countries as potential sites for investment, combined with rising labour costs, eroded Ireland's attractiveness. Its pull as a low-wage export platform for US firms wanting access to the EEC had been undermined by the accessions of Greece, Portugal, and Spain.

This deterioration in the international environment occurred at a time when demographic changes were putting increasing pressure on the economy's job-creating capacity. The census of 1971 registered the first increase in the population for the twenty-six counties since partition and this trend was maintained in 1981, when the census showed an annual rate of increase of 14.4 per 1,000 compared with 5.5 during the 1960s. The improved economic conditions of the 1960s and early 1970s encouraged more people to remain in the country, and former emigrants and their children also began to return to Ireland resulting in a net immigration figure of 100,000 for the 1970s. A late Irish 'baby boom' was another by-product of economic optimism which weakened the unique Irish pattern of very late marriage.[7] Ireland's rate of natural increase was six times that of the EEC average during the 1970s and by the beginning of the 1980s the Irish birth rate at 21 per 1,000 was far in excess of the European average, which was 12.[8] By the end of the 1970s it was calculated that 20,000 new jobs a year were needed just to deal with new entrants to the labour force. This compared with the annual average of 17,200 new jobs created during the decade.[9] The Fianna Fáil government, which came to power in 1977, sought to deal with the shortfall by expanding public sector employment, financing this through borrowing and creating a major problem of state indebtedness by the beginning of the 1980s. The sense of a national crisis that gripped the country at the time was reflected in a period of unprecedented political instability.

The National Coalition 1973–7

The initial response of Fianna Fáil to the signs of deteriorating conditions was to maintain the optimistic assumption of the 1960s that all the economic problems would be solved by a new and long-lasting expansion, which it was the responsibility of the state to kick-start. George Colley, who had replaced Haughey as Minister of Finance after the Arms Crisis, ignored the warning of T. K. Whitaker, now Governor of the Central Bank, and, despite the existence of rising inflation, made a radical departure from financial orthodoxy in his budget of 1972 by running a deficit on current account. His justifications were that the economy was running well below capacity, that unemployment was high, and that 'economic buoyancy' was needed to deal with the demands of adaptation to EEC membership, and these arguments were unlikely to be contested by the Labour Party.

More surprising was Fine Gael's enthusiastic endorsement of the new principle.[10] Although the party had been rescued from its dire condition in the 1940s by the experience of coalition government, the radical shift in Fianna Fáil's economic policies had removed one of the party's main areas of policy distinctiveness. Lemass's proclaimed desire for a more positive engagement with the North had a similar effect. The departure from the scene of increasing numbers of politicians from the Civil War generation raised fundamental questions for a party that seemed to have increasingly little left to define it, apart from a widespread perception that it was in politics to defend the interests of big farmers, merchants, and professionals. This unfavourable image was complemented by the part-time and often amateurish ethos of many of its TDs.

When de Valera retired, Fine Gael's leadership was still an uneasy duopoly with Richard Mulcahy as president of the party in the country and John A. Costello as leader in the Dáil when his busy professional life as a barrister permitted. When Mulcahy retired in 1959, a majority of the party in the Dáil rebuffed Costello's plea that he should now combine the two roles while maintaining his legal practice and James Dillon was elected leader. Dillon had been a critic of the many part-timers in the upper reaches of the parliamentary party and favoured a modernized and professional party organization. However, his modernizing ideas did not extend much beyond party organization. Although he would have preferred Ireland to move from isolation towards a 'White Commonwealth Alliance' with the Britain, the USA, Canada, and the other dominions, his past record of opposition to neutrality and his staunch anti-communism made him a supporter of moves to join the EEC which, its critics claimed, would ultimately involve Ireland in some sort of military alliance. On issues of economic and social policy he was, as an American diplomat put it, 'cast in an Edwardian mould'.[11] He was ideologically and temperamentally profoundly out of tune with the Lemassian themes of industrial development and the need for planning. His position as Minister of Agriculture in both the inter-party governments reflected his deep, almost philosophical, conviction that agriculture would always be Ireland's prime source of wealth and his scepticism about whether a country with few natural resources for industrial development could sustain the ambitious vistas set out by Lemass. He was also resolutely pre-Keynesian in his views on the role of the state in the economy and of anything that smacked of the welfare state or 'socialism'.

Dillon's leadership was seen as damagingly conservative by an influential group of younger party members led by Declan Costello. Like his leading acolyte, Garret FitzGerald, Costello was a son of the party's aristocracy: his father was a former Taoiseach while FitzGerald's had been Minister of External Affairs in the first Cumann na nGaedheal government. Costello was one of that rare breed: an intellectual in Dáil politics. He had created the Fine Gael Research and Information Centre in 1957 and through it and the *National Observer*, a newspaper that he had founded, he promoted the idea that Fine Gael needed a new, left-of-centre identity.[12] Fine Gael's defeat in two by-elections in 1964 weakened Dillon's capacity to resist the left and Costello was able to persuade the Fine Gael parliamentary party to adopt a resolution supporting a 'more just social order' and 'a more equitable distribution of the nation's wealth'.[13] The party accepted Costello's *Just Society* programme during the 1965 election campaign. It upstaged Fianna Fáil with its proposals for a new Department of Economic Affairs, an incomes policy, state control of the credit policies of the commercial banks, and a social development strategy to complement economic modernization with proposals for a free medical service and higher spending on housing and education.

Although the *Just Society* caught the popular imagination, especially among younger voters, there remained a fundamental question mark over the extent and the depth of the party's commitment to Costello's philosophy. Dillon assured journalists on the day the *Just Society* document was published that Fine Gael remained 'a party of private enterprise' and many in the party would have agreed with Senator

E. A. McGuire, the owner of Brown Thomas, Dublin's major department store, that Costello's proposals were 'pure socialism of the most dictatorial kind'.[14]

If radical policies demanded a radical leader, then Dillon's successor was an undoubted improvement. Liam Cosgrave, son of W. T. Cosgrave, had played an important role in the process by which the party had adopted the *Just Society* programme. At the same time he was trusted by many of the party traditionalists because of his strongly conservative views on moral issues and his identification with the classically Fine Gael values of law and order and the defence of the institutions of the state against any subversive threats.

Cosgrave's support for Costello's proposals reflected, not any left-of-centre disposition, but his strong belief that they would provide a more coherent basis for co-operation with the Labour Party in order to displace Fianna Fáil from power. He was prepared to be radical in the pursuit of this goal and had even proposed a merger of the two parties in 1968, which had been rejected by Labour's leader, Brendan Corish, as had Cosgrave's suggestion of a pre-election pact between Fine Gael and Labour in 1969.[15] Labour's failure to make an electoral breakthrough in 1969 put an end to the go-it-alone strategy. Visions of the 1970s as being socialist and as having a Labour Party with sufficient Dáil seats to form a government on its own gave way to a more realistic assessment that, together with the 'social democratic' element of Fine Gael, Labour in coalition could make a real difference to the lives of its working-class supporters.

The 1969 election had produced an important shift in the balance between pro- and anti-coalitionists in the party. Traditionally it had been the rural deputies who were strongly in favour of coalition while those from urban areas, particularly Dublin, tended towards a rejectionist position based on socialist principles. The 1969 election had brought in a group of new Dublin deputies, including Dr Conor Cruise O'Brien and Justin Keating, who combined an impressive amount of intellectual fire-power with the conviction that 'principled socialist opposition' was a recipe for impotence. The Arms Crisis and its revelation of the links between sections of Fianna Fáil and the Provisionals added the argument that the two main opposition parties had a national duty to provide a stable and democratic alternative to Fianna Fáil. A special delegate conference held in Cork in December 1970 allowed the leadership to complete what Conor Cruise O'Brien called 'Operation Houdini' by voting to allow the leader and the members of the Parliamentary Labour

Party to make the decision to go into coalition when they were convinced this would allow the implementation of Labour's policies.[16] This was more than enough latitude for a parliamentary party that, with the exception of Dr Noel Browne, was determined to get into government at the earliest opportunity.

When Jack Lynch dissolved the Dáil in February 1973, Labour and Fine Gael hastily concluded a coalition agreement and issued a joint fourteen-point programme that contained few specific promises and which Labour's historian described as 'consisting largely of platitudes'.[17] Due to the success of vote transfers between the two parties, Labour won an extra seat, although it had lost votes compared to 1969, particularly in Dublin where anti-coalition supporters transferred to Official Sinn Féin, which had fought the election on a fairly left-wing set of policies. But it was Fine Gael who benefited most from the transfer pact, pushing up their number of seats by four to fifty-four. Thus despite the fact that Fianna Fáil increased its share of the vote slightly on 1969, it lost the election and the two opposition parties were able to form a stable coalition government.[18]

To many observers the most remarkable thing about the National Coalition was its unity. It faced economic problems and challenges on the security and Northern Ireland fronts that were far greater than those that the previous inter-party governments had to endure. Key to this unity was the absence of any major divisions on left–right lines between Labour and Fine Gael members of the government. Much of the credit for this must go to Liam Cosgrave, who from his initial decision to offer Labour five ministries—one more than their electoral performance strictly warranted—had operated as a considerate and fair chairman of government meetings.[19] However, it also reflected the fact that the Labour ministers did little to put a distinctive imprint on the key areas of domestic policy during their time in office.

As Tánaiste and Minister of Health and Social Welfare, Brendan Corish at 60 was running out of steam and lacked the inclination or time to give a clear direction to his colleagues. Three of them were particularly forceful personalities; Justin Keating at Industry and Commerce, Conor Cruise O'Brien at Posts and Telegraphs, and Michael O'Leary at Labour. They had their own departmental agendas and, in the case of Keating and O'Leary, leadership ambitions that took priority over any notion of a common Labour strategy. This would, in any case, not have been easy to develop, given the buffeting that the Irish economy was receiving from the end of 1974. The 1973 manifesto had promised that a 'programme of planned economic development' would be a central feature of the government's policy and that an immediate aim was a stabilization of prices, a halt in redundancies, and a reduction of unemployment. The five-fold increase in oil prices removed any possibility of these ambitions being realized. Prices rose by about 90 per cent during the first four years of the Coalition's term, an average rate almost twice that experienced during the previous four years of Lynch's government. The combined effect of freer trade and recession caused many firms to cease production or cut their workforces. The number of unemployed rose from 71,435 when the Coalition took power in March 1973 to 115,942 four years later, from 7.9 per cent to 12.5 per cent of the insured labour force.[20]

These dismal figures undermined any possible electoral benefit Labour might have had from the achievements of the Coalition in the areas of social expenditure and taxation. Expenditure on social welfare rose from 6.5 per cent of GNP in 1973 to 10.5 per cent four years later and most benefit rates rose by 125 per cent, considerably more than wages and prices. The rate of house building increased by 50 per cent and expenditure on health services increased almost three-fold.[21] Taxation was an area in which Fine Gael's left made common cause with Labour. The election manifesto had committed the Coalition to a wealth tax, and Garret FitzGerald, who was a member of the cabinet's economic sub-committee, supported his Labour colleagues on the need for taxation of capital gains and wealth.[22] A White Paper published in February 1974 proposed a capital gains tax of 35 per cent and an annual wealth tax on estates of over £40,000. In an attempt to lessen criticism from the large propertied and middle-class element in Fine Gael's traditional support, death duties were to be abolished. The intensity of the reaction, led in the Dáil by the only recently rehabilitated Charles Haughey, resulted in the dilution of the package with the introduction of a higher threshold of £100,000 and a lower rate of 1 per cent. Such redistributive policies alienated the middle class, whilst their only marginal contribution to the public purse did little to compensate Labour's working-class supporters, many of whom experienced a real drop in their living standards in the last two years of the Coalition. Labour's presence in government had made it easier for the leadership of the Irish trade union movement to be persuaded of the need for 'responsible' wage demands. Real pre-tax incomes rose in 1974 and 1975 but then National Wage Agreements were amended to introduce pay curbs, which, together with a heavily regressive tax system, led to a squeeze on working-class living standards.[23]

The apparent lack of division within the Coalition on the economy, the issue that would lose them the election in 1977, was in contrast to the open tensions over how best to deal with the reverberations of the northern conflict. Cosgrave, along with Conor Cruise O'Brien, had favoured a low-key approach to Northern Ireland, aimed at a largely internal power-sharing deal between the Ulster Unionists and the SDLP. Garret FitzGerald had been appointed to Foreign Affairs by Cosgrave, who had an uneasy relationship with his voluble and super-confident colleague and had hoped that the many ramifications of EEC membership would result in the minister being out of Ireland a lot. This ignored FitzGerald's formidable energy and his conviction that having a mother from a northern Presbyterian background gave him a particular insight into the mentalities of both communities in the North.

FitzGerald soon asserted a key role in Northern Ireland policy and used it to support the more activist policies favoured by John Hume. O'Brien, who was an increasingly scathing critic of the conventional Irish nationalist analysis of Northern Ireland, was kept on as Labour Party spokesman on Northern Ireland and at Sunningdale had tried in vain to argue for a deal more palatable to Faulkner's supporters. After the UWC strike he became the first Irish government minister to state publicly that he was not working actively for Irish unity as it was not a practicable goal. In a document prepared for his party colleagues and leaked to the press, he argued that to prevent a 'doomsday situation' in the North the government in Dublin should adopt a relatively low profile.[24]

O'Brien was criticized at the time and since for an unbalanced approach that demanded from Irish nationalists an intellectual maturity and generosity of spirit that he never demanded from Unionists.[25] Yet it was precisely O'Brien's point that much of the rigidity, lack of imagination, and the simple bigotry associated with the Unionist cause was a result of nationalism's refusal to accept that there could be any democratic validity to partition. He was convinced that reform in the North and better North–South relations were a real possibility if the unity issue were put on one side. This inevitably meant that he concentrated his attentions on those best placed to unlock this progressive potential in the North by abandoning positions that, no matter how appealing in Dublin, strengthened the hands of the most reactionary opponents of change in Belfast.

O'Brien's most vociferous critics were in his own party. Justin Keating was in the forefront of those wedded to the republican socialist mantras of James Connolly, demanding British withdrawal at a time when the North was as near to a sectarian civil war as at any time since the 1920–2 period. Anti-partitionists were soon joined in the ranks of critics of 'The Cruiser' by civil liberties groups and a substantial sector of the Dublin print and broadcast media as O'Brien and Cosgrave became identified with a heavy-handed approach to the activities of the IRA in the South.

Cosgrave had outraged his more liberal colleagues and threatened to split the Fine Gael parliamentary party when, in December 1972, he had indicated that he would support Fianna Fáil's amendment to the Offences Against the State, which allowed the indictment of those suspected to be terrorists by a senior police officer. The explosion of two bombs in the centre of Dublin, killing two people and injuring over a hundred, which was probably the work of loyalist terrorists, led to the withdrawal of Fine Gael's opposition to the amendment and saved Cosgrave's leadership. However, his government was soon faced with intensifying and often sickening reminders that neither republicans nor loyalists would respect the border when the exigencies of the 'war' in Northern Ireland demanded it.

Within a fortnight of the Coalition coming into office, the *Claudia*, a fishing boat filled with an IRA arms shipment and with the senior Belfast IRA man Joe Cahill on board, was captured off the Waterford coast as a result of joint British–Irish intelligence work. Over the next two decades the IRA's 'southern command' would use the Republic as the major location for its arms dumps, for the training of its 'volunteers', and as a source of funds through bank robberies, kidnappings and other forms of extortion. In the autumn of 1973 all the members of the government were informed that they and their families were under direct threat of kidnapping by one or other of the republican groups. In 1975 a Dutch businessman, Tiede Herrema, was taken by the IRA, who demanded the release of its prisoners in Irish jails. The government refused to negotiate. As Conor Cruise O'Brien puts it in his account of the Coalition, 'We and Herrema got lucky': police interrogation of a suspected member of the gang revealed where the victim was being held and he was released without physical harm.[26] Others were less lucky. In March 1974 a Fine Gael Senator, Billy Fox, was visiting his fiancée in the border county of Monaghan when he was shot dead by the Provisionals. Fox, like the family he was visiting, was a Presbyterian, and the motive for the murder was apparently sectarian.[27] Although the IRA had attempted to deny its involvement in Fox's murder, it openly admitted responsibility for the murder of the British ambassador Christopher

Ewart Biggs, whose car was blown up by a landmine near his official residence on the outskirts of Dublin on 23 July 1976.

The Dáil was recalled for a special emergency sitting and Cosgrave proposed a state of national emergency with a substantial increase in the powers of the state in its 'anti-subversive' struggle. A politically embarrassing conflict with the President, Cearbhall O'Dalaigh, occurred when he referred one of the proposed pieces of legislation to the Supreme Court in September. The Minister of Defence, Paddy Donegan, a strong Cosgrave loyalist, departed from his script in a speech to troops at Mullingar to refer to O'Dalaigh as a 'thundering disgrace', provoking the President's resignation. It is hard not to agree with the knowledgeable political journalist Bruce Arnold in his judgement that Cosgrave overresponded to the murder, in part to wrong-foot Fianna Fáil with the objective of an early election on the law-and-order issue.[28] It is difficult otherwise to explain why similar measures had not been proposed after the appalling atrocity committed by the Ulster Volunteer Force (UVF) when it exploded car bombs in the centres of Dublin and Monaghan on 17 May 1974, killing thirty-three people in the worst single loss of life of the Troubles.

If Cosgrave did have an undeclared electoral agenda, the President's resignation frustrated it and intensified the authoritarian and repressive image of the government. Newspaper reports of police brutality in the interrogation of terrorist suspects by what was described as the 'Heavy Gang' were taken so seriously by FitzGerald that he considered pressing for an inquiry and resigning from the government if it were not granted.[29] O'Brien's role as the minister responsible for the implementation of section 31 of the Broadcasting Authority Act of 1960, which banned the use of radio and television by those linked to the IRA or other terrorist organizations, added to the government's 'law-and-order' image. In 1976 he amended the Act to allow the Minister to proscribe groups whose members could not be interviewed. This meant that for the first time Sinn Féin was formally proscribed.

If, as Garret FitzGerald claims, the Coalition lost the 1977 election because 'the people were tired of us,'[30] then what Professor Lee calls the 'constipated' image of Cosgrave as opposed to the amiability of Jack Lynch may well have played a role.[31] His obvious relish in the fight against subversion and O'Brien's 'anti-national' views on Northern Ireland have been seen by some analysts as key elements in the Coalition's defeat.[32] The repressive image of the government may have damaged it among younger voters. The voting age had been reduced to

18 for the first time and a quarter of the electorate was under 26. The Coalition's appeal to this group had been hurt by Cosgrave's decision to vote against his own government's legislation on contraception. This had been prompted by a Supreme Court ruling in the McGee case in December 1973, which declared the ban on the importation of contraceptives under the 1935 Act to be unconstitutional. The government's legislation, which aimed to regularize the situation by allowing chemists to sell contraceptives to married couples, was hardly a charter for promiscuity, but worried a number of Fine Gael TDs with rural seats to defend.[33] Cosgrave's vote and a number of other Fine Gael defections killed the bill. Yet, if some younger voters were dismayed by the Coalition's failure on contraception, they were hardly likely to turn to Fianna Fáil, which took an unabashedly traditional line on the issue. It is also unlikely that Northern Ireland played a significant role in Cosgrave's defeat. It featured little in the campaign and if the defeat of Conor Cruise O'Brien was seen by some as a blow struck by the electorate against revisionist views on the North, what then was the significance of Justin Keating's loss of his seat, given his unreconstructed anti-partitionism?

But if the Irish media's fixation on the repressive and authoritarian features of the Coalition and O'Brien's revisionist agenda had little impact on the electorate, it did dent the morale of many of the government's members and contribute to the decision to go to the country in June 1977. This was despite the fact that the government had another six months to run and despite signs that the economy was moving back to rapid growth and inflation was falling.[34] Cosgrave was proud of the Coalition's ability to hold together for four and a half years, longer than any government since the Emergency, and hopeful that a radical redrawing of constituency boundaries by the Labour Minister of Local Government, James Tully, would damage Fianna Fáil. In fact, while the infamous 'Tullymander' might have been effective against a moderate swing to the Opposition, what occurred in June 1977 was a massive surge to Lynch's party. For the first time since 1938, Fianna Fáil won over 50 per cent of the vote and eighty-four seats, an extra fifteen. The combined vote for the Coalition parties dropped from 49 per cent to 42 per cent and from seventy-three seats to sixty.[35]

The key to Lynch's success was a sharp turn of working-class voters towards Fianna Fáil. In 1969, 40 per cent of skilled workers voted for Fianna Fáil and 26 per cent for Labour. By 1977 the gap had widened to 54 per cent for Fianna Fáil and 11 per cent for Labour.[36] Disillusion with the Coalition on unemployment and falling incomes was decisive. However, it was transformed into a surge of support for Lynch through Fianna Fáil's first ever election manifesto, *Action Plan for National Reconstruction*, which was the most extravagant and reckless collection of economic pledges ever made in an Irish election. It promised to create 25,000 jobs a year, when the previous average had been around 4,000 a year. Income tax was to be cut and domestic rates abolished along with road tax. First-time house buyers were to receive a grant of £1,000.

Conor Cruise O'Brien has claimed that this audacious programme 'bore all the hallmarks of C. J. Haughey, now again the rising star of Fianna Fáil'.[37] In fact, the manifesto was designed to ensure such a margin of victory that Lynch would once and for all be able to put the 'unconstitutional element' in the party in its place. In this sense Northern Ireland did play a subtle and subterranean role in the election. Haughey had maintained a strong body of support within the party and after the collapse of the power-sharing executive and the apparently bleak prospects for further political reform in the North, there was an upsurge of traditional anti-partitionist sentiment within Fianna Fáil. Michael O'Kennedy, the party's new spokesman on Northern Ireland, was in awe of Haughey and in March 1975 the party published a distinctly more hawkish policy document on Northern Ireland, which called for a British commitment to implement an 'ordered withdrawal' from the North.

Haughey's post-1970 public posture of loyalty to the party and his strong performance in the Dáil as a critic of the Coalition's wealth tax had led to his return to the Opposition front bench in 1975 as spokesman on Health and Social Welfare. He had used his time in the political wilderness to cultivate the party's grass-roots. There was no 'rubber chicken' function in a rural backwater that he was not prepared to grace with his presence. Lynch, aware of Haughey's popularity with the party's foot-soldiers, hoped that a major election victory would allow him to re-establish his authority in the party. It was with this in mind that he had asked Martin O'Donoghue, Professor of Economics at Trinity College, to be a candidate in the election and write the sort of expansionist manifesto that would copper-fasten his leadership.[38] Against his better economic judgement, O'Donoghue delivered the victory. Unfortunately for Lynch, the influx of new TDs included many who would look to Haughey for the strong leadership deemed necessary when O'Donoghue's strategy appeared to threaten national bankruptcy.

Charles Haughey and the Fracturing of Fianna Fáil

The strong passions that Haughey aroused in his opponents and allies have tended to result in a version of the political history of the South in the 1980s that pays too much attention to the role of individuals and not enough to the profound economic problems that the Republic faced. If one individual has to be singled out as responsible for the crisis years of the early 1980s, then it has to be Jack Lynch. One Irish historian's comment that Lynch 'stood for nothing in particular except a kind of affable consensus' has been criticized by Professor Lee for not recognizing that such a consensus was an achievement if the alternative was the 'breakdown of civilized discourse or government by the elect instead of the elected'.[39] Yet, Lynch had displayed severe hesitancy during the Arms Crisis and an unwillingness to confront Haughey and his fellow conspirators until forced to do so by Liam Cosgrave.[40] The consensus he prioritized was that within Fianna Fáil and in 1977 he showed a marked inclination to sustain that consensus with an electoral triumph whatever the ultimate economic cost.

This was apparent to some leading members of the party at the time, with Haughey's ally Brian Lenihan commenting on the manifesto, 'Blessed are the young for they shall inherit the national debt.'[41] Martin O'Donoghue was now in the cabinet heading a new Department of Economic Planning and Development. He set out the government's economic strategy in a White Paper, *National Development 1977–1980*. It was, he admitted, a gamble, relying on a vigorous pump-priming exercise by the state that would create the expansionist environment in which private enterprise would take over, allowing for a reduction in the role of the state and in the level of public expenditure. Two of the basic assumptions underpinning the strategy were dangerously optimistic. One was that the oil price shock of 1973 was a once-and-for-all event and that international economic conditions would continue to recover. The other was that the trade union movement would be prepared to exchange 'responsible' wage demands for job creation.

The second large increase in oil prices at the end of 1978 and the consequent deep international recession dealt a severe blow. Growth of GDP, which had averaged 6 per cent in 1977 and 1978, dropped to 1.5 per cent in 1979 and unemployment and redundancies began to increase sharply. Lynch had said that he would resign if the number of unemployed could not be brought below 100,000—it was 106,000 when the Coalition left office. In the first two years of the new administration over 60,000 new jobs were created and the number of unemployed had fallen to 90,000 by 1979. It then began to rise and reached 100,000 in 1980. By 1983 it would have soared to 200,000, or 16 per cent of the workforce, the highest rate in the EEC.[42] The jobs that were created were mostly in a fast-growing public sector and were paid for by a sharp rise in public expenditure financed by government borrowing. By the time Haughey succeeded Lynch as Taoiseach in December 1979, the Exchequer borrowing requirement had doubled and the national debt was more than two-thirds higher than when the Coalition had left office.[43]

To imported inflation was added the inflationary effect of trade union wage demands. The 1970s had seen a shift towards more centralized collective bargaining between ICTU and the employers' organizations through a series of national wage agreements. In the second half of the decade the government began to play a formal role in these negotiations. This culminated in the *National Understanding for Economic and Social Development* in 1979, aimed at eliciting union restraint on wages in return for government action on a wide range of issues that included health, education, taxation, and employment.[44] However, the fragmentation of the Republic's trade union movement made it difficult for the ICTU leadership to deliver its members' compliance in wage restraint. In 1978 a plea from the Minister of Finance, George Colley, for a national wage settlement of 5 per cent had little effect as average industrial earnings rose by 17 per cent.[45]

Wage discipline was made less likely because of an eruption of urban/rural conflict over taxation. Membership of the EEC had given a major boost to farm incomes. The Common Agricultural Policy (CAP) provided Irish farmers with a golden harvest. Guaranteed prices and highly favourable price increases due to green pound movement following the substantial devaluations of sterling had brought Irish farmers unprecedented prosperity. By 1978 real incomes in agriculture had doubled compared with 1970.[46] The fact that farmers were not subject to taxation on their incomes seemed increasingly intolerable as more and more urban workers were brought into the higher income tax brackets because of inflation. The exclusion of farmers from the income tax base of the state, together with very a favourable tax regime for companies, meant that during the 1970s there was a considerable increase in the tax burden for those subject to income tax. The proportion of their income taken from individuals on average earnings increased by half during the decade.[47] George Colley had attempted to deal with growing criticism of his government's inaction on farm incomes with a proposal for a 2 per cent levy on farmers' turnover in his 1979 budget. However, by this time the CAP-induced boom had come to an end. Ireland's decision to join the European Monetary System when it was created in 1978 meant the end of the favourable green pound movements as the link with sterling was broken. EEC concern with over-production under the CAP led to a reduction in the rapid rate of increase in agricultural prices and ushered in a slump in agriculture. A strong reaction from farmers' organizations led to the proposed farm levy being dropped. The result was an explosion of protest from trade unionists, who took to the streets in marches and demonstrations for tax equity, culminating in a one-day national strike on 20 March 1979 with 150,000 protesters in Dublin and another 40,000 in Cork. George Colley, who had criticized the strike as 'unproductive' on the day before it took place, probably sealed his fate in the forthcoming battle for the leadership of the party.

With unemployment and inflation rising, tax protesters on the streets, and a prolonged and bitter strike by postal workers, 1979 was the year in which the direction of economic policy by a small 'inner cabinet' of Lynch's closest supporters sparked off a revolt in the parliamentary party. Some of those involved were new TDs with a background in business and accountancy, including Albert Reynolds and Charlie McGreevy. Others were aghast at the party's poor electoral performance. In the first elections for the European Parliament in June, Fianna Fáil's vote slumped to 34 per cent and it won only five of the Republic's fifteen seats. Most galling for Lynch was the election of one of his most virulent republican critics, Neil Blaney, as an Independent in the Connaught/Ulster constituency.[48] Then in November the party lost disastrously in two by-elections in Cork, one of them in Lynch's own constituency.

To the economic reverses and electoral rebuffs were added the legacy of the Arms Crisis and Lynch's unpopularity with the more unreconstructed republicans in the party. On 27 August 1979 the IRA blew up a yacht belonging to the Queen's cousin, Lord Mountbatten, who was holidaying in county Sligo. Mountbatten and three others of the party were killed. At Narrow Water in county Down on the same day another IRA attack killed eighteen soldiers. Lynch agreed to requests from Margaret Thatcher to allow British military aircraft brief incursions into the Republic's airspace in pursuit of terrorists. When news of the 'air corridor' agreement appeared in the press, it produced a paroxysm of traditionalist rage against such 'collaboration' with a Tory government. An attempt to discipline a TD who had claimed that Lynch had lied about the agreement backfired badly and then Sile de Valera, a grand-daughter of de Valera, made an only slightly veiled attack on Lynch's northern policy in an address to a Fianna Fáil commemoration. Lynch, shocked by the extent and bitterness of the back-bench revolt, announced that he would resign. It is unlikely that the government's failures on the economy and the election reverses would in themselves have led to Lynch's decision. His administration had another two years to run and previous governments had recovered from similar reversals. It was the extra dimension of bitterness that came from the legacy of the Arms Crisis, the 'sulphurous' atmosphere that a journalist detected in the parliamentary party,[49] that propelled Lynch, a leader who had prided himself in his ability to bring together the different wings of the party, out of politics. In the contest for the leadership that followed Haughey defeated Colley by forty-four votes to thirty-eight.

Haughey's victory has been depicted by one of his numerous critics as the opening up of 'the most sordid and diseased chapter in Irish political life since the end of the civil war'.[50] One of a number of tribunals of inquiry established at the end of the 1990s to investigate corruption in Irish politics since the 1960s established that Haughey had run up a debt of £1.14 million with the Allied Irish Bank during the 1970s and that he had used his position as Taoiseach to persuade the bank to settle for £750,000.[51] At the time rumours about how he had acquired his fortune in the 1960s abounded, as did those about his current financial problems. It was to these that Garret FitzGerald alluded in his speech on Haughey's nomination as Taoiseach when he referred to a 'flawed pedigree' and a man who, while his abilities were undeniable, should be disqualified from high office as he wanted 'not simply to dominate the state but to own it'.[52]

With a self-image that seemed to blend the Renaissance prince and the Gaelic chieftain, Charles Haughey did not regard himself as bound by the conventional values that applied to ordinary mortals. Just as, in the late 1970s, bank officials were threatened with his displeasure if they dared to apply the same standards to him as to other debtors, Ben Dunne, one of Ireland's leading businessmen, was approached to bail him out of an even deeper hole of indebtedness in 1987 and provided him with payments amounting to £1.1 million over the next four years.[53] The many rumours about how he financed such a lavish lifestyle did not damage his immense popularity with a substantial section of the party and the electorate. Like the 'whiff of cordite' associated with the Arms Trial, such rumours made him seem appealingly dangerous. As the respected Irish political journalist Stephen Collins has noted, Haughey's popularity revealed the continuing influence of almost primordial sentiments: 'deep ambivalence to politics and law, coupled with the atavistic anti-English strain in Irish nationalism' amongst many Irish people.[54]

Haughey had always been dismissive of Lynch's consensual and relaxed leadership style and his own was characterized by the encouragement of a deferential and at times fearful loyalty among his supporters, who called him 'Boss', and the implacable desire to marginalize his opponents. Although some of these, including Colley, who refused to offer Haughey loyalty as leader of the party and demanded a veto on the appointment of the Ministers of Justice and Defence, were resolute in opposition, others, including Des O'Malley, were open to persuasion.[55] Instead, Haughey looked towards a victory in the next general election as the prerequisite for a final purge of his most irreconcilable critics.

The fixation on obtaining a Fianna Fáil majority was in part responsible for his rapid volte-face on the economy. In his first televised address to the nation on 9 January 1980, he had sounded a stern note: 'as a community we have been living beyond our means . . . we have been living at a rate which is simply not justified by the amount of goods and services we are producing.'[56] Having sacked Martin O'Donoghue and abolished his department, Haughey now proposed cuts in government expenditure and a reduction in borrowing. A large part of the business and financial community, virtually all of the media, and most professional economists were enthused at the prospect of a Celtic Thatcherism. It was not to be, at least not yet. A right-wing turn in economic policy made good economic sense but was politically perilous for a party whose recovery from the post-war doldrums had been based on Lemass's mixture of economic expansion and co-operation with the unions. Working-class resentment on the taxation issue had been manifest two weeks after Haughey's television address, in what the BBC referred to as 'the largest peaceful protest in postwar Europe'.[57] An ICTU-organized national strike for tax reform was supported by 700,000 workers, with a mass demonstration of 300,000 in Dublin. For many of those TDs who had supported Haughey, fiscal rectitude seemed a recipe for political suicide.

Haughey's own lavish and debt-financed lifestyle may have made him uncomfortable with demands that the largely working-class electorate of his north Dublin constituency put on hair shirts while his own were tailor-made in Paris.[58] His political career and personal fortune had been built in the expansionary 1960s when the building industry had begun to have an increasingly powerful influence on Fianna Fáil.[59] This was a major sector of the economy that stood to lose badly from neo-liberal policies. Big cuts in public expenditure might be seen as necessary to get the economic fundamentals right by those sections of Irish industry that had successfully made the transition to free trade and selling abroad. However, there remained many Irish manufacturers who were uncompetitive, relied on the domestic market, and were directly threatened by the shrinkage in demand that deflationary policies would inevitably produce. Haughey's backtracking reflected the real pressure of major sections of the middle and working class who were reluctant to pay the high price of economic adjustment. Within months the government had agreed another National Understanding with the unions, which involved an increase in welfare benefits and job creation targets along with a promise of more investment in infrastructure and a continuation of high levels of government borrowing. Haughey's former business allies despaired as the budget deficit rose from £522 million in 1979 to £802 million in 1981 and the Exchequer borrowing requirement from 13.8 per cent of GNP to 16.8 per cent,[60] with the Department of Finance forecasting that it would reach 21 per cent by 1982.[61]

With all the main economic indicators deteriorating, Haughey attempted to maintain support by a robustly nationalist line on Northern Ireland. Describing it as a 'failed political entity', he announced that he wanted to raise the issue to a 'higher plane' by seeking a solution through direct negotiations with the British government.[62] Despite his public disdain for Thatcher's neo-liberal economic policies, he was obviously attracted by her imperious mode of government and her impatience with the inherited policy of power-sharing devolution. There were hints of a willingness to consider a defence deal with the UK and, more immediately, after his first meeting with Thatcher when he presented her with a silver Georgian teapot, it was announced that there would be a meeting between the Chief Constable of the RUC and the Garda Commissioner.[63] The British hoped that Haughey's solid republican credentials would allow him to act decisively against the IRA. As a result, Haughey did remarkably well in the major Anglo-Irish summit held in Dublin on 8 December 1980. In their joint communiqué after the talks, Thatcher acknowledged Britain's 'unique relationship' with Ireland and permitted the establishment of joint study groups to find ways of expressing this uniqueness in 'new institutional relations'. The two

Prime Ministers agreed to devote their next meeting to considering 'the totality of relations within these islands'. Haughey's subsequent dema- gogic exploitation of this phrase infuriated Thatcher and differences over the IRA hunger strikes and the Falklands War further soured rela- tions between the two. However, the logic of Haughey's approach—that the two governments should act over the heads of the northern parties, particularly the Unionists—would come to partial fruition in the Anglo- Irish Agreement.

In the short term the credibility of Haughey's approach to the North was damaged by the hunger strikes and his failure to have an influence on Thatcher's handling of them. Nevertheless, unsure of the electorate's verdict on his economic stewardship, he dissolved the Dáil on 21 May 1981, claiming that he was calling the election 'because of the grave and tragic situation in Northern Ireland'.[64] This was the first time Northern Ireland had been proclaimed the central issue in a southern election. Although Bobby Sands had died on 5 May and other hunger strikers were nearing death, the bulk of the electorate continued to focus dog- gedly on the domestic issues of taxation, inflation, and unemployment. Haughey, who was about equal in popularity with FitzGerald when the election was called, paid a hefty price for such a clumsy diversionary tactic. By giving a high profile to Northern Ireland he provided Sinn Féin with the best opportunity for advance in southern politics since the 1950s. Nine republican prisoners were nominated for the election and the two that were successful took seats that would otherwise have gone to Fianna Fáil.

Any vestigial claim to economic competence or responsibility that his government might have made was undermined by his descent into crude vote-buying in key constituencies, with a commitment to an inter- national airport in a remote part of county Mayo to bring pilgrims to the Marian shrine at Knock and a deal with workers in the Talbot car assembly plant in his constituency that guaranteed them state salaries for life when the plant closed. Both commitments were made without any consultation with his colleagues or the Department of Finance.[65]

The result of the 1981 election was a substantial victory for Fine Gael, whose percentage of the vote increased from 30.5 to 36.5 and seats from forty-three to sixty-five, its best ever result. Under Garret FitzGerald's leadership since 1977, Fine Gael's archaic structure had been modernized and its culture of genteel amateurism transformed. Youth and women's wings were established and it was the first of the major parties actively to promote women candidates, becoming home to some of those who had played a prominent role in the development of the Irish women's movement in the early 1970s.[66] The party had waged a professional and aggressive campaign and its promise of large cuts in income tax had allowed it to make significant inroads into working-class support for Fianna Fáil. FitzGerald's public persona—that of an amiable and loquacious academic—contrasted sharply with Haughey's tight-lipped and imperious aura.

Fianna Fáil's vote dropped from 50.6 to 45.3 per cent and its seats from eighty-four to seventy-five in a Dáil where the number of seats had been increased from 148 to 166.[67] The Lynch/Haughey inheritance of debt and inflation led to a sharp decline in middle-class support, while rising unemployment and lack of tax reform produced an only slightly less sharp drop in working-class support.[68] However, its vote in 1977 had been exceptional and, given the worsening economic situation, its losses were not unexpectedly high. In 1969 Fianna Fáil had won an overall majority of seats with a slightly smaller share of the votes. It was the agreement between Fine Gael and Labour to urge their supporters to give their lower preferences to the other party that proved decisive. Without the transfer arrangement Fianna Fáil would have won five extra seats, which, given the absence of the two hunger strike TDs, would have given it a clear overall majority.[69] Haughey made use of this to claim that he had not really lost the election: a quirk of the electoral system and the intervention of the hunger strikers had robbed him of victory.[70] The fact that the new government was a minority administration dependent on the votes of three leftist independents encouraged him and his supporters to believe that their loss of office would be brief.

Although still convinced that Fine Gael's only secure future was as a 'social-democratic' party, FitzGerald was soon forced to apply a radical deflationary programme to deal with what his Minister of Finance, the wealthy county Meath farmer John Bruton, termed the threat to national economic independence that was the legacy of the previous government.[71] An emergency budget was introduced in July with increases in indirect taxation and spending cuts aimed at reducing the Exchequer borrowing requirement from 20 to 16 per cent of GNP.[72] The draconian budget created major problems for the junior partner in the Coalition: Frank Cluskey, the gruff Dublin trade unionist who had been elected Labour leader in 1977, would probably have led his ministers out of government. However, Labour had lost two seats in the election and one of those was Cluskey's. His successor was the altogether smoother Michael O'Leary, a former student radical who had been a research officer for ICTU before becoming Minister of Labour in the 1973–7 Coalition, where he was seen as the most successful of the Labour ministers.[73]

Labour's performance in the election had been dismal. Given a bad result in 1977 and the fact that it was in Opposition at a time of very high unemployment and inflation, it had expected to make gains. In fact its share of the vote fell to under 10 per cent for the first time since 1957 and its number of seats to fifteen in a much larger Dáil. Its performance in Dublin was particularly bad with a reduction of three seats leaving it with only three, a sad decline on the ten it had won in 1969. The party remained divided over the leadership's support for a coalition strategy. Anti-coalition feeling and a more ideological socialism were strong amongst party members in Dublin, but continued support for coalition was guaranteed by the support of rural members. Critics argued that the pursuit of coalition with Fine Gael had blurred Labour's distinctiveness and weakened its independent appeal: 'since a vote for Labour was a vote for a Fine Gael-dominated coalition, then in many ways it may make more sense simply to vote for Fine Gael *per se*.'[74] It now faced a challenge from a number of smaller parties to its left. Dr Noel Browne had changed his party affiliations yet again and was elected as a Socialist Labour Party TD in Dublin; Jim Kemmy an Independent socialist with strongly anti-nationalist views on Northern Ireland won Limerick East; and Joe Sherlock won East Cork for Sinn Féin—The Workers' Party, as the increasingly successful political arm of the Official IRA was now known.

Labour entered the 1981 Coalition from a position of weakness. In 1969 it had won half as many votes as Fine Gael; now it had barely a quarter. Its share of the total Coalition vote was 21 per cent and of Dáil seats, 19 per cent. With four cabinet seats out of fifteen, the Labour ministers could do little to blunt the edges of Bruton's draconian budget except prevent the income tax cuts that would have intensified the regressive effects of the taxation changes. Dissent within the party increased and in October its ruling Administrative Council declared that the Labour ministers had exceeded their mandate in agreeing to the July budget. However, worse was to come when in January 1982 Bruton proposed an even tougher second budget with cuts in food subsidies, rises in indirect taxation, and new taxes on clothing and footwear, with FitzGerald refusing to consider the exemption of children's shoes in case it was exploited by women with small feet. This was the last straw for Jim Kemmy, who subordinated his strong dislike of Haughey's position on

Northern Ireland to his rejection of such a regressive measure and voted with the Opposition against the budget, thus ensuring the government's defeat by eighty-two votes to eighty-one.

Despite its commitment to austerity, Fine Gael marginally increased its vote in the subsequent general election in February 1982, although its number of seats fell by two to sixty-three. Fianna Fáil increased its vote from 45.3 to 47.2 per cent and its seats from seventy-eight to eighty-one. The Labour Party's vote had declined slightly but it held its fifteen seats, although it now faced a sharp left-wing challenge in the Dáil after Sinn Féin The Workers' Party (SFWP) made a breakthrough to win three seats. The three SFWP TDs and four Independents held the balance of power.[75]

Haughey's failure to win a majority for the second time precipitated a period of intense convulsion in his party. The Opposition front bench was already clearly divided over economic policy when the election was called. In an attempt to mend his fences with some of his most prominent critics in the party, Haughey had appointed Martin O'Donoghue as the party spokesman on Finance and had agreed that a more 'responsible' attitude be adopted to the government's proposals for dealing with the dire economic situation. However, as soon as the campaign started he reverted to populist mode with attacks on the Coalition's 'Thatcherite' approach. FitzGerald, he claimed, was 'hypnotized' by the issue of the national debt and Fianna Fáil would find 'a more humane way' of running the economy even if it did mean borrowing money. Just as this failed to convince many of his colleagues, it had little impact on the electorate. At the beginning of the campaign 51 per cent of those polled chose FitzGerald as Taoiseach compared to 31 per cent for Haughey; by the end the respective figures were 56 and 36 per cent.[76]

Even before a new government could be formed, Desmond O'Malley had declared his intention to stand against Haughey for the leadership of the party. O'Malley's distrust of Haughey dated from the Arms Crisis when he had been a key supporter of Lynch. It was now accentuated by his wholehearted commitment to neo-liberal economics and an identification of Haughey as an irresponsible populist. However, O'Malley's aloof and prickly personality made him an unappetizing alternative to that sizeable section of Fianna Fáil TDs who were wavering in their allegiances and when Martin O'Donoghue, who had been his campaign manager, at the last moment called for unity behind Haughey, O'Malley withdrew his challenge. Haughey then outbid FitzGerald for the support of Tony Gregory, an Independent TD of republican-socialist leanings, who represented an inner-city constituency in Dublin. The 'Gregory deal' involved a government commitment to spend over £80 million in job creation, new housing, environmental works, and schooling.[77] The support of the three SFWP TDs for Haughey was a major surprise, given that party's shift to a position on Northern Ireland that accepted the need for Unionist consent for constitutional change. The party supported the proposals of James Prior, the Northern Ireland Secretary, for the election of a Northern Ireland Assembly. While Haughey believed the proposals to be unworkable, he agreed to adopt a public position of neutrality. Together with his promise of opposition to the privatization of state-owned companies and his anti-Thatcherite rhetoric, this was sufficient to obtain SFWP support.[78]

The government's short life was dominated by rumours of plots and the unorthodox methods adopted by some of Haughey's supporters to deal with his critics. George Colley was dropped from the cabinet and, with his veto on appointments to the Ministries of Defence and Justice removed, Haughey filled the positions with two of his loyalists, Sean Doherty and Paddy Power. Power was a very traditional republican and when the *Belgrano* was sunk during the Falklands War he embarrassed Haughey by making a speech accusing the British of being the aggressor. However, it was the appointment of Doherty that would have the most devastating long-term effects on Haughey's career. Only 37 when appointed, the county Roscommon TD had been one of Haughey's most strident supporters. An ex-Garda, he showed little inclination to respect the law when it came into conflict with his political or personal priorities. In January 1983 the Garda Commissioner and his deputy were forced to resign when it emerged that they had agreed to Doherty's request for the tapping of the telephones of two journalists. In both cases the purpose of the taps was to discover which of Haughey's critics in the party had been talking to the press. Doherty also supplied Ray MacSharry, the Tánaiste and Minister of Finance, with Garda equipment to bug a conversation with Martin O'Donoghue. When in August a suspected murderer was found living in the Dublin flat of the Attorney General, who then departed on holiday to New York knowing of the arrest of his guest, Haughey described the sequence of events as 'grotesque, unprecedented, bizarre and unbelievable'. Conor Cruise O'Brien, Haughey's most coruscating critic, turned the description into a telling acronym that has since become the government's epitaph: GUBU. The débâcle was to lead to another failed attempt to oust Haughey in the autumn, although this time twenty-two TDs openly opposed him. However, the fate of the government had already been decided by yet another turn in economic policy.

Ray MacSharry had initially dismissed the economic policies of the Coalition as 'gloom and doom' and promised 'boom and boom'. However, as 1982 progressed, the economic crisis deepened with more companies collapsing, more redundancies, and rising unemployment. At the same time net foreign debt rose from £3,451 million at the end of 1981 to £5,114 a year later.[79] In response MacSharry announced a radical shift in policy in July with a postponement of an already agreed rise in public sector pay along with a series of spending cuts. The government's apparent conversion to economic realism was complete by October when it published a major economic policy document, *The Way Forward*, which committed it to phasing out the budget deficit by 1986. The promise of austerity ahead brought an end to SFWP support. The party had already been annoyed by Haughey's denunciation of the Prior proposals for a northern Assembly when they were made public in April. When Garret FitzGerald put down a vote of no confidence in November, the government fell.

The FitzGerald Coalition 1982–7

The second general election in less than a year saw Fianna Fáil's vote fall from 47.3 per cent to 45.2 per cent, while Fine Gael's rose from 37.3 per cent to 39.2 per cent, and Labour's increased marginally from 9.1 per cent to 9.4 per cent. In terms of seats, Fianna Fáil lost six, while Fine Gael gained seven and Labour one. Michael O'Leary had resigned as leader of the Labour Party in October after failing to persuade its annual conference to adopt a pre-electoral commitment to coalition. His successor was Dick Spring, a 32-year-old barrister who had been elected to the Dáil for the first time in the 1981 general election. Spring's father, Dan, from whom he inherited his North Kerry constituency, had been typical of the rural TDs who had dominated the party until the 1960s influx of Dublin intellectuals such as O'Brien and Keating. His son's horizons had been widened through the still unusual choice of Trinity College, Dublin as his university and by two years working in the US. The result was that although Spring maintained his father's distrust of the intellectual left in the party, as personified by the eloquent Galway TD and Chairman of the party, Michael D. Higgins, he was much more sympathetic to those arguing for a liberal agenda on such issues as divorce and contraception than many of his rural-based colleagues.[80]

With Fine Gael's seventy seats and Labour's sixteen, the Coalition had a clear working majority in the 166-seat Dáil. Spring was Tánaiste and Minister of Environment; Frank Cluskey, Minister of Trade, Commerce, and Tourism; Liam Kavanagh, Minister of Labour; and Barry Desmond, Minister of Health and Social Welfare. Although Spring developed a good personal relationship with FitzGerald, he came into frequent and sometimes public conflict with Alan Dukes, the Minister of Finance. Like Spring, Dukes had entered the Dáil for the first time in 1981. A former student of FitzGerald's, he had been an adviser to the Irish Farmers' Association and was on the right of Fine Gael. Dukes gave strong support to the view of Department of Finance officials that the major task of the government was to cut the budget deficit by the maximum amount possible, almost regardless of the political consequences. Dukes's right-wing radicalism allowed FitzGerald to present himself to Spring and his Labour colleagues as a moderate social democrat trying to contain the Thatcherites in Fine Gael ministerial group and parliamentary party. He supported Labour's demand for a residential property tax and for a National Development Corporation to deal with the problem of the growing number of young unemployed.[81]

The unease that this apparent alliance between the Taoiseach and Tánaiste produced within Fine Gael has led some commentators to claim that FitzGerald's government failed to confront the public of the public finances.[82] In fact, by taking some account of Labour's concerns in both the 1983 and 1984 budgets, FitzGerald was able to implement what remained quite draconian cuts in public expenditure accompanied by substantial rises in taxation. The result was that well over half of the reduction in the Exchequer borrowing requirement from a threatened 21.5 per cent of GNP in 1982 to 1.5 per cent in 1989 was accomplished by the two Fine Gael–Labour Coalitions of 1981–2 and 1982–7.[83] Inflation was cut from 17 per cent to 4 per cent. The cost was high for many of Labour's traditional supporters. Real personal income after tax fell by 12 per cent between 1980 and 1986 and emigration, after net inflows in the 1970s, averaged 25,000 a year during the 1980s.[84] The Labour Party paid a high electoral price for FitzGerald's economic achievement. It lost its four seats in the European Parliament in the 1984 elections, and in the local government elections of 1985 it did badly nationally and was humiliated in the capital where the Workers' Party, as the SFNP was now known, won six seats to its two.[85] Spring finally decided to leave the government in January 1987 rather than support significant cuts in health expenditure.

In the general election that followed, Labour's support dropped to 6.4 per cent—its worst result since 1933—although it managed to retain twelve seats. Fine Gael dropped from 39.2 per cent to 27.1 per cent and from seventy to fifty-one seats. Despite the unpopularity of the government parties, Fianna Fáil under Haughey failed for the fourth time to win a majority. Its vote fell marginally to 44.1 per cent although its number of seats increased from seventy-five to eighty-one. The biggest shock of the election was the performance of a new party, the Progressive Democrats, who replaced Labour as the third-largest party, winning 11.8 per cent of the vote and fourteen seats. The party had been formed in early 1986 after a schism from Fianna Fáil led by Des O'Malley. Although its main figures were prominent ex-Fianna Fáilers, including Bobby Molloy and Mary Harney, it was able to attract support from sections of Fine Gael who had disapproved of the 'contamination' of the party's traditional conservative stance by the coalition arrangement with Labour.[86]

Haughey and the Origins of the Celtic Tiger 1987–92

The recession had promoted new left–right polarization in Irish politics, pitting Labour and the Workers' Party against Fine Gael and the Progressive Democrats. Fianna Fáil had fought the election on a centrist platform, renewing its commitment to economic growth, welfarism, and social partnership while accepting the need for some degree of fiscal balance. A trade union movement that had felt spurned and neglected by the Coalition was happy to have Haughey back in power. In opposition, Haughey had assiduously cultivated trade union leaders. A Fianna Fáil Trade Union Committee was established in 1986 and through it a series of meetings with key union officials laid the basis for the government–union concordat, *The Programme for National Recovery*, concluded in October 1987. As Kieran Allen has pointed out, Haughey was the beneficiary of the decline in trade union strength and militancy which the soaring redundancies, unemployment, and rocketing emigration of the early and mid 1980s had produced.[87] Shut out of any role in the framing of public policy on the economy under FitzGerald and Spring, and with the Progressive Democrats keen to import a pure neo-liberal model, it was little wonder that the trade union leadership accepted Haughey's offer to participate in what he skilfully presented as a national stabilization programme based on partnership rather than Thatcherite dog-eat-dog philosophy.[88] In return for an agreement for modest wage increases over a three-year period, the unions were tied into co-operation with a government that proceeded to implement a cuts package of £485 million.

The size of the cuts proposed by Ray MacSharry, Haughey's Minister of Finance, so impressed the new leader of Fine Gael, Alan Dukes, that he announced that he would not oppose the government as long as it stuck to its commitment to slash expenditure. The so-called 'Tallaght Strategy' meant the arrival of a dominant ideological consensus from which only Labour and the Workers' Party were excluded. MacSharry's economic shock therapy implemented in two harsh budgets cut public expenditure by £900 million, or 8 per cent, between 1987 and 1989. Within a short period of time the harsh medicine appeared to work. Economists started to talk about 'expansionary fiscal contraction'. The dominant consensus on putting the public finances in order had apparently restored the confidence of investors and from the second half of the 1980s the Irish economy began to grow at rates that far outpaced the rest of Europe.[89]

Irish GDP rose by 36.6 per cent between 1987 and 1993 compared with an increase of 13.3 per cent in the EU as a whole.[90] Growth accelerated in the period from 1994 to 1999, when GDP rose by 8.8 per cent a year. Ireland had surpassed even the emerging 'Tiger' economies of Asia in terms of high growth rates, industrial production, and low inflation. Unemployment, which had stood at 17 per cent in the mid 1980s, the second highest in the EU, had fallen to 6 per cent—below the EU average—in 1998 and was reduced further to 4.4 per cent in July 2000.[91] By the end of the decade the Republic's per capita income surpassed Britain's and was set to exceed the EU average by 2002.[92] The success of the 'Celtic Tiger' won the plaudits of the world's financial press and the OECD, notoriously a severe judge of national economies, said of the Republic in 1999:

It is astonishing that a nation could have moved all the way from the back of the pack to a leading position within such a short period, not much more than a decade, in fact.[93]

The more euphoric accounts of the Republic's 'economic miracle' need to be deflated. Gross National Product (GNP), which is the final output attributable to Irish workers, firms, and government, has consistently grown less quickly than Gross Domestic Product (GDP). This is because an increasing proportion of production within the country accrues to foreigners, mainly in the form of profits going to foreign investors and as interest on the foreign debt. GDP was also overstated because of transfer pricing by multinational corporations who exploited the fact that Ireland was a low-tax jurisdiction for most corporations (10 per cent on the profits of manufacturing firms) by inflating the proportion of their overall profits that they claimed to have been generated in Ireland. Disposable income per head also grew much more slowly, in part a result of unfavourable movements in the terms of trade and also because of a fall in the transfer payments from the EU as the Republic's economic success made it less eligible for such assistance.[94]

Ulster Unionist critics made much of the role of these transfers in generating the 'Celtic Tiger'. The EU had created Structural and Cohesion funds to deal with the difficulties that the less developed and poorer members would experience in the process of creating a Single Market that began with the Single European Act in 1987 and was completed with the Maastricht Treaty in 1992. The strong endorsement of both by the Irish electorate reflected government promises of Euro bounty to come. In 1992, promoting a 'yes' vote in referendum on Maastricht, the Taoiseach, Albert Reynolds, claimed that the Republic would receive £8 billion in the next allocation of Structural and Cohesion funds. Although this claim was inflated and was received frostily in Brussels, Ireland did eventually get over £6 billion and this was reckoned to have raised GNP by between 2 and 3 per cent. Although small in gross terms, the funds did make a very significant contribution to public expenditure in infrastructure projects, which were important in the 1990s take-off.[95]

Despite this, all serious accounts of the 'Celtic Tiger' agree that it was a product of a number of factors, of which EU funding was a real but in no way decisive one. The Single Market was much more directly important as it made the Republic an even more attractive location for foreign investors, particularly US ones. The Republic's Industrial Development Agency was already offering high grants, tax breaks, and a young and skilled workforce. It had also proved adept at 'picking winners'—setting out to expand particular industrial sectors, including electronics, pharmaceuticals, chemicals, software, and, more recently, financial services and tele-services. By the end of the 1990s, leading-edge companies such as Intel, Microsoft, IBM, Hewlett Packard, and Kodak were all represented in Ireland. The Republic was also benefiting from the substantial increases in investment in education and training dating from the 1960s. As one US commentator noted, 'Ireland's well-educated workforce today offers multinational businesses perhaps Europe's best ration of skills to wages'.[96]

For all the complexity of the debate on the causes of the unprecedented levels of economic growth, there is little doubt that the reinvigoration of social partnership between unions, employers, and the state played a fundamental domestic role: something recognized particularly by left-wing critics of the 'Tiger' phenomenon.[97] The National Economic and Social Council (NESC), an offspring of Lemass's corporatist initiatives in the 1960s, had in 1986 worked out an agreed strategy to escape from the vicious circle of stagnation, rising taxes, and exploding debt. Haughey had used this as the basis for his negotiation of the *Programme for National Recovery* in 1987, which ran to 1990. It was the first of four agreements that brought the Republic through more than a decade of negotiated economic and social governance.[98] The *Programme for National Recovery* was followed by the *Programme for Economic and Social Progress* (1991–3), the *Programme for Competitiveness and Work* (1994–7), and *Partnership 2000* was agreed in 1997.

In exchange for trade union support for corrective measures in fiscal policy, the government committed itself to maintaining the value of social welfare payments. In return for moderate pay rises, take-home pay was increased through tax reductions. The agreements fixed pay increases and established common ground on a range of issues from tax reform and measures to tackle poverty to exchange-rate policy and measures Ireland was to adopt to prepare for membership of a European Single Currency. Although there was some rank-and-file dissatisfaction with evidence of rocketing corporate profits while wage increases lagged behind, a dramatic drop in the number of strike days from an average of 316,000 a year in the eight years to 1987 to an average of 110,000 a year in the nine years to 1996 was an indication of the success of social partnership.

The evidence that the economic gloom of the Coalition years was fast dissipating and the Opposition's tacit support for the main lines of his government's economic policy encouraged Haughey to call another general election in June 1989. Although Fianna Fáil's vote dropped only marginally, it lost two seats and, more importantly, while its support among middle-class voters increased significantly, there were major losses of working-class support to Labour and the Workers' Party. With fifteen Labour Party TDs and seven from the Workers' Party, together with two left-wing independents, the Irish left had won its highest share of Dáil seats ever. Richard Sinnott noted that 'The story of the election is undoubtedly the polarisation of the voters along class lines.'[99] Fine Gael had improved its position somewhat with an increase in its vote from 27.1 per cent to 29.3 per cent and its seats from fifty to fifty-five. The Progressive Democrats had lost a slice of its support to Haughey's new-found economic respectability. Its vote had dropped from 11.8 per cent to 5.5 per cent and its seats from fourteen to six.

Haughey attempted to persuade the Fine Gael and the Progressive Democrats to continue with the 'Tallaght Strategy' but both now demanded a share in government and he was forced to abandon what had hitherto been proclaimed as a central value of Fianna Fáil: its refusal to consider forming a coalition with another party. By entering into government with the Progressive Democrats in July 1989, Haughey finally ended the pretence that Fianna Fáil was a 'national movement' and not a 'mere political party'. At the time, the deal with their former colleagues that brought Desmond O'Malley and Bobby Molloy into the cabinet represented a deep 'cultural shock' to many in Fianna Fáil.[100] Yet by jettisoning the traditional imperative to form only a single party government, Haughey had placed his party in a better position to maintain a dominant role in what had become a much more fragmented party system. Now it could tack to the right or left, forming alliances with the Progressive Democrats or Labour and the Workers' Party. Ironically, the only remaining obstacle to the full development of this new flexibility was Haughey himself. He remained anathema to many on the Irish left. This was not for his economic viewpoint, which, apart from his 'Thatcherite' lapse in 1980, was rhetorically Keynesian, even Peronist. Rather it reflected the fact that the 1980s had witnessed intense debates on moral issues and Northern Ireland, during which Haughey had positioned his party on the side of traditional Catholic values and irredentism.

A Church under Pressure

Two decades of rapid economic growth after 1959, urbanization, a new openness to the outside world, and fairly sweeping cultural change created the conditions for fierce debates over the Catholic Church's teachings on sexual behaviour and morality. An important factor in promoting change was the significant increase in the participation of women in the labour force. From partition to the 1960s, the opportunities for female participation in paid employment had been restricted by the South's lack of a significant manufacturing sector, particularly one with industries that tended to employ women.[101] In 1961, 28.5 per cent of women and only 5.2 per cent of married women were economically active in the South compared with 35.3 per cent and 19.5 per cent in the North. By 1995 the respective figures were 62 per cent of women and 64.2 per cent of married women in the North and 38.5 per cent of women and 36.6 per cent of married women in the South. Although even in the 1990s the proportion of women in the labour force in the South was still below the EU average of 45 per cent, there had been a very dramatic increase in married women's participation, particularly in the two decades after 1971.[102]

The mass entry of married women into the labour market and the expansion of higher education formed the background in Western developed countries to the impressive expansion of feminist movements from the 1960s on.[103] Ireland's participation in these developments was later and more muted but significant none the less. Together with an urbanized, better educated, and younger population in a society less insulated from the materialist values of consumer capitalism, they represented a major challenge to the defenders of traditional Catholic values.

The Irish Catholic Church had shown only very limited signs of responding to the far-reaching alterations in liturgy, theology, church government, and ecumenism promoted by the Second Vatican Council (1962–5). There was a process of liturgical renewal and a limited expansion of a lay role in church government. There was no objection when, in 1972, the government proposed the deletion of Article 44 of the Constitution, which had accorded a 'special position' to the Catholic Church. However, despite the radicalism of Vatican II on inter-church relations, Ireland experienced no ecumenical revolution, with inter-church activity often restricted to 'rarefied theological discussion'.[104] The Irish Church's conservatism was most obvious in its undeviating support for *Humanae Vitae*, the encyclical of Pope Paul VI, in 1968, which had come out against all artificial means of contraception. The hierarchy was relentless in its opposition to any change in the law on contraceptives despite the Supreme Court decision in the Magee case in 1973 and the fact that opinion polls showed a growing level of public support for legalisation.[105]

It was the Irish hierarchy's rigid adherence to the Vatican line on contraceptives that was mainly responsible for the weakening of the Church's moral authority in the 1970s and 1980s. It provided the impetus for the development of the Irish women's movement when, in 1971, feminists took a train from Dublin to Belfast in order to buy contraceptives and import them into the Republic in defiance of the 1935 Criminal Law (Amendment) Act, which proscribed their sale, importation, advertisement, and distribution.[106] The failure of the Coalition's attempt to reform the law in 1974 led to the formation of a Contraception Action Programme, a pressure group composed of women's groups and Labour Party activists, including Senator Mary Robinson who forced the Coalition's hand by introducing her own, much more liberal bill in the Seanad. It was their activist campaign that began to influence the public mood and made reform an issue in the 1977 election, inducing Fianna Fáil to give a commitment to introduce legislation. The Health (Family Planning) Bill was introduced by Charles Haughey in December 1978 and declared by him to be 'an Irish solution to an Irish problem'. It was a minimalist response to a situation where couples were increasingly using birth-control methods without concern for the law. It provided for the availability of contraceptives on prescription where the doctor was satisfied that they were sought '*bona fide* for the purpose of family planning'.[107]

Despite its restrictive nature, the legislation contributed to a growing traditionalist backlash. Following the example of new right pressure groups of a 'pro-life' sort in the USA and Britain, the initiative came from lay Catholics rather than the clergy or the hierarchy. The fundamentalists had been given major encouragement by the visit of Pope John Paul II to Ireland in 1979, which the Irish hierarchy had organized with the purpose of stemming what it perceived as the rising tide of materialism and secularism. The Polish Pope, smarting after an Italian referendum in favour of divorce and with an ongoing campaign to legalize abortion in Italy (which would be successful in 1981), depicted Ireland as a proud centre of the faith but warned that forces were at work in tempting it to forsake this historic role. In his address at Limerick, the Pope called for a continuing Irish witness to 'the dignity and sacredness of all human life, from conception to death'.[108]

Abortion was illegal in Ireland under the 1861 Offences Against the Person Act but the religious right feared that a successful campaign by feminists and Dublin liberals and leftists might result in its legalization. An Irish branch of the British Society for the Unborn Child was established in the aftermath of the Pope's visit and in 1981 the Pro-Life

Amendment Campaign (PLAC) was founded to lead a campaign for a constitutional amendment to prohibit abortion. Taking advantage of the unprecedented degree of governmental instability in the early 1980s, the PLAC had no problems in getting pledges from both FitzGerald and Haughey that they would support the holding of a referendum on abortion. Before it left office in 1982, the Haughey government introduced its proposed wording for an amendment to the constitution: 'The State acknowledges the right to life of the unborn and, with due regard to the right to life of the mother, guarantees in its laws to respect, and as far as is practical by its laws to defend and vindicate that right.' Back in government in 1983, FitzGerald rejected the Fianna Fáil wording but this was eventually endorsed by the Dáil with the support of Fine Gael and Labour Party defectors.

Voting took place on 7 September 1983 following a campaign that reached levels of acrimony 'probably not witnessed in Ireland since the post-Treaty campaigning by rival sides in 1922'.[109] Despite this, the result of the referendum was a disappointment for the Church. Although of those who voted 66.5 per cent were in favour of the amendment, only 54.6 per cent of those eligible had actually voted, reflecting a feeling among a significant sector of the population that the referendum was an unnecessary distraction from more pressing economic and social issues.

At the time some argued that the low turnout and the fact that the amendment was carried with only the slimmest of majorities in Dublin boded ill for the future of traditional Catholic values.[110] It was true that there was continuing evidence of large-scale rejection of the Church's position on contraception, particularly amongst the young and the university-educated, urban middle class. It was this that induced the Coalition government to introduce new family-planning legislation in 1985. Its most notable provision allowed for the sale of contraceptives to anyone aged over 18. It was passed by the Dáil despite the opposition of the Catholic hierarchy opportunistically tail-ended by Fianna Fáil. Desmond O'Malley refused to vote against the bill, arguing that the Dáil had to prove itself free to legislate on such matters regardless of the teaching of the Catholic Church. For this and his declaration that he would stand by the concept of a secular republic, he was expelled from Fianna Fáil. Within a year he was leading the Progressive Democrats, a party whose main dynamic came from the secularizing impulses of the urban middle class.[111]

That such a secularizing trend was still relatively weak was shown in 1986 when the Coalition failed in its attempt to introduce divorce, which was outlawed under Article 41 of the 1937 constitution. The hierarchy made clear its opposition to the proposed constitutional amendment and the associated divorce legislation in a leaflet delivered to every home in the country. The Archbishop of Dublin, Dr Kevin McNamara, warned that 'divorce would generate a social and moral fallout as lethal as the effects from the recent accident at the Chernobyl nuclear power station'.[112] As in 1983 the traditionalist campaign was spearheaded by a coalition of lay Catholic groups headed by the Family Solidarity organization. It amplified the Church's moral arguments, with an appeal to material insecurities connected with property and inheritance rights and visions of deserted and impoverished mothers with starving children.[113] The result was a second defeat for the liberal agenda. On a turnout of 60.5 per cent the amendment was rejected by 63.5 per cent to 36.5 per cent. There was little consolation to be drawn from the fact that the amendment was supported by a small majority of Dublin voters. Optimists argued that the low turnout in both referenda and the fact that concerns about land and property ownership as well as succession rights were important influences in the divorce referendum showed that traditionalism was on the wane. Yet when a further referendum was held in 1995, the amendment in favour of divorce was only carried by a paper-thin majority.[114]

This was hardly a ringing endorsement of pluralism. This was especially the case given that there had been a number of major blows to the religious right and the moral authority of the Catholic Church in the early 1990s. In 1992 a 14-year-old girl who was pregnant as a result of rape was prevented from seeking an abortion in Britain by an injunction obtained by the Irish Attorney General and a subsequent High Court decision that forbade her to leave the jurisdiction for nine months. An appeal to the Supreme Court produced a ruling that the 1983 amendment did in fact provide for abortion when, as in this case, there was a real threat to the life of the mother through a possible suicide.[115] The 'X' case complicated the 1992 referendum on the Maastricht Treaty as the government had previously obtained a protocol in the Treaty designed to ensure that future EU law could not override the 1983 amendment. An attempt to regularize the situation with a further and more restrictive amendment failed to satisfy either side of the debate and was rejected.

To the disarray of the religious right was added the discomfiture of the Church as a result of a series of clerical sex scandals that dominated the media and fascinated and repulsed the public. In 1992 the *Irish Times* revealed that the high-profile Bishop of Galway, Eamonn Casey, had fathered a child when he was Bishop of Kerry in the 1970s. He had pressurized the mother to have the child adopted and then used dio- cesan funds to make payments to ensure the mother's silence.[116] Even more damaging for the Church was a deluge of charges that there had been the institutional cover-up of the sexual and physical abuse of chil- dren by priests and members of religious orders. The dam broke in the autumn of 1994 when Father Brendan Smyth was convicted in a Belfast court of sexually abusing children. A subsequent television documentary revealed that he had a record of paedophilia in Ireland, the US, and Britain that had been known to his own order and other Church author- ities who had shielded him by moving him to another parish when- ever complaints arose. Exposures of the physical and sexual abuse of children by members of religious orders, male and female, who had been responsible for running residential institutions quickly followed.

The author of a historical sociology of the Irish Catholic Church described the results of these scandals: 'The media have driven a stake into the heart of the institutional church from which it will recover, but never fully. We will never see the likes of the Catholic Church's moral monopoly again.'[117] Mass attendance rates had remained impressively high throughout the 1970s and 1980s, especially by international stand- ards. As late as 1990, 85 per cent of those surveyed went to mass at least once a week. By 1997 this had dropped to 65 per cent.[118] This was still high by international standards and, as one historian noted, 'it would be wrong to write off the Catholic Church's grip upon the mores and the outlook of its Irish members.'[119]

Yet the Church's capacity to defend its power and influence was even more profoundly sapped by a sharp decline in vocations. Ordinations for the priesthood dropped from 412 in 1965 to forty-four in 1998, while even starker declines occurred in those entering the religious orders. Between 1967 and the 1998 the total number of priests, brothers, and nuns in Ireland fell from almost 34,000 to just under 20,000, or by 41 per cent.[120] An ageing, shrinking Church was unable to staff the schools, hospitals, and other public services that provided much of the insti- tutional basis of its power as late as the 1960s. The political significance of this was twofold. First, it removed the 'Catholic card' from electoral politics to the disadvantage of the party that had been most proficient in using it—Fianna Fáil. Second, it revealed the hollowness of the argu- ment that the main motivation behind Ulster Unionist resistance to Irish unity was a fear of Catholic power as the growing secularization of the Republic did little to undermine support for partition in the northern majority. Despite this, the political leader identified with this analysis, Garret FitzGerald, was responsible for the most significant political advance for Irish nationalism since partition.

The Republic and the Anglo-Irish Agreement

The marginalization of those in the Fianna Fáil leadership identified with a more conciliatory line on Northern Ireland provided Garret FitzGerald with an opportunity to establish Fine Gael as the sensible, moderate alternative on the North and Anglo-Irish relations. At a time of considerable tension over the hunger strikes and the Falklands War, this was an approach that appealed to an electorate that ranked Northern Ireland far down on the list of issues that would influence its vote. It also made FitzGerald seem more the sort of Taoiseach with whom Mrs Thatcher might do business.

In September 1981 FitzGerald had announced that he wanted to launch a crusade to create a 'genuine republic' with which northern Protestants would wish to have a relationship. Criticizing the Republic, he declared 'If I were a northern Protestant today, I cannot see how I could be attracted to getting involved with a state that is itself sectarian.'[121] Although FitzGerald's willingness to criticize the Catholic ethos of the Republic and his desire to open up dialogue with Unionists, rather than appeal over their heads to London, raised his popularity ratings in Belfast, the honeymoon was short-lived. His 'constitutional crusade' did not survive the pressures of the abortion debate. The victories of Sinn Féin candidates in the Assembly elections put paid to his earlier objective of seeking a solution to the northern conflict through dialogue with the Unionists: 'I had come to the conclusion that I must now give priority to heading off the growth of support for the IRA in Northern Ireland by seeking a new understanding with the British government'.[122]

FitzGerald's decision to establish the New Ireland Forum in 1983 was clearly related to an immediate political crisis: the threat posed by Sinn Féin to the SDLP. However, it was also prompted by Hume's idea that all the main constitutional nationalist parties on the island needed to produce an agreed statement of the principles believed to be at stake in the Northern Ireland conflict. This statement would then be the basis for an approach to the British government. The Forum comprised representatives of the SDLP, Fianna Fáil, Fine Gael, and the Irish Labour Party.

Although unlike Hume's original idea it was open to Unionist participation, its stated purpose of unifying and revivifying the non-
violent nationalist tradition ensured that none of the Unionist parties
participated, although some Unionists gave evidence as individuals.

Professor John Whyte noted that the Forum, with government funding and a full-time staff, was in a position to make a weightier contribution to the discussion on Northern Ireland than any previous body on
the nationalist side since the All-Party Anti-Partition Conference in
1949.[123] Given that the latter resulted in little more than a restatement of
old nationalist attitudes, this was not a very exacting criterion of success.
In fact the final Report was an unimpressive document. This in part
reflected the need to ensure that Charles Haughey was kept on board.
The demands of pan-nationalist unity among the constitutional parties
ensured that the historical section was untainted by any of the 'revisionist ideas' that had increasingly influenced the professional writing
of Irish history. Similarly, it was Haughey's veto power that resulted
in all the party leaders agreeing to a unitary thirty-two county state
as the Report's preferred constitutional option. It is true that the
Report referred to two other options—a confederal Ireland and joint
authority—and that the latter implied an acceptance that a total British
withdrawal might not be necessary for a solution of the Northern
Ireland problem. However, as neither constitutional nationalism nor
physical force republicanism was any nearer to achieving British withdrawal in 1984 than they had been in 1949, the retraction of ambition
might be interpreted as a not very substantial concession.

This was certainly the predictable Ulster Unionist response. However,
despite Mrs Thatcher's vigorous rejection of all three options at a press
conference after her summit meeting with FitzGerald in November 1984,
the Anglo-Irish Agreement, while not joint authority, for the first time
did provide the Irish state with considerable leverage on the governance
of Northern Ireland. Public opinion in the Republic was supportive of
the Agreement and Charles Haughey's denunciation of it as 'copper-
fastening partition' was not well received. As leading members of Fianna
Fáil announced that the party was proud to be 'the sole party with the
nationalist forces', Haughey appeared to take a position on the Agreement that was indistinguishable from that of Gerry Adams. Such
extremism was damaging. Support for the Agreement rose from 59 per
cent, with 32 per cent supporting Haughey's position in its immediate
aftermath, to 69 per cent in favour by February 1986.[124] It was becoming
increasingly clear that public opinion in the Republic, while still robustly

nationalist, saw the Agreement as achieving a shift in the balance of power in Northern Ireland that favoured the SDLP and Dublin, while still maintaining northern passions and violence at arm's length.

The unpopularity of Haughey's negative reaction to the Anglo-Irish Agreement had forced him to backtrack,[125] and by the time of his resignation in 1992, his ambitions for the North did not seem to go beyond joint authority, a position he had execrated when it was supported by Garret FitzGerald in the 1980s. In an analysis of public attitudes in the Republic towards Northern Ireland written two years after the Agreement, Peter Mair demonstrated that while the aspiration to unity was pervasive, less than a third of the electorate was prepared to pay extra taxes to achieve it. Elections were fought and lost on economic issues. He concluded: 'Irish voters will be primarily concerned about their pocket-books for the foreseeable future while Northern Ireland will remain a foreign country.'[126] While the Agreement would do much to increase the involvement of the Irish government in the day-to-day governance of the North, it did little to undermine popular aversion to the 'Black North' and what were seen as its two squabbling and murderous tribes.

The Republic in the 1990s

Although the birth of the 'Celtic Tiger' in the 1990s had its roots in the resurrected social partnership that Haughey's governments had developed from 1987, it did not provide his party with the electoral boost that Lemass's investment in economic programming and corporatism had given Fianna Fáil in the 1960s. Haughey was forced to resign in January 1992 when his former Minister of Justice, Seán Doherty, revealed his complicity in the phone-tapping of two journalists in 1982. However, even before the Doherty revelation, his leadership had been under renewed pressure because of increasing public concern at what became known as the 'Golden Circle': prominent businessmen who had used various sharp practices to make multi-million pound deals and whose accountants and lawyers had created complex structures to conceal their identities and reduce or eliminate their tax liabilities. The 'Golden Circle' had close personal and political connections with leading politicians.[127] At the centre of these concerns was Larry Goodman, the dominant figure in the Republic's meat-processing industry. Goodman was a friend of Haughey's and other leading members of Fianna Fáil, and after Haughey returned to power in 1987 his business had received substantial assistance from the IDA and also from the Ministry of Industry and Commerce for an export credit insurance scheme to cover its beef exports to Iraq.[128] The beef industry had long been the subject of allegations of corruption and in May 1991 the ITV programme *World in Action* alleged that serious malpractices were commonplace in Goodman's plants. The PD leader in the coalition, Des O'Malley, insisted on a tribunal of inquiry, which revealed that many of the allegations, including millions of pounds of tax evasion, were true.

Haughey's successor, Albert Reynolds, had as Minister of Industry and Commerce been extremely relaxed in granting Goodman's group large amounts of export credit insurance for their extremely risky venture into the Iraqi market. A self-made millionaire from Longford who made his money in dancehalls and dog food, there was never any suggestion of personal corruption on his part. Nevertheless, the tribunal led to the collapse of the government when Reynolds accused O'Malley of committing perjury in his evidence and the PDs withdrew from the government. The subsequent general election produced a spectacular result for Dick Spring and the Labour Party, whose vote increased by almost 10 per cent to 19.3 per cent—its highest since 1922—and whose number of seats increased from fifteen to thirty-three. Fianna Fáil's vote declined to 39 per cent, its worst since 1927, while Fine Gael, which had been shaken by the emergence of the PDs, saw its vote decline by almost 5 per cent to 24.5 per cent.[129]

Labour's victory had been anticipated in the 1990 presidential elections when, for the first time since the inauguration of the office, Fianna Fáil's candidate had been defeated. Spring had persuaded the constitutional lawyer and champion of divorce and contraception Mary Robinson to stand, even though she had resigned from Labour over the Anglo-Irish Agreement. The first woman candidate for the post, Robinson also gained the support of the Workers' Party, the Greens, and many women's groups. Her declarations of support for gay rights and for the active promotion of contraception did not endear her to many male voters in rural Ireland, although her gender and some of the crasser attacks on her by male Fianna Fáil politicians may have led their wives and daughters to a different conclusion. The one region where she triumphed over Brian Lenihan, the Fianna Fáil candidate, was Dublin City and County and there was a strong correlation between support for Robinson and a 'progressive' stance in the abortion and divorce referenda, leading one commentator to claim that 'the "new Ireland" had emerged victorious after two referenda defeats'.[130] This 'new Ireland', a constituency of the young, educated, urban middle class, was well represented among Fine Gael voters and large numbers of them had voted for Robinson rather than Austen Currie, the former SDLP politician who was the party's candidate. Currie's vote at 17 per cent was a major setback for Fine Gael and led to the resignation of Alan Dukes and his replacement by John Bruton. Despite this, it was the distribution of Currie's second preferences that ensured Robinson's victory, as she was trailing Lenihan by 38.9 per cent to 44.1 per cent after the first count.

Labour's surge in 1992 was in part a product of the 'Robinson effect' but it was also a reflection of widespread public perception of a Fianna Fáil political class embroiled in sleaze. Neither of these factors would continue to favour the party once Spring shocked many of his party supporters by entering into a coalition with Reynolds. After the collapse of the Reynolds government in 1992, Spring had told the Dáil it was impossible to envisage entering into partnership with a party that 'has gone so far down the road of blindness to standards and blindness to the people they are supposed to represent'.[131] However, after the election Spring displayed no real enthusiasm for John Bruton's proposal of a 'rainbow coalition' including Fine Gael, Labour, and the Progressive Democrats. This reflected the deep-rooted hostility of Spring to Bruton, which had its origin in bitter clashes between the two when they were in the 1983–7 coalition. Spring was also concerned that neither Fine Gael nor the Progressive Democrats would countenance the participation of Democratic Left in the coalition. This party had been formed when six of the seven Workers' Party TDs had split from the organization in March 1992 over their disquiet about revelations of the continuing links between leading members of the WP and the Official IRA in Northern Ireland.[132] Labour, watchful of its left flank, went through the motions of negotiating a platform with Democratic Left to construct a centre-left government with Fine Gael but this became academic when after a series of recounts it was confirmed that the Democatic Left had lost its Dublin South-Central seat, robbing the centre-left option of sufficient Dáil support.

Although some of Reynolds's colleagues were hostile to the idea of a coalition with Labour, Brian Lenihan welcomed the possibility of a return to Fianna Fáil's social republican past when it had initially governed with the support of the Labour Party. Spring had sent Reynolds a paper drawn up by Labour and the Democratic Left during their negotiations and Fianna Fáil's response was drafted by the Taoiseach's special adviser, the Oxford-educated historian Dr Martin Mansergh. Although

the perceived incongruity between his Protestant, Anglo-Irish background and his strong republican line on Northern Ireland was to
make him a figure of fascination for many journalists, another side to
Mansergh's intellectual make-up was important in the formation of
the Coalition. This was his firm conviction that Fianna Fáil's social-
republican and corporatist tendencies had been the real source of its
hegemony in Irish politics.[133] Such a leftist portrayal of the party eased
Labour's way into government but the process was undoubtedly greatly
assisted by Reynolds's apparent success at the Edinburgh EU summit,
where he claimed to have secured £8 billion for Ireland in structural
and cohesion funds up to 1999. This made it easier to implement those
elements of Labour's programme that involved a commitment to extra
expenditure on health and social welfare, which in turn enabled
Reynolds to insist that Labour accept the budgetary constraints imposed
by the Maastricht Treaty. All of the Labour demands on the 'liberal
agenda' and the issue of sleaze were included in the programme for
government with commitments to an Ethics in Government Bill, Dáil
reform, the introduction of divorce, abortion legislation, and the
decriminalization of homosexuality. Labour's stunning electoral performance was also recognized in an unprecedented profile in government. It had six of the fifteen cabinet posts and a special office of the
Tánaiste was created, situated in government buildings, with its own
staff and budget.

Despite such an apparently auspicious beginning, including a Dáil
majority of 42, the largest in the history of the state, the Coalition was
characterized by internal conflict almost from the start. In part this
reflected a serious personality clash between Reynolds and Spring: 'The
two men were like chalk and cheese and seemed always prepared to
think the worst of each other. In contrast to Reynolds's bright and
breezy style, Spring was thoughtful and reserved and quick to take
offence.'[134] Such tensions were exacerbated by Labour's increasing dissatisfaction with Reynolds's failure to rein in Fianna Fáil's proclivity to
favour its business allies and his tendency, when the need arose, to
behave as if he were leading a single-party government. Spring, conscious of the shock that his move into government with Fianna Fáil had
caused many of those who had voted Labour in 1992, was determined
that Labour would play a high-profile and assertive role in government.
Labour insisted on a new system of ministerial programme managers
whose job it was to ensure that the coalition deal was implemented. The
programme managers appointed by the six Labour ministers were all

Labour Party activists and Labour surprised even Reynolds and shocked some of its supporters in the media by the extent to which political and familial nepotism influenced its appointments from special advisers to secretaries and drivers.[135]

In 1993 Reynolds insisted on a new amnesty for tax evaders, the second in five years, which was opposed by his own Minister of Finance Bertie Ahern and which deeply troubled many Labour supporters already annoyed by the government's first budget in 1993, which had increased taxes and imposed a 1 per cent income levy.[136] Further concessions to the rich came in the 1994 Finance Bill, which relaxed the tax regime for wealthy expatriates, and in the so-called 'Masri affair'. This arose from the granting of Irish citizenship to two members of the Masri family from Saudi Arabia under a Business Migration Scheme. It transpired that the two businessmen had invested £1 million in an Irish pet food company that was owned by Reynolds. Reynolds in turn was exasperated with what he regarded as Labour's refusal to face up to hard economic decisions—the budget was a response to a difficult economic situation, which included a significant rise in unemployment and a currency crisis that had forced a devaluation of the Irish pound.

He and his colleagues were also deeply resentful about Labour's 'holier-than-thou' pose as the moral mudguard of the coalition. This was the context in which Reynolds ignored a cabinet decision that the forthcoming report of the Beef Tribunal would be studied before the government issued its collective response. Instead, fearing that Labour would use the report to undermine him, Reynolds had the report scrutinized by his own legal and political advisers and then issued a statement that the report had vindicated his role in the affair. Spring was furious at having been ignored—the Taoiseach refused to accept his phone calls while the report was being studied—and his supporters claim he only remained in government because of the delicate state of the peace process in Northern Ireland.[137]

It was in the area of Northern Ireland policy that the Reynolds/Spring coalition registered its major success. Reynolds had inherited the ongoing contacts that Haughey had initiated with Sinn Féin but was able to develop these within the context of a new engagement with John Major, the British Prime Minister. Taking up John Hume's idea that a joint declaration by London and Dublin on the basic principles of a settlement could create the conditions for an IRA cease-fire, he displayed a ruthless pragmatism and a willingness to accommodate the constitutional concerns of Ulster Unionists. The result was the Downing Street

Declaration of December 1993, with its subtle combination of 'green' language and democratic content. Further inducements were proffered to republicans, including an end to their banishment from the airwaves and an Irish version of a proposed Anglo-Irish Framework document that provided a 'dynamic' set of North–South institutions that republicans could envisage as 'transitional' to a united Ireland. Reynolds persuaded President Clinton to allow a visa to Gerry Adams for a visit to the US. In return, Reynolds made it clear that the only response he would be satisfied with was a permanent end to violence. The alternative he made clear was a deal with Major, the Unionists, and the SDLP, which would leave republicans isolated.[138] The IRA's announcement of a 'complete cessation of military operations' on 31 August 1994 was to a very significant extent Reynolds's achievement: his blunt businessman's approach with its lack of ideological baggage on the North and above all his willingness to take major risks had paid off.

However, even this success was double-edged for it was very much the Taoiseach's and Spring, despite his role as Foreign Minister and a history of Anglo-Irish involvement going back to 1984/2, was marginalized. In fact, it is doubtful whether Spring's background and his political base in 'republican' Kerry would have allowed him to deal as robustly with Sinn Féin as Reynolds had done. A radical deterioration in relations between the coalition partners had occurred over Reynolds's treatment of the Beef Tribunal report. A terminal blow was struck in November 1994, when Reynolds insisted on appointing Attorney General Harry Whelehan as President of the High Court. Spring had opposed Whelehan, who was a conservative with no judicial experience, and when it transpired that the Attorney General's office had been responsible for a delay in the processing of an extradition warrant for a paedophile priest and that a similar case had occurred in 1993, the Labour ministers resigned from the government and Reynolds stepped down as leader of Fianna Fáil.

Fine Gael, Labour, and the Democratic Left, whose Dáil strength had increased to six TDs after two by-election victories, were able to form a 'rainbow coalition' in December 1994 with John Bruton as Taoiseach. Labour retained six cabinet seats while the Democratic Left leader, Proinsias de Rossa, became Minister of Social Welfare and three of the party's TDs were appointed Ministers of State. The three parties established a good working relationship and there was no repeat of the divisions that had been a feature of the previous administration. Tensions did exist between Spring and de Rossa on Northern Ireland because of the latter's hostility to Sinn Féin and his clear sympathy for mainstream

Ulster Unionism. This was particularly so after the coalition's greatest setback: the ending of the IRA cease-fire in February 1996. Republicans blamed Major for allegedly using the question of IRA weapons as an obstacle to 'conflict resolution' and, supported by Albert Reynolds, they criticized Bruton and de Rossa for being accomplices in 'British intransigence'. Spring's most influential adviser, Fergus Finlay, publicly established clear green water between Spring and his government partners by declaring that talks without Sinn Féin were 'not worth a penny candle'.[139]

One of the most significant effects of the peace process after 1992 was the increasing 'Ulsterization' of politics in the Republic, as there was a qualitative leap in the amount of time and energy that the Republic's political class had to invest in the developing political situation in the North. Public opinion in the Republic was also affected as, for the first time since 1969, there appeared to be a real possibility of an end to violence. The effects were complex. On the one hand there was a willingness to jettison more traditional forms of irredentism and, in 1998, support what was essentially a 'two states—one nation' settlement. On the other there was an upsurge in uncritical support for northern nationalism, once it appeared that its violent cutting edge could be discarded. The fact that the IRA went back to war in February 1996 was put down to John Major's indulgence of Ulster Unionist intransigence, an interpretation that was then considered vindicated by the sectarian stand-off over the Portadown Orange Order's desire to march down the mainly nationalist Garvaghy Road. During the 1997 general election campaign Bertie Ahern attacked Bruton's handling of the peace process, asserting that it was the duty of the Taoiseach to act as leader of 'Nationalist Ireland'. Sinn Féin won its first seat since 1957 when its candidate topped the poll in Cavan-Monaghan. Although its overall vote at 2.5 per cent was still small, it had overtaken the Democratic Left and good polls in Kerry and inner-city Dublin showed a substantial potential for growth. This potential was all the greater given the increasingly fragmented nature of party support in the Republic.

Fianna Fáil's performance was not impressive in terms of votes: it was only marginally up on 1992 at 39.3 per cent, although a more effective vote management strategy brought it an extra nine seats. Fine Gael had been rescued from the doldrums by Bruton's performance in government and its share of the vote increased from 24.5 per cent to almost 30 per cent, gaining it an extra nine seats. Labour paid the price for its embrace of Reynolds with its vote almost halved to 9 per cent and its number of seats dropping from thirty-three to seventeen. Although the Progressive Democrat vote held up at just under 5 per cent, it lost six of its ten seats. Bertie Ahern was able to construct a minority coalition government with the PDs depending on the support of some of the plethora of independents who had been elected.[140]

Fine Gael had consolidated its position as the second major party in the state and in opposition had begun to portray itself as the leader of a social democratic alternative to a conservative Fianna Fáil/PD alliance. Bertie Ahern, who had been a trade union activist before entering full-time politics, was unlikely to accept such a right-wing designation for his party and the strong performance of the economy in the closing years of the century made it easier to avoid the traditional tough choices between expenditure and tax cuts. His government's position was also strengthened by his role in the Northern peace process and, above all, by the Good Friday Agreement. Fianna Fáil's choice of a northern Catholic, the Queen's University Law Professor, Mary McAleese, as its presidential candidate when Mary Robinson resigned in 1997 was the first clear indication of how 'Ulsterization' could benefit Fianna Fáil. McAleese, whom some members of the SDLP regarded as a Sinn Féin sympathizer, was an example of a new breed of younger, upwardly mobile Catholics who had benefited from reformist direct rule. Self-confident in their nationalism, they regarded a non-violent republican movement as a more effective voice than the increasingly tired and middle-aged SDLP.

The peace process had dominated the Irish media for most of the 1990s. After the IRA cessation Sinn Féin's leaders had many less occasions to appear as apologists for violence and instead projected themselves as calm, reasonable, and earnest men who talked about peace. For younger voters with no direct experience of atrocities like Enniskillen, Teebane Cross, or the Shankill Road bombing, Sinn Féin became an increasingly attractive anti-establishment political force. A survey of school students carried out by the National Youth Council of Ireland in 2000 showed that it was the second most popular party after Fianna Fáil and had almost as much support as Fine Gael, Labour, and the Greens put together.[141]

Sinn Féin, despite the IRA's bloody history and the organization's involvement in criminal activities including armed robberies and smuggling, did not hesitate to denounce the 'immorality' of the Republic's political élite. Certainly the scale of corruption involving senior political figures, most of whom were members of Fianna Fáil, proved substantial, as evidenced by the results of the two tribunals of inquiry set up to investigate, first, the finances of Charles Haughey and second, the way the physical planning process had been distorted by developers' payments to Dublin-based TDs and councillors. What is surprising was its relatively muted political impact.

Although Fianna Fáil did not win any of the five by-elections held during the new Dáil, it did reasonably well in the local and European elections held in 1999 and there was little evidence of a revival of the main opposition parties. Labour under a new leader, Ruairi Quinn, had merged in 1998 with the Democratic Left. The new organization turned out to be less than the sum of its constituent parts, as the smaller party's more radical, campaigning edge and its commitment to those excluded from the benefits of the Celtic Tiger were absorbed without trace in Labour's parliamentarist blandness.[142] The merger opened up a space in the most deprived working-class neighbourhoods, which was soon filled by Sinn Féin with the potent mixture of populist nationalism and vigilante justice for local drug dealers and petty criminals which it had perfected in the North. Fine Gael, which had fought the 1997 election on left-of-centre commitments to a more equitable tax system and the need for radical improvements in public services, did not sustain this dynamic in opposition. As its support in opinion polls slumped,[143] a sizeable section of the party in the Dáil blamed John Bruton's leadership style, stiff and didactic, and his alleged 'pro-Unionist' bias on the North. However, his successor, Michael Noonan, more populist and more nationalist, did not produce any significant improvement in the party's poll ratings.

Bertie Ahern's 'Teflon' quality, his ability despite his former close links to Haughey not to be seriously damaged by the tribunal's revelations, must be linked to the astonishing performance of the Republic's economy in the first three years of the coalition (1997–2000). Growth rates at 10 per cent a year were unprecedented and unemployment fell from 10 per cent to under 4 per cent for the first time in the history of the state. The result was that, as one financial journalist put it, 'normal rules of budgetary policy did not seem to apply, every budget brought lower taxes, higher spending and the promise of more to come.'[144] The Minister of Finance, Charlie McCreevy, was able over four budgets to make substantial cuts in direct taxation. The main beneficiary was the business community and high earners: corporation tax was cut from 36 per cent to 16 per cent and capital gains tax was halved, while probate tax was abolished. The large surpluses generated by the Celtic Tiger did permit substantial tax benefits to workers as well: there were substantial cuts in the standard and top rates of income tax and a widening of the standard rate band.[145] Increasing private affluence, while it greatly strengthened the government's ability to insulate itself from the revelations of sleaze, did not prevent it from being criticized for ignoring the evidence that while the Republic was now one of the richest countries in the EU it was also one of the most unequal, with a crumbling infrastructure and seriously under-funded public services. Social spending fell as a share of GDP during the period 1997–2001 and, according to the United Nations Human Development Report, the Republic had the second highest level of poverty in the developed world.[146]

Issues of who benefited from the Celtic Tiger became more pressing when, in 2001, it became evident that the years of spectacular boom were over. The economic downturn reflected the global slowdown in the information and communications technology sector on which Ireland was particularly dependent. Even before the events of September 11, the Republic had been hard hit by the recession. As the IDA calculated that 6,500 multinational jobs were lost in 2001 and the economy's rate of growth slumped from 11 per cent in 2000 to 3 per cent,[147] the Governor of the Central Bank declared the era of the Celtic Tiger was over.[148]

The coalition's response to the end of the boom was unsure. Some ministers, including McCreevy and the Tánaiste and PD leader Mary Harney, continued to articulate a strong neo-liberal response, criticizing the EU for its 'outmoded philosophy of high taxation and heavy regulation' and declaring that the Republic was 'spiritually closer to Boston than Berlin'.[149] Others, including the Taoiseach, rediscovered Fianna Fáil's social democratic vocation and Ahern even called himself a socialist.[150] The conflicting messages contributed to the government's major defeat on the Treaty of Nice Referendum in June 2001. The Treaty was designed to make the institutional reforms to EU decision-making structures necessary for enlargement. Supported by all the main parties, the trade unions, employers, farmers' organizations and the Irish Catholic bishops, it was nevertheless rejected by 54 per cent of the third of the electorate who bothered to vote.

The two parties that had been active in the anti-Nice campaign, the Greens and Sinn Féin, put a radical, anti-militarist gloss on the result. However, it appears that the biggest factor leading to a 'No' vote was what one academic labelled a 'growing independence sentiment: the feeling that Ireland should do all that it can to protect its independence from the EU'.[151] With the Republic now too rich to enjoy 'objective one' status and the access to structural funds that it provided and with the prospect of having to compete for EU resources with the prospective new members from the former Soviet bloc, Irish Euro-scepticism reflected insular self-interest more than some radical anti-system agenda. The darker side of Irish Euro-scepticism was also seen in increasing evidence of racism and antagonism to foreign workers and asylum seekers attracted during the Tiger years.

Ahern suffered another significant reversal when the government held a referendum on abortion in March 2002. The government's proposal aimed at 'tidying up' the situation created by the 'X' case: it proposed to remove the threat of suicide as a justification for a termination. Ahern had given a pledge to deal with the issue during the 1997 campaign and had made a post-election commitment to hold a referendum to four of the Independent TDs who supported the government. Despite the support of the Catholic Church and the main 'pro-life' groups, the government's amendment was narrowly defeated: 49.58 per cent to 50.42 on a turnout of 42.89 per cent. Although there was a clear urban–rural divide with Dublin, Cork, Galway, and Limerick voting 'No' and the predominantly rural constituencies voting 'Yes', the turnout in urban areas was higher than that in the countryside, indicating the waning of traditional Ireland. As one commentator noted, 'Never before has the electorate refused to yield before the full force of Rome and the Republican Party.'[152]

Despite his defeats on Nice and abortion, and despite the economic downturn, Ahern's reputation for competence, even statesmanship, which had been gained through his role in the peace process, remained a major asset to Fianna Fáil. It helped to cement Fianna Fáil's success in the Republic's general election in May 2002. Fighting on the slogan, 'A Lot Done, More to Do', the party portrayed itself as the only political force large enough and coherent enough to protect the prosperity generated by the Celtic Tiger in a more unstable international environment and at a time of increasing evidence that there had been a serious deterioration in the public finances during 2001.[153]

Fine Gael, which had alienated some of its core support with Noonan's more nationalist stance on the North, further disconcerted them with a manifesto full of spending commitments which allowed Fianna Fáil to attack it for irresponsibility. Fine Gael's incoherence and its low poll ratings led to large-scale defections by its supporters to Labour, Fianna Fáil and the Progressive Democrats who appealed to the electorate to deny Fianna Fáil an overall majority and ensure that they could continue to act as a governmental restraint on the larger party. Labour refused Noonan's plea for a pre-election pact but, like Fine Gael, it underestimated the majority of the electorate's preference for governmental stability over specific spending commitments. It calculated on a post-election deal with either Fine Gael or Fianna Fáil, but Fine Gael's weakness and Fianna Fáil's buoyancy in the opinion polls during the campaign made either prospect unlikely. However, Labour's implicit commitment to a centrist coalition meant that it failed to benefit from the substantial 'anti-establishment' vote that went to Sinn Féin, the Greens, and Independents.

The result was a triumph for Ahern and a disaster for Noonan. Fianna Fáil's vote rose by over 2 per cent to 41.7 per cent and its number of seats from seventy-seven to eighty-one. Fine Gael's vote fell by 5.5 per cent to 22.5 per cent while its seats plummeted from fifty-four to thirty-one. In Dublin it was left with only three TDs, putting it in fifth place. Labour's vote fell by 2 per cent to 10.77 per cent although it returned with the same number of seats: twenty-one. The Progressive Democrats, despite a small decline in their vote (0.72 per cent to 3.96), doubled their number of seats to eight. Sinn Féin's vote increased by 4 per cent to 6.5 per cent and its number of seats from one to five. The Green vote increased by 2 per cent to 3.85 and its seats from two to six. There would be a record number of Independents in the new Dáil: fifteen.[154]

For all the immense economic, social, and cultural changes that the Republic had undergone since the 1960s, its party system remained largely unaffected. The 2002 election seemed to some commentators to portend radical change.[155] Although 'Civil War politics' had long since diminished in significance in terms of the issues on which Irish elections were fought, it had continued to structure the party system. Now there was much talk of a terminal crisis for Fine Gael as that party lost its historic position as the core of any potential anti-Fianna Fáil coalition. While this opened up the possibility of a clearer right–left divide in Irish politics, the left was more fragmented than ever as Labour faced a strong and growing challenge from Sinn Féin (which had performed best of all in Dublin) and the Greens.

Sinn Féin had benefited from its role in the northern peace process but its election campaign had stuck doggedly to economic and social issues and there was little to support its hope that the focus of national-ism in the Republic would begin to transcend a twenty-six county framework. The Republic in 2002 was a more prosperous and self-confident country but the height of the ambitions of its people in rela-tion to Northern Ireland was a good deal for its Catholics and, even more importantly, that its violent potential to disrupt normality in the South be switched off once and for all.

10

Between War and Peace:
Northern Ireland 1985–2002

Direct Rule with a Green Tinge 1985–93

The argument had surfaced from the Irish side in the negotiation of the Agreement that one positive effect of the accord would be to 're-educate' Unionism by making it clear that only by accepting power-sharing devolution could it minimize the role of the Dublin government in the affairs of the North. This thesis had been doubted by the British but it was in fact borne out, even though changes in the disposition of the SDLP made it of dubious significance.

The early life of the Agreement was dominated by the theme of confrontation: Paisley versus Thatcher. It soon became clear, however, that the Unionist campaign against the Agreement—in its most intense form including strikes and attacks on the homes of members of the RUC for alleged 'collaboration'—lacked the resources to win. In particular the widespread sense of material dependence on the UK Exchequer was profoundly debilitating and prevented mass militancy. The Agreement's fundamental unpopularity with Protestants was to remain one of the core facts of Northern Irish political life, but this was to coexist with a growing awareness that the Agreement was a more-or-less permanent fixture in the governance of Northern Ireland. In January 1986 the mass resignation of Unionist MPs, by far the most striking of the anti-Agreement strategies, had led to only a slight increase in the Unionist vote in the subsequent by-elections.[1]

Another notable feature of the post-Agreement landscape was the weakening of the DUP, which appeared powerless in the face of the Agreement. Indeed the DUP's intransigence could be credibly presented as part of the reason for the imposition of the accord itself. The DUP's practice of resistance to relatively marginal concessions to the Catholic community was in any case rendered futile when such a substantial concession as the Agreement was already in place. The party entered hesitantly into a pact with the Unionist Party from which it emerged in a weakened state, shorn of some of its best-known leaders. In the 1992 general election it achieved a mere 13.7 per cent of the poll, although its decline stabilized somewhat at 17.2 per cent in the May 1993 local government elections.[2] The DUP's difficulties went hand in hand with a steady rise in Protestant paramilitarism: loyalist paramilitaries killed only two people in 1984, but by 1991–2 they were more active agents of death than the IRA.

While the Agreement led to a significant increase in support for integrationist ideas amongst the Protestant middle class, James Molyneaux advocated a strategic minimalism based on twin perceptions of the need to maintain Unionist Party unity and of increasing Conservative disenchantment with the Agreement. Aware of the weakening of the Unionist position that the Agreement had so graphically established, and while deeply averse to the more traditional NIO objective of power-sharing devolution, Molyneaux was nevertheless determined that mainstream Unionism would not be imprisoned within a public posture of inflexibility. If the British government was to raise the possibility of a new and more broadly based agreement, the Unionist Party would not adopt a rejectionist stance.[3]

But if there was to be increasing evidence of a new-found Unionist Party flexibility, it could not disguise the profound divisions that still existed with constitutional nationalism. This was only partly because the leadership of the Unionist Party still found it publicly unpalatable to talk of power-sharing devolution. For the SDLP had, by 1988, shown clear signs of moving decisively beyond the demands of Sunningdale. This was, in part, the result of the failure of the Agreement to marginalize Sinn Féin. For although that party's support had peaked before the Agreement, it had consolidated at around 11 per cent of the electorate. While the Agreement had accelerated those tendencies that made direct rule the 'best possible shell' for an expanding Catholic middle class, it had delivered neither the final decisive defeat for Unionism nor the concrete economic benefits for the impoverished urban Catholic ghettos that might have reduced republican support in a more substantive way. It was also a reflection of the failure of Hume's own belief in the early phase of the Agreement—from November 1985 to mid 1987—that since Mrs Thatcher had 'lanced the Protestant boil' by imposing the Agreement on the majority community, the Unionists would have no alternative but to negotiate with him. He had predicted in an *Observer* interview that this would occur by the end of 1986.[4] The failure of the prediction produced, with the lack of a Sinn Féin meltdown, a radical turn away from the vista of Sunningdale—a marginalization of the men of violence through a coming together of constitutional nationalism and Unionism. The 'pan-nationalist front' was beginning to emerge.

The first sign of this was the seven-month-long dialogue between the SDLP and Sinn Féin in 1988. This was facilitated by Sinn Féin's desire to avoid the political isolation and marginalization that were the objective of the Agreement. Despite the political breakthrough of 1982 and 1983, Gerry Adams recognized that as long as the Sinn Féin vote was contained at around 30 to 40 per cent of the Catholic electorate—as seemed likely—the impetus of the 1982 electoral surge might well dissipate. Adams was also concerned that Sinn Féin's attempt to build up an electoral base in the Republic had so far proved fruitless. The breakthrough of their bitter enemies, the Officials—now known as Sinn Féin The Workers' Party—into Dáil politics was noted with some envy by Adams and his comrades, particularly after the three SFWP deputies had forced Haughey to cut a deal with them in order to form a government in 1982.[5] Convinced that the party's maintenance of the traditional policy of refusing to take their seats in the Dáil was a major obstacle to political advance in the Republic, Adams and his allies had waged a campaign against abstentionism, which culminated in the Sinn Féin árd fheis in 1986 voting to remove the ban on attendance at the Dáil from the party's constitution.

The removal of the ban had provoked a final break with the traditionalists led by Ruairí Ó'Brádaigh and Daithi O'Connaill, who resigned from the party and created Republican Sinn Féin. Adams's critics claimed that despite his continued public support for the 'armed struggle', the logic of increasing political involvement would eventually lead the Provisionals down the same road as the Officials and Fianna Fáil towards incorporation in the 'partitionist system'. In 1981, when Adams was starting the process of building up the political side of the movement, Danny Morrison had brilliantly anticipated the complaints of the more militarist elements in a speech to the Sinn Féin árd fheis in which he proclaimed 'Who here really believes that we can win the war through the ballot box? But will anyone here object if, with a ballot paper in one hand and an Armalite in the other, we take power in Ireland?'[6] In fact, although tremendously effective as rhetoric, the 'armalite and ballot box strategy' did put a severe limit on Sinn Féin's capacity to grow electorally in both states. Adams was soon criticizing IRA 'mistakes' that killed ordinary people and deterred northern Catholics from voting for his party. In the first general election in the Republic after the decision to get rid of abstentionism, support for Sinn Féin was a mere 1.9 per cent.[7] The connection with northern violence was clearly a formidable obstacle to Adams' aim of Sinn Féin acquiring a pivotal role in the Dáil.

It also made impossible the creation of a broad 'anti-imperialist alliance' proposed by Adams and including the SDLP and Fianna Fáil. The aims of such an alliance were to pressurize the British government to declare in favour of a united Ireland and use its influence to move the Unionists in that direction. For although the Anglo-Irish Agreement had been denounced by Sinn Féin as an attempt to build up the SDLP and marginalize republicans, there was a clear recognition that the British state had made a substantial concession to constitutional nationalism and undermined the Unionist position in Northern Ireland.[8] Using his friend Alex Reid, a redemptorist priest from the Clonard Monastery in West Belfast, as intermediary, Adams informed Haughey that he would support an IRA cease-fire if the Irish government would pursue the issue of Irish unification.[9] During 1988 Adams was involved in secret discussions with Martin Mansergh, Charles Haughey's adviser on Northern Ireland. However, the price for pan-nationalist negotiations was an IRA cease-fire and this was, publicly at least, said to be out of the question by Adams, who declared that the 'British will leave only when they are forced to leave'.[10] However, behind this public reiteration of the continued centrality of 'armed struggle' an intense debate on future strategy had opened up amongst the republican leadership.

By the mid 1980s the conflict between the IRA and the British state was stalemated. The reorganized, slimmed-down, and militarily proficient terrorist organization—the result of the 'Long War' strategy promoted by Adams and his supporters from 1977—was far from being defeated by the security forces. Yet, its campaign was increasingly obviously containable. Its main victims had long ceased to be British troops: as a result of the policy of 'Ulsterization', it was local Protestants in the police and the Ulster Defence Regiment who bore the brunt of Provisional attacks. In the year of the Anglo-Irish Agreement, of the sixty-four deaths from the conflict only two were of British soldiers whereas twenty-seven were of members of either the RUC or the UDR.[11] Adams has subsequently described the situation in which republicans found themselves after the Agreement: 'There was a political and military stalemate. While republicans could prevent a settlement on British government terms, we lacked the political strength to bring the struggle to a decisive conclusion. Military solutions were not an option for either side.'[12] In fact there were still those in the leadership of the IRA who believed that the 'war' could be won.[13] A serious attempt was made to break the stalemate with the help of three shipments of arms and explosives from the Libyan leader Colonel Gaddafi in 1985–6. These included two tons of the powerful plastic-explosive Semtex, surface-to-air missiles, heavy machine-guns, and rocket launchers. The more militaristic of the IRA's leadership, including its Chief of Staff, saw in the Libyan material the possibility of a major shift in the balance of forces that would lead to an end to British rule.[14] In July 1986 the list of IRA 'legitimate targets' was widened to include civil servants, building contractors, caterers, and British Telecom employees, so far as any of these did work for the security forces. Republicans had killed forty-two people in 1985, while in 1987 they killed sixty-nine and in 1988, sixty-two.[15] But if the intensification of 'armed struggle' gained it some gruesome headlines, with the murder of a leading Northern Irish judge and his wife in a car-bomb attack in April 1987 and a landmine at Ballygawley, county Tyrone, in August 1988 that killed eight off-duty soldiers, it also had high military and political costs.

The 'Long War' strategy by reducing the number of IRA activists had made it easier for the security forces to concentrate their resources against known activists. The Special Air Services (SAS) was first publicly committed to action in Northern Ireland in 1976 to combat the IRA in South Armagh, an area with a centuries-old tradition of anti-state activities and a republican stronghold which the security forces could only enter in strength and with helicopter backup. Now its activities were expanded to Fermanagh and Tyrone where the IRA was attempting to create another 'free zone' like South Armagh. In May 1987 it wiped out an eight-man IRA unit that was in the process of attacking the RUC station at Loughgall. This was the IRA's largest loss of 'volunteers' in a single incident since the Civil War and a major blow to its East Tyrone brigade, one of its most effective units. The same brigade was dealt another blow in August 1988 when the three IRA men responsible for the Ballygawley landmine were killed in an SAS ambush as they attempted to kill a lorry driver who was a part-time member of the UDR. In March 1988 three of the IRA's most experienced operatives had been shot dead in Gibraltar while unarmed. It was alleged that they were preparing a bomb attack on a British Army band.[16]

Controversy over the use of the SAS and their tactics, particularly over whether it was necessary to kill those whom they had ambushed, was inevitable. However, Sinn Féin's ability to exploit it was limited by the IRA's spiralling list of 'mistakes' in which it had to admit that it had killed the wrong people. Most politically damaging was the detonation of a bomb at the Remembrance Day ceremony in Enniskillen on 8 November 1987, which killed eleven people. The IRA admitted that this had dealt a 'body blow' to hopes of a 'broad-based front against imperialism'.[17] The 1988 eight-month dialogue with the SDLP, so important for Adams in his quest for pan-nationalist unity, was called off by John Hume when the IRA accidentally killed two of his constituents.[18] By the end of the decade hopes of military victory had been relinquished, although the republican movement was far from discarding the application of violence or the threat of it as a tool for political bargaining.

The intensification of republican violence after 1986 showed the limitation of any attempt to combine the armalite with the search for more electoral support. Sinn Féin lost sixteen seats in the 1989 local government elections and some of its councillors began to point out publicly the contradiction between its criticisms of direct rule's failure to deal with unemployment levels in West Belfast while the IRA's bombing campaign continued to put people out of work and scare off new investors.[19] The impasse of the 'armalite and ballot box' strategy and the knowledge of internal republican debate gained by intelligence services led to a two-track approach on the part of the British, by which hints of flexibility in the event of a cease-fire were combined with the threat of inter-party talks aimed at a centrist settlement that would isolate and marginalize republicans.

As early as the end of March 1987, Margaret Thatcher felt that the security returns following the Agreement were inadequate: 'I told Tom King [Northern Ireland Secretary] there must be a paper brought forth setting out all the options. I was determined that nothing should be ruled out.'[20] The election of the Haughey government served to cool the atmosphere even further, as did the announcement in January 1988 by the Attorney General Sir Patrick Mayhew that there would be no prosecutions arising out of an inquiry into an alleged 'shoot-to-kill' policy of the RUC that led to the deaths of six unarmed men in county Armagh in 1982. John Stalker, Assistant Chief Constable of Manchester, who had been brought in to conduct the inquiry, complained of resistance and sabotage by some in the RUC and was taken off the inquiry in suspicious circumstances.[21] Although he did find that there was no official policy of 'shoot-to-kill', the controversy surrounding his replacement and the Mayhew decision led to the resurgence of the megaphone diplomacy between London and Dublin that the Agreement was supposed to have consigned to the history books.

Thatcher and Mayhew had little sympathy with an approach to policing that seemed to them to impose standards appropriate to a liberal democracy untroubled with a terrorist campaign on a society in which the IRA's main target was the RUC. Thus in the year that the 'shoot-to-kill' incidents took place, republicans had killed eight members of the RUC and four of the RUC Reserve. In the year that the Anglo-Irish Agreement was signed twenty-three members of the RUC and RUC Reserve had been murdered, nine of them in one IRA mortar attack on Newry RUC station. In the 1982–5 period republicans were responsible for 70 per cent of the deaths from political violence while the security forces were responsible for 13 per cent.[22] Although even the most right-wing members of Thatcher's cabinet would have accepted that the state should not debase its standards to those of the terrorists, there was little inclination to see the issues raised by Stalker as more than blemishes on what was fundamentally a disciplined and lawful response to an organization which, as John Hume pointed out, had killed twice as many Irish Catholics as the security forces in the first twenty years of the 'Troubles'.[23]

Thatcher's annoyance with Dublin grew as Irish politicians condemned the decision of the Court of Appeal to reject the appeal of the six men convicted of the 1974 Birmingham pub bombings. Convinced that she had signed the Agreement to facilitate more Irish co-operation against the IRA in such key areas as policing and extradition, she now complained that Haughey's government provided less co-operation in the security field than any other European country: 'Our concessions had alienated the Unionists without gaining the level of security cooperation we had a right to expect.'[24] This was the context in which she directed her new Secretary of State for Northern Ireland, Peter Brooke, to begin the search for a new and more broadly based agreement.

As the republican movement both intensified its military campaign and gave public hints of a new-found flexibility over the next five years, British policy assumed an increasingly pro-Union public posture while at the same time giving substantive private signs of an interest in republican revisionism. Peter Brooke launched the search for a new agreement through inter-party talks in January 1990 and managed to achieve some progress by the eve of the 1992 general election. An offer to suspend temporarily the workings of the Anglo-Irish Agreement proved enough to ensure the participation not only of the Ulster Unionists but also of the DUP. After the election the talks continued in a more serious vein with a new Secretary of State, Sir Patrick Mayhew. The Unionists approached the talks in a slightly more confident frame of mind: their proposals were certainly considerably more advanced and elaborate. Under John Major, who had succeeded Margaret Thatcher in late 1990, the government gave even more explicit signs that it wished to reduce the Unionist sense of isolation and anxiety. The Foreign Secretary, Douglas Hurd, told the 1991 Conservative Party Conference that the debate on partition was over. The Anglo-Irish inter-parliamentary tier was presented in early 1992 with a critical British analysis of the working of the Agreement. In the run-up to the election in April 1992, a Tory Prime Minister rediscovered the Union as a political theme. After the election there was the appointment of a team at the NIO that was just about as Unionist in political sympathy as the current Conservative Party could produce.

However, the talks process foundered on the rock of the SDLP's refusal to depart from its original policy document, which argued for a form of joint authority with an added European dimension. It was clear during the talks that the NIO was impressed with the flexibility of the Ulster Unionists. Although they had originally insisted on an agreement in 'strand one', which dealt with the internal structures of the North's governance before the start of 'strand two', dealing with North–South relations, they proved willing to make the crucial transition without agreement having been reached in 'strand one'. The unprecedented willingness of the Ulster Unionists to go to Dublin to discuss North–South relations was made possible by a private letter from Mayhew to Molyneaux indicating the former's lack of enthusiasm for the SDLP document. Nevertheless, Dublin's apparent unpreparedness to respond to the Unionist flexibility, together with Hume's refusal to budge from the original document, led to the collapse of the talks.

Deeply ingrained distrust of Unionist motivation and an acute awareness of the potential republican cries of 'sell-out' for anything smacking of an 'internal solution' strongly impelled the SDLP against a historic compromise with Unionism. The Anglo-Irish Agreement had created a context in which it became logical, almost compellingly so, for constitutional nationalists to argue for a form of joint authority. British dissatisfaction with the Agreement's domestic failures—nobody questioned its international success in fire-proofing British policy in Northern Ireland—produced the usual frenetic tactical ingenuity, but this simply served to obscure the fundamental shift in terrain that the

Agreement had produced. Even if a Sunningdale-type agreement were now possible, it was too 'internalist', too dependent on Unionist goodwill, to be attractive from the SDLP's point of view. Both constitutional and revolutionary nationalism were convinced that the Agreement was a clear indication that the tide of history was running their way.

The failure of the talks and Major's increasingly precarious position in the House of Commons encouraged the Ulster Unionists as, dependent on their nine votes at Westminster, the public tone of government statements intensified in their Unionism. Yet the failure of the talks also pushed the government back towards an Anglo-Irish approach and into the intensification of private communications with the republican movement that had been initiated in October 1990.[25] Republican interest had been stimulated by hints of a new flexibility in speeches by Brooke. In an interview to mark his first 100 days as Secretary of State, Brooke had conceded that it was difficult to imagine a military defeat of the IRA. The following year he made a more direct appeal to republican strategists when he declared that the British government had 'no selfish strategic or economic interest in Northern Ireland'.[26] This produced a number of public indications of possible republican flexibility on some of their more fundamentalist postures—particularly that Britain should withdraw in the lifetime of one parliament. A 'scenario for peace' emerged in which an IRA cease-fire might be forthcoming for a British commitment to withdraw in a 'generation' whilst, in the interim, structures of joint authority would operate. Ultimately it appears that, despite the intensification of IRA activities in the North and Britain in 1991 and 1992, it was republican rather than Unionist flexibility that was found most impressive.

Only the impact of serious intelligence work can explain British willingness to wager on these hints of a new republican flexibility at a time when IRA violence was intensifying. The IRA launched a renewed campaign in England in the early 1990s. At first aimed at 'Establishment' figures and institutions—Ian Gow MP, a close friend of Mrs Thatcher and former adviser on Ireland, was murdered in a car-bomb attack in July 1990 and, in January 1991, 10 Downing Street was mortared while a cabinet meeting was taking place—the campaign developed into devastating bomb attacks on key financial and commercial centres. On 10 April 1992, the day after the British general election, two IRA bombs exploded at the Baltic Exchange in London, killing three people and causing £800 million of damage. More attacks followed over the next year. In March 1993 a bomb in a shopping centre in Warrington killed two young boys and in April a massive explosion at the NatWest Tower in the City of London killed one person and caused over £1 billion in damage.[27] There was also an upsurge of IRA attacks in Northern Ireland. In 1991 the IRA planted more incendiary devices in commercial premises than it had in the previous nine years, as well as launching some massive car-bomb attacks in Belfast. The year 1992 began with the slaughter of eight Protestant building workers whose van was destroyed by a bomb at Teebane Cross in county Tyrone as they returned from working at an army base. During the year that followed the centres of a number of predominantly Protestant towns were destroyed by IRA car-bombs.

The Provisional campaign was increasingly matched in murderous intensity by the main loyalist paramilitary organizations. The UDA had experienced a palace revolution in the late 1980s as a leadership considered too middle-aged and corrupt had been pushed aside by a younger and more single-mindedly ruthless cadre. Working under the *nom de guerre* of the Ulster Freedom Fighters (UFF), they had responded to the Teebane Cross atrocity by an attack on a bookmaker's business on Belfast's Lower Ormeau Road in which five Catholics were murdered. In 1992 and 1993, for the first time since the outbreak of the 'Troubles', loyalists were responsible for more deaths than republicans.[28] The campaigns of the UFF and UVF, although ordinary Catholics were still the main victims, were also notable for their targeting of Sinn Féin activists and because for the first time some of their victims were successfully targeted IRA members. Claims of security force 'collusion' soon became a major issue. However, the main result of the intensification of loyalist violence was a further weakening of electoral support for Sinn Féin. It lost ground to the SDLP in the 1992 general election and Adams lost his West Belfast seat to Joe Hendron of the SDLP. Although the immediate cause of his defeat was the decision of a substantial section of the 3,000 Unionists in the constituency to vote tactically for Hendron, there could be no disguising the fact that republican complicity in the violent sectarian atmosphere of the early 1990s had cost them votes. However, Adams' disappointment at his loss of West Belfast was mitigated by ongoing negotiations with John Hume to construct a pan-nationalist alliance that would pressurize the British government for a radical shift in policy on Northern Ireland.

The Origins of the Peace Process

During the 1988 discussions between Sinn Féin and the SDLP the core difference between the parties, apart from the issue of violence, was the SDLP's interpretation of the Anglo-Irish Agreement as establishing Britain's neutrality on the partition issue: 'that she has no military or economic interests and that if the Irish people reached agreement among themselves on, for example Irish unity, Britain would facilitate'.[29] Although even in 1988 the extent of the British financial subvention made it difficult for republicans to argue that Britain had an economic interest in maintaining partition, they claimed that a strategic interest did exist:

Strategic interests are now the most important consideration in Britain's interference in Ireland. Quite apart from the very real, if somewhat exaggerated fear among the British establishment, that an Ireland freed from British influence could become a European 'Cuba', even the prospect of a neutral Ireland is regarded as a threat to British and NATO's strategic interests.[30]

The fall of the Berlin Wall and the collapse of 'actually existing socialism' in Russia and Eastern Europe instituted a new world order within which only one hegemonic power, the USA, existed. The end of the Cold War removed any lingering credibility from the notion that Britain remained in Northern Ireland for strategic reasons. It had a related effect noted by Michael Cox: 'it was inevitable that as the global tide of radicalism began to retreat after 1989, this would feed into republican thinking.'[31] With former 'anti-imperialist' and 'national liberation' forces in Central America, the Middle East, and South Africa opting for negotiations rather than the continuation of armed struggle, the international context helped to foster hitherto heretical thoughts among leading republicans. Thus the republican propagandist Danny Morrison reflected on the fall of the Berlin Wall in a letter from prison:

If there is one thing last year in Eastern Europe should have taught us it was the bankruptcy of dogmatism ... The lesson has certainly helped me rethink my politics and become more pragmatic and realistic in terms of our own struggle. If we all lower our demands and our expectations a peg or two we might find more agreement.[32]

But this new realism did not mean that republicans had come anywhere near accepting that there was a democratic basis for partition, nor even that they were prepared to countenance John Hume's argument that the British state was neutral on the issue. During their discussions with republicans in 1993, the British had specifically rejected the republican demand that, in return for an IRA cease-fire, they should adopt the role of 'persuading' the North's majority population of the merits of a united Ireland.[33] However, this notion would be central to what became known as the 'Hume–Adams' negotiations.

John Hume had approached Gerry Adams in October 1991 with a proposal, the idea for which had come from the same Catholic cleric who had opened up contacts between republicans and Charles Haughey in 1987, for a joint declaration to be made by the British and Irish governments. This would set out the agreed principles that must underlie any final settlement and was aimed to be open enough to republican aspirations to allow for an IRA cessation of its campaign. Republicans were unhappy with Hume's reformulation of the principle of Irish self-determination, which made it dependent upon 'the agreement and consent of the people of Northern Ireland'. This was flawed from a republican point of view as it gave Unionists, who were a majority in Northern Ireland, a 'veto' on the achievement of national unity.[34] Yet, the fact that Hume had obtained the support of Charles Haughey for the draft of the joint declaration encouraged Adams' leadership group to envisage the construction of a pan nationalist front that might be able to shift the British towards a more proactive position.

A crucial development that affected republican calculations was the election of Bill Clinton as the new President of the USA in 1992. The end of the Cold War had drained the 'special relationship' of much of its significance for Washington and made it easier for Clinton to intervene in what had up until then been regarded as London's business. During the presidential campaign Clinton had supported the granting of a visa to Gerry Adams and also the idea of an American 'peace envoy' to be sent to Northern Ireland. Central to this more interventionist approach was the emergence of a new élite Irish-American lobby that aimed to transcend the existing division between Noraid and other pro-IRA groups and the 'Friends of Ireland', for instance Senator Robert Kennedy, who were closely allied with John Hume.[35] 'Americans for a New Irish Agenda' was a powerful group of well-funded, business-oriented Irish-American opinion,[36] whose leaders included ex-Congressman Bruce Morrison, Niall O'Dowd, editor of the *Irish Voice*, and two millionaire businessmen, William Flynn and Charles Feeney. A native of Drogheda, O'Dowd had links with republican supporters in

Noraid but believed that Irish-American leverage was weakened by its association with support for IRA violence. A leading member of 'Irish-Americans for Clinton and Gore', he travelled to Belfast early in 1992 to talk to the Sinn Féin leadership about the developing American scene.[37]

Republican enthusiasm for the injection of an American dimension into the situation was a reflection of the leadership's calculation that Clinton's support might make it easier to sell a compromise to the more fundamentalist elements of the IRA. The price of the creation of a pan-nationalist front with the blessing of the White House would be a cease-fire and this was bound to remind the 'republican base' of the last nearly disastrous cease-fire of 1975. In 1986 Martin McGuinness had declared 'Our position is clear and it will never, never, never change. The war against British rule must continue until freedom is achieved.'[38] Yet by the early 1990s it was clear to Adams and his closest allies that, as Danny Morrison put it in a letter to Adams in 1991, 'I think we can fight on forever and can't be defeated. But, of course that isn't the same as winning or showing something for all the sacrifices.'[39] The purpose of the 'Irish peace process', as Sinn Féin described its deepening involvement with constitutional nationalist parties in both states, was to obtain a settlement amounting to joint sovereignty that could be presented as transitional to the final goal of a thirty-two-county democratic socialist republic. In return the IRA would deliver an open-ended cessation of violence. The devastating bombs in London in 1992 and 1993 were aimed, not at moving the British towards talks[40]—the republicans were convinced during their 'back-channel' contacts that the Major government was amenable—but at increasing republican leverage once all-party talks about a settlement got underway.

US involvement was important as a compensatory device that allowed the republican leadership to recover from its profound disappointment with the Downing Street Declaration produced by John Major and Albert Reynolds on 15 December 1993. When Reynolds had dispatched his amended version of the Hume–Adams document to Major in June 1993 it was still heavily republican in content, with references to Britain as a 'persuader' and the demand for a specific time-frame within which unity was to be attained.[41] However, this was little more than an opening gambit as Reynolds had accepted that the notion of 'persuasion' was incompatible with the principle of consent. Despite his frustration with Major's much more cautious approach to the possibility of an IRA cessation, Reynolds did not shift on this fundamental point and he was also concerned, as was Major, that mainstream Unionism in the person of figures such as James Molyneaux and the Church of Ireland Primate Robin Eames would not reject any joint declaration.

Republican violence made it all the more necessary for the two Prime Ministers to distance themselves from 'Hume–Adams'. On 23 October an IRA attempt to kill the leadership of the UDA in a bomb attack on the Shankill Road resulted in the death of ten people, nine of them shoppers or passers-by who were killed when the Provisionals' bomb went off prematurely. The day before the carnage John Hume had told the House of Commons that his talks with Adams provided 'the most hopeful dialogue and the most hopeful chance of lasting peace that I have seen in twenty years'. He called on the two governments to 'hurry up and deal with it'.[42] Hume now seemed dangerously isolated in his partnership with the republican movement and Adams further shredded the tattered moral credibility of 'Hume–Adams' by helping to carry the coffin of the IRA bomber killed in the attack. On 30 October the UDA, using its *nom de guerre* of the Ulster Freedom Fighters, wreaked its revenge for the Shankill bombing when two of its men machine-gunned customers in the *Rising Sun* bar in Greysteel, county Londonderry, killing six Catholics and one Protestant.

On 27 October Dick Spring had announced to the Dáil six democratic principles that should underpin any settlement. These included a rejection of talks with those who used, threatened, or supported violence and no change in the North's constitutional position without the consent of the Unionist majority.[43] Two days later, after a meeting between Major and Reynolds at an EU summit in Brussels, the Prime Ministers developed the six principles as a seemingly explicit alternative to the Hume–Adams document. In fact, as Reynolds privately informed his press secretary, 'Hume–Adams was being declared dead, in order to keep it alive, in the same way as Adams carried the bomber's coffin, because otherwise he couldn't deliver the IRA.'[44] Despite further embarrassment when, in November, news of the 'back-channel' discussions with republicans leaked to the press, Major was still prepared to continue with discussions aimed at producing an IRA cease-fire.[45] At the same time he intensified the process of consultation with Molyneaux and other Unionist leaders to attempt to ensure that any joint declaration would at least have the acquiescence of the majority community.

The Joint Declaration was signed at a ceremony at 10 Downing Street on 15 December 1993. It was a relatively brief document of eleven paragraphs but underneath a certain opaqueness of style there was considerable originality and sophistication. This was particularly so in the complex language of the Declaration's fourth paragraph, in which the British government agreed 'that it is for the people of the island of Ireland alone, between the two parts respectively, to exercise their right of self-determination on the basis of consent, freely given, North and South, to bring about a united Ireland, if that is their wish'.

After the Downing Street Declaration, 'Hume–Adams' phraseology continued to dominate the political scene, but its content was dramatically altered. One of the most effective slogans of Irish nationalism had been given a new, decidedly softer conceptual content, and this had been done by a Fianna Fáil government. The self-determination of the Irish people was conceded by Britain, but only on the basis that the Irish government wished to operate that principle in favour of Irish unity with the support of a majority in the North. Superficially, the rhetoric of the 'Hume–Adams' process had been conceded but, in essence, the process had been stripped of its content in a quite dramatic way. The British were now 'facilitators', though not for Irish unity but for an agreed Ireland, and an 'agreed' Ireland, by definition, could not be a united Ireland until there was majority consent in the North.

Divisions among republicans over how to evaluate the Declaration were soon apparent. Mitchell McLaughlin, the prominent Sinn Féin leader from Derry, claimed that the general reaction of republicans was one of disappointment. At a meeting of around 400 republican activists, many of them ex-prisoners, at Loughmacrory in county Tyrone in December there was no support for the Declaration.[46] Yet Gerry Adams insisted that the Declaration did represent a significant shift by the British, who had for the first time, if in a heavily qualified manner, recognized the right of the Irish people as a whole to self-determination. He was even to claim that it 'marked a stage in the slow and painful process of England's disengagement from her first and last colony'.[47] Tensions within the republican movement were exacerbated by Major's talk of a 'decontamination period' for Sinn Féin before they could enter into dialogue with the governments and the other parties about the way ahead. It was also made clear by the British government that the IRA would have to decommission before Sinn Féin would be admitted to all-party talks.[48] Dick Spring compounded the republican leadership's problems when he also announced that republican participation in talks would necessitate movement on the arms issue.[49]

Yet if many rank-and-file republicans saw in the Declaration little more than the 'Unionist veto' disguised in more 'green' verbiage, Adams and his supporters in the leadership detected real possibilities of political advance for Sinn Féin, North and South. Reynolds did all he could to play on Adams's desire for a republican political breakthrough in the Republic. The ban on Sinn Féin from radio and television in the Republic was removed in January 1994 and Reynolds announced that a Forum for Peace and Reconciliation would be set up to allow all the parties in the Republic to consider ways in which 'agreement and trust' could be developed between the 'two traditions on the island'. If republicans were being invited into the mainstream in the Republic, Reynolds also ensured that Adams would be elevated to the status of an international statesman provided he gave clear evidence that he was committed to 'conflict resolution'. Crucial here was Clinton's decision in January, against the wishes of Major and the US State Department and the Department of Justice, to grant a visa to Adams to allow him to attend a high-profile one-day conference on Northern Ireland in New York, organized by leading figures in the corporate wing of Irish-America. Clinton's decidedly 'green' Irish ambassador, Jean Kennedy-Smith, was also important in impressing upon Adams and his colleagues the powerful allies that Sinn Féin could look to in Washington.

When the leadership of the republican movement set out to prepare the IRA activists for an indefinite cease-fire, they conjured up visions of a powerful pan-nationalist alliance supported by the White House. In a document revealingly titled 'The Tactical Use of Armed Struggle', circulated in the summer of 1994, the main factors that were argued to favour an initiative were:

Hume is the only SDLP person on the horizon strong enough to face the challenge.
Dublin's coalition is the strongest government in 25 years or more.
Reynolds has no historical baggage to hinder him and knows how popular such a consensus would be among the grassroots.
There is potentially a very powerful Irish-American lobby not in hock to any particular party in Ireland or Britain.
Clinton is perhaps the first US President in decades to be substantially influenced by such a lobby.[50]

But the involvement of Reynolds and Clinton was clearly conditional on a radical shift in the IRA's position. Both reacted angrily when, in pursuit of the 'tactical use of armed struggle' in the forlorn hope that the British could still be coerced into acting as 'persuaders' for unity, the IRA mortared Heathrow Airport in March 1994.[51] Back at the time of the spat with Major over Adams's visa, Reynolds had privately declared that 'Sinn Féin will pay a price for going to Capital Hill. A lot of powerful people went out on a limb for Adams. If he doesn't deliver, they'll have him back in the house with steel shutters [Sinn Féin headquarters on the Falls Road] so fast his feet won't touch the ground.'[52] When the IRA declared a three-day cease-fire in March, it was received with cold contempt by Adams's 'allies' in Dublin and Washington and by the beginning of the August, after some more gruesome loyalist murders of Catholics and with rumours of an imminent IRA cessation that would be time-limited and reserve them the right to defend nationalist communities, Reynolds let Adams know that republicans could be as quickly consigned to the margins as they had been recently brought in from the cold:

I've told them that if they don't do this right, they can shag off. . . . Otherwise I'll walk away. I'll go off down that three-strand talks/framework document road with John Major, and they can detour away for another 25 years of killing and being killed – for what?[53]

The IRA declaration of a 'complete cessation of military operations' on 31 August 1994 was therefore in part the product of a carrot-and-stick strategy on the part of the Irish government aided by the White House. Fear of political isolation if London and Dublin proceeded with the inter-party talks process from which they were excluded was a factor. So was the realistic assessment that 'republicans at this time and on their own do not have the strength to achieve the end goal'.[54] At the core of the leadership's optimism about 'the new stage of struggle' was the information it had obtained from Reynolds about the ongoing discussions with the British on the Framework Document which the two governments were drafting as a basis for a new and decisive round of all-party talks. The document, laden with cross-border institutions, was given an all-Ireland ethos designed to be seductive to republicans. From this perspective a 'transitional' settlement combining strong North–South institutions and a process of radical reform of the northern state would create conditions for unity over a period of fifteen to twenty years. Central to this process was the further fragmentation and weakening of Unionism. But could republicans continue to count on Unionism remaining inertly divided between Paisleyite rejectionism and Molyneaux's crab-like adjustment to the strategic initiatives of others?

Unionism and the Peace Process

James Molyneaux had tried to counter the lurid doom-mongering of Paisley by stressing his ability to have the Unionist position respected at the highest levels in Westminster and Whitehall. His 'friends in high places' approach came near to foundering in 1985 and only the disarray of the DUP in the aftermath of the Agreement saved him. The publication of the Framework Document seemed to many in the Unionist Party to show that their leader had been fooled again because of a naïve faith in the good will of a British Prime Minister.

The Framework Document dealt a fatal blow to Molyneaux's leadership. In March 1995 Lee Reynolds, an unknown 21-year-old student, obtained 15 per cent of the votes in an audacious leadership challenge to Molyneaux. In the summer his party lost the North Down by-election, a prime Unionist seat, to an arch Molyneaux critic, Robert McCartney QC, and Molyneaux resigned.

North Down was referred to in media parlance as the North's 'gold coast' because of its high concentration of prosperous Protestants. These were the so-called 'contented classes': those who had in material terms done very well under direct rule. A major factor in the well-being of this group was the growth of the public sector, which had been expanded as a fire damper against political violence. By the 1980s public sector employment accounted for 42 per cent of the total workforce compared to 27 per cent a decade earlier.[55] Even under Thatcher, government policy in Northern Ireland remained strongly interventionist and quietly Keynesian. The result was a massive expansion in the size of the subvention: the fiscal transfer that was paid by the Treasury to the region and reflected the difference between what was raised locally in taxes and the amount of public expenditure injected into the region. While the subvention was tiny in the early 1970s, by the mid 1990s it had become huge, standing at about £3.7 billion annually.[56]

The economic dependence of the North on the British Exchequer raised a serious practical obstacle to Irish unity and also provided a strong prudential argument against the 'little Ulster' vision of the DUP. The material well-being of the Protestant middle class in the UK was another factor that British policy-makers might have hoped would buttress moderate Unionism. However, the problem with this economic underpinning of the Union was that it tended to encourage a largely privatized lifestyle that wanted to insulate itself as much as possible from politics. For most middle-class Protestants the lives of their working-class co-religionists in North and West Belfast were as much an unknown and alien territory as those of the inhabitants of the Falls Road and Ardoyne. The problem facing any attempt to develop a more politically rational and proactive Unionism had its social roots here. As the Church of Ireland leader, Robin Eames, explained to the Opsahl Commission: 'To many the political process in Northern Ireland is already irrelevant. The opting out of the middle class is a definite factor at play. For those whose work, recreation or social life is untouched by the community of fear, there is a reluctance to get involved.'[57]

The 'community of fear' reflected not simply ongoing violence but a broader perception of decline and retreat amongst Protestants. It was the obverse of rising nationalist and republican self-confidence and reflected demographic and electoral trends. The Catholic share of the North's population increased from a third to at least 40 per cent between 1971 and 1991 and the 2001 census may well show the Catholic share as 46 per cent.[58] Although demographers disagreed on the likelihood of a future Catholic majority because of declining Catholic birth-rates since the 1980s, such qualifications did little to calm more atavistic interpretations of imminent victory or defeat in an ethnic breeding contest. A rising nationalist and republican share of the vote—from 31 per cent in the early 1980s to 43 per cent in 2001—had a similar effect. Even those tendencies that might have been seen as providing sections of the Catholic community with a material stake in partition were read through Orange spectacles. Thus the strengthening of Fair Employment legislation in 1989, which by the mid 1990s was contributing to an increase in the Catholic share of employment in virtually every occupational grouping,[59] was read as a Dublin government-inspired stratagem for discrimination against Protestants. Such fearful pessimism would remain a major influence in Unionist politics throughout the 1990s.

In the leadership contest that followed Molyneaux's resignation, David Trimble was seen as the most articulate and dangerous candidate of the right. This in part reflected his role in the major confrontation between the security forces and Portadown Orangemen who were blocked from marching from Drumcree Church down the Garvaghy Road in July 1995. The Garvaghy Road was one of a number of areas where Catholic residents claimed that changing demography demanded that 'offensive' parades be curtailed. Sinn Féin had played an important role in the establishment of these committees, in part as an example of 'unarmed struggle'.[60] The increasing confrontation over marches also reflected the new interventionist role of the Irish state in the North through the institutions and rights agreed at Hillsborough in 1985.[61] As tens of thousands of Orangemen came to give support and others blocked roads and the port of Larne, Trimble, in whose constituency the conflict was taking place, was intensively involved in attempts to resolve the issue. However, the undoubtedly positive role he played in bringing the stand-off to a peaceful conclusion was obliterated by his indulgence in a piece of triumphalist street theatre with Ian Paisley.

His role at Drumcree would certainly have appealed to the many Orangemen who were delegates to the Ulster Unionist Council that met to elect Molyneaux's successor. Yet those in the upper reaches of the NIO who were aghast at Trimble's election misread both the man and the circumstances of his victory. In a party as bereft of intellectual ballast as the Ulster Unionists, it was no great compliment to Trimble to point out that he was by far the most cerebral of the candidates for the leadership. He was the only mainstream Unionist figure who had the intellectual and strategic capacity to enter into a serious contest with Hume and Adams.

Trimble had been in Bill Craig's Vanguard movement and had supported the idea of an emergency coalition with the SDLP in 1976. This willingness to share power with nationalists was one indication of Trimble's basic political realism: his acceptance of the fact that no British government would return devolved institutions to Northern Ireland except on the basis of power-sharing. At the same time he found Molyneaux's trust in the pro-Union pieties of Margaret Thatcher dangerously naïve. A law lecturer at Queen's University until he won the Upper Bann seat in 1989, Trimble was also an omnivorous reader of books on Irish history and had published two serious works of amateur history.[62] This historical perspective provided him with a useful corrective to the overly pessimistic view of the British state that gripped many in the Unionist community in the early 1990s. For if Unionists were mistaken to rely on Thatcher's supposed 'innate' sympathy for their cause, it was equally mistaken, if more understandable because of the Anglo-Irish Agreement, to become consumed by fear of British betrayal.

For Trimble the IRA cease-fire was an admission of the failure of armed struggle, although he had no doubt that for 'tactical' reasons it would continue to play a role in republican strategy until the decommissioning issue was adequately addressed. His views were set out clearly in an interview soon after he became leader:

Even though the cease-fire may be merely a tactic, the fact that they have had to change their tactics is an admission that the previous tactic (armed struggle) has failed. Although there are elements in the republican movement that desire a return to violence, they will be returning to a tactic that was not working. . . . So, in that sense the republican movement is being defeated slowly. It is a slow process but that is what is happening. From our point of view, what we have to ensure is that while their campaign is winding up it does not cause any political or constitutional change which is contrary to the interests of the people of Northern Ireland. And we also want to do everything possible to ensure that the Union is strengthened.[63]

This was a sophisticated analysis, too sophisticated for many Unionists who still preferred the Paisley/McCartney vision of a republican movement with almost demonic powers that was moulding Anglo-Irish policies to its will through the continuing threat of force. Such views were strengthened by the end of the first cease-fire in February 1996 with the exploding of a massive bomb at Canary Wharf in London.

In the autumn of 1995 Major and Bruton had agreed to establish an international body to find a way forward on the arms issue. Chaired by a close Clinton ally, Senator George Mitchell, its report in February 1996 suggested waiving the British government's precondition—the beginning of decommissioning before republicans got into talks—and instead put forward the notion of decommissioning in conjunction with the talks. There had already been signs that the balance of forces within the republican movement had shifted against the cease-fire as exaggerated hopes in rapid movement towards all-party talks and the creation of 'transitional' structures were disappointed. Despite a demand by President Clinton, on a visit to Belfast in November 1995, for an end to paramilitary 'punishment' beatings and shootings, by the end of the year the IRA, using the *nom de guerre* 'Direct Action against Drugs', had killed six alleged drug dealers. Major's luke-warm acceptance of the Mitchell Report and his emphasis on the way forward being through an election produced a bitter denunciation from John Hume in the House of Commons and, within days, the bomb at Canary Wharf.

Despite Canary Wharf, Trimble maintained that for Unionists to retreat into a posture of resistance to dialogue would be disastrous. Neither London nor Dublin had given up on the republican movement and a simple denunciatory response from Unionists would guarantee that they became the passive victims of political change. He could also point out that one of the main reasons for the republican relapse was anger at his success in persuading Major of the need for elections as an alternative way into dialogue with republicans.

In the elections for a Northern Ireland Forum held in May 1996, the UUP vote at 24.2 per cent had declined by 5 per cent compared to the local government elections of 1993, while support for the DUP at 18.8 per cent had increased by less than 2 per cent.[64] The limited rise in the DUP vote reflected inroads made into its support base by the two parties linked to Protestant paramilitary organizations: the Progressive Unionist Party (PUP), linked to the UVF, and the Ulster Democratic Party (UDP), linked to the UDA. Both organizations had responded to the IRA's cease-fire with one of their own, declared on 13 October 1994. Then the 'Combined Loyalist Military Command' had declared that assurances had been sought from the British government that no secret deal had been done with the IRA and that 'the Union is safe'. They also offered 'abject and true remorse' to the families of their many innocent victims.[65] Although members of both, particularly the larger and more Balkanized UDA, would soon be involved in sectarian attacks on Catholics and, like the IRA, continue to use violence to defend their many profitable criminal activities from drugs to cross-border fuel smuggling, the cease-fire did enhance the credibility and political acceptability of the PUP and the UDP among the Protestant working class.

Concerned that politics could be seen to work for the loyalist paramilitaries, the Northern Ireland Office provided a mixed electoral system for the Forum, which allocated an extra twenty seats to be filled on a regional list system, giving two to each of the ten parties with the highest votes. The PUP with 3.5 per cent, the UDP with 2.2 per cent, and the Northern Ireland Women's Coalition with a mere 1 per cent were all allocated seats. However, the Forum elections also gave a major boost to Sinn Féin, which won its largest-ever share of the vote: 15.5 per cent. The narrowing of the gap with the SDLP and the party's strong performance in the Republic's general election made a second cease-fire very likely. At the same time it was clear that republicans were waiting for a British general election to deliver a Labour government with a secure majority which, they hoped, would push forward with a settlement that could be portrayed as transitional to Irish unity.

Trimble was untroubled by the prospect of a substantial Labour victory. He had established good relations with elements of 'new Labour'. Tony Blair had sacked Labour's 'green' Northern Ireland spokesman and replaced him with Dr Marjorie ('Mo') Mowlam. His first trip outside London as Prime Minister was to Northern Ireland where, on 16 May at

Balmoral, he declared that Unionists had nothing to fear from his government: 'A political settlement is not a slippery slope to a united Ireland. The government will not be persuaders for unity. The wagons do not need to be drawn up in a circle.' He also declared that he valued the Union and that 'none of you in this hall today, even the youngest, is likely to see Northern Ireland as anything but a part of the United Kingdom.' [66] Such sentiments were profoundly distasteful to republicans yet they were soon given a very practical compensation when the government declared that a renewed cease-fire would get Sinn Féin into talks within six weeks. The decommissioning precondition had gone.

From the earliest days of Blair's administration the attractive and repulsive aspects of the deal on offer to Unionists were relatively clear. Central to any settlement was an acceptance of the consent principle. This was to be copper-fastened by full constitutional recognition of Northern Ireland by the Republic. There would be a return of devolution to the North, now in the context of Labour's commitment to constitutional change in the rest of the UK. This would spell the end of the Irish government's 'interference' in the governance of the North in the form of the Anglo-Irish Agreement. The price to be paid for these political and constitutional gains was an Irish dimension embodied in a North–South Ministerial Council and the determination of Dublin, London, and John Hume that republicans must be integral to any settlement.

The Good Friday Agreement

The IRA did not return to full-scale 'armed struggle' during the sixteen months between Canary Wharf and its declaration of a second cease-fire on 21 July 1997. This was little consolation for the families of Detective Garda Gerry McCabe, shot dead in June 1996 during an IRA robbery of a mail van in county Limerick, or Stephen Restorick, a British solider shot dead by a sniper in south Armagh in February 1997. Most IRA activity occurred in Britain with a series of bombs in London and the devastation of the centre of Manchester by a 3,500 pound lorry-bomb in June 1996. As the general election approached, the attacks focused on disrupting road and rail networks as well as the Grand National. Such violence served a number of purposes. It reminded the British government that if a cease-fire was restored, republican demands had to be seriously addressed if the peace process were not to be put in crisis again. Gerry

Adams' 'peace strategy' continued to have a coercive element. It maintained the unity of the republican movement by showing restive elements in the IRA that involvement in negotiations had not made them redundant. By keeping the level of violence low and mostly outside Northern Ireland, it did not damage the continuing electoral expansion of Sinn Féin. In the 1 May general election Adams won back West Belfast from the SDLP and Martin McGuinness won Mid-Ulster from the DUP's William McCrea. Three weeks later in the local government elections Sinn Féin increased its vote to 17 per cent, cutting the margin between it and the SDLP from 75:25 of the nationalist vote in the 1993 local government elections to 55:45 in 1997.[67]

But if republican violence, or the threat of it, continued to perform important functions for Adams' strategy, it was difficult to see it as more than a means of increasing the 'green' façade of what was clearly a partitionist settlement. Adams was now writing about 'renegotiating the Union' rather than ending it.[68] The new Irish Taoiseach, Bertie Ahern, had already declared that 'Irredentism is dead' and that it was not 'feasible or desirable to attempt to incorporate Northern Ireland into a united Ireland against the will of a majority there, either by force or coercion'. He also rejected joint authority as a realistic option.[69] It was possible for republican leaders to depict the North–South institutions as mechanisms for creeping integration but there was no guarantee that their version of North–South links would be the accepted one.

Republican optimism was encouraged by the way the new Labour government downplayed the decommissioning issue. There was also a commitment to 'confidence-building measures' in areas such as the reform of the RUC and the strengthening of Fair Employment legislation. Although the government had initially proposed to deal with the arms issue along the lines of the Mitchell Report—by decommissioning in conjunction with political negotiations—this was dropped after a flexing of IRA muscle. On 17 June two community policemen were shot dead by the IRA in Lurgan, county Armagh. Within days an Anglo-Irish paper on decommissioning made it clear that all Sinn Féin would have to do was agree to discuss the issue during the talks.[70] This approach, while it permitted the successful completion of negotiations, could not prevent the issue returning to haunt the early life of the new devolved institutions.

Some on the Tory right had denounced the internationalization of the search for a settlement involved in British acceptance of Senator George

Mitchell as chair of the talks process, claiming that American involvement would simply strengthen the nationalist cause.[71] In fact for Mitchell as well as his sponsor, Clinton, it was accepted that the talks could only be successful if, as well as bringing in republicans from the cold, they did not drive the majority of Unionists into the rejectionist camp. At the centre of Gerry Adams' pan-nationalist strategy there had been the over-optimistic assumption that Clinton's involvement would follow an Irish-American agenda. While there was no doubting the deeper emotional sympathy of the Democratic administration with nationalist Ireland, Clinton's substantive political interest was the attainment of a deal that could be trumpeted as 'historic' and this necessitated keeping Trimble's party on board.

Paisley and McCartney had led their parties out of the talks when Sinn Féin entered in September 1997, thus making the negotiation of an agreement possible.[72] While the leadership of Sinn Féin claimed a victory over Unionist 'intransigence' and British 'prevarication', some members of the IRA, at both leadership and rank-and-file levels, were increasingly apprehensive about the implications of the peace process for traditional republican objectives. To gain entry to the talks process, Sinn Féin had to sign up to the 'Mitchell Principles', which committed them, amongst other things, to 'democratic and exclusively peaceful means of resolving political issues and to the total disarmament of all paramilitary organizations'. They were also committed to urge an end to punishment killings and beatings—the main rest and recreation activity of IRA volunteers on cease-fire—and to take effective steps to prevent them taking place.[73] Decommissioning was to be treated as an issue to be addressed during the talks and although Unionist sceptics predicted that it would be fudged, there were some in the republican movement who feared that the military integrity of the IRA would be sacrificed on the altar of Sinn Féin's electoral and governmental ambitions. To quieten such voices a senior IRA spokesman had told *An Phoblacht* that the IRA 'would have problems with sections of the Mitchell Principles' and that the IRA was not a participant in the talks.[74] This was a fiction, as senior members of the political wing of the republican movement were also members of the Army Council of the IRA, but it did reflect real tensions in the movement created by the political leadership's increasing envelopment by the process of political bargaining.

Already the Continuity IRA, the military wing of Adams's former comrades who had seceded in 1986 to form Republican Sinn Féin, were attempting to attract disgruntled Provisionals by a series of car-bomb attacks on RUC stations. In November an attempt by Adams' supporters in the IRA to centralize control over the ultimate disposition of arms with the IRA Army Council resulted in a split when the IRA's Quartermaster General and a number of other senior IRA figures in the border area resigned from the movement and went on to form the 'Real IRA'.[75] The dissidents established their own political wing, the 32-County Sovereignty Movement, which, although it initially had the support of only a few disillusioned members of Sinn Féin, made up for this in 'movement' credibility by having the support of a sister of Bobby Sands. Given the epochal significance of the deaths of Sands and his comrades for the Provisional movement, it was acutely embarrassing for Adams to be condemned by Bernadette Sands-McKevitt for entering a talks process that could only result in a 'modernized version of partition'. As she witheringly put it, her brother did not die for cross-border tourism authority.[76]

If republicans were going to embrace a settlement that left the North inside the UK for at least the medium term and accept the principle of consent—the 'Unionist veto' in the movement's traditional language— then it was important that it could be presented to their supporters as 'transitional'. Acceptance of new devolved structures of government at Stormont needed to be balanced by a set of strong, free-standing North–South institutions along the lines set out in the Framework Document. But in January 1998 even these consolatory structures were put in question with the British and Irish governments' joint document, 'Heads of Agreement', which, in setting out their understanding of the likely parameters of any final deal, proposed North–South institutions that would be mandated by and accountable to the Northern Ireland Assembly and the Irish parliament. A Belfast-based journalist knowledgeable about republicanism described 'Heads of Agreement' as a triumph for Trimble and a disaster for republicanism.[77] In fact, as Trimble himself pointed out, the process of bargaining, which led to an agreement and subsequently to the formation of an 'inclusive' government for Northern Ireland, was a 'white-knuckle ride' in which an apparent victory for one side produced such a bitter response from the other that it was soon provided with a compensatory 'victory' of its own.

Republican displeasure was soon evident in another 'tactical use of armed struggle' when first an alleged drug dealer and then a prominent loyalist were shot dead. Although the violence resulted in Sinn Féin being temporarily excluded from the talks, it may have contributed to the determination of Bertie Ahern's government to press the British for a return to the bolder version of cross-borderism of the Framework Document. The result was a final frenetic four days of negotiation, kick-started by George Mitchell's presentation to the parties of a draft of the agreement on 7 April. This included a section on strand two (North–South institutions) that the governments had drafted, which returned to a maximalist version of the Framework vision. Mitchell himself recognized that this would be unacceptable to Trimble and, with the leader of the Alliance Party, John Alderdice, predicting disaster if the proposals were carried out, Blair and Ahern descended on Stormont for three days and nights of what James Molyneaux disparagingly referred to as 'high-wire act' negotiations.

The final Agreement allowed Trimble to claim that the Union was not only safe but actually stronger because of Unionist negotiating successes in strand two and on constitutional recognition. Unionist focus on strand-two issues during the final days of the negotiations had got a result: the North–South ministerial council and its cut-down list of 'implementation bodies' in areas including animal and plant health and teacher qualifications were difficult to portray either by republicans or Unionist rejectionists as 'creeping reunification'. For the first time an Irish government had committed itself to the constitutional recognition of Northern Ireland through the amendment of Articles 2 and 3 of its constitution and all signatories of the Agreement were committed to accepting the principle of consent.

But the strong belief of the two governments and the SDLP that republicans were essential to any final settlement inevitably meant that Unionists would have to pay a price for these victories. On devolution itself there was little attempt to defend the original Unionist Party position of administrative devolution, with committee chairs allocated by the d'Hondt rule—a mathematical device normally used for the allocation of seats in legislatures under the additional-member system of proportional representation. The SDLP demand was for a power-sharing cabinet while republicans still ideologically opposed to devolution had made no contribution to the negotiations in this area while of course demanding 'inclusion' in whatever structures eventuated. The result was described by Robin Wilson: 'Rather like the camel that emerged from a committee designing a horse, a power-sharing executive with positions distributed by d'Hondt was the outcome.'[78]

Unionists had agreed to what was in essence compulsory coalition with republicans. If there was a calculation that this would be easier to sell to their supporters than a voluntary form of power-sharing, this was soon undermined by the lack of a clear linkage between participation in government and decommissioning. As republicans could point out, IRA action on weapons was not a precondition for Sinn Féin's participation in government. It was this issue that led some of the members of Trimble's negotiating team, most importantly the MP for Lagan Valley, Jeffery Donaldson, to refuse to support the Agreement. Ambiguity on the issue of decommissioning was part of the price that Unionists had to pay to allow republicanism a soft landing given that, as one of their leading strategists admitted, the Agreement had legitimized the British state in Ireland.[79] Another last-minute concession to republican unhappiness with the North–South and constitutional dimensions of the deal was the reduction of the period—from three years to two—before which prisoners belonging to paramilitary groups on cease-fire would be released. This and what Sinn Féin referred to as the 'Equality Agenda', involving human rights legislation and safeguards, commissions on policing and criminal justice, and a British commitment to demilitarization, were to act as consolation for what a considerable number of republicans considered as an Agreement that enshrined the 'Unionist veto'.

These were the issues that dominated the intra-Unionist debate on the Agreement in the period leading up to the two referenda on 20 May through which the electorate North and South were to express a judgement on what had been agreed on Good Friday. It soon became clear that while nationalists and republicans overwhelmingly supported the deal, Unionists were split. At first roughly half were in favour, a quarter against, and a quarter undecided. In the weeks leading up to the referendum in Northern Ireland attention focused not on the constitutional aspects of the deal and Trimble's success on domesticating the North–South institutions but on the more emotive issues of early prisoner releases, the presence of 'terrorists' in government, and the supposed threat to the future of the RUC. Unionist rejectionists benefited from the spectacle of the triumphal reception given at a special Sinn Féin árd fheis to recently released IRA men who had been involved in bombings and kidnapping in London in the 1970s. The choreography of this event was staged to give the imprimatur of those who suffered two decades of imprisonment for the 'struggle' to a radically revisionist republican strategy. But it produced a wave of repulsion in the Unionist community and threatened major damage to the pro-Agreement cause.

The fact that just over a half of Unionists did vote 'Yes' in the referendum was in large part the product of frequent trips to the North during the last two weeks of the campaign by Blair, who gave numerous reassurances, particularly on the issue of decommissioning. He was backed up by a cavalcade of British political leaders and international figures including Nelson Mandela. A strong sense of the 'historic' nature of the choice on offer was also encouraged by an unprecedented presence of the national and international media and by a heavily funded 'Yes' campaign that could rely on the support of Saatchi & Saatchi and even teamed up the staid, besuited, and middle-aged figures of Trimble and Hume with the Irish 'mega-band' U2 at a rock concert in Belfast in the final days of the campaign.

The result was the mobilization of the Protestant 'comfortable classes' in an unprecedented fashion. Turn-out at 81 per cent (in the Republic it was a mere 56 per cent) was the highest ever in Northern Ireland: 160,000 more had voted than in the last Westminster election.[80] This surge was disproportionately drawn from the majority Unionist areas east of the Bann where turn-out was traditionally the lowest in the North. Thus although the 71 per cent 'Yes' vote gave the Agreement a strong boost, its basis in the Unionist community was relatively precarious. As a leading member of the DUP put it of those who had broken a habit of a lifetime: 'They came out to vote for what they saw as peace and now they will return to political hibernation for another 30 years. But those who voted "No" are not so apathetic.'[81]

The DUP man's prediction appeared vindicated at the election for the new Northern Ireland Assembly on 25 June. Many of those Unionists who had voted 'Yes' in May now stayed at home and Trimble's party turned in its worst-ever performance, coming second to the SDLP with 21.3 per cent of the first preference vote to the DUP's 18 per cent. Although pro-Agreement parties won 73 per cent of the vote and eighty of the Assembly's 108 seats, there was no disguising the precarious nature of Unionist support in the Assembly where pro-Agreement Unionists held thirty seats while the 'antis' had twenty-eight. Nationalist and republican concern with the supposed danger of a Unionist majority abusing its position had led to mechanisms for cross-community validation on key decisions that required, at minimum, the support of 40 per cent of each communal bloc. This was now an ever-present threat to pro-Agreement Unionism.

Movement on the arms issue by the IRA would have given a substantial boost to Trimble's position both in his party and the wider Unionist community. The political wing of republicanism had never seemed stronger. The Assembly elections had been a major victory for Adams' pan-nationalist strategy. The SDLP topped the poll with 22 per cent and the aggregate vote of the nationalist/republican bloc was at its highest ever with a Sinn Féin vote of 17.7 per cent. The peace process had put Adams and Martin McGuinness at the centre of national and international attention. Received respectfully in Downing Street, Leinster House, and the White House, they were listened to deferentially when they continued to complain of being marginalized. They had before them the heady vision of being the first transnational party in the European Union with seats in the Dáil, Stormont, and Westminster and the possibility of being in government in both Belfast and Dublin.

If the massive political benefits of flexibility, compromise, and *realpolitik* were obvious, the dire futility of a return to armed struggle was made awfully clear on 15 August in Omagh when twenty-eight people were murdered in a Real IRA car-bomb attack. This was largest loss of life in Northern Ireland during the Troubles. In the words of one former IRA hunger striker, Omagh was 'the end of an era for a certain school of republican thought. What little sympathy was remaining for the physical force element evaporated on that dreadful Saturday afternoon.'[82] The Omagh atrocity offered the leadership of the republican movement the best possible conditions to address the arms issue. However, nothing was done for another year and a half, by which time Trimble's position was substantially weaker within his party and the electorate.

In part this reflected Adams' long-standing caution in edging the movement in a more flexible and political direction while doing his utmost to prevent a split. It was also the case that the substantively partitionist nature of the deal that republicans had accepted made action on arms more difficult: giving ground on political fundamentals made even a gesture on arms more difficult to sell within the IRA. There was also a major obstacle in the strong element of solipsistic self-righteousness so strongly developed in the republican mentality. Republican violence was from this perspective a legitimate response to state and loyalist violence. This was despite the fact that of the 3,633 violent deaths during the Troubles, republicans were responsible for 2,139, or 58.8 per cent, of the total. In comparison the reviled RUC, whose disbanding Sinn Féin put near the top of its post-Agreement demands, was responsible for fifty-two deaths.[83] Only a tiny element of the most sophisticated in the leadership would even hint at the possibility that the armed struggle had made an independent and powerful contribution to making Northern Ireland in 1998 more polarized, more segregated, and more embittered than it was thirty years before. From this perspective the cease-fire was the fundamental concession made by the IRA and pressure for it to move on decommissioning was an attempt to 'humiliate' an 'undefeated army'.

Gerry Adams had recognized that most Unionists 'quite rightly' would not feel any gratitude towards the IRA: 'We are not thanking these people for stopping what they should never have done in the first place.' Yet he did expect an understanding from Unionists that any action on weapons would wait until all the aspects of the Agreement had been implemented, particularly the provision for an international commission on policing. Until then the IRA would remain 'on the sidelines'.[84] It did not take a particularly negative cast of mind for many in the Unionist community to interpret this as 'the politics of threat'.

From June 1998 to December 1999 Trimble maintained a position of refusing to form an administration that included Sinn Féin until the weapons issue was seriously addressed. A tactically ingenious 'sequencing' proposition was put forward by the two governments at Hillsborough in April 1999, by which a 'shadow executive' would be formed and within a month, during a 'collective act of reconciliation', some arms would 'be put beyond use on a voluntary basis' and powers devolved to the Executive. Martin McGuinness rejected the proposals as an ultimatum imposed by the British military establishment and Trimble.[85] With republicans talking of the danger of a split, the Unionists came under intense pressure to make a 'leap of faith' on the basis of 10 Downing Street's belief that there had been a 'seismic shift' in the republican position. Blair, buoyed up by his central role in the Kosovo conflict and keen to announce an Ulster deal to coincide with the inauguration of the Welsh and Scottish Assemblies, set a deadline of 30 June. If Trimble had felt any inclination to oblige a Prime Minister with whom he had an extremely good personal relationship, this was undermined by another bad election performance. In the European Elections in June the Ulster Unionist candidate got 17.6 per cent of the vote, the party's lowest ever share, and it narrowly avoided an ignominious fourth place behind Sinn Féin.[86]

Trimble's rejection of the two governments' new attempt at sequencing in *The Way Forward* proposals in July led to a reinvolvement of George Mitchell in a review of the Agreement that started in the autumn. Despite a recrudescence of IRA punishment beatings and killings during the summer, Mitchell achieved a breakthrough with an agreement by Trimble to recommend to his party that, in return for a commitment by republicans to address the decommissioning issue by the end of January 2000, an Executive could be formed. However, the souring of the atmosphere as a result of the publication of the Patten Report on policing in September made Trimble's offer conditional. The international commission headed by the ex-Tory politician and former Governor of Hong Kong produced a report that, while it did not recommend the disbanding of the force, as republicans demanded, put forward proposals for radical restructuring that most controversially proposed a change of name and insisted that the symbols should not reflect those of the British and Irish states. The report produced fierce denunciations from all shades of Unionism.

Believing that he might not win a majority in the Ulster Unionist Council for his proposal to form a government including Sinn Féin, Trimble promised to recall the Council in February to report on what progress there had been on weapons and deposited a post-dated letter of resignation as leader of the party with its President. Adams now claimed that Trimble had added a new precondition to what had been agreed in the talks chaired by George Mitchell. The result was that while Northern Ireland had its first government since 1974 in January 2000, it lacked even the rudiments of a common understanding on what was a central issue—after all, under the Agreement the decommissioning of para-military weapons was supposed to be completed by May 2000. This experience of devolved government lasted less than two months. While Unionists had to get used to two republicans running the departments of Health and Education (one of them, Martin McGuinness, popularly believed to have been a member of the IRA's Army Council until very recently) republicans appeared to have calculated that once the institutions of government were functioning, Unionists would be reluctant to bring them down.

However, with the support of a more Unionist-friendly Secretary of State, Peter Mandelson, who had replaced Mowlam in October 1999, Trimble did not hesitate to use his threat of resignation to force Mandelson to suspend the institutions in February. This hard-nosed approach outraged nationalists, who claimed that Mandelson's assertion of British sovereignty over Northern Ireland violated the spirit of the Agreement. However, it steadied nerves in his own party and forced republicans to move on arms. On 6 May an IRA statement committed it to put its arms 'completely and verifiably beyond use' in a manner that would be acceptable to the International Commission on Decommissioning, headed by the Canadian General John de Chastelain. The return of devolution on 27 May 2000 took place after Trimble had got the support of 53 per cent of the 800 or so delegates to the Ulster Unionist Council, the party's ruling body. His margin of support in the council had narrowed substantially from the 72 per cent of the UUC who had voted in favour of the Good Friday Agreement in April 1998. However, neither nationalists nor republicans appeared to have much concern about this attenuation of pro-Agreement Unionism. After two IRA arms dumps were independently inspected by a leading member of the ANC and a senior Finnish politician in June, there was little more of substance for General de Chastelain to report. Meanwhile, Sinn Féin and the SDLP criticized the British government for allegedly eviscerating the Patten Report while Trimble used his powers as First Minister to ban Sinn Féin ministers from attending meetings of the North–South ministerial council and the implementation bodies.

With a senior republican claiming that Trimble's action and the failure of the British government to deliver on Patten and 'demilitarization' (the closing down of British army installations in strategic border areas such as south Armagh was particularly emphasized) were threatening the peace process,[87] 2001 began gloomily for pro-Agreement Ulster Unionists. The IRA had formally disengaged from contacts with the international decommissioning body and the UUP's continued involvement in government with Sinn Féin was a source of increasing intra-party conflict as activists faced a general election with a high probability of losses to the DUP. Reacting to this pressure, Trimble lodged a letter with the Speaker of the Northern Ireland Assembly on 23 May resigning as First Minister with effect from 1 July 2001 if by then the IRA had not begun to decommission. Despite this action, the UUP lost three seats in the general election while the DUP gained two. Without it, it is possible that the UUUP would have lost two more seats: Trimble's own in Upper Bann, where he was hard-pressed by a fairly unknown DUP candidate, and East Antrim. The overall result—UUP: 26.8 per cent and six seats; DUP: 22.5 per cent and five seats; Sinn Féin: 21.7 per cent and four seats; SDLP: 21 per cent and three seats—was interpreted by many commentators as a triumph for the extremes.[88]

This was an oversimplification. Such a judgement was based on a comparison with the 1997 election, thus ignoring the radical effects of the Belfast Agreement on the political environment in Northern Ireland, particularly its destabilizing influence on Unionism. A better comparison is with the 1998 Assembly elections, and here the picture for pro-Agreement Unionism was not quite so bleak. The UUP vote increased from 21.3 to 26.8 per cent; the DUP's victories were also accompanied by a shift in its discourse towards a more subtle and less hysterical critique of the Agreement. This was most ably accomplished by its victor in North Belfast, Nigel Dodds, who focused not on the influence of Dublin or the Vatican but on the alleged unbalanced nature of the workings of the Agreement, which he alleged was hollowing out the 'Britishness' of the North. This took up emotionally powerful issues such as the 'destruction of the RUC' and Sinn Féin ministers' refusal to allow the Union Jack to fly over their buildings.

If decommissioning had begun it might have been easier to deal with these criticisms, particularly as the DUP was heavily involved in the institutions of the Agreement: sitting on Assembly committees with republicans and participating in the Executive although refusing to sit around the cabinet table with 'Sinn Féin-IRA' ministers. The election result, which saw Sinn Féin out-poll the SDLP for the first time, demonstrated the gains from the 'peace strategy'. Yet senior republican figures were still telling the rank-and-file that there would be no decommissioning.[89] Attempts to justify republicans' refusal to move on arms pointed to an ongoing campaign of pipe-bomb attacks on Catholic homes by elements of the UDA and the challenge of republican dissidents. These justifications were shown to be less than convincing when, in October 2001, the IRA began to decommission despite the continuation of sectarian attacks and the scorn of fundamentalists who claimed the Provos had finally surrendered. That the weapons issue was at last addressed was a product of events in Colombia and New York that put irresistible pressure on the leadership of Sinn Féin.

Despite Irish fears that the new US President, George Bush, would adopt a more distant approach to Northern Ireland, US strategic concerns ensured an engagement that, for the first time since 1994, republicans would find unwelcome. The arrest of three Irish republicans in Bogota on 6 August 2001 and the claim of the Colombian authorities that they had been training FARC guerrillas was acutely embarrassing for Gerry Adams, who was unable to give a satisfactory explanation to either the Bush administration or those wealthy Irish-Americans who had raised millions of dollars for the party in the 1990s. The events of 11 September put irresistible pressure on Adams to demonstrate, beyond contradiction, that republicans were not part of the 'international terrorist network'. Despite the instinctive anti-imperialism of many republicans, Adams moved quickly to accommodate the White House and corporate Irish-America and on 26 October the IRA announced that it had begun the process of decommissioning.[90]

The IRA's action enabled Trimble to get the support of the UUC to return to government and with no elections due until 2003, pro-Agreement Unionists hoped that having secured the principle of consent, the abandonment of the Republic's territorial claim, and the beginning of a process that republicans had claimed would never happen, ground lost to the DUP could be regained. However, the prolonged nature of the conflict over arms and the lack of transparency involved in its beginning undermined its positive effects, as did the British government's acceptance that the process might take years to complete.

Protestant 'alienation' became a central theme in the speeches of NIO ministers and had a particularly ugly manifestation in a blockade of a Catholic primary school in North Belfast, which began in the autumn of 2001, where declining working-class Protestant communities in areas such as Ardoyne and Tiger Bay felt themselves losing out in a zero-sum territorial conflict with Catholics. A much broader section of the Unionist community found it difficult to accept a republican presence in government, even with increasing signs that there was little chance of the Provos going back to war. This did not stem simply, as some commentators claimed, from an unwillingness to accept equality with Catholics. Rather, it rested on a perception that the new dispensation was based on the steady dilution of the North's Britishness as reflected in changes in the name and symbols of the RUC, and disputes over the flying of the Union flag on public buildings.

The end of Unionist hegemony within the northern state and the associated rise in nationalist and republican self-confidence both contributed to a prevalence of what Steve Bruce has called the 'dismal vision' in the Unionist community:[91] a vision of inexorable decline in terms of demography and economic clout. Yet, looked at from the perspective of the period covered in this book, this seems an overly black picture. The massive economic and social changes that had transformed the Republic since the 1960s, culminating in the 'Celtic Tiger', have consolidated a twenty-six-county-state patriotism that prioritizes stability over unity. The end of the IRA's armed struggle and the acceptance by Irish nationalists of the 'consent' principle contributed powerfully to the stabilization of the northern state, which, for the first time in its history, has the possibility of becoming a fully legitimate entity.

However, the Good Friday Agreement was an élite-brokered settlement that balanced precariously on deep reserves of communal distrust and antagonism. The fact that political élites North and South have been prepared to take risks for a historic compromise, rather than indulge populist ethnic agendas, represents not the 'end of Irish history' but the opening of a new phase, where northern sectarianisms lack the legitimization given to them for much of the twentieth century by the states and dominant parties in Belfast and Dublin. Yet the virulence of sectarianism in the North remains a major threat to the newly devolved institutions. With Sinn Féin's predominant position in nationalist politics in the North likely to be consolidated by a good performance in the Republic's May 2002 general election, there is the prospect of a crisis of the institutions after the Assembly elections in 2003. For even if the Ulster Unionist Party withstands the challenge from the DUP, the prospect of its members accepting Gerry Adams as Deputy First Minister of Northern Ireland is slight. So although the maintenance of the North's uneasy peace seems relatively certain, the possibility of its politics moving away from the struggle for ethnic supremacy is much less so.

NOTES

Chapter 1

1. David Officer, 'In Search of Order, Permanence and Stability: Building Stormont, 1921–32', in Richard English and Graham Walker (eds), *Unionism in Modern Ireland* (Dublin, 1996), 142.
2. Paul Bew, Peter Gibbon, and Henry Patterson, *Northern Ireland 1921–1996: Political Forces and Social Classes* (London, 1996), 28.
3. Paul Bew, *Ideology and the Irish Question: Ulster Unionism and Irish Nationalism 1912–1916* (Oxford, 1994).
4. Enda Staunton, *The Nationalists of Northern Ireland 1918–1973* (Dublin, 2001), 7.
5. Austen Morgan, *Labour and Partition: the Belfast Working Class, 1905–1923* (London, 1991), 269.
6. Michael Farrell, *Arming the Protestants* (London, 1983), 168.
7. Graham Ellison and Jim Smyth, *The Crowned Harp: Policing Northern Ireland* (London, 2000), 23.
8. Ibid. 23.
9. Memorandum by S. G. Tallents, Colonial Office Papers, Public Record Office, CO 906/24.
10. Paul Bew, 'The Political History of Partition: The Prospects for North–South Co-operation', in A. F. Heath, R. Breen, and C. T. Whelan (eds), *Ireland North and South: Perspectives from Social Science* (Oxford, 1999), 408–9.
11. Bew, Gibbon, and Patterson, 241–2.
12. J. J. Lee, *Ireland 1912–1985: Politics and Society* (Cambridge, 1989), 238.
13. Tallents' report, CO 906/30.
14. Michael Farrell, *Northern Ireland: The Orange State* (London, 1976), 84.
15. Letter from Adrian Robinson to F. M. Adams, Press and Publicity Officer, Stormont Castle, 21 November 1944, PRONI, HA/32/1/649.
16. Dominions Office comment on Home Office views, 18 November 1938, PRO, DO 35/893.
17. Bew, Gibbon, and Patterson, 49.
18. Ibid. 57.
19. Quoted in Patrick Buckland, 'The Unity of Ulster Unionism', *History*, 60 (1975).
20. W. A. Maguire, *Belfast* (Keele, 1993), 136.
21. Henry Patterson, *Class Conflict and Sectarianism: The Protestant Working Class and the Belfast Labour Movement 1868–1920* (Belfast, 1980), 20–3.

22. D. S. Johnson, 'The Northern Ireland Economy 1914–39', in Liam Kennedy and Philip Ollerenshaw (eds), *An Economic and Social History of Ulster 1820–1939* (Manchester, 1985), 192.

23. Ibid. 199.

24. David Fitzpatrick, *The Two Irelands 1912–1939* (Oxford, 1998), 208, and Johnson, 190–1.

25. Fitzpatrick, 178.

26. Bew, Gibbon, and Patterson, 69.

27. Christopher Norton, 'Creating Jobs, Manufacturing Unity: Ulster Unionism and Mass Unemployment 1922–1934', *Contemporary British History*, Vol. 15, Summer 2001, 9–10.

28. Graham Walker, 'Protestantism before Party: The Ulster Protestant League in the 1930s', *The Historical Journal*, Vol. 28, 1985, 961.

29. Brian Barton, *Brookeborough: The Making of a Prime Minister* (Belfast, 1988), 84.

30. Ibid. 85–7.

31. Bew, Gibbon, and Patterson, 58.

32. Dennis Kennedy, *The Widening Gulf: Northern Attitudes to the Independent Irish State 1919–1949* (Belfast, 1988), 143.

33. Oliver P. Rafferty, *Catholicism in Ulster 1603–1983* (Dublin, 1994), 230.

34. Sean T. O'Kelly, Vice-President of the government, declared in March 1932: 'We will make every effort to establish a republic of 32 counties. This is our aim and if the gun is necessary, the people have the government to direct the army and they have the volunteer force behind them.' Kennedy, 199.

35. Bew, Gibbon, and Patterson, 70.

36. 'The Impact of Ethnic Violence: The Belfast Riots of 1935', in A. C. Hepburn, *A Past Apart: Studies in the History of Catholic Belfast 1850–1950* (Belfast, 1996), 183.

37. John M. Regan, *The Irish Counter-Revolution 1921–1936* (Dublin, 1999), 378.

38. Ibid. 377.

39. Ibid. 374.

40. Paul Bew, Ellen Hazelkorn, and Henry Patterson, *The Dynamics of Irish Politics* (London, 1989), 26.

41. Dermot Keogh, 'The Role of the Catholic Church in the Republic of Ireland', in *Building Trust in Ireland: Studies Commissioned by the Forum for Peace and Reconciliation* (Belfast, 1996), 103.

42. Peter Hart, *The IRA and its Enemies* (Oxford, 1998), 286.

43. Regan, 254.

44. Ibid. 137.

45. Nicholas Mansergh, *The Unresolved Question: The Anglo-Irish Settlement and Its Undoing 1912–72* (New Haven and London, 1991), 136.

46. Ibid. 237.

47. Peter Mair, *The Changing Irish Party System* (London, 1987), 20.

48. Richard Dunphy, *The Making of Fianna Fail Power in Ireland 1923–1948* (Oxford, 1995), 83.
49. Bew, Hazelkorn, and Patterson, 33.
50. Mair, 17.
51. Dunphy, 82.
52. Ibid. 79.
53. K. A. Kennedy, T. Giblin, and D. McHugh, *The Economic Development of Ireland in the Twentieth Century* (London, 1988), 45.
54. Enda Delaney, 'State, Politics and Demography: the Case of Irish Emigration, 1921–71', *Irish Political Studies*, Vol. 13, 1998, 30.
55. Bew, Hazelkorn, and Patterson, 75.
56. Dunphy, 178–9, and Lee, 193.
57. Lee, 193.
58. Between 1933 and 1939 the number of Irish industrial concerns quoted on the Dublin stock exchange trebled and their aggregate capital doubled: Cormac O'Gráda, *A Rocky Road; The Irish Economy since the 1920s* (Manchester, 1997), 109.
59. Emmet O'Connor, *A Labour History of Ireland* (Dublin, 1992), 130.
60. Ibid. 130.
61. Delaney, 30.
62. In 1935–7, some 75,150 emigrated to the UK: Dunphy, 163.
63. James Meenan, *The Irish Economy since 1922* (Liverpool, 1970), 41.
64. Arthur Mitchell, *Labour in Irish Politics 1890–1930* (Dublin, 1974), 246.
65. Ibid. 258.
66. Mair, 20.
67. Enda McKay, 'Changing the Tide: The Irish Labour Party 1927–1933', *Saothar Journal of the Irish Labour History Society*. Vol. 11, 1986.
68. Mansergh, 304, and Paul Canning, *British Policy towards Ireland 1921–41* (Oxford, 1985).
69. Canning, 201–2.
70. Ibid. 233–5.
71. Dermot Keogh, *Twentieth-Century Ireland: Nation and State* (Dublin, 1994), 104.
72. Lee, 215–16.

Chapter 2

1. Brendan Lynn, *Holding the Ground: The Nationalist Party in Northern Ireland, 1945–72* (Aldershot, 1997), 4.
2. Oliver P. Rafferty, *Catholicism in Ulster 1603–1983: An Interpretative History* (Dublin, 1994), 223.
3. Michael Farrell, *Northern Ireland: the Orange State* (London, 1976), 143.

4. The Prime Minister departed for a family holiday in Scotland in the month of the riots and did not return until September: A. C. Hepburn, *A Past Apart: Studies in the History of Catholic Belfast 1850–1950* (Belfast, 1996), 196.

5. Letter from Cahir Healy to the secretary of the County Cavan Executive of Fianna Fáil, 28 October 1938, 'An Taoiseach wants the pressure to be from within the Six Counties rather than from without at the moment', PRONI, Cahir Healy Papers, D/2991/B/98/1–2.

6. Brian Barton, *Northern Ireland in the Second World War* (Belfast, 1995), 123.

7. *The Round Table*, Vol. XXXII, No. 125, December 1951.

8. Chris Norton, 'The Politics of Exclusion: Nationalism in Northern Ireland' (unpublished paper).

9. Hepburn, *A Past Apart*, 193.

10. *An Phoblacht*, 20 August 1932, and Ronaldo Munck and Bill Rolston, *Belfast in the Thirties: An Oral History* (Belfast, 1987), 184.

11. Neil Jarman and Dominic Bryan, *From Riots to Rights* (Coleraine, 1998), 28.

12. Laura K. Donohue, 'Regulating Northern Ireland: The Special Powers Acts, 1922–1972', *Historical Journal*, 41, 4, 1998, 1094.

13. Jarman and Bryan, 46.

14. Sir Charles Wickham to the Secretary, Ministry of Home Affairs, 3 December 1938, PRONI, Ministry of Home Affairs, HA/32/1/1649.

15. Brian Barton, *Brookeborough: The Making of a Prime Minister* (Belfast, 1988), 129.

16. Barton, *Northern Ireland in the Second World War*, 124.

17. *Irish News*, 5 September 1939.

18. *Irish News*, 17 September 1940.

19. J. J. Lee, *Ireland 1912–1985: Politics and Society* (Cambridge, 1989), 267.

20. *Irish News*, 24 June 1940.

21. Barton, *Northern Ireland in the Second World War*, 120.

22. Rafferty, *Catholicism in Ulster 1603–1983*, 242.

23. *Belfast Newsletter*, 20 June 1940.

24. One journalist claimed that in parts of Northern Ireland 'Catholics have joined the army at the rate of anything from eight to fourteen Catholics to one Protestant'; see Gertrude Gaffney's comments in *Orange Terror* by 'Ultach': A Reprint from the *Capuchin Annual*, 1943 (Dublin, 1998), 39.

25. *Irish News*, 21 September 1940.

26. J. Bowyer Bell, *The Secret Army: A History of the IRA 1916–1970* (London, 1972), 239.

27. Barton, *Northern Ireland in the Second World War*, 44.

28. Denis Sampson, *Brian Moore: The Chameleon Novelist* (Dublin, 1998), 47.

29. T. D. Williams, 'A Study in Neutrality' (V), *The Leader*, 28 March 1953.

30. Barton, *Northern Ireland in the Second World War*, 200.

31. Graham Walker, *The Politics of Frustration: Harry Midgley and the Failure of Labour in Northern Ireland* (Manchester, 1985), 132.
32. Brian Lacy, *Siege City: The Story of Derry and Londonderry* (Belfast, 1990), 238–43.
33. Barton, *Northern Ireland in the Second World War*, 123.
34. Lacy, *Siege City*, 243.
35. PRONI, Cahir Healy Papers, D/2991.
36. MacEntee's criticisms were in a speech on 15 April 1944 that provoked protests from leading northern nationalists: see correspondence in PRONI, Cahir Healy Papers, D 2991/B/23/46.
37. Spender was to end his days as an integrationist: a supporter of Northern Ireland's total political and administrative assimilation into the rest of the UK; see Paul Bew, Kenneth Darwin, and Gordon Gillespie, *Passion and Prejudice: Nationalist–Unionist Conflict in Ulster in the 1930s and the Founding of the Irish Association* (Belfast, 1993), x.
38. Bew, Darwin, and Gillespie, *Passion and Prejudice*, 50.
39. Farrell, *Northern Ireland: the Orange State*, 147.
40. Barton, *Brookeborough*, 209.
41. Barton, *Northern Ireland in the Second World War*, 17.
42. Ibid., 18–19.
43. Barton, *Brookeborough*, 159.
44. *Belfast Newsletter*, 19 June 1940.
45. Quoted in Barton, *Northern Ireland in the Second World War*, 116.
46. *Belfast Newsletter*, 29 May 1940.
47. See letter from Dr James Little MP, *Belfast Newsletter*, 23 June 1940.
48. Barton, *Brookeborough*, 159–162.
49. Thus in his resignation speech Warnock denounced the government as 'pathetic, with the exception of the Minister of Agriculture they had done nothing', *Belfast Newsletter*, 19 June 1940.
50. Bew, Darwin, and Gillespie, *Passion and Prejudice*, 40.
51. Robert Fisk, *In Time of War: Ireland, Ulster and the Price of Neutrality* (London, 1983), 51.
52. Ian Budge and Cornelius O'Leary, *Belfast: Approach to Crisis* (London, 1973), 194.
53. W. A. Maguire, *Belfast* (Keele, 1993), 147.
54. Walker, *The Politics of Frustration*, 127, and Paul Addison, *The Road to 1945* (London, 1975).
55. Letter from Maynard Sinclair, Brian Maginess, and Wilson Hungerford, quoted in John Ditch, *Social Policy in Northern Ireland 1939–1950* (Aldershot, 1988), 68.
56. 'Northern Ireland's Manpower Resources', a report by Mr Harold Wilson, 17 December 1940, PRONI, COM61/440.
57. Ibid.

58. D. S. Johnson, 'The Northern Ireland Economy 1914–39', in Liam Kennedy and Philip Ollerenshaw (eds), *An Economic History of Ulster 1820–1939* (Manchester, 1985), 194.

59. 'The Manpower Position in Northern Ireland', 24 March 1941, PRONI, Ministry of Commerce, COM 61/440.

60. M. Moss and J. R. Hume, *Shipbuilders to the World: 125 Years of Harland and Wolff, Belfast, 1861–1986* (Belfast, 1986), 347.

61. Johnson, 'The Northern Ireland Economy', 201, and Barton, *Northern Ireland in the Second World War*, 81.

62. Barton, *Northern Ireland in the Second World War*, 189.

63. 'When Peace Breaks Out in Ulster', *The Bell*, No. 5, February 1943.

64. For intellectual life in the North in the period, see Robert Greacen, *The Sash My Father Wore: An Autobiography* (Edinburgh, 1997); John Boyd, *The Middle of My Journey* (Belfast, 1990); and 'Regionalism: The Last Chance', in Tom Clyde (ed.) *Ancestral Voices: The Selected Prose of John Hewitt* (Belfast, 1987).

65. Johnson, 'The Northern Ireland Economy', 208.

66. Paul Bew, Peter Gibbon, and Henry Patterson, *Northern Ireland 1921–1996: Political Forces and Social Classes* (London, 1996), 82.

67. Ditch, *Social Policy in Northern Ireland 1939–50*, 80.

68. Barton, *Brookeborough*, 213.

69. R. R. Bowman to Cabinet Secretary, 6 April 1945, PRONI, Cabinet, 9C/22/2.

70. See Malachy Gray, 'A Shop Steward Remembers', *Saothar Journal of the Irish Labour History Society*, Vol. 11, 1986.

71. Barton, *Brookeborough*, 186–7.

72. E. H. Cooper, Ministry of Commerce, to H. R. Chapman, Ministry of Aircraft Production, 14 October 1942, in file on 'Labour Disputes', PRONI, Ministry of Commerce, COM 61/655.

73. Mike Milotte, *Communism in Modern Ireland* (Dublin, 1984), 201.

74. *Belfast Newsletter*, 15 October 1942.

75. During a dispute at Short and Harland, Tommie Watters, a Communist Party militant, deplored the strike 'during this critical period for freedom loving people of the world', *Belfast Newsletter*, 19 October 1942.

76. Minutes of Cabinet Committee on Manpower, 6 August 1942, PRONI, Ministry of Commerce, COM 61/266.

77. Minister of Labour to Prime Minister, 5 November 1942, PRONI Cabinet Secretariat, 'Arbitration in Strikes and Industrial Dispute', Cab 9C/22/1.

78. Emmet O'Connor, *A Labour History of Ireland 1824–1960* (Dublin, 1992), 187.

79. Andrews and the Minister of Labour supported the reduction of fines on strikers at Short and Harland and Harland and Wolff against the advice of Brooke and the Inspector General of the RUC. See letter from Gransden, Cabinet Secretary to Montgomery of Home Affairs, 3 April 1942, PRONI, Cabinet Secretariat, Cab 9C/22/1.

80. See file on Labour Disputes in PRONI, Ministry of Commerce, COM61/655.
81. Barton, *Brookeborough*, 203.
82. Letter from Hugh Douglas to Prime Minister, 27 March 1943: 'the current of abuse against the government from the business and middle class people of the Province', PRONI, Cabinet Secretariat, 'Arbitration in strikes and industrial disputes', Cab 9C/22/2.
83. W. D. Scott, Regional Controller of Ministry of Supply, Belfast, to E. M. Bowen, Ministry of Supply, London, 31 March 1944, PRONI, Ministry of Commerce, 'Labour Disputes', COM 61/655, and *Belfast Newsletter*, 4 April 1944.
84. Telegram from Brooke to Churchill, 9 March 1944, and Churchill's response, 15 March, on this 'most serious and lamentable strike', PRONI, Cabinet Secretariat, 'Arbitration', Cab 9C/22/2.
85. *Northern Whig*, 7 April 1944.
86. See Lowry's report of a meeting with a deputation from Belfast Trades Council on 24 May 1944, PRONI, Cabinet Secretariat, 'Arbitration', Cab 9C/22/2.
87. Letter from J. F. Gordon, Minister of Labour, to Andrews, 15 January 1942, PRONI, 'Infiltration of workers from Eire', Ministry of Finance, FIN 18/22/37.
88. Conclusions of Cabinet Sub-committee on Infiltration, 5 February 1942, PRONI, FIN 18/22/37.
89. Letter from Dawson Bates to Herbert Morrison, 26 March 1942, PRONI, FIN 18/22/37.
90. PRONI, Cabinet Secretariat, 'Infiltration of Eire Workers', Cab 9C/47/2.
91. Memorandum from Minister of Labour on labour for stone quarries, 18 April 1942, PRONI, FIN 18/22/37.
92. Letter from F. A. Clarke, Ballinamallard, to Sir Basil Brooke, 11 March 1944, and Cabinet Conclusions, 6 April 1944, PRONI, Cabinet Secretariat, 'Infiltration of Eire Workers', Cab 9C/47/2 (3).
93. Figures from memorandum on the Residence in Northern Ireland (Restriction) Order, October 1946, PRONI, Cabinet Secretariat, Cab 9C/47/3.
94. Terry Cradden, *Trade Unionism, Socialism and Partition* (Belfast, 1993), 46. In the 52-seat parliament, the Unionist Party had 33 seats and the Nationalists 10. Sydney Elliott, Northern Ireland Parliamentary Election Results 1921–1972 (Chichester, 1973), p. 92.

Chapter 3

1. Speech to the Dáil, 18 June 1936, Public Record Office (PRO), 'Notes on the work of the Irish section of the Security Services 1939–1945', KV 4/9 59761.
2. Peter Mair, *The Changing Irish Party System* (London, 1987), 20.
3. T. Ryle Dwyer, *De Valera: The Man and the Myths* (Dublin, 1992), 219.

4. T. D. Williams, 'A Study in Neutrality', *The Leader*, 31 January 1953.
5. Speaking on supplementary army estimate in the Dáil, *Irish Times*, 17 February 1939.
6. G. R. Sloan, *The Geopolitics of Anglo-Irish Relations in the 20th Century* (Leicester, 1998), 184.
7. Eunan O'Halpin, 'The Army in Independent Ireland', in Tom Bartlett and Keith Jeffery (eds), *A Military History of Ireland* (Cambridge, 1996), 419.
8. Tony Gray, *The Lost Years: The Emergency in Ireland 1939–45* (London, 1998), 49.
9. Dermot Keogh, *Twentieth Century Ireland: Nation and State* (Dublin, 1994), 109.
10. Maurice Moynihan (ed.), *Speeches and Statements by Eamon de Valera* (Dublin and New York, 1980), 418.
11. O'Halpin, 418.
12. Garret FitzGerald, 'Myth of Irish Neutrality not Borne out by Historical Fact', *Irish Times*, 24 April 1999.
13. O'Halpin, 'The Irish Army in Independent Ireland', 420.
14. 'Notes on the work of the Irish Section of the Security Services 1939–1945'.
15. J. J. Lee, *Ireland 1912–1985: Politics and Society* (Cambridge, 1989), 234.
16. Sloan, 201.
17. David O'Donoghue, *Hitler's Irish Voices: The Story of German Radio's Wartime Irish Service* (Belfast, 1998), 19.
18. C. S. Andrews, *Man of No Property* (Dublin, 1982), 162.
19. O'Donoghue, 19.
20. Lee, 247.
21. Brendan Barrington (ed.), *The Wartime Broadcasts of Francis Stuart 1942–1944* (Dublin, 2000), 32.
22. Eunan O'Halpin, *Defending Ireland: The Irish State and its Enemies since 1922* (Oxford, 1999), 239–45.
23. Conor Foley, *Legion of the Rearguard: The IRA and the Modern Irish State* (London, 1992), 191.
24. Lee, 223.
25. Ibid.
26. *The Round Table*, No. 119, June 1940.
27. Account of Plant's trial by Military Court, National Archives, Dublin (NAD), Department of the Taoiseach, S 12682.
28. John Horgan, *Seán Lemass: The Enigmatic Patriot* (Dublin, 1997), 108.
29. 'Notes on the work of the Irish section of the Security Services 1939–1945'.
30. *The Round Table*, No. 119, June 1940.
31. Letter from Maurice Moynihan to Patrick Kennedy in the Department of the Taoiseach with enclosures detailing the extent of wartime co-operation with the British government, included as an Appendix in Tim Pat Coogan, *De Valera: Long Fellow, Long Shadow* (London, 1995), 748–9.

32. Coogan, *De Valera*, 549.
33. 'Notes on the work of the Irish section of the Security Services 1939–1945'.
34. Ibid.
35. Sloan, 210.
36. Ibid. 227.
37. Geoffrey Roberts, 'Three Narratives of Neutrality: Historians and Ireland's War', in Brian Girvin and Geoffrey Roberts (eds), *Ireland and the Second World War: Politics, Society and Remembrance* (Dublin, 2000), 167.
38. Ibid. 173.
39. See for example O'Halpin, *Defending Ireland*, 151.
40. The Irish Association, established in 1938 largely on the initiative of some liberal unionists, published a pamphlet on neutrality, 'Ireland and the War', in 1940, which took up this theme. It is included in Bew, Darwin, and Gillespie, *Passion and Prejudice: Nationalist–Unionist Conflict in Ulster in the 1930s and the Founding of the Irish Association* (Belfast, 1993), 84–104.
41. The Earl of Longford and Thomas P. O'Neill, *Eamon de Valera* (Dublin, 1970), 354.
42. Brian Girvin, 'Politics in Wartime: Governing, Neutrality and Elections', in Girvin and Roberts (eds), *Ireland and the Second World War*, 27.
43. *The Round Table*, No. 121, December 1940.
44. Maurice Manning, *James Dillon: A Biography* (Dublin, 1999), 172.
45. Robert Fisk, *In Time of War: Ireland, Ulster and the Price of Neutrality* (London, 1983), 160.
46. Ibid.
47. Ibid. 165.
48. Memorandum signed by James Dillon and T. G. O'Higgins, 14 June 1940, NAD, Department of Justice, 'Fine Gael and Neutrality', S 14213.
49. John Bowman, *De Valera and the Ulster Question* (Oxford, 1985), 229.
50. Lee, 248.
51. Fisk, 186.
52. 'Notes on the work of the Irish section of the Security Services 1939–1945'.
53. Longford and O'Neill, 349.
54. Manning, 163.
55. Notes on a conference held in the Taoiseach's room, 16 July 1940, NAD, Department of Justice, 'Fine Gael and Neutrality', S 14213.
56. Moynihan (ed.), 373.
57. Report of contents of German Foreign Office documents in *Irish Independent*, 3 August 1957.
58. Lee, 247.
59. T. D. Williams, 'A Study in Neutrality', *The Leader*, 28 March 1953.
60. *The Round Table*, No. 126, March 1942.
61. Hempel reported to Berlin that de Valera's 'democratic principles' were

sympathetic to Britain: German Foreign Office documents reported in the *Irish Times*, 18 October 1958.

62. *The Round Table*, No. 120, September 1940.
63. Arrland Usher, *The Face and Mind of Ireland* (London, 1949), 68.
64. Manning, 160.
65. *The Irish Times*, 14 November 1941.
66. Donal O Drisceoil, *Censorship in Ireland 1939–1945* (Cork, 1996), 121–5.
67. *The Round Table*, No. 125, December 1941.
68. *Irish Times*, 14 November 1941.
69. Roberts, 176–7.
70. F. S. L. Lyons, *Ireland Since the Famine* (London, 1973), 557–8.
71. Brian Fallon, *An Age of Innocence: Irish Culture 1930–1960* (Dublin, 1998), 214.
72. 'One World', *The Bell*, Vol. 7, No. 4, January 1944.
73. *Parliamentary Debates: Dail Eireann* (PDDE), Vol. LXXXII, col. 1118, 2 April 1941.
74. *The Bell*, Vol. 2, No. 4, July 1941.
75. Ibid.
76. 'Notes on the work of the Irish section of the Security Services, 1939–1945'.
77. Lee, 224.
78. Richard Dunphy, *The Making of Fianna Fáil Power in Ireland, 1923–1948* (Oxford, 1995), 220.
79. Enda Delaney, 'State, Politics and Demography: the Case of Irish Emigration 1921–71', *Irish Political Studies*, Vol. 13, 1998, 33.
80. O Drisceoil, 257.
81. Special Branch report of unemployed workers' meeting, 4 April 1941, NAD, Department of Justice, JUS8/46, 'Unemployed Workers' Organisations'.
82. Dunphy, 223.
83. Fallon, 8, and O Drisceoil, 100.
84. One example from Garda reports was a Belfast militant who told a meeting of the Dublin unemployed that anti-partitionism would have to engage with economic realities: 'since the unemployed in Northern Ireland were better treated than those in Eire, it made their lot of convincing them to unite with Eire more difficult': NAD, Department of Justice, S42/39 Part 1, 21 January 1940.
85. Dunphy, 180–1.
86. Lee, 216, and Kieran Allen, *Fianna Fáil and Irish Labour: 1926 to the Present* (London, 1997), 77.
87. Alan, 77.
88. Cormac O'Gráda, *A Rocky Road: The Irish Economy since the 1920s* (Manchester, 1997), 17, and Emmet O'Connor, *A Labour History of Ireland 1824–1960* (Dublin, 1992), 136.
89. O'Gráda, 16.
90. Lee, 233.

91. O'Gráda, 6, and Tony Gray, *The Lost Years: The Emergency in Ireland 1939–45* (London, 1997), 143.
92. Special Branch report of public meeting held by Dublin Central Branch of the Irish Labour Party, 17 September 1942, where the government was attacked for allowing fuel merchants to charge high prices for turf, NAD: Department of Justice, JUS 8/884.
93. Greta Jones, *'Captain of all these men of death': The History of Tuberculosis in Nineteenth and Twentieth Century Ireland* (Amsterdam and New York, 2001), 188.
94. Police report of a meeting of 200 labourers at Foynes, Newcastlewest, 6 March 1941, NAD, Department of Justice, JUS 8/746.
95. Horgan, 121.
96. Emmet O'Connor, 133.
97. Ibid. 134.
98. Special Branch report of meeting at College Green, 22 June 1941, NAD, Department of Justice, JUS 8/884.
99. Allen, 77.
100. Mair, 20.
101. Cornelius O'Leary, *Irish Elections 1918–1977* (Dublin, 1979), 35.
102. Terry Cradden, *Trade Unionism, Socialism and Partition* (Belfast, 1993), 65.
103. John P. Swift, 'The Last Years', in Daniel Nevin (ed.), *James Larkin: Lion of the Fold* (Dublin, 1996), 86.
104. O'Leary, 35.
105. Dunphy, 288.
106. Dunphy, 285, and John de Courcy Ireland, 'As I remember Big Jim', in Nevin (ed.), 454.
107. Horgan, 124.
108. Brian Girvin, 'Politics in Wartime: Governing, Neutrality and Elections', in Brian Girvin and Geoffrey Roberts (eds), 39–41.
109. *Irish Press*, 20 January 1944, in Special Branch report, NAD, Department of Justice, JUS 8/917.
110. Mike Milotte, *Communism in Modern Ireland* (Dublin, 1984), 199.
111. Report on Communists in the Labour Party, 20 April 1944, in papers deposited by John Horgan with the Irish Labour History Museum, Dublin. My thanks to Paddy Gillan for bringing this report to my attention.
112. Alan, 80.
113. Mair, 20.
114. The most reliable estimate is of 72,000 members for the ITUC and 53,000 for the CIU: Cradden, 112.
115. Debate on the Beveridge Plan, 13 December 1942, NAD, Department of the Taoiseach, S13053a.
116. Andrews, 171.
117. Flinn was in charge of the emergency turf campaign for the Turf Develop-

ment Board. He was a detested figure among those of the unemployed who had been forced to experience the low wages, military discipline, and poor food in the labour camps set up on Clonsast and other boglands in county Kildare. Andrews refers to the 'atmosphere of labour unrest in the camps', 174–8, and Peader Cowen, later a leader of Clann na Poblachta, who was a Labour Party organizer at the time, claimed to have set up more than 60 labour branches in turf-producing counties: see his speech denouncing Flinn at a meeting of the Central Branch of the Labour Party, 3 July 1940, NAD, Department of Justice, JUS 8/884.

118. Brian Girvin, *Between Two Worlds: Politics and Economy in Independent Ireland* (Dublin, 1989), 150.
119. Memorandum on Full Employment Policy, 17 January 1945, NAD, Department of the Taoiseach, S13101a.
120. Dunphy, 231.
121. *The Round Table*, No. 121, December 1940.
122. Charles Townshend, *Ireland: The 20th Century* (London, 1999), 155.
123. See, for example, Lee, 334. An editorial in *The Bell* in April 1941 provided an early critique: 'We tried to establish a network of decentralised factories. . . . we had an idealised vision of little industries in the small towns and villages . . . The census returns replied in the name of realism with the flow from the fields to the cities, the decay of small villages and our smaller towns.'.
124. Mair, 25.
125. See his suggestion for the 'displacement' of the worst farmers in 'Memorandum on Full Employment Policy', 17 January 1945, NAD, Department of the Taoiseach, S13101a.
126. Sheila May, 'Two Dublin Slums', *The Bell*, Vol. 7 No. 4, 1944.
127. Deirdre McMahon, 'John Charles McQuaid of Dublin, the Politician: A Reassessment', *Studies*, Winter 1998, Vol. 87, No. 348, and J. H. Whyte, *Church and State in Modern Ireland 1923–1979* (Dublin, 1984), 76–9.
128. Whyte, 78.
129. Paul Bew and Henry Patterson, *Seán Lemass and the Making of Modern Ireland* (Dublin, 1982), 30.
130. Whyte, 102.
131. Lee, 234.

Chapter 4

1. Enda Delaney, 'State, Politics and Demography: the Case of Irish Emigration, 1921–71', *Irish Political Studies*, Vol. 13, 1998, 36.
2. *Mayo News*, 10 January 1931.
3. 'Post-War Policy and the Programme for the Land Commission', 21 August 1942, NAD, Department of the Taoiseach, S1301a.

4. Paul Bew and Henry Patterson, *Seán Lemass and the Making of Modern Ireland* (Dublin, 1982), 5.
5. See his dialogue with Lemass in Cabinet Committee on Economic Planning, NAD, Department of the Taoiseach, S13026b.
6. 'Memorandum on Full Employment Policy', 17 January 1945, NAD, Department of the Taoiseach, S13101a.
7. 'Position of the Minority in the 26 Counties', NAD, Department of Foreign Affairs, 305/14/35 IA.
8. Cormac O'Gráda, *A Rocky Road: The Irish Economy since the 1920s* (Manchester, 1997), 22.
9. O'Gráda, 22.
10. *Economic Development* (Dublin, 1958), PR 4803, 153.
11. Terence Brown, *Ireland: A Social and Cultural History* (London, 1981), 184.
12. K. H. Connell, 'Catholicism and Marriage in the Century after the Famine', in K. H. Connell, *Irish Peasant Society* (Oxford, 1968).
13. James Meenan, *The Irish Economy since 1922* (Liverpool, 1970), 112.
14. Richard Dunphy, *The Making of Fianna Fáil Power in Ireland 1923–1948* (Oxford, 1995), 211–12.
15. 'Discussions with Eire Ministers on UK–Eire Economic Relation', Note by Commonwealth Relations Office, 17 September 1947, PRO, Prem 8/824.
16. Bew and Patterson, 40.
17. 'Eire and Western Europe', June 1948, PRO, Prem 8/824.
18. 'Working Party on the Irish Republic', 1957, PRO, MAF 40/471.
19. 'Memorandum on Full Employment Policy'.
20. Liam Skinner, *Politicians by Accident* (Dublin, 1946), 63.
21. *Irish Times*, 12 February 1947.
22. Alvin Jackson, *Ireland 1798–1998: Politics and War* (Oxford, 1999), 308.
23. Ironically, McCaughey blamed MacBride for his capture for he was arrested soon after he had reluctantly agreed to meet MacBride at his office in Dublin to show him extracts from the confession he had recently helped to beat out of the alleged informer Stephen Hayes: see Raymond J. Quinn, *A Rebel Voice: A History of Belfast Republicanism* (Belfast, 1999), 71.
24. Kevin Rafter, *The Clann: The Story of Clann na Poblachta* (Dublin, 1996), 25.
25. Eithne MacDermott, *Clann na Poblachta* (Cork, 1998), 61, and David McCullagh, *A Makeshift Majority: The First Inter-party Government* (Dublin, 1998), 10.
26. M. J. Kennedy to Frank Gallagher, 18 December 1946, National Library of Ireland, MS 18336.
27. Rafter, 39.
28. MacDermott, 19.
29. Dunphy, 39.
30. Rafter, 35–6.
31. MacDermott, 35.

32. McCullagh, 26–9.
33. Peter Mair, *The Changing Irish Party System* (London, 1987), 54.
34. McCullagh, 30.
35. *Irish Times,* 18 May 1944.
36. *The Round Table,* No. 136, September 1944.
37. MacDermott, 33.
38. McCullagh, 182.
39. See Ronan Fanning, *The Irish Department of Finance* (Dublin, 1978), 456–60, and Patrick Lynch, 'More Pages from an Irish Memoir', in Richard English and J. M. Skelly (eds), *Ideas Matter* (Dublin, 1998), 133.
40. Brian Girvin, *Between Two Worlds: Politics and Economy in Independent Ireland* (Dublin, 1989), 170.
41. Lynch, 133.
42. McCullagh, 145.
43. F. S. L. Lyons, *Ireland since the Famine* (London, 1971), 571.
44. McCullagh, 158–9.
45. Greta Jones, '*Captain of all these men of death': The History of Tuberculosis in Nineteenth and Twentieth Century Ireland* (Amsterdam and New York, 2001), 230.
46. Noel Browne, *Against the Tide* (Dublin, 1986), 35.
47. Browne, 124.
48. McCullagh, 205–6.
49. Ruth Barrington, *Health, Medicine and Politics in Ireland 1900–1970* (Dublin, 1970), 182–8.
50. J. H. Whyte, *Church and State in Modern Ireland 1923–1979* (Dublin, 1980), 305.
51. The letter of 10 October 1952 is reprinted in Paul Blanshard, *The Irish and Catholic Power* (London, 1954), 76–7.
52. McCullagh, 217.
53. Blanshard, 74.
54. McCullagh, 223.
55. J. J. Lee, *Ireland 1912–1985: Politics and Society* (Cambridge, 1989), 318.
56. McCullagh, 198.
57. Whyte, 238.
58. McCullagh, 199.
59. Ronan Fanning, 'McQuaid's Country on Bended Knee', *Independent on Sunday,* 12 April 1998.
60. Ibid.
61. Whyte, 43.
62. Ibid. 158.
63. Enda Delaney, 'State, Politics and Demography: the Case of Irish emigration 1921–71', *Irish Political Studies,* Vol. 13, 1998, 39.
64. Emmet O'Connor, *A Labour History of Ireland 1824–1960* (Dublin, 1992), 136.

65. Whyte, 166.
66. Ibid. 173.
67. Ibid. 268.
68. McCullagh, 157.
69. 'The Year in Retrospect', *The Irish Times*, 1 January 1954.
70. McCullagh, 230.
71. Quoted in Blanshard, 15.
72. Rafter, 77.
73. *The Round Table*, No. 136, September 1944.
74. Commonwealth Relations Office to Attlee, 23 October 1947, PRO, Prem 8/824/4487.
75. Report by Lord Rugby, 28 October 1947, PRO, Prem 8/824/4487.
76. Troy D. Davis, *Dublin's American Policy: Irish American Diplomatic Relations, 1945–52* (Washington DC, 1998), 151.
77. Lynch, 127.
78. They regularly breakfasted together in MacBride's office in Iveagh House: Rafter, 108.
79. Davis, 96.
80. Ibid. 127.
81. *Belfast Newsletter*, 8 March 1951.
82. McCullagh, 114.
83. Dermot Keogh, *Twentieth Century Ireland: Nation and State* (Dublin, 1994), 186.
84. Conor Cruise O'Brien, *Memoir: My Life and Themes* (Dublin, 1998), 146.
85. 'Mr Blythe's suggestions for a revised policy on partition', Memorandum by Conor Cruise O'Brien to the Secretary, Department of External Affairs, 12 August 1949, NAD, Department of Foreign Affairs, 305/14/62.
86. Speech by Colonel Topping, Unionist Chief Whip, on 18 September 1950, reported in 'Position of the Minority in the 26 Counties', NAD, Department of Foreign Affairs, 305/14/351 A.
87. Letter from R. C. Geary, Central Statistical Office, to the Secretary, Department of External Affairs, 23 October 1951, in 'Position of the Minority in the 26 Counties'.
88. Whyte, 169.
89. Dennis Kennedy, *The Widening Gulf: Northern Attitudes to the Independent Irish State* (Belfast, 1988), 182–4.
90. 'Protestants Denied Positions in Eire', *Belfast Newsletter*, 17 January 1951.
91. Annual Report of the Ulster Unionist Council, 1951, PRONI, Ulster Unionist Council Papers, D 1377/20/2/34.
92. Report on a meeting at the London Embassy, 8 August 1952, NAD, Department of Foreign Affairs, 313/3.
93. Boland to the Secretary, Department of External Affairs, 23 October 1953, NAD, Department of Foreign Affairs, 313/3.

94. Lord Brookeborough, *Diaries*, 4 April 1956, PRONI, Ulster Unionist Council Papers, D 3004/E/21.
95. O'Gráda, 25.
96. Meenan, 112.
97. Barry Brunt, *The Republic of Ireland* (London, 1988), 13.
98. O'Gráda, 27.
99. 'Economic Relations with the Irish Republic', February 1960, PRO, Cab 129/100.
100. Liam Kennedy, *The Modern Industrialisation of Ireland* (Dublin, 1989), 9.
101. Girvin, 197.
102. Kennedy, 9.
103. Meenan, 112.
104. Bew and Patterson, 56–8.
105. Seamus Cody, John O'Dowd, and Peter Rigney, *The Parliament of Labour: 100 Years of the Dublin Council of Trade Unions* (Dublin, 1986), 200.
106. Bew and Patterson, 61.
107. Cody, O'Dowd, and Rigney, 201.
108. Girvin, 184.
109. *The Round Table*, Vol. 44, October 1953.
110. Bew and Patterson, 69.
111. Garret FitzGerald, 'Turning Point', *Irish Times*, 1 January 1957.
112. Bew and Patterson, 87.
113. *Irish Times*, 23 February 1957.
114. Mair, 32.
115. Horgan, *Seán Lemass: Enigmatic Patriot* (Dublin, 1997), 175.
116. *The Times*, 17 September 1957.
117. T. K. Whitaker, 'Capital Formation, Saving and Economic Progress', *The Journal of the Statistical and Social Inquiry Society of Ireland*, Vol. 19, 1955–6.
118. Horgan, 165.
119. *Irish Press*, 12 October 1955.
120. Lee, 343.
121. Girvin, 192.
122. Lee, 344, and Bew and Patterson, 115.
123. Girvin, 192–3.
124. Lee, 354.

Chapter 5

1. A. J. Kelly (Home Office) to A. Gransden (Cabinet Office, Stormont), 2 April 1946, PRONI, Cab 9J/53/1.
2. Peter Rose, *How the Troubles Came to Northern Ireland* (Basingstoke and New York, 2000), 2.

3. 'Note of a meeting with Rt. Hon. Herbert Morrison MP', 15 September 1946, PRONI, Cab 9J/53/2.

4. G. C. Duggan, 'Northern Ireland: Success or Failure?', *Irish Times*, 19 April 1950. Duggan was Comptroller and Auditor General at Stormont.

5. Memorandum on 'The Constitutional Position' by R. Nugent, 6 January 1946, PRONI, Cab 9J/53/1.

6. Memorandum by Minister of Health and Local Government, 9 July 1946, PRONI, Cab 9J/53/2.

7. John Ditch, *Social Policy in Northern Ireland 1939–1950* (Aldershot, 1988), 105.

8. Letter from Lieutenant Colonel J. M. Blakiston-Houston, Beltrim Castle, Gortin, to Basil Brooke, 9 April 1948, PRONI, Cab 9J/53/1.

9. *Belfast Newsletter*, 27 November 1947.

10. Note on Dominion Status from Robert Gransden, Cabinet Secretary to the Prime Minister, 31 October 1947, PRONI, Cab 9J/53/2.

11. Sir Alexander Maxwell to the Home Secretary, 25 October 1945, included in a file on 'Infiltration of Éire Workers into Northern Ireland', PRONI, Cab 9C/47/3.

12. Paul Bew, Peter Gibbon and Henry Patterson, *Northern Ireland 1921–1996 Political Forces and Social Classes* (London, 1996), 107.

13. Letter from Henry McCay, Secretary of the City of Londonderry and Foyle Unionist Association, to McCoy, 29 March 1951, PRONI, McCoy Papers, D333/A/1.

14. Madge MacDonald to McCoy, 24 February 1948, PRONI, McCoy Papers, D333/A/1.

15. May Knox-Browne, Aglinton Castle, Fivemiletown, to McCoy, 9 September 1952, PRONI, McCoy Papers, D333/A/1.

16. *Belfast Newsletter*, 22 December 1945.

17. Bew, Gibbon, and Patterson, 103.

18. Sabine Wichert, *Northern Ireland since 1945* (London, 1991), 72.

19. F. H. Boland, Irish Ambassador, London, to Seán Nunan, Secretary, Department of External Affairs, 6 January 1954, NAD, Department of Foreign Affairs, 305/14/249.

20. Sir Basil Brooke, *Diaries*, 18 February 1951, account of Ulster Unionist Council Meeting, PRONI, D 3004/D/44.

21. Letter from Maginess to Brooke, 21 August 1951, PRONI, Cab 9J/53/2.

22. 'Roman Catholic Electors Seeing the Light', *Northern Whig*, 20 October 1951.

23. *Belfast Newsletter*, 13 July 1946.

24. Statement showing scope and amount of social services in Northern Ireland and Éire, October 1946, PRONI, Cab 9C/47/3.

25. F. S. L. Lyons, *Ireland since the Famine* (London, 1971), 742.

26. *The Ulster Year Book 1947* (Belfast, 1948), 76, and *The Ulster Year Book 1963–64* (Belfast, 1965), 213.

27. From 2,026 in 1945–6 to 4,708 in 1963–4, *The Ulster Year Book 1963–64*, 234.

28. John Ditch, *Social Policy in Northern Ireland 1939–1950* (Aldershot, 1988), 107.
29. *The Ulster Year Book 1960–62* (Belfast, 1963), 229.
30. J. H. Whyte, 'How much discrimination was there under the Unionist regime 1921–68?' in I. T. Gallagher and James O'Connell (eds), *Contemporary Irish Studies* (Manchester, 1983), 20.
31. Graham Gudgin, 'Discrimination in Housing and Employment under the Stormont Regime', in P. Boche and B. Barton (eds) *The Northern Ireland Question: Nationalism, Unionism and Partition* (Hampshire, 1999), 103.
32. Memorandum by the Minister of Home Affairs on the Civil Authorities (Special Powers) Act, 22 February 1950, PRONI, Cab 4/846/10/.
33. See Henry Patterson, 'Party versus Order: Ulster Unionism and the Flags and Emblems Act', *Contemporary British History*, Vol. 13, No. 4, Winter 1999, 104–29.
34. *Belfast Newsletter*, 13 July 1946.
35. Report of the Proceedings of the half-yearly General Meeting of the Grand Lodge of Ireland, Sandy Row Orange Hall, 14 December 1949, in the Library of the Orange Order, Belfast.
36. Michael McGrath, 'The Narrow Road: Harry Midgley and Catholic Schools in Northern Ireland', *Irish Historical Studies*, Vol. XXX, no. 119, May 1997, 439.
37. Ibid. 440.
38. Oliver P. Rafferty, *Catholicism in Ulster 1603–1983: An Interpretative History* (Dublin, 1994), 247.
39. Belfast LOL 958 resolution, which protested against grants to sixteen Catholic schools under the 1947 Act, Meeting of Grand Lodge of Ireland, 8 June 1949, the Library of the Orange Order, Belfast.
40. *Ulster Protestant*, October 1957.
41. 'Position of the Minority in the 26 Counties', 24 October 1950, NAD, Department of Foreign Affairs, 305/14/35 IA.
42. *Ulster Protestant*, August 1951.
43. Memorandum from the Inspector General of the RUC, 30 December 1953, PRONI, HA/32/1/ 956.
44. Patterson, 120.
45. Ibid. 108.
46. Sir Basil Brooke, *Diaries*, 6 June 1956, PRONI, D 3004/D/45.
47. Ibid., 13 September: 'Deputation headed by Teddy Jones (MP for Londonderry City) on industries. They are anxious that we should not get an invasion from the other side.'
48. This was after a letter from Teddy Jones that warned that if the position 'falls into the wrong hands, the situation in Londonderry City will go from bad to worse and ultimately destroy us'. Letter from Jones to A. J. Kelly, Cabinet Office, PRONI, Cab 9C/5/4.
49. Harry Diamond, a Republican Labour MP quoted in *Irish News*, 15 October 1953.

50. Whyte, 10.
51. Sir Basil Brooke, *Diaries*, 24 February 1956, PRONI, D 30004/D/45.
52. Ibid. 5 September 1956.
53. Paul Teague, 'Discrimination and Segmentation Theory: A Survey', in Terry Cradden and Paul Teague (eds), *Labour Market Discrimination and Fair Employment in Northern Ireland: International Journal of Manpower*, Vol. 13, Nos. 65/7, 1992.
54. The seminal article on the topic is E. A. Aunger, 'Religion and Occupational Class in Northern Ireland', *Economic and Social Review*, Vol. 7, No. 1, 1975.
55. Whyte, 21–3.
56. Letter from Brian Maginess to R. A. Butler, 15 December 1954, PRONI, Cab 4A/38/21.
57. Memorandum of the Minister of Commerce on Advanced Factories, 28 March 1956, PRONI, Cab 4A/38/25.
58. Letter from Brian Maginess to R. A. Butler, 15 December 1954, PRONI, Cab 4A/38/21.
59. This depressing story is, not surprisingly, easier to follow in the Prime Minister's diaries than in the cabinet papers: 30 April 1957, 'Cabinet sub-committee on Derry employment problem in new industries. There are two lines we can help—getting good labour relations people into the factories . . . Housing is important and getting Derry men from other parts of the Province and from England to return to the city.' 17 May 1957: 'Met Executive of the party at Glengall Street and told them we had made arrangements for Derry about new industries.' 26 June 1957: 'Teddy Jones saw Labour and Commerce about employment in Derry. He says there is a row with the Apprentice Boys that no Protestants are being employed in the building operations (for Dupont plant). Extracts from *Diaries*, PRONI, D 3004/D/45.
60. Campaign for Social Justice in Northern Ireland, *The Plain Truth* (Dungannon, 2nd edition, 1969).
61. Niall O'Dochartaigh, *From Civil Rights to Armalites, Derry and the Birth of the Irish Troubles* (Cork, 1997), xvi–xvii.
62. Sir Basil Brooke, *Diaries*, 23 September 1958, PRONI, D 3004/D/45.
63. Copy of telephone message from Brookeborough to the Home Secretary, 7 February 1958: 'The unemployment rate in Londonderry is 17% and the closing of the station will completely cancel the volume of additional work being provided by new industry in the area', PRONI, Cab 4A/38/29.
64. Brendan Lynn, *Holding the Ground: The Nationalist Party in Northern Ireland, 1945–72* (Aldershot, 1997), 4.
65. 1951 election address of Gerald Annesley, APL candidate in South Down, NAD, Department of Foreign Affairs, 305/14/109/4/1.
66. In a memorandum on the state of northern Nationalism, 1 May 1958, NAD, Department of Foreign Affairs, 305/14/2/4.
67. Lynn, 37.

68. Ibid. 55.
69. Visit by Dr Conor Cruise O'Brien to anti-partitionist centres in Northern Ireland, 23–5 March 1953, NAD, Department of Foreign Affairs, 305/14/2/3.
70. Ibid.
71. J. Bowyer Bell, *The Secret Army: A History of the IRA 1916–1970* (London, 1972), 296.
72. Report by F. H. Boland to Seán Nunan, Department of External Affairs, 26 November 1953, NAD, Department of Foreign Affairs, 305/14/249.
73. Conor Cruise O'Brien report on a visit to Ulster, 21–2 June, NAD, 305/17/2/3.
74. *The Round Table*, No. 177, December 1954.
75. Report on a visit to Ulster, 21–2 June, NAD, 305/17/2/3.
76. Bowyer Bell, 313–15.
77. Thus Seán Rafferty to a Sinn Féin meeting in Belfast, 'They had a far greater weapon in the ballot box than in bullets, bayonets and bombs.' *Irish News*, 16 May 1955.
78. An intercepted communication from Eamon Timoney, an IRA officer in Derry, to his commanding officer was revealing: 'Our boys are anxious to let the 'B' patrols have it, but I have objected . . . If you say the word "let them have it" we will not say "no".' Quoted at his trial, *Belfast Newsletter*, 20 June 1957.
79. Examples were the killing of Seargent Ovens by a booby-trap in August 1957 and the shooting of an off-duty RUC constable by an IRA team in Fermanagh in January 1961. Bowyer Bell, 367 and 391.
80. Seán Cronin, *Irish Nationalism* (Dublin, 1980), 171.
81. Target list included in documents found on IRA man tried in Belfast, *Belfast Newsletter*, 16 March 1957.
82. 'Belfast Man Jailed for Possessing IRA Documents', *Belfast Newsletter*, 11 December 1956.
83. Inspector General's office, Crime Branch Special, 'Subversive Activities: Reports and Correspondence', PRONI, HA/32/1/1349.
84. Department of External Affairs memorandum on meeting with Michael O'Neill, 19 May 1955, NAD, Department of Foreign Affairs, 305/14/2.
85. Conor Cruise O'Brien, report on visit to Ulster, 21–2 July 1954, NAD, Department of Foreign Affairs, 305/17/2/3.
86. J. G. Nelson, RUC Headquarters, to R. F. R. Dunbar, Ministry of Home Affairs, 26 September 1958, PRONI, HA/32/1/1349.
87. Henry Patterson, *The Politics of Illusion: A Political History of the IRA* (London, 1997), 92.
88. 'Subversive incidents in Northern Ireland since 12 December 1958', PRONI, HA/32/1/1349.
89. 'Proposed winding up of the APL in the Six Counties', NAD, Department of External Affairs, 305/14/2/4.
90. Memorandum on Publicity by Eric Montgomery, Director of Publicity, 7 April 1957, PRONI, Cabinet Publicity Committee, Cab 4A/26/75.

91. Government of Northern Ireland, *Report of the Joint Working Party on the Economy of Northern Ireland*, Cmnd 446, (Belfast, 1962) (hereafter referred to as the *Hall Report*, after Sir Robert Hall, who chaired it), para. 23.

92. G. P. Steed, 'Internal Organization, Firm Integration and Locational Change; The Northern Ireland Linen Complex 1954–64', *Economic Geography*, No. 47, 1971.

93. Report by officials on employment policy, December 1960, PRONI, Cabinet Employment Sub-Committee, Cab 4A/38/43.

94. *Hall Report*, para. 21.

95. Ibid. para. 26.

96. Ibid. para. 44.

97. Bew, Gibbon, and Patterson, 119.

98. *Hall Report*, para. 25.

99. Bew, Gibbon, and Patterson, 118.

100. *Hall Report*, para. 26.

101. Minute from the Prime Minister to the Home Secretary, 29 December 1949, in 'Industrial Development and Employment in Northern Ireland, Measures by British Government', PRONI, Cab 9F/188/1.

102. Note by Sir Frank Newsam of the Home Office of a meeting to discuss unemployment in Northern Ireland, PRONI, Cab 9F/188/3.

103. PRONI, Cab 4/970/830 April 1955.

104. 'Employment Policy: Report by Officials', December 1960, PRONI, Cab 4A/38/43.

105. Ibid.

106. 'Industrial Development and Employment in Northern Ireland, Measures by British Government', PRONI, Cab 9F/188/72.

107. Terry Cradden, *Trade Unionism, Socialism and Partition* (Belfast, 1993), 179.

108. 'The Economic Survey of Northern Ireland', memorandum by the Minister of Commerce, 16 October 1957, PRONI, Cab 4/1049.

109. Bew, Gibbon, and Patterson, 126.

110. See O'Neill's comments at meeting of Cabinet Employment Committee, 3 April 1958, PRONI, Cab 4A/38/21.

111. 'Observations on the 1953 election', Ulster Unionist Council Papers, PRONI, D1327/16/3/51.

112. Cabinet Employment Committee, 19 November 1958, PRONI, Cab 4A/38/34.

113. Personal note from Minister of Finance to Cabinet Employment Committee, 12 February 1958, PRONI, Cab 4A/38/29.

114. Bew, Gibbon, and Patterson, 128.

115. Sydney Elliott, *Northern Ireland Parliamentary Election Results, 1921–1971* (Chichester, 1973), 43.

116. *Belfast Newsletter*, 2 June 1962.

117. This was the opinion of Jack Sayers, the liberal editor of the *Belfast Tele-*

graph, who in his column in the *Round Tables* noted, 'It begins to appear that Northern Ireland's failure to recruit to the political field men and women of greater stature, capacity and breadth of vision is at last coming home to roost', *The Round Table*, No. 185, December 1956.

118. 'Future of Messrs. Short Brothers and Harland', memorandum by Minister of Defence and Minister of Aviation, 2 October 1962, PRO, Cab 127/110. Wilson's remark is from a meeting with Terence O'Neill and other members of the Stormont cabinet, 4 November 1968, PRONI, Cab 4/1413/10.

Chapter 6

1. 'Economic Relations with the Irish Republic', 5 February 1960, PRO, Cab 129/100, 5 February 1960.
2. Symposium on *Economic Development, Journal of the Statistical and Social Inquiry of Ireland*, Vol. XIX, Part II, 1958/59.
3. Paul Bew and Henry Patterson, *Seán Lemass and the Making of Modern Ireland* (Dublin, 1982), 114.
4. 'Economic Relations with the Irish Republic', PRO, Cab 129/100, 5 February 1960.
5. John Horgan, *Seán Lemass: The Enigmatic Patriot* (Dublin, 1997), 216.
6. Garret FitzGerald, *All in a Life: An Autobiography* (Dublin, 1991), 58.
7. Bew and Patterson, 136.
8. Ibid. 184.
9. 'The Political Implication of an Anglo-Irish Free Trade Area', 1 January 1965, NAD, Department of the Taoiseach, S16674 Q/95.
10. Peter Mair, *The Changing Irish Party System* (London, 1987), 182.
11. Susan Baker, 'Nationalist Ideology and the Industrial Policy of Fianna Fáil', *Irish Political Studies*, Vol. 1, 1986, 61.
12. Ibid. 64.
13. Lemass in a speech to the Dublin South-Central branch of Fianna Fáil, *Irish Times*, 13 May 1961.
14. Report of a meeting between the Minister of Industry and Commerce and the Linen, Cotton and Rayon Manufacturers' Association, 13 July 1961, NAD, Department of the Taoiseach S6272 C/61.
15. Cormac O'Gráda, *A Rocky Road: The Irish Economy since the 1920s* (Manchester, 1997), 29.
16. All the figures in this paragraph are from Liam Kennedy, *The Modern Industrialisation of Ireland 1940–1988* (Dublin, 1989), 14–16.
17. Liam Kennedy, 15.
18. Kieran Allen, *Fianna Fáil and Irish Labour: 1926 to the Present* (London, 1997), 108.
19. Allen, 109.

20. Niamh Hardiman, *Pay, Politics, and Economic Performance in Ireland 1970–1987* (Oxford, 1988), 48.
21. Horgan, 230.
22. Bew and Patterson, 173.
23. Horgan, 229.
24. Finola Kennedy, *Public Social Expenditure in Ireland*, Economic and Social Research Institute, Broadsheet No. 11, February 1975.
25. Mair, 30.
26. F. S. L. Lyons, *Ireland since the Famine* (London, 1971), 623–24.
27. J. J. Lee, *Ireland 1912–1985* (Cambridge, 1994), 629.
28. Jonathan Bardon, *A History of Ulster* (Belfast, 1992), 629.
29. *New York Times*, 29 April 1957.
30. Martin Mansergh, 'The Political Legacy of Seán Lemass', *Études Irlandaises*, No. 25-1, Printemps 2000, 160.
31. Lemass in his Presidential Address to árd fheis, 20 November 1962, in 'Partition: Government Policy', NAD, Department of the Taoiseach, S 9361 K/63.
32. In 1956–7 when ill with phlebitis he sent a note to T. K. Whitaker: 'Dev wants me to brush up my Irish—please send me some books on economics and finance' in Horgan, 302. The same book records his view on the afterlife: 'This is all nonsense. When it's over, it's over' (325).
33. *The Round Table*, No. 196, September 1959.
34. Henry Patterson, 'Seán Lemass and the Ulster Question 1959–65', *Journal of Contemporary History*, Vol. 34, No. 1, 1999, 151–2.
35. After a meeting with northern nationalist MPs and senators on 19 July 1962, Lemass asked the Minister for Transport and Power, Erskine Childers, to raise these issues with the two state companies: NAD, Department of the Taoiseach, 'Government Policy on Partition', S 9361 K/62.
36. Presidential address to árd fheis, 20 November 1962.
37. *Irish Times*, 16 October 1959.
38. At his first meeting in November 1963 with Sir Alec Douglas-Home, the British premier suggested a meeting with Lemass: Andrew Gailey, *Crying in the Wilderness: Jack Sayers; A Liberal Editor in Ulster 1939–69* (Belfast, 1995), 81–2.
39. Gransden, who was Cabinet Secretary from 1939 to 1957 and Northern Ireland Agent in London from 1957 to 1962, had become friendly with Hugh McCann, then Irish Ambassador in London and subsequently Secretary of the Department of External Affairs. His views were expressed during a holiday in Ireland in June 1963 and recorded in a note by McCann on 15 July 1963, NAD, Department of Foreign Affairs, 'Partition: Government Policy', DFA 313/31K.
40. *Irish Times*, 30 July 1963.
41. Robert Savage, *Seán Lemass* (Dublin, 1990), 40.
42. *Irish Press*, 12 September 1963.

43. Letter from Seán Lemass to all cabinet ministers, 10 September 1963, NAD, Department of the Taoiseach, S 1627 E/63.

44. 'Suggested Civil Service Level Discussions with Six County Representatives', 28 September 1963, NAD, Department of the Taoiseach, S 1627 E.

45. *Irish Times*, 17 October 1963.

46. *Irish Press*, 18 October 1963.

47. See his 1962 speech to árd fheis: 'I am convinced that British action in expanding freedom throughout Africa and Asia will eventually have its effect in bringing partition to an end', NAD, Department of the Taoiseach, 'Government Policy on Partition', S 9361 K/62.

48. Patterson, 150

49. 'Suggested Civil Service Level Discussions with Six County Representatives', 28 September 1963, NAD, Department of the Taoiseach, S 1627 E.

50. *Irish Times*, 2 November 1967.

51. Horgan, 267.

52. NAD, Department of External Affairs 305/14/360, 5 July 1967.

53. Horgan, 267.

54. Ibid. 197.

55. Erskine Childers to Seán Lemass, 1 March 1961, NAD, Department of External Affairs, 305/14/360.

56. Comments by B. Gallagher on proposed discrimination pamphlet, 12 August 1964, NAD, Department of External Affairs, 305/14/303.

57. Memorandum by B. Gallagher, 6 July 1967, NAD, Department of External Affairs, 305/14/360

58. Horgan, 298.

59. Allen, 123.

60. Aidan Kelly and Teresa Brannick, 'The Changing Contours of Irish Strike Patterns, 1960–84', *Irish Business and Administrative Research*, Vol. 8. pt. 1, 1986, 84.

61. Allen, 127–33.

62. Kieran Allen's analysis is a good example of this approach: see p. 123 of *Fianna Fáil and Irish Labour*.

63. Michael Gallagher, *The Irish Labour Party in Transition: 1957–82* (Dublin, 1982), 4.

64. Emmet O'Connor, *A Labour History of Ireland: 1824–1960* (Dublin, 1992), 172.

65. Gallagher, *The Irish Labour Party in Transition*, Appendices 1 and 2.

66. Ibid. 42.

67. Conor Cruise O'Brien, *Memoir: My Life and Themes* (Dublin, 1998), 317.

68. Figures from Mair, 117 and 120, Appendix 3.

69. Gallagher, 87.

70. Ibid. 89.

71. Ibid. 95.

72. Cruise O'Brien, 321.

73. James Wickham, 'The Politics of Dependent Capitalism: International Capital and the Nation State', in Austen Morgan and Bob Purdie (eds) *Ireland: Divided Nation Divided Class* (London, 1982), 62.

74. J. H. Whyte, *Church and State in Modern Ireland 1923–1979* (Dublin, 1984), 195.

75. Tom Garvin, 'Patriots and Republicans: an Irish Evolution', in William Crotty and David E. Schmitt (eds), *Ireland and the Politics of Change* (London, 1998), 150.

76. Christopher Whelan, 'Class and Social Mobility', in Kieran Kennedy (ed.), *Ireland in Transition* (Dublin, 1986), 85.

77. Garvin, 152.

78. John Cooney, *John Charles McQuaid: Ruler of Catholic Ireland* (Dublin, 1999), 338–9 and 358.

79. John Sheehan, 'Education and Society in Ireland 1945–1970', in J. J. Lee (ed.), *Ireland 1945–70* (Dublin, 1979), 62.

80. The figures for the North are from *The Ulster Year Book 1947* (Belfast, 1947), 76 and *The Ulster Year Book 1963–64* (Belfast, 1964), 213, and Sheehan, 65.

81. Whyte, 343–6.

82. Robert J. Savage, *Irish Television: The Political and Social Origins* (Cork, 1996), 46.

83. J. J. Lee, 'Continuity and Change in Ireland 1945–70', in J. J. Lee (ed.), *Ireland 1945–70* (Dublin, 1979), 172.

84. Bew and Patterson, 168.

85. Maurice Manning, *James Dillon: A Biography* (Dublin, 1999), 380.

86. James Downey, *Lenihan: His Life and Loyalties* (Dublin, 1998), 55.

87. T. Ryle Dwyer, *Charlie* (Dublin, 1987), 8–9.

88. 'The Berry Papers: The secret memoirs of the man who was the country's most important civil servant', *Magill,* June 1980, 48.

89. Feargal Tobin, *The Best of Decades: Ireland in the 1960s* (Dublin, 1996), 159–60.

90. Horgan, 333–6.

91. *Irish Times,* 4 November 1966.

92. 'GAA Salutes Lynch's Unique Sporting Record', *Irish Times,* 21 October 1999.

93. Horgan, 330.

94. Ryle Dwyer, 67.

95. *Irish Times,* 3 October 1968.

96. *Irish Times,* 6 December 1968.

97. Cornelius O'Leary, *Irish Elections 1918–1977* (Dublin, 1979), 68.

98. Maire Geoghegan-Quinn, 'Lynch, Gentle Leader with a Core of Tempered Steel', *Irish Times,* 23 October 1999.

99. 'Government Information Bureau—Future Activities in Relation to the 6 Counties', NAD, Department of the Taoiseach, 25 January 1969, 2000/6/497.

100. John Bowman, *De Valera and the Ulster Question* (Oxford, 1982), 324.

101. Ronan Fanning, 'Playing it Cool: The Response of the British and Irish Governments to the Crisis in Northern Ireland, 1968–9', *Irish Studies in International Affairs*, Vol. 12 (2001), 68.

102. Horgan, 342.

103. Ronan Fanning, 'Living in those Troubled Times', *Sunday Independent*, 2 January 2000.

104. Ronan Fanning, 'Bank Chief was Architect of Government's NI Policy', *Sunday Independent*, 16 January 2000.

105. The address is printed in full in the inquiry of Lord Scarman, 'Violence and Civil Disturbances in Northern Ireland in 1969', Report of a Tribunal of Inquiry, HMSO Belfast, Cmnd. 556, 1972, Vol. 2, 43–4.

106. 'The Berry Papers: the secret memoirs of the man who was the country's most important civil servant', *Magill*, June 1980, 48.

107. See his speech to the London Irish Club banquet: 'the prosperity of these islands as a region is indivisible', *Irish Times*, 18 March 1965.

108. Rachel Donnelly, 'Haughey seen as "shrewd and ruthless"', *Irish Times*, 1 and 3 January 2000.

109. Ryle Dwyer, 3.

110. The comment was made in an interview for RTE's epic history of the Irish state, *Seven Ages*, *Sunday Tribune*, 26 March 2000.

111. Horgan, 335.

112. Denis Coghlan, 'Lack of Political Direction on North Ended in Arms Trial', *Irish Times*, 10 January 2000.

113. Details of the men and of the expanded activity of the Irish state in Northern Ireland can be found in 'Government Information Bureau—Special Section arising out of Distress in 6 Counties', NAD, Department of the Taoiseach, 2000/6/497.

114. The report is quoted in Justin O'Brien, *The Arms Trial* (Dublin, 2000), 58.

115. Quoted in O'Brien, *The Arms Trial*, 222.

116. Bruce Arnold, *What Kind of Country? Modern Irish Politics 1968–1983* (London, 1984), 78.

117. Ryle Dwyer, 88.

118. Ronan Fanning, 'Bank Chief was Architect of Government's NI Policy', *Independent on Sunday*, 16 January 2000.

119. Arnold, 46–7.

120. Memorandum on 'Policy in Relation to Northern Ireland', 28 November 1969, NAD, Department of the Taoiseach, 2000/6/658.

121. Report of a discussion on the Northern Ireland situation between the Minister of External Affairs and the Chancellor of the Duchy of Lancaster, George Thompson, at the Foreign and Commonwealth Office, 20 February 1970, NAD, Department of Foreign Affairs, 2000/14/185.

122. Report on Six Counties by Eamonn Gallagher, 7 April 1970, NAD, 2000/14/185.

123. Arnold, 89–90.
124. Address to árd fheis, 17 January 1970 in 'Partition: Government Policy', 29/12/69—23/4/70, NAD, Department of the Taoiseach, 2000/6/151.

Chapter 7

1. *Irish Times*, 12 October 1959.
2. 'Changes in Unionist Thinking', *Irish Times*, 3 November 1959.
3. 'Will Nationalists ever Join Unionists?', *Northern Whig*, 2 November 1959.
4. Brooke, *Diaries*, 4 November 1959, PRONI, D 3004/D/45.
5. *Belfast Telegraph*, 10 November 1959.
6. Brooke.
7. Ed Moloney and Andy Pollak, *Paisley* (Dublin, 1986), 82.
8. Denis P. Barritt and Charles F. Carter, *The Northern Ireland Problem: A Study in Group Relations* (Oxford, 1962), 93.
9. Although the RUC Special Branch kept National Unity under close observation, it had to report that it had no subversive intent: 'Report on National Unity Organization' by D. I. Fanin for Inspector General of RUC, 21 January 1960, in PRONI, Ministry of Home Affairs papers, HA32/1/1361.
10. Barritt and Carter, 76. Gerry Adams, who would have been 12 in 1960, records that people from Catholic West Belfast shopped on the Protestant heartland of the Shankill Road for bargains and that his new racing bike was bought there. He also relates that the early sexual experiences of himself and his friends from the Catholic Ballymurphy estate were with Protestant girls from neighbouring estates. Gerry Adams, *Before the Dawn: An Autobiography* (London, 1996), 47 and 49.
11. 'Belfast Letter', *Irish Times*, 16 January 1960.
12. See the discussion of the 1962 Stormont election in PRONI, Ulster Unionist Council Papers, D 1327/16/13/61.
13. W. A. Maguire, *Belfast* (Keele, 1993), 169. As early as the 1953 election an analysis of loss of support in Belfast by Glengall Street refers to this factor. See 'Observations on the 1953 election', in PRONI, Ulster Unionist Council Papers, D 1327/16/3/51.
14. See Robert J. Savage, *Irish Television: The Political and Social Origins* (Cork, 1996), 434–45, and Rex Cathcart, *The Most Contrary Region: The BBC in Northern Ireland 1924–1984* (Belfast, 1984).
15. Cathcart, 146.
16. John Boyd, *The Middle of My Journey* (Belfast, 1990), 163–7.
17. He persuaded his colleagues in the cabinet's publicity committee to have an analysis made of the content of questions asked on *Your Questions* and of the political complexion of the panel: Minutes of Cabinet Publicity Committee, 8 March 1961, in PRONI Cab 4A/26/103.
18. Cathcart, 190–3.

19. Barritt and Carter, 61.
20. *Belfast Newsletter*, 2 June 1962.
21. David Bleakley, *Faulkner: Conflict and Consent in Irish Politics* (London, 1974), 26.
22. Michael Farrell, *Northern Ireland: The Orange State* (London, 1976), p. 208.
23. This was how Sayers saw him: Andrew Gailey, *Crying in the Wilderness: Jack Sayers, a Liberal Editor in Ulster 1939–69* (Belfast, 1995), 51.
24. Farrell, 222.
25. *Irish Times*, 7 November 1959.
26. At a cabinet meeting on 2 November 1960 a request by the President of the Association, the prominent Ulster linen industrialist Sir Graham Larmour, that its annual meeting pay its respects to the Governor, the monarch's representative in Northern Ireland, was considered and rejected after Faulkner claimed that both Larmour and the Association favoured a united Ireland PRONI, Cab 4/1143.
27. Letter from Connolly Gage to Jack Sayers, 16 September 1963. Gailey, *Crying in the Wilderness*, 90.
28. Marc Mulholland, *Northern Ireland at the Crossroads: Ulster Unionism in the O'Neill Years* (London, 2000), 25.
29. Thus at the height of the Dominion Status controversy he wrote to the Prime Minister criticizing the way some ministers were dealing with grass-roots concerns. Letter from O'Neill to Sir Basil Brooke, 23 November 1947, and Brooke's positive response, 26 November 1947: PRONI, Cabinet Secretariat, 'Relations with Labour Government (Dominion Status)', Cab 9J/55/2.
30. Ken Bloomfield, *Stormont in Crisis: A Memoir* (Belfast, 1994), 27.
31. Ibid. 26–89.
32. Gavan McCrone, *Regional Policy in Britain* (London, 1969), 120.
33. Government of Northern Ireland, *Belfast Regional Plan*, Cmnd. 451 (Belfast, 1963).
34. *Belfast Newsletter*, 6 April 1963.
35. Ibid.
36. Interview with Mervyn Pauley, *Belfast Newsletter*, 12 January 1965.
37. *Economic Development in Northern Ireland*, Cmnd 479 (Belfast, 1964).
38. Ibid., para 14.
39. The key role of Derry Unionists in sabotaging the city's bid for the university was first publicly stated by the maverick Unionist MP for North Down, Robert Nixon, and set out fully in an article by Ralph Bossence in the *Belfast Newsletter*, 19 February 1965.
40. Gerard O'Brien, '"Our Magee Problem": Stormont and the Second University', in G. O'Brien and W. Nolan (eds), *Derry and Londonderry: History and Society* (Dublin, 1999), 681–2.
41. *Belfast Newsletter*, 14 August 1964.
42. Ibid. 23 and 24 July 1964.

43. *The Autobiography of Terence O'Neill* (London, 1972), 61.
44. *Belfast Newsletter*, 5 March 1965.
45. Ibid. 21 January 1965.
46. A point made by the right-wing Unionist MP for Shankill, Desmond Boal, in the Stormont debate on the summit, *Belfast Newsletter*, 4 February 1965.
47. *Belfast Newsletter*, 15 January 1965.
48. Within a few weeks of the meeting Lemass made a speech offering Unionists a 'realistic' recognition of the continued existence of a Northern government and parliament in a united Ireland and praised Labour's Foreign Secretary for declaring that the British government had no longer any desire to intervene in Ireland. *Belfast Newsletter*, 27 January 1965.
49. His chief critic was the iconoclastic former minister Edmond Warnock, who issued a statement criticizing O'Neill 'for doing within a couple of months what all our enemies failed to achieve in 40 years. He has thrown the whole Ulster question back into the political arena.' *Belfast Newsletter*, 6 April 1965.
50. *The Autobiography of Terence O'Neill*, 47.
51. J. A. V. Graham, *The Consensus Forming Strategy of the NILP*, MSc thesis, Queen's University of Belfast, 1972, 183.
52. *The Round Table*, 216, March 1964.
53. *Belfast Telegraph*, 3 April 1964.
54. Mulholland, 63–4.
55. The quotation is from a *Guardian* article by Charles Brett that is included in a British Labour Party Research Department document prepared for discussions between the Wilson government and an NILP delegation: PRONI, HO 5/186.
56. Barritt and Carter, 57.
57. The claim that was made by Brett in his *Guardian* piece: 'Today there are very many respectable Catholics including professions men, members of the business community and trade union officials who are both qualified and willing to serve . . . lists of suitable names have been submitted to the authorities and even to the Cabinet secretariat, without result.'
58. *Belfast Newsletter*, 15 March 1965.
59. Ibid.
60. Bob Purdie, *Politics in the Streets: The Origins of the Civil Rights Movement in Northern Ireland* (Belfast, 1990), 82–102.
61. John Whyte, 'How Much Discrimination Was There under the Unionist Regime, 1921–68?', in Tom Gallagher and James O'Connell (eds), *Contemporary Irish Studies* (Manchester, 1983), 30–1.
62. Purdie, 83.
63. Graham Gudgin, 'Discrimination in Housing and Employment under the Stormont Administration', in P. Roche and B. Barton (eds) *The Northern Ireland Question: Nationalism, Unionism and Partition* (Hampshire, 1999), 103.

64. The system was described in the Campaign for Social Justice's pamphlet, 'Northern Ireland: The Plain Truth', second edition, 1969. The town was divided into three wards, each of which returned seven councillors. East Ward: 1,729 electors, comprising 543 Catholics and 1,186 Protestants; seven Unionist councillors. West Ward: 1,031 electors, comprising 844 Catholics and 187 Protestants; seven Nationalist councillors. Central Ward: 659 electors, comprising 143 Catholics and 516 Protestants; seven Unionist councillors.

65. 'Northern Ireland: The Plain Truth', 27.

66. Brendan Lynn, *Holding the Ground: The Nationalist Party in Northern Ireland, 1945–72* (Aldershot, 1997), 165.

67. Conn McCluskey quoted in *Holding the Ground*, 171.

68. Purdie, 104.

69. Ibid. 105.

70. Memorandum on 'Allegations of religious discrimination in Northern Ireland. The position of the United Kingdom government in respect of matters transferred to the government of Northern Ireland', by A. J. Langdon of the Home Office, 5 November 1964, in 'Northern Ireland: Religious Intolerance'.

71. Peter Rose, *How the Troubles Came to Northern Ireland* (Basingstoke and New York, 2000), 26.

72. A copy of the report, 'An assessment of Irish Republican Army activities from 10 December to date', was sent by the Home Office to Cecil Bateman, Secretary to the Northern Ireland Cabinet. It was sent by Bateman to the Ministry of Home Affairs on 24 November 1964, PRONI, HA/32/1/1349: 'Subversive Activities—Reports and Miscellaneous Correspondence'.

73. Rose, 17–18.

74. Thus he was the first British Prime Minister since partition to address the Irish Club's St Patrick's Day banquet in London, infuriating O'Neill by his support for a tripartite meeting between himself, Lemass, and the Northern PM in London. *Irish Times*, 18 March 1965.

75. See Purdie, 107–20.

76. Rose, 44.

77. 'Discussions at Downing Street on 5th August', PRONI, Cab 4/1338.

78. 'Irish concerns raised in Lynch-Wilson meeting', *Irish Times*, 1 and 2 January 1997.

79. All the quotes are from Eamon Phoenix, 'Growing hostility of Labour MPs put Stormont under pressure', *Irish Times*, 1 and 2 January 1998.

80. Purdie, 118.

81. Henry Patterson, *The Politics of Illusion: A Political History of the IRA* (London, 1997), 108

82. Government of Northern Ireland, *Disturbances in Northern Ireland*, cmnd. 532, Belfast 1969, 15.

83. Bew, Gibbon, and Patterson, *Northern Ireland 1921–1996: Political Forces and Social Classes* (London, 1996), 150–1.
84. Lynn, 129.
85. Ibid. 177.
86. Purdie, 133.
87. Lynn, 201.
88. The woman was engaged to be married but her husband-to-be was a resident of Monaghan and hence ineligible for the council waiting list. She did live in overcrowded conditions with the rest of her family and the case was not such a glaring injustice as Currie alleged but, given that she was the secretary of a solicitor who was a Unionist parliamentary candidate, the council's decision was even more blinkered than usual. See Purdie, 135, and Graham Gudgin.
89. Purdie, 136.
90. Devlin quoted in Paul Kingsley, *Londonderry Revisited* (Belfast, 1989), 133.
91. Eamonn McCann, *War and an Irish Town* (London, 1980), 41.
92. The Sunday Times Insight Team, *Ulster* (London, 1972), 52.
93. Michael Farrell, 'The Long March to Freedom', in M. Farrell (ed.), *Twenty Years On* (Dingle, 1988), 56.
94. See his contribution to the *New Left Review*'s special issue on Ulster, where he refers to 'Catholic-based power of a socialist form', *New Left Review*, 55, May/June 1969.
95. PRONI, CAB 4/1406, 14 October 1968.
96. In a cabinet discussion on 23 October, Craig claimed that a change in the local government franchise 'could have disastrous political repercussions' while Faulkner claimed that he 'did not share the reservations which some members of the Party felt'. PRONI, Cab 4/1409.
97. PRONI, Cab 4/14013/10, 4 November 1968.
98. PRONI, Cab 4/14013, 7 November 1968.
99. PRONI, Cab 4/1418, 20 November 1968.
100. PRONI, Cab 4/1418, 20 November 1968.
101. PRONI, Ulster Unionist Council Papers: Secretary's Correspondence, May 1968, D 1327/18/496.
102. PRONI, Ulster Unionist Council Papers: Secretary's Correspondence, Report on discussion forum at Unionist Headquarters with rank and file members, September 1968, D 1327/18/500.
103. The speech was given to a packed Ulster Hall, *Belfast Telegraph*, 29 November 1968.
104. The text of the broadcast can be found in *The Autobiography of Terence O'Neill*, 145–9.
105. See letter from Miss Noreen Cooper, a leading Unionist in Enniskillen, to J. O. Bailey, Secretary to the Ulster Unionist Council, January 1969: 'It is

very easy to be snug in and around Belfast by virtue of superiority in numbers but the lean counties have no such security and they already feel abandoned. It was made quite clear to me at the last standing committee that the feeling was that our three western counties were lost anyway and therefore the concentration from Belfast would be on winning over the moderate Nationalists.' PRONI, Ulster Unionist Council Papers: Secretary's Correspondence, D 1327/18/504.

106. Paul Arthur, *The People's Democracy 1968–73* (Belfast, 1974), 40.
107. The author was present at a meeting of PD leftists in Farrell's house in the Stranmillis area of Belfast in December 1968 when the prediction was made.
108. *The Autobiography of Terence O'Neill*, 112–13.
109. Arthur, 41.
110. Jonathan Bardon, 'O'Neill Warning Went Unheeded', *Irish Times*, 1 and 2 January 2000.
111. The interchange of letters can be found in *The Autobiography of Terence O'Neill*, 150–4.
112. Bew, Gibbon, and Patterson, 179.
113. Bloomfield, 106.
114. Niall Ó Dochartaigh, *From Civil Rights to Armalites* (Cork, 1997), 40–7.
115. Ibid. 51.

Chapter 8

1. Henry Patterson, *The Politics of Illusion: A Political History of the IRA* (London, 1997), 123.
2. The Sunday Times Insight Team, *Ulster: A Penguin Special* (London, 1972), 116.
3. Eamonn McCann, *War and an Irish Town* (London, 1974), 57–8.
4. *Ulster: A Penguin Special*, 119.
5. Ken Bloomfield, *Stormont in Crisis: A Memoir* (Belfast, 1994), 112.
6. Niall Ó Dochartaigh, *From Civil Rights to Armalites* (Cork, 1997), 122.
7. Bloomfield, 114.
8. See Gerry Adams, *Before the Dawn: An Autobiography* (London, 1996), 109 10.
9. Rachel Donnelly, 'Wilson Weighed up Direct Rule in North', *Irish Times*, 1 and 2 January 2000.
10. Ronan Fanning, 'Living in those Troubled Times', *Independent on Sunday*, 2 January 2000, and his 'Playing it Cool: The Response of the British and Irish Government to the Crisis in Northern Ireland, 1968–9', *Irish Studies in International Affairs*, Vol. 12 (2001), 62.
11. Paul Bew and Gordon Gillespie, *Northern Ireland: A Chronology of the Troubles 1968–1999* (Dublin, 1999), 21.

12. Kenneth O. Morgan, *Callaghan: A Life* (Oxford, 1997), 352.
13. Ronan Fanning, 'New Despatches from the 1969 Frontline', *Independent on Sunday*, 27 February 2000.
14. Brian Faulkner, *Memoirs of a Statesman* (London, 1978), 66.
15. Fanning, 'New Despatches from the 1969 Frontline'.
16. Ibid.
17. *Irish Times*, 27 March 1970.
18. Report of a discussion of the Northern Ireland situation between the Minister of External Affairs and the Chancellor of the Duchy of Lancaster, 20 February 1970, NAD, Department of Foreign Affairs, 2000/14/185.
19. Anthony McIntyre, *A Structural Analysis of Modern Irish Republicanism 1969–73*, DPhil, Queen's University (Belfast, 1999), 96. Dr McIntyre provided me with access to a copy of his thesis.
20. R. H. S. Crossman, *The Diaries of a Cabinet Minister*, Vol. III, 1968–70 (London, 1977), 636.
21. Ciaran De Baroid, *Ballymurphy and the Irish War*, revised edition (London, 2000), 37.
22. Desmond Hamill, *Pig in the Middle: The Army in Northern Ireland 1969–1985* (London, 1985), 28.
23. De Baroid, 5. At the height of the riots 1,000 soldiers saturated an area of one square mile.
24. Peter Taylor, *Provos: The IRA and Sinn Féin* (London, 1997), 77–83.
25. Morgan, 353.
26. Hamill, 35.
27. Ibid. 36.
28. De Baroid, 47.
29. 'Consequently, the potential for IRA recruitment amongst the nationalist young could only be enormous': Anthony McIntyre, *A Structural Analysis of Modern Irish Republicanism 1969–73*, 151.
30. Faulkner, 78–80.
31. Meeting between Northern Ireland Cabinet and GOC, 6 July 1971, G2.20–G 2.623, material released by Ministry of Defence for Saville Inquiry into Bloody Sunday.
32. Ó Dochartaigh, 234.
33. Faulkner, 110.
34. Ibid. 119.
35. Meeting at Downing Street on 5 August 1971, G5.50–G5.55, material released by Ministry of Defence for Saville Inquiry into Bloody Sunday.
36. Hamill, 60–1.
37. John McGuffin, *Internment* (Tralee, 1973), 119–20.
38. Bew and Gillespie, 37.
39. Meeting to consider briefing for Mr Faulkner's visit, 6 October 1971, G15.87–G15.91.

40. Future Military Policy for Londonderry. An Appreciation of the Situation by the Commander of the Land Forces, 14 December 1971, G41.263.

41. Ford's analysis of the situation in Derry on 7 January 1972 is quoted in Professor Paul Bew's 'Report to the Saville Commission' as one of its two historical advisers.

42. Quoted in Professor Bew's 'Report to the Saville Commission'.

43. Visit of Chief of the Defence Staff, 24 January 1972, G70.433.

44. Eamonn McCann, 'Post-Bloody Sunday, it was all to play for', *The Sunday Tribune*, 26 September 1999.

45. Sydney Elliott and W. D. Flackes, *Northern Ireland: A Political Directory 1968–1999* (Belfast, 1999), 681–5.

46. Seán MacStiofain, *Revolutionary in Ireland* (Farnborough, Hants, 1974), 243.

47. *Belfast Newsletter*, 21 March 1972.

48. *Ulster a Nation* (Belfast, 1972). This was a pamphlet produced by Craig's Vanguard movement.

49. Bloomfield, 137.

50. Paul Bew and Henry Patterson, *The British State and the Ulster Crisis: From Wilson to Thatcher* (London, 1985), 62.

51. See interview with Smyth in David Hume, *The Ulster Unionist Party in an Era of Conflict and Change*, D.Phil, University of Ulster, 1994, Vol. II, 325.

52. Bew and Gillespie, 46.

53. Bew and Patterson, 49.

54. Ulster Vanguard, *Ulster a Nation* (Belfast, 1972).

55. Sarah Nelson, *Ulster's Uncertain Defenders: Loyalists and the Northern Ireland Conflict* (Belfast, 1984), 94–8.

56. Steve Bruce, *The Red Hand: Protestant Paramilitaries in Northern Ireland* (Oxford, 1992), 14–22.

57. Bew and Gillespie, 39.

58. Bruce, 55.

59. See Alvin Jackson, *Ireland 1798–1998* (Oxford, 1999), 402.

60. Bruce, 42.

61. Clifford Smyth, *The Ulster Democratic Unionist Party: A Case Study in Political and Religious Convergence*, PhD thesis, Queen's University, Belfast, 1983, 36.

62. Smyth, 31.

63. Paul Bew, Peter Gibbon, and Henry Patterson, *Northern Ireland 1921–1996: Political Forces and Social Classes* (London, 1996), 170.

64. Bew and Gillespie, 56.

65. The poll, intended to be taken every ten years, was held on 8 March 1973. The SDLP and republicans urged a boycott and the bulk of nationalists did not vote. The result was that out of an electorate of 1,030,084, some 591,820 voted in favour of the Union and 6,463 in favour of a United Ireland. Thus 57.5 of the total electorate link—probably an under-recording of the pro-Union

vote as pro-Union Catholics in largely nationalist areas might have felt reluctant to be seen entering a polling station. Elliott and Flackes, 186.

66. Bew and Gillespie, 61.
67. For a 'class analysis' of Vanguard see Belinda Probert, *Beyond Orange and Green: The Northern Ireland Crisis in a New Perspective* (London, 1978), 117–28.
68. For the account of a liberal Unionist who rejected the Alliance option see Basil McIvor, *Hope Deferred: Experiences of an Irish Unionist* (Belfast, 1998), 58.
69. Faulkner, 174.
70. Bloomfield, 168–9.
71. Faulkner, 194.
72. This was certainly the objective of Ken Bloomfield who drafted the oath. *Stormont in Crisis*, 180–1.
73. Elliott and Flackes, 533.
74. Garret FitzGerald, *All in a Life* (Dublin, 1991), 200.
75. Bloomfield, 152.
76. Francis Mulhern, *The Present Lasts a Long Time: Essays in Cultural Politics* (Cork, 1998), 13.
77. Gerard Murray, *John Hume and the SDLP* (Dublin, 1998), 4.
78. Paul Routledge, *John Hume* (London, 1997), 78.
79. Paddy Devlin, *Straight Left: An Autobiography* (Belfast, 1993), 140.
80. Eamonn Gallagher, Report on conversation with John Hume, 16 February 1970, NAD, Department of Foreign Affairs, 2000/14/185.
81. Routledge, 98.
82. Murray, 6–7.
83. Routledge, 112.
84. Barry White, *John Hume: Statesman of the Troubles* (Belfast, 1984), 127.
85. Murray, 18.
86. *Republican News*, 2 January 1972.
87. *The Times*, 23 June 1972.
88. Patterson, 153–5.
89. Taylor, 142.
90. Bew and Patterson, 54.
91. Election results from Elliott and Flackes, 533.
92. *Irish News*, 3 July 1973.
93. White, 142.
94. Bew and Patterson, 72.
95. Basil McIvor, *Hope Deferred: Experiences of an Irish Unionist* (Belfast, 1998), 93.
96. FitzGerald, 215.
97. McIvor recalls a conversation with the Taoiseach and his ministerial colleague, Conor Cruise O'Brien towards the end of the conference: 'Both of

them sadly agreed that . . . we Unionists were not going to sell Sunningdale to our people at home', *Hope Deferred*, 91.

98. Bew and Gillespie, 77.
99. Faulkner, 251.
100. Nelson, 157.
101. Bloomfield, 219.
102. Faulkner, 276.
103. Nelson, 157–8.
104. Elliott and Flackes, 541.
105. Hume, Vol. 1, 105.
106. Ed Moloney and Andy Pollak, *Paisley* (Dublin, 1986), 288–9.
107. Smyth, 112.
108. Elliott and Flackes, 532–3 and 550–1.
109. Smyth, 143.
110. Padraig O'Malley, *The Uncivil Wars: Ireland Today* (Belfast, 1983), 170–1.
111. Paul Bew, Henry Patterson, and Paul Teague, *Between War and Peace: The Political Future of Northern Ireland* (London, 1997), 42, and Julia Langdon, 'Labour Thought of Ulster Pull-out', *The Guardian*, 19 July 1983.
112. Quoted in Taylor, 171.
113. Taylor, 191.
114. Elliott and Flackes, 681–5.
115. Taylor, 175.
116. Brice Dickson, 'Criminal Justice and Emergency Laws', in Seamus Dunn (ed.), *Facets of the Conflict in Northern Ireland* (London, 1995), 64–71.
117. Kevin Boyle and Tom Hadden, *Northern Ireland: The Choice* (London, 1994), 85.
118. See Sean O'Callaghan, *The Informer* (London, 1998), 118.
119. Bew and Patterson, 85.
120. *The Times*, 28 September 1976.
121. Taylor, 211.
122. *Irish Times*, 30 December 1977.
123. Roy Mason, *Paying the Price* (London, 1999), 218.
124. Bew, Patterson, and Teague, 88.
125. Bob Rowthorn and Naomi Wayne, *Northern Ireland: The Political Economy of Conflict* (Oxford, 1988), 117.
126. Bew and Patterson, 90.
127. Mason, 219.
128. Hume in a *Radio Eireann* interview on 25 May, reported in *The Ulster General Strike: Strike Bulletins of the Workers Association* (Belfast, 1974).
129. Murray, 37.
130. Ibid. 48.
131. *Irish Times*, 16 February 1978.
132. Adams, 266.

133. David Sharrock and Mark Devenport, *Man of War, Man of Peace: The Unauthorised Biography of Gerry Adams* (London, 1997), 168.

134. Patterson, 193–4.

135. Bew and Gillespie, 146.

136. Sharrock and Devenport, 182–92.

137. Margaret Thatcher, *The Downing Street Years* (London, 1993), 385.

138. Seán Donlon, 'Bringing Irish Diplomatic and Political Influence to Bear on Washington', *Irish Times*, 25 January 1993, and see also Andrew J. Wilson, *Irish America and the Ulster Conflict* (Belfast, 1995).

139. 'US Speaker O'Neill's Role on Ulster is Highlighted', *Belfast Telegraph*, 1 July 2000.

140. *Irish Times*, 16 November 1985.

141. Quoted in Paul Bew, 'Agreement or a Booby Prize?', *Irish Times*, 22 April 1995.

Chapter 9

1. Philip J. O'Connell, 'Sick Man or Tigress? The Labour Market in the Republic of Ireland', in A. F. Heath, R. Breen, and C. T. Whelan (eds), *Ireland North and South: Perspectives from Social Science* (Oxford, 1999), 219.

2. Liam Kennedy, *The Modern Industrialisation of Ireland 1940–1988* (Dublin, 1989), 48–9.

3. Peter Mair, *The Changing Irish Party System* (London, 1987), 211.

4. Paul Bew, Ellen Hazelkorn, and Henry Patterson, *The Dynamics of Irish Politics* (London, 1989), 103.

5. J. J. Lee, *Ireland 1912–1985: Politics and Society* (Cambridge, 1989), 462.

6. Bew, Hazelkorn, and Patterson, 104.

7. D. A. Coleman, 'Demography and Migration in Ireland, North and South', in Heath, Breen, and Whelan (eds), 83–4.

8. D. A. Gillmor, *Economic Activities in the Republic of Ireland: A Geographical Perspective* (Dublin, 1985), 27.

9. OECD, *Economic Surveys, Ireland*, May 1978, 30.

10. Lee, 465.

11. Maurice Manning, *James Dillon: A Biography* (Dublin, 1999), 329.

12. Garret FitzGerald, *All in a Life: An Autobiography* (Dublin, 1991), 68.

13. Mair, 186.

14. Manning, 362.

15. Bruce Arnold, *What Kind of Country? Modern Irish Politics 1968–1983* (London, 1984), 85.

16. Michael Gallagher, *The Irish Labour Party in Transition 1957–82* (Dublin, 1982), 186.

17. Ibid. 118.

18. Michael Gallagher, *Political Parties in the Republic of Ireland* (Dublin, 1985), 156–8.
19. Conor Cruise O'Brien, *Memoir: My Life and Themes* (Dublin, 1998), 342.
20. Gallagher, *The Irish Labour Party in Transition*, 198.
21. Ibid. 200.
22. FitzGerald, 298.
23. Niamh Hardiman, *Pay, Politics, and Economic Performance in Ireland 1970–1987* (Oxford, 1988), 99.
24. Gallagher, *The Irish Labour Party in Transition*, 210.
25. Lee, 477–8.
26. O'Brien, 355.
27. FitzGerald, 311: the raiders threw family bibles into the fire.
28. Arnold, 122.
29. 'I allowed myself to be persuaded to leave this sensitive issue over for several months', FitzGerald, 313.
30. FitzGerald, 320.
31. Lee, 483.
32. Kieran Allen, *Fianna Fáil and Irish Labour: 1926 to the Present* (London, 1997), 149–50.
33. O'Brien, 345–6.
34. FitzGerald, 320.
35. Mair, 30 and 33.
36. Allen, 150.
37. O'Brien, 357.
38. The anti-Haughey agenda behind the 1977 manifesto was first pointed out by the political journalist Olivia O'Leary: 'How Haughey Swung the Forum', *Magill*, August 1984.
39. Lee, 498.
40. Vincent Browne, 'Lynch Partly Responsible for the 1970 Arms Crisis', *Irish Times*, 27 October 1999.
41. James Downey, *Lenihan: His Life and Times* (Dublin, 1998), 105.
42. Bew, Hazelkorn, and Patterson, 121.
43. FitzGerald, 353.
44. Bill Roche, 'Social Partnership and Political Controls: State Strategy and Industrial Relations in Ireland', in M. Kelly, L. O'Dowd, and J. Wickham (eds), *Power, Conflict and Inequality* (Dublin, 1982), 63.
45. *Irish Banking Review*, December 1978.
46. Lee, 474.
47. Bew, Hazelkorn, and Patterson, 115.
48. Arnold, 136.
49. Dick Walsh, *The Party inside Fianna Fáil* (Dublin, 1986), 142.
50. Kevin Myers in an obituary of Jack Lynch, *Irish Times*, 27 September 1999.

51. Stephen Collins, *The Power Game: Fianna Fáil since Lemass* (Dublin, 2000), 123.
52. FitzGerald, 340.
53. Vincent Browne, 'Conduct Unbecoming', *Magill*, September 1997.
54. Collins, 127.
55. Walsh, 146.
56. Allen, 158.
57. Ibid. 159.
58. The Moriarty Tribunal heard evidence in 1999 of how he spent over £16,000 a year on shirts from the exclusive Charvet shop in Paris: Collins, 125.
59. Dick Walsh, 'Next Election Most Significant since 1930s', *Irish Times*, 12 August 2000.
60. Lee, 502–3.
61. Garret FitzGerald, 'Some Perspectives on the Economic Records of Governments in the 1980s', *Irish Times*, 26 June 1999.
62. Downey, 110.
63. Eunan O'Halpin, *Defending Ireland: The Irish State and its Enemies since 1922* (Oxford, 1999), 332.
64. Arnold, 158.
65. Joe Joyce and Peter Murtagh, *The Boss: Charles J. Haughey in Government* (Dublin, 1983), 33.
66. Stephen O'Byrnes, *Hiding Behind a Face: Fine Gael under Garret FitzGerald* (Dublin, 1986), 73.
67. Mair, 30–3.
68. Ibid. 41.
69. Gallagher, *The Irish Labour Party in Transition*, 240.
70. Joyce and Murtagh, 14.
71. Arnold, 166.
72. FitzGerald 367.
73. Bew, Hazelkorn, and Patterson, 156.
74. Mair, 56–7.
75. Joyce and Murtagh, 31.
76. Ibid. 22.
77. FitzGerald, 404.
78. Joyce and Murtagh, 53–4.
79. Lee, 508.
80. Stephen Collins, *Spring and the Labour Story* (Dublin, 1993), 97.
81. FitzGerald, 435–6.
82. This is Stephen Collins' opinion: see *Spring and the Labour Story*, 107.
83. Garret FitzGerald, 'Some perspectives on the economic records of governments in the 1980s', *Irish Times*, 26 June 1999.
84. John Kurt Jacobsen, *Chasing Progress in the Irish Republic* (Cambridge, 1994), 161.

85. Collins, *Spring and the Labour Story*, 130.
86. Brendan O'Leary, 'Towards Europeanisation and Realignment? The Irish General Election, February 1987', *Western European Politics*, Vol. 10, No. 3, July 1987.
87. Allen, 171.
88. See Paul Teague and John McCartney, 'Industrial Relations in the Two Irish Economies', in Heath, Breen, and Whelan (eds), 349.
89. Cormac O'Grada, *A Rocky Road: The Irish Economy since the 1920s* (Manchester, 1997), 32–3.
90. Ibid. 33.
91. *The Irish Times*, 5 August 2000.
92. Robert Kuttner, 'Ireland's Miracle: The Market Didn't Do It Alone', *Business Week*, 7 July 2000.
93. Paul Sweeney, *The Celtic Tiger: Ireland's Continuing Economic Miracle* (Dublin, 1999), 8.
94. Jonathan Haughton, 'The Dynamics of Economic Change', in W. Crotty and D. E. Schmitt, *Ireland and the Politics of Change* (London, 1998), 29–30.
95. Sweeney, 87.
96. Kuttner, 'Ireland's Miracle'.
97. Denis O'Hearn, *Inside the Celtic Tiger* (London, 1998) is an example.
98. Rory O'Donnell, 'The New Ireland in the New Europe', in Rory O'Donnell (ed.), *Europe: The Irish Experience* (Dublin, 2000), 177.
99. *Irish Times*, 19 June 1989.
100. The term was used by one of the party's negotiators, *Irish Times*, 14 July 1999.
101. Yvonne Galligan, *Women and Politics in Contemporary Ireland: From the Margins to the Mainstream* (London, 1998), 31.
102. Pat O'Connor and Sally Shortall, 'Variations in Women's Paid Employment, North and South', in Heath, Breen, and Whelan (eds) 288–9.
103. Eric Hobsbawm, *Age of Extremes: The Short Twentieth Century 1914–1991* (London, 1994), 311.
104. James S. Donnelly, Jr, ' A Church in Crisis: the Irish Catholic Church Today', *History Ireland*, Vol. 8, No. 3, Autumn 2000, 13.
105. Basil Chubb, *The Government and Politics of Ireland* (London, 1982), 29.
106. Galligan, 53.
107. Ibid. 149–50.
108. M. A. Busteed, *Voting Behaviour in the Republic of Ireland: A Geographical Perspective* (Oxford, 1990), 182.
109. Dermot Keogh, 'The Role of the Catholic Church in the Republic of Ireland 1992–1995', *Building Trust in Ireland: Studies Commissioned by the Forum for Peace and Reconciliation* (Belfast, 1996), 177.
110. Lee, 654.
111. Galligan, 152–3.

112. Cited in Busteed, 201–2.
113. Emily O'Reilly, 'The Legion of the Rearguard', *Magill*, September 1986.
114. Brian Girvin, 'The Irish Divorce Referendum, November 1995', *Irish Political Studies*, Vol. 11, 1996.
115. Gene Kerrigan and Pat Brennan, *This Great Little Nation. The A-Z of Irish Scandals and Controversies* (Dublin, 1999), 310.
116. Kerrigan and Brennan, 53.
117. Tom Inglis, *Moral Monopoly: The Rise and the Fall of the Catholic Church in Modern Ireland* (Dublin, 1998), 257.
118. Niamh Hardiman and Christopher Whelan, 'Changing Values', in William Crotty and David E. Schmitt (eds), *Ireland and the Politics of Change* (London, 1998), 79.
119. K. Theodore Hoppen, *Ireland since 1800: Conflict and Conformity* (London, 1999), 283.
120. James S. Donnelly Jr, 'A Church in Crisis: The Irish Catholic Church Today', *History Ireland*, Vol. 8, No. 3, Autumn 2000.
121. FitzGerald, 378.
122. Ibid. 462.
123. John Whyte, *Interpreting Northern Ireland* (Oxford, 1991), 138.
124. Brian Girvin, 'Nationalism and the Continuation of Political Conflict in Ireland', in Heath, Breen, and Whelan (eds), 381.
125. Ibid.
126. Peter Mair, 'The Irish Republic and the Anglo-Irish Agreement', in Paul Teague (ed.), *Beyond the Rhetoric: Politics, the Economy and Social Policy in Northern Ireland* (London, 1987), 109.
127. Kerrigan and Brennan, 134.
128. Collins, *The Power Game*, 182.
129. Paul Mitchell, 'The 1992 Election in the Republic of Ireland', *Irish Political Studies*, Vol. 8, 1993, 116.
130. Eoin O'Sullivan, 'The 1990 Presidential Election in the Republic of Ireland', *Irish Political Studies*, Vol. 6, 1991, 96.
131. Collins, *The Power Game*, 242.
132. Henry Patterson, *The Politics of Illusion: A Political History of the IRA* (London, 1997), 258.
133. He once explained to me that this was the reason why the best books on Fianna Fáil had been written by Marxists.
134. Collins, *The Power Game*, 257.
135. Seán Duignan, *One Spin on the Merry-Go-Round* (Dublin, 1996), 88.
136. Fergus Finlay, *Snakes and Ladders* (Dublin, 1998), 170–1.
137. Ibid. 235.
138. Duignan, 147.
139. Paul Bew and Gordon Gillespie, *Northern Ireland: A Chronology of the Troubles 1968–1999* (Dublin, 1999), 328.

140. Gary Murphy, 'The 1997 General Election in the Republic of Ireland', *Irish Political Studies*, Vol. 13, 1998, 131.

141. Fintan O'Toole, 'How the Celtic Tiger's Cubs Find Sinn Féin Reassuring', *Irish Times*, 14 January 2001.

142. Richard Dunphy, '"A group of individuals trying to do their best": the dilemmas of the Democratic Left', *Irish Political Studies*, Vol. 13, 1998, 50–75.

143. Garrett FitzGerald, 'A Duty to Show Upheaveal was Worthwhile', *Irish Times*, 3 February 2001.

144. Cliff Taylor, 'Value for Money in Public Finances Key in Mind of Voters', *Irish Times*, 15 April 2002.

145. Denis Coghlan, 'Low-tax Low-spend Policy Leaves Social Service in its Wake', *Irish Times*, 16 April 2002.

146. Kieran Allen, 'Hypocrisy of Social Partnership, *Irish Times*, 14 February 2001.

147. John Murray Brown, 'Celtic Tiger Aged as US Technology Sector Falters', *Financial Times*, 19 December 2001.

148. *Irish Times*, 8 November 2001.

149. Dick Walsh, 'Crucial Debate on How We Run our Country,' *Irish Times*, 23 September 2000.

150. Mike Allen, 'Attempt to Steal Labour's Clothes Will Not Work', *Irish Times*, 10 January 2001.

151. Jane O'Mahony, '"Not So Nice": The Treaty of Nice—The 2001 Referendum Experience', *Irish Personal Studies*, Volume 16, 2001, 208.

152. Fintan O'Toole, 'No Longer Yielding to Party or Pulpit', *Irish Times*, 8 March 2002.

153. Garret FitzGerald, 'We Need a Tough Minister of Finance to Sort out the Financial Mess', *Irish Times*, 11 May 2002.

154. 'Election 2002', *Irish Times*, 20 May 2002.

155. Michael Marsh, 'The End of Politics as We've Known It', *Irish Independent*, 20 May 2000.

Chapter 10

1. Arthur Aughey, *Under Siege: Ulster Unionism and the Anglo-Irish Agreement* (Belfast, 1989), 69–81.

2. Sydney Elliott and W. D. Flackes, *Northern Ireland: A Political Directory 1968–1999* (Belfast, 1999), 572 and 575.

3. Ann Purdy, *Molyneaux: The Long View* (Antrim, 1989) 147.

4. The interview is quoted in Paul Bew and Henry Patterson, 'The New Stalemate: Unionism and the Anglo-Irish Agreement', in Paul Teague (ed.), *Beyond the Rhetoric: Politics, the Economy and Social Policy in Northern Ireland* (London, 1987), 46.

5. Ed Moloney, 'Adams Played a Pivotal Role for Peace', *Sunday Tribune*, 28 May 2000, where he recalls a conversation in 1983 with a key Adams aide to this effect.

6. Paul Bew and Gordon Gillespie, *Northern Ireland: A Chronology of the Troubles 1968–1993* (Belfast, 1993), 157.

7. Henry Patterson, *The Politics of Illusion: A Political History of the IRA* (London, 1997), 206.

8. Ibid. 200.

9. Gerard Murray, *John Hume and the SDLP* (Dublin, 1998), 171.

10. *Irish Times*, 24 February 1989.

11. Elliott and Flackes, 681.

12. Gerry Adams, *Free Ireland: Towards a Lasting Peace* (Dingle, 1995), 194–5.

13. Murray, 176.

14. Sean O'Callaghan, *The Informer* (London, 1999), 281.

15. Elliott and Flackes, 683.

16. Patterson, 211.

17. *An Phoblacht/Republican News*, 26 January 1989.

18. Paul Bew, Peter Gibbon, and Henry Patterson, *Northern Ireland 1921–1996: Political Forces and Social Classes* (London, 1996), 220.

19. Patterson, 215–16.

20. Margaret Thatcher, *The Downing Street Years* (London, 1993), 402–15.

21. Graham Ellison and Jim Smyth, *The Crowned Harp: Policing Northern Ireland* (London, 2000), 132.

22. Kevin Boyle and Tom Hadden, *Northern Ireland: The Choice* (London, 1994), 71.

23. Hume's attack on the IRA was made at the SDLP's annual conference in 1988, *Irish Times*, 28 November 1988.

24. Thatcher, 415.

25. The republican version of this exchange is in *Setting the Record Straight: A Record of Communications between Sinn Féin and the British Government, October 1990–November 1993* (Belfast, 1993).

26. Patterson, 226.

27. Bew and Gillespie, 298.

28. Elliott and Flackes, 683.

29. *Irish Times*, 19 September 1988.

30. From Sinn Féin document 'A Strategy for Peace', *Irish Times*, 7 September 1988.

31. Michael Cox, 'Cinderella at the Ball: Explaining the End of the War in Northern Ireland', *Millennium: Journal of International Studies*, Vol. 27, No. 2, 1998, 325–42.

32. Danny Morrison, *Then the Walls Come Down: A Prison Journal* (Cork, 1999), 91.

33. Patterson, 244.

34. Eamonn Mallie and David McKittrick, *The Fight for Peace: The Secret Story behind the Irish Peace Process* (London, 1996), 120.
35. Conor O'Clery, *The Greening of the White House* (Dublin, 1996), 61.
36. John Dumbrell, ' "Hope and History": the US and Peace in Northern Ireland', in Michael Cox, Adrain Guelke, and Fiona Stephen (eds), *A Farewell to Arms? From 'Long War' to Long Peace in Northern Ireland* (Manchester, 2000), 216.
37. Mallie and McKittrick, 280.
38. Bew and Gillespie, 294.
39. Morrison, 241.
40. A point made by Reynolds' principal adviser on Northern Ireland: Martin Mansergh, 'Secrecy on the Road to Peace', *Sunday Tribune*, 5 May 1996, in which he dismisses the republican 'myth that the Bishopsgate bomb in April 1993 had in some way moved the British'.
41. Peter Taylor, *Provos: The IRA and Sinn Féin* (London, 1997), 335–6.
42. Bew and Gillespie, 277.
43. Mallie and McKittrick, 207.
44. Sean Duignan, *One Spin on the Merry-Go-Round* (Dublin, 1998), 106.
45. Anthony Seldon, *Major: A Political Life* (London, 1997), 422–3.
46. Bew and Gillespie, 286.
47. Patterson, 250–3.
48. In an interview in the *Irish News* on 8 January 1994, Adams criticized Sir Patrick Mayhew's post-Declaration statement that talks between the government and Sinn Féin would be concerned with decommissioning.
49. Duignan, 136.
50. The TUAS document is printed as an appendix in Mallie and McKittrick, 381–4.
51. Duignan, 137 and 40.
52. Ibid. 139–140.
53. Ibid. 147.
54. Quote is from the TUAS document.
55. Paul Bew, Henry Patterson, and Paul Teague, *Between War and Peace: The Political Future of Northern Ireland* (London, 1997), 91–2.
56. Ibid. 90.
57. Andy Pollak, *A Citizens' Inquiry: The Opsabel Report on Northern Ireland* (Dublin, 1993), p. 7.
58. Kevin Boyle and Tom Hadden, *Northern Ireland: The Choice* (London, 1994), 30–2, and Graham Gudgin, 'A Catholic Majority is Far from Certain', *Belfast Telegraph*, 15 February 2002.
59. Bew, Patterson, and Teague, 144–5.
60. Ruth Dudley Edwards, *The Faithful Tribe: An Intimate Portrait of the Loyal Institutions* (London, 1999), 283.
61. Eamon Delaney, *An Accidental Diplomat: My Years in the Irish Foreign Service 1987–1995* (Dublin, 2001), 289.

62. Henry McDonald, *Trimble* (London, 2000), 87–90.
63. Rogelio Alonso, *Irlanda del Norte: Una historia de guerra y la busqueda de la paz* (Madrid, 2001), 390–1 (translation by Henry Patterson).
64. Elliott and Flackes, 580.
65. Bew and Gillespie, 298.
66. The text of the Balmoral speech can be found in Bew, Patterson, and Teague, 217–24.
67. Elliott and Flackes, 594.
68. Patterson, 289.
69. Speech to the Irish Association, 2 February 1995, reprinted in Bew, Patterson, and Teague, 225–31.
70. Paul Bew, 'Decommissioning', in Robin Wilson (ed.), *Agreeing to Disagree? A Guide to the Northern Ireland Assembly* (Norwich, 2001), 139–42.
71. 'But Is There an Agreement on Northern Ireland?', *Daily Telegraph*, 17 April 1998.
72. 'Reaching an agreement without their presence was extremely difficult, it would have been impossible with them in the room.' George Mitchell, *Making Peace* (London, 1999), 110.
73. Bew and Gillespie, 318.
74. Ibid. 348.
75. Deaglan De Breadun, *The Far Side of Revenge: Making Peace in Northern Ireland* (Cork, 2001), 74.
76. Ibid. 84–5.
77. Ed Moloney, 'Triumph and Disaster', *Sunday Tribune*, 18 January 1998.
78. Robin Wilson, 'The Executive Committee', in Wilson (ed.), *Agreeing to Disagree*, 76.
79. Mitchell McLaughlin in an interview in *Parliamentary Brief*, May/June 1998, quoted in Thomas Hennessey, *The Northern Ireland Peace Process* (Dublin, 2000), 171.
80. Richard Sinnott, 'Historic Day Blemished by Low Poll', *Irish Times*, 25 May 1998.
81. Suzanne Breen, 'United No Parties Set their Sights on Assembly', *Irish Times*, 25 May 1998.
82. Tommy McKearney, 'There is No Support for IRA Physical Force Any More', *Sunday Tribune*, 15 August 1999.
83. Paul Bew, 'Reckoning the Dead', *Times Literary Supplement*, 28 January 2000.
84. 'Keep IRA on Sidelines, Says Adams', interview of Adams by Geraldine Kennedy, *Irish Times*, 20 May 1998.
85. *Irish Times*, 8 April 1999.
86. Frank Millar, 'No Way to Soften the Impact of Paisley's Defiant Triumph', *Irish Times*, 15 June 1999.
87. Anne Cadwallader, 'Peace Deal on its Last Legs, Says IRA', *Ireland on Sunday*, 24 December 2000.

88. For a good critique see Jyrki Ruohomaki analysis of the election results in a Democratic Dialogue discussion paper: http://www.democraticdialogue.org/working/Elect.htm

89. Jim Cusack, 'Decommissioning Pace Forced by IRA's Colombian Links', *Irish Times*, 27 October 2001.

90. Ibid.

91. Steve Bruce, *The Edge of the Union: The Ulster Loyalist Political Vision* (Oxford, 1994) 37–71.

INDEX

INHUMAN RESOURCES

Also by Pierre Lemaitre in English translation

Pierre Lemaitre

INHUMAN
RESOURCES

Translated from the French by
Sam Gordon

MACLEHOSE PRESS
QUERCUS · LONDON

First published in the French language as *Cadres noirs* by Editions Calmann-Lévy, Paris, in 2010
First published in Great Britain in 2018 by MacLehose Press
This paperback edition published in 2019 by

MacLehose Press
an imprint of Quercus
Carmelite House
50 Victoria Embankment
London EC4Y 0DZ

This book is supported by the Institut Français (Royaume Uni)
as part of the Burgess programme

ISBN (PB) 978 1 84866 890 4
ISBN (Ebook) 978 1 84866 889 8

10 9 8 7 6 5 4 3 2 1

Designed and typeset in Minion by Libanus Press Ltd, Marlborough
Printed and bound in Great Britain by Clays Ltd, Elcograf S.p.A.

To Pascaline.
To Marie-Françoise, with all my affection.

"I belong to an unlucky generation,
swung between the old world and the new,
and I find myself ill at ease in both.
And what is more, as you must
have realised by now, I am without illusions."

G. Tomasi di Lampedusa, *The Leopard*
tr. Archibald Colquhoun

BEFORE

1

I've never been a violent man. For as long as I can remember, I have never wanted to kill anyone. The odd flare of the temper, sure, but never any desire to inflict proper pain. To destroy. So, when it did happen, I suppose it took me by surprise. Violence is like drinking or sex – it's a process, not an isolated phenomenon. We barely notice it set in, quite simply because we are ready for it, because it arrives at precisely the right moment. I was perfectly aware that I was angry, but I never expected it to turn to cold fury. That's what scares me.

And to take it out on Mehmet, of all people . . .

Mehmet Pehlivan.

The guy's a Turk. He's been in France for ten years, but his vocabulary is worse than a ten-year-old's. He has only two settings: either he's shouting his head off, or he's sulking. When he's angry, he lets rip in a mixture of French and Turkish. You can't understand a word, but you never doubt for a second what he means. Mehmet is a supervisor at Pharmaceutical Logistics, my place of work. Following his own version of Darwin's theory, the moment he gets promoted he starts disparaging his former colleagues, treating them like slithering earthworms. I've come across people like him throughout my career, and not just migrant workers. No, it happens with lots of people who start out at the bottom. As soon as they begin climbing the ladder, they align themselves wholeheartedly with their superiors, and even surpass them in terms of sheer determination. The world of work's answer to Stockholm Syndrome. The thing is, Mehmet doesn't just think he's a boss. He becomes the boss incarnate. He *is* the boss as soon as the boss is out the door. Of course, at this company, which must employ two hundred staff, there's not a big boss as such, just managers. But Mehmet is far too important to be a humble manager. No, he subscribes to an altogether loftier, more intangible concept that he calls "Senior Management", a notion devoid of meaning (round here, no-one even knows who the senior managers are) yet heavy with innuendo: the Way, the Light, the Senior Management. In his own way, by scaling the ladder of responsibility, Mehmet is moving closer to God.

I start at 5.00 a.m. It's an odd job (when the salary is this low, you have to say it's "odd"). My role involves sorting cardboard boxes of medication that are then sent off to far-flung pharmacies. I wasn't around to see it, but apparently Mehmet did this for eight years before he was made "supervisor". Now he is in the proud position of heading up a team of three office drones, which is not to be sniffed at.

The first drone is called Charles. Funny name for a guy of no fixed abode. He is one year younger than me, thin as a rake and thirsty as a fish. I say "of no fixed abode" to keep things simple, but he does actually have an abode. An extremely fixed one. He lives in his car, which hasn't moved for five years. He calls it his "immobile home". That's typical of Charles' sense of humour. He wears a diving watch the size of a satellite dish, with dials all over the place, and a fluorescent green bracelet. I haven't got a clue where he's from or how he ended up in these dire straits. He's a funny one, Charles. For instance, he has no idea how long he's been on the social housing waiting list, but he does keep a precise tally of the time that has passed since he gave up renewing his application. Five years, seven months and seventeen days at the last count. Charles counts the time that has elapsed since he lost any hope of being rehoused. "Hope," he says, as he raises his index finger, "is a pack of lies invented by the Devil to reconcile men with their lot." That's not one of his, I've heard it before somewhere else. I've searched for the quote but never managed to track it down. Just goes to show that behind his veneer of drunkenness, he is a man of culture.

The other drone is Romain, a young guy from Narbonne. Following a few prominent turns in his school drama club, he dreamed of becoming an actor and, straight after passing his baccalaureate, moved to Paris. But he failed to make even the smallest of splashes, not least because of his Gascon accent. Like a true young D'Artagnan, or Henri IV arriving at court, his provincial drawl – all *r*'s and *ang*'s – prompted sniggers among the drama school elite with all its urbane courtiers. It amuses us all no end, too. He had elocution lessons for it, but to no avail. He took on a series of part-time jobs, which kept a roof over his head while he attended castings for roles he never had a hope in hell of landing. One day, he understood that his fantasy would never come true. Red-carpet Romain was done. What was more, Narbonne had been the biggest city he had known. It didn't take long for Paris to flatten him, to crush him to dust. He grew homesick, yearning for the familiar surroundings of his childhood. Problem was that he couldn't face going back empty-handed. Now he works hard to pay his way, and the only role he aspires to is that of the prodigal son. With this aim in mind, he does any piecemeal job he can find. An ant's vocation. He spends the rest of his time on Second Life, Twitter, Facebook and a whole load of other networks – places where no-one can hear his accent, I suppose. According to Charles, he's a tech wizard.

I work for three hours every morning, which brings in 585 euros gross (whenever you talk of a part-time salary, you have to add the word "gross", because of the tax). I get home around

9.00 a.m. If Nicole is out the door a bit late, we might run into each other. Whenever that happens, she says "I'm late" before giving me a peck on the nose and closing the door behind her.

This morning, Mehmet was seething. Like a pressure cooker. I suppose his wife had been giving him grief, or something. He was pacing angrily up and down the aisle where all the crates and cardboard boxes are stacked, clutching his clipboard so tightly his knuckles had turned white. He gives the impression of being burdened with major responsibilities, exacerbated by personal strife. I was bang on time, but the moment he set eyes on me he yelled out a stream of his gibberish. Being on time, apparently, is not sufficient to prove your motivation. He arrives an hour early at least. His tirade was fairly unintelligible, but I got the gist, namely that he thinks I'm a lazy arsehole.

Although Mehmet makes such a song and dance about it, the job itself is not very complicated. We sort packets, we put them in cardboard boxes, we lay them on a palette. Normally, the pharmacy codes are written on the packets in large type, but sometimes – don't ask me why – the number is missing. Romain reckons the settings on one of the printers must be wrong. If this does happen, the correct code can be found among a long series of tiny characters on a printed label. The numbers you want are the eleventh, twelfth and thirteenth. It's a real hassle for me because I need my glasses for this. I have to fish them out of my pocket, put them on, lower my head, count the characters ... A loss of precious time. And if Senior Management were to catch me doing this, it would annoy them greatly. Typical, then, that the first packet I picked up this morning didn't have a code. Mehmet started screaming. I leaned over. And at that precise moment, he kicked me right in the arse.

It was just after five in the morning.

My name is Alain Delambre. I am fifty-seven years old. And four years ago, I was made redundant.

2

Initially, I took the morning job at Pharmaceutical Logistics as a way of keeping myself occupied. At least that's what I told Nicole, but neither she nor the girls fell for it. At my age, you don't wake up at 4.00 a.m. for 45% of the minimum wage just to get your endorphins going. It's all a bit more complicated. Well, actually it's not that complicated. At first, we didn't need the money – now we do.

I have been unemployed for four years. Four years in May (May 24, to be exact).

This job doesn't really make ends meet, so I do a few other bits and bobs too. For a couple of hours here and there, I lug crates, bubble-wrap things, hand out fliers. A spot of night-time industrial cleaning in offices. A few seasonal jobs, too. For the past two years, I've been Father Christmas at a discount store specialising in household appliances. I don't always give Nicole the full picture of my activities, since it would only upset her. I use a range of excuses to justify my absences. As this is harder for the night jobs, I have magicked up a group of unemployed friends with whom I supposedly play poker. I tell Nicole that it relaxes me.

Before, I was H.R. manager at a company with almost two-hundred employees. I was in charge of staff and training, overseeing salaries and representing the management at the works council. I worked at Bercaud, which sold costume jewellery. Seventeen years casting pearls before swine. That was everyone's favourite gag. There was a whole load of extremely witty jokes that went around about pearls, family jewels, etc. Corporate banter, if you like. The laughter stopped in March, when it was announced that Bercaud had been bought out by the Belgians. I might have been in with a shout against the Belgian H.R. manager, but when I found out that he was thirty-eight, I mentally started to clear my desk. I say "mentally" because, deep down, I know I wasn't at all ready to do it for real. But that was what I had to do – they didn't hang about. The takeover was announced on March 4. The first round of redundancies took place six weeks later, and I was part of the second.

In the space of four years, as my income evaporated, I passed from incredulity to doubt, then to guilt, and finally to a sense of injustice. Now, I feel anger. It's not a very positive emotion, anger. When I arrive at Logistics, and I see Mehmet's bushy eyebrows and Charles' long, rickety silhouette, and I think about everything I've had to endure, a terrible rage thunders inside me. Most of all, I have to avoid thinking about the years I have left, about the pension payments I'll never receive, about the allowances that are withering away, or about the despair that sometimes grips Nicole and me. I have to avoid those thoughts because – in spite of my sciatica – they put me in the mood for terrorism.

In the four years we have known each other, I have come to count my job centre adviser as one of my closest friends. Not long ago, he told me, with a degree of admiration in his voice, that I was an example. What he means is that I might have given up on the idea of finding a job, but I haven't given up looking for one. He thinks that shows strength of character. I don't want to tell him he's wrong; he is thirty-seven and he needs to hang on to his illusions for as long as possible. The truth is I've actually surrendered to a sort of innate reflex. Looking for work is like working, and since that is all I have done my whole life, it is ingrained in my nervous system; something that drives me out of necessity, but without direction. I look for work like a dog sniffs a lamp post. No illusions, but I can't help it.

And so it was that I responded to an advertisement a few days ago. A headhunting firm looking to recruit an H.R. assistant for a big company. The role involves hiring staff at executive level, formulating job descriptions, carrying out assessments, writing up appraisals, processing social audits, etc., which is all right up my street, exactly what I did for years at Bercaud. "Versatile, methodical and rigorous, the candidate will be equipped with excellent interpersonal skills." My professional profile in a nutshell.

The moment I read it, I compiled my documents and attached my C.V. Needless to say, it all hangs on whether they are willing to take on a man of my age.

The answer to which is perfectly obvious: it'll be a "no".

So what? I sent off my application anyway. I wonder whether it was just a way of honouring my job centre adviser's admiration.

When Mehmet kicked me in the arse, I let out a yelp. Everyone turned around. First Romain, then Charles, who did so with greater difficulty as he was already a couple of sheets to the wind. I straightened up like a young man. That's when I realised that I was almost a head taller than Mehmet. Up to now, he had been the big boss. I'd never really noticed his size. Mehmet himself was struggling to come to terms with kicking me in the arse. His anger seemed to have abated entirely, I could see his lips trembling and he was blinking as he tried to find the words, I'm not sure in which language. That was when I did something for the first time in my life: I tilted my head back, very slowly, as though I were admiring the ceiling of the Sistine Chapel, and then whipped it forward with a sharp motion. Just like I'd seen on television. A head-butt, they call it. Charles, being homeless, gets beaten up a lot, and knows all about it. "Nice technique," he told me. For a first-timer, it seemed a very decent effort.

My forehead broke Mehmet's nose. Before feeling the impact on my skull, I heard a sinister crack. Mehmet howled (in Turkish this time, no doubt about it), but I couldn't ram home my advantage because he immediately took his head in his hands and sank to his knees. If I had been in a film, I almost certainly would have taken a run-up and laid him out with an almighty kick in the face, but my skull was aching so much that I also took my head in my hands and fell to the ground. Both of us were on our knees, facing each other, heads in hands. Tragedy in the workplace. A dramatic scene worthy of an Old Master.

Romain started flapping around, no idea what to do with himself. Mehmet was bleeding everywhere. The ambulance arrived within a few minutes. We gave statements. Romain told me that he'd seen Mehmet kick me in the arse, that he would be a witness and that I had nothing to worry about. I kept silent, but my experience led me to believe that it definitely wouldn't be as simple as all that. I wanted to be sick. I went to the toilets, but in vain.

Actually no, not in vain: in the mirror, I saw that I had a gash and a large bruise across my forehead. I was deathly pale and all over the place. Pitiful. For a moment, I thought I was starting to look like Charles.

3

"Oh my goodness, what have you done to yourself?" Nicole asked as she touched the enormous bruise on my forehead.

I didn't answer. I handed her the letter in a way that I hoped would seem casual, then went to my study, where I pretended to rummage through my drawers. She looked long and hard at the words: "Further to your letter, I am delighted to inform you that your application for the role of H.R. assistant has been accepted in the first instance. You will shortly be invited to take an aptitude test which, if successful, will be followed by an interview."

I think she had to read it several times before it registered. She was still wearing her coat when I saw her appear at the door of my study, resting her shoulder against the frame. She was holding the letter in her hand, head tilted to the side. This is one of her classic mannerisms and, along with two or three others, by far my favourite. It's almost like she knows it. When I see her in that position, I feel comforted by the extreme grace she has. There is something doleful about her, a litheness that's hard to explain . . . a languor that is extraordinarily sexual. She was holding the letter in her hand and staring at me. I found her extremely beautiful, or extremely desirable, and was overcome by a furious urge to jump her. Sex has always been a powerful antidepressant for me.

At first, when I didn't regard unemployment as a fatal situation, just a calamitous, worrying one, I was constantly jumping

Nicole. In the bedroom, in the bathroom, in the corridor. Nicole never said no. She is very perceptive, and understood that it was my way of affirming that I was still alive. Since then, anxiety has given way to anguish, and the first visible effect of this is that I'm practically impotent. Our lovemaking has become rare, challenging. Nicole is very kind and patient, which only makes me more unhappy. Our sexual barometer is all over the place. We pretend not to notice or that it's not important. I know Nicole still loves me, but our life has become much more difficult and I can't help feeling that it cannot carry on like this for ever.

But back to her clutching the letter from B.L.C. Consulting.

"Sweetheart, this is unbelievable!" she said.

I reminded myself that I really needed to track down the author of Charles' quotation about the Devil and hope. Because Nicole was right. A letter like this was out of the ordinary, and at my age, having not worked in my field for more than four years, I didn't have the faintest chance of landing the job. A glimmer of optimism stirred in Nicole and me that very second. As though the months and years that had passed had taught us nothing. As though the two of us could never be cured of our hope.

Nicole moved towards me and gave me one of those wet kisses that make me go wild. She's brave. There is nothing harder than living with a depressive. Apart from being depressed yourself, of course.

"Do we know who they're recruiting for?" Nicole asked.

I turned around my screen to show her B.L.C. Consulting's website. The name comes from its founder, Bertrand Lacoste. Serious pedigree. The type of consultant who charges himself out at 3,500 euros a day. When I first joined Bercaud, with my whole future ahead of me (and even several years later, when I signed up for a lifelong learning course to get a coaching qualification), becoming a high-level consultant like Bertrand Lacoste was exactly what I dreamed of: efficient, always one step ahead of my opposite number, producing lightning-quick analyses and a barrage of managerial solutions whatever the situation. I never finished the course because our girls arrived around then. That's the official version. Nicole's version. In reality, I never had the talent for it. Deep down, I have the mindset of an employee: I am the prototypical middle-manager.

I said:

"The ad is vague. They talk about an 'industry leader with a global presence'. Apart from that . . . the job's based in Paris."

Nicole watched me scroll through web pages on employment regulations and new laws on continuing professional development that I had spent the afternoon reading. She smiled. My desk was strewn with Post-its and notes-to-self, and I had taped various sheets of paper to my bookshelves. She seemed to realise at that moment that I had worked relentlessly all day. She is one of those people who immediately picks up on the slightest domestic detail. If I move something, she notices as soon as she enters the room. The only time I've been unfaithful, a long time ago (the girls were still very young), she rumbled me that very evening, despite all the precautions I'd taken. At first, she didn't say anything. It was a tense evening. In bed, she simply said to me in a tired manner:

"Alain, never again . . ."

Then she curled up next to me in bed. We have never exchanged another word on the subject.

"I don't have a chance in a thousand."

Nicole places the letter from B.L.C. Consulting on my desk.

"You never know," she says, taking off her coat.

"Someone my age . . ."

She turns towards me.

"How many applications do you reckon they received?" she says.

"Maybe three hundred and something."

"And how many do you think have been called up for the test?"

"I'd say . . . around fifteen?"

"So explain to me why they have chosen *your* application out of more than three hundred. Do you think they didn't notice your age? Do you think that passed them by?"

Of course not. Nicole is right. I spent half the afternoon turning the theories round in my head. Each time I come up against the same impossible point: my C.V. stinks of "man in his fifties" from a mile off, so if they're calling me in, there must be something about my age that interests them.

Nicole is very patient. While she peels the onions and potatoes, she listens to me as I detail all the technical reasons they might have for selecting me. She can hear the excitement bubbling up in my voice despite my attempts to contain it. I haven't received a letter like this for more than two years. At worst, I never hear back; at best, I get told to bugger off. I never get called to interview anymore, because a guy like me is of no interest to anyone. So I've come up with all sorts of hypotheses about the response from B.L.C. Consulting, and I reckon I have fallen on the right one.

"I think it's because of the scheme."

"What scheme?" Nicole asked.

The rescue plan for seniors. It turns out that seniors are not working long enough anymore. If only the government had got in touch, I could have saved them the expense of some very costly studies. In this case, we're obviously talking about people who are still in work. It seems they stop working even though the country still needs them. And if that's not terrible enough, it gets worse. Apparently, there are seniors who want to work, but can't find a job. Whether they're not working enough or are no longer working at all, the older generations represent a serious problem to society. The government has therefore agreed to help by providing cash incentives for companies that agree to employ the elderly.

"It isn't my experience that interests them, it's because they want tax exemptions and other benefits."

Sometimes Nicole does this thing with her mouth to feign scepticism, jutting out her chin slightly. I love it when she does that, too.

"The way I see it," she says, "these sorts of companies have no shortage of cash, so they don't give a damn about government reward schemes."

The second part of my afternoon had been dedicated to clarifying this whole reward scheme business. And, once again, Nicole is right – it's a weak argument. The tax exemptions only last a few months, and the scheme only covers a small part of the salary of an employee at this level. And, what's more, it's on a sliding scale.

No, in the space of a couple of minutes Nicole has come to the same conclusion it has taken me a day to reach: if B.L.C. are calling me in, it's because they are interested in my experience.

For four years I have exhausted myself explaining to employers that a man of my age is just as dynamic as a younger person, and that experience leads to savings. But that's a journalist's argument, fine for the "Jobs" supplements in the broadsheets; it just pisses off employers. Now, for the first time, I get the impression that someone has properly read my cover letter and studied my application. This makes me feel like I might have hit a home run.

I want the interview to happen right here, right now. I want to scream.

But I keep it cool.

"Let's not mention anything to the girls, O.K.?"

Nicole agrees that's for the best. It has been tough for the girls seeing their parents living hand to mouth. They never say a word, but they can't help it – the image they have of me has worn away. Not because of unemployment, but because of the effects unemployment has had on me. I have aged, I have shrunk, I have grown gloomy. I've become a pain in the arse. They don't even know about my job at Pharmaceutical Logistics. Raising their hopes that I might have landed something, only to announce later that I have blown it, is another flop I cannot face.

Nicole cuddles up against me. She delicately places a finger on the bump on my forehead.

"Care to explain?"

I do my best to relate the story in a neutral tone. I'm pretty sure I even put a humorous spin on it. But the idea of me being kicked in the arse by Mehmet does not amuse Nicole in the slightest.

"He's wrong in the head, that bloody Turk!"

"That's not a very European reaction."

But again, my attempt at humour falls flat.

Nicole strokes my cheek pensively. I know full well that she feels bad for me. I try to seem philosophical, despite my heavy heart, and despite realising from the mere touch of her hand that we are entering into fragile emotional territory.

"Are you sure this business ends here?" Nicole asks, looking at my forehead.

That's it: next time I'm marrying an idiot.

But Nicole places her lips on mine.

"Screw it," she says. "I'm sure this is the job for you. I'm certain of it."

I close my eyes and pray that, with all his talk of hope and the Devil, my friend Charles is just being a tedious piece of shit.

4

This letter from B.L.C. Consulting has been a real bombshell. I can't sleep anymore. My mood swings between euphoria and pessimism. Whatever I'm doing, my mind constantly comes back to it and creates all sorts of scenarios. It's exhausting.

On Friday, Nicole spent part of the day on her resource centre's website and printed off dozens of pages of legal information. After four years out of the game, I'm badly behind. The regulations in my field have changed a lot, especially regarding dismissals (things have become far more relaxed in that department). As for management, there have been plenty of innovations too. Fashions are changing at breakneck speed. Five years ago, everyone was mad about transactional analysis, but that's seen as deeply antiquated today. Current trends include "transition management", "sectorial restructuring", "corporate identity", the development of "interpersonal relations", "benchmarking" and "networking". But above all, businesses champion their "values". It's no longer enough to work . . . now you have to "adhere". Before you just had to agree with the business, nowadays you have to amalgamate with it. To become one with it. Suits me just fine: they employ me, I amalgamate with them.

Nicole sorted and selected the documents, I did some revision cards, and since this morning she has been firing questions at me. We're cramming. I am pacing around my study, trying hard to focus. Having composed various mnemonics to help, I'm now muddling them all up.

Nicole makes tea and flops back onto the sofa with papers all around her. She's still in her dressing gown, as is often the case, especially in winter, when she doesn't have anything planned for the day. Wearing her old T-shirt and odd woollen socks, Nicole smells of sleep and tea; cosy as a croissant and beautiful as spring. I adore her abandon. If I weren't so stressed by all this job stuff, I would take her straight back to bed. Given my current performance in the sex stakes, I desist.

"No touching," Nicole says, on seeing me finger my bruise.

I don't think about the knock often, but I'm cruelly reminded of its presence the moment I step in front of a mirror. This morning it turned a ghastly colour. Mauve in the middle and yellow on the sides. I'd hoped it would make me look manly, but the effect is more grubby. The paramedic told me I would have it for about a week. As for Mehmet, he's off for ten days with his broken nose.

The teams for day-night shifts were swiftly reshuffled to compensate for our absences. I pick up the phone and call my colleague Romain. I get Charles.

"The shifts are a mess," he explains. "Romain did the night and I'm on afternoons for two or three days."

A supervisor is doing overtime to stand in for Mehmet, who has already informed the company that he would like to get back to work sooner. Now there's someone who doesn't need management seminars to learn about adhering to values. The overseer who has temporarily replaced him told Charles that Senior Management cannot tolerate brawling in the workplace. "What is the world coming to when team leaders wind up in hospital for reprimanding a subordinate?" the guy would have said. I don't know the significance of that, but it's of no value to me. I decide not to say anything to Nicole so as not to worry her: if I get lucky with the job through B.L.C. Consulting, I can deal with all the crap from before with a big grin on my face.

"I'll put some foundation on you tomorrow," Nicole jokes as she inspects my forehead. "No, seriously! Just a bit, you'll see."

We'll see. I tell myself that tomorrow is just an aptitude test, not an interview, by which point the bruise will have more or less disappeared. If I make it that far, of course.

"Well of course you'll make it that far," Nicole assures me.

True faith is confusing.

I try to hide it, but my excitement is sky high. It's not the same as yesterday or the day before: the closer the test gets, the more my nerves overwhelm me. On Friday, when we started revising, I had no idea how badly behind I was. When I did realise, it sent me into a panic. All of a sudden, the girls coming round doesn't seem like such a welcome distraction. The thought of losing prep time sends me into a fluster.

As soon as he enters, Gregory points at my forehead and says, "What happened here, Grandpa? Starting to get a bit wobbly on your feet?"

The "grandpa" is his in-joke. In these cases, Mathilde, my elder daughter, usually digs an elbow into his ribs, because she thinks I'm touchy about it. In my opinion, she'd do better to smack him in the fucking face. I say this because she has been married to him for four years, and for four years I've wanted to do it for her. Imagine, a guy with the name "Gregory" . . . Plus, he has slicked-back hair, which is another dead giveaway. Mating with a mug like this clearly doesn't bother my daughter, but I'm sorry, it pisses me off. Nicole is right. I do feel touchy. She says it's a result of inactivity. I love this word, even if it's not the first that springs to mind when my alarm goes off at 4 a.m. to go and get my backside kicked.

Mathilde is an English teacher. She is a very normal girl. She reserves an inexplicable passion for the quotidian. She adores doing the shopping, wondering about what she's going to cook, thinking six months in advance about finding a good place to go on holiday, remembering the first names of all her friends' children and everyone else's birthdays, planning her pregnancies . . . This ability to fill up her life amazes me. There is something genuinely fascinating about generating such joy from the administration of the banal.

Gregory is a branch manager at a consumer credit firm. He lends to people so they can buy loads of stuff, like hoovers, cars and televisions. Conservatories. In the brochures, the interest rates seem completely fine, but in actual fact you end up having to repay three or four times what you borrowed. And if you are having trouble repaying, it's perfectly straightforward: you get another loan, but this time you need to repay thirty times what you borrowed. Standard. My son-in-law and I have spent entire evenings at each other's throats. He represents pretty much everything I hate. It's a real family drama. Nicole is of much the same opinion, but she has better manners than I have, and since she has work, she doesn't spend hours on end thinking about it, whereas an evening with my son-in-law can leave me seething inside for three days straight. I always end up replaying the conversations like a football pundit after a match.

When she's at home, Mathilde often comes for a chat in the kitchen while I finish the cooking. This is usually a pretext for tackling any washing-up left in the sink (she just can't help herself). At her place she's at it constantly; even at her girlfriends' houses she knows where all the glasses go and where the cutlery lives. It must be some sort of sixth sense. I find it quite remarkable.

She passes behind me and plants a kiss next to my ear, like a lover.

"So you bashed yourself?"

Her pity might have made things worse, but it is expressed with such kindness that actually it helps.

I'm about to answer, but the doorbell goes. It's Lucie, my

second daughter. She is very flat-chested, which causes her great distress. Nice guys find it cute, but try telling that to a girl of twenty-five. She's thin, nervous, skittish. With her, reason doesn't always prevail – she's a passionate girl, quick to anger, more than capable of saying things she immediately regrets. She has a lot more childhood friends than her sister, who never gets cross with anyone. Lucie's the kind of girl who would head-butt Mehmet, after which Mathilde would be waiting with the foundation.

Lucie is flying solo tonight. Her life is complicated. She kisses her mother hello and whirls into the kitchen like a domestic hurricane. She lifts up the lid.

"Did you add a squeeze of lemon?"

"I don't know, your mother's in charge of the blanquette."

Lucie sticks her nose into the saucepan. No lemon. She offers to make the béchamel.

"I'd rather do it myself," I decline politely.

Everyone is well aware that béchamel is the only thing I can make. Don't take that away from me . . .

"I think we've finally found one," Mathilde says, ready to burst.

Lucie raises an eyebrow in surprise. She has absolutely no idea what her sister means. To buy her a bit of time, I feign bewilderment.

"No?!"

Lucie pretends to feel aggrieved, but inside she finds it funny.

Our daughters are a true cross of their parents. Lucie resembles me physically, but she has her mother's temperament; Mathilde's the opposite. Lucie is lively and adventurous. Mathilde is hard-working and resigns herself to things easily. She is courageous and energetic, and does not ask for much from life. Just look at her husband. She was good at English, didn't look much beyond that, and became an English teacher. Chip off the old block. Lucie, however, is more out there. She studied history of art, psychology, Russian literature and I don't know what else – she couldn't settle on one subject because she found everything so interesting. She did well in studies that she never completed, changing plans as quickly as she did boyfriends. Mathilde did well in her studies because she'd started them, then married a friend from secondary school.

To everyone's surprise, even though we considered her to be unaccomplished in intellectual activities requiring rigour and detail (or perhaps it's because of this), Lucie became a lawyer. For the most part, she defends women who have been abused. Like with funerals or tax, there won't be any shortage of work in this field, but she's hardly about to make a fortune.

"It's a three- or four-room apartment in the nineteenth," Mathilde continues, completely in her element. "Near Jaurès. It's not exactly the neighbourhood we were after, but . . . all the same, it's nice and bright. And it's on Gregory's line, which is handy."

"How much?" Lucie asks.

"Six hundred and eighty thousand."

"Wow, there you go . . ."

I find out that they only have 55,000 euros for their deposit and that, despite Gregory's connections in the banking sector, getting a mortgage will be tricky.

This sort of thing hurts. Once upon a time I was in charge of the "Bank of Maman and Papa". They would ask without any hesitation, I would play hard to get, then give in with mock frustration, lending them sums they would never repay, and we all knew I was delighted to do it. It's nice to be useful. Nowadays, Nicole and I have cut back our lifestyle to the bare minimum, which is plain to see everywhere: in what we have, what we wear, what we cook. We used to have two cars, partly because that seemed more practical, but mainly because we never queried it. Over the years, our level of living rose through a combination of successive promotions and pay rises for both of us. Nicole landed deputy manager at her resource centre, and I became head of

H.R. at Bercaud. We used to look to the future with confidence, sure that we'd manage to pay off the mortgage on our flat. For example, when the girls moved out, Nicole wanted to do some work on the flat: keep just the one spare room, knock through the dividing wall between the living room and the second bedroom to turn it into a double-sized living room, then shift the water pipes so the sink could go under the window. That sort of thing. So we put some money aside. The plan was simple. We'd put the mortgage repayments on hold, pay for the works in cash, and go on holiday. We were so confident; it was a no-brainer. It would still be a few years before we'd pay off the mortgage on our flat, but we had money, and we went ahead with the works, starting with the kitchen. In terms of dates, that's very easy to remember: the builders started tearing everything down on May 20, and I was fired on May 24. We stopped the works immediately. After that, the engine tanked, the nose-dive began, and we've been in free fall ever since. As the kitchen had already been ripped up, from the plumbing to the tiles, I had to enter D.I.Y. mode. I erected a sink on two bits of plasterboard and reconnected some makeshift plumbing. Since it was temporary, we bought three kitchen units that I attached to the wall. We went for the cheapest ones, which unsurprisingly meant the ugliest ones. And the least sturdy. I'm always petrified of putting too many dishes in them. I also laid some lino directly onto the cement. We replace it every year. I usually do it to surprise Nicole. I open the door with a grand gesture and say: "We've got a new kitchen!" And she usually says something along the lines of: "Let's crack open a half bottle!" We both know it's not the most hilarious of jokes, but we do our best.

Since my unemployment benefits weren't enough to pay the bills, we dipped into the savings earmarked for the works. And when these reserves dried up, we realised that we still had four years of mortgage to pay off before the flat was ours, and Nicole said we'd have to sell it to buy somewhere smaller that we could pay for in cash. I refused. I've worked for twenty years to get this flat, and I cannot bring myself to sell it. The longer it's gone on, the less Nicole feels able to say anything about it. For now. She'll be right in the end. Especially if this Mehmet business turns sour. I'm not sure if we'll manage to save face in front of our daughters. Nowadays they are coping just fine by themselves. They can't even do me the good turn of asking for money.

I have successfully completed the béchamel. Just like normal. Same for everyone around the table – we're just like normal. Before, our predictable conversations and repetitive jokes were fine, but in the last year or two everything has irritated me. I've lost my patience, I freely admit it. This evening especially . . . I am desperate to tell the girls that I've been called in for a job that is absolutely perfect for me, that I haven't had a break like this for four years, that in two days I'm going to pass the aptitude test with flying colours before storming the interview, and in one month, kids, your disappointment of a father will be nothing but a distant memory. But instead of that I say nothing. Nicole smiles at me. She is superstitious. And happy. There is so much confidence in those eyes.

"So this guy," Gregory is saying, "enrols to read law. And the first thing he does . . . any guesses?"

No-one guesses. Except Mathilde, who doesn't want to ruin her husband's show. I haven't really been listening, I just know that my son-in-law is a prick.

"He took his uni. to court!" he announces with adulation. "He compared his enrolment fees to those from the year before and deemed the increase to be illegal because it hadn't been matched by a 'significant rise in the loans available to students'."

He bursts out laughing in a manner intended to highlight the brilliance of his story.

An intimate blend of right-leaning convictions and leftist fantasies, my son-in-law adores this kind of story. He teems with anecdotes about patients suing their therapists, or twin brothers laying into each other before a tribunal, or mothers with large families attacking their children. In certain variations, customers might get compensation from a contravention by their local supermarket or a car manufacturer. But Gregory verges on the orgasmic when the rulings go against the public sector. Perhaps S.N.C.F. has been found guilty because of a broken ticket machine, or the tax office has been forced to hand out a rebate to someone who's filed their return. Another time it might be the Ministry of Education losing against a parent who, after carrying out a comparison of students' marks for an essay on Voltaire, feels that their child has been the victim of some grave act of discrimination. Gregory's jubilation is directly proportionate to how inane the issue is. It's his way of showing that the law allows for the perpetual recurrence of the noble David versus Goliath struggle. In his mind, there is something grandiose about this fight. He is convinced that the law enforces democracy. Once you get to know him a bit, you are mighty relieved that he works in finance. Had the guy been a lawyer, he would have done unimaginable damage.

"That's a bit troubling," Lucie says.

Gregory, not fazed by the idea of giving a law lecture in front of Lucie, a lawyer, pours himself another glass of the Saint-Émilion he brought, visibly delighted to have provoked a heated debate, over the course of which his hypothesis will be demonstrably, indisputably superior.

"On the contrary," he says. "It's reassuring to know that we can still win even if we are the weaker party."

"Does that mean you could sue me just because you think the blanquette was under-seasoned?"

Everyone turns to me. Maybe it was my voice that alerted them. Mathilde silently implores me. Lucie looks triumphant.

"Does it need more salt?" Nicole asks.

"It's an analogy."

"You might have chosen a different one."

"Well, it's a bit trickier with the blanquette," Gregory concedes. "But it's the principle that counts."

In spite of the look on Nicole's face, which is one of extreme unease, I decide to hold my ground.

"But the principle is what bugs me. It's idiotic."

"Alain . . ." Nicole urges, laying her hand flat on top of mine.

"What do you mean 'Alain'?"

Nobody understands why I'm so annoyed.

"You're wrong," Gregory replies, not a man to back down when he thinks he has the initiative. "This story shows that anyone" – he leans into the "anyone" so that each of us is aware of the weight of his conclusion – "absolutely *anyone* can win if they have enough energy to do it."

"Win what?" Lucie says, to calm things down.

"Well" – Gregory stutters, thrown by such a basic jab – "well, win . . ."

"I'm sceptical of anyone who has the energy to chase a tax rebate or thirty euros' worth of enrolment fees . . . surely that energy could be better spent on less selfish causes?"

Here's how this usually pans out. Mathilde jumps to the defence of her prat of a husband, Lucie perseveres, and within a couple of minutes the two sisters are at each other's throats. Then Nicole slams her fist on the table, never quite at the right moment. When the others have gone, she sulks until she can't contain herself any longer, at which point she explodes at me: after the children, it's the parents turn to have a blazing row.

"You're a real pain in the arse!" Nicole says.

In her underwear, she slams the wardrobe door and disappears into the bathroom. I can see her bum through her knickers, which is a great start.

"I was on fire," I say.

But my joshing hasn't got a laugh out of her for twenty years.

When she returns to the bedroom, I'm once again immersed in my notes. Nicole comes back to earth. She knows that we have reached a critical point with this miraculous news. This is pretty much my last chance, and seeing me revising my notes in bed calms her down. She smiles.

"Ready for the big moment?"

She lies down next to me, picks up my notes and moves them slowly to one side, the way a parent might take off their sleeping child's glasses. Then she slips her hand under the sheets and finds me straight away.

Ready for the big moment.

From: Bertrand Lacoste [b.lacoste@BLC-Consulting.fr]
To: Alexandre Dorfmann [a.dorfmann@Exxyal-Europe.com]
Sent: Monday, April 27, 09:34

<u>Subject</u>: Selection and recruitment

Dear Monsieur Chairman,

Please find below an outline of the main points covered in our recent meeting.

In the course of the coming year, your group is to proceed with the closure of its Sarqueville site and the subsequent wide-ranging redundancy plan.

You wish to select one of your current executives to take charge of this difficult mission.

As such, you have asked me to devise a method of assessment to identify the individual who is the most steadfast and reliable: in short, the most competent.

You approved my Hostage-Taking Simulation Plan, over the course of which the executives under assessment will – without prior warning – be ambushed by an armed commando.

The ensuing test will make it possible to measure the candidates' ability to remain calm under pressure, their conduct in an extremely stressful scenario, and their loyalty to company values, above all when they are pressed by the hostage-takers to betray them.

With your agreement, we will link this operation with our own recruitment process for an H.R. assistant: <u>the candidates for this</u> <u>H.R. position will be required to conduct the role play</u>, thereby allowing us to assess their professional aptitude.

Combining these two operations can only be of benefit: at the same time as your executives are being assessed, the candidates for the H.R. role will be able to showcase their skills as assessors.

I have taken it upon myself to recruit the necessary personnel and to make the material arrangements for the role play. This is, as you can imagine, a rather complex process: we require weapons, actors, a site, a plausible scenario, a concrete plan of action, behaviour observation criteria, etc.

In addition we require a watertight premise for calling in candidates to carry out aptitude tests. For this, Monsieur Chairman, your valuable insight will be necessary. And your participation. All in due course.

I suggest we schedule this double operation for Thursday, May 21 (we must choose a day when the offices are closed, and that Thursday – Ascension Day – strikes me as appropriate, if you agree).

I will be submitting a proposal in the near future.

Yours,
Bertrand Lacoste

5

Nicole tells me that I'm very negative and that things always turn out better than expected. She's right again. Two days ago I was extremely depressed. Fine, eleven adults in a room, beavering away like schoolchildren, is hardly a massive deal. After all, in life we're constantly being assessed. No, what got to me was the realisation on entering the room that I was the oldest. Or rather the only old person. Three women, seven men, aged between twenty-five and thirty-five, all looking me up and down as though I was a casting error or some prehistoric curiosity. It was predictable, but still demoralising.

We were shown in by a girl with a Polish name, Olenka or something. Pretty girl – sparkling. Icy. Chilling. I don't know what her job is at B.L.C. (she didn't say), but judging by her authoritative attitude and her pushy manner, you got the sense that she gives it everything, that she would sell her soul to be taken seriously. Must have been an unpaid intern. Behind her was a pile of papers, the tests she'd be handing out in a few minutes' time.

She started by briefing us: the eleven of us had been selected from one hundred and thirty-seven candidates. For a millisecond, a silent yet palpable air of triumph filled the room. Then she introduced the position, omitting to name the recruiting company. The job she described suits me so well that during the course of her short announcement, I pictured myself wholeheartedly and delightedly accepting the offer.

But I came back down to earth with a crash when we were handed a 34-page pack of questions that were either open-ended, closed, semi-open, half-closed or three-quarters-open (not sure how they're going to pick through all that) and given three hours to complete it.

I was caught seriously off guard.

I had mainly mugged up on legislation, but the questions were very much geared towards "management, training and assessment". I had to summon all my reserves as I tried to recall information that seemed to date back to the Flood. Since I was side-lined I have lost my reflexes. The new techniques and last-ditch gimmicks I'd discovered two days earlier with Nicole had not stuck. I didn't manage to apply them to the practical examples we were given. At times I found myself just ticking and hoping for the best. That's all I am good for – autofill.

Over the course of the test I realised that my handwriting is terrible, at times barely legible. I had to try harder with the open-ended questions. I was almost relieved when I had to answer with a tick. A real chimp. Or an old chimp, more like.

To my right there was a girl of about thirty who looked vaguely like Lucie. At the start I attempted a complicit smile. She looked at me like I was trying to shag her.

By the end I was exhausted. All the candidates filed out and we just gave each other a nod, like distant neighbours who sometimes bump into each other by accident.

Outside it was a beautiful day – it would have been perfect weather to celebrate a victory.

I walked towards the *métro* station, each step leaving me more desperate. It was like a gradual dawning, one layer at a time. I'd left a whole load of questions unanswered. As for the others, the right answers came to me afterwards, each one different to the one I'd given. In this sort of game, the youngest ones are like ducks to water. Not me. It was a competition aimed at an age bracket that I don't belong to. I tried to tally up the precise number of questions I'd got wrong, but I lost count.

When I left I was just tired, but by the time I'd arrived at the *métro* I had sunk into a terrible depression. I could have cried. I realised that I'd never escape this. In the end, head-butting Mehmet seems like the only good solution, the only one that fits what is happening to me. There are terrorists who crash lorries full of explosives into schools; others who plant nail bombs in airports. I felt a strange connection with them. But instead of doing that, I've fallen for something else. Each time, I play the bastards' game. A job ad? I respond. Tests? I pass. Interviews? I attend. Have to wait? I wait. Have to come back? I come back. I'm obliging. For guys like me, the system is there, for all eternity.

It was the end of the afternoon and the *métro* carriages were filling up. Normally I move down the station by walking along by the ticket machines, but this time, I don't know why, I made my way down the edge of the platform, along the white line that you can't cross without putting yourself at risk of being hit by the approaching train. I was like a drunkard, my head spinning. Suddenly there was a great gust to my left. I hadn't been aware of the incoming train, not even heard it enter the station. Each one of its carriages rushed past me, missing me by a few centimetres. Nobody made a start towards me. I suppose everyone here is living dangerously. My mobile vibrated in my pocket. It was Nicole calling for the third time. She wanted some news, but I didn't have the strength to answer. I spent an hour on a bench at the station, staring at the thousands of passengers piling in to get home. Finally, I decided to board a train.

A youngish man got on just behind me but remained standing at the end of the carriage. As soon as it left, he started yelling to contend with the sound of the train as it whistled round the bends. He relayed his story at such a speed that no more than a few words could be made out: "hostel", "work", "illness". He smelt of booze, rattled on about meal vouchers and *métro* tickets, said he wanted work but work didn't want him. A few other words emerged from his garbled speech: he had children, he wasn't "a beggar". The commuters stared at their shoes or suddenly became immersed in their free newspaper as he passed before them with a polystyrene Starbucks cup in his outstretched hand. Then he left the carriage to get onto the next one.

His display got me thinking. Sometimes we give, other times we don't. Of all the homeless people, we give to the ones who touch us the most, those who find the words capable of stirring us. The conclusion hit me smack in the face: ultimately, even with the destitute, it's the survivors who perform best, since they're the ones who succeed in undermining the competition. If I end up homeless, I'm not at all sure I'll be one of the survivors. Not like Charles.

At home in the evening, I was meant to be tired because – having risen at 4 a.m. – I'd done my morning shift at Logistics before going on to nail the test at B.L.C. Consulting. The truth is I haven't told Nicole that I won't be going back to Logistics anytime soon. The Monday after head-butting Mehmet and my two-day suspension from work, I was greeted by a letter that arrived by recorded delivery. I'd been fired. It was a shocker, because we badly need the money.

I took myself to the job centre immediately to see if my adviser had anything up my street. Normally I fall under A.P.E.C.'s remit, the recruitment agency for people at executive level, but they don't offer part-time work. I prefer the employees and workers section. It's a couple of notches down the pecking order, where you have a slightly greater chance of survival.

Since I didn't have an appointment, he saw me in the corridor between the waiting room and the cubicles that serve as offices. I told him that Logistics no longer needed me.

"They haven't called me," he said with surprise.

He's young enough to be my son, but frankly I'm relieved he's not. But he is kind to me – he treats me like a father.

"They will call you. In the meantime, you haven't got something quick for me?"

He nodded at the noticeboard.

"They're all there. Right now there's pretty much nothing."

If I had a forklift licence or vocational training as a cook, I'd have a better shout at landing something. I had to search the unskilled jobs, but my sciatica counts me out of the rare vacancies on that front. As I left I made a small gesture at him through his office screen. He was interviewing a girl of about twenty. He responded with an irritated look, as though he half-recognised me but was struggling to place me.

The following day I received a letter by registered post from Logistics' lawyers. I'd read around this case to get a better understanding, and there's nothing complicated: I hit my manager, and he denies kicking me. He's saying he was walking past and "brushed" me. Getting fired is not the worst of it: I could end up in court for assault. Mehmet has cast-iron evidence recording his gravely incapacitating injuries and the potential after-effects they could cause. The letter detailed his balance and wayfinding issues, and of his severe post-traumatic stress, the long-term repercussions of which will be hard to predict.

He is demanding 5,000 euros in damages.

Just shy of sixty years old, I got kicked in the backside by my superior, yet it seems I have "seriously violated the principle of hierarchy in the company". That's it. I have disrupted the social order. For their part, Logistics are demanding 20,000 euros in damages. That's fifty times the monthly salary that I'm no longer receiving.

Nicole, my love, her patience is wearing thin. She's had her fill. I decided not to bring this up with her. The report I gave her of the test required her to draw on every last drop of energy and encouragement she had left at the end of the day: wait for the results, we're never in a strong position to judge ourselves, you don't know for sure that the young guns did better, just because they seemed so confident doesn't mean they gave the best answers, especially with the open-ended questions it's all about experience, something they lack, and what's more if the recruitment people called you in then it's because they're looking for a more considered approach, someone more tried and tested. I know the spiel by heart. I love Nicole more than anything, but the spiel . . . the spiel I hate.

Later on she finally fell asleep. I got up as quietly as possible so as not to wake her. I do that when I can't sleep: I get dressed and go out for a stroll round the neighbourhood. These last few years it's become something of a ritual. After traumatic experiences like the one at the *métro* earlier on, I need to steady my thoughts. This time I walked a bit further than usual. I was far from home, near the R.E.R. station. The gates were open and the cold wind was rushing through the pedestrian tunnels. The bins were overflowing and cans of beer lay strewn across the cement. A heavy neon light flooded the station. I pushed at a metal sheet that read "Staff Only" and went down a flight of stairs. I was on the well-lit platform. I didn't feel as if I was crying, but all the same the tears started to flow. I was standing up, feet planted on the track ballast, legs apart. I waited for the train.

All that for nothing.

In the morning, I'm shocked to see the envelope with the B.L.C. Consulting logo. I hadn't expected anything for a week, and it's not even been three days. I open it in such a hurry that I tear off part of the letter.

Holy fuck.

I sprint up to the apartment and then back down again, and very soon it's midday and I've been pacing back and forth outside Nicole's resource centre for an hour, jittery as a cat, until finally she comes out. She sees me from a distance and can tell from my body language that it's good news; she smiles as she comes towards me, I hold out the letter, she scans it and straight away says "my love", and her voice catches. I am overwhelmed by the certainty that a miracle has just taken place in our life. Both of us have tears in our eyes. I know I must resist the temptation, but I already have a strong urge to call the girls. Mathilde in particular, I don't know why. Probably because she's the more normal of the two, the one who'll process it quicker.

Against all expectations, I have passed the tests. I've made it through.

Individual interview: Thursday, May 7.

This is unbelievable . . . I made it through!

Nicole hugs me tight, but she doesn't want us to make a scene outside her workplace. I kiss a few of her colleagues and shake some hands in greeting as they head out for lunch. Everyone knows I'm looking for work, so when I go round there I try hard to look my best, to appear like I'm bearing up and not letting things get on top of me. For an unemployed person, being there when people are leaving the office is always tough. It's not jealousy. The unemployment itself isn't the hard part: what's difficult is continuing to exist in a society based on labour economics. No matter where you turn, you are defined by what you don't have.

But now everything's different. I feel as though my chest has burst open, that for the first time in four years I can breathe. Nicole says nothing; she is jubilant, holding my arm and squeezing it as we make our way down the street.

In the evening we go to Chez Paul to celebrate, even though we both know this is a real extravagance. We act as though it's no big deal, but that doesn't stop us from selecting our dishes via the price column on the menu.

"I'll have a main course and a dessert," Nicole says.

But when the waitress arrives I order two starters (*œufs en gelée*, which I know Nicole loves), and a half-bottle of Saint-Joseph. Nicole swallows hard, then smiles with resignation.

"I'm so proud of you," she says.

I don't know why she says that, but it's always good to hear. I hurry to get round to what I consider the most important point.

"I've thought about how I'm going to handle the interview. I reckon they'll have called in three or four of us. I have to stand out. My idea . . ."

And off I go. I'm like an excited teenager recounting his first triumph over a grown-up.

Every now and then Nicole places her hand on mine to let me know I'm speaking too loudly. I lower my voice, but within five minutes I've forgotten again. It makes her laugh. Good God, it's been years since we were as happy as we are tonight. At the end of the meal, I realise that I virtually haven't drawn breath. I try to tone it down, but I can't control myself.

Rue de Lapp is buzzing as though it were summer. We walk arm-in-arm, in love.

"And you'll be able to stop working at Logistics," says Nicole.

It takes me by surprise, and Nicole raises a quizzical eyebrow. I pull a face that would seem credible enough to me, looking rather ashen in the process. If I don't get this job and end up in court with 25,000 euros to pay in damages . . . Thankfully Nicole doesn't notice anything.

Instead of taking the *métro* at Bastille, I'm not sure why, she carries on walking, stops at a bench and sits down. She rummages in her bag, takes out a little package, and hands it to me. I open it to find a little roll of fabric with an orange pattern, held together by a small piece of red string, at the end of which is a tiny bell.

"It's a lucky charm. It's Japanese. I bought it the day you were called in to take the test. So far it seems to be doing the trick."

It seems silly, but it makes me very emotional. Not the gift itself. At least . . . I don't really know anymore, but I feel emotional. I must have polished off the Saint-Joseph more or less on my own. It's our life that I find moving. This woman, after everything we've been through, deserves every good fortune. As I stuff the talisman into my trouser pocket, I feel indestructible.

From now on, I'm on the home straight.

No-one's going to stand in my way anymore.

Charles often used to say: "The only certainty is that nothing happens as planned." That's classic Charles. He loves nothing more than a momentous phrase or a lofty stance. I wonder whether he might be an orphan. Long story short, I had horrendous nightmares in the run-up to the interview, but in the end it went pretty well.

I had been invited to B.L.C. Consulting's headquarters in La Défense. I was biding my time in the waiting room, a large space with a luxurious carpet, uplighting, a stunning Asian receptionist and discreet background music. A place tailor-made for boredom. I was quarter of an hour early. Nicole had applied a very thin layer of foundation to my forehead to hide any trace of my bruise. I had a constant feeling that it was running, and I had to resist the temptation to check. In my pocket, I played the Japanese charm through my fingers.

Bertrand Lacoste came striding in and shook me by the hand. At fifty years of age, he came across as absurdly sure of himself, but quite affable.

"Would you like a coffee?"

"No thank you, I'm fine," I said.

"Nervous?"

He asked this with a little smile. Slipping coins into the machine, he added:

"Yup, it's always difficult finding work."

"Difficult, but honourable," I said.

He looked up at me, as if seeing me properly for the first time.

"So no coffee?"

"Thank you, no."

And we stayed there, in front of the machine, with him sipping his synthetic coffee. He turned his back and considered the reception area around him with an air of glum resignation.

"Fucking decorators – can't trust them to do anything!"

Straight away that set down the marker for me. I don't know exactly what happened after that. I was so pumped up it came out automatically.

"I see," I said.

This made him start.

"What do you see?"

"You're going to play it all 'casual'."

"Sorry?"

"I said you're going to play it all 'relaxed', sort of 'the circumstances are professional, but at the end of the day we're all human beings'. Am I right?"

He shot me a look. He seemed livid. I told myself I'd got off to a decent start, then continued:

"You're playing on the fact that we're more or less the same age to see whether I fall into the trap of being overfamiliar. And now I think you're giving me this look to see if I panic and start back-pedalling."

His glare softened and he smiled:

"Right . . . well, we've succeeded in clearing the air, wouldn't you say?"

I didn't answer.

He chucked his plastic cup in the bin.

"So, let's get on with the serious stuff."

He walked ahead of me down the corridor, still with that long stride. I felt like a confederate soldier a few minutes before the enemy charge.

He'd done his job well and studied my application carefully, incisively. The moment he came across a weakness in my C.V., he pounced on it, exploiting the first sign of frailty in the candidate.

"He carried on testing me, but the tone was different now."

"Did he tell you who he was recruiting for?" Nicole asks.

"No, not at all . . . There were just two or three clues. It's all pretty vague, but maybe I'll manage to find out more. It's in my interest to get ahead of the game. You'll see why. At the end of the interview, I said to him:

'I must say that I'm very surprised that you should be interested in a candidate of my age.'

Lacoste pretended to be nonplussed, but eventually he placed his elbows on the table and stared at me.

'Monsieur Delambre,' he said to me, 'we are just another company in a competitive market. Everyone needs to stand out from the crowd. You with your employers, me with my clients. You are my wild card.'"

"But . . . what does that even mean?" Nicole asks.

"'My client is expecting young graduates, which is what I'm going to give them; they're not expecting an applicant like you – I'm going to surprise them. And then, between you and me, when push comes to shove in the next round, I reckon the decision will make itself.'"

"Is there another round?" Nicole asks. "I thought — "

"'There are four of you on the shortlist. The final decision will be based on one further test. I'm going to be open with you: you are the oldest of the four, but it's not at all beyond the realms of possibility that your experience will make all the difference.'"

Nicole begins to look suspicious. She cocks her head to one side.

"And what is this 'further test'?"

"'Our client intends to assess a selection of their top execs. Your mission is to conduct this assessment. You will be tested, if you will, on your ability to test others.'"

"But . . ." Nicole still doesn't see where this is going. "How does that work?"

"'We are going to simulate a hostage-taking . . .'"

"What?!"

Nicole looks as if she's about to choke.

"'. . . and your task involves placing the candidates under sufficient duress for us to test various criteria: their coolness under pressure, their conduct in an extremely stressful scenario, and their loyalty to the values of the company to which they belong.'"

Nicole is struck dumb.

"But that's outrageous!" she cries. "You have to make these people think they've been taken hostage? At work? Is that what you're telling me?"

"'There will be a commando unit played by actors, weapons loaded with blanks, cameras to film their reactions, and you will lead the interrogations and direct the commandos. You will need to use your imagination.'"

Nicole is on her feet, disgusted.

"That's sick," she says.

There's Nicole in a nutshell. You'd think that her capacity for indignation would have lost its edge over time, but not a bit of it. When she feels scandalised, she can't help herself – nothing will stop her. In these situations, you have to try to calm her down straight away, to step in before her reaction gets out of control.

"You shouldn't look at it like that, Nicole."

"How should I look at it? An armed commando unit comes bursting into their office, threatens them, interrogates them, for how long? An hour? Two hours? They think they might die, that these people will kill them? All that just so their boss can have a bit of a laugh?"

Her voice is trembling. I haven't seen her like this for years. I try to be patient. Her attitude is understandable. But I'm already fast-forwarding ten days, and it hits me: everything hinges on one single, palpable fact: I have to pass this test.

I try to smooth things over.

"I know it's not very . . . But you have to look at the situation from a different angle, Nicole."

"Why? Because you think this approach is acceptable? Why don't we just shoot them too, while we're at it?"

"Wait — "

"Or better still! Put some mattresses on the pavement without telling them, then hang them out the window! Just to see their reaction! Alain, have you gone completely mad?"

"Nicole, don't — "

"And you're really prepared to go along with this?"

"I understand where you're coming from, but you have to see things from my side, too."

"No way, Alain. I can understand anything, but that doesn't mean I can forgive it!"

She has moved into our train wreck of a kitchen.

I see the two bits of plasterboard that have been holding up the sink for years. The current lino is even less resistant than last year's, already curling up at the corners in pitiful fashion. Nicole, livid as she stands in the centre of this mess, is wearing a woollen cardigan that she can't afford to replace. It makes her look diminished. It makes her look poor. And she doesn't even realise. I take it as a personal insult.

"For Christ's sake, all I know is that I'm still in the running!"

I'm shouting now. The violence of my tone roots her to the spot.

"Alain . . ." she says, panic in her voice.

"Don't 'Alain' me! Fucking hell, can't you see we're turning into bloody tramps? We've been slowly running aground for four years . . . soon enough we'll be *in* the ground! So yes, it's disgusting, but so is our life – our life is disgusting! Yes, those people are sick, but I'm going to do it, you hear me? I'm going to do what they ask. Everything they ask! Even if I have to bloody shoot them to get the job, I'll do it because I'm fed up . . . I'm sixty years old, and I'm fed up of having my arse kicked!"

I am beside myself.

I grab the wall unit beside me and yank it so violently that it comes away completely. Plates, mugs – everything comes tumbling down with a terrible crash.

Nicole cries out and then starts sobbing into her hands. But I don't have the strength to console her. I can't. Deep down that's the worst thing about it. We've been fighting together for four years just to keep our heads above water, and one fine day we realise it's over. Without knowing it, each of us has folded. Because even with the best couples, each one has a different way of seeing reality. That's what I am trying to say to her. But I am so furious that I get it wrong.

"You're able to have scruples and morals because you have a job. For me, it's the opposite."

It's not the best way of putting things, but in the circumstances I can't do any better. I think Nicole has got the general gist, but I don't have time to make sure. I pull the door shut as I leave.

At the bottom of our building, I realise I have forgotten to put on a coat.

It's raining and cold, so I turn up my shirt collar.

Like a tramp.

6

It's May 8, a public holiday. We are celebrating Mother's Day round at our place because next Sunday, Gregory wants to be with his own mother. Nicole has told Mathilde twenty-thousand times that she doesn't give a damn about Mother's Day, but to no avail. Mathilde, however, sticks to it. I reckon it's because later on she doesn't want her children to overlook it. She is in training.

The girls are supposed to be arriving at midday, but at 9 a.m., Nicole is still in bed, facing the wall. Since her horrified reaction to the selection test that I intend to pass, we've barely exchanged three words. For Nicole, it is simply unacceptable.

I think she was crying this morning. I didn't have the courage to touch her. I got up and went to the kitchen. Last night she didn't pick up the broken dishes, just pushed them into a pile in the corner of the room. It's very large – I must have broken most of our dishes. I can't tidy it up now, it would make a dreadful racket.

I turn around, not knowing what to do, so I go and switch on my computer to see if I have any messages.

I gauge my usefulness to society by the number of emails I receive. Back in the day, my ex-colleagues from Bercaud would send me a few lines that I'd reply to straight away. Just chatting. And then I realised that the only ones who still wrote to me were the ones who had been fired too. Fellow reduced-to-clear friends. I stopped replying, and they stopped writing. In fact, everything around us got scarcer. We had two old friends: a school pal of Nicole's who lived in Toulouse, and a guy I knew from military service who I had dinner with from time to time. The others were friends from work or holidays, or the parents of the girls' friends from when they lived at home. Maybe people got a bit tired of us. And we of them. When you don't share the same concerns, you don't share the same pleasures. Nowadays Nicole and I are rather lonely. Only Lucie still sends me emails, at least one a week. These messages are practically devoid of content, just a way for her to let me know she's thinking of me. Mathilde rings her mother – that's another way.

My inbox consists of newsletters from various job centres and recruitment agencies, and a few reminders from management or H.R. publications that I haven't subscribed to for three years.

When I open my browser, Google gives me some headlines from around the world. ". good news: only 548,000 job losses in the United States this month." Everyone was expecting far worse. It doesn't take much to celebrate these days. "Financial crime reaches all-time high. Business leaders explain it is a natural phenomenon . . ." I click onto the next page, not in the least disturbed: I have every confidence in business leaders and their ability to explain away the natural effects of economics.

I hear a noise in the bedroom and move towards it. Nicole appears at last.

Without uttering a word she pours herself some coffee into a Duralex glass. The mugs are in bits over by the door, with the broom resting on top.

Her attitude infuriates me. Rather than supporting me, she's being all sanctimonious.

"Scruples don't pay the bills."

Nicole doesn't answer. Her face is sullen and she looks exhausted. What have we become . . .

She puts her glass in the sink, takes out some large bin bags and fills up four because each one gets so heavy. The jagged porcelain is sharp and cuts through the plastic here and there. You'd normally expect to see plate-smashing antics for the audience's amusement in some *vaudeville* farce. Here it seems so prosaic.

"I couldn't give a damn about being poor. I don't want to be immoral."

I don't have an answer for that. I take the bin bags downstairs while Nicole has a shower. Two trips. When we're back in the room together, we don't manage a conversation and the minutes pass by. The children are going to arrive and nothing is ready. And we need to go and buy some dishes. Short on time, but more importantly, what with this leaden atmosphere, short on strength.

Nicole is sitting down, bolt upright, looking outside as though there was something to see.

"It's the company that's immoral," I say. "Not the unemployed."

When the girls ring the bell, each of us waits for the other to act. I give in first. I provide a few lame excuses that demand no further explanation, and we take everyone to a restaurant. The girls are surprised and find it odd that, bearing in mind the circumstances, their mother doesn't seem to be at the party. And what makes it worse is that Nicole is pretending to be happy. I can tell that it's upsetting them. No, not upset . . . They feel that whatever's wrong with us might overwhelm them too, and it scares them. Mathilde gives her a mother a cardigan. A cardigan, for fuck's sake. I can't remember when it started, but for months now they have been giving us useful presents. If they find out that I've broken all the dishes, I can expect six soup bowls for my birthday.

During dessert, Mathilde announces that they have signed a purchase agreement for their flat. There are still a few question marks with the bank, but Gregory breaks into a smug smile: he's got it all under control. Their solicitor is putting together the paperwork and it will be theirs by the holidays. Inside, I hope they manage to pay for it.

When I go to settle the bill, I realise that Lucie has beaten me to it without anyone noticing. Both of us pretend not to make a big deal out of it.

"I can help you with anything, Alain," Nicole says before bedtime, "but this . . . this hostage-taking doesn't fit with who I am. I don't want to hear any more of it. Don't make me live with that."

She turns towards the wall immediately. I can't expect to persuade her, and it makes me sad.

But I don't leave it there. I start thinking about this final test. Because if I pass, even if it involves methods she finds objectionable, our differences of opinion will be nothing but a distant memory.

That's the way to look at it.

David Fontana
F.A.O. Bertrand Lacoste
Subject: "Hostage-taking" role play – Client: Exxyal

As discussed, this is where the operation currently stands.

For the commando unit, I have recruited two colleagues with whom I have worked on several occasions in the past and for whom I can vouch entirely.

   As regards the role of Exxyal's clients, I have shortlisted two men: a young Arab and a fifty-year-old Belgian actor.

   In terms of weaponry, I have opted for:
   –   3 × Uzi submachine guns (under three kilograms in weight, rate of fire of 950 rounds/min., 9 × 19 cartridges);
   –   2 × Glock 17 pistols (635 grams, same calibre, 31-cartridge magazines);
   –   2 × Smith & Wesson pistols.

   All weapons will of course be loaded with blank rounds.

The space I am proposing is in a prestigious location, as Exxyal is "inviting important clients" there. It has a meeting room and four offices, with toilets, etc. The site is situated on the outskirts of Paris, with large glass windows overlooking the Seine (see photos and map – Appendix 3).

   The premises offer a very favourable layout for what you have planned. We will need to carry out several run-throughs, and so we must finalise a scenario as soon as possible. You will find my proposal in Appendix 4.

Overview: your client's executives will be summoned to a highly important but confidential meeting, which will explain why it is taking place on a public holiday and why they have been notified at such short notice.

The pretext is that they will be meeting important overseas clients.

The commando unit will intervene at the start of the meeting.

The head of Exxyal Europe, Monsieur Dorfmann, will be evacuated immediately, thereby creating an intensely stressful atmosphere conducive to the aims of your test. It will also give him the opportunity to observe the ensuing sequence of events from elsewhere.

The remaining executives, having been relieved of their personal effects and mobile telephones, will be held in the office and interrogated in turn. The scenario can if necessary accommodate the option of isolating the hostages for several minutes in order to gauge their capacity for organising themselves, or indeed for offering resistance, as per your request. The commando head will conduct the individual interrogations as per the assessors' instructions.

The role play will be monitored via cameras and screens.

It is my belief that this fulfils the terms of the brief you assigned me. Thank you for your confidence and for the valuable assistance offered by Madame Olenka Zbikowski.

Respectfully yours,
David Fontana

7

Now that I've stopped working at Logistics, you would think the 4 a.m. wake-up would start to wear, but not a bit of it. In fact, I feel so charged up that I barely sleep, and getting out of bed almost comes as a relief. Most nights, Nicole clings to me in her sleep, something to do with holding on to me – it's a game between us. We hold each other, pretend to let go, then grab each other again. We've done this for twenty years and not once spoken about it.

This morning, I know full well that she's awake and that she's just bluffing. But we both remain in our bubbles. A tacit agreement not to touch one another.

As planned, I get to Logistics a little ahead of time. I know the guys from the other teams, and since I have no desire for their questions or their pity, I find a corner where I can survey the entrance without being seen, keeping an eye out for the big, gangling frame of Romain. But it's the unsteady frame of Charles that appears at the end of the street. I have no idea how he does it – the guy must drink in his sleep – but it's not even 5 a.m. and already his breath smells like a brewery. But I know my boy Charles . . . tanked up or not, he's always hale and hearty. Although that said, he does seem to be struggling to place me this morning.

"Well I never . . ." he says, looking as if he's seen a ghost.

He slowly lifts his left hand, in a little salute. It's a gesture born of shyness that he makes quite often. A shy, restrained gesture. It makes his enormous watch slide down to his elbow.

"How are you doing, Charles?"

"The golden days are behind us," Charles replies, as enigmatic as ever.

"I'm waiting for Romain."

Charles' face brightens. He is visibly happy that he can be of service.

"Ah, Romain's switched teams!"

Over the past four years, I have become hyper-sensitive to cock-ups. Just one word and I can feel them looming – it's become a reflex.

"Meaning?"

"He's on full nights. Thing is he's supervisor now."

It is very hard to know what someone like Charles is thinking. The trancelike state he is permanently in lends him a certain unfathomability. You can't tell if a great deal of comprehension is going on, whether the blank delivery of this harmless news is belying a sort of creeping reflection, or whether booze has addled every last brain cell.

"What do you mean, Charles?"

There's no doubt he registers my concern. He becomes all philosophical, shrugging his scrawny shoulders.

"He's been promoted, Romain. Been made supervisor and we . . ."

"When exactly?"

Charles purses his lips, as if things are about to come to a head.

"Monday after you left."

I ought to be congratulating myself for my intuition, but this is too much of a cock-up. Charles pats me on the shoulder like a Good Samaritan, as if he were offering me his condolences. Maybe his mind does work faster than I've given him credit for, because he says:

"If you need me I was there too and I saw everything."

That I did not see coming. For further encouragement, Charles raises a solemn finger:

"When the woodcutter enters the forest with his axe on his shoulder the trees say the handle is one of ours."

The bit about the axe bamboozles me, but however he chooses to phrase his offer of help, you only need to look at Charles to see how much he means it.

"That's kind, Charles, but I'm not about to make you lose what little work you have."

A sudden look of weariness and regret descends on Charles.

"You don't think I make much of a witness, not presentable enough that it? Well hear you me that's bang on. If you tip up in court with a bum like me as your only witness that risks being quite . . . quite . . ."

He searches for the word.

"Counter-productive?" I suggest.

"That's the one!" Charles bursts out. "Counter-productive!"

He is over the moon. Finding the *mot juste* classes as a major victory. So much so that he forgets the need for any commiseration on my part. He bobs his head, in a state of marvel at this word. It's my turn to pat him on the shoulder. But with me, the condolences are sincere.

I get ready to leave and Charles grabs me by the arm:

"Come and have a drink at my place one evening, if you'd like . . . I mean . . ."

As I attempt to imagine the meaning of "at my place", and the significance of the invitation, Charles is already walking off with his long, lolloping gait.

I mull it over on the way home.

On the *métro*, I check I still have Romain's mobile number. Logistics seem to be taking this whole matter very seriously. They are iron-cladding their case. They won't stop at the shirt – I'm going to end up stark bollock naked.

A quick calculation tells me that if he's on nights, Romain might not even be asleep yet.

I call.

He picks up straight away.

"Hi, Romain!"

"Oh, hi!"

He recognises me at once. Makes me wonder if he was expecting me. His voice is chirpy but faint. I detect a little irritation. Nicole says that unemployment has made me paranoid, and she may well be right. Romain confirms his sudden promotion.

"What about you, old man?" he asks straight after.

The more of this "old man" I get, the less I can handle it. Nicole says that unemployment has made me touchy, too.

I tell him about Logistics and the letter from the lawyers. I allude to the threat of a trial.

"No way!" Romain says, flabbergasted.

No point going any further. He's pretending to be surprised by a piece of news that everyone knows already. No doubt it's been a hot topic of discussion for the last three days. If he's trying to pull the wool over my eyes then he's flunked it.

"If I find myself in court, your witness statement will help me out a lot."

"Well, of course, old man!"

No doubt about it this time. If he said it would be tricky to testify in my favour, I might still been in with a chance. But no, Romain's mind is made up. He won't be picking up two days before he takes the stand.

"Thanks, Romain. Really, thanks a lot, too kind!"

Touché. He clocked the irony. That millisecond of silence before his response confirms my every fear.

"Don't mention it, old man!"

I hang up, feeling pretty downbeat. For a moment, I entertain the thought of going back to Charles. If I ask him, he'll lose his job, but he'll come all the same. I don't think he will have an ounce of credibility and it would all be for nothing. That said, if it's all I have, I will do it. No choice.

The sword of Damocles is hanging over me, and the higher it gets the greater the destruction when it's finally released. I feel wild thoughts running through me.

Why do they want to do this to me?

Why do they feel this need to hold my head underwater?

Romain, I understand. I don't hold it against him. In his position, if I had to choose between helping a friend and keeping my job, I'd have no hesitation either. But the company?

I run through the various options available to me. Given the circumstances, I choose the remorseful approach. I'm going to write a letter of apology. If they want, they can pin it up around the workplace or send it to the employees with their next payslip . . . I couldn't give a stuff. Losing this job is hard to take, but it's nothing compared to a trial that might see me stripped of everything.

Back home, I run up to my office. A courier must have arrived first thing since Nicole was still in to take delivery of a thick envelope with the B.L.C. Consulting logo. My heart is pounding. They didn't hang around.

Normally, when we leave something for each other at home, Nicole and I will pop a little note alongside, make a joke if we're in good spirits, or something frisky if we're in the mood. Or something loving if none of that applies. This morning, Nicole just left the envelope on my desk. No comment.

Before opening it, I grab the letter from Logistics' lawyer that I have hidden in my study and call the number. A girl picks up and puts me through to a guy who explains that the lawyer can't speak to me. It takes ten minutes of negotiating to arrange a telephone meeting with the lawyer's assistant. I have to call back this afternoon at 3.30 p.m. and she'll give me five minutes of her time.

8

The B.L.C. Consulting envelope contains a dossier entitled "Recruiting an H.R. Assistant". Inside, a document with the heading "Role-play exercise: hostage-taking at the workplace".

Page one announces the objective: "Your mission: to assess senior executives subjected to violent and sustained stress."

Page two details the broad outline of the scenario. Since the hostage-taking will be conducted by candidates for the H.R. position (my competitors and myself), the document sets out the protocols to ensure each of us has an equal chance.

The candidates for one position select the candidates for another: how very in line with the times. The system doesn't even need to exercise authority anymore – the employees take care of that themselves. In this case it's pretty extreme, since we get to fire the worst-performing execs on the spot before they've even secured the job.

The incoming generate the outgoing. Capitalism has just achieved perpetual motion.

I scan the dossier as quickly as possible but, as feared, all the documents are stock, anonymous. We are not therefore supposed to have any way of guessing which company is involved, and more importantly of identifying the execs that have been put forward for the test, which would have opened the way for all sorts of secret negotiations among the H.R. candidates charged with assessing them.

The system does have some moral standing.

We are to assess five execs. Their ages have been rounded to the nearest five.

<u>Three men</u>:
- Thirty-five, Ph.D. in Law, legal department
- Forty-five, top credentials in economics, finance manager
- Fifty, top degree in civil engineering, senior project manager

<u>Two women</u>:
- Thirty-five, H.E.C. business school graduate, sales executive
- Fifty, top degree in structural engineering, senior project manager

These are senior execs with serious responsibilities. The cream of the company. Champions of the M&M machine: "Marketing & Management", the two heaving breasts of modern business. The principles are simple: marketing involves making people buy what they don't want to buy, while management involves making executives do what they don't want to do. In short, these people are very active in the running of the company and must adhere passionately to its values (otherwise they'd have been weeded out long ago). I wonder why they are assessing these five ahead of any others. Clarifying that will be crucial.

The dossier contains details of everything: their studies, their career paths, their responsibilities. I estimate their annual salaries to fall in the 150,000- to 210,000-euro bracket.

I go for a walk to think all this through. That's one of my things. My thoughts have a tendency to simmer away. Walking doesn't so much calm them down as channel them. And right now I'm boiling over. I stop in my tracks as I consider how fast everything around me is unravelling. Nicole, Romain, Logistics … Getting this job is becoming all the more essential. I am reassured by the fact that I've worked for more than thirty years, and I can confidently say I'm good at what I do. If I carry on being good at it for ten more days then I'll be able to eradicate all these threats. This helps me regain my focus. I fall back into my stride, but I'm still struggling to silence the little voice running through my head. Nicole's voice. Not so much her voice as her words. Acting against her will is unbearable, and I've been in doubt ever since she set out her categorical disapproval. I never hesitate to do what needs to be done, and that's something she'll never comprehend. Life in her job is a cosy one. Nicole, lucky thing, will never know what it takes to survive in a competitive commercial field. What worries me about her reaction is that ultimately she doesn't believe in my chances; she thinks I'm getting worked up over something that's more virtual than real. My gut's telling me to join the fray, right now. But . . .

I turn all this over and over, unable to think about anything else. My anxiety is like a roly-poly – it always rights itself. I make up my mind.

It's the young Polish girl who picks up. I like her slightly husky tone very much. I find it sexy. I introduce myself. No, Bertrand Lacoste cannot take my call, he's in a meeting. Is it anything she can help me with?

"It's rather complicated."

"Try anyway."

Pretty abrupt.

"I'm just about to get under way with my preparation for the final recruitment test."

"Yes, I'm aware of that."

"Monsieur Lacoste assured me that each candidate's chances were the same, but — "

"But you're not so sure."

The girl's not cutting me much slack, here. I'm going to trip up, but I go for it anyway.

"That's exactly it. I find it odd."

Lacoste may well be in a meeting, but she disturbs him nonetheless. My tactic's turning out alright. An evaluation and recruitment firm's image must be rooted in its integrity. That justifies disturbing the boss. He comes on the line.

"How are you?"

You would swear he'd been expecting my call and that he was overjoyed to hear from me. That said, there's still a slight edge to his voice.

"I'm in a meeting right now, but my assistant tells me you have some concerns."

"A few, yes. In fact, no – just the one. I am sceptical about the chances of a man my age in a recruitment process at this level."

"We've been through this already, Alain. And I've given you my answer."

He's good, the wily dog. I'm going to have to keep my wits about me. The whole "Alain" thing is a classic ruse, but still it works: he's playing it all matey, even though both of us know full well I can't call him "Bertrand" in return.

My silence speaks volumes.

He knows that I know. At last, we have some sort of understanding.

"Listen," he continues, "I was clear with you before and I'll be clear with you again. There won't be many of you. Each profile is fairly different from the other. Your age is a handicap, but your experience is a bonus. What more is there to discuss?"

"Your client's intention."

"My client is not after looks, he's after skills. If you feel up to the mark, as your test results indicate, your application will stay live. If not . . ."

He picks up on my hesitation.

"I'm going to take this on another line. One minute . . ."

The switchboard fobs me off with forty seconds of music. Hearing this version of Vivaldi's *Spring* makes it hard to hold out much hope for the summer.

"Excuse me," Bertrand Lacoste picks up again.

"Not at all."

"Listen, Monsieur Delambre."

No more Alain. The mask slips.

"The company for which I am recruiting is one of my most important clients. I cannot allow myself to make an error of judgement."

His intimate tone has given way to seriousness. Now he's playing the sincerity card. When you're dealing with managers at his level, it's impossible to know where the lying stops.

"This position requires a high level of professionalism and I have not found a huge number of candidates who are *really* up to the mark. I cannot prejudice the outcome, but between you and me, you would be wrong not to stay in the running. I'm not sure if I'm being clear . . ."

Now this . . . this is new. Very new indeed. I barely heard the rest of his speech. I should have recorded it to play to Nicole.

"That's all I needed to know."

"I'll see you soon," he says as he hangs up.

My heart is pounding. I start walking again to vent my frazzled neurons. And then I get back to work. That has done me the world of good.

First up, focus on the objective facts.

I reckon we are three or four candidates: any more than that would be unmanageable. I base my calculations on three since it doesn't alter things dramatically.

So I must beat two rivals to land the job. To manage that, I must perform the best when selecting the five executives. I must eliminate the weakest candidates. Whichever of us registers the most scalps will have been the most selective and therefore the most effective. Five to start with, get rid of four and finish with a bullseye. That's the objective.

I'll have a job if one of them (or preferably several) loses theirs.

As I was thinking all this through I had slipped into autopilot and taken a left, ending up down in the *métro*. I have no idea where I'm going. My feet have led me here. I look up and focus on the map. From where I live, every train goes via République. I trace the multicoloured lines and can't stop myself smiling: my subconscious is guiding me. I sit down and wait for the connection.

I have to load all the dice in my favour. That involves choosing the best strategy, the one that will result in the greatest number of losers.

I leave République behind and push on to Châtelet.

I'm applying management rule no. 1: an executive can only be defined as competent when he is capable of anticipation.

As far as I can see, there are two possible strategies.

The first is the one prompted by the dossier: read the anonymous files, study the scenario and imagine, in absolute or approximate terms, how to make the execs surrender to the terrorists' demands, to lose control, to come across as cowards, to betray their company and colleagues – to betray themselves. Classic. Each of them will trust his or her intuition, knowing that in a similar situation, the question is not *whether* they will betray (with a gun to their head!), but *how much* they will betray.

If I were younger, that's the strategy I would use to prep for the task. However, thanks to Lacoste, I know that all my competitors are younger than me – they will definitely approach it that way too.

I have no choice but to opt for the second strategy. I kick my brain into gear.

Management theory states the following: to attain a goal, set interim objectives. I establish three: it is essential I discover the identity of B.L.C. Consulting's client and of the five execs; then I will need to investigate each one to find out everything about their lives, hopes, expectations, strengths and – most importantly – weaknesses; and finally I have to work out how to give myself the best chance of bringing them down.

I have ten days to go, not long at all.

My subconscious has brought me this far. To the gates of B.L.C. Consulting headquarters.

The heart of La Défense, that vast space bristling with buildings, riddled with motorway and *métro* tunnels, and banked up by wind-battered walkways teeming with myriads of panic-stricken ants just like me. The sort of place where, if I'm victorious, I'll have the opportunity to see out my career. I enter the building's vast lobby and scope out the lie of the land, before making for a set of armchairs with a good view of the lifts.

Even though time is of the essence, I bed in for several hours of (fruitless) surveillance dedicated to the arrival of a person who won't lead me anywhere . . . It's not the right strategy, but it does allow me some time to think, and it's in a place where there's a chance – however slim – of finding something useful. I station myself sideways on so that I'm invisible to anyone exiting the lift, and I take out my booklet. Every twenty seconds I glance over at the lifts. I never thought there'd be so much coming and going at this time of day. People of all shapes and sizes.

I try to focus on my primary objective. B.L.C. Consulting's client is a major company (in terms of scale and resources) operating in a strategic industry (if its executives require regular assessment, that means their responsibilities are more important than they are). But then there are any number of strategic industries. They range from the military to the environment, via international organisations or any area linked to the State, which covers trade secrets, defence, pharmaceuticals, security . . . It's all too wide. I strike them off and retain two key points: a very big company operating in a strategic industry.

Waves of people roll in and out of the interminable lifts. An hour passes. I carry on taking notes.

Administering a hostage-taking role play is no simple task. You need actors, fake weapons . . . what else? A few vague images come to me from the movies: people burst into a bank, police sirens wailing outside, they barricade the doors, yelling to each other as they run behind the counter, employees and customers looking on in terror. Everyone's on the floor. What then?

Another hour later, the intern arrives. She really is very pretty. Her blonde hair is unbelievable. She exits the lift with an assured step, her eyes focused straight ahead. The sort of girl who wants to show that she never deviates from her path. She's wearing a light-grey suit and very high heels. Half a dozen sets of men's eyes follow her as she crosses the lobby towards the revolving doors. Mine not included. A few seconds later I start tailing her, then watch from the pavement as she strides into the *métro*. I'm left feeling rather frightened by her. I have no way of knowing whether she'll be present on the day of the hostage-taking, or which bit she'll be overseeing, but I just hope I don't come up against an adversary of her calibre, because this girl is razor-sharp: too young to have done the damage she's capable of, but her time cannot be far off.

At the precise moment I come through the revolving door back into the lobby, I see Bertrand Lacoste leaving the lift right opposite me.

Struck by panic, I lower my head and do a complete circuit in the door, then cross the street. My heart is pounding and my legs turn to cotton wool. If he saw me and recognised me I can kiss my hopes goodbye. But I get away with it. In my haste, I had failed to take stock of the details. In fact, Lacoste had got out of the lift alongside a man of about fifty, not very tall but with a muscular, athletic build. His walk is so fluid that he has an almost liquid quality to him.

The two men talk as they make their way across the lobby.

I check that my observation post shelters me from their line of sight. A few seconds later and they are on the pavement shaking hands. Lacoste re-enters the building and heads back to the lifts, while the other man stands outside.

He scans left and right, perfectly upright, his legs slightly apart.

I look him up and down. Rectangular face, thin mouth, crew cut. I stop in the middle, armpit-level, where his pecs are. I could swear he's wearing a gun. All I know about this stuff is what I've seen in the movies, but I think I can make out the bulge of a weapon. His hand goes to his right pocket and he takes out a piece of chewing gum that he unwraps as he looks around.

He feels he's being watched. His eyes comb the area and settle on me for a microsecond. Then he stuffs the wrapper in his pocket and makes his way to the *métro*.

That short moment has left me petrified.

This guy might have been anybody, but that one fraction of a second is enough to convince me – beyond any doubt – that he isn't.

I flick through my professional memory in search of a match for a man like that. The spectral face, the economical movements, the very short grey hair . . . the walk.

A type comes to the surface from the depths of my mind: ex-military. What else, though? The answer smacks me in the face: mercenary.

If I'm not mistaken, Lacoste has enlisted a specialist to organise this hostage-taking situation.

Time to leave.

I need to call the lawyer.

On my notepad I have written down the gist of what I'm going to say. My watch indicates that it is 3.30 p.m. when a girl answers with a firm voice:

"Monsieur Delambre? Maître Christelle Gilson. What can I do for you?"

She's young. It feels like I'm talking to the intern at B.L.C. Consulting. For a moment, I picture my daughter Lucie, in her lawyer's outfit, answering the telephone to an unemployed guy like me, with the same peremptory tone, the same air of disdain. Why do all these young people seem so similar? Maybe because wimps like me are so similar too.

In a few seconds she confirms that I've been dismissed for misconduct.

"What misconduct?"

"Striking your superior, Monsieur Delambre. You would be fired for that at any company."

"And at any company would a superior have the right to kick a subordinate in the backside?"

"Oh yes, I read that in your statement. But that's not how it happened."

"How can you say that?" I snap. "I was kicked in the backside at 5.00 a.m. What were you doing at 5.00 a.m. that morning?"

The short silence that follows establishes that the interview will be over very soon. I have to iron this out, I absolutely have to find a way in. I glance at my notes.

"Maître Gilson, excuse me for asking, but . . . can I ask how old you are?"

"I don't see what that has to do with anything."

"That's what bothers me. You see, I'm fifty-seven years old. I've been unemployed for over four years and . . ."

"Monsieur Delambre, this is not the time for pleas."

". . . I lose the only job I have. You summon me to court . . ."

My voice has risen very high again.

"It's not me you should be telling this," she says.

". . . and you demand damages that amount to four years of my salary! Are you trying to kill me?"

I'm not sure if the girl is listening to me, but I think she is. I switch to Plan B.

"I am prepared to make a formal apology."

"In writing?" she says after a pause. I have piqued her interest – we're on track.

"Absolutely. Here's what I propose. Your version isn't right at all, but that's fine. I apologise. I won't even ask for my job back. All I want is for this to stop here. Do you understand? No trial, that's all."

The girl thinks for a second.

"I think we can accept your apology. Can you submit it straight away?"

"Tomorrow. No problem. Then it's over to you to terminate proceedings."

"Everything in its own time, Monsieur Delambre. You address a detailed apology to Monsieur Pehlivan as well as your former employer, and then we'll take it from there."

I will need to think all this through, but I've bought some time. I am about to hang up, but there's still something I want to know.

"Actually, Maître Gilson. What makes you so sure that the events occurred as Monsieur Pehlivan described them?"

The girl weighs up whether or not to take the bait. Her silence already speaks volumes. In the end, she bites.

"We have a witness statement. One of your colleagues who was present at the scene guarantees that Monsieur Pehlivan only brushed past you and that . . ."

Romain.

"O.K., O.K., we'll drop it. I'll submit my apology and we'll leave it there. Deal?"

"I look forward to receiving your letter, Monsieur Delambre."

Less than two minutes later I'm in the *métro*.

A few months ago, I went to Romain's place to pick up a hard drive he was lending me. I don't remember the exact address, but I think I'll be able to find it again. I can picture the street pretty well, with a pharmacy on the corner and his building a bit further down on the right. I struggle to remember the number, but then it comes back to me – 57, same as my age. There's an intercom, I press Romain Alquiler's button, and a sleepy voice answers.

As it happens, Romain is not sleepy at all. I find him pale, anxious, his hands shaking. I had forgotten how small his place is. A shoebox. A sliding door shields the "kitchen space", half a square metre lined with stuffed cupboards above a sink the size of a hand. In the main room, his desk – pushed up against the wall and overloaded with computer equipment – occupies half the space. The other half consists of a sofa that must fold out for the night. That's where Romain is sitting. He motions towards an amorphous mass of red plastic on the floor that might be some sort of stool, but I prefer to stay standing. Romain gets to his feet too.

"Listen," he begins, "let me explain . . ."

I silence him with a curt gesture. We are face to face in this tiny space like two rabbits in a hutch. He stops talking and looks at me with blinking eyes. He is scared about what might happen, and with good reason, because I'm not leaving until I get what I came for. Everything depends on him, and that makes me nervous. I spot some beads of sweat on his brow. I shake my head, trying hard to stay calm. I know that this episode between him and me is just a small part of a greater story, the story of our lives. His is easy to understand. Romain comes from a rural, provincial background, and the mentality that stems from those origins governs all his actions and reactions. He has learnt to hold on to whatever he has, to guard it jealously. This applies to jobs as well as everything else. Whether he likes it or not, it's a part of him, his property. And I shake my head again, despite agreeing with him wholeheartedly.

To prove the extent of my detachment, I turn to admire his desk, which is dominated by an enormous flatscreen computer monitor. Technology like that sticks out in a hutch like this. I come back to him. He blinks. His shovel-like hands dangle at the end of his long arms. He'd rather be killed on the spot than back down from something that doesn't matter. Bollocks to it. This is an emergency.

"Keeping your job is vital, Romain. I understand. And I don't hold it against you. In your position, I'd be doing the same. But I have a favour to ask you."

He frowns, as if I were trying to sell him a tractor for an unfeasibly low price. I jab my thumb at the monitor:

"It's for a job, to be precise. I'm on to something. I need you to do a little bit of research for me . . ."

His face brightens. He looks mightily relieved to have escaped so lightly and reaches for his keyboard with a broad smile. Everything in this place is within arm's reach. An electronic jingle welcomes us to the virtual world, and I explain to Romain what I need.

"This might be trickier than you think," he says, his provincial prudence getting the better of him.

But his fingers are already dancing over the keyboard. The B.L.C. Consulting website appears, he spends a second browsing three separate windows that are immediately relegated to the corner of the screen. He's like a conductor. A few clicks later and one, two, three, eight windows burst open in succession. He's only just begun and already I'm lost.

"It's virtually unprotected. What are they, idiots?" Romain says.

"Maybe they don't have anything to protect."

He turns to me, intrigued by such a novel concept.

"Well looking at it from my point of view," I continue, "I can't see what I would need to protect on my computer."

"Err, how about your privacy?"

Romain is horrified. The idea that you wouldn't protect your data, even if it was of no interest, is complete anathema to him. As for me, I find his indignation astonishing.

"If you had access to my private stuff, what would you do with it? It's the same as yours, same as everybody's."

Romain sits there, stubbornly shaking his head.

"Maybe," he says. "But it's yours."

Like talking to a brick wall. I drop it.

His fingers carry on dancing.

"Here, this is their client file."

A list. One second later, the printer beneath his desk stirs into action. Romain emails me some ZIP files. He's disappointed that it was all so easy.

"Anything else you want?"

I have more or less everything. The list, with the heading "Current Clients", is short, and leads to eight sub-files. I skim through their names on my way home. I'm at République now. I get off the train and duck into a corridor towards my connection, all the while scanning the list in my hand. *Exxyal.* I stop abruptly. A girl walks into the back of me and lets out a cry, so I move to the side. I quickly go back through the list to check. Exxyal Europe is the only company that fits the brief. Right scale, strategic industry . . . it's all there. I continue slowly down the corridor – all my energy is focused on this name.

Even for someone like me who knows nothing about oil and gas, Exxyal brings to mind one of those monstrous machines, with thirty-five-thousand employees stationed across four continents and a turnover greater than the Swiss federal budget, enough hidden profit in its coffers to pay off Africa's debt twice over. I don't know where Exxyal Europe sits in the multinational rankings, but it's a heavyweight. I'm on the right track. I go back through the list again: the other companies are relatively hefty small- and medium-sized enterprises, along with a few other big companies of no great consequence working in the manufacturing or tertiary sectors. Additional detail: a hostage-taking is a much more plausible scenario for a firm working in the oil and gas industry than it is for, say, a company manufacturing cars or garden gnomes.

The day ends on a crucial success, the achievement of my first objective: I am almost certain about the identity of the recruiting company.

I drift off for a moment. Head of H.R. at one of Exxyal Europe's offices! It doesn't get any better. I step on it with renewed enthusiasm and arrive home a few minutes later.

As I turn the key in the lock and open the door, I immediately grasp the magnitude of the difficulty that awaits me. A glance at my watch: 7.45 p.m.

I go in.

On the kitchen table I see two large paper bags with the words "Discount Dishes" on the side. Nicole is still wearing her coat. She passes me in the corridor without a word. I've screwed up.

"I'm sorry."

Nicole hears me but she doesn't listen to me. She must have got home at around 6 p.m. Nothing ready for dinner. We've improvised the last three days, but today I had promised to go and buy new dishes. So she must have gone out and done the shopping herself, hence the markedly tense atmosphere at my homecoming. Nicole, without a word, places the new plates, mugs and glasses in the sink. All of it is horrid.

"I know what you're thinking, but it's the cheapest they had," she says, reading my mind.

"That's why I'm looking for a job."

It's like a broken record. We are starting to resent each other. What is so painful is that we have stuck together, stayed in love, through the hardest times, and just as we're coming out the other side, we start pushing each other away. She has bought something in a container with a brown sauce that looks Chinese. It's all ready – we eat it in silence. The atmosphere is so heavy that Nicole turns on the television. The muzak to our marriage. "*Tagwell announces 800 job cuts at Reims factory.*" Nicole chews, looking at her plate, which seems even uglier now that it's full. I pretend to be engrossed in the news, although it's not telling me anything new ("*. . . is soaring. Tagwell was up 4.5% at the close of the markets . . .*").

After dinner, exhausted by the bitterness driving us apart, we go our separate ways without a word: Nicole to the bathroom after doing the washing-up, me to my study. She seems to be in a particularly stubborn mood.

My screen doesn't display any of the balletic movement or graceful orchestration of opening and moving windows: just a businesslike webpage with the B.L.C. Consulting logo. A little envelope indicates the arrival of Romain's emails. In the B.L.C. Consulting client files, I consult the correspondence between Bertrand Lacoste and his client, Alexandre Dorfmann.

This from the C.E.O. of Exxyal Europe: "*Let's be frank: our initial estimates forecast that the 823 redundancies at Sarqueville will, directly or indirectly, involve more than 2,600 people . . . The entire pool of employees will be gravely and permanently affected.*"

A bit later on: "*This complex redundancy programme will add much value: the executive who gains the opportunity to run this confidential mission will find it to be not just an exceptional experience, but no doubt an emotional adventure too. He or she will have to be psychologically sound, reactive, and will have to demonstrate a great capacity for shock-resistance. Moreover, we must be certain of his or her unfailing adherence to our values.*"

On a pad I jot down:
Sarqueville = strategic challenge for Exxyal
∴ *Essential selection of highly efficient executive*

to manage the issue
∴ *Hostage-taking as test to choose the best*
from potential candidates.

All I need to do now is identify the candidates. But rummaging through Lacoste's client file reveals no sign of a list of executives for assessment. I comb through everything again from the start, reviewing files in other folders in case they were simply in the wrong order, but I already know it's futile. Maybe Lacoste doesn't have it yet. I'll need to look for it myself.

The only thing on the Exxyal homepage aside from a diagrammatic overview of the group's structure is a photograph of the C.E.O., Alexandre Dorfmann, sitting pretty in the centre of the page. Roughly sixty years old. Thinning hair, a fairly strong nose, a flinty expression, and a discreet smile at the camera that betrays the unwavering self-assurance of a powerful man at the pinnacle of his career, reaping the rewards that his success is due. Sometimes arrogance can be so blatant it makes you want to throw a punch. I study the photograph. If I cock my head to the right, I can see my reflection in the mirror hanging above the corner chimney. I come back to the photograph. I observe my negative. At fifty-seven, I still have all my hair, albeit with a few grey strands, a rounded face, and a boundless capacity for self-doubt. Apart from our determination, we are complete opposites.

In Lacoste's client files, I find a detailed prospectus for the whole of Exxyal Europe, which I print off. Armed with the criteria I derived from my B.L.C. document, I go through all the Exxyal executives that might correspond with my research, ending up with a list of eleven potential candidates. That's good going, but it's still too many, and that's the problem: the first sift is always the easiest. From now on, I can't afford any mistakes. Every time I eliminate a candidate, my risk of failure is at its maximum. I open a document, copy and paste the eleven names, and rub my hands as though I were placing a bet at the roulette table.

The door opens. It's Nicole.

Is it because of her intense fatigue, or because she's wearing a T-shirt for bed? Is it because she leans her shoulder against the doorframe and tilts her head in that way that always makes me want to cry? I pretend to massage my forehead, but I'm actually checking the time in the corner of the screen – 22:40. Too wrapped up in my own business to notice the evening pass by. I look up.

Normally in these situations, if she's happy she'll speak to me. If she isn't, I stand up and walk over to her. This time, both of us hold our ground in our respective corners of the room.

Why won't she understand?

In all the time we have lived together, this is the only question I have never asked myself. Not until today. Never. Today there is an ocean between us.

"I know what you're thinking," Nicole says. "You think I don't understand how important this is to you. You're telling yourself that I have my own little life, my little job, and that I've grown used to having an unemployed husband. And that I think you're incapable of finding a job that's worthy of you."

"It's a little of all those things. Not entirely, but a little."

Nicole walks up to my desk and stops in front of me. I'm sitting down, she's standing. She takes my head and holds it against her belly. I move my hand under her T-shirt and let it rest on her bottom. We've done this for twenty years and still the sensation is nothing short of miraculous. The desire is still there, even today. Except that today the ocean separating us is not between us but within us. We are a couple.

I pull away from her. Nicole contemplates the dancing fish of my screensaver.

"What do you want me to do?" I say.

"Anything but this. It's just . . . it's not good. When you start doing things like this . . ."

This would be the moment to explain to her that Mehmet's

kick in the arse will be forcing an additional humiliation on me later tonight: writing a formal apology. But I would be ashamed to admit to it. Same with telling her that the job centre is going to have fewer and fewer jobs for me thanks to my dismissal for gross misconduct. And that compared to what we have in store, buying ugly and cheap tableware will feel like the crowning glory of our many years of blissful happiness. I decide against it.

"O.K."

"O.K. what?"

She takes a step back and holds me by the shoulders. I'm still cupping her hips in my hands.

"I'll drop it."

"Seriously?"

I'm a bit ashamed of this lie, but like all the others, it's necessary.

Nicole holds me tight. I can feel the relief in every part of her embrace.

"None of this is your fault, Alain," she says, trying to express herself. "There's nothing you can do about it. But this whole job hunt . . . We won't come out of it in one piece if we stop respecting each other. Don't you agree?"

There's too much to say to that. I think I've played my cards right. I nod. Nicole runs her fingers through my hair, her tummy hugging against my shoulder, her buttocks tensed. This is what I'm fighting for, to keep all this. Getting her to understand is impossible. I have to do it without her and then present her with the finished article. I want to be the hero in her life again.

"Are you coming to bed?" she says.

"Five minutes. One email and I'm there."

She turns and smiles at me from the door.

"Will you be quick?"

There can't be more than two men in a thousand capable of turning down an offer like that. But I'm one of them.

"Two minutes."

I think about writing the letter to the lawyer, but tell myself I'll have time to do it tomorrow. My attention is drawn inexorably back to the list. One click and the fish give way to the Exxyal Europe website.

Eleven potential candidates that I need to narrow down to five: three men, two women. I go back through the list cross-referencing ages and degree subjects, then I take them one by one and focus on retracing their careers. I find them on different networks or alumni associations where some people give summaries of their careers. To head up the massive redundancy programme at Sarqueville, they will need to have solid leadership experience and have already carried out difficult or sensitive assignments that have caught the eye of senior management. This approach helps me reduce it to eight. Still three too many. Two men and one woman. But I can't do any better. It would already be an enormous stroke of luck if the five I'm looking for are in these eight.

I do a bit of flicking between the Exxyal site and the professional networks where I found a few of them and draw up a profile for each one.

My desk isn't that big, so for one of my birthdays Nicole gave me a set of cork boards to pin documents to: six large boards attached to the back of the door which fan open like the pages of a giant book.

I tear down the stuff that's been there for an age: yellowing job ads, lists of potential employers or training schemes that I'm too old to be eligible for, details of colleagues working in H.R. for other companies and whom I came across frequently in a professional association that I am no longer a member of. I run off large mugshots of each candidate along with their career profiles, leaving plenty of room for notes, and pin the whole thing on the cork boards.

I take a step back to admire my work. Now I can browse my full-size dossier. I have left the outer boards blank, so when I close it you can't see anything.

I don't hear the door behind me open. But the sound of Nicole's tears does attract my attention. I turn around, and there she is in her big white T-shirt. It's been two, maybe three hours since I promised to join her. Since I promised to relinquish everything. She takes in the series of colourful portraits and blown-up C.V.s, and without a word she moves her head from left to right. It's the most devastating thing she could have done.

I open my mouth, but there's no point.

Nicole has already left. I quickly load the files from Romain onto a U.S.B. stick, plug in my laptop to charge the battery, shut down my P.C., close the cork boards that make up my wall display, head into the bathroom, and arrive in the bedroom to find it empty.

"Nicole!"

My voice echoes strangely through the night. It sounds like loneliness. I go to the kitchen, the sitting room . . . no-one. I call out again, but Nicole doesn't reply.

A few steps further and I'm outside the door of the guest room, which is closed. I grab the handle.

Locked.

I didn't just make a mistake, I lied too. I feel terrible. But I have to stay philosophical. When I've nailed down this job, she'll realise I was right.

I take myself to bed. Tomorrow is a big day.

9

My head didn't stop spinning with the same questions all night. If I were in Lacoste's shoes, how would I handle this? There is a hell of a difference between deciding to do a role play and actually staging one. Nicole's questions come back to me: commandos, weapons, interrogations . . .

Soon it'll be 5.00 a.m. I left for "work" like normal and am now settled in a giant brasserie by Gare de l'Est. At the counter, I pick up a copy of *Le Parisien*: "*Paris Bourse booming. Ninth consecutive week of growth.*" I flick through as I wait for my coffee: "*. . . Tansonville factory cleared by police. The 48 employees occupying the premises . . .*"

Having settled at a table at the very back of the largest room, my laptop lies open in front of me as I drink a revolting coffee, waiting for the system to start up. This is a proper rail station cafeteria. Besides a handful of Togolese street sweepers joking around on their break, the other early birds include insomniac drunkards, night workers finishing their shifts, taxi drivers, exhausted couples and wasted kids. This dawn underworld makes for a depressing sight. I'm the only person in the room slogging away, but I'm not the only one in distress. I open the files saved on the U.S.B. stick from last night.

In amongst Lacoste's correspondence, I find two notes written by a certain David Fontana, possibly the bloke I saw at B.L.C.

headquarters. The first is about hiring Arab actors and acquiring weapons loaded with blanks. The second contains a map of the premises where the hostage-taking is to be held. Judging by his style and given his field, this Fontana must be ex-military. I log on to the brasserie's WiFi and look him up. My failure to find him confirms my suspicions. So discreet he doesn't feature anywhere, at least not under that name. I jot down a mental reminder: establish his identity, find out where he comes from.

Right from the off, I know I'll need help. Another essential quality for any H.R. manager is the ability to assemble skill sets. That's management rule no. 2.

I love the Internet. You can find anything on it, however vile. The Web really is made in the image of Western society's subconscious.

It takes me a little over an hour to find the site I need. It has police officers, former police officers, future police officers, police fans – and there's a whole lot more of them than you might think. I spend a while chatting with the other users online, but without much success. At this time of day there's just the drop-outs and the unemployed. No interest. The safest bet would be to place an ad. I'm a novelist searching for very precise information on hostage-taking. I need a user with experience in this type of situation. I give an email address created specially for the occasion, but I change my mind. Time is of the essence: I give my mobile number and cross the first item off my pad.

The following part of my research brings very bad news. Private detective rates vary from 50 to 120 euros per hour. I do the numbers – it's disastrous. Yet I'm struggling to come up with an alternative solution. I have to investigate these eight execs, not just their professional bios but their private lives too. I gather three or four addresses of detective firms offering their services to businesses, and which don't seem either overly prestigious or patently dodgy. Even if it is a bit of a lottery, I choose the ones located closest to where I am now. It's just before 8.00 a.m. when I hit the road.

It doesn't matter what office or company, the manager I meet with always resembles the person I was before, back when I was confident in my skills and still had somewhere to apply them.

"I see," he says.

Philippe Mestach. Mid-forties, calm, organised, methodical, normal build. Basically the sort of person who goes unnoticed. I decide to tell it to him straight. I talk about a job opportunity, but I don't mention the nature of the role play, simply explaining the aims of the assessment the five employees are to undergo. He clocks exactly what I'm up to.

"So you're definitely loading the odds in your favour," he says. "But the timescale's not on our side. We often investigate people on behalf of their employers – it's a growth market for us. Unfortunately, in our line of work, the quality of the result is often contingent on the time invested in it."

"How much?"

He smiles. Let's cut to the chase.

"You're right," he says, "that is what it comes down to. Shall we run through everything?"

He tallies up all my requirements, does some calculations on a little pocket calculator, and pauses for a long moment's reflection. He stares at the figures, returns the gadget to his pocket, then looks up at me.

"All in: 15,000 euros. No hidden costs. Thirteen thousand if you pay in cash."

"What can you guarantee?"

"Four full-time investigators and — "

I cut him off.

"No, I mean results! What can you guarantee?"

"You give us the names of your 'clients', we find their addresses and then for each one we give you their marital status, detailed family history, information on assets, the salient aspects of their private and professional lives, as well as a broad outline of their current financial situation (obligations, availabilities, etc.)."

"That's it?"

He raises a perplexed eyebrow. I carry on:

"What do you expect me to do with general stuff like that? I'll end up with a whole bunch of Mr Averages."

"The country is populated entirely by average people, Monsieur Delambre. Me, you, them – everyone."

"I'm looking for something more targeted."

"Like?"

"Debts, professional misconduct at a previous job, family problems, younger sister in the hospice, alcoholic wife, naughty habits, speeding fines, orgies, lovers, mistresses, secret lives, Achilles heels … That sort of thing."

"Anything's possible, Monsieur Delambre. But there again, the clock's against us. What's more, to dig this deep, we must use very specific channels, nurture relationships, follow up leads, not to mention get lucky."

"How much?"

He smiles again. It's not so much the wording he enjoys as the directness of the request.

"We must be methodical, Monsieur Delambre. Here's what I suggest. Two days after your first payment, we will provide you with the main information pertaining to each of your clients. You study these, you focus your research criteria so that we can target our approach, and I give you a quote."

"I'd rather pay a flat rate."

He takes out his little calculator and taps in some numbers.

"For an additional two days' investigation: 2,500 euros per client. Including bribes."

"And in cash?"

"That's the price in cash. By invoice, that would be …"

More number-crunching.

"Don't bother. I get it."

It's colossal. If I only pay the additional fee for half my execs, I'm still looking at 23,000 euros. Even with the entire remainder of our savings, I'm 95% shy of the sum.

"Think it through, but don't take too long. Once you confirm, I will need to assemble a team very quickly . . ."

I stand up, shake his hand and get back on the *métro*.

This is the moment of truth. I've known it since the start. The arguments with Nicole, the nerves of the last few days, the tension surrounding the aptitude tests and the interview with Lacoste . . . everything has just been a precursor to this final stage, which rests on one single, critical issue: the question of how far I am willing to go.

To succeed, I must take every risk.

I can't make up my mind.

I feel terribly depressed.

My eyes skim over the adverts on the *métro*, over the relentless boarding and disembarking of passengers. My feet carry me up the escalator automatically, and here I am at the street where we live, in this neighbourhood that we fell in love with immediately from the second we first saw it.

It was 1991.

Everything was going well for us. We had been married for more than ten years. Mathilde was nine and Lucie seven. I called them all sorts of silly names, "my princesses", and all that. Even then Nicole was radiant, you just need to look at the photos. We were a very French couple, with fixed jobs and reasonable, climbing salaries. Our bank informed us that we could make it onto the property ladder. Acutely aware of the responsibility, I took a map of Paris and marked out the areas where it was realistic to look, and almost at once we found somewhere right on the other side of town.

That's where I am now. I leave the *métro*. I remember. I can replay the scene perfectly in my mind.

The charm of the place struck us straight away. The neighbourhood sits on a little hill, the streets weaving up and down; the buildings, like the trees, have been there a century. Ours is a tidy, red-brick job. Without saying anything, we hoped that our apartment would be one of those with bow windows. As the lift juddered I swiftly estimated that we'd be able to fit all the household appliances in it except the sofa. The estate agent looked at his feet, very professional, opened the door, and the apartment was incredibly light because it was so high up, and it only cost 15% more than what we could borrow. We were eager and panicky in equal measure. It was exhilarating. The bank manager rubbed his hands and offered us additional funding. We bought it, we completed, we picked up the keys, dropped off the girls with some friends, and returned just the two of us, and the apartment seemed even bigger to us. Nicole flung open the windows that look out behind over a schoolyard with three plane trees. The rooms echoed with the emptiness to be filled and the fun to be had, with the life that was smiling on us, and Nicole grabbed me by the waist and pinned me against the kitchen wall, taking my breath away with a ferocious kiss, buzzing with excitement, but I realised I'd have to hold fire until later because she was off again, walking from room to room, outlining her grand plans with big, birdlike waves of her arms.

We were in debt up to our necks, but despite the impending disaster, by some miracle, by some fate we weren't even aware of, we got through those years unscathed. The secret to our happiness in those days was not love (we've always had that), nor was it the girls (we still have them too); no, the secret to our happiness was that we had work, that we could, no questions asked, enjoy the innumerable positive consequences of our unimaginable good luck: paid bills, holidays, outings, university enrolment fees, cars and the certainty that our diligent, determined work would reward us the way we deserved.

I am at this same place again almost twenty years later, but I feel a century older.

I hear Nicole's tears, I'm in my study, I see her tattered cardigan, the discount dishes, and I dial a telephone number and ask for Gregory Lippert. The lino in the kitchen is curling up again (it'll need changing), and I say "Hi, it's Grandpa", trying to apply a jocular tone, but my voice betrays my true intentions. The makeshift sink is more desperate than ever, and I need to find a unit to stick on the wall, and he says "Huh?", surprised because I don't call him often, and I say "I need to see you", and he says "Huh" again. It disgusts me already but I need him, I'm insistent – "immediately" – and he realises it's really, truly urgent, so he says: "I can manage a few minutes, shall we say eleven?"

10

The café is called Le Balto. There must be about two or three thousand just like it in France. Typical of my son-in-law to choose a place like this. I bet he has his lunch here every day, first-name terms with the waiters, enjoying a quick scratch-card with the secretaries while cracking hilarious jokes about "lucky dips". There's a *tabac* in the corner of a large room with knackered seats, Formica furniture, shiny tiles on the floor, and on the terrace window a roll-down menu with pictures of hot dogs and sandwiches for the dipshit customers who can't assimilate the words "hot dogs" and "sandwiches".

I'm early.

A big flatscreen, positioned very high on the wall, is tuned to a rolling-news channel. The volume is right down. Even so, the customers propping up the bar are glued to the screen, watching the headlines streaming across the bottom: *"Business profits: 7% to employees and 36% to shareholders – Forecast: 3 million unemployed by end of year."*

I reflect on how lucky I am to be job-hunting in this climate.

Gregory is keeping me waiting. I'm not convinced there is any particular reason – I can picture him deliberately making himself a little late, his way of showing me what a big deal he is.

On the next-door table, two young guys in suits, insurance types, not unlike my son-in-law, are finishing their coffee.

"No, no I promise you," says one, "it's ridiculously funny! It's called 'On the Streets'. You play a homeless guy. The aim of the game is to survive."

"What, like integrate back into society?" asks the other.

"Don't be so fucking stupid! No, the aim is to survive. You have these three key factors – three compulsory things . . . You can't avoid them, you just do what you can to keep them in check. There's cold, hunger and alcoholism."

"Brilliant!"

"It's hilarious, I swear! Shit, we had fun! You play with dice, but it's a game of tactics. You can earn free meals, nights in hostels, a spot in a heated *métro* entrance (those are the hardest to get!), cardboard boxes for when it's cold, access to railway station toilets to wash … No, I promise, it's fricking hard!"

"But who do you play against?"

The guy hesitates for a second.

"You play for yourself, buddy! That's the beauty of the game!"

Gregory arrives and shakes hands with the two guys (I called it). They leave as Gregory sits down opposite me.

He's wearing a steel-grey suit with one of those pastel shirts that always bring to mind a kitchen colour scheme, all sky blue or pale mauve. Today it's waxy yellow with a beige tie.

When I left Bercaud, I had four suits and a shedload of shirts and ties. I loved it, the whole dressing-up thing. Nicole used to call me an "old tart" because I had more clothes than she did. I was the only dad you could give a tie to for Father's Day two years running without being reprimanded. The only ties I never wore were the ones from Mathilde. She has appalling taste: her husband is living, breathing proof.

So, I used to have four suits. Shortly after I was made redundant, Nicole started insisting that I throw away the oldest ones, but I refused. From my first day of unemployment, I wore a suit every time I left the house. And not just for appointments at the job centre or the occasional interviews I managed to line up. No, I went to Pharmaceutical Logistics at 5.00 a.m. wearing a suit and tie. A bit like a prisoner who shaves every morning to hold on to a shred of the self-respect they feared they had lost. But one day, on my way home, the stitching on my favourite suit came undone on the *métro*. It ripped open from the armpit to the pocket. Two girls standing next to me burst out laughing. One of them held up her hand in apology, but she couldn't help herself. I maintained an air of dignity. All of a sudden, a few of the other passengers started giggling too. I got off at the next station, removed my jacket and slung it over my shoulder, like a trendy businessman on a hot day, even though we were in January. When I arrived home, I threw away everything that was more than four or five years old. All I kept was one clean suit and a few shirts, which I'm saving. They still have the see-through plastic cover from the last trip to the dry-cleaner's. My clothes are wrapped in cotton wool, like antiques. The first thing I'll do if I land this job is get measured up for a tailored suit. That wasn't even a luxury I allowed myself when I was in work.

I'm tense.

"You seem tense," Gregory says, with his usual subtlety.

As he scrutinises me more closely, however, he notices my desolate expression and remembers how I'd told him that I needed to see him, something that has never happened in all the time we've known each other. He gathers himself, clears his throat, and offers a little supportive smile.

"I need a loan, Gregory. Twenty-five thousand euros. Today."

I realise this is a lot of information for him to take in. But after thinking through all the possible approaches, I'd come to the conclusion that it was better to get straight to the heart of the matter. It works. My son-in-law's mouth hangs open in silence. I feel an urge to shut his lower jaw with my fingertips, but I resist.

"It's vital, Gregory. It's for a job. I have a one-off opportunity to land my perfect job. All I need is 25,000 euros."

"You're buying a job for 25,000 euros?"

"Something like that. It's too complicated to explain everything in detail, but — "

"No chance, Alain."

"What, buying a job?"

"No, lending you that amount. No way. In your situation . . ."

"Exactly, son! That's why I'm a reliable customer. I'll be able to repay you easily once I've got the job. It's a very short-term loan I need. A few months, that's it."

He's struggling to keep up, so I clarify.

"O.K., you've got me . . . I'm not literally buying a job. It's . . ."

"A bribe?"

I make a pained expression and reluctantly agree.

"That's shameful! They can't make you pay to get a job. It's illegal, apart from anything else!"

This makes my blood boil.

"Listen, my boy. What's allowed and what's illegal is another matter entirely! Do you know how long I've been unemployed?"

I'm shouting. He tries to simmer things down:

"It's been . . ."

"Four years!"

My voice has become very shrill. This is driving me close to the edge.

"*Have you ever been unemployed?*"

I'm bellowing now. Gregory looks around the room, afraid of making a scene. I have to ram home this advantage, so I raise my voice a notch higher. I want this loan, I want him to back down, I want a memorandum of understanding. I'm determined he will give me his word.

"You can shove your stupid morals up your arse! You've got a job, and all I'm asking you is to help me find one! Is it that complicated? Hey – is it that complicated?"

He motions at me to calm down. I try a different tactic. I move closer and talk in a hushed tone.

"You could lend me 25,000 euros for whatever, a car, a fitted kitchen . . . There we go, that'll work, a fitted kitchen – you've seen ours. And then I repay in twelve months. One thousand seven-hundred euros per month plus interest is not a problem, I'm telling you, there's no risk for you."

He doesn't answer but looks me in the eye with renewed self-assurance. The look of a professional. In just a few seconds my status has changed. Now I'm negotiating a loan. Before I was his father-in-law. Now I'm a client.

"It's out of the question, Alain," he says firmly. "To lend an amount like that, we need guarantees."

"I'll have a job."

"Yes, maybe, but right now you don't."

"The job title is H.R. manager. It's for a very big company."

Gregory frowns. Another change of status: now he's taking me for a fool. The situation is slipping away from me. I attempt a reboot.

"Fine, what do people need to get 25,000 euros from you lot?"

"Sufficient income."

"How much?"

"Listen, Alain, this is no way to go about it."

"O.K., what if I have a guarantor?"

His eyes light up.

"Who?"

"I dunno. You."

His eyes close.

"It's impossible! We're buying a flat! Our debt ratio will never stretch –"

I grab his hands across the table and grip them in mine.

"Listen to me, Gregory."

I realise I've only got one round left, and I'm not sure I have the courage to fire it.

"I've never asked you for anything."

This is going to require a lot of energy. A whole lot.

"The thing is, I don't have any other options."

I look down at our intertwined hands and rally my thoughts. Because this is tough, really tough.

"You're my only hope."

I gather my strength between each word, trying hard to focus elsewhere, like a first-time prostitute limbering up for her debut blowjob.

"I must have this money. It's vital."

Good God, I'm not going to have to stoop this low, am I?

"Gregory . . ."

I swallow back my saliva. Fuck it.

"I'm begging you."

There, I said it.

He's as stunned as I am.

His profession as a usurer has led to countless family disputes, and now here I am, sitting in front of him begging for the charity of a loan. The situation is so improbable that it leaves us both feeling dizzy for a while. I took the gamble that this surprise strategy would make him do a U-turn, but Gregory shakes his head.

"If only it were down to me . . . You know I would. But there's no way I can fast-track a case. I have bosses. I don't exactly know what your income is, Alain, or Nicole's, but I doubt . . . If you needed three thousand, or even five thousand, we could see, but . . ."

What happens next is, I think, attributable to just one word. Begging. I shouldn't have begged him. I did something that can never be undone. I realised it was a mistake before I'd even said it, but I did it anyway. As I lean back in my chair and twist round to my right, like I'm about to scratch my arse, I am not completely conscious of my actions, but I am sure that they are the inevitable consequence of a single word. Ghastly wars must have been waged like this, because of a single word.

I wind up, gather all my strength, and slam my fist into his face. He wasn't expecting that at all. It's instant chaos. My clenched fist strikes him between the cheekbone and the jaw, his body is flung backwards, and his hands reach out in a desperate reflex to grab hold of the table. He's flung back two metres, crashing into another table and taking two chairs with him, his arms flailing around for support as he falls, his head smacking into the post behind him and his throat letting out a rasping, bestial yelp. All the regulars turn around as the din of shattered glass, broken chairs and upturned tables is replaced by stunned silence. The space in front of me is clear. I clutch my fist so hard against my stomach that it hurts. Then, to everyone's bewilderment, I stand up and leave.

I have gone from never flooring anyone in my entire life to doing it twice in the space of a few days: first my Turkish supervisor, now my son-in-law. There's no escaping it. I have become a violent man.

I'm back in the street.

I am yet to grasp how damaging the results of my actions will be.

But before worrying about that, I intend to solve my one problem, my one and only problem: finding these 25,000 euros.

11

Having laid my son-in-law out for the count, I continue on my way. From the outside, anyone might think I've lost all feeling. Once upon a time, I knew myself well. I mean that my behaviour rarely surprised me. When you've experienced most situations, you also learn the correct responses to them. You even notice the circumstances where self-control isn't necessary. Family scuffles with pricks like my son-in-law, for example. Past a certain age, life starts repeating on itself. The thing is, anything you do or don't acquire through experience alone you can learn in two or three days' worth of management seminars, with the aid of grids that class people according to their character. The process is practical, it's playful, it boosts your spirits at little cost, and it makes you feel clever. It even lets you imagine you might become more efficient in the workplace. In short, it soothes you. Over the years, trends have changed, and so have the criteria. One year you get tested to see if you are methodical, energetic, cooperative or determined. The next it might be to check if you're hard-working, precocious, pioneering, persistent, empathetic or blue-sky-thinking. If you have a new coach, it turns out you are protective, directive, putative, emotive or responsive, while the next session you attend helps discern whether you're action-, method-, idea- or procedure-oriented. The whole thing's a hoax, but no-one can get enough of it. It's like with horoscopes, where you always end up identifying traits that match your own. The reality is that you never know what you're truly capable of until you find yourself in extreme circumstances. Right now, for example, I'm surprising myself a lot.

My telephone rings as I'm leaving the *métro*. I'm always wary when things are moving too fast, and things are moving too fast now.

"My name is Albert Kaminski."

A pleasant, open voice, but it's too soon. Come on, I only posted the ad this morning and already . . .

"I believe I can offer you what you're looking for," he tells me.

"And what is it I'm looking for?"

"You're a novelist. You're writing a book that revolves around a hostage-taking and you need practical, concrete advice. Precise information. Unless I misread your advertisement?"

He is well-spoken and not at all fazed by my direct question. Seems solid. I get the impression he is calling from a public place where he has to keep his voice down.

"And you have personal experience in this field?"

"Of course."

"That's what everyone says."

"I've experienced several real hostage situations, all with different circumstances and in the recent past. Last few years. If your questions are about how this sort of operation unfolds, then I think I'll be able to answer most of them. If you want to meet me, here's my number: 06 34 . . ."

"Wait!"

There's no doubt he's skilled. He speaks calmly, he doesn't get annoyed by my deliberately aggressive questions, and he's even managed to wrest back the initiative, since I'm the one requesting a meeting. This could well be my guy.

"Are you free this afternoon?"

"Depends what time."

"You tell me . . ."

"From 2.00 p.m."

It's a date. He suggests a café near Châtelet.

What will have happened since my departure? It must have taken my son-in-law some time to get back on his feet. I picture him spreadeagled on the floor right in the middle of the room. The owner comes running up, slips his hand under his head, and says: "Wow, my man, you seem pretty shaken up! Who was that guy?" Ultimately, though, I don't know Gregory that well. I have no idea whether he's brave, for example. Maybe he stands up and dusts himself down to salvage some dignity. Or maybe he starts yelling: "I'll kill him, the bastard!" That line always seems pathetic. The big question, of course, is whether he'll call Mathilde now or wait until this evening. My entire strategy hinges on that decision.

The entrance to the *lycée* where Mathilde teaches English is located down a side street. At lunchtime, there are always loads of kids loitering on the pavement outside. Plenty of heckling, noise, rowdiness – boys and girls spilling over with white-hot hormones. I keep my distance, huddled in the doorway to an apartment block. Mathilde picks up quickly. There's a racket going on at her end as well as mine. She's surprised. I can tell that her husband hasn't called her yet. The window of opportunity is very narrow, and it is essential I don't let it close.

"Here? Now? Is it Maman, is something wrong? Where am I? Outside, but where?"

"No, it's not Maman, don't worry, nothing serious, I need to see you that's all, yes it's urgent, in the street, just here . . . If you've got five minutes … Yes, straight away."

Mathilde is prettier than her sister. Less beautiful, less alluring, but definitely prettier. She's wearing a delightful printed dress, the sort of dress you notice on a woman straight away. She has an attractive, swaying walk that reminds me a bit of Nicole, but her expression is anxious, fearful.

It's so hard to explain, but I get there in the end. My request is hardly crystal clear, but Mathilde latches onto the bottom line: 25,000 euros.

"But, Papa! We need it for the flat. We've signed the preliminary contract!"

"I know, my angel, but the sale's not for another three months. I'll have paid you back well before then."

Mathilde is very flustered. She starts pacing around the street, three angry steps this way, three mortified steps back.

"Why do you need this money?"

I tried the same tactic on her hubby an hour ago, and I know it won't go down well this time either, but right now it's all I have.

"A bribe? Twenty-five thousand euros for a bribe? That's crazy!"

I nod bitterly.

Four more nervous paces along the pavement, then she turns to me:

"Papa, I'm sorry, but I can't."

She has a lump in her throat, and she's looking me straight in the eye. She has summoned up all her courage. I'll have to tread carefully.

"Angel . . ."

"No Papa, don't 'angel' me! No emotional blackmail, I'm warning you!"

Looks like I'll have to tread very, very carefully. I put forward my argument as calmly as I can.

"How do you intend to pay me back in two months?"

Mathilde is a practical woman who never strays from concrete fact, and she always asks the right questions. Even when she was little, the moment we needed to plan anything – a trip, a picnic, a party – her hand would be the first to go up. Her wedding required almost eight months' preparation. Everything was arranged with military precision . . . I've never been so bloody bored in my whole life. Maybe that's why she seems so distant from me sometimes.

She's standing in front of me. I suddenly ask myself what I'm *really* doing here. I shoo away the image of Gregory sprawled across the café floor, his cheek pressed up against the pillar.

"Are you sure they'll pay an advance to someone they've only just hired?"

Mathilde has agreed to discuss the matter. She doesn't realise it yet, but her refusal is now long gone. She's still prowling up and down the pavement, just more slowly now, keeping nearer and returning quicker.

She's hurting, and it's starting to make me hurt too. I've been so caught up in my own helter-skelter situation that I've lost all qualms. If I had to lay out her cretin of a husband again, I'd do it in a flash, but now, suddenly, I feel bereft. My daughter is before me, torn apart by her conflicting obligations, a genuine moral dilemma: her home or her father. She has saved up this money; it is the sum of her life's hopes and dreams.

It's her printed dress that rescues me: I realise that the shoes and bag are matching. The sort of outfit that Nicole should be able to afford.

Mathilde is canny when it comes to hitting the sales, one of those women who goes on scouting missions two months in advance and who, by sheer force of preparation and strategy, one day manages to purchase her dream skirt suit despite it being wildly beyond her means. Mathilde must be the result of some freak genetic quirk, since neither of her parents are capable of such an achievement. I'm sure it's what attracted her husband to her.

Speaking of whom . . . I picture him back in his office. A secretary will have brought him a freezer bag full of ice cubes as he considers whether or not to sue his father-in-law. He'll be fantasising about a judge – the long arm of the law – issuing the sentence loud and clear. Gregory gleefully immerses himself in the scenario: he leaves the courtroom in triumph, his wife weeping by his side.

Mathilde looks down, forced to recognise that her husband's values are superior to her father's. She is torn. But not Gregory. Awash with sanctimony and righteous anger, fearless and upstanding, Gregory sweeps down the steps of the Palais de Justice, which has never before been so deserving of its name. Behind him is me, his father-in-law, broken and battered, gasping for breath, begging . . . There's that word again. Begging. I had to beg him.

Me.

I press on:

"Mathilde, I need this money. Your mother and I both need it. To survive. I'll pay back whatever you're able to lend me. But I'm not going to beg you."

Then I do something terrible: I bow my head and walk away. One step, two steps, three . . . I walk quickly because the momentum is in my favour. I'm ashamed, but I have to be resilient. To get this job, to save my family, to save my daughters, I have to be resilient.

"Papa!"

Score!

I close my eyes as the scale of my deceit dawns on me. I turn back. I will never forgive the system for what it is doing to me. Fine, it's me who is rolling around in the mud, me who is being vile, but in exchange, may the gods of the system give me what I'm due. May they let me back in the game, back in the world. Let me be human again. Be alive. May they give me this job.

Mathilde has tears in her eyes.

"How much exactly do you need?"

"Twenty-five thousand."

The die is cast. It's over. The rest is just formalities, and Mathilde knows how to take care of those. I have won.

My ticket to hell is guaranteed.

I can breathe.

"You have to promise me," she begins.

She detects so much confidence in me that she can't help but smile.

"I can swear to whatever you want, my angel. When do you exchange?"

"We don't have an exact date. Two months . . ."

"I'll have paid you back, angel, cross my heart."

I pretend to spit on my hand.

She hesitates.

"Because . . . I'm not going to say anything to Gregory, alright? So I'm counting on you . . ."

Before I can even answer, she has grabbed her mobile to ring the bank.

All around us the schoolchildren are yelling, jostling, taking the piss out of each other, drunk with the joys of being alive and fancying each other. For them, life is nothing but one huge prospect. We are here, my daughter and I, standing in the midst of them, both of us bolt upright as the tide of youthful enthusiasm pitches up from side to side. All of a sudden Mathilde seems less pretty, somewhat faded in her dress that now seems less elegant, more ordinary. I have a think and it comes to me: my daughter looks like her mother. Because she's afraid of what she is doing, because her father's situation is wearing down her resistance, Mathilde seems jaded. Her chic outfit even takes on the appearance of a tired cardigan.

She's on the telephone, and gives me an inquisitive look.

"In cash, yes," she confirms.

It's a wrap. She raises an eyebrow at me and I close my eyes.

"I can be there around 5.15 p.m.," she says. "Yes, I realise twenty-five thousand is a lot in cash."

The bank manager is not taking this lying down. He likes his money.

"The sale won't be happening for another two months at least . . . By then . . . Yes, no problem. Five o'clock, yes, perfect."

She hangs up, terrified at having crossed the point of no return. My daughter resembles me, now. She's broken.

We stay there without saying anything, just looking. A wave of love rolls right through my body. Without thinking I say, "Thank you." It hits Mathilde like an electric shock. She helps me, she loves me, she hates me, she's scared, she's ashamed. No father should provoke so many powerful emotions in a daughter, or take up so much space in her life.

She returns to the school in silence, her shoulders limp.

I have to be back at 5.00 p.m. to accompany her to the bank. In the meantime, I call Philippe Mestach, the detective.

"You'll get your advance tomorrow morning. Nine a.m. at your office? Go ahead and assemble your team."

Châtelet.

It's sort of a brasserie, but with leather armchairs. The chic end of shabby-chic. The kind of place I would have loved when I had a salary.

When I see him, the first thing that comes back to me is his voice. It seemed borrowed, as if speaking irritated him. He barely stirs, or if he does it's very subtle, like slow-motion. He's thin. I find him very strange-looking. Like an iguana.

"Albert Kaminski."

He hasn't stood up, just leaned forward a little, holding out his hand indifferently. First impression: -10. It's a poor start, a major handicap, and I don't have much time to lose. I have objectives.

I sit straight-backed at the edge of the armchair, no intention of staying for long.

He's the same age as me. We sit in silence as the waiter takes our order. I try to figure out what is bothering me about him, then it hits me. He's a druggie. This is a tricky area for me, because, as astonishing as it might sound, I've never touched them. For a man of my generation, that's nothing short of miraculous. So when it comes to drugs, I'm not exactly a natural, but I think I've put my finger on it. Kaminski is all over the place. He's in free fall. We could be cousins. Our fall might not be the same, but our desperation is. I back away. I need strong people: skilful, operational.

"I used to be a commandant in the police," he begins.

His face is creased, but his eyes are dry. Nothing like Charles. Alcohol ravages you in a different way. What's he on? I don't have a clue, but it's clear that this inspector has lost none of his self-esteem.

Latest score: -8.

"I spent most of my career doing special operations at R.A.I.D. That's why I answered your ad."

"Why aren't you there anymore?"

He smiles and looks down.

"I don't mean to pry, but how old are you?" he says.

"More than fifty, less than sixty."

"Roughly the same as me, then."

"What's that got to do with anything?"

"By the time you get to our age, you can spot certain types right away: gays, racists, fascists, hypocrites, alcoholics. Drug addicts. And you, Monsieur . . . ?"

"Delambre. Alain Delambre."

". . . I can tell you see me for what I am, Monsieur Delambre. So that's my answer to your question."

We smile at each other. -4.

"I used to be a negotiator. I was struck off from the police eight years ago. Professional misconduct."

"Anything serious?"

"There was a fatality. A woman, a desperate case. I was a little high. Ecstasy. She threw herself out the window."

Anyone who can cancel out a ten-point deficit in just a few minutes is someone capable of faking compassion, proximity, similarity. In short, a good cheat. In the Bertrand Lacoste mould. Either that or they're extremely sincere.

"And you think I can trust someone like you?"

He thinks for a moment.

"That depends on what you're looking for."

He must be taller than me. Standing up, I reckon five foot nine. He's broad-shouldered, but everything tapers in the further down you get, like someone from the nineteenth-century with consumption.

"If you really are a novelist and you're looking for information about hostage-taking scenarios, then I meet your needs."

The subtext is clear: he's no fool.

"What does R.A.I.D. stand for?"

He frowns in total despair.

"No, seriously . . ."

"Research, Assistance, Intervention, Dissuasion. I was in charge of the dissuasion bit. At least I was until I was given the heave-ho."

He's not bad. Even if the two of us do make for a right old pair of sad cases. How does he make his living? He's poorly dressed. Seems an opportunist type, in poor health: can't imagine he turns much down work-wise. Sooner or later, this guy will end up in the slammer or in a dealer's wheelie bin. In terms of rates, that gives me some bargaining power. The thought of money overwhelms me with sadness. Mathilde's face enters my mind, followed by Nicole, my wife who doesn't want to sleep by my side. I am tired.

Albert Kaminski looks at me with concern and offers me the jug of water. I'm struggling to catch my breath. I'm taking this too far, it's all going too far.

"Are you alright?"

I down a glass of water and shake myself.

"How much do you charge?"

David Fontana
May 12

F.A.O. Bertrand Lacoste
Subject: "Hostage-taking" role play – Client: Exxyal

The preparation of the location is under way. We will be employing two main zones.

Firstly, the larger room (Sector A on the diagram) will be where the hostages are held. It is separated from the corridor by a partition with a glass window that the commando can cover should you wish to carry out any isolated interrogations.
Secondly, there are the offices.
D marks a rest area and debriefing room. B denotes the interrogation chamber. As outlined in the scenario, the executives will be interrogated in turn, with the interview based on their individual areas of expertise.
The interrogation will be viewed by the assessors, who will be monitoring events on screens located in Sector C.
In the current configuration, the candidates for the H.R. position (marked in grey on the diagram) will be sitting in front of their screens.
We have carried out some tests: the soundproofing between the rooms is satisfactory.

Two sets of cameras will relay the footage live to the assessors. The first camera will be in the hostage "waiting room"; the second will be in the interrogation chamber. As soon as these rooms are fitted out, we will begin full trial runs.

Finally, I feel I must reiterate that it is not always possible to predict how participants will react in a role-play scenario.

Regardless of the outcome, the parties commissioning the operation will be held responsible.

Please find attached in Appendix 2 the disclaimers to be signed by you or your client.

Yours sincerely,
David Fontana

"HOSTAGE-TAKING" ROLE PLAY – MASTER PLAN

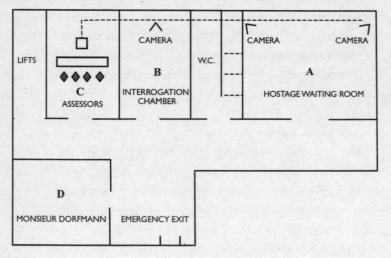

12

At 5.00 p.m., the first thing Mathilde sees as she leaves the *lycée* is her father. Me. There I am, standing stock still as the youths flood out from every angle, shouting, running, barging. She doesn't say a word to me – doesn't even break her stride – tight-lipped as though heading to the slaughter.

Iphigenia,

I think she's over-doing it a bit.

We enter the branch and up pops her "customer adviser". A dead ringer for my son-in-law: same suit, same hairstyle, same bearing, same voice. Heaven knows how many clones have come off the same production line. But it's best I avoid thinking about Gregory, because he might yet be the precursor to some colossal problems.

Mathilde sees the bank manager by herself for a moment and then comes back. It's crazy how simple it is. My daughter hands me a fat envelope.

I go to hug her but she mechanically offers me her cheek. She regrets her coldness, but it's too late now. She thinks I'm cross: I look for something to say, but it doesn't come. Mathilde squeezes my forearm. Now that she has relinquished half of what she owns to me, she seems calmer. She simply says:

"You promised, remember . . ."

Then she smiles, as if ashamed of repeating herself, of showing me so little trust. Or so much fear.

We go our separate ways outside the *métro*.

"I'm going to walk for a bit."

I wait for her to leave, then go down into the station myself. I didn't have the courage to prolong the contact. I put my phone on vibrate mode and slide it into my trouser pocket. By my count, Mathilde will be home in less than half an hour. One station follows another, I change and walk through the corridors, my phone slapping against my thigh. At the interchange, instead of boarding the train, I take a seat and scoop up a crumpled copy of *Le Monde*. I browse the article: "*Employees currently represent 'main threat' to businesses' financial security.*"

I look at my watch nervously as I continue to leaf through. Page 8: "*Auction record: Emir Shahid Al-Abbasi's yacht to sell for 174 million dollars.*"

My feet are on hot coals and I can barely concentrate.

I don't have to wait long. I fumble for my phone and look at the screen. It's Mathilde. I swallow hard and let it ring through. No message.

I try hard to focus on something else. Page 15: "*After four months of strike action at factory, Desforges employees lift blockade after accepting 300-euro payout.*"

But two minutes later she calls again. A glance at my watch and I do a quick calculation. Nicole won't be home yet, but she will get back before me and I do not want Mathilde leaving a message on our machine. The third time I pick up.

"Papa!"

Her words catch. So do mine.

"How could you . . ."

But that's all she can manage. She's back home. She has just discovered her husband's face all smashed up and heard that I had gone to her because I'd failed with him.

Mathilde must have confessed to her husband that she'd given their flat money to her father.

They are livid, I understand that.

"Listen, angel, let me explain . . ."

"STOP!"

She yells this with all her strength.

"Give me back my money, Papa! Give it back RIGHT NOW!"

I reply before I lose my courage.

"I don't have it anymore, angel. I just put it towards the job."

Silence.

I'm not sure if she believes me, because all that I used to represent in her eyes has now melted away to form a new image of me, one that is unimaginable and unbearable.

It's not only that she has to revise everything she thought she knew about her father. It's worse: she has to live with it.

Right, I must reassure her. Tell her she has nothing to worry about.

"Listen, my angel, you have my word!"

Her voice is serious, measured. This time, the words come easily. She is able to distil all her thoughts into a few simple syllables.

"You are a bastard."

This is not an opinion, it's a fact. As I leave the station, I hold the envelope tight against me. My ticket for the top spot in the pantheon of bastard fathers.

13

Mathilde did not call back. She was so furious that she came in person. The finger she pressed on the buzzer seethed with such rage it felt as though it were still ringing when she was upstairs and hurling abuse at me in front of her mother. She demanded I give back the money she lent me, yelling at me like I was a crook. I didn't want to dwell on the fact that the envelope containing her money was in the top drawer of my desk, and that it would have taken me a second to put her mind to rest, to restore order. I focused, drawing on all my reserves of courage, like when you're at the dentist and he's wrestling with a tricky tooth.

Everything went terribly. It was to be expected, of course, but it was painful all the same.

Why won't they understand? It's a mystery. Actually, it isn't really. In the beginning, for Mathilde and for Nicole, unemployment was an abstraction, a concept: something written about in the papers or spoken about on television. Later, reality caught up with them: as unemployment spread, it became impossible to avoid contact with someone personally affected, or someone with a close relation out of work. Yet the reality was still foggy, an undeniable presence, but one you could live with; you know it exists, but it only concerns others, like world hunger, homelessness or Aids. Or haemorrhoids. For those not directly involved, unemployment is background chatter. Then one day, when no-one is expecting, it comes knocking on your front door. Just like Mathilde, it presses its fat finger on the buzzer, except the sound doesn't carry on ringing in everyone's ears for the same length of time. Those who go to work in the morning, for example, stop hearing it there and then, only to be reminded of it when they get home in the evening. If at all. That's if they live with someone unemployed, or if it makes a brief appearance on the news. As for Mathilde, she only ever heard it mentioned on the odd evening or weekend when she came to visit. That's the big difference: unemployment bored into my eardrums, and it's never stopped. Try explaining that to them.

As soon as Mathilde gave me the chance, I tried to reason that this was an unprecedented opportunity (a job I had a genuine hope of securing), but one word in she started yelling again. I wondered for a second whether she might re-smash all our new crockery. Nicole said nothing. Slumped in a corner of the room, she looked at me and wept in silence, as if I were the sorriest specimen she had ever witnessed.

Eventually, I gave up explaining myself. I went back to my study, but that wasn't good enough. Mathilde flung open the door with a fresh volley of insults – nothing would appease her. Even Nicole started trying to reason with her, to tell her that shouting and screaming wouldn't change anything, that she had to take a more constructive approach, see what can be done in practical terms. Mathilde's anger then turned on her mother.

"What do you mean 'what can be done'? Can you pay back what he took from me?"

Then she turned to me:

"Do you REALLY want to pay me back, Papa! Do you REALLY want to give back the money before we buy the flat, because . . ."

At that point she stopped dead.

She had been so overwhelmed by fury that it hadn't dawned on her until now: there was nothing she could do about it. If I don't pay her back, the sale will fall through and she will lose most of her deposit. Nothing can be done. She choked. I said:

"I gave you my word, angel. I will repay you, in full, before your deadline. Have I ever lied to you?"

It was a low blow on my part, but what other option did I have?

Once Mathilde had gone, a long, droning silence filled the flat. I heard Nicole moving from one room to another, then finally she came to me. Her anger had given way to utter despondency. She had dried away her tears.

"What was it for, this money?" she asked.

"To load the dice in our favour."

She waved this aside with furious disbelief. For several nights now, ever since she's been sleeping in the spare room, I've been wondering whether I'd be brave enough to say when she asked me that question. I'd devised plenty of theories. Of all the possible solutions, however, it was Nicole who unwittingly chose one.

"You said to Mathilde that it was for . . . a bribe?"

"Yes," I said.

"Who for?"

"The recruitment firm."

Nicole's face changed. I thought I detected a glimmer of hope in it. I went for it. I know I shouldn't have gone this far, but I was in need of some comforting too.

"B.L.C. Consulting is in charge of the recruiting. They're the ones who will choose. That's what I paid for. I bought the job."

Nicole sat down on my desk chair. The computer screen woke up and displayed the Exxyal website, with its oil wells, helicopters, refineries and all the rest.

"So . . . it's certain?"

I would have given all my remaining years not to have to answer that, but none of the gods came to my rescue. I was left alone to consider Nicole's burgeoning hope, her wide-open eyes. The words wouldn't come. I smiled and spread my arms as a token of proof. Nicole smiled too. She found it utterly marvellous. She started crying again and laughing at the same time. All the same, she carried on looking for the catch.

"Maybe they asked the other candidates to do the same?"

"That would be stupid. There's only one job up for grabs! Why get the others to do it if it only means repaying them after?"

"It's so weird! I can't believe they suggested this."

"It was my idea. There were three candidates whose profiles matched. We were neck and neck. I had to stand out from the others."

Nicole was stunned. I felt some small relief, but it had an extremely bitter taste to it: the more I presented this version of events as infallible, the more menacing the uncertainties of my plan seemed. I was jettisoning my last chances of ever being understood, even though victory wasn't even guaranteed.

"And how are you going to pay Mathilde back?"

As anyone knows, the first lie spawns the second. In management, we learn to lie as seldom as possible, to stay as close as we can to the truth. That's not always feasible. In this case, I had no choice but to escalate it a notch.

"I negotiated 20,000 euros. But for 25, they'll do what they can to convince their client to pay me an advance."

I wondered where I was going with this.

"They'll give you an advance while you're still on probation?"

In any negotiation, there is a tipping point. Make or break. I was there. I said:

"Twenty-five thousand euros . . . it's just three months' salary."

A veil of scepticism continued to linger between us, but I felt that I was on the brink of persuading her. And I knew why. Because of hope – inescapable, rotten hope.

"Why didn't you tell Mathilde all this?"

"Because Mathilde can't see beyond her anger."

I went up to Nicole and took her in my arms.

"So," she said, "this hostage-taking . . . what's that all about?"

All that remained was to play this bit down. I felt good, as though I had started believing my own lie.

"It's nothing more than a charade, my love! In fact, it's utterly pointless now because the game's already been decided . . . We're talking about a couple of guys with plastic guns who'll scare everyone for a bit and then it's finished. The role play will last about fifteen minutes, just a way of seeing whether or not the folks completely lose their cool, and then the client will be happy. Everyone will be happy."

Nicole carried on thinking for a second, then said:

"So, there's nothing more you have to do? You've paid and you've got the job?"

I answered:

"Correct. I've paid. All we have to do is wait."

If Nicole had asked one more question, just one, it would have been my turn to break down in tears. But she had nothing left to ask – she was satisfied. I was tempted to point out that she didn't have such a big problem with the hostage-taking now that she knew I would get a job out of it, but I'd already tried my luck and, in all honesty, I was exhausted with myself, with all my lies and trickery.

"I know that you're a very brave man, Alain," she said. "I know how desperate you are to get out of this. I know full well that you do menial jobs that you never talk about because you're afraid I'm ashamed of you."

I'm astonished she knows all that too.

"I've always admired your energy and willpower so much, but you have to leave our daughters out of this. It's up to us to over-come this, not them."

In principle I agree, but if they hold the only solution, then what? We pretend not to see? Does solidarity work only one way? Of course, I don't say any of this aloud.

"This money thing, about buying your job, you have to explain all this to Mathilde," Nicole continued. "Reassure her. I'm telling you, you have to call her."

"Listen, Nicole, all of us are caught up in anger, emotion and panic. In a few days, I'll have a job, I'll give back her money, she'll buy her flat and everything will be back to normal."

Deep down, we were each as exhausted as the other.

Nicole relented to my scummy reasoning.

14

I've more or less finished my research into Exxyal Europe's activities.

I know the European group's organisation chart by heart (as well as the major shareholders in the American group), and I'm proficient in the key growth figures from the last five years, the backgrounds of all the top dogs, the detailed breakdown of their capital, the main dates relating to the group's market history and their future plans, especially the initiative to trim back production sites and close down several refineries across Europe, including the one at Sarqueville. The hardest was getting acquainted with the sectors in which Exxyal operates. I spent two whole nights familiarising myself with the principal aspects of the industry: deposits, exploration, production, drilling, transport, refining and logistics. At first it all frightened me because I'm not that hot on the technical side, but I'm so pumped up that I'm ready for the challenge. It's weird, but every now and again, I feel like I'm already there, already in the company. I even think that some of the execs might be less well informed about the group than I am.

I've made myself revision cards. Almost eighty of them. Yellow for the group's finances and stock market history; blue for technical aspects; white for partnerships. I wait for Nicole to leave, then recite them to myself as I pace around the living room. I'm completely in the zone – the immersion technique.

Four days now I've been cramming. This is always the most thankless part, where the ideas have registered but are still muddled. A bit longer and everything will start settling in my brain. I'll be as ready as anything when the test day arrives. Nothing to worry about from that perspective.

According to their role in the group, I start envisaging the questions I'm going to put to the exec hostages, ones that are likely to derail them. The lawyers must have access to confidential information on previous arrangements with subcontractors, partners or clients; the finance guys must know about various bits of foul play in the negotiation of major contracts. That side of things is still a bit vague . . . I need to dig deeper, prepare more, be match fit for the big day. I'm also making notes about hostage-taking, which I then revise with Kaminski.

Yesterday I received the first investigation reports from Mestach's agency. Reading them terrified me: in terms of their private lives, these people are perfectly ordinary. I mean representative-sample ordinary. Degrees, marriages, a few divorces; children who get degrees, get married, get divorced. Humanity can be so bloody depressing sometimes. Looking at their details and track records, these people are commonplace. Even so, I have to find their faults, to lay them bare.

I'm waiting for Kaminski. Despite being on the ropes himself, he managed to take advantage of my urgent situation to negotiate favourable terms. He's expensive, and I'm scraping the financial barrel, but I like the guy, he's decent. I couldn't keep the novelist act up for long. I told him the real story, which has simplified our working relationship no end.

Yesterday he read the "hostage" profiles, which I find so lacklustre, and he saw my concern.

"If you were to read your own profile," he said, "it would look like that. But you're not just some average unemployed guy: you're planning a hostage-taking."

I knew this, but in Nicole's absence, I don't have anyone to tell me the simple things I need to hear.

So I read and reread the profiles. As Kaminski said, "However exhaustively you prepare, when it comes down to it you're always forced to follow your intuition."

If I bear in mind the possible mistakes in my list of hostages, my chances of success are moderate at best. But even if I slip up in my preparations, I'm still banking on the fact that none of my competitors will have the same level of insight into the hostages' private lives.

I only need to crack two or three to come out on top. And to achieve that, I need to source some "hard-hitting" information.

I can afford supplementary investigations into five people, no more. After a huge amount of deliberation, I kept two men (the economics specialist Jean-Marc Guéneau, forty-five years old, and the civil engineer in his fifties, Paul Cousin) and two women (Évelyne Camberlin, fifty, structural engineer, and the business school grad, Virginie Tràn, thirty-five). And I threw in David Fontana, the organiser from Bertrand Lacoste's emails.

With Paul Cousin, there wasn't a shadow of a doubt: his bank accounts show that his wages are not paid into either his personal account or his family account. Very mysterious indeed. His wife has an account that he tops up himself each month. He doesn't transfer huge amounts – smells like separation. Or if their relationship is stable, she must be in the dark about the real situation. The fact is that Cousin's salary (he's a civil engineer in his fifties with more than twenty years under his belt, so it's hardly inconsiderable) doesn't show up anywhere: it's stashed elsewhere in an account under a different name.

Very promising indeed.

Bonus information.

I examined Jean-Marc Guéneau's file in microscopic detail. He is forty-five years old. At the age of twenty-one, he married one of the Boissieu girls – tidy little fortune. They have seven children. I found virtually nothing on Guéneau's family, but on the flip side, his wife's father is none other than Dr Boissieu, a fervent Catholic and a very vocal anti-abortion lobbyist. As such, they're at it like rabbits at Guéneau H.Q., firing out a sprog every five minutes. You don't need to be too cynical to suspect he's got a few beauties waiting in the wings. The moment people start wearing their morals on their sleeves, you can be positive there's something unmentionable going on behind closed doors.

Bonus information.

Out of the ladies, I kept Évelyne Camberlin. Fifty, single, high-ranking . . . scratch away at a woman like that and something is bound to come up. My decision to keep her was very much based on her photographs: I'm not sure why, but I find her interesting. When I told Kaminski as much, he smiled and said: "Well spotted."

I rounded off my line-up with Virginie Tràn. She's in charge of several major accounts, Exxyal's biggest clients. She's ambitious, calculating, moves up the ladder quickly: I don't think this girl is held back by scruples. Surely some leverage somewhere in there.

There's every possibility that these additional investigations won't come to anything, but I'm making progress.

How am I ever going to get out of this shitstorm? Sometimes the thought makes me dizzy. Not least because the rest of the landscape is looking so bleak.

I've not heard a peep on the Pharmaceutical Logistics front since sending off my letter to the lawyer. Every morning as I pretend to come home from work, I empty the letterbox to find that nothing has come. I've called Maître Gilson two or three times a day but never managed to get hold of her. A gnawing sense of anxiety has set in. So when the postman makes me sign for a letter sent by recorded delivery, and I see the Gilson & Fréret firm heading, I feel an unpleasant tingle run down my spine. Maître Gilson informs me that her client has decided to uphold their complaint against me and that I will receive a court summons to make a statement on the assault committed against my supervisor, Monsieur Mehmet Pehlivan. To my astonishment, Maître Gilson picks up this time.

"There's nothing I can do, Monsieur Delambre, I've done everything I can. What more do you want? My client is taking this complaint seriously."

"But didn't we have an agreement?"

"No, Monsieur Delambre. It was your idea to write a formal apology. We didn't ask you for anything. You did that on your own initiative."

"But . . . why go to court if your client has accepted my apology?"

"My client has accepted your apology, true. He then forwarded it to Monsieur Pehlivan who, by my understanding, was quite satisfied with it. But you must be aware that this letter represents a comprehensive confession."

"So . . . ?"

"So . . . insofar as you acknowledge the facts fully and freely, my client feels he is within his right to claim for the damages he is due in court."

When I offered to write this letter of apology, it did occur to me that things might turn out this way, but I didn't think it was possible for an employer and his lawyer to be capable of such a craven move towards someone in my situation.

"You're a fucking bitch."

"I understand your point of view, but I'm afraid that won't stand up in court, Monsieur Delambre. I advise you to find a stronger line of defence."

She hangs up. This hasn't made me as angry as I expected it to. I only had one card to play and I played it. No point beating myself up about it, and I can't even blame them: it's hard to leave the table when you know you have a winning hand.

That doesn't stop me from hurling my mobile against the wall, where it explodes. When I realise I need a new one (in other words about five minutes later) I start looking for the bits underneath the furniture. Patched up with sticky tape, it now looks like a ragdoll, or an old fogey's glasses down at the hospice.

I've spent everything Mathilde gave me and, even though Kaminski has agreed to lower his rate from 4,000 to 3,000 euros for the two days' work, I've still had to withdraw 1,000 euros of the 1,410 left in our savings account. Let's hope Nicole doesn't feel inclined to check the balance before all this is over.

Right at the start, Kaminski suggested a plan of action: day one would be dedicated to the nuts and bolts of the hostage-taking; day two, we would tackle the psychological side of the interrogations. Kaminski doesn't know David Fontana, but having read the organiser's messages, he tells me that the guy knows exactly what he's doing. Bertrand Lacoste and I each have our adviser, our expert, our coach – we're like a pair of chess players the day before the world championships.

As far as Nicole is concerned, everything's still fine. She has calmed down and, despite my reservations, I suspect she's phoned Mathilde to reassure her and explain the ins and outs of the situation.

So when Kaminski arrives just before 10.00 a.m., I don't imagine for a second that I'm on the brink of disaster.

As agreed, he's brought along a camera and tripod that we can connect to the television so we can look back over what he calls the "respective positions", and for rehearsing the interrogations.

To help me get to grips with the technical side of things, he's also brought two firearms: an 18-round 4.5mm Umarex pistol, which is a copy of the Beretta; and a Cometa-Baikal-Q.B. 57 to stand in for the Uzi submachine guns that, according to Fontana's email, will be used in the real thing. Kaminski proposes replicating the layout of the two main rooms, as per the site map from the email, to show me where the pivotal action spots will be, and we've rearranged the sofa, table and chairs to create the zone where the hostages will be held.

It's just gone 12.15 p.m.

Kaminski tells me how the commando will manoeuvre itself in the premises to ensure it retains overall control of the situation. He's sitting on the floor – back against the partition wall, legs folded – impersonating a hostage.

I'm standing in the doorway with the little submachine gun slung across my shoulder like a bandolier, the barrel trained in his general direction, when Nicole arrives home.

It's quite a spectacle.

If she'd walked in on me shagging the next-door neighbour then that would have been absurd, and therefore easier to process. But this . . . The sight that greets Nicole belongs in the realm of hyperrealism: the weapons Kaminski brought are terrifyingly present. This is training. The man hugging his knees and staring up at her from the ground is a professional.

Nicole is speechless. She holds her breath in bewilderment. I'd pretended to her that the interview was just a formality. Now she's fathoming the extent of my duplicity. Her eyes dart over the gun in my hands, the furniture pushed into the corners. It is such a calamity that neither of us can find anything to say.

In any case, my lies spew out so loudly that they're unintelligible. Nicole just shakes her head and leaves without a word.

Kaminski's being decent about it. He manages to find something to say. Later on I defrost some food in the microwave and we eat standing up. I reflect on the horror of the situation. Nicole hardly ever comes back for lunch. It would be quite extraordinary if she did it twice a year. And she always rings ahead to make sure I'm there. Of all the days! Everything is conspiring against me. Kaminski smiles and tells me that it's in situations like this that true strength of character shines through.

It's now early afternoon and the atmosphere is heavy. I need to dig deep to summon the energy to get back to work. The image of Nicole in the doorframe, her eyes – it's giving me hell.

He's a good guy, Kaminski. He's going the extra mile, telling me real-life anecdotes so I can envisage all the possible scenarios. He's very cagey about his own life, but one thing leads to another and I end up pretty well piecing together the details of his career. He did clinical psychology before joining the police, then he became a negotiator with R.A.I.D. My guess is that he wasn't a user by then, or at least that the effects weren't so visible.

As the day draws on, he gets more nervous. Withdrawal. From time to time he claims he needs a cigarette to recharge his batteries. He goes downstairs for a few minutes and comes back calmer, eyes gleaming. His tipple remains a mystery to me. His addiction doesn't bother me in the slightest; what pisses me off are his diversion tactics. In the end I snap:

"Do you think I'm stupid?"

"Screw you!"

He's furious, a mutinous look in his eyes. I hesitate for a second before carrying on:

"I know you're high as a kite all day long, but at this price I'd hope for more than a wreck!"

"What difference does it make?"

"Every difference. Do you think you're worth what I'm paying for you?"

"That's your call."

"Well, I'd say no. The girl you killed, she jumped out the window while you were shooting up behind some truck . . ."

"So what?"

"So that wasn't your only fuck-up! Am I wrong?"

"That's none of your business!"

"It's not the same in the police as it is in the private sector. You don't get fired the first time you mess up. How many were there before? How many deaths had you been drugged up for before they decided to chuck you out?"

"You've got no right!"

"And while we're at it, this girl . . . did you see her fall or did you just see her body on the pavement? I've heard it makes a nasty sound. Young girls especially. Am I right?"

Kaminski slumps back in his chair and pulls out a pack of cigarettes. He offers me one. I await his verdict.

"Not bad at all," he says with a smile.

I feel mightily relieved.

"Not bad: you held your line, remained focused on impactful subject matter, and proceeded with short, incisive, well-chosen questions. No, I'm telling you, for an amateur, that wasn't bad at all."

He stands up and stops the camera. I hadn't realised it was filming.

"We'll keep that for tomorrow and go back over the sequence when we discuss the interrogations."

Good day's work.

He leaves the house at around 7.00 p.m.

Evening falls and I'm alone in the flat.

Before he went, Kaminski suggested we put all the furniture back in place. I told him it wasn't necessary; I knew Nicole wasn't coming home. I scraped some change together and went to buy a bottle of single malt and a packet of cigarettes. I'm on my second whisky when Lucie arrives to collect her mother's things. I open the windows wide because it's warm and the smoke from my first fag is going to my head. When she comes in, I must look like I'm completely off the rails, which I'm not. But appearances matter. She doesn't comment. All she says is:

"I can't stay, I have to look after Maman. How about lunch tomorrow?"

"I can't do lunch. Tomorrow evening?"

Lucie nods and hugs me with great tenderness. It hurts.

But I still have plenty of work to do.

I light a second cigarette, grab my notes, and start revising, pacing around the big, deserted sitting room: "Capital – 47 million euros. Composition – Exxyal Group: 8%, Total: 11.5% . . ."

Over the course of the evening, Mathilde leaves two short, violent messages.

At one point she says: "You're the exact opposite of what I expect my father to be."

It breaks my heart.

Olenka Zbikowski
B.L.C. Consulting

F.A.O. Bertrand Lacoste
Subject: End of internship

As you will no doubt be aware, my second internship finishes on May 30. This six-month period followed an initial four-month internship.

You will find enclosed with the present note a full report on my activities at B.L.C. Consulting since you were kind enough to place your confidence in me. I would like to take this opportunity to offer my sincere thanks for the roles you have allocated me in these ten months, roles which, in several cases, have far exceeded the responsibilities ordinarily attributed to an intern.

Almost ten months of unpaid activity, during which I have demonstrated constant willingness and unfailing loyalty, represents a sufficient trial period for me to expect a decision on your part regarding permanent employment.

Allow me to take this opportunity to declare once again my dedication to the company's business activities, and my strong desire to continue to collaborate alongside you.

Best,
Olenka Zbikowski

15

Charles said: "I live at number 47." Which really means that his car is parked opposite number 47.

Number 47 is the only number on the street, along with 45, which is three hundred metres away. Between the two lies the enormous brick wall of a factory, the neighbourhood's only attraction. Opposite, construction hoarding and scaffolding. The street is straight as a die, dark, with lamp posts at thirty- or forty-metre intervals.

Charles greets me with the little sign he makes with his left hand.

"Before," he tells me, "I was over there right under the street lamp. Forget about sleeping! Had to wait for a space to free up in the shade."

Charles had burst out laughing when I called him.

"Is that drink still going?" I said.

His joy was genuine, despite having already drunk enough for both of us that day:

"Seriously? You want to come to my place?"

And so here we are, almost 11.00 p.m., standing outside his place: a bright-red Renault 25.

"1985," Charles says, proudly patting the roof. "Six-cylinder 2.5-litre turbo V6!"

The fact it hasn't been driven for more than ten years doesn't faze him in the slightest. The car is up on blocks to avoid flat-spotting the tyres, which lends it the impression of floating above the ground.

"I've got a pal who comes round every few months to pump them up for me."

"That's great."

What's really astonishing are the bumpers. Front and rear. Huge great chrome bars, way too big, that rise to about a metre off the ground. The sort more commonly seen on American trucks. Charles notes my amazement.

"It's my neighbours in front and behind. The last ones. Every time they came home from a ride they'd bash into my motor. One day I got fed up. So here we go."

Here we go indeed. Quite something.

"Down there further along," he says, pointing to the other end of the street, "there used to be another Renault 25. An '84 G.T.X.! But the guy moved."

His voice is tinged with the regret of lost friendship.

A good part of the street is occupied by knackered old vans and other cars up on blocks, all housing families of immigrant workers. The postman leaves the mail under the wipers, like fines.

"There's a good atmosphere in this neighbourhood, you can't complain," says Charles.

We go inside for drinks. It's very organised, Charles' apartment, ingeniously arranged.

"Well it has to be!" he answers when I remark on it. "It's not very big so it has to be . . ."

"Functional . . ."

"Yes! Functional!"

As ever, Charles is bowled over by my vocabulary.

He places a tray between the seats to serve as a sort of drinks trolley for the bottle and the peanuts. It's mild outside so I lower my window, and I feel the night air caressing the back of my neck. I brought a drinkable whisky: nothing too swanky, but not grotty either. And a few packets of crisps and nibbles.

We barely speak, Charles and I. We look at each other, smiling. Not that there's any ill will between us. It's a moment of calm. We're like two old friends in our rocking chairs on the terrace after a family meal. I let my mind drift and it fixes on Albert Kaminski. I look at Charles. Which of them do I feel closer to? Not Charles. He sips his whisky, his lost eyes gazing through the windscreen, past the huge bumper and beyond to his peaceful neighbourhood. Charles is a victim; that's the only profile he fits. Kaminski and I are severe cases, car crashes: either of us could end up a murderer. It's a serious point. We are dabbling with radicalism. Having abandoned all hope, Charles might just be the wisest of the three of us.

On the second whisky, Romain's shadow looms before me, a reminder of the long procession of grievances I have in store. I've made my decision. I won't ask Charles to testify.

"I reckon I'm going to take care of this myself," I say.

This comes right out of the blue, and it's obvious Charles doesn't fully grasp what I am talking about. He inspects the bottom of his glass in a dreamlike state, before grumbling a few words that might amount to an agreement, but who knows. Then he thinks and shakes his head, as if to say that it's better this way, that he understands. I turn to the line of cars, the tarmac glistening under the yellow smudges of the street lamps, and the factory wall that looks like a prison. I'm on the verge of the Big Test, the one that I've dedicated all my energy to, more than all of it. I savour this moment of peace as though I might die tomorrow.

"Funny when you think about it . . ."

Charles agrees that yes, it's funny. This is the moment where, helped along by the whisky, I ask myself the question: why am I here? It terrifies me to think that I came to gather my strength. If I miss my shot, this may well be what I can look forward to – a car up on blocks in a derelict suburb. That's a bit harsh on Charles.

"That wasn't very nice of me . . ."

Without hesitating, Charles places his hand on my knee and says:

"Don't worry."

I'm still ashamed. I try to change the subject.

"So, have you got a radio?"

"Well, now you're talking!" says Charles.

He reaches out and hits the button: "*. . . with the C.E.O. receiving a golden handshake of 3.2 million euros.*"

Charles turns it off.

"Good system, hey?" he says proudly.

I don't know if he's talking about the news or if he's just happy to be showing me his home comforts. We stay there for a good while.

Then I tell myself it's time to go back. I've got revision to do, I must stay focused.

I didn't say anything, yet Charles motions to the bottle:

"A little one for the road?"

I pretend to think about it. I actually do think about it. It's not a good idea. I decline, saying I need to be sensible.

Several more sedate, gentle minutes pass by. The calm makes me want to cry. Charles pats me on the knee again. I focus on the bottom of my glass. It's empty.

"Right, time to call it a night . . ."

I turn to grab the door handle.

"Let me show you out," says Charles, opening his side.

We shake hands in silence at the back of the car.

As I walk to the *métro*, it occurs to me that Charles might be the only friend I have left.

16

Five days until I'm up against the wall on Thursday. The count-down is both reassuring and frightening. For now, all I want is reassurance.

Despite the half-bottle of whisky I knocked back last night, I'm up and ready for battle at dawn. As I drain my coffee I realise that my revision notes are starting to stick. On Monday or Tuesday I should be receiving the results from the additional investigations, leaving me a day or two to come up with a strategy, provided there's even an ounce of dirt to go on.

Since Nicole left, the flat has been desperately sad.

Mathilde has stopped giving me grief via the answering machine. She'll be having a tough time stopping her husband from suing me straight away. Maybe he already has.

Kaminski arrives on time, to the second. On the agenda: reading and analysing several R.A.I.D. training documents focusing on the psychological aspects of hostage-taking and interrogation.

First he refers to an itemised list of manoeuvres that make hostages confess – so long as they've been held for long enough – and the precautions the commando would have to take. That gives me a better understanding of the various psychological phases the victims go through, not to mention the points at which they'll be at their most vulnerable.

We summarise what we've covered at the end of the morning session, then dedicate the afternoon to the interrogations. My management experience has already given me a solid grounding in manipulation techniques. Interrogating hostages is simple: take a job interview, multiply it by an annual performance review, then add weaponry. The principal difference is that in business, your fear is latent, whereas in a hostage-taking, the lives of the victims are in danger. On second thoughts, it's the same in business. Ultimately, the only real difference lies in the nature of the weapons and the length of time they're left to stew.

In the evening, as planned, I have dinner with Lucie.

Her treat, so her choice of restaurant. Sooner or later, as we grow older, we become our children's children. They're the ones who take charge. But I'm in denial that that moment has already come, so I insist on a change of restaurant. We go to the Roman Noir, which is just down the road. It's warm. Lucie looks as pretty as a flower, even though she's making out that this dinner isn't a special occasion. The fact is that by talking about other things, the occasion becomes an event. Lucie tries the wine (it's common consensus that she has the best nose in the family, not that there's ever been any proof of it). Perhaps she doesn't know where to start. In any case, she opts to talk about everything and nothing, about the flat she wants to move out of because it's so dingy, her work at her firm, the low pay that's forcing her to live hand to mouth. Lucie only talks about her love life when she's not having any joy. She's avoiding the subject, so I ask the question:

"What's his name?"

She smiles, takes a glug of wine, and looks at me as though she's announcing bad news:

"Federico."

"Of course, you always go for the exotic ones! What was the last guy called, again?"

"Papa!" she says, smiling.

"Fusaaki?"

"Fusaaki."

"Wasn't there an Omar, too?"

"You make it sound like there have been hundreds!"

It's my turn to smile. Bit by bit we keep pretending to forget why the two of us are here. To put her at ease, as soon as we've ordered dessert I ask her how her mother is doing.

Lucie doesn't answer straight away.

"She's sad," she says eventually. "Very stressed."

"It's a stressful time."

"Are you going to tell me why?"

Sometimes you have to prepare for a meeting with your children the same way you do a job interview. Of course I don't have the energy or the inclination this time round, so I improvise, keeping it very general.

"Come on, spell it out," Lucie says after my bungled account.

"Well, your mother refused to listen, and your sister refused to understand."

She smiles.

"What about me – where do I fit in?"

"There's room in my camp, if you're keen."

"Wow, it's a pitched battle, is it?"

"No, but it is a battle, and right now I'm fighting it alone."

So I have to explain. More lies.

As I repeat what I said to Nicole, I realise how many lies I've heaped one on top of the other. I'm keeping the whole, wobbling lot together, but the slightest knock and it'll come crashing down, bringing me with it. The ad, the tests, the bribe . . . That's where it snags. Lucie's more perceptive than her mother and doesn't fall for it for a second.

"A well-established recruitment firm is entertaining a bull-shit idea like this for a few thousand euros? That's really quite astonishing . . ."

You'd have to be blind not to detect her scepticism.

"It's not the *whole* firm. The guy's doing it solo."

"That doesn't mean it's not risky. Doesn't he care about his job?"

"I've no idea, but once I have my contract, he can go to the slammer for all I care – I couldn't give a toss."

There's a lull as the waiter arrives with the coffees, and afterwards the conversation struggles to pick up again. I know why. So does Lucie. She doesn't believe a word of what I'm telling her. As if to prove it, she drinks her coffee and places her two hands on the table.

"I've got to make a move . . ."

She's surrendering, no doubt about it. She could have scratched away at the sore point, but she chooses not to. She'll still come up with a few platitudes to say to her sister and her mother; she'll think of something. As far as she's concerned, I'm caught up in some tawdry affair, and she's not in any hurry to find out the details. Lucie is running away.

We walk together a little. Eventually she turns to me:

"Right, well, I hope everything turns out how you want. If you need me . . ."

And there's so much sadness in the way she squeezes my arm and kisses my cheek.

After this, my weekend takes on an eve-of-battle feel.

Tomorrow in the battle think on me.

Except that I'm alone. I don't just miss Nicole because I'm alone, but because my life without her has no direction, no sense. I'm not sure why I've been unable to explain all this to her, how things have become so knotty. This has never happened to us. Why would Nicole not hear me out? Why did she not believe in my chances of success? If Nicole no longer believes in me, I'm already dead.

I need to hold on for a few more days.

Until Thursday.

The following day, I revise my notes and run through my accounts to see how much I've spent, nausea overwhelming me at the thought of what might happen if I screw this up. I study the photographs and biographies of the hostages. I go for a walk to keep my concentration fresh. I bring all my notes, my beginner's guide to the oil and gas industry, and a photocopy of the R.A.I.D. document from Kaminski.

When I get back, there are three messages from Lucie. Two on my mobile, which I'd left at home, and another on the landline. After our futile dinner last night, she would like an update. She's a bit worried, she doesn't say why. I don't want to call her back – I can't afford to lose my focus. In four days, I'll be back in the race, and I'll be able to explain how hard it was bearing up without them.

17

Mestach called last night to say that the additional investigations were now available. As I still owe him half his fee, he doesn't miss the opportunity to remind me that his investigators have worked to a very tight deadline and that it is miraculous that they've obtained so many results – a classic technique to make me think I'm getting value for money. I don't fall for it.

Mestach counts the money twice before handing me an A4 envelope. He makes to show me out, but I take a seat in the armchair in the corridor leading up to his office.

It dawns on him that if I don't feel I have enough bang for my buck, then he'll know about it straight away. This is my daughter's money, and I have no intention of frittering it away on nothing.

To be honest, given the time constraints, it's good. In places, it's even very good. I don't want to let this on, so as soon as I've taken stock of the first few results, I slip out of the building. Seems he won't have to know about it after all.

Back at home, I clear my desk and line up the findings.

Jean-Marc Guéneau. Forty-five years old.

This guy is straight out of the nineteenth century. People from Catholic families like his have been intermarrying for generations. The men are all generals, priests, professors; the women are all housewives, little more than laying hens. His family tree is more of an elaborate tropical shrub. Like the rest of the spineless upper middle classes, his little clique has been diligently leaching income from land and property ever since the start of the industrial revolution, a term they hold in particular disdain because it reeks of the proletariat. Predictably enough, the last few generations have been especially hard-line. They live in the sixteenth, the seventh, the eighth, Neuilly – only the classiest neighbourhoods. Our Guéneau marries at twenty-one and proceeds to produce a brat every eighteenth months for the next ten years. They called it a day at seven. Madame must be taking her temperature every five minutes between Hail Marys, insisting on the withdrawal method too because you can never be too careful. So it's unsurprising that Guéneau needs to come up for air; rather seedy air, as it happens. I have two photographs of him: the first is taken at 7.30 p.m. as he enters a side door on rue Saint-Maur; the second, taken at 8.45 p.m., shows him leaving. That means getting home around 9.15 p.m. For his trip to the "gym", he's carrying a sports bag.

This is a real stroke of luck. His credit card shows that he spends two hours a week on rue Saint-Maur, usually on Thursdays. He's bound to have some friends among the regulars. That cracks me up. This one's a done deal – dead man walking.

Paul Cousin, fifty-two, is less classic, and all the more exciting because of it.

A man with a C.V. like this is untouchable. He's got nothing that will let me stand out from the rest of the pack. I'll need to ensure that his interrogation falls to one of my rivals. That's the plan, at least.

In the photographs, he has a worrying physique: an unbelievably voluminous head with eyes that bulge out of their sockets. He goes to work every day at Exxyal, he has his own underground space in the company car park, he's a senior project manager, he travels, he submits reports, he attends meetings, he visits facilities … and yet for more than four years he's been signed up to A.P.E.C. and receiving unemployment benefits. I check his employment record and, with the help of an accompanying note with precise details, dates and facts, I manage to piece together his strange career.

Paul Cousin worked for Exxyal for twenty-two years until he was fired four years ago (victim of a staff cut in the department he'd been assigned to a few months previously). At that point, he was forty-eight years old. What happened in his head? Was it a mental block or a desperate tactic? He decided to continue coming in to work, as if nothing had happened. His superiors cited him and the case went right to the top, where the powers-that-be ruled in his favour. If he wanted to carry on coming in to work, that was fine with them. He doesn't get a salary, he works, performs well, but there's no other way of putting it: for four years, he's been volunteering!

He must be holding out some hope that he can prove himself. He is working to get his job back.

In doing so, Paul Cousin is embodying capitalism's oldest dream. Even the most imaginative of bosses couldn't hope for better. He's sold his flat because he can't afford the repayments, traded in his car for a cheaper model, and receives a minute sum in unemployment benefits, and all the while he's got loads of responsibility. It's not hard to see why he's so interested in the Sarqueville redundancy plan: if he does a good job heading up this round of staff cuts, then he'll be back in the fold once and for all. This is his return ticket to the giddy heights of the Exxyal Group. A man with this level of ambition will give up his life without flinching – he is unstoppable. He will never surrender, not even when he's staring down the barrel of a submachine gun.

Then there's Virginie Tràn, the Vietnamese girl. Now she's a fine customer.

Mestach and his team couldn't be sure when her affair with Hubert Bonneval began. Judging by her telephone records and various hits on her credit card statements, you could hazard a guess that they've been together for eighteen months. I have several photographs taken two days ago showing the couple at the food market on rue du Poteau: eying each other up lustfully in front of the cheese; snogging next to the peppers. The final shot shows them entering Mademoiselle Tràn's flat, arm-in-arm. Must be less than eighteen months if you ask me – either that or they're genuinely in love. The notes suggest they met in professional circumstances: a seminar, trade fair, or something. Possible. But even more interesting than Mademoiselle Tràn is her lover. He's thirty-eight and a senior project manager at Solarem, a subsidiary of Exxyal's main business rival. She is quite literally in bed with the competition. Excellent.

I get straight online and in no time at all I've found the big sites run by Solarem. I have a very clear idea of the situation I'll put little Virginie in to crack her, to show her what sort of an assessor I am; I will push her to betray her lover for her company, forcing her to reveal technical information pertaining to the offshore rigs installed by Solarem. She will have to ring her man and explain that, for work purposes, she *must* have certain bits of confidential information about her competitor's sites. To demonstrate her loyalty to her employer, she'll have to make him be unfaithful to his. Perfect. Textbook.

As for Évelyne Camberlin, nothing. Odds and sods. Money farted into the breeze.

They saved the best until last.

David Fontana. The pro brought in by B.L.C. Consulting to organise the hostage-taking. I recognise him in the photograph: definitely the man I saw with Lacoste.

Six years ago he set up an agency specialising in security. Checks, installations, surveillance. His company is kosher. Nothing wrong with cashing in on the latest wave of collective paranoia. Every year, he and his team install more cameras than you can shake a stick at. His balance sheet is not entirely positive:

the investigator's theory is that a decent amount of his profit is stashed away with the help of some creative accounting, before being paid to the boss on the sly. The hidden part of his business activities is more opaque, almost as much as his past. Business intelligence for companies, debt collection, protection in all its forms. His clients only see the agreeable side of his C.V. He began his career in the army, the paras, before making a long transition into the D.G.S.E. intelligence services. As far as his clients are concerned, his official pedigree ends there. He keeps shtum about his "freelance" (read "mercenary") activities. Scratch below the surface and in the past twenty years we see David Fontana popping up in Burma, Kurdistan, Congo, former Yugoslavia . . . The man likes to travel. After that, he jumps on the modern bandwagon by joining various private military contractors, whose client lists include governments, multinational corporations and organisations, and diamond merchants. His main job is combat training, his skills getting plucked by the most famous agencies: Military Professional Resources Inc., DynCorp, Erinys, and the rest. Seems he's been more than happy to lend a hand in several different theatres. You get the feeling that this guy is full of goodwill.

In the end, Fontana is forced into early retirement following a slight hiccup: he's suspected of involvement in the massacre of seventy-four people in South Sudan at a time when the company employing him was propping up the Janjaweed, the government-supported militia.

After that he sensibly decides to settle down and establish his own surveillance and security company.

No doubt Bertrand Lacoste knows nothing of all this. Neither do Exxyal. His company brochure is squeaky clean, his C.V. meticulously sugar-coated. Not that they'd give two hoots anyway: no matter what domain they're dealing with, they want skilled people, and there can be no doubt that David Fontana is an expert.

I think back to my fear at being rumbled by him outside the B.L.C. Consulting building. My intuition wasn't wrong.

I create a sheet for each of the three execs with my personal notes. As I imagine the questions I'm going to put to them and how I'm going to conduct the interviews, I can't help feeling apprehensive. My selection process was rigorous, but if the execs who turn up on the day are different to the ones I've investigated and invested in, it will be catastrophic – I would be going in empty-handed.

This prospect makes me so anxious that I instantly chase it from my mind. In life, you need luck too. Having had my fair share of bad fortune over the years, it's reasonable to suppose that I'm due some favourable odds. All the same, I go back over my selection criteria, and I'm relieved to reconfirm my choices. Now that the flat is empty and I'm all alone, I have to resort to self-congratulation.

Bertrand,

So. After blanking my message about my internship finishing and the permanent position you promised me, I hear you've awarded an unpaid internship to Thomas Jaulin, a friend of mine from college.

I notice that the role he's been offered is absolutely identical to the one I've been carrying out for the past ten months at B.L.C. (you just copy and pasted my contract when you drew up his!).

I'm keeping things "professional" for now, but I seriously hope that I've misread the situation.

Call me at home tonight, pls.
I don't care what time.

Olenka

P.S. I left my little necklace in your bathroom, please keep an eye out for it . . .

Bertrand Lacoste
B.L.C. Consulting
May 18

F.A.O. Olenka Zbikowski
Subject: Your internship

Madame,

I give our various discussions due consideration and can confirm that we cannot foresee a situation whereby you are granted permanent employment.

A number of recent contracts have allowed us to secure the company's short-term future, but they are not sufficiently longstanding to enable us to take on new colleagues on a lasting basis.

With the exception of one or two isolated incidents, your time at B.L.C. Consulting can on the whole be described as satisfactory, and we are glad to have been able to offer you the opportunity of such a worthwhile experience that will strengthen your curriculum vitæ as you approach potential employers.

I appreciate your surprise with regard to the approval of Monsieur Thomas Jaulin's application for a five-month unpaid internship at B.L.C. Consulting. Our acceptance followed your categorical refusal to extend your internship beyond May 30. It goes without saying, however, that, given your intimate understanding of our activities and the seamless manner in which you have engaged with your fellow team members, Monsieur Jaulin's offer would immediately be withdrawn should you wish to extend your current internship.

I very much look forward to hearing your response.

    Kindest regards,
    Bertrand Lacoste

18

The situation couldn't be clearer: the odds are in my favour.

I can't imagine any of the other candidates being better prepared. I'll be the best because I've worked the hardest.

This thought is running through my head when, at around 7.00 p.m., the telephone rings.

It goes to the answering machine, but it's not Lucie's voice on the speaker again. I know this voice. It's a woman. A young woman.

"My name is Olenka Zbikowski."

I approach the speakerphone with a combination of intrigue and suspicion.

"We met at B.L.C. Consulting when you came in for your tests. I was the one who . . ."

When I realise who she is, I rush to the telephone so quickly that I knock it over. I have to run my hand under the sofa to recover the handset.

"Hello!"

I've only taken three steps and done one squat but I'm as breathless as if I'd run a marathon. I am terrified by this call – it is not at all in the ordinary running of things.

"Monsieur Delambre?"

I confirm that yes, that's me: my voice betrays panic, the girl apologises, and I realise that it's definitely her, the girl who handed out our test papers.

She wants to meet me. Immediately.

This isn't normal.

"Why? Tell me why!"

She can hear how shaken I am by this call.

"I'm not very far from where you live. I can be there in twenty minutes."

These twenty minutes feel like twenty hours, twenty years.

The meeting takes place in the little garden by the square. We're sitting on a bench. The street lamps light up one by one. There aren't many people around. She's not as pretty as I remember, perhaps because she's not wearing any make-up. She composes herself and, in very simple words, informs me that the world has ended.

"Officially, you're one of four candidates, but three of you are just there to make up the numbers. The position is going to be allocated to a candidate named Juliette Rivet. You don't stand a chance. You're just a foil."

This information whirls around my brain, but it doesn't break through the cortex. It carries on its journey before worming its way between my two synapses. The scale of the calamity starts to dawn on me.

"Juliette Rivet is a very close friend of Bertrand Lacoste," the young woman continues. "She's the one he will pick. So he has chosen three candidates for show. The first because he has an international profile that will satisfy the client, and another with a vaguely similar C.V. But Lacoste is going to make sure they get marked down. As for you – you were chosen on account of your age. According to Lacoste, 'it looks good to have an old guy in the picture these days'."

"But Exxyal choose the candidates, not him!"

She's taken aback:

"How do you know that it's Exxyal recruiting?"

"Answer me . . ."

"I have no idea how you know that, but Exxyal won't contest Lacoste's verdict. They're looking for someone with a similar skillset and will be happy to take the candidate favoured by the firm they've hired for the recruitment. End of story."

I look around but it's like a mist has descended. I'm about to faint. My stomach is in knots, my kidneys aching.

"This job is not for you, Monsieur Delambre. You have absolutely no chance."

I am so disorientated, so bewildered that she wonders if she was right to warn me. I must be a frightening sight.

"But . . . Why are you telling me this?"

"I've informed the other two candidates as well."

"What's in it for you?"

"Lacoste used me, squeezed me, drained me, then discarded me. I'm doing everything in my power to make sure his glorious operation fails because no-one is there to take part in it. His candidate will be the only one who turns up. It will be a personal kick in the teeth and, as far as his client is concerned, an absolute disaster. I appreciate it's a bit childish, but it makes me feel better."

She stands up.

"The best thing you can do is not go, I guarantee. I'm sorry to have to tell you, but your test results were very poor. You are no longer in the running, Monsieur Delambre, you shouldn't have even been called in for interview. Lacoste kept you for show, so even if by some small miracle you manage to pull something out the bag, you don't stand a chance. I'm sorry . . ."

She makes a vague hand gesture.

"I admit that I'm doing this mainly for selfish reasons, but I'm also telling you so that you don't have to go through a fruitless and potentially humiliating experience. My father must be roughly the same age as you, and I wouldn't want . . ."

She's sufficiently thin-skinned to realise that her attempt at demagoguery might be taking it one step too far. She purses her lips. My desolate expression is enough to tell her that she's found her target.

I feel like I've had a lobotomy.

My brain has ceased to react.

"Why should I believe you?"

"Because you've known from the start that it was too good to be true. That's why you called Bertrand . . . I mean Monsieur Lacoste a few days ago. You wanted to believe it, but it defied all logic. I think you know it . . ."

I wait for my brain to kick back into action.

When I look up, the girl is gone, she's already at the edge of the square, heading slowly towards the *métro*.

It's dark now. The lights are still off in the flat. The window in the sitting room is wide open and the dim glow of the street lamps is trickling in.

I'm alone in my chaotic flat. Nicole is gone. I've beaten up my son-in-law. He and my daughter are waiting to get their money back. The Logistics trial will be under way in a few weeks.

Suddenly the intercom rings.

Lucie. She's downstairs.

She has called and called and now she's worried.

I stand up but I barely make it to the door. I collapse to my knees and start crying.

Lucie's voice is imploring.

"Open up, Papa."

She knows I'm there because of the open window. I can't even move now.

It's finished. Time to bow out.

Tears come and keep on coming. Crying like this is my first real respite for a long time. The only thing that's been absolutely true. Tears of disarray. I am devastated, inconsolable.

Lucie eventually leaves.

I have been crying, crying so much.

It must be very late. How long have I stayed here, slumped against the front door, sobbing? Until the tears run dry.

Finally, I summon the strength to get up, despite my exhaustion.

A few thoughts pick their way through my head.

I take a deep breath.

Anger overwhelms me.

I look up a telephone number and dial. I apologise for calling so late.

"Do you know where I can get myself a weapon? A real one . . ."

Kaminski leaves me hanging for a few seconds, unsure how to respond.

"In theory, yes. But . . . What exactly is it you need?"

"Anything . . . No! Not anything. A pistol. An automatic pistol. Can you? With real ammunition."

Kaminski concentrates for a second.

"When do you need it for?"

DURING

19

An hour before the start of the operation, Monsieur Lacoste came to me and said:

"Monsieur Fontana, there's been a slight change of plan. There will just be two candidates for the H.R. post, rather than four."

His tone suggested that this was a minor detail that had no bearing on proceedings; but the tense expression I'd noted a few minutes earlier when he received his second text message of the morning led me to believe otherwise. His client, Exxyal, had requested four candidates, and it was hard to imagine that reducing this by half would be without consequence. Monsieur Lacoste didn't give me any indication as to why these two candidates had pulled out at the last minute, and it wasn't my place to ask.

I kept quiet. Not my problem. My job exclusively involved organising the technical aspects of the operation: finding the premises, sourcing personnel, etc.

The fact is, I've run a fair few operations in my time – many of them a lot more complex than this – and if my experience has taught me one thing, it's that they are as vulnerable as living organisms. They're like a chain: all the links must hold. So when little hitches start stacking up in the minutes before lift-off, alarm bells ring. You always have to trust your intuition. Except by the time your intuition tells you something's wrong, it's usually too late.

From a distance, I saw Monsieur Lacoste deep in discussion with Monsieur Dorfmann, the C.E.O. of Exxyal Europe. He had that air of detachment that people affect when they're delivering bad news as though it was of little importance. If Monsieur Dorfmann was annoyed by this, he didn't show it. Now there's a man who knows how to stay cool under pressure; there's a man I can respect.

A little after 9.00 a.m., someone rang to say that two people had arrived, so I headed downstairs. The deserted main lobby made for a truly depressing sight, with twenty or so enormous armchairs and two lone people. They were sitting more than ten metres apart and hadn't even dared greet one another.

It took me a split second to recognise Monsieur Delambre. As I approached him, I rolled back the tape in my head, pausing on a frame from a few days earlier. I had just come out of a meeting with Monsieur Lacoste. I was on the pavement, about to move out, when I sensed I was being watched. It's a very particular feeling, and years of hazardous exercises have taught me to pay great attention to it. It has saved my life on more than one occasion. So I stopped right where I was, took out a piece of chewing gum to buy myself some time, and while I was unwrapping it I mentally scoured the area to identify the enemy's position. As soon as my intuition turned to certainty, I looked up with a snap. On the corner of the building opposite, a man was watching me. He pretended to look at his watch, before – just by chance – his mobile decided to ring. He took out the device and clamped it to his ear, turning round as though he was engrossed in the call. It was Monsieur Delambre. He must have been on a reconnaissance mission. But the person in front of me was unrecognisable from the man I'd seen on the pavement that day.

From the off, his anxiety struck me as disproportionate. A real bundle of nerves.

His face was haggard, almost deathly pale. He had clearly cut himself shaving as there was an unpleasant red scab on his right cheek. A nervous tic made his left eye twitch intermittently, and his palms were sweaty. Any one of these symptoms would have been enough to suggest that he was feeling extremely out of his depth in this situation, and that he had little chance of seeing it through to the end.

Picture it: two withdrawals in quick succession, Mademoiselle Zbikowksi A.W.O.L. (Monsieur Lacoste was leaving her endless messages, and with greater and greater urgency), and one candidate on the brink of cardiac arrest ... The whole adventure was threatening to be a lot more perilous than expected. But that was none of my business. The premises met the brief and were suitably equipped, the devices all worked, and my team had been well trained. I had done my bit, and whatever the reasons for their monkeying around, they didn't concern me. All I cared about was receiving the balance of my fee.

Having said that, part of my brief did involve "consultancy" services, so I decided to cover my back: after shaking hands with Monsieur Delambre and Madame Rivet (sorry, *Mademoiselle* Rivet), I asked them if they'd be so kind as to wait a moment. I went over to the reception desk and put an internal call through to Monsieur Lacoste to explain the situation.

"Monsieur Delambre strikes me as being in very poor shape. I think he's a non-starter."

Monsieur Lacoste didn't react straight away. After the series of mishaps he had sustained since our arrival, this news seemed to knock him further. It even occurred to me that if Monsieur Lacoste himself were to show signs of weakness, then that would be game over; but he pulled himself together just in time.

"What do you mean, poor shape?"

"He strikes me as very nervous."

"Nervous? Of course he's nervous! Everyone's nervous! Me included – I'm nervous!"

In my head, I added the raw tension in Monsieur Lacoste's voice to the growing list of calamities blighting this affair. He quite literally wouldn't hear another word said about it. The wheels were in motion, and even though the operation was starting to resemble the mad runaway train from "*La Bête humaine*", he could see no way of halting it without losing face in front of his client. He was making these problems out to be nothing but minor inconveniences. I've seen a lot of this since I started working with businesses. Like heavy machinery, these projects gather so much momentum (in terms of energy, capital and time) that no-one has the balls to stop them. You see it with advertising or marketing campaigns, or big events. When their backs are against the wall, the people in charge always acknowledge in hindsight that the warning signs were there – they just chose not to acknowledge them. But they only admit this to themselves, never out loud.

"We'll manage just fine," Lacoste said to me with a reassuring tone. "And anyway, there's nothing to say that Delambre won't come good and prove himself a much stronger candidate than we're giving him credit for."

Faced with such wilful blindness, I decided to hold my tongue.

At the far end of the lobby, Monsieur Delambre's shrunken figure seemed apprehensive; a bomb ready to blow. Barring a technical cock-up (which would have brought my role into question), I didn't foresee any danger. This was just a little role play exercise.

If I'm honest, it didn't bother me much to see the operation scuppering. To begin with, at least, it even amused me. Understand that I've spent twenty years in various theatres of operation. I've risked my life as many as twenty times, and I've seen a lot of people die. So when a company shows up wanting to stage a virtual hostage-taking . . . Fine, I'm sure they had their reasons (linked to their balance sheet, undoubtedly), but over the course of the planning, I noticed the *Schadenfreude* they were taking from it. Monsieur Dorfmann and Monsieur Lacoste have mind-blowing levels of responsibility, but this hostage-taking escapade had gone further: it frightened them, and they relished the fear. The consequence of this was now plain to see.

Monsieur Lacoste joined us downstairs soon after. It was hard to tell whether his nervousness was merely down to the situation or whether, like me, he had an inkling that the exercise was entering a tailspin. This is typical of successful people: they don't have a shred of self-doubt and consider themselves capable of overcoming any difficulty. They think they're untouchable.

Monsieur Delambre's whole demeanour jarred with that of the svelte, ethereally pretty Mademoiselle Rivet, in her figure-hugging grey flecked suit. She knew what she was doing when she picked that outfit. Slumped in his sizeable lobby armchair, Monsieur Delambre suddenly appeared old and jaded. It seemed like an unfair contest. Not that it was a fashion competition . . . No, this was a test in which the participants would need to demonstrate considerable interpersonal skills and genuine proficiency, and on this front, Monsieur Lacoste was right: Monsieur Delambre still had every chance. In fact, now that there were two of them instead of four, on paper his chances had doubled.

The two candidates stood up in a single movement. Monsieur Lacoste made the introductions:

"Monsieur Delambre, Mademoiselle Rivet . . . and Monsieur David Fontana, who is our noble stage manager."

A warning light immediately started flashing in my head: there was something about the woman's collectedness and Monsieur Lacoste's insistence; a certain manner about them . . . I remember being convinced that these two were already – what's the word? – *acquainted.* And I couldn't help feeling sorry for Monsieur Delambre, because if I was right, he was in danger of being nothing more than a walk-on part.

I also noticed that Monsieur Delambre was carrying a brief-case, while Mademoiselle Rivet had just her handbag, which only served to highlight their difference further. It looked like he was on his way to work, while she was on her way home.

"It's just the two of us?" Monsieur Delambre asked.

The tone of his voice stopped Monsieur Lacoste in his tracks. It was low and shaky. The voice of a man under intense pressure.

"Yes," Monsieur Lacoste replied. "The others have withdrawn. Your chances are all the higher . . ."

The news didn't seem to please Monsieur Delambre in the slightest. He had a point: even if it did improve his chances, it still seemed . . . all this rigmarole and only two candidates? Monsieur Lacoste sensed his misgivings.

"Forgive me for speaking frankly," he added, "but the fundamentals of this operation have nothing to do with you!"

He glared at Monsieur Delambre, realising the importance of wresting back control of the situation.

"Our client needs to select the most suitable candidate from five executives to carry out a vital restructuring process. This is the primary objective of the exercise. However, an H.R. assistant will be recruited simultaneously over the course of the assessment; after all, the main role of an H.R. executive is, of course, to evaluate personnel. We are simply killing two birds with one stone."

"Thank you, understood," Monsieur Delambre said.

It was difficult to tell whether his tone carried bitterness or a thinly veiled anger. Whatever the case, I felt it better to change the subject, so I showed the candidates to the lift and took them upstairs.

We entered the meeting room at precisely 9.17 a.m. Yes, I'm certain of that. In my line of work, precision is paramount. Over the years, I've managed to internalise my timekeeping: at any hour of the day, I can tell you the exact time, correct to within a few minutes. But that morning I also had my eye on the clock. The meeting had been called for 10.00 a.m. and the Exxyal Europe execs were scheduled to arrive at least ten or fifteen minutes in advance: all the final arrangements needed to be made before then.

I introduced Monsieur Delambre and Mademoiselle Rivet to the team, starting with the two actors who would be playing the role of the clients. Malik was wearing a large, brightly coloured djellaba and a violet keffiyeh with geometric patterns, while Monsieur Renard was wearing a traditional suit.

"At the start of the role play," I explained, "Malik and Monsieur Renard will play the clients that the Exxyal Europe execs are invited to meet. Malik will exit right away; Monsieur Renard will stay until the end."

Throughout this presentation, I paid particular attention to the candidates' reactions because, while Monsieur André Renard may not be an actor of any great renown, a few years ago he did appear in a fairly successful advert for a household product, and I was worried that the participants might recognise his face. But Monsieur Delambre and Mademoiselle Rivet's concentration was already fixed on the three members of the commando. It's important not to understate their impact, complete with their fatigues, balaclavas and combat boots, and their three Uzi submachine guns lined up on the table alongside rows of ammunition. Even though everyone knew full well that this was a role play, the whole thing made for quite a spectacle, not least because (without wanting to brag) I had picked my teammates well. Kader, the commando chief, has a calm, determined face; and Yasmine is capable of looking terrifyingly stern. Both of them started their careers in the Moroccan police, and their records speak for themselves. As for Mourad, in spite of his shortcomings, I'd decided to keep him on because of his rugged features: with his full, unshaven cheeks, he has a brutal face that suits his role down to the ground.

Everyone greeted each other with a simple nod of the head. The atmosphere was fairly tense. That's always the way in the minutes before the start of an operation – it can be misleading.

Next I showed them the three rooms: the meeting room where the role play would begin and where the group of hostages would be held; then the interrogation chamber where the executives would be called individually or in pairs, should Monsieur Delambre or Mademoiselle Rivet want to play them against each other. There was a laptop computer connected to the Exxyal Group system sitting open on a small table. Lastly, I took them to the observation room, from where the two candidates would administer the interrogations. One monitor would display images from the waiting room recorded on two different cameras; and on another, images from the table in the interrogation chamber. The final room, from where Monsieur Dorfmann and Monsieur Lacoste would oversee the operation, was none of their concern.

Monsieur Lacoste left us at that point. We could see that he had some concerns. My guess is that he went to call Mademoiselle Zbikowski yet again, even if, given the time, we both knew she wouldn't be coming. I've no idea what happened between the two of them, but it wasn't hard to guess that his assistant had stood him up, leaving him to take care of things on his own.

Mademoiselle Rivet attempted a smile at Monsieur Delambre, probably as a way of easing the tension, but he seemed far too anxious to respond. They sat down next to each other and turned to the screens that were relaying live footage from the meeting room.

That was when Monsieur Dorfmann arrived. I had only met him once before, a few days earlier at our only rehearsal. He had been very gracious and very receptive to my suggestions; both of which were effective ways of emphasising his authority. For a man of his age, he is remarkably flexible – it took him no time at all to learn how to collapse the right way.

We went into the rest area so that I could bring him up to speed. I reminded him of his instructions, but Monsieur Dorfmann was less accommodating than at the rehearsal. It irritated him hearing information for a second time, so I kept it short, and he promptly returned to the meeting room. Everyone was on edge.

As per the plan, Monsieur Renard was seated to his right. He seemed to be getting in the zone for his role as an important client, while Malik was sipping a very strong coffee to Monsieur Renard's right.

And we began the wait.

20

The images relayed by the cameras were clear. I was happy with everything from a technical perspective.

Monsieur Lacoste was stationed just behind Monsieur Delambre and Mademoiselle Rivet with a pad of paper. I pulled up a chair and watched them. I was a bit nervous myself. Not because of what was at stake, no – there was nothing in it for me – but because I like a job well done. And because I was still owed a third of my fee, to be paid on completion of the operation. The mission was very well paid, I have to admit. The truth is that business role plays come with a serious price tag, but they're not all that interesting. They're there for the amusement of companies and managers. I like my missions a bit more real.

In any case, I always get nervous before the start of a mission, regardless of how major it is. But nothing compared to Monsieur Delambre. He was staring straight into the monitors, as though he was expecting them to reveal some hidden truth, and when he switched from one screen to the other, it wasn't just his eyes that moved, but his entire head, a bit like a chicken. Mademoiselle Rivet seemed more concerned with her neighbour than with the test itself. She was looking at him surreptitiously, the way you might eye a messy eater at the next-door table in a restaurant. Monsieur Delambre didn't even seem to notice her, and carried on with his mechanical actions. I found his behaviour so worrying (it's normal to be nervous in this kind of situation, but *this* nervous?) that I touched him on the shoulder and asked him if everything was alright. I hadn't even finished my sentence when he leapt up as if I'd just electrocuted him.

"Huh? What?" he said, spinning round abruptly.

"Is everything alright, Monsieur Delambre?"

"Huh? Yes, fine . . ." he replied, but he was somewhere else entirely.

That's what is so hard to take: right then, I had all the confirmation I needed that everything was about to go pear-shaped. My concern had given way to certainty. Yet still I did nothing. Monsieur Delambre had a screw loose. We could easily have cancelled the test for the H.R. candidates without interfering with the assessment of the execs. It was just that the two operations had always been linked in my mind, and so the idea never occurred to me. And from then on, everything went too fast.

As the start of the operation approached, Mademoiselle Rivet seemed less and less composed. In fact, she hadn't regained her colour since seeing the members of the commando with their black, shiny guns – little did she know that her tribulations were far from over. I stood up to show the two of them how to use the microphone to speak into the earpieces of the different members of the commando. Monsieur Delambre answered with a series of groans, but he had clearly understood the instructions because he operated the controls correctly when it was his turn for a trial run.

The Exxyal execs were beginning to trickle in: Monsieur Lussay first, followed by Mademoiselle Tràn.

Monsieur Maxime Lussay is a legal executive. Just as well if you ask me, because he looks like a natural born lawyer: immaculately turned out, every movement underpinned by a certain stiffness. His eyes seemed to twitch in staccato fashion, as if they had to revert to their original position before moving to the next spot. I had read their files closely: I remembered that Monsieur Lussay had a doctorate in law, and had drawn up and overseen numerous Exxyal Group contracts.

As for Mademoiselle Tràn, you could tell straight away that she worked in sales. A very dynamic woman – a little too dynamic, if you ask me, almost like she was on something. She walked with assurance, standing square in front of people. She gave off the impression that nothing could faze her, and that if you dithered at all, she would finish your sentences for you. With her physique and her six-figure salary, she must be highly attractive to men her age.

These young executives . . . you could tell how modern and confident they were just by the way they swaggered into the waiting room. Every shake of the hand screamed: "We are powerful, productive, happy people."

The Exxyal executives went up in turn to greet their boss, Monsieur Dorfmann, and he treated each of them with that sort of familiar attitude you see all too often in business. I find it so puzzling. From the top of the ladder to the bottom, everyone is friends with everyone, calling each other by their first name even though traditionally it should be *Monsieur* this or *Madame* that. I think this confuses the picture. In that sort of environment, people end up mistaking their office for the local café. I spent part of my career in the army, and things there are a lot more clear-cut. You know why you are there. Your colleagues are either superiors or subordinates, and when you meet someone, you know straight off whether he's one or the other: whether he's above you or below you. In business, it's all become blurred. You play squash with your boss, you go for a jog with your line manager . . . it's a mess, quite frankly. If people aren't careful, there won't be any leaders left; companies will be controlled by spreadsheets alone. Although sooner or later, there'll be a return to hierarchy – make no mistake. And quite right too . . . when the spreadsheets show that someone's performance isn't up to scratch, and the powers-that-be demand answers, they can't feel hard done by just because they've spent too long mistaking their bosses for school friends.

That's how I see it, at least.

Anyway, there was Monsieur Dorfmann holding court at the end of the table. One by one, his colleagues came in and, amid all the back-slapping, advanced straight past "Go" and landed on the square marked "Power", shaking their C.E.O.'s hand before schmoozing with Monsieur Renard and Malik, who Monsieur Dorfmann took a moment to introduce. Then they took their seats.

Back where we were in the observation room, Monsieur Lacoste named each executive as he or she arrived, pointing out each one in turn to Mademoiselle Rivet and Monsieur Delambre against the list they had been given. For example, he'd say: "Maxime Lussay, Ph.D. in Law, thirty-five, legal department"; or "Virginie Tràn, thirty-five, H.E.C. graduate in business, sales executive."

Monsieur Delambre had clearly done his homework. He had sheets for each candidate and was taking lots of notes, on their behaviour I suppose, but his hand was shaking so much I wondered if he'd manage to read them later on. Mademoiselle Rivet's approach was less intensive: she was working directly on the document she'd been sent, and was marking the names of the people with a cross as they entered. The overall impression was that she hadn't taken her preparation so seriously.

Monsieur Jean-Marc Guéneau and Monsieur Paul Cousin arrived within a few minutes of each other.

The former is an economist, and the first thing that struck you was how pleased he was with himself. He strutted around with an air of entitlement, puffing out his chest, reeking of self-confidence. His lazy eye was irritating – you couldn't tell which one was true.

His neighbour, Monsieur Paul Cousin, was the exact opposite. I remember noticing that Monsieur Cousin had a very large head, at the same time as being frighteningly thin. He had a fanatical look in his eyes, like an overzealous churchgoer. A raft of engineering degrees, a decent part of his career spent in the Persian Gulf, followed by a return to H.Q. four years ago with considerable levels of responsibility. This guy is Captain Technical, the Emperor of the Oil Well.

Madame Camberlin is around fifty, a senior project manager. She was sufficiently sure of herself not to mind arriving last.

Monsieur Dorfmann seemed keen to make a start, so he tapped his fingers on the table before turning to Monsieur Renard and Malik.

"Alright then. First of all, allow me to wish you a warm welcome on behalf of Exxyal Europe. The introductions were a little swift, so if I may . . ."

The atmosphere in the observation room had hardly been light in the first place, but at that point it became oppressive.

The voices we heard through the speakers seemed to come from a far-away and sinister world. I looked over at Monsieur Lacoste, who responded with a small nod of the head.

I left the room to join my team in the area next door. Out in the corridor, I could hear Monsieur Dorfmann's voice filtering through from the meeting room.

(". . . *with this highly promising synergy, which we are absolutely thrilled about . . .*")

All three of them were prepared. True professionals. All I had to do was adjust the angle of Yasmine's submachine gun, a reflex on my part. Then I held my arms out to the side.

The signal was clear: it is time.

Kader gave a nod.

They were on the move immediately. I watched them file down the corridor (". . . *and represents a major turning point in global strategy for stakeholders across our sector. This is why . . .*"). I followed them before making a sharp turn and falling back in behind Monsieur Delambre and Mademoiselle Rivet.

In under seven seconds, the commando reached the meeting room and burst through the door.

"Hands on the table!" Kader screamed, while Mourad headed to his right and stalked round the perimeter of the room.

Yasmine nimbly circled the table, banging her Uzi barrel loudly on the desk to make sure everyone obeyed the order.

They were all so shocked that no-one moved a muscle. Not a sound was uttered as everyone held their breath. The Exxyal execs looked aghast at the submachine gun barrels mere centimetres from their faces. They were too hypnotised to register who was holding them.

In front of his screen, Monsieur Delambre tried to write something on his pad, but his hand was trembling too much. He glanced to his right, where Mademoiselle Rivet was trying to keep a certain distance. Everything happened so suddenly that her face had gone almost as white as her neighbour's.

Using the remote control, I activated the camera recording the scene and panned around the table: the five execs were wide-eyed with terror, no-one attempting even the smallest movement. They were petrified.

On our screens, we saw Kader approach Monsieur Dorfmann.

"Monsieur Dorfmann," he began, with his thick Arabic accent.

The Exxyal boss slowly looked up. He suddenly seemed smaller, older. His mouth hung open and his eyes looked like they might burst out of their sockets.

"You're going to help me clarify the situation, if you don't mind," Kader continued.

Even if someone had been crazy enough to intervene, he wouldn't have had time to lift a finger. In less than two seconds, Kader took out his SIG Sauer pistol, extended his arm towards Monsieur Dorfmann, and fired.

The sound was deafening.

Monsieur Dorfmann's body was flung backwards, his chair

tipping back for a moment into thin air before snapping forward and throwing his upper body onto the table.

Then the action sped up. Malik stood, his huge djellaba billowing around him, and started yelling at the leader of the commando in Arabic. There was an urgency to his words as he unleashed a stream of furious, panic-stricken insults, the sentences flooding from his mouth. The torrent dried up when Kader fired a bullet into his chest, striking him near his heart. Malik did a quarter turn that he didn't have time to complete, as the second bullet hit him full in the stomach. He folded under the impact and collapsed to the ground with a thud.

Hostage behaviour falls into three categories: physical resistance, verbal resistance and non-resistance. As a matter of course, we favour non-resistance, since it helps the remainder of the operation run more smoothly. During the preparations, I had selected a hostage to "symbolise" a losing strategy (Malik had just achieved this task perfectly) in order to demonstrate that non-resistance represented the group's best chance of survival. Our client had asked us to test their employees' shock resistance, which requires – as Monsieur Lacoste had reminded me on several occasions – assessing their level of cooperation with the enemy on a scale that runs from total resistance at one end, to barefaced collaboration at the other. In order for this to happen, it was essential that they agreed to negotiate, and the best way to do this was effectively to show that it was the only option available to them.

But let me return to the action.

With the first bullet, everyone let out a muffled cry. Try to imagine . . . by that point the room was shuddering with the sound of the three explosions, which completely dominated the room, and two men were lying on the ground, each of them with a bloodstain spreading around their bodies.

Madame Camberlin clasped her hands to her ears, while

Monsieur Lussay – eyes screwed shut, palms flat on the table, completely disorientated – thrashed his head from left to right as though he was trying to bounce his brain from one side of his skull to the other.

"I think the rules have been made clear. My name is Kader. But we have plenty of time to get to know each other."

His voice seemed muffled to them.

Kader looked down at Monsieur Guéneau and frowned with mild disdain.

There was a clear sound of dripping liquid; a large, dark puddle was forming beneath Monsieur Guéneau's chair.

Despite the fact that all people have distinct characters and temperaments, hostages always respond in more or less the same way. The brain reacts to suddenness, terror and threat in a fairly narrow way. It is common for hostages – as seemed to be the case with Monsieur Cousin, who was clasping his head and gazing directly ahead of him – to remain in a state of incredulity due to the suddenness of the attack, as though refusing to believe it, preferring to think they've fallen victim to some sick practical joke. But it doesn't take long for them to come round to a more rational state, especially when you kill one or two people in front of them. That was why I'd chosen to "take out" Monsieur Dorfmann immediately, since he represented a figure of authority in their eyes. This manoeuvre served to flip the pyramid on its head, and consequently, the commando's message was clear: we're in charge. The fact that Monsieur Dorfmann had played his role to perfection, bursting the pouch of blood I had provided him with and falling just like I had shown him, only added to the effect. I'd reassured him beforehand: at the end of the day, no-one would notice if he didn't pull it off perfectly, since people's brains are so frazzled by the unexpected nature of the situation.

Monsieur Delambre and Mademoiselle Rivet didn't move a millimetre. A hostage-taking on television and a hostage-taking in real life are not at all the same thing. I know, I know, this wasn't exactly "real life" but, without wanting to blow my own trumpet, it was bloody realistic. The two candidates experienced the action as though they were in the meeting room themselves. The reason I say that? Their reactions. Going back to what I was saying about the different behaviours exhibited by victims in this sort of situation, they encompass nine key emotions: shock, astonishment, anxiety, terror, frustration, vulnerability, powerlessness, humiliation and isolation. Monsieur Delambre's reaction corresponded with anxiety and isolation, while Mademoiselle Rivet was displaying shock and terror.

In the event that the murder of the Arab client didn't have the desired deterrent effect, my plan was to cut short any attempt at physical resistance by the hostages.

"Everyone over here!" Mourad shouted, gesturing towards the wall opposite the windows.

Struck dumb with fear, they all stood up and started shuffling around uncertainly, as though they were afraid they might knock over a valuable object, keeping their heads down to avoid any missile that might come their way.

"Hands against the wall, legs apart!" Mourad shouted.

Monsieur Lussay, who had no doubt seen this done before on television, spread his arms and legs wide, his buttocks tensed as he waited to be frisked. Next to him, Mademoiselle Tràn's tight skirt was inhibiting her legs. Yasmine approached her from behind and yanked up the material with the tip of her gun, before kicking her feet apart harshly. Mademoiselle Tràn placed her hands against the wall too, fingers splayed. Having her skirt hitched up like that was degrading, especially with men around: another effective technique to emphasise a hostage's vulnerability. As for Monsieur Guéneau, his trousers were sodden down to his knees and his whole body was shaking, while Monsieur Cousin's eyes were screwed shut as though he were expecting a bullet to shatter his skull at any second. Wedged between the Exxyal execs, Monsieur Renard, our actor, was murmuring away softly and incomprehensibly. Madame Camberlin, at the end of the line, seemed all the more unnerved when she realised he was reciting a prayer (just as I'd instructed him). The sound of someone praying for their life is another good way of guaranteeing cooperation in hostage situations.

A few seconds later, their backs still turned, everyone heard footsteps, then a door opening and closing again. Each of them must have sensed a figure moving back and forth behind them. They could make out the sound of tables being dragged, and then some panting. The members of the commando were busy removing the two bodies.

After two or three minutes, Kader ordered them to turn around. The tables had been lined up along the partition wall, and the bloodstains on the carpet were glistening black. The centre of the room was entirely empty; in situations like this, nothing is more unsettling than emptiness.

When Mourad came back into the room, his submachine gun hanging limply in his hands, it was clear he had wiped his bloodied chest with the back of his sleeve. Like a carefully choreographed routine, each member of the commando assumed position in front of the line of hostages: Kader in the middle, Yasmine to the right, Mourad to the left.

A few seconds went by, during which the only sound was Monsieur Guéneau's sobbing as he stared at the floor.

"Right," Kader said. "Everyone empty their pockets!"

Wallets, bunches of keys, music players and mobile phones were collected into the two women's handbags on the big conference table.

Yasmine walked down the ranks and began searching them with her expert hands. She left nothing to chance: pockets, belts . . . the whole lot. Mademoiselle Tràn felt the young woman's hands skim dextrously over her breasts and between her thighs. Madame Camberlin wasn't paying attention to anything; she was simply trying to keep herself upright, even though it was obvious that all she wanted was to collapse in a heap. Yasmine then frisked the men, running her skilful hands over their buttocks and the inside of their legs. Even Monsieur Guéneau's drenched trouser legs were patted down without any compromise, before she took a few steps back and signalled to the leader that all was in order.

The hostages were lined up again, still on their feet, with the commando fanned out in front of them.

"We are here for a sacred cause," Kader said calmly, "a cause worthy of every sacrifice. We require your cooperation, and we are prepared to lay down our lives to get it. Yours too, should that be necessary. We will leave you to reflect on this for a moment. *Allahu akbar!*"

The other two members of the commando repeated "*Allahu akbar*" after him in unison. Then the leader walked out, followed by Yasmine, leaving big Mourad to guard them on his own.

No-one knew what to do.

No-one moved.

Monsieur Guéneau fell to his knees and huddled on the floor, sobbing.

21

Malik had changed out of his costume into jeans and a pullover, and his sports bag was sitting next to him on the floor. I gave him his envelope, we shook hands, and he disappeared off to the lift while I went back to Monsieur Delambre and Mademoiselle Rivet.

After putting on a fresh shirt and suit in the rest area, Monsieur Dorfmann poked his head in. I gave him a thumbs up to confirm that he had played his part wonderfully. He smiled at me, and I realised at that moment that I'd never seen him smile before.

He slipped away and, along with Monsieur Lacoste, went back to the rest area where the monitors were showing footage from both the meeting room where the hostages were being held, and from the interrogation chamber where his executives would soon be taking it in turns to sit down across the table from Kader.

From then on, Monsieur Dorfmann and Monsieur Lacoste worked away in their room. They were the sleeping partners: it was their job to discuss the test and comment on the execs' performance. I was alone with the other two candidates to oversee the technical developments of the hostage-taking. It's funny, but despite the extensive (and, as it would emerge, memorable) operation I'd put together for Monsieur Dorfmann, I don't think I'd exchanged more than twenty sentences with him. I had no idea what state of mind the man was in. He must have been certain that it was necessary and in the best interests of his company.

He was the God of his world. But who was his God? What did he worship? His board of directors? His shareholders? Money? I was still pondering on this when Monsieur Delambre started fidgeting in his chair. I assumed he needed the toilet. Mademoiselle Rivet was deathly pale, jotting down the odd word on her pad, clicking her biro and pulling her suit jacket around her as though she were suddenly cold.

"We'll get them into position. Then it's up to you how you play it," I said. My voice made them jump. They both turned towards me, which meant I could see them face on. They were no longer the same as just before. I've seen it so many times: strong emotions contort people's appearances, as though their true faces, their true selves, come to the surface in extreme circumstances. Monsieur Delambre was the worst – his grimace looked like a death mask.

"Mourad, arrange them in a circle as planned, please," I said into the microphone.

As I was speaking to him, Mourad cupped his hand around his ear like a singer. He nodded, standing in the middle of the room, but as he moved away the earpiece fell out.

"Right," he said.

Six pairs of frantic eyes turned on him, then on the earpiece dangling comically on the end of its wire.

"We're going to, er . . ." Mourad said. "We're going to change. Position. We're going to change it."

The message didn't register. Right from the start, I'd never been a hundred per cent sure about him: even in the practice runs, he hadn't covered himself in glory. I'd brought him on board because of his physical presence, but frankly the guy's as thick as two short planks, which ensured I kept his involvement to a minimum. He's cousins with Kader, and I agreed to have him on the basis that this was a role play – I wouldn't have given his C.V. more than three seconds if this had been a real operation. In fact, if you want the truth, he kind of cracked me up. But I have to admit he'd surpassed himself with the earpiece gaffe. If the situation hadn't been so fraught, I would have burst out laughing, but in the circumstances, all I could do was join the others in watching the scene anxiously.

The hostages were aware that they had to act, but the "position" instruction had baffled everyone. Madame Camberlin looked at Mademoiselle Tràn, who was examining Monsieur Cousin. Monsieur Renard had stopped praying, while the snivelling Monsieur Lussay stared at Monsieur Guéneau. Nobody knew what was going on.

"O.K., you," Mourad said.

He pointed at Monsieur Cousin, who straightened up immediately. In the face of adversity, that's what he does: he straightens. I made a mental note that he'd be a tough one to crack.

"You come here," Mourad said (he motioned to where Madame Camberlin was standing) ". . . you, there . . ." (gesticulating to Monsieur Renard) ". . . and you, round here . . ." (somewhere between Madame Camberlin and Mademoiselle Tràn) ". . . next to you . . ." (pointing at Monsieur Guéneau) ". . . and you . . ." (Mademoiselle Tràn) ". . . you come and stand here . . ." (this time the intended destination was very unclear, a spot somewhere near Madame Camberlin, but it was hard to tell) ". . . and you, er . . ." (Monsieur Lussay was on tenterhooks) ". . . O.K., you, here . . ." (he was pointing at his feet) ". . . but in a circle!" Mourad blurted out for good measure.

The hostages didn't feel remotely threatened. Mourad's orders lacked any edge – he came across as finicky, almost relishing the moment, like a greedy teenager picking out his favourite treats at the patisserie counter. And to top it off, he now stood there looking pleased to bits with his job. Except no-one had moved. In the hostages' defence, even I – the person responsible for designing the desired configuration – had no idea what he was trying to get them to do.

"Come on, move!" Mourad said, in the most convincing voice he could manage.

Understand that when a character like Mourad tries to act all assertive with a submachine gun slung over his shoulder and the barrel swinging around in front of him, it makes the weapon considerably less manoeuvrable. So despite his attempt at vigour, the order fell flat – everyone hesitated yet again.

That was Monsieur Cousin's cue. As I've said, it's in situations like this that a person's true character comes through. No-one knew what to do, but Monsieur Cousin kicked into action. In retrospect . . . no, let's not get ahead of ourselves.

Monsieur Cousin stepped forward and stood in the space he had been designated, as did Mademoiselle Tràn, followed by Monsieur Guéneau. Then Madame Camberlin moved to her right and Monsieur Renard headed left, before everyone stopped, uncertainly. Monsieur Lussay bumped into Monsieur Cousin, who sent him back towards Madame Camberlin.

Mourad was disappointed: he thought his orders had been nice and clear. But what he did next was inexplicable. I'm telling you, this guy was full of surprises . . . He put down his Uzi and walked up to the hostages. He grabbed Madame Camberlin by the shoulders and peered at the floor as if he was looking for specific markers on the carpet. It was like he'd invited Madame Camberlin to partner him in a tango lesson and was desperately trying to remember his steps. He shoved her a metre along and said: "There." He was so absorbed in his task that it didn't even occur to him that the hostages might take the opportunity to seize the submachine gun and attack him. Mademoiselle Tràn, her body extremely tense, took a step towards the weapon . . . I felt an icy chill run down my spine. But Mourad turned round just in time, busily taking Monsieur Renard by the shoulders and positioning him a little further away. Then it was Mademoiselle Tràn's turn, followed by Monsieur Lussay, Monsieur Guéneau and Monsieur

Cousin. The hostages were arranged back-to-back in a broad semi-circle, each one about a metre apart. No-one was facing the door.

"Sit down."

Mourad had picked up his weapon again.

"That's good like that," he announced with a satisfied tone, before turning to the camera, as though hoping the lens might congratulate him on his outstanding performance.

Then the hostages heard the door open and close again.

Silence fell. Two or three minutes passed by.

Mademoiselle Tràn risked a sideways glance.

"He's gone," she said, blankly.

22

"I . . . I have a telephone . . ." Monsieur Renard said, turning to the others. His face was very white, and he had to swallow back his saliva a number of times. "It's my wife's, I'd forgotten about it . . ." he went on, speaking in a bewildered tone.

He sank his hand into his inside pocket and pulled out the tiny mobile.

"I've . . . They didn't find it . . ."

He examined the mobile lying flat on his palm.

The revelation fell like a bombshell.

"You'll get us killed, you bastard!" Monsieur Guéneau cried, beside himself.

"Calm down," Madame Camberlin said.

Monsieur Renard looked thunderstruck, his eyes flicking between the telephone and the faces of the execs.

"They're watching us," Monsieur Lussay added through pursed lips, his voice hushed.

With a discreet movement of his chin, he indicated the top corner of the room where a small, black camera had been installed. Everyone turned either left or right to look at the ceiling.

"When the red light's blinking, it means it's not working," Mademoiselle Tràn said.

"You can't be sure of that," Monsieur Lussay replied.

"It's true! When it's on, there's a green light; if it's red it's off,"

Mademoiselle Tràn said with a tone of pure disgust, even hatred.

"These cameras . . ." Madame Camberlin cut in, "they don't have sound. They can't hear us."

Only Monsieur Cousin remained silent. He was still ramrod straight, inflexible, as stiff as a corpse.

"So what do I do?" Monsieur Renard asked.

He made his voice quiver to perfection. It was a remarkable performance, which I found reassuring after Mourad's woeful display.

"We've got to call the police," Madame Camberlin said, who was trying to sound calm.

"We have to give them the phone!" Monsieur Guéneau shouted.

"Shut your face for a second!"

All eyes turned to Mademoiselle Tràn, who was glaring at Monsieur Guéneau.

"Try thinking for a second, you bloody idiot," she snapped, turning to Monsieur Renard and holding out her hand. "Give it to me."

It was my turn to intervene.

"Mourad! Quick, get back to the hostage room!" I hissed into the microphone, and a second later I heard him crashing down the corridor.

Monsieur Renard had put the handset on the floor and was about to slide it over to her like a puck across an ice rink. He drew it back and forth on the ground, summoning all his concentration, before releasing it with a flourish. The telephone careened across the carpet towards Mademoiselle Tràn, whirling around like a spinning top, but his aim wasn't good.

On the screens, we saw Mourad open the door right at the moment the mobile came to rest at Monsieur Guéneau's feet. Caught by surprise, he slipped it up his right sleeve and tried to look calm, as if he hadn't moved a muscle since his captor had left.

In front of me, Monsieur Delambre was furiously taking notes, which at the time I found encouraging, I suppose. Perhaps at the start he was only suffering from pre-match nerves. Now he was in the zone, fully focused. Mademoiselle Rivet was scribbling away too.

A long silence ensued. Mourad was fiddling with his earpiece, struggling to keep it in place. In fact he was so consumed with his earpiece-insertion manoeuvre, that he seemed to have forgotten about the hostages. All eyes (with the exception of Mourad's) were bearing down on Monsieur Guéneau, who looked like he might expire at any moment. I zoomed in on his arm momentarily: he was clearly holding the little mobile in his sleeve and trying to cup it there, before clearing his throat.

"Excuse me . . ." he said.

As Mourad turned towards him, the earpiece fell out.

"The toilet . . ." Monsieur Guéneau said, his voice barely audible. "I need the toilet."

Not only was he failing to demonstrate any sangfroid, but he wasn't being very creative either. His trousers were as wet as a mop, and there he was asking for the toilet . . . But Mourad is not the sort of person who thinks like this. In fact, he seemed delighted at the opportunity that had presented itself.

"We've got a plan for this," he said. "You need to be accompanied," he added, reeling off the lines he had learnt by heart.

Monsieur Guéneau immediately realised that he'd made a strategic error, and so he made eye contact with Madame Camberlin, who cottoned on straight away:

"Me too! I need the toilet too."

Mourad closed his eyes then opened them again.

"O.K., there's a plan for that too," he said triumphantly. "You have to go one at a time. You asked first, so you get to go first," he said to Monsieur Guéneau, while putting the earpiece back in.

I breathed a "very good" into Mourad's earpiece and he smiled like a giant baby. Monsieur Guéneau hesitated, unsure what to make of this sudden show of happiness.

"On you go," Mourad said, holding out his hand as reassuringly as possible, before opening the door. Standing there was Yasmine, stony-faced, her legs set, as though they were planted in the ground. She looked Monsieur Guéneau in the eyes without blinking.

"Go!" Mourad repeated.

So Monsieur Guéneau stood up, both fists clenched at the end of his straightened arms, the only way he could prevent the mobile from slipping out of his sleeve.

Monsieur Delambre looked up. He seemed to be mulling over an intriguing idea, made a few notes on his pad, then laid down his pen.

And we waited. A few minutes passed. Provided my instructions were being carried out to the letter, I knew that Monsieur Guéneau had made it down the corridor, all the while under close guard. He'd entered a cubicle, turned and tried to shut the door, but the barrel of Yasmine's Uzi had blocked him.

"Do you mind . . ." Monsieur Guéneau said, scandalised that she was standing there facing him.

"Up to you. I could always take you back?" Yasmine said coldly.

Monsieur Guéneau turned and lifted the toilet seat with a frustrated motion, before opening his fly, rummaging around a little, and then urinating noisily. He kept his eyes down as he slid the telephone along his wrist. On his own mobile, he could have written a text with his eyes closed. They're all the same, he told himself: same functions, same keys. Head still lowered, he clutched his tummy to gain a few more precious seconds, then ran his index finger down the keypad to find the button at the bottom, and started typing discreetly.

That was when the mobile started ringing. The volume was so loud we could hear it all the way down the corridor.

On hearing the blaring ringtone echo round the toilet cubicle, the blood drained from Monsieur Guéneau. He fumbled for the phone as it vibrated in his sleeve and only just managed to catch it in his fingertips. Then he froze for a second, his eyes closed, probably waiting for his captor to unleash a burst of gunfire into his kidneys. But nothing happened. He blinked and turned towards Yasmine. What was he expecting? A blow to the face? A bullet in the head? A kick in the bollocks? He had no idea, but his whole body trembled. Yasmine didn't move, even when the phone rang a second time. She pointed to it with her submachine gun as it continued buzzing in his hand. He shivered from head to toe as though he was being electrocuted.

Yasmine jerked her weapon towards his waist.

Monsieur Guéneau looked down and closed his fly, blushing, then held out the device to Yasmine, who simply repeated the same, categorical gesture.

He looked at the flashing screen – unknown number – pressed the green button, and heard a man's voice. Kader's voice.

"Do you think this is acceptable behaviour, Monsieur Guéneau?"

23

The first thing Monsieur Guéneau saw as he entered the room was the Uzi on the table by Kader. Submachine guns always make so much more of an impression than a simple pistol. And should a hostage try his luck and grab it, they're just that little bit harder to manoeuvre, allowing the captor plenty of time to intervene. Kader is very experienced: these amateurs didn't pose any threat, not least because the weapons were loaded with blanks. Plus I had the utmost confidence in Kader and Yasmine, having enlisted their services for several challenging operations. I was aware of their quality. Kader just sat there holding the SIG Sauer he had used to "kill" two men a few minutes earlier. Monsieur Guéneau turned in a panic, only to meet the steely expression of Yasmine, who shoved him in the back with her Uzi towards an empty chair.

This was the moment of truth.

The first interrogation would set the tone for the remainder of the role play. If it went well, it would mean that the strategy was right for the task. Up to that point, my scenario had proved effective, and everything had gone according to plan. That's experience for you. But now we were entering the "active" phase, in which Monsieur Delambre and Mademoiselle Rivet had to interrogate the execs to assess their behaviour, and which would involve a certain amount of improvisation. I therefore remained attentive to every little detail.

Mademoiselle Rivet approached the microphone between herself and Monsieur Delambre, and let out a faint, dry cough.

Monsieur Guéneau sat down. He was shaking violently – his sodden trousers must have made him cold. On the screen, we could see him mouthing words, but we couldn't hear anything through the speakers.

Without waiting for any instructions, Kader leant towards him and asked:

"Sorry?"

"Are you going to kill me?" Monsieur Guéneau mumbled.

His voice was barely audible, which made his fear seem even more pathetic. Mademoiselle Rivet must have picked up on this, because she kicked into action:

"That is not our primary intention, Monsieur Guéneau. Unless, of course, you leave us with no other option."

Kader interpreted the words very well and relayed them carefully. Coming from his mouth, the word "intention" sounded like a threat – maybe because of his accent, or maybe because of his controlled, convincing tone. Mademoiselle Rivet could hear her own words being echoed. It gave all three of us the peculiar impression of being in both places at once.

Monsieur Guéneau shook his head, eyes closed.

"Please . . ." he murmured through his tears.

He thrust his hand into his pocket and slowly withdrew the mobile, placing it on the table as though it were a stick of dynamite.

"I'm begging you . . ."

Mademoiselle Rivet turned to Monsieur Delambre and indicated the microphone so that he could have his turn to intervene, but he didn't move and carried on staring at the screen. I realised that he was sweating, which was surprising bearing in mind how cool the air conditioning was. Mademoiselle Rivet ignored him and continued:

"Were you going to call the police?" she said into the microphone for Kader to repeat. "You're seeking to undermine our cause, is that it, Monsieur Guéneau?"

Monsieur Guéneau looked up at Kader, ready to swear by Almighty God, but he thought better of it.

"What . . . what do you want?" he said.

"No Monsieur Guéneau, that's not how this is going to work. You're a member of the finance department at Exxyal Group. As such, a lot of confidential information passes through your hands: contracts, agreements, transactions . . . So, my question to you is this: what are you willing to do for our cause in exchange for your life?"

Monsieur Guéneau was stunned.

"I don't understand . . . I don't know anything . . . I don't have anything . . ."

"Come on, Monsieur Guéneau, we both know perfectly well that in the oil and gas industry, a contract is like an iceberg: most of it is under the surface. You've negotiated several contracts yourself, if I'm not mistaken?"

"What contracts?"

Monsieur Guéneau thrashed his head from side to side, as if he were pleading for help from some invisible bystander.

Wrong move. From the start of the interrogation, there was a feeling that Mademoiselle Rivet hadn't taken into account Monsieur Guéneau's current circumstances; that she didn't have the measure of the situation. She'd gone fishing for information, but Monsieur Guéneau hadn't bitten, and now he seemed to have guessed her strategy, even if he was yet to pin it down completely. A few uneasy seconds passed.

"What exactly do you . . . want from me?"

"You tell me," Mademoiselle Rivet said.

The interview was foundering.

"But you do – you do want something from me, don't you?" Monsieur Guéneau asked.

He was extremely distressed. The questions he was being asked seemed at odds with the brutality of the situation. It was as if the commando didn't know what they wanted.

I never like it when things start drifting. I swallowed hard.

That was when Monsieur Delambre snapped out of his lethargic state, stretching out a hand and taking the mic for himself:

"You're married, are you not, Monsieur Guéneau?" he said.

Kader was taken aback, not only by the change of voice in his earpiece, but no doubt by Monsieur Delambre's deathly tone.

"Er, yes . . ." he replied to Kader's forceful question.

"And that's going well?"

"Pardon?"

"I'm asking you whether everything's going well with your wife."

"I don't understand . . ."

"Sexually . . . with your wife?" Monsieur Delambre persisted.

"Listen . . ."

"Answer me."

"I don't see . . ."

"Answer me!"

"Yes, er . . . everything's fine."

"You're not . . . hiding anything from her?"

"Pardon?"

"You heard me."

"Well, er . . . I don't see . . . no . . ."

"And your employer, too – you're not hiding anything from him?"

"What . . . that's not the same . . ."

"It often amounts to the same thing."

"I don't understand . . ."

"Take off your clothes."

"What?"

"I said take off your clothes! Now! Hurry up!"

Kader realised the objective and put down the SIG Sauer and picked up the Uzi instead. Monsieur Guéneau looked on in horror, babbling incoherently.

"Please, no," he implored.

"You have ten seconds," Kader added, standing up.

"No, I beg you . . ."

Two or three long seconds passed.

Monsieur Guéneau wept, looking in turn at Kader's face and the submachine gun. At a guess, he was trying to utter the words, "Please, please, I'm begging you . . ." But at the same time, he was taking off his jacket, which fell to the floor behind him as he started to unbutton his shirt.

"Trousers first," Monsieur Delambre barked. "And take a step back . . ."

Monsieur Guéneau stopped and did as he was told.

"Further back!"

He was in the middle of the room, in full view. He set to work on his belt, letting out a groan as he went. He wiped his eyes clumsily.

"Faster . . ." Kader urged him, under Monsieur Delambre's instructions.

Monsieur Guéneau had taken off his trousers and was hanging his head. He was wearing a pair of women's knickers. Bright red ones. With cream lace. The kind you might see in the window of a sex shop.

If you want the absolute truth, I was disgusted by him. I'm no fan of homos at the best of times, but there's something about deviant homos that I find even harder to stomach.

"The shirt," Monsieur Delambre said.

When Monsieur Guéneau had taken everything off, we could see that he'd been wearing the full kit beneath his suit: matching bra and knickers. He made for a truly pathetic sight. His arms dangling at his side, his head bowed, sobbing more violently than ever. He was fuller in the chest than his bra size could cope with, and the bright-red material was slicing into his tubby, hairy body. His stomach was white and saggy, and the piss-soaked knickers were wedged right up his fat buttocks.

It was impossible to say where Monsieur Delambre's intuition had come from, but it had come from somewhere. How had he suspected Monsieur Guéneau of his dirty secret? Mademoiselle Rivet did not know what had hit her: this first interrogation had gone way beyond anything she could have imagined.

Monsieur Delambre took to the floor again:

"Monsieur Guéneau!"

The man looked at Kader in a state of bewilderment.

"Do you think anyone can trust a man like you, Monsieur Guéneau?"

He was doubled up with the humiliation, his shoulders drooping forward and downward, his chest heaving and his knees almost knocking against each other. Monsieur Delambre took his time before moving in for the kill.

"For political reasons that we don't have time to go into, we would like Exxyal Group to hit the headlines. Our cause requires us to damage the reputation of various large European corporations. Exxyal Group must be made to look its absolute worst, if you follow me. To achieve this, we need to provide the press with tangible proof. We know that you have access to information that can aid us in our cause: confidential clauses, bribes, backhanders, secret deals, undisclosed backing, aid, sweeteners . . . You know what I'm talking about. So you have a choice. I can either kill you now. Or if you'd rather take some time to think through my proposal, I can send you back to your colleagues for a couple of hours. No doubt they'll be amused to see you in this – what's the word? – *decadent* outfit."

"No . . ." Monsieur Guéneau murmured, whimpering now.

He was in an awful way – totally and utterly humiliated.

He must have been aware of Yasmine looking at him from behind. Even though she was in uniform, she was still a young woman. He clawed at his sides as though he were trying to rip his skin off.

"Unless, of course, you are prepared to support us in our cause?"

It all happened very quickly.

Monsieur Guéneau fell on the pistol, and before Kader could move a muscle, he'd grabbed it and jammed the barrel into his mouth. Yasmine's reflexes were excellent. She caught his arm and jerked it towards her. The pistol bounced onto the floor.

Everyone froze.

Monsieur Guéneau, in his red lingerie, was lying spreadeagled on his back across the table, one arm flung over his chest, the other hanging in mid-air. He had the air of a wretched victim on a sacrificial altar, like something out of a Fellini film. You couldn't help thinking that the man had just lost a part of his self-esteem that he would never recover. He wasn't moving and was struggling to breathe. Eventually, he rolled onto his side, huddled into the foetal position, and started crying again, silently this time.

It was clear that Monsieur Guéneau wanted to die.

Monsieur Delambre leant into the microphone again.

"Time to do it," he whispered to Kader. "Get his Blackberry."

Kader said something in Arabic to Yasmine, who went to fetch the little box into which the hostages' telephones, watches and other personal effects had been put, then laid it by Monsieur Guéneau's face.

"Over to you, Monsieur Guéneau," Kader said. "What do you choose?"

The wait was interminable. Monsieur Guéneau was numb, his actions very slow. He seemed dazed, but managed to roll over, prop himself up and, with great difficulty, stay upright. He tried to unhook his bra, but Monsieur Delambre rushed to the microphone:

"No!"

Not a chance.

Monsieur Guéneau shot a look of pure hatred at Kader. But once again, it was futile: he was dressed in women's underwear, soaked to the bone, terrified of losing a life he no longer had. He was crushed. He rummaged through the box and picked out his Blackberry, which he switched on with a familiar hand. The scene was all the more pitiful because it was so drawn out. Monsieur Guéneau connected his device to the laptop computer linked to the Exxyal Europe system. Kader was behind him to keep a close eye on things. Monsieur Guéneau punched in his code and started digging around the files of various contracts, I suppose – on our screens we couldn't see what was happening in any detail.

After that, I believe opinions differ.

As far as I'm concerned, I heard Monsieur Delambre say: "Bastard." Whether it was one "bastard" or several "bastards", I'm not a hundred per cent sure. He didn't say it loudly – it was more like he was saying it to himself. Mademoiselle Rivet said she didn't hear anything, herself. But I'm certain that's what he said. The interrogation was over, Monsieur Guéneau was finished – how it had come to this, we weren't even sure ourselves – and Monsieur Delambre turned his head and said "Bastard" (I'm sure of it). The operation he was conducting was far from complete, but the impression we got was that he'd lost all interest in it. Kader turned towards the camera, waiting for his instructions. Monsieur Guéneau, slumped over the laptop keyboard, continued to sob like a baby in his skimpy red lingerie. After a bit, Yasmine looked up at the camera too.

It was amid this general confusion that Monsieur Delambre decided to stand up. I was looking at him from behind, so I couldn't tell you what his expression was like. My guess is that there was an element of – what do I mean? – *relief* about it . . . Like a calmness. Of course, it's always easy to say that in retrospect, but you can check, I said this in my first statement.

Anyway, Monsieur Delambre was on his feet throughout this weird silence, during which Mademoiselle Rivet's disquiet was plain to see. Then he picked up his briefcase, turned and left the room.

The effect was odd. You'd have sworn he was heading home at the end of a day's work.

As soon as he left, I knew I had to act. In the interrogation chamber, Kader was still wondering what to do as the wretched Monsieur Guéneau blubbed over his keyboard. I grabbed the microphone and said hastily: "Stop that and get dressed!" before switching the mic. to Mourad's earpiece, causing him to crane his neck with great concentration. "Keep an eye on them," I said. I turned to run after Monsieur Delambre before he did anything stupid, but I'd barely taken a step before Monsieur Dorfmann and Monsieur Lacoste came into the room.

They were standing stiffly upright and staring straight ahead. Next to them, Monsieur Delambre was clutching his briefcase in his left hand. In his right hand, he was holding a pistol, a Beretta Cougar, which was pressed against Monsieur Dorfmann's temple. I could tell at once that he wasn't playing around – there was a wild look in his eye and he was determined. And when you see one man holding a gun to another man's head, it's always best to assume he's prepared to pull the trigger.

"Everyone into the meeting room!" Monsieur Delambre yelled.

He yelled because he was afraid, and his eyes were wide open, which made him look like he was hallucinating.

Mademoiselle Rivet let out a cry.

"What's going on?" I started saying, but Monsieur Delambre cut me off. He swung the gun over to Monsieur Lacoste's head, aimed just in front of him, closed his eyes and fired. Not a moment's hesitation. The bang was horrific: two screens exploded

(Monsieur Delambre had fired at random), glass was everywhere, smoke, a stench of burning plastic; Mademoiselle Rivet fell to her knees screaming; the two men he was holding at gunpoint buckled under the blast, hands to their ears.

I held up my hands as high as I could to show that I wasn't going to put up any resistance, because with the exploding screen and the foul smell of cordite, there was no doubt he could have killed any one of us; all of us.

Monsieur Delambre was using live ammunition.

24

"Hands up! Move! Step on it!"

Monsieur Delambre was shouting constantly, filling the space with sound to prevent us from thinking, and making the most of the element of surprise.

In a few seconds, he made us cross the corridor, picking up Kader, Monsieur Guéneau and Yasmine on the way, and – still screaming – shoved us violently in the back as far as the meeting room, where the fake hostages had just become real ones.

For good measure, he then turned to the right-hand camera, took aim and fired. The device disintegrated in a cloud of smoke. Next he swung to the other side and let off another bullet, but he had less luck: it struck well wide of the camera, making a hole the size of a football in the partition wall. But Monsieur Delambre was not about to lose face. "Fucking hell!" he yelled, before firing at the camera again, this time striking his target.

It's impossible for you to imagine the effect of three gunshots from a 9mm Beretta pistol in a forty-square-metre room. Everyone felt as though their head had just exploded like the cameras themselves. This Beretta had a 13-round clip. That meant he still had nine left to shoot, and whether or not he had a back-up magazine, this was no time for mucking about.

What struck me most was Monsieur Delambre's *professionalism*. Sure, he was screaming like a man possessed and had lost all his composure (you could tell from his nervous, jerky motions – precisely what made him so dangerous). But he was continuously scanning around him, and each gesture was measured and deliberate. Kader shot me a glance to see if I was on the same page as him: there was method to Monsieur Delambre's madness. It suggested some sort of coherent security protocol, and it was a sign that he'd received some training from a professional. For starters, he was holding his weapon with two hands. Amateurs often keep their arms locked, like they've seen on television, instead of simply tensing them (and more often than not, they place their weaker hand further back on the weapon). Monsieur Delambre, however, was holding his weapon perfectly: poised and ready for the recoil should he need to shoot. It was surprising, but at the end of the day, I was there as Monsieur Lacoste and Monsieur Dorfmann's adviser – why shouldn't Monsieur Delambre have his advisers, too? And if he had sought guidance, then it was a necessary precaution, because there was nothing simple about what Monsieur Delambre was preparing to do.

You see, waving a Beretta around in front of a couple of people is one thing, but taking twelve or so people hostage is another matter. And I must confess, Monsieur Delambre had made a pretty decent start, and our response needed to take this into account. I don't mean to brag, but if he hadn't shown such discipline or method, if he hadn't made some of the right moves, then me or Kader would have eaten him for breakfast.

Deep down, I have to admit, I knew the tables had turned.

It was as though the man on stage was entirely different from the one who'd been waiting in the wings. I had the unpleasant feeling that I'd been outplayed by a fellow professional and, for a man of my experience, that was extremely hard to take. For the purposes of the operation, and as per our orders, until now we'd been "playing" at hostage-taking, and just like that, someone had changed the rules of the game. I didn't take it well. I don't like being challenged, over and above the fact that Monsieur Lacoste was paying me to ensure everything ran smoothly. He'd agreed to my very high rates so that everything *would* run smoothly. And for some pathetic, unemployed little middle manager, prompted by God knows who, to come along and start brandishing a gun at us and thinking he'd get away with it . . . No, I didn't like it one bit.

Monsieur Delambre was holding a Beretta, a gun I know very well.

Kader, Yasmine and I looked at each other in silence and came to the same conclusion. The smallest window, the slightest error, and Monsieur Delambre was a dead man.

By that point, everyone in there must have thought they'd gone mad. Those who'd known that this was a simulation realised that we'd switched from a role play to the real thing. The others must have been totally bemused to see the commando who'd taken them hostage moments before were now prisoners themselves. That must have been quite hard for them to process. The Exxyal execs, who had seen Monsieur Dorfmann shot dead a few minutes before, must have been surprised to find him alive and well, at the same time as discovering they'd been the victims of a hoax. Various new people had now entered the fold, including a man holding a gun to their boss's head and blowing cameras to smithereens. This state of astonishment played into Monsieur Delambre's hands.

Before anyone could take stock of the situation, he made all of us lie flat on our stomachs, arms and legs spread apart.

"Fingers too, spread them! Anyone tries anything and I shoot!"

That's not something you make up on the spot. You've really got to know your stuff to say the "spread the fingers" thing. That said, despite the shrewd pointers he'd been given, you could tell from his technique that he was a first-timer. He must have clocked his error when he went to search the newcomers: everyone was lying down all over the place, and there was no way he could properly frisk everyone at the same time as keeping them all in his field of vision. This is the lone gunman's primary problem. Working alone requires a lot of technical organisation and anticipation, and if one aspect doesn't go according to plan, you can be sure you'll run into problems. What's more, Monsieur Delambre's mental state was not up to the task. He was still yelling things like: "Don't move! First person to move gets it!" Deep down, he didn't mean it. At least that was my impression when I felt him stand over me and pat me down. His movements weren't so cack-handed that I had reasonable cause to intervene, but they weren't as systematic and precise as they should have been. He might slip up, I remember thinking – in fact I was sure he would. Stretched out in the middle of the room like a customer caught in a run-of-the-mill supermarket hold-up, I resolved to show no mercy should I gain the upper hand.

Little did he know, but Monsieur Delambre had never been so close to death.

When he searched me, even if his technique was a little graceless, he had an advantage: he knew what he was looking for. Mobile telephones, mainly. One for each person. And then watches, to deprive us of any time markers. He had no difficulty relieving us of these objects, which he stashed in a drawer he'd pulled out of the table.

After that, he went to the windows and shut the blinds, before proceeding to the next phase of the operation, namely reconfiguring the room:

"You!" he shouted in Monsieur Cousin's direction. "Yes, you! Get up, KEEP your hands in the air, and move over there! HURRY UP!"

He was still shouting, but some words he was screaming. It was hard to tell whether this was a sign of increased panic or whether he was still filling the space with sound to prevent us from thinking. The problem was, it was preventing him from thinking too. I was one of the first he ordered to stand up, and this gave me the chance to observe him for a second. I remember noting how agitated he was. The idea that he was so impatient, so irritable, made us all scramble. We felt he wasn't far from committing a blunder of some sort, or being seized by a murderous impulse at any point.

When you look back on events as I am now, everything seems to play back in slow motion. You take in every gesture, every intention, but the fact is it all happened very fast. So fast that I didn't even have time to consider the fundamental question: why was Monsieur Delambre doing this? What did he want? Why was an exec who'd been called in for a recruitment test taking his future employers hostage? And why with real bullets? Behind all this there were stakes that were beyond my understanding, and I realised that the best thing was to wait for the dust to settle.

He made each of us get back up in turn, and assigned us all a space. Then he ordered us to place our hands flat on the ground and sit on top of them, with our backs to the wall. The opportune moment was not going to be presenting itself any time soon, because this position is one of the hardest to get out of. I've used it myself in countless operations.

It was clear he hadn't planned this in minute detail, because he'd often point to someone, hesitate and snap "There!" before changing his mind with a "No, there!" The effect was unsettling.

Eventually everyone was in position. I'm not sure if it was deliberate, but there was a certain logic to the order we were in. To his right, he had the Exxyal Europe lot: Madame Camberlin, Mademoiselle Tràn, Monsieur Cousin, Monsieur Lussay and Monsieur Guéneau (who'd had time to slip his trousers and suit jacket back on). To his left, he had my team: Mourad, Yasmine,

Kader, Monsieur Renard and myself. And finally, alone in the middle, wedged between the two groups, were Monsieur Dorfmann, Monsieur Lacoste and Mademoiselle Rivet. The result, though improvised, was impressive, because these two men immediately took on the appearance of a pair of defendants before a tribunal. They must have felt it: they were deathly pale. It was maybe more striking in Monsieur Lacoste's case, who's naturally suntanned (all that time on the ski slopes, at a guess).

Contrary to what people might think, in such circumstances it's not the women who cry the most or the loudest. Monsieur Guéneau, who was maxed out on the tear front, stared at the ground between his legs, his jacket wrapped firmly around him. Monsieur Lussay, on the other hand, had picked up the baton and was now whimpering, like a puppy afraid of being smacked. Madame Camberlin was crying in silence, her make-up a total mess, with black streaks down her cheekbones and only a small bit of rouge left on her lower lip. I always find it a little off-putting when middle-aged women look such a state. Mademoiselle Tràn was very pale. She looked like she'd aged ten years in the space of a few minutes, all the volume gone from her hair. I notice this a lot. When people are under duress, the first thing they reject is their appearance – their life is the only thing that matters any more. And generally speaking, they become quite ugly.

Most impressive of all was Monsieur Cousin. Normally, his extreme skinniness was extraordinary enough, but sitting there he was as upright as an altar candle, and his hawk-like eyes seemed to be scanning for obstacles. Unlike the others, who were prepared to abandon all dignity if it meant saving their lives, he was glaring at Monsieur Delambre as though he were a mortal enemy: unblinking, unflinching. It was like they were on an equal footing, and his obedience to Monsieur Delambre's every order betrayed a silent yet radical opposition, while his shrinking co-hostages moved as little as possible.

The ones we could hear most clearly were Monsieur Lussay, who was moaning relentlessly, and Monsieur Renard, our actor, who looked as though he wanted to melt into the carpet to escape what was, undoubtedly, the most challenging role of his career.

There was a thirty-second silence.

Monsieur Dorfmann had managed to stay poker-faced. As I've said before, his composure was quite remarkable.

Monsieur Lacoste was just about regaining his senses. He looked over at me and raised his eyebrows, proof that he was prepared to stage an intervention. But this was my responsibility, not just because I was the organiser of the operation, but also because I had the longest track record in this field. I caught Yasmine's eye, as I was aware of her experience in the psychological aspects of crisis situations. She responded with an ambiguous look – it was hard to read her opinion. I felt I was able to take the initiative, and so I made the most of this short lull to establish first contact:

"What do you want, Monsieur Delambre?"

I did my best to keep my voice serene, composed, but in retrospect I realise this wasn't the best opening gambit. Monsieur Delambre came hurtling towards me, and we all recoiled, starting with me.

"What about you – what do *you* want, you bastard?"

He struck me with his gun, square in the forehead, near my hairline, and since I'd not seen him apply the safety catch, I'll admit I was alarmed. I shut my eyes as tight as possible.

"Nothing, I don't want anything . . ."

"That's why you're giving me shit, you bastard? *For nothing?*"

A bead of cold sweat pricked at me, and I was overcome with nausea. You know, in my line of work, I know what the fear of death feels like, and I can assure you it's unmistakable . . .

The best thing was not to answer, to avoid agitating him any further.

The barrel of his gun was pointed at my brain. The man was verging on pure insanity, and I told myself that at the first opportunity, I'd have no hesitation lodging a bullet in that same spot, right in his brain.

25

There was no doubt my intervention had been premature, but it was too late for regrets. I had presented Monsieur Delambre with a breach, and he'd charged right into it.

"Right then, big guy!" he said to me. "Where's all your wonderful organisation, now? Where is it now eh, you prick?"

I can't tell you how the others reacted to this, because I kept my eyes closed.

"It was all going so well . . . such a shame. Your little team, your little cameras, your shitty little machine guns!"

He drilled the gun into my forehead, as if he wanted the barrel to pierce my skull.

"But this one . . . this is a real one, my friend. With real bullets, that make real holes. We're not playing 'Cowboys and Indians' now. In fact, speaking of Indians, where's the big chief?"

Monsieur Delambre was standing up again, hand on hip, pretending to search around.

"That's a very good point . . . where's the head honcho?"

He knelt down in front of Monsieur Dorfmann, just as he had with me. He placed the tip of his Beretta in exactly the same position, right in the middle of his forehead. He was fizzing with hatred. He wanted to belittle us, humiliate us. This answered my question about his motives, and went a long way to explaining what would happen in the future: deep down, Monsieur

Delambre didn't want anything. He wasn't after money; he wasn't demanding a ransom. No: he wanted revenge. Bitterness and resentment had driven him to these lengths. He was craving retribution of the symbolic kind.

This ageing, jobless executive was starting to take a perverse pleasure in brandishing a gun in the face of a major European C.E.O., so much so that a bloodbath had become a plausible outcome.

"Well then . . ." he continued. "He's so discreet, our generalissimo. He seems worried sick. Of course he does – he's got such mighty responsibilities! Must be tough, eh? Eh? Yes it is, it's tough . . ."

Monsieur Delambre had adopted a theatrical, mocking, sympathetic tone.

"Mass redundancies . . . Now that really is tough. But wait! That's not even the toughest part, is it now? No, no, no . . . the toughest part is planning them all. Now that really is complicated. They're just coming so thick and fast, aren't they? You've hit your stride. It takes some expertise to manage all this sacking – some real willpower. Got to bargain with the bastards, don't you. And for that you need men; good ones at that. Soldiers, boots on the ground for the great capitalist cause. You can't just pick any old so-and-so, can you, O mighty Caesar? And when it comes to choosing the best, nothing does it quite like a good old-fashioned hostage-taking. Well: you're in luck, dear leader. You've got one."

He leant forward, turning his head to the side, as if he were about to kiss him on the lips, and I managed to catch a glimpse of Monsieur Dorfmann's face. He was keeping his cool, holding his breath and thinking about what to say. But he never got the chance – Monsieur Delambre was on a roll.

"In fact, your higher-than-highness, tell me about Sarqueville: how many exactly are you firing there?"

"What . . . what do you want?" Monsieur Dorfmann managed to say.

"I want to know how many people you are firing from that plant. I could easily kill everyone here for you, right here, right now. That would make twelve. A decent start. But I'm just a lowly sole trader. You – you work on an industrial scale. How many are you planning to mow down at Sarqueville?"

Monsieur Dorfmann felt it wise not to venture down that road, and he decided to keep quiet. Good job too, if you ask me.

"I remember reading the number 823 somewhere," Monsieur Delambre continued. "But I don't know if that last count's up to date. How many is it, exactly?"

"I . . . I don't know . . ."

"Oh, but you do, you do know!" Monsieur Delambre insisted, brimming with confidence. "So come on, enough false modesty . . . How many!"

"I don't know, I'm telling you!" Monsieur Dorfmann shouted. "Just tell me what you want!"

Monsieur Delambre ignored him.

"It'll come back to you. You'll see," he said.

He turned, raised his arm and fired at the water cooler, smashing it to smithereens and sending twenty litres of water cascading onto the floor.

Eight bullets left. And nobody was in any doubt that he was capable of inflicting far more damage with that much ammo.

Once again he leant towards Monsieur Dorfmann.

"Where were we? Oh yes. Sarqueville. So, how many exactly?"

"Eight hundred and twenty-five," Monsieur Dorfmann whispered.

"There you go – it did come back. So let me see . . . that's two more. But, two doesn't mean anything to you, does it? My guess is that those two people see it rather differently."

Up to that point, Monsieur Delambre had been organised and

meticulous, but since he'd started addressing Monsieur Dorfmann, his strategy seemed less coherent, as though he had lost track of what he wanted to achieve. This backed up my theory that his sole aim in taking us hostage was to frighten or humiliate us. As hard as it was to believe, this was the most likely explanation judging by his behaviour.

Stress. It's sort of like a thread that each of us carries inside; a thread whose resistance we can never really predict. Everyone has their own threshold. Madame Camberlin must have reached her breaking point, because she'd started moaning, quietly at first, then louder and louder. As though this were a signal or a form of consent, all the others started wailing too. The collective effect reminded me of a pressure valve being released. With this cry, everyone gave free rein to their fear and anguish, and as it drew out, the voices of the men and women melded into a single, bestial lowing that filled the room, and I thought it would never stop.

In the midst of this astonishing cacophony, Monsieur Delambre couldn't meet anyone's eye, since they all had their chins pressed into their chests, their eyes screwed tight shut. He staggered back into the centre of the room and started yelling himself, and his shriek was so powerful, so harrowing, that his pain seemed to stem from somewhere far deeper . . . The others fell silent, cut off in their stride, and looked up at him. It was a curious scene, you know: this man standing in the middle of a meeting room, pistol in hand, his eyes raised to the heavens as he howled like a wolf, as though he were on the brink of death. In a split second, Kader and I reached an agreement. We flung ourselves at him, Kader at his legs, me at his waist. But Monsieur Delambre dropped to the floor, like a house of cards, the best possible way to check our attack. His bullet struck me in my right leg, and Kader held up his hands in surrender after Monsieur Delambre had cracked him over the head with the butt of his pistol.

"Nobody move! Stay where you are!" I shouted through the pain. I was afraid somebody else might try to attack and make him start spraying bullets all over the place.

Kader and I crept back towards the wall, me clutching my leg, him his head. The sight of blood marked a new stage in events, and everybody was aware of the escalation. Until this point, there had been noise and fear, but the blood made things more physical, more visceral. It took us one step closer to death, and drew another collective whine from the hostages.

I've thought long and hard about whether I did the right thing. Kader assures me I did. He reckons we couldn't have let the situation unravel without trying something, and that had been the most opportune moment. The way I see it, a course of action is only correct if it's successful. This episode heightened my frustration and made me all the more determined to show Monsieur Delambre that he wouldn't escape so lightly for ever.

Back against the wall, Kader and I established that neither of us was seriously injured. He only had a slight gash on his scalp, but it was still bleeding freely, quite spectacularly, in fact; as for me, I was clasping my leg and grimacing, but as soon as I ripped open my trouser leg, I realised that the bullet had grazed me without causing much damage. But Monsieur Delambre was oblivious of this, and so without exchanging a word, Kader and I exaggerated our pain.

Monsieur Delambre had come round and was back in the middle of the room. He retreated within himself, not knowing what to do.

"You need to call an ambulance," I murmured.

He was disoriented, lost, unhinged. It fell to us to provide him with solutions.

He didn't answer, so I pressed on, trying hard to keep my voice level.

"Things aren't too bad for now, Monsieur Delambre. You

can still come out of this O.K. It's fine, we're only wounded. But you see, I'm losing a lot of blood. Kader too . . . You need to call an ambulance."

I didn't have my watch anymore, but I knew that the real hostage-taking had only been going on for about twenty minutes so far. Monsieur Delambre had fired five shots, but the building was in a business park, and on a public holiday like this, there was little chance that anyone had raised the alarm. There was only one remaining solution: for Monsieur Delambre to give himself up. Our wounds provided good leverage for this outcome, but Monsieur Delambre was showing no sign of going down without a fight. He shook his head over and over, as if hoping the problem would take care of itself.

"Wounds . . . Anyone here know first aid?" he said after a brief silence.

No-one answered. Everyone knew instinctively that a new power struggle was about to unfold.

"So? Anyone? O.K., let's try this another way!" Monsieur Delambre said. "Fuck, if we're going to cause irreparable damage, we might as well do it properly!"

Two strides and he was in front of Monsieur Dorfmann, crouching down and resting the barrel of his gun on the C.E.O.'s knee.

"Come on then, The Great Helmsman. Time for some heroics!"

Judging by the speed with which he'd made his decision, there was no doubt whatsoever that he was going to shoot, but a loud voice stopped him short.

"I'll do it."

Monsieur Cousin was on his feet. He looked like a ghost, there's no other way to describe it. He had a milky-white complexion, almost translucent, and a wild look in his eyes. Even Monsieur Delambre was thrown.

"I know a bit of first aid. I'll have a look."

And Monsieur Cousin was on the move. It was so surprising that he seemed to be walking in slow motion. First he approached Kader.

"Look down," he said, leaning down next to him and fiddling with his hair for a second.

"It's nothing," he said, "just an abrasion to the scalp. It's superficial. The bleeding will stop on its own."

He spoke with immense authority, as if he himself had become the hostage-taker. His assurance and gravitas meant that he had switched roles with Monsieur Delambre, who stayed kneeling in front of the Exxyal chairman, unsure what to do.

Then Monsieur Cousin stooped down to inspect my leg. He lifted it from underneath the tibia like paramedics do, and moved the fabric to one side.

"Snap – this one's not serious either. It'll be just fine," he said.

He stood up and turned towards Monsieur Delambre.

"Right, so . . . What do you want exactly? Let's get this over with! Who are you, anyway?"

Monsieur Cousin was holding his captor to account.

In the space of a few seconds, this hostage-taking had become a battle of two wills. The hostages were still sitting around the room, forming a sort of ring around the two men glaring at each other in the middle. Monsieur Delambre was at a major advantage: he had a gun. He had used it six times, making several holes in the wall, injuring two people and annihilating a water cooler. And he had seven bullets left. Monsieur Cousin, however, was not about to feel intimidated by his opponent. His hackles were up, and he looked ready for a fight.

"Aaaaaah!" sighed Monsieur Delambre. "The model exec swoops in to rescue his boss – how touching!"

He had taken a backwards step, so that he was pressed against the door, his pistol still held in both hands. He swung towards Monsieur Dorfmann again.

"Congratulations, your Excellency, for what you've achieved with this man. He's almost the prototype! You fire him, but he carries on working for free, hoping you'll take him back on. Isn't that just wonderful?!"

As he spoke he pointed his gun skywards like he might fire at the ceiling, or as though calling everyone to witness. Then he thrust it towards Monsieur Cousin, nodding his head in admiration.

"And you, you want to defend your company, is that it? Risk your life for it, if need be? It's your family, your gang! They've been running you into the ground for months . . . no qualms whatsoever about giving you the chuck. But that doesn't mean a thing to you: you're willing to die for them! That's not just submission – that's martyrdom."

Monsieur Cousin looked him square in the eyes, not in the least bit shaken:

"I repeat," he said. "Who are you and what do you want?"

He didn't seem at all fazed by Monsieur Delambre's performance, nor by the weapon training at him.

Monsieur Delambre brought his arms to his sides with a false air of remorse:

"But, the same thing as you, old boy. All I want is a job."

He then stalked up to Monsieur Lacoste, whose face contorted with fear. This time, instead of resting the barrel on his forehead, he aimed it directly at his heart.

"I did everything to get this job."

"Listen . . ." Monsieur Lacoste stammered. "I think you have . . ."

But Monsieur Delambre silenced him by pressing the weapon further into his chest. His voice was calm now, and that's what was so frightening – how measured his tone was:

"I worked harder than anyone to get this job. You led me to believe I had every chance. You lied to me, because in your mind, I'm not even human."

He started tapping Monsieur Lacoste's chest again with the barrel of the gun.

"The truth is, I'm better than her! Miles better!" he yelled, jerking his head towards Mademoiselle Rivet, whose presence only seemed to add to his fury, because suddenly he shouted:

"I deserved this job! And you stole it from me! You hear me: you stole it from me and it was *all I had left*!"

He fell silent. He leant in close to Monsieur Lacoste's ear and, loud enough for all of us to hear, said:

"So, because you won't give me what I am due, I have come to take my pound of flesh."

Suddenly we heard the sound of hurried footsteps.

As soon as he realised that Monsieur Cousin had fled down the corridor, Monsieur Delambre swung round and shot at the main entrance, but his aim was too high and he only managed to make a hole in the partition wall. He started running, careered into a chair that Monsieur Cousin had knocked over on his way past, nearly crashing to the floor with his gun, but making it to the corridor. We saw him raise his weapon with both hands, hesitate, then lower his arms. It was too late.

He now only had two bad solutions to choose between: running after Monsieur Cousin and leaving us unguarded with our telephones, or staying with us and letting Monsieur Cousin go and call for help.

He was trapped.

There was still no shortage of possible outcomes, but at that point it ceased to matter what happened, or whether some people came out dead or alive: one way or another, it was over.

The experience taught me that it only takes a couple of seconds for a man to become a maniac. The basic ingredients (a sense of humiliation or injustice, extreme loneliness, a weapon and nothing to lose) all resulted in Monsieur Delambre's decision to barricade himself in with us as the police arrived outside.

When he re-entered the room, his gun dangling by his side and his head bowed in defeat, I thought it was Monsieur Delambre's turn to start crying.

26

Monsieur Delambre could have chosen to back down, but I don't think he had the strength. He had reached a point of no return, and he clearly had no idea how things were going to finish. That's always the hardest bit – finishing.

He pulled up a chair and just sat there, back to the door, facing the hostages.

He was no longer the same man. He was beaten, spent. Worse than that, he was crushed. With his elbows resting on his knees, he held his pistol limply in his right hand, gazing at the floor. In his left hand, he was fingering a small piece of orange cloth, which had a sort of miniscule bell that made a sharp ringing sound. It looked like a lucky charm.

Monsieur Delambre had positioned himself at the opposite end of the room, too far away for anyone to reach him before he could raise his gun.

What was I thinking at that moment? Well, I was wondering what he had been hoping would happen. He had brought a loaded gun, which suggested he had always been prepared to use it, but what was his objective? No matter how much I turn it over in my head, the vision he presented at that instant confirmed everything: Monsieur Delambre had acted out of desperation. So desperate, so devoid of hope, that he was willing to kill.

As Monsieur Cousin had predicted prior to his escape, Kader's bleeding had effectively stopped. As for me, I'd made a tourniquet to stem the flow of blood, and now it was just a matter of patience.

A calm composure had settled over the group. It felt like a vigil. The tears had stopped, along with the groans, moans and grievances. The whole thing had lasted well under an hour, but enough had happened to leave everyone traumatised.

The stage was set for the final act.

Everyone was apprehensive, retreating within themselves to summon as much strength as they could. If Monsieur Delambre's will to keep us there appeared to be faltering, then there was some hope, but you only needed to look at him to see that he was in it for the long haul, and there was no telling how long.

And so when the first police sirens were heard a short while later, everyone was wondering what the next twist in the saga would be. Would Monsieur Delambre surrender or make a stand? Heads or tails? Everyone placed their bets; everyone waited for the outcome.

When the sirens drew nearer, Monsieur Delambre did not look up; he did not make even the slightest movement. His spirits had been sapped. I listened closely and discerned at least five police cars and two ambulances. Monsieur Cousin must have been efficient and persuasive, since the authorities had taken him seriously. We could hear the heavy tramping of boots in the car park. The police were assessing the scale of the problem. First the building had to be secured. In a few minutes' time, vanloads of R.A.I.D. counter-terrorist teams would arrive. We would then enter into a negotiation process lasting five minutes or thirty hours depending on how comprehensive, skilful and resistant Monsieur Delambre proved to be. As he was still looking at his feet, lost in thought, the hostages stared at each other, communicating silently as their personal uncertainty accumulated to form a collective anxiety. Monsieur Dorfmann, collected as ever, tried to calm everyone down by looking reassuringly at each person in turn. Monsieur Lacoste, however, had been found wanting from the start of the ordeal and still hadn't managed to get back on track. He looked defeated.

A megaphone crackled to life, and a voice was heard:

"*The building is surrounded . . .*"

Still slumped in his chair and his head still lowered, Monsieur Delambre held his arm aloft and – without a second's hesitation – fired a bullet into the window. The glass behind the blind shattered with an almighty crash, and all the hostages instantly rolled into a ball to protect their heads from the falling shards.

Then Monsieur Delambre stood up, went over to his briefcase and opened it, taking no precautions whatsoever with regard to us, as if we were no longer an issue. He removed two Beretta magazines – enough for a siege – and returned to his seat, laying the fresh ammunition at his feet. This didn't bode well at all for the final phase.

After their first announcement on the megaphone, the police didn't push it. A few minutes later, more sirens. R.A.I.D. had just arrived. They would need about twenty minutes to consult the building's architectural plans, establish eyes and ears where possible to observe what was happening in our room, and assemble teams at the key access points with a view to sealing the premises. At the same time, elite R.A.I.D. snipers would be positioned opposite the windows, each one of them capable of slamming two bullets into Monsieur Delambre's head should he make the smallest slip.

I estimated first contact from the negotiator to come after about ten minutes, and I reckon I wasn't far off. He called on an internal line that was located on the floor near the wall to Monsieur Delambre's right.

All eyes converged on the device, but it took a good twelve rings before Monsieur Delambre decided to react. He seemed exhausted. The handset was a standard-issue thing with buttons and a digital screen.

"Hello," Monsieur Delambre said picking it up, but without initial success. Then he pushed a button, then a second, before getting very angry very quickly and pushing almost all of them, following which all of us could hear the person speaking at the other end – he'd pressed the loudspeaker button by mistake, not that this seemed to bother him.

"Monsieur Delambre, this is Captain Prungnaud."

"What do you want?"

"I want to know how the hostages are doing."

Monsieur Delambre looked around the room.

"Everyone's fine."

"You have wounded two of them."

The conversation adhered to normal protocol and advanced as predicted. It didn't take long at all for Monsieur Delambre to declare that he wouldn't let anyone go, and that they would have to "come and fetch him". To punctuate this announcement, he took aim and shattered two more windows. The laminated blinds he'd pierced now had large holes burnt out of them, which gave a solid impression of what might happen if Monsieur Delambre decided to start firing at us instead of the windows. At that moment, the R.A.I.D. snipers would no doubt be squirming in the hope of catching a glimpse of Monsieur Delambre through the gaping holes in the blinds, but he was too far from the windows for them to risk anything.

Neither Kader nor myself could wait any longer to intervene. While we were waiting for the police, I had stolen a glance at Yasmine, who until now had been keeping a low profile, which was quite out of character for her. Throughout the long wait, she had – millimetre by millimetre – managed to change position, stealth-ily bringing a foot beneath her backside, shifting her opposite arm: on her marks, set, and ready to pounce. A true pro. She was sitting about seven metres from Monsieur Delambre, and I knew that she was ready to take him out at the first sign of weakness. A little earlier, when Monsieur Delambre had gone to get his extra ammunition, I signalled to her that it wasn't the right moment. The perfect window would be just after he fired his final bullet. In the few seconds it would take him to realise his magazine was empty, get a new one and replace it, Yasmine would have all the time in the world. I wouldn't have given Monsieur Delambre a one in a hundred chance against that perfectly trained live wire. For the moment, he had three bullets left and seemed primed to fire at anything that moved; paradoxically, this was good news for us, since it meant our opportune moment would arrive sooner. We therefore had an unexpected chance to take action before R.A.I.D.

And to be perfectly honest, that was my sole objective.

I felt thwarted, and I'd vowed to resolve the situation myself before the security forces arrived. It was a matter of honour. I was all the more determined since Monsieur Delambre was armed: I could kill him in cold blood without any fear of the consequences and claim self-defence. In front of the other hostages, I would let off a quick burst, pretending I didn't have time to take aim, even though in truth I'd need just a few tenths of a second to lodge a bullet right in the middle of his forehead. Which was precisely my intention.

But things didn't quite pan out like that, you might say.

Monsieur Delambre seemed more confused than ever, and was trying to remember all the advice he'd been given. He was back on his chair, facing the group, but as we waited for him to fire his last round, he ejected his current magazine and replaced it with a fresh one. The whole thing took him less than four seconds, and before we knew it Monsieur Delambre was holding a newly loaded pistol with thirteen good bullets, ready for action.

Yasmine kept her cool, but inside I could tell she was devastated. We were heading for a R.A.I.D. assault, with all the consequences that entailed.

Our room was on the fourth floor of the building. Three of the four windows had been shattered by gunshots, and the wind was blowing in through the gaps. At first the air had been rather pleasant, but now it was making things extremely uncomfortable. Would the R.A.I.D. team opt for this entry point? Not impossible . . . My money was on a simultaneous double offensive targeting the corridor and the exterior: a two-pronged attack that Monsieur Delambre would be incapable of resisting by himself. And after seeing him blast out three windows without warning and with real bullets, the security forces would never give a man holding twelve people hostage (including two injured) any chance of escaping with his life.

From an investigation point of view, the police and R.A.I.D. had moved very quickly: Monsieur Delambre had been identified, allowing the negotiator to call him by his name from first contact. In fact, from the information supplied by Monsieur Cousin, it must have been a doddle for them to pull up Monsieur Dorfmann and Monsieur Lacoste, and maybe even collar Mademoiselle Zbikowski, who surely held the keys to this mystery.

The first round of negotiations had been over and done with very quickly – the three gunshots made sure of that. It wouldn't be long until R.A.I.D. turned up the heat again. Only ten minutes, as it happened.

Monsieur Delambre stood up at the second ring. Yasmine watched his every movement. So did I. Would he look away while he was talking? Where would he leave his weapon during the conversation? Would he move as far as the telephone cable let him? He jabbed at the buttons again, one undoubtedly cancelling out the other, and the loudspeaker stayed activated.

"Monsieur Delambre, what do you want?"

Captain Prungnaud again, whose clear, calm voice oozed professionalism.

"I don't know . . . Can you find me a job?"

"Yes, I had a feeling the problem might have been along those lines."

"That's correct, just a small problem. 'Along those lines.' I have a proposal for you."

"Go ahead."

"The people here with me all have jobs. If I kill one of them – any of them – and free the rest, can I have their job?"

"We can talk about anything, Monsieur Delambre, and I mean anything, including your job hunt, but before that we'll need you to release some hostages."

"Talk about money, for example?"

The negotiator let that one lie for a second, just to size up the problem.

"You want money? How m — ?"

But before he could finish his sentence, Monsieur Delambre had fired at the last window, sending more glass crashing onto the crouched hostages.

We'd barely opened our eyes before Monsieur Delambre had hung up and resumed his position. A huge commotion could be heard downstairs in the car park. The fact they were dealing with someone hell-bent on exterminating windows at random intervals was not making the security forces' job any easier.

The telephone rang again about five minutes later.

"Alain . . ."

"That's *Monsieur Delambre* to you! It's not like we're old pals from the job centre!"

"O.K. Monsieur Delambre, as you wish. I'm calling because I have someone next to me who wants to speak to you. I'll pass her over."

"NO!"

Monsieur Delambre shouted and smashed the handset down. But he stayed put, paralysed in front of the phone, mute and motionless.

Yasmine stared intently at me, asking whether now was the moment, but I was sure the negotiator wouldn't pass up a response like that. Indeed, a few seconds later the telephone rang again, but this time it wasn't the R.A.I.D. negotiator at the other end. It was a woman. Young, no more than thirty, I don't think.

"Papa ...?"

Her voice was trembling with emotion, while Monsieur Delambre squirmed uneasily.

"Papa, answer me, please ..."

But Monsieur Delambre couldn't speak. He held the handset in his left hand, the gun in his right, and it seemed nothing could pull him out of the turmoil the woman's voice had just plunged him into. Hearing that voice was harder for him than firing a bullet into Monsieur Dorfmann's head, but maybe it boiled down to the same thing: unambiguous proof of the desperate stalemate he was in. For a second – just a second – I felt sorry for him.

There was confusion on the line. No-one knew where to go from there.

Another woman's voice on the line, older this time.

"Alain?" she said. "It's Nicole."

Monsieur Delambre was absolutely rooted to the spot.

The woman was crying uncontrollably, choking and unable to speak. We could barely hear anything over her sobbing. And it was upsetting to us, because she wasn't just crying for our sake, but the sake of her husband, the man who'd taken us prisoner and been threatening to kill us for over an hour.

"Alain," she said. "I'm begging you ... answer me."

That voice, those words had a devastating effect on Monsieur Delambre.

"Nicole ... Please forgive me," he said in a very low voice. That was it. Nothing else.

After this, he replaced the handset and grabbed the drawer with all our mobiles and watches. Then he went up to the window, lifted the blind and flung the contents out of it. One motion, everything at once. I have no idea why he did that – I'm telling you, it was very odd. In any event, I didn't have long to speculate.

The first bullet whisked millimetres past his left shoulder, and the second went right through the space where his head had been half a second earlier. He fell to the ground and turned towards us, holding his gun in his outstretched hand. Which was just as well, because Yasmine was already on her feet, ready to spring on him.

"Get down!" he cried at her.

Yasmine did as she was told. Monsieur Delambre crawled on his belly and stood up a few metres away. He went to the door, opened it and turned to us.

"You can go," he said. "It's over."

Astonishment all round.

Did he just say it was over? No-one could believe it.

Monsieur Delambre stayed like that for a few seconds, his mouth hanging open. He was right – it was over. I think he wanted to say something to us, but it didn't come, the words catching in his head. The telephone carried on ringing, but he didn't even flinch at it.

He turned and left.

The last sound we heard was the key turning in the lock from outside in the corridor.

We were locked in, but we were free.

It's hard to describe what happened next. All the hostages leapt to their feet and rushed to the windows. Once the blinds had been torn open, it took a good amount of persuasion and effort from me and my team to stop them from clambering onto the ledges and throwing themselves out. It was pure panic.

On seeing the hostages congregated at the windows, the police officers in the car park were not immediately sure what had happened. The negotiator called on the internal line. Yasmine answered and informed the police of the apparent situation, because we still weren't sure whether Monsieur Delambre would change his mind or not. It was deeply uncertain, and I shared the officers' concern. We didn't know, for example, where he was with his loaded gun and all that spare ammunition. Had he genuinely stood down? Was he not waiting in ambush somewhere else in the building?

Kader was struggling to calm Monsieur Lussay, Madame Camberlin and Monsieur Guéneau. Monsieur Renard was the most agitated. He kept yelling: "Come and get us! Come and get us!" Yasmine had no other choice but to let off two deafening whistles that quietened him down in an instant.

Limping as best I could, I took hold of the phone and introduced myself, before having a brief conversation with the R.A.I.D. captain.

Ten or so minutes later, ladders were placed against the outside wall of the building. Two R.A.I.D. teams wearing bulletproof vests and helmets, and armed with assault rifles, scaled them in seconds flat. The first made sure we were protected, while the second went down to open the inside doors to make way for the other teams, which immediately scoured the building for Monsieur Delambre.

Moments later we were down in the car park, wrapped in those foil blankets . . .

There – that's more or less what I told the police and repeated to the investigating magistrate.

It emerged that Monsieur Delambre had laid down his weapon and the remaining full magazine on the floor by the entrance of the office where he'd shut himself in. The R.A.I.D. team discovered him crouching at the foot of a desk, head between his knees and his hands clutching the back of his neck.

He didn't put up any resistance.

I must have taken part in a good fifteen or so operations that were considerably more dangerous and complicated than this one. Yasmine, Kader and myself carried out a thorough debriefing the following day. Every operation has its learning outcomes, so it's always worth playing back the film in slow motion, frame by frame, pulling out every detail, however insignificant, to feed into our experience. After all, experience is what earns us our bread and butter. Then we move on to new destinations, new missions.

Except this time, it didn't work out that way.

The images from that half-day whirled through my head on repeat, as if they contained some subliminal message that had eluded me.

I told myself this was pointless, that I should focus on other things, but to no avail – for days later the images were still coming back to me.

Always the same.

We were in the car park. An air of relief had descended on everyone. The R.A.I.D. team that discovered Monsieur Delambre in an office radioed down to the agents positioned outside to inform them that the operation was over. My leg was receiving attention. Paramedics were all around us. The R.A.I.D. captain came to shake my hand and we exchanged a few passing comments.

I could see the freed hostages from where I was standing. Each person's reaction matched his or her temperament. Monsieur Guéneau was wearing his full suit again, in complete disarray; Mademoiselle Tràn had already touched up her make-up; Madame Camberlin had also regained some colour and wiped away the smudges that had covered her cheeks just moments before. They were all in a circle around Monsieur Dorfmann, who was answering their questions with a smile. Authority hadn't taken long to restore itself. It even seemed like the hostages needed it, as though it were a vital touchstone. What was extraordinary was that none of them resented the Exxyal Europe boss for organising the hostage-taking, an ordeal that had been cruel and violent in equal measure. To the contrary, everyone seemed to find the whole thing perfectly worthwhile. For some of them, this was to garner credit for their performance; for others, to atone for their weaknesses. It was remarkable how quickly normal life resumed. Monsieur Cousin's hulking frame stood out from the others. The verdict was clear: he was the man of the moment, the embodiment of altruism and courage, the day's big winner. He wasn't smiling. He looked like an election candidate whose victory had just been announced, but who was pretending to take the result in his stride to demonstrate mental superiority. Yet all you had to do was consider the position he occupied alongside Monsieur Dorfmann, or gauge the invisible, admiring circle his colleagues had formed around him – colleagues who just a few hours before must have scorned him – to understand that he was the undisputed champion of this adventure. No-one was in any doubt that he'd just sealed his ticket to the Sarqueville refinery.

Monsieur Lacoste was already on the telephone. Animal reflex, without a doubt. He was speaking animatedly. I think he had a lot on his plate. He'd have to answer to his client, Monsieur Dorfmann, and with that I wished him luck . . .

A little further away, Monsieur Renard was already relaying the details of our incarceration and release to the press, his measured movements becoming increasingly flamboyant. His finest role to date. I remember feeling that he'd have been quite happy to die in his sleep that night.

The flashing lights were turning slowly, engines purring, lending the entire scene a reassuring sense that the crisis was over.

That's how I remember it.

And then there were the two women I didn't know. Mother and daughter. Monsieur Delambre's wife is a very pretty woman. I mean, really lovely. Her daughter, thirty or so, had her arm wrapped around her mother's shoulder. Neither of them were crying. They gazed at the entrance to the building. They'd been told that Monsieur Delambre had been apprehended without resistance, and that he hadn't been injured. A third woman arrived, also around thirty. Her face, although very pretty, was drawn and aged. The three of them held each other's hands tight as the R.A.I.D. team left with Monsieur Delambre.

There you have it – these are the recurring images that have come back to me since that day.

I'm at home, by myself. All this happened about six weeks ago. It's Tuesday. I have some work to do, but nothing urgent.

Yasmine called me from Georgia the day before yesterday for an update. She asked if I was still "mulling over" the affair. I laughed it off, but the fact is that I was. This morning again, as I was stirring my coffee and looking out on the tall trees in the square, I replayed Monsieur Delambre's exit.

It's funny sometimes how it plays on repeat. It was 10.00 a.m. Again I watched the R.A.I.D. agents bringing out Monsieur Delambre.

As soon as they had secured him in the interrogation chamber, they fastened him into a straitjacket made of black material. This was not a method I was familiar with, but Captain Prungnaud assured me it was highly practical. In short, Monsieur Delambre was handcuffed underneath, and the straitjacket formed a sort of hammock to carry him on his back. The R.A.I.D. officers were holding him up by four straps, his body swinging to the rhythm of their running as they headed for the vehicle. We could only see his face. He passed by a few metres from the three women, who started crying when they saw him in this position. His wife made a futile gesture in his direction. The police were running so fast that he was past us in less than a second.

This is what's been lingering in my mind since the end of the ordeal. The look in his eyes. His face . . . It was almost impassive, which was hardly out of the ordinary for anyone who saw it. It was even to be expected that Monsieur Delambre's expression should be so relaxed, so relieved after this saga.

But it was the way he looked at me as he went by. It lasted a fraction of a second. It wasn't the defeated, loser's look I might have anticipated.

He held my stare very deliberately.

It was the look of a winner.

And beneath it, I could have sworn there was the hint of a smile.

The image is vague, but it's there nonetheless.

Monsieur Delambre departed the scene with an air of triumph, satisfaction, and the faintest of smiles. He may as well have winked at me. It was bizarre . . .

I played back the film one more time.

Now I'd put my finger on the right memory, I could see his face clearly. That smile – it wasn't the final revenge of a loser; it was the smile of a winner.

The image had become crystal clear.

I rewound the film even further. R.A.I.D. swooped in throwing smoke-grenades. Before that, the hostages flocked to the window. And before that, Monsieur Delambre said: "It's over."

Shit.

Monsieur Delambre was alone in that room waiting to be arrested. *The R.A.I.D. team discovered him crouched at the foot of a desk, head between his knees and his hands clutching the back of his neck.*

That's the reason I highlight the coincidence, because it was at that precise moment my telephone rang.

It was Monsieur Dorfmann.

I had never spoken to him on the phone. He was the end-client. My only point of contact had been my employer, Monsieur Lacoste, a point I tried to make to him.

"There's no more Lacoste," he replied.

His tone was direct. As you have no doubt noticed by now, Monsieur Dorfmann is not a man who takes kindly to being contradicted.

"Monsieur Fontana, would you be willing to accept a new mission? It follows on from the one you were previously assigned."

"In principle, yes. It's a matter of — "

"Money won't be an issue," he said, cutting me off with disdain.

After a moment, Monsieur Dorfmann said:

"You see, Monsieur Fontana, we have . . . a serious problem."

Yes they did, as I'd just realised myself.

"This is not coming as a great surprise," I responded. "With all due respect, sir, I do believe we've been fucked. Hard."

Silence.

"You could say that, yes," Monsieur Dorfmann concluded.

AFTER

27

I used to think I'd stop at nothing to get a job, but that was because prison had never crossed my mind.

I realised I had none of the necessary genetic traits for survival in this habitat. In Darwinian terms, my capacity to adapt to the prison environment placed me at the bottom of the hierarchy. Like me, there are some who have landed here by chance, accident or lunacy (all three, in my case), and who are struggling with the deep anxiety of their situation. They may as well stroll around wearing a placard with the words: "Easy pickings: help yourselves!" This condition is known as "cell shock", and it's the primary cause of early suicide.

To establish which sub-species you belong to, you just need to take one step outside your cell. It turns out I belong to the group that gets punched in the face straight away, and then relieved of any possessions that the officials haven't already taken. I didn't even see the guy coming, but there I was sprawled across the floor with my nose split open. He crouched over me, took my watch and my wedding ring, then entered my cell and swiped everything that took his fancy. As I got to my feet, I realised that my altercation with Mehmet had anticipated my new circumstances very accurately, but with two crucial differences: firstly, I was on the losing side this time; and secondly, for a single agent like myself, there were plenty more potential Mehmets out there. The opening exchange had not gone well for me. All the others were watching me with their arms folded. Taking one in the face like that (the first time I step out of my cell) wasn't the most humiliating thing; in one way or another, it's what I've had to endure since day one of unemployment. No: the humiliating thing was being the victim of an action that had been predictable to everyone except me. The guy who nicked everything I owned just happened to be at the front of the queue. In the space of a few seconds, he taught me that this place is a zoo, that at some point everything ends up with a fight.

Since I've been here, I have seen about thirty new prisoners arrive, and the only ones who avoid this initiation are the re-offenders. Being a first-timer at my age didn't let me off the hook. Now I'm part of the club: I fold my arms and watch the show.

Nicole visited me at the start of my detention. My nose looked like a pig's snout. We made an odd couple, because unlike me Nicole had made herself as pretty as a picture, with lovely make-up and the beautiful patterned dress that crosses over at the front, and which I love because I always used to pull at the little cord . . . In short, she wanted to project confidence, desire; she wanted to do me a good turn, to put on a brave face despite the circumstances, because she felt it was necessary for enduring the long road ahead of us. When she saw me, she acted as though everything was normal, which was impressive. The nurse, a brutish fellow, had just changed the dressing, leaving me with large wads of bloodied cotton wool up each nostril so I had to breathe through my mouth, and the scar running beneath the two sets of stitches was still covered in dried blood. I was also struggling to open my right eye as the lid had tripled in size. The antiseptic cream was a pissy yellow and gleamed beneath the neon lights.

And so it was that Nicole sat down in front of me and smiled. She swallowed back the "How are you?" question and started talking about the girls, all the while staring at an imaginary point in the middle of my forehead. She talked about the house, day-to-day stuff, and a few minutes in, silent tears began streaming down her cheeks. She carried on talking as though she hadn't noticed them. Finally, the words stuck in her throat and, afraid of seeming weak when I needed her to be strong, she said: "sorry". Simply "sorry", just like that. And then she lowered her head, devastated by the scale of the catastrophe. She decided to get a tissue out of her bag, fumbling around for an eternity. We were both dejected, defeated.

It occurred to me that this was the first time we'd been so apart since we met.

That "sorry" from Nicole unsettled me deeply. Things have been hard enough for her already, and it's only just getting started. There's stacks of paperwork – the whole thing is a bloody mess. I told her that she mustn't feel she has to come and see me, but she replied:

"It's already enough that I have to sleep without you . . ."

Those words suffocated me.

After that, in spite of her distress, Nicole managed to compose herself. She had some questions for me. There was so much she didn't understand. What had happened to me? I no longer resembled her husband, not even physically. The man she'd lost would never have done those things.

This was the essence of her question: what have I become?

A bit like in accidents, her brain was fixated on peripheral details. She was in shock.

"How did you find a gun with real bullets?"

"I bought it."

She wanted to ask me where, how much, how, but her real question was too pressing:

"Did you want to kill people, Alain?"

Now that was a tricky one. Yes, I think I did.

"No! Not at all . . ." I answer.

Nicole clearly didn't believe a word coming out of my mouth.

"So why did you buy it?"

I got the impression that this gun was going to stay between us for some time.

Nicole started crying again, but this time she didn't try to hide it. She took my hands in hers, and there was no hiding the proof anymore: my wedding ring had disappeared. Our wedding ring had probably already changed hands for a blowjob from a young rent boy, who'd worn it in his ear for a few days before trading it for some weed, a couple of subbies or some methanol . . . Nicole said nothing. She simply filed the information away in the spreadsheet that one day will calculate the sum total of our shared losses. Or perhaps in our statement of affairs when we file for bankruptcy.

I'm now aware that the one question burning on her lips was also the one she'd never ask me:

Why have you abandoned me?

Chronologically speaking, however, the first visit was from Lucie. Not unexpectedly, in fact. The police remanded me in custody and asked if I had a lawyer. And I said Lucie. She was willing enough to come. The second R.A.I.D. arrested me, she knew I'd call her first. She squeezed me in her arms and asked me how I was, without a single word of judgement or criticism. It was incredibly comforting. That's why I would have called her ahead of her sister even if she hadn't been a lawyer.

The police installed us in a little room and hit the timer. We cut short the gushing to avoid being overwhelmed by the emotion of it all, and I asked Lucie how everything would pan out, and in what order. After giving me a broad outline of all the procedures, the penny dropped.

"Oh, no! No Papa, not a chance!" she protested.

"Why not? Come on: I'm in prison and my daughter's a lawyer . . . it makes perfect sense!"

"I might be a lawyer, but I can't be *your* lawyer!"

"Why, is it illegal?"

"No, it's not illegal, but . . ."

"But what?"

Lucie aimed a gentle smile at me that reminded me of her mother. Given the circumstances, this made me enormously depressed.

"Listen," she said with as much composure as possible, "I don't know if you realise, Papa, but what you did was really . . . disturbing."

She spoke to me like I was a toddler. I pretended not to notice because at that stage in the conversation, it seemed a fair assessment on her part.

"It all depends on the charges the magistrate decides to press. At the very least, he'll get you for 'false imprisonment', maybe 'aggravated', and because you fired at the police — "

"I didn't fire at the police, I fired at the windows!"

"Yes, fine, but the police were on the other side of the windows, and that's known as 'armed assault against a police officer in the execution of his duty'."

For someone who doesn't know the first thing about law, this was a terrifying expression. It raised just one question:

"So how long are we talking? Worst case scenario . . ."

My throat was dry, as was my tongue, and I felt like my vocal cords were lined with sandpaper. Lucie stared at me for a moment. She had the hardest task, namely giving me a reality check. And she did it very well. My daughter is a mighty fine lawyer. She spoke slowly and clearly.

"What you did is about as serious as it gets, Papa. Worst-case scenario: thirty years in prison."

Until then, the number had been hypothetical. On Lucie's lips, it became real and terrifying.

"Any chance of a reduced sentence . . . ?"

"We're a long way from that, believe me." Lucie sighed.

Thirty years! She could tell that the prospect shattered me. Things had been desperate enough before, but this news finished me off. I must have seemed shrunken in my seat, and I couldn't hold back the tears. I knew I mustn't, because nothing is worse than seeing old men cry, but it was beyond my control.

Two days before the hostage-taking, before throwing myself into the fray, I spent a mere hour weighing up the legal risks. I consulted two or three law books, reading them in the mad grip of my fury. I knew I was embarking on something desperate, but the consequences were far less tangible than my anger.

As I gazed at Lucie, I felt convinced I would die in prison. And the look in her eyes indicated that she thought the same. Even half this sentence, a measly fifteen years, was unthinkable. How old would I be when I got out? Seventy-five? Eighty?

Even if I managed to avoid getting my face smashed in on a bi-monthly basis, it would still be impossible.

I sobbed like a baby, and Lucie swallowed hard.

"We'll fight this, Papa. Firstly, that's the maximum sentence, and there's nothing to say that the jury will . . ."

"What do you mean 'jury'? Won't I be tried by a magistrate?"

"Nooo, Papa."

She found my ignorance bewildering.

"Your actions mean you'll be tried in the high court."

"High court? But I'm not a murderer! I didn't kill anyone!"

My tears had reached the next level, fuelled by my indigna-tion. For Lucie, the situation was becoming more and more complicated.

"That's why you need a specialist. I've done some research and I've f — "

"I don't have the money to pay for a specialist."

I wiped my eyes with the back of my hand.

"We'll find the money."

"Oh yeah? How's that, then? Hold on, how about this for an idea: let's ask Mathilde and Gregory if we can dip into their savings!"

That pissed her off. I carried on:

"Forget it. It's fine, I'll defend myself."

"Don't even think about it! In this sort of case, naivety will only go one way: the maximum sentence."

"Lucie . . ."

I took her hand and stared her in the eye.

"If it's not you, it's me. No-one else."

My daughter saw there was no point persisting. Her arguments would fall on deaf ears, and the realisation left her despondent.

"Why are you asking me to do this, Papa?"

I'd calmed myself down. I had a huge advantage over her: I knew what I wanted. I wanted my daughter to be my lawyer. I'd thought of nothing else over the last few hours. As far as I could see, there was no other solution. My decision was made.

"I'm going to be sixty, Lucie. That is what's at stake for me – the rest of my time on this earth. I don't want that to be in the hands of someone I've never even met."

"But Papa, this isn't psychotherapy, it's a high court trial! You need a professional, a specialist!" she said, grappling for the words. "I don't know how it all works. The high court is . . . it's very particular. It's . . . it's . . ."

"Here's what I'm asking you, Lucie. If you don't want to, I understand, but if it's not you . . ."

"Yes, so you've said! This is blackmail!"

"Absolutely. I'm banking on you loving me enough to agree to help me. If I'm wrong, then please let me know!"

The tone settled as quickly as it escalated. We'd come to an impasse, neither of us saying anything. She blinked nervously. I thought she might back down. There was light in the tunnel. There was still a chance.

"I have to think about it, Papa, I can't give you an answer just like that . . ."

"Take your time, Lucie, there's no hurry."

But the truth is, there was a hurry. We needed to go through a whole lot of processes, and soon: the investigating magistrate will need to elect a suitable interlocutor, I'll need counsel to establish my line of defence, and several other grim complications besides.

"I'll think about it. I don't know . . ."

Lucie hit the buzzer. There was nothing left to discuss. We said our goodbyes quickly. I don't think she had any hard feelings against me. Not yet, at least.

28

My case hit the headlines in no time. Even the eight o'clock news ran it, which wouldn't sit well with the investigating magistrate – they never take kindly to media exposure. Two days after my arrest, I'd hoped against hope that the spotlight on me would fade when the C.E.O. of some big company had wound up in prison for embezzling an eye-watering sum of money (he's in the same jail as me, but in the V.I.P. wing). Maybe it's because guys like him are ten a euro cent nowadays, or just because their cases aren't considered that newsworthy anymore, but the diversion was short-lived and the cameras were back on me soon enough. My story was more media-friendly than his. After all, more folk out there can identify with an unemployed guy blowing his fuse than with some bigwig who siphons off six times the value of his share options.

The journos have treated my hostage-taking like one of those nasty news items where a U.S. teenager shoots up his school. They're making out as though I were in some sort of unemployment-induced stupor. A fanatic. Reporters rushed to question a few idiots on my street ("Oh, well, you know, he was an easy-going sort of neighbour. If I'd had any idea . . ."), a few guys from work ("Oh, well, you know, he was an easy-going sort of colleague. If I'd had any idea . . ."), even my adviser from the job centre ("Oh, well, you know, he was an easy-going sort of unemployed person.

If I'd had any idea . . ."). It's funny to see such unanimity on the matter. It feels like you're attending your own funeral, or reading your own obituary.

On the Exxyal front, there's been plenty of noise too, not least regarding the hero of the day, Crown Prince Paul Cousin. His display of courage did more than enough to restore the company's faith in him. He's back in the fold. Everything I'd dreamed of for myself. I can just picture him, already back at Sarqueville heading up a round of redundancies that will affect several hundred families. Perfect man for the job.

In front of the cameras he seemed genial enough, a bit like he'd been with me once the hostage-taking was over: rigid, ruthless, upright. Never one to gush. He's like the epitome of an early Calvinist, or one of those puritans who set sail for the New World. Paul Cousin is to capitalism what Torquemada was to Catholicism. The Grim Reaper's got nothing on him. As I said, the perfect man for the job.

"We could not stand by and watch the workplace turn into a crime scene," he said to camera. Just picture it: if every unemployed person were to take their potential employer hostage . . . Imagine. Tremble at the thought. His message was clear: senior executives like him are acutely aware of their duty, and any wrongdoer seeking to harm their employer can expect to find a Paul Cousin blocking the way. All a bit terrifying when you think about it.

Throughout, Alexandre Dorfmann has been taking an Oscar-winning turn as "The Victim". Sober, solemn and greatly saddened by these horrific circumstances. Let it be known that Alexandre Dorfmann is a C.E.O. full of humanity, a C.E.O. who has stood shoulder-to-shoulder with his execs in the face of terror. He has shown himself to be stoic, which is no surprise considering the burden of his responsibility. And had it behove him to lay down his life for his employees, let there be no doubt: he would have done so gladly and without hesitation. As for me, he had some stern words. I threatened his senior execs, which is not something he could ever forgive. The underlying message was clear: business chiefs are not going to be messed around by some unemployed middle manager, gun or no gun. They will never be defeated. All bodes well for the trial . . .

When he stared into the camera, I had the impression that Dorfmann was looking directly at me. There was another, deeper message he was communicating: "Delambre, taking me for a prick was a very bad idea, and I'm not about to wait thirty years to string you up by the balls." All bodes well for the next few months behind bars . . .

Seeing him speak to me like that made me realise I'll be hearing from him very soon. Let's not dwell on that for now. Suffice to say that when it does happen, I have no idea how I'm going to escape unscathed.

Next up, the report focused on me, on my life, showing shots of the windows to our apartment and the entrance to our building. Our letterbox. It sounds silly, but the sight of our name written like that on the little yellowed label, which dates back almost to the time we moved, was painful. I imagined Nicole shut away inside the house, talking to our daughters on the telephone in tears.

The thought still tears my heart to pieces.

It's incredible how far apart we are.

Lucie has explained to Nicole what to do when she's bombarded by journalists on the telephone, in the *métro* station, at the supermarket, on the pavement, or the stairwell, the foyer at the resource centre, the lift. The toilets of her bloody cafeteria. Her view is that if we ignore them, the newspapers will leave us alone until the start of the trial, which shouldn't be for at least another eighteen months. When the date was announced, I reacted as bravely as possible. I've done my sums. Take the most clement verdict, subtract any special remissions I might hope for, then subtract the time spent on remand. Even then, the resulting sentence is unthinkably long. My age has never seemed like such a threat.

Besides all that, the telly coverage has let me enjoy my fifteen minutes of fame in jail: people discuss my case, everyone expresses their opinion, I'm asked questions. There are a lot of know-it-alls in here. Some reckon I'll have extenuating circumstances working in my favour, which amuses those of the opposite persuasion: that I'll be held up as an example to other unemployed people who might be tempted by an idea as absurd as mine. Everyone measures my situation against their own, factoring in all their hopes and fears, their pessimism or optimism. They each have their own definition of the word "lucidity".

Some people call this "preventive detention", and that seems about right: if you forget the endless forms of wheeling and dealing that go on here, you're prevented from doing pretty much anything. The only thing they take a liberal attitude to are the numbers. Instead of the four hundred detainees there should be, there are seven hundred. If you take the exact figure, it works out at almost 3.8 prisoners per cell. In other words, you'd need a miracle to avoid sharing a two-man cell with three others. At the start, it was really tough: in eight weeks, I changed cells or cellmates eleven times. Who would have thought that such a sedentary population could be so unstable? I've had a bit of everything: psychos, loonies, depressives, fatalists, armed robbers, druggies, suicide risks, druggy suicide-risks . . . It's like a trailer for what prison has in store for me.

The spirit of enterprise is alive and well. Everything here is bought, sold, swapped, exchanged and valued. Jail is a non-stop marketplace for basic valuables. My flattened snout taught me a lesson: since then, I haven't kept anything, cutting my wardrobe down to two unspeakably ugly outfits that I wear on alternate weeks. I'm keeping a low profile.

Charles is my adviser. Apart from the girls (by which I mean Nicole and Lucie), he was the first to make contact with me. My letters to Charles arrive in three days tops, but when he writes to me, it takes over a fortnight – his letter has to be screened by the investigating magistrate's office, who lets it through in his own sweet time. I picture my pal Charles in his car, pad resting on the steering wheel. The image of him deep in concentration comes naturally. The effort must be monumental. In his first letter, he wrote: "If you answer don't feel you have to but just tell me if Morisset is still there Georges Morisset he's a good guy I knew him from my time inside."

Reading Charles' literary output is much like listening to him speak. Free of punctuation, extremely long-winded, stream-of-consciousness stuff.

A little later on, he wrote: "I will come and see you soon it's not that I can't where there's a will there's a way and all that but it brings back awful memories so I'd rather not but I do want to see you so I'll come anyway." The advantage to his prose style is that you can follow his line of thought nice and easily.

The Georges Morisset he mentions has one of the best reputations of all the guards. He has gradually worked his way up the rungs of the penitentiary ladder. I told Charles he'd been made a prison officer, and in his last letter he wrote: "Morisset officer doesn't surprise me cause he's a workhorse he's hungry and he's got the talent you'll see he's not going to leave it at that I wouldn't be surprised if he makes senior officer at the next round of exams you'll see."

There were a few other admiring lines. Charles was ecstatic about the meteoric rise of Officer Morisset. Of course it took going to jail myself to find out that my best friend – my only friend, in fact – had been sent down twice himself. And this was the very place he'd been remanded the first time. I have so far resisted the urge to ask him what he did.

In one of his letters, he also wrote: "As I know the lie of the land sort of I can help you see how it works cause at the start it's definitely hard and you're at a bit of a loss and maybe when you arrive you get smacked in the face so when you know things sometimes you can manage to avoid the most shitty problems."

This offer was timely, since I'd just been given two extra stitches beneath my left eyebrow following a contretemps (of the sexual sort, this time) in the showers with a somewhat simpleminded bodybuilder who hadn't been turned off by my age. Charles is now my mentor, and I follow his advice to the absolute letter.

The advice about the clothes was one of his, along with a stack of other little things that have, by turn, let me: hold on to the best part of my lunch; not stray inadvertently into any of the different factions' "restricted areas", whose size and location seem to vary according to a baffling set of rules and customs; not be robbed of items the second I buy them; and not be flipped out of my bunk by new inmates too quickly.

Prompted by the news that I'd already had my face smashed in twice, Charles also explained that the worst thing of all was to be seen as a punchbag, the sort of guy you can rough up: "You will need to put a stop to that and reverse the tide and to do that there are two solutions first crack the biggest guy on your wing in the face or if you can't do that no offence but maybe that'll be the case with you then find protection from someone who can get you some respect."

Charles is right. These might be chimpanzee tactics, but that's how prison works. I've been keeping this in mind and have started trying to butter up the big guns in the hope that one of them will offer me protection.

First up I set my heart on Bébétâ. He's a guy of about thirty who must have been lobotomised at a very young age, with the result that he functions exclusively in binary mode. When he's pumping iron, he can only process two instructions: up/down. If he's eating: chew/swallow. Walking: right foot/left foot. Et cetera. He's waiting to be sentenced for beating a Romanian pimp to death (fist forward/fist back). He must be about six foot six, and if you removed all his bones, there'd still be more than twenty stone of muscle. Interacting with him requires a scientific approach that borrows from the field of animal cognition. I have made preliminary contact, so he can register my face, a process that might take several weeks. I'm not even holding out hope that he'll remember my name. These initial moves have gone well. I've managed to effect a preliminary reflex: he smiles when he sees me. But it's going to be a long, long road.

For some reason, Charles' words about Officer Morisset kept simmering away in the background. At various points in the day, I would catch myself thinking about him, or notice him walking past my cell or in the yard during exercise time. He's about fifty years old, strongly built despite a slight paunch, and you get the feeling he's been at the prison for a while, and that if push came to shove, he wouldn't be afraid of a confrontation. He surveys everything with a keen eye. I even saw him reprimand Bébétâ once, who must be three times his weight. There was something in his manner with the big guy, his way of explaining to him what he was unhappy about, that intrigued me. Even Bébétâ can grasp that this is a man who breathes authority. That was when I had the idea.

I hotfooted it to the library and tracked down the details of the competitive examinations for becoming a senior prison officer. I checked that my intuition wasn't leading me up the garden path and that my plan had a vague chance of success.

"So, Officer, these exams . . .? Not easy, from what I hear."

It was the following day, in the yard. The weather was nice, the inmates calm, and Morisset didn't seem the sort to throw his baton about. He smokes light cigarettes with meticulous concentration, as if each one is worth four times his annual salary. He holds his fag between thumb and index finger, cupping it with an almost maternal devotion. Quite odd, really.

"No, not easy," he answered, drawing delicately on the filter, where a little fleck of ash had settled.

"And what have you chosen for the written part: general dissertation or executive summary?"

That made him look up from his cigarette.

"How do you know about all that?"

"Oh, I know these civil service exams well. I've coached people preparing for them for years. All the government departments: health, labour, local authorities . . . The courses are all pretty similar – the core issues don't vary much."

I was worried I'd overplayed my hand with the "core issues" bit. Too impatient. I almost bit my lip, but I managed to restrain myself. The officer returned to his cigarette and kept silent for a long while. Then, smoothing over the fold in the paper with a fingernail, he said:

"You know what, I do struggle with the executive summary . . ."

Bingo! Delambre, you're a genius. You may well be looking at thirty big ones, but you've still got it when it comes to manipulation. All those years of management have really paid off. I let a few seconds pass before saying:

"I hear you. But the problem is that almost every candidate chooses the dissertation. Because almost every candidate is the same as you – they're afraid of the executive summary element. So basically, if you play the percentage game, you can stand out in the eyes of the examiners. The numbers would work in your favour. And what's even better is that the executive summary, once you get the hang of it, is far more straightforward than the dissertation. It's more clear-cut."

This gave Officer Morisset plenty to think about. I had to be careful not to take him for a fool: I wouldn't gain anything by pushing him and risk losing the little ground I'd made. So I said:

"Right then, best of luck, Officer."

And off I went into the courtyard. I'd hoped he would call me back, but nothing. The bell sounded, and after falling in line with the others, I turned to see that Morisset had disappeared.

29

In summer it gets very hot in prison. The air doesn't circulate, bodies sweat, the atmosphere grows heavy, electric, and the guys become even more aggressive. Prison life has started to gnaw away at me like a cancer. I don't know how I'm going to endure the misery of finishing my days here.

Twice a week I go and correct Officer Morisset's executive summaries. He works like a Trojan. Every Tuesday and Thursday, he uses three hours of his time off in lieu to do his homework under exam conditions. Luckily for me, he's still way off the money, and his technique is appalling. He's fallen for the whole thing about making him stand out from his rival candidates.

The last topic I gave him was about the state of prisons in France. No less an authority than the European Committee for the Prevention of Torture had published a report on our prisons. When I handed it to him, he asked if I was taking the piss, even though he knows full well that this is the sort of thing that might come up in the exam. I take care to drip-feed my pointers nice and slowly so that he requires my services for as long as possible. He's more than happy with the set-up. Twice a week, he summons me to his office and we work on technique. I give him plans, advising him on how to structure his summaries. He doesn't get any support from the administration, so he's bought a flipchart and some felt-tips out of his own pocket. We work in two-hour sessions. When I leave his office, the other inmates joke around and ask me whether I've taken it up the arse from him or just sucked him off, but it doesn't bother me: Officer Morisset is respected, everyone knows where they stand with him. Most importantly, though, I've found my protection. For the moment.

Lucie was a good call, too. She's very proactive. There have obviously been a few issues with the investigating magistrate, who's a little sceptical about seeing such an inexperienced lawyer taking a case to the high court. She must be putting the hours in, because at every meeting with the magistrate she has the answer to any question put to her, expressing her views clearly, taking endless notes and citing case law. Plus, her face looks almost as tired as mine, even though we've still got months and months to go. The slow pace of the investigation suits her because it means she can keep up to speed. She's enlisted the support of a certain barrister, Maître Sainte-Rose, and speaks about him regularly. If I express any doubt or start quibbling, she invokes him like some incontrovertible authority – must be a bigwig. He may well know his stuff, but he's not my lawyer. To him, my case is nothing but theory. Anyway, apparently he's got lots of experience and knows what he's doing. I'd be grateful if he could throw some of his legal jargon at the co-prisoner in the canteen who insists on devouring half my tray while his two cronies look on indifferently.

Lucie is going to an extraordinary amount of trouble. She's working even harder than when she was training, and she's never been under so much pressure.

She alone can save her father. It reads like a tragedy. And I trust no-one but her, which is a drama in itself.

What's worrying her is the Pharmaceutical Logistics kerfuffle.

"The prosecution will be quick to point out that you floored your supervisor – head-butted him, no less – just a few days before taking these people hostage. He was off work for ten days. You'll come across as a violent man."

Hardly a shocking revelation to a guy who held twelve people at gunpoint with a loaded Beretta . . .

"Depends on your approach," I suggest.

"There is a chance," she says, flicking through her yellow folder, "that we'll go down the Logistics route. It would all be much easier if your former employer withdrew their claim. Sainte-Rose says . . ."

"They'll never agree. They even extracted a formal apology from me, the bloody vampires. They're the sort who'll bleed a corpse dry before ditching it . . ."

Lucie has found the document she was looking for:

"Maître Gilson," she says.

"Yeeees . . ."

"Maître Christelle Gilson?"

"Maybe, I don't know, we were never that close . . ."

"Well, I was . . ."

I look at her.

"She was a friend of mine at uni."

My heart skips a beat.

"A good friend?"

"Yes, best friends, in fact. Close enough to 'borrow' each other's boyfriends," Lucie says, grimacing.

"Who borrowed whose boyfriend?"

"I borrowed hers."

"You can't be serious . . . You didn't!"

"Oh, I'm sorry Papa, but at the time I didn't know my father was planning on becoming a gun-toting maniac and that I'd need to defend him at the high court!"

"O.K., O.K.!" I say, holding up my hands in surrender. Lucie calms down.

"Anyway, I did her a favour. That guy was a complete tosser."

"Yes, but he was her tosser . . ."

This is a perfect example of the sorts of conversations Lucie and I have.

"Well then," she says. "I guess I'll have to pay her a visit."

Lucie explains that if she manages to convince her ex-best friend to mediate on her client's behalf to drop the charges and the damages claim, then I'll need to try the same tactic with Romain, our key witness. I hold my tongue. I make out that I understand, but for the moment, I'd prefer it if Romain was still officially an adversary. Keep it under wraps that he gave me a massive helping hand. It mustn't get out that he was complicit.

Over the course of our conversations, Lucie gives me news about her mother, who is terribly lonely. Early on I managed to call her on the phone. Lucie tells me she's worried because I don't anymore. I pretend that it's harder now, but the fact is that when I call Nicole, just hearing her voice makes me want to cry. It's unbearable.

Lucie informs me that her sister will be visiting soon. I don't believe it for a second. But it unsettles me, because I'm dreading the moment I have to confront her.

It's not easy to feel so ashamed in front of your children.

I have decided to start writing my story. It's not been easy, because it takes concentration, and wherever you are in this place, the telly's blaring all day long. At 8.00 p.m. it's a bloody racket, with everyone switching on their favourite news show at full volume. The headlines overlap and become virtually incomprehensible. France 2 (*"With annual salaries of 1.85 million euros, French C.E.O.s are the best paid in Europe"*) vies with T.F.1 (*"Unemployment is expected to reach 10% by the end of the year"*). It's a complete shambles, but at least it gives you the overall picture.

It is almost impossible to escape the endless torrent of series, clips and game shows. They drill into your head and follow you everywhere you go. Television ends up as part of your being. I don't get on well with earplugs, so I've bought a full-on pair of ear defenders. I forgot to specify a colour, so I've ended up with a bright-orange set, which makes me look like one of those people who directs planes at the airport. The guys call me the "air traffic controller", but it doesn't bother me . . . I work better with them.

I'm not a great writer – always been better at speaking rather than writing. (My hope is that this skill will come in handy at the trial, even though Lucie tells me I have to let her do all the talking and that I can only say what I've learnt by heart in the run-up to the hearings.) I'm not writing my memoirs, I'm merely trying to tell my story. Mainly for Mathilde's sake, though I'm doing it for Nicole, too, since she doesn't understand the full extent of it. And for Lucie, because not even she knows everything. Seeing it on paper, it's unbelievable how mundane I find my story. It is original, though, I'll give it that. Not everyone turns up to a job interview with a fully loaded Beretta.

Maybe that's a shame in itself. Surely one or two people have thought about it.

30

Ever since my arrival, and since Alexandre Dorfmann's first appearance on T.V. the day after the hostage-taking, I've found the lack of word from Exxyal dispiriting.

It doesn't feel right. There's no way they can stay quiet for months on end.

Those were my exact thoughts when the word finally did arrive, as I was heading into the laundry at about 10.00 a.m. this morning.

The inmate in charge took my bundle and disappeared into the bowels of the room.

And a few seconds later, he was replaced by the hulking Bébêtâ. I smiled at him and raised my right hand, as if I were taking an oath, which had become my way of greeting him. But my mind started racing when the figure of Boulon emerged from behind him. The guy they call Boulon is much smaller than Bébêtâ, but infinitely more disturbing. A real sicko. He gets his nickname from the bolts he fires from his weapon of choice, a slingshot: a highly sophisticated piece of kit with a tubular, elastic arm-rest, which he likes to load with stones. But bolts are his favourite. When he was a free man, he carried bolts of every size around in his various pockets, and could hit targets dead on from incredible distances. His final exploit was to bury a 13mm bolt right in the middle of a man's forehead from fifty metres. The bolt lodged itself in the centre of his brain – a nice, clean shot. He is known to have committed countless unspeakable acts, but boasts that he's never spilt a drop of blood. Deep down, despite appearances, maybe he does have some heart.

As soon as I saw him emerge alongside Bébétâ in the laundry room, I realised I was about to receive some news from my ex-future employer. I turned to flee but Bébétâ's outstretched arm grabbed me by the shoulder. I tried to scream but in a fraction of a second he had spun me round and pinned me against him, his hand across my mouth like a gag. He lifted me off the ground without any effort whatsoever and squeezed me tight. I flailed my arms and legs in every direction as I tried to cry out. These men were going to kill me, I knew it. My efforts were in vain. Bébétâ carried me as though I were a living-room cushion. We were behind the counter, between the rows of sheets and blankets. He tried to put me down but I was so terrified that my legs couldn't bear my weight, and he had to support me. I carried on screaming with his hand over my mouth, emitting an inhuman wail in which I couldn't even recognise my own voice. I was like a car at the scrapheap waiting to get crushed. Bébétâ held my head in place with one arm, still gagging me, and with the other he grabbed my left wrist and thrust it towards Boulon, who stared at me calmly, not saying a word. I thrashed my elbows, arms, legs, but all resistance was futile. I kept trying to scream. It was an utterly desperate situation. I felt appallingly alone. I was willing to give anything, to surrender. Anything. Nicole's face suddenly flashed before me. I held on to her image but the Nicole before me was crying, about to watch me suffer and die as her tears fell. I tried to beg but no sound came from my mouth. Everything was happening in my head. Boulon said:

"I have a message for you."

That was it.

A message.

Bébétâ forced my hand flat on a shelf. Boulon took my thumb and snapped it back on itself. The pain was searing. I screamed. I felt like I was going mad. I tried to fight back, kicking my feet everywhere, especially behind me to make Bébétâ loosen his grip a bit, but Boulon had already taken my index finger and snapped it back too. He grasped the finger and bent it until it reached the back of my hand. It made a sinister sound. The pain was blinding, nausea overwhelmed me and I vomited, but Bébétâ kept hold of me, as if the capacity to be disgusted didn't enter his excuse for a brain. When Boulon took my third finger, I fainted. I think I fainted. But no, I was still conscious when the next finger was snapped back, sending an electric shock right through me. I couldn't even scream – I was well beyond that. My body was like a wet rag in Bébétâ's vicelike grip. I was sweating like a forsaken soul. I think that was when I shat myself. But Boulon wasn't finished. There were still two fingers. I thought the pain would kill me. It was so complete I thought I was going mad. Waves of it ran from my head to my feet; even the agony was wild and panic-stricken. When Boulon did the little finger, the last one, my mind fled, my stomach churned, and it hurt so badly I wanted to die. Bébétâ let me go, and I collapsed to the ground screaming. I tried to clasp my hand. I couldn't even hold it against me, couldn't even touch it. I wailed. I was nothing but a giant surge of pain. I could no longer control myself – I'd been undone.

Boulon leant down to me and, his voice still calm, said:

"That's the message."

I don't know what happened next because I fainted.

When I woke up, my hand was swollen like a pumped-up football. I was still crying, stretched out on a bed in the infirmary. I don't think I'd stopped crying since they'd taken me.

The pain was terrible, terrible, terrible.

I turned onto my side and curled up like a baby, my bandaged hand pressed into the hollow of my stomach. I cried. I was afraid. Horribly afraid. I didn't want that. I must get out of here. I don't want to die here.

Not like that.

Not here.

31

The good thing about prison is that the hospital stints are short. Four days. Reduced service. My disarticulated metacarpophalangeals, fractures and dislocations were operated on and reset by a perfectly pleasant surgeon (as pleasant as the surgeon species permits, at least).

Several months of splints and casts lie ahead before I can expect a return to normality, something the specialist thinks unlikely anyway. I will live with the after-effects.

As I come into my cell, a young man stands up and holds out his hand. He can't resist a smile as he notices the mass of bandages, and offers me the other one. We shake the wrong way round – great start.

The only thing I want is to lie down.

Until yesterday, my hand was giving me unbearable shooting pains, and the nurse didn't have any painkillers that were sufficiently powerful. Either that or he didn't want to give them to me. Officer Morisset didn't just secure me a transfer, he brought me some tramadol too. It makes me drowsy, but at least it eases the pain and lets me sleep every now and then. Morisset assured me they'll open an inquiry and told me I must hand over the names of my attackers, but he didn't even wait for an answer before leaving my cell.

Jérôme, my new roomie, is a professional conman of about thirty. He's got a handsome face, wavy hair, a reassuringly natural bearing, and if you picture him in a suit, he'd be the consummate exec. Face on, he's your bank manager; from behind, your estate agent; right-hand side, your new G.P.; and from the left, your childhood friend who's nailing it as a stockbroker. He's got fewer qualifications than a shepherd from Sierra Leone, but he is very well-spoken and has bags of personality and charisma. There's a bit of the young Bertrand Lacoste about him, perhaps by virtue of the fact they're both crooks. Since I have more than twenty years of management experience, we get on pretty well despite the age difference. He's a talented chap. Not talented enough to avoid prison, but a wily one nonetheless. He already has plenty on his C.V.: dozens of forged cheques, tonnes of imaginary commodities sold for cash, genuine fake documents traded for an absolute fortune, fictitious jobs complete with bribes and state subsidies, and even shares transferred to foreign markets. What landed him in here was the pre-sale of some non-existent apartments just to the north of the Riviera – property of a hitherto-unseen luxury, quite literally in this case. He explained the whole ruse, but it was all far too clever for me. The guy is loaded. He could buy anything he wanted (well, with the exception of his freedom). His line of work must have been lucrative. I feel like a hobo by comparison.

I don't say anything.

Jérôme observes my head and my right hand, which is still very swollen indeed. He wants to know how I managed to get myself into such a bloody mess. It intrigues him. He's sniffing out a good business opportunity. I have to be careful of what I say and how I say it; what I don't say and how I don't say it.

My encounter with Boulon and Bébétâ has left me with post-traumatic stress, and I am terrified the moment I leave my cell. I scan my surroundings with apprehension, watching my back and all around me, permanently on the lookout. From a distance, I see Boulon going about his business, his dealings. He turns but doesn't seem to notice me. As far as he's concerned, I'm nothing but another transaction. I won't exist in his eyes until he receives a new order, at which point the only question he'll ask himself is how far he'll have to go, and whether he'll be paid enough for it. As for Bébétâ, when we cross paths he smiles, raises his hand with the palm facing me, the way I showed him, delighted to say hello to me, as if pulverising each finger on one of my hands had somehow created a new emotional bond between us. What happened in the laundry room has already been driven out of the hole at the top of his spinal cord that serves as a brain.

Jérôme doesn't find me at all talkative. He, on the other hand, is extremely chatty. He needs to talk all the time. My thoughts are dark (possibly a side-effect of my medication), and I obsess about the "message". The thing that worries me, of course, is the follow-up. That was the essence of the message: this is just the beginning.

Good Lord, I have absolutely no idea what to do.

Right from the start, I've been acting without any real notion of how this will finish. I'm improvising. I react when I'm staring a situation in the face.

I got a fist right between the eyes the second I arrived, but afterwards I found Officer Morisset and earned his protection. They broke my fingers, but I managed to get a transfer into a two-man cell in a safer section.

At worst, I'll have to endure my fate.

At best, I'll manage to shorten my sentence.

But fundamentally, from the moment I realised that Exxyal were screwing me over, when I discovered that everything I'd done to get a job had been in vain, that I'd stolen my daughter's money for nothing . . . ever since I felt myself overwhelmed by that dark fury, I have been reacting, trying hard to come up with solutions, but without ever having an overarching strategy. No plan that could factor in the consequences. I'm no crook. I've got no idea what to do.

I'm in a real bind.

The fact is that if I had had a broad strategy, and it had brought me here, then at least I could say I'd had a strategy, albeit a piss-poor one.

The first message has very much arrived. What now?

One thing is for sure: I must find a way to prevent the second message from reaching me.

Curiously enough, it's the psychiatrist charged with my assessment who sets me on the right track.

He's fifty, and a proper, open kind of guy, despite all the buzzwords. Every sentence he utters is infused with meaning, betraying a lofty opinion of his function. While none of it rings false, the problem with my case is that it's pretty self-explanatory. You just need to put my file next to my C.V. and there's your diagnosis. I don't go to too many pains to convince him of what he already knows.

What does strike me is the question he uses to kick off the session: "If you were to tell me your life story, what would you say first?"

After the interview, I launch myself wholeheartedly into my work.

As I can't write, I ask Jérôme to help: I dictate, he writes, I reread, he corrects. It's going fairly quickly, though never quick enough for me. I'm trying to disguise the fact that I've entered a race against the clock.

If everything goes to plan, the manuscript will be done in four or five days. I embellish my adventure, making no shortage of additions and inserting plenty of symbolic violence. I write in the first person, and I mix up the tenses to give it impact and pace.

And then I look into which newspapers might be interested.

*

Relations with Nicole have become strained. She is very depressed, living in a precarious state of limbo, and can see me getting it full in the neck. She is lonely and in a terrible way, and there's nothing I can do for her.

She came to visit last week.

"I'm selling the flat," she said. "I'll send you the paperwork. You have to sign it and send it straight back."

"Sell the flat? Why?" I said, stunned.

"Your trial against your former employer is about to start, and I want to be able to pay damages if it comes to it."

"We're not there yet!"

"No, but we will be. And anyway, I don't need it – it's too big for me on my own."

It was the first time I'd heard Nicole so clearly state the incontrovertible fact that I would never be coming back to live with her. I didn't know what to say. I could tell she was sad to have resigned herself to that truth.

"And then there are the legal fees," she continued, clouding the issue.

"But there are hardly any fees – we're not paying for a lawyer!"

Nicole seemed utterly dismayed, I wasn't sure why.

"Alain, I know things can't be easy for you here, but seriously, you've lost all sense of reality!"

I must have looked confused by these words.

"*I don't want Lucie working for nothing,*" Nicole said, hammering the point home. "I want her to be paid. She's quit her job to defend you, using her savings to replace the salary she's lost. And ..."

"And what?"

After everything I've been through ...

"And Maître Sainte-Rose is expensive," Nicole persisted. "Very expensive. And I don't want her to keep on paying."

This shocked me. First Mathilde, now Lucie plunged into debt by their father.

I couldn't look her in the eye any longer, and she couldn't look into mine.

Lucie's approach with Maître Gilson, her ex-pal from university, has clearly been unsuccessful. Lucie didn't offer anything in exchange. All she did was ask for a bit of goodwill and clemency. No matter how much I told her that these were not qualities that Pharmaceutical Logistics possessed in spades, she couldn't resist trying her luck. Lucie is a very good lawyer, but she's also naive. Must be a family trait. As it happened, the conversation soon turned to humiliation. Lucie's old friend seemed to revel in this opportunity for revenge, as if a simple refusal from her client weren't enough, and without showing the faintest compassion for what I'm going through and what I have at stake. As if pinching someone's boyfriend was really on a par with consigning a sexagenarian to thirty years in prison. It beggared belief. In short, Lucie now wants me to approach Romain. If he agrees not to testify, Logistics will lose their only witness, which she reckons will bring their whole case crashing down. She would then step into the breach and get all the charges dropped. I find it a bit silly to focus on this issue when I'm headed for the high court, but it seems that Sainte-Rose, her henchman, is adamant about this.

"He wants to clean up the case," Lucie explains to me. "We have to present you as a peaceable person. Show that you're not a violent man at all."

A non-violent, Beretta-wielding man.

Terrific.

Anyway, I promise to send Romain a letter, or ask Charles to pay him a visit to talk about it, but I know I won't do anything of the kind. To the contrary: all my fortunes, not to mention Romain's safety, hinge on everyone regarding him as my foe.

32

Yesterday I found out that the second message was arriving.

I didn't sleep a wink.

"Visits" are announced the day before, but you're never told who's coming. Sometimes it's a surprise, and not always a pleasant one.

As is the case with me this morning. It's the messenger, I'm sure of it. Nicole isn't meant to be coming this week, and I gave up expecting Mathilde weeks ago. Lucie is welcome any time (the procedure is different for lawyers). And anyway, she's working far too hard on my case right now to have any time to visit.

It's exactly 10.00 a.m.

We're standing in line in the corridor waiting for our names to be called. Some are excited, others despondent. As for me, I'm shit-scared. Feverish. That was the word chosen by Jérôme, my main conman, when he saw me leave the cell. An inmate I know is staring at me. He's worried for me. So he should be.

David Fontana is wearing a suit and tie. Almost smart. If I didn't know what he was capable of, I'd think he was just a normal middle manager. He's a lot more than that. Even sitting in a chair, he's threatening. The sort of guy who picks Boulon as his messenger, though he'd much rather do the job himself given half a chance.

His eyes are gleaming. He hardly ever blinks.

His presence fills the atmosphere of the tiny booth, behind which a guard passes every forty seconds. Fontana radiates terrifying levels of power and violence. He could kill me with his bare hands in the interval between the guard's rounds, no doubt about it.

Just seeing him brings back the sound of my snapping fingers, and a shiver runs down my spine.

I sit down opposite him, and he smiles at me calmly. I'm not wearing a bandage anymore, but my fingers are still very swollen, and the ones that were fractured are still being supported in grubby splints. I look like someone who's had a terrible accident.

"So you received my message, Monsieur Delambre?"

His voice is cold, abrupt. I wait. Don't make him angry. Let him come to you. Play for time. But most of all – most of all – don't do anything to annoy him; don't make him give Boulon and Bébétâ the order to drag me into the workshop and crush my head in a vice.

"I say 'my message'. I really mean my client's message," Fontana corrects himself.

Sounds like there's been a change of client. Exit Bertrand Lacoste. The great consultant has been tried, tested and found wanting. His little Polish intern has cast him into the abyss, and he's not getting out any time soon. It doesn't look pretty for the Lord High Headhunter. He needs to think long and hard about his fall from grace, and remember that you can never be too wary of the small fish, the mediocre ones. His ingenious hostage-taking idea was an H.R. catastrophe of historic proportions. Exxyal will make sure everyone knows it. His career path has taken a major diversion, and his firm's future looks about as rosy as mine.

So exit Lacoste, enter The Mikado. Alexandre Dorfmann himself is in the seat. Ex officio.

We're in a new category, now. Until now it's been the semi-professionals – now we're into the big time.

The difference in approach between Lacoste and Dorfmann is

immediately noticeable. The former makes promises about jobs, so no real consequences there. The latter engages Fontana, who deploys Bébétâ and Boulon like a commando. Dorfmann will have said: "I don't want to know details." The gloves are off, but his hands are going to stay clean. Not that Fontana will mind: the need for total discretion in this operation means he can triple his fee, plus it gives him *carte blanche* to run things his own way (and I've already had a taster of what that entails).

Fontana waits as I piece the puzzle together. With the fake hostage-taking for Exxyal, his role was largely organisational. Now he's in his element. He seems at ease taking me to task; like an athlete returning to the track after a niggling injury.

Did I receive his message? You don't say . . .

I swallow hard and nod in silence.

Not that the words would come, anyway. Seeing him reminds me of my anger, of Exxyal, Bertrand Lacoste – everything that's landed me here in this mess. The vision of Fontana pouncing at me, teeth bared, comes flooding back. If he'd had the chance to kill me then, he would have done it. But he just hobbled to the window, his leg bleeding. Here in the visiting room, I can smell the cordite again, and in my hand I can feel the cold, heavy weapon I used to shoot the windows. I wish I still had that gun in my hand; wish I could hold it in my outstretched arm and slam two bullets into Fontana's head. But he's not here to get himself killed by my fury. He's here to take back what little I've won.

"Little . . .?" he asks. "I hope you're joking!"

So here we are.

I don't move.

"We'll get onto that, but first, congratulations Monsieur Delambre. Very nice move. Really, very fine work. I certainly fell for it . . ."

The admiring tone was at odds with his expression. His lips are pursed, his eyes boring into mine. Subliminal messages are oozing from every pore, and I'm picking up on each and every one of them. They all revolve around the same theme: I'm going to crush you like a piece of shit.

"A rookie would say that you'd planned everything well, but I think the exact opposite. Otherwise you wouldn't be here . . . You're not a strategist. You're improvising, making it up as you go along. You should never do that, Monsieur Delambre," he says, wagging his finger. "Never."

I'm itching to remind him that his magnificent planning didn't prevent his hostage-taking from going tits up. But I'm spending all my energy on giving nothing away: poker face. My heart is beating at a hundred miles an hour. I hate him with an intensity that scares me. The man is capable of sending murderers to my cell, even at night.

"Although that said," he continues, "for an improvisation, it was a decent spot, I must admit. It took me a while to figure it out. And of course, by the time I did figure it out, it was too late. Well, I say 'too late' . . . We'll make up for the lost time, Monsieur Delambre. You can be sure of that."

I don't even flinch, breathing from my stomach. Not a movement – mustn't let any emotion show. Stony-eyed.

"Monsieur Guéneau was the first man you interrogated. That was your stroke of luck, I think. Because, despite appearances," he says, with a sweeping gesture that takes in the surrounding décor, "you have had some luck, Monsieur Delambre. Until today, that is."

I swallow hard.

"If Monsieur Guéneau had been interrogated later," Fontana continues, "your plan would have worked, but I'm not sure you would have gone through with it. You would have weighed up the situation more carefully. And ultimately, you wouldn't have risked it . . . But it was served up to you on a plate, so you couldn't help yourself. You couldn't resist the temptation. Do you remember how scared he was, Monsieur Guéneau?"

Jean-Marc Guéneau, eyes darting all over the place. I picture him sitting bolt upright as the young Arab fired him questions. And next to me, Lacoste's turkey, who . . .

But Fontana was front row for all that.

"Monsieur Guéneau's interrogation went badly wrong. You saw Mademoiselle Rivet wasn't up to the mark with her clumsy questions. She lost her footing, never managed to assert herself, and sure enough, Monsieur Guéneau started having his doubts, thrashing his head from side to side, not quite figuring out the game. The whole thing was seconds away from collapsing on itself. Then you decided to intervene . . ."

I remember approaching the microphone. And a few minutes later, Monsieur Guéneau had stripped down to his red-lace lingerie and was sobbing. Then he fell on the gun and swallowed the barrel.

"The man was desperate. You might not be much of a forward-planner, but you're not short of intuition."

There's that admiring tone again. Fontana's main aim is to shatter the icy wall I've put up against him. He's trying every trick in the book.

"You ruined him. He was willing to sell out his company, hand it to you on a plate. He was willing to give you anything: financial secrets, hidden deals, slush funds . . . And that's what you were hoping for."

True, that was what I was waiting for, even if I wasn't expecting it to come so quickly. And the fact that the first man to be interrogated was the one I'd been banking on was indeed a stroke of luck.

He had sat down at the desk indicated by the commando leader, and plugged his Blackberry into the laptop computer before logging into the Exxyal Europe system.

He clicked once, twice, and opened the finance folder.

I waited a few seconds, watching him very closely.

He entered his personal passwords: the first, then the second.

I was looking out for that classic bit of body language that we all exhibit when our password is accepted. When the path is open at last and you can finally get to work; a minute reflex in the hands and shoulders that represents release.

"Then you stood up, and you said: 'Bastard'. Although I haven't stopped wondering whether I misheard and it was actually plural: 'Bastards'?"

I don't move.

He carries on:

"The rest was all for show. You were terrified by what you were doing, and that played into your hands. Your fear was your trump card. Because your emotions were genuine, your terror was genuine – what you were doing took serious balls. Everyone read your fear at face value: an exec goes ballistic and ends up staging a spontaneous hostage-taking. Of course he's scared! But the whole point was that this was a diversion."

I lined up the hostages, following Kaminski's instructions to the letter. I frisked them, spinning them round clockwise, fingers fully splayed. With my back to the door, I shot at the windows . . .

"And finally, the opportunity came to you through Monsieur Cousin. Ah, how he wanted to be the hero of the day, that guy! But if he hadn't provided you with your chance, it would have been someone else. It didn't matter to you. My cameo could have given you your opportunity – the only reason you repelled me was to give weight to your 'plan'. By that point, all you wanted was to fail. That's what no-one could understand."

Paul Cousin, the spectre. The colour of chalk. He got to his feet and squared up to me. He was perfect. Precisely what I needed, it's true. When he intervened, he was the epitome of the company's values. Like a genre painting: *Outraged executive making a stand against Adversity*.

"You needed to appear defeated. That way you could keep us

contained. You could pretend you were giving up and surrendering. Ultimately, you could do what you were planning from the start: go and tuck yourself away in the other room, where the laptop was still logged on thanks to Monsieur Guéneau. Open goal. The hostage-taking gave you free rein over Exxyal's accounts. All you had to do was sit down, tap the keyboard, and help yourself."

David Fontana stops. He seems genuinely impressed. There's something dodgy about his admiration – it's going to cost me dear. It's intended to cost me . . .

"Ten million euros, Monsieur Delambre! You weren't messing about!"

I'm stunned.

Not even his client is telling him the truth.

I took 13.2 million.

I can't help but let the mask slip a little, and a glimmer of a smile crosses my lips. By now Fontana is over the moon:

"Bravo, Monsieur Delambre. No really, bravo! I couldn't care less about the technical details. According to the I.T. specialist who examined the leak, you arranged a transfer to an offshore account without leaving a trace."

It was actually a lot cleverer than that.

When I left the hostages and sat down at the laptop, I only had fifteen minutes to spare, and my computer skills are minimal to say the least. I know how to do spreadsheets and word processing. But anything beyond that? Well, I do know how to insert a U.S.B. stick and send an email. Romain told me that would be enough. He'd worked almost thirty hours straight to sort everything out. The software he'd installed on the U.S.B. stick did all the hard work as soon as it was plugged in. Once I'd given him the access, it took Romain (working from his desktop at home) less than four minutes to release a Trojan horse into the Exxyal system. The malware he installed would allow him to re-enter the system during business hours: enough time to access their accounts, secure the transfer to a tax haven, then delete every trace.

Fontana was right on this one point – the details don't affect the result.

"Especially well played, given you're acting with total impunity. Cleaning out an oil company's slush fund, one that's used for paying out bribes and kickbacks here, there and everywhere . . . You can be sure they won't press charges against you."

No reaction.

He doesn't have the whole story, but he's got most of it.

The details don't matter at all.

Fontana doesn't budge. The seconds tick on.

"But ultimately, despite appearances, you haven't thought about a thing. What you did was motivated by pure anger. You took off with the cash, ran for forty metres, then stopped. And now here we are sitting opposite each other, Monsieur Delambre. What a miscalculation . . . In all honesty, I find it a complete mystery. Well, I have my theories. I don't think you were out to benefit yourself by taking this money. You're keeping it warm for your little family, not for yourself. After a hostage-taking like that, you can't be under any illusions: best-case scenario, you'll be out in fifteen years. That's if you don't get cancer first."

Fontana leaves a heavy silence hanging.

"Or if I don't have you killed first. Because my client is very, very, very angry, Monsieur Delambre."

I can picture the fallout. The board of directors at Exxyal Europe won't have been given the details, but major shareholders can't be left in the dark. However much you love your C.E.O., a thirteen-million hole in the finances is going to ruffle some feathers. Of course, a thirteen-million hole in the finances isn't enough to get the boss of a big multinational fired – that would be absurd – but it's in everyone's interests for order to be restored. Capital on one side, unemployment on the other. Dorfmann must have given his shareholders some guarantees. He will have promised to recover the slush fund, to bring it home.

Fontana looks at my hand, and it starts hurting terribly.

"How much do you want?"

My throat is so dry that my voice doesn't carry. I'm forced to repeat the question.

"How much do you want?"

Fontana looks surprised.

"But, all of it, Monsieur Delambre. Absolutely all of it."

O.K. Now I see why Exxyal didn't give him the real number.

If I pay back the ten million they're asking for, that leaves me with three.

That's their offer.

Forget the bit after the decimal point. Let's not split hairs. Give back the slush fund, keep three million euros, save your life, and everything can go back to normal. Wipe the slate clean. That's what profits and losses are all about. If I deduct Romain's share, that leaves me with two million. Two million: easily enough to pay back Mathilde and Lucie, and to make Nicole change her mind about selling the flat.

But I reckon I'm entitled to a bit more than that. I've crunched the numbers in my head several times. The sum I took from Exxyal Europe is less than three years' salary for one of the top dogs. O.K., it's a millennium's worth if you're on the minimum wage, but fuck, I'm not the one who sets the rates.

I play my final card.

"And what about the payee list?"

My tone is the same. Fontana raises his eyebrows, but his question is a silent one. He hunches his shoulders a bit, like someone expecting a brick to land on his head.

I don't move. I wait.

"Explain that one to me, Monsieur Delambre."

"I understand your proposal regarding the cash. I just want to know what to do with your client's contact list. You know, the payees from this fund. Along with the details of the accounts their fees are transferred into for services to your client. There are all sorts in there: French deputy ministers, foreign politicians, sheikhs, businessmen . . . I'm just wondering what to do with it, since you brought it up."

Fontana looks extremely animated. Not only because of me, but because his client hasn't told him everything, which he finds very irritating. He clenches his jaw.

"I'll need some tangible proof for my client. A copy of your document."

"I'll forward you the first page. Give me an email address to send it to."

I've sown some more doubt. Fontana's a prudent man. He'll look into this, and if I'm telling the truth, his client will have to tread very carefully with me. I've bought myself some time.

"Fine," he says at last. "I'll need to discuss this with my client."

"That seems very sensible. Discuss away."

I make my final play. I smile, full of self-confidence:

"Keep me posted, will you?"

Fontana hasn't moved a millimetre, but I'm already on my feet.

I walk down the corridor, legs like jelly.

In two days, three at most, Fontana will find out I'm bluffing and that there's no list whatsoever.

He's going to be livid.

If my new strategy doesn't yield any results in the next two days, Bébêtâ and Boulon are going to quite literally make a killing themselves: my insides will be emptied onto the concrete of the exercise yard.

33

Day one: nothing.

As I move around, I keep an anxious eye on Boulon. As far as he's concerned, I don't exist. He hasn't received an order concerning me. I'm still alive today.

Keep faith.

It should work. It has to work.

Day two: nothing.

Bébétâ is pumping iron in the gym. He sets down his dumbbells to hold up his hand at me, because nodding hello while he's doing something else is beyond his capabilities.

You can tell straight away with him: he hasn't received an order concerning me either.

The day goes slowly. Jérôme wants to chat, but he can see that now's not the time.

I only venture out of my cell once. I try to bargain for a blade from a guy I know. I want to be able to defend myself, even if I won't know what to do should the situation arise. He's not interested in anything I have to exchange, and I return to my cell empty-handed.

I stop eating. Not hungry.

I can't stop running through everything in my head. It might work. Tomorrow's another day.

I hang on to that.

*

Day three: the last.

I can't see Boulon or Bébétâ.

Not a good sign.

Generally speaking, I know where I might find them. I don't want to bump into them, but not seeing them makes me even more anxious. I do a broad sweep of their usual hangouts as discreetly as possible. I look for Officer Morisset and remember that he's away for a few days. One of his friends is dying, and he's gone to his bedside.

I return to my cell and stay put. If they are looking for me, they'll have to come here.

I've been sweating since early this morning.

Midday arrives and still there's no news. Tomorrow, I'm a dead man. Why didn't it work?

And then it's 1.00 p.m.

T.F.1.

My face is on the front page. It's a work mugshot that dates back to the Jurassic era. God knows how they got their hands on that one.

Straight away, two, three, four inmates come rushing in to watch the rest of the story in our cell. They slap their thighs in excitement. Others say "Shhhh!!" so they can hear the newsreader better. There's a real crackle of excitement.

The journalist reports that this morning, *Le Parisien* published a double spread on me and my story, printing an extract from the first few pages of the manuscript I'd sent them. They went for the juiciest bits. I'm announcing the imminent release of my book, which tells the full story.

And my word if it isn't just the most heart-rending testimony of a real-life victim of the crisis! Pitch perfect.

First, some background. Delambre. That's me. One of the inmates gives me a comradely slap on the back.

Delambre – an out-of-work senior in search of a job – and his professional background, his story, the good years followed by the scourge of unemployment later in life. The sense of injustice; the years in the doldrums. This man has been to hell and back. The humiliation before his children. His hopes of working again constantly frustrated, then the slide into hardship, and finally depression.

The hostage-taking? An act of desperation.

The moral of the story? He's facing thirty years in prison.

The country's heart bleeds. My testimony is deemed "shattering". Archive images follow from a few months before: Exxyal Europe headquarters, the car park full of police, flashing lights, the hostages safe and sound in their foil blankets, then there's me, the guy they've trussed up and captured, being marched off at pace. The inmates in our cell howl with joy, and from elsewhere there's another "shhh!".

The guest analyst is a sociologist who has come in to comment on depression in executives and on social violence. The current system discourages and demotivates people, pushing them to extremes. The weakest feel like only the strongest can succeed. Older employees increasingly face the threat of exclusion. He has a question for the viewers: "In 2012, we'll have ten million seniors. Does that mean ten million thrown onto the scrapheap?"

My story becomes symbolic; the drama of my unemployment a fact of society.

Well played.

Fuck you, Fontana.

An inmate hugs me round the neck, delighted to be pals with a T.V. star.

Vox pops . . .

Ahmed, 24, warehouse assistant: "I read the article in *Le Parisien* . . . I get it, I'm behind him all the way. Yeah, I'll read the book. It's all we can talk about at work. An unemployed guy in jail just for being unemployed . . . it's not right. Isn't the suicide rate high enough as it is?"

Françoise, 45, secretary: "I'm scared of being made redundant one day. It terrifies me, in fact. I don't know where I'd go. And when you've got kids . . . I read the article in *Le Parisien* and I understood. In the office, we can barely talk about anything else. I'm going to buy a copy for my husband."

Jean-Christian, 71, retired: "It's all a load of tosh. People who really want work can find it. They do whatever, but a job's a job, even if it's just packing boxes at a warehouse."

All the guys around me jeer. If I ever see Jean-Christian in the flesh, I'll shove my Pharmaceutical Logistics payslip up his arse. Tosser. Not that it matters.

I catch Jérôme's eye. He's laughing. He gets it.

The T.V. and the papers all close with the announcement of the book's release: "A devastating account that is sure to turn political heads." I haven't found a publisher yet, but the last five minutes have left me confident that there won't be any trouble on that front.

From now on, I'm the most famous unemployed person in France.

A paragon. Untouchable.

I stretch. I breathe.

Boulon and Bébétâ are going to have to look for work elsewhere.

I stand up. I'm going to demand to see the warden.

Anything happens to me now, the prison administration are going to get it in the neck. They'll have to protect me. I'm a celebrity.

It's like I've committed insider trading: I've bought myself a ticket to the V.I.P. wing.

34

Usually, Lucie takes out the huge files and the reams (I mean *reams*) of notes filled out with her pretty, precise handwriting. Today, nothing. She doesn't move, her eyes fixed on the table. Her fury is bubbling with a delirious intensity. If I wasn't her father, she'd have smacked me outright.

"If you were a client, Papa, I'd be calling you a bloody bastard."

"I'm your father. And you did just call me that."

Lucie is white as a sheet. I wait, but she's waiting too. I launch in.

"Listen, let me explain . . ."

That was all she was waiting for. A trigger, a word. Her rage floods out like a river that's broken its banks.

Here are the highlights:

"This is a betrayal . . . You couldn't have done anything in the world more shitty . . . I don't want to defend you anymore . . . I caved in to your shameless emotional blackmail . . . Ever since, I've worked day and night to give us the best chance when it comes to the trial and you, behind my back, you write your fucking *memoirs* and go and send them to the press . . . Shows how little you appreciate my work . . . How little you appreciate me . . . Because you can't have written that shit overnight! . . . Days, weeks even . . . Days and weeks when you were seeing me, speaking to me regularly . . . You've made a complete *mockery* of me . . . But it's not even that . . . You did it without telling me, because in your eyes, I'm of no importance whatsoever . . . I'm just a little cog in the machine . . . Sainte-Rose doesn't want anything to do with this case now . . . He's ditched me . . . He said: 'Your client's more of a threat than the jury. He's a loose cannon. You don't stand a chance, leave it.' . . . The investigating judge asked me if I'm trying to put pressure on him or the jury by exposing the case in the media . . . 'Maître, you gave me your word that the investigation would proceed without any disturbance, and you've just broken that promise. From now on, I know where things stand with you.' . . . You've ruined my reputation . . . And Maman clearly wasn't in on this either. Well guess what – she is now! . . . Since seven this morning there's been a mob of journalists downstairs screaming at her if she so much as opens the curtains . . . And there's no hope they'll leave her alone any time soon . . . The telephone's ringing off the hook . . . She'll have to put up with this for months . . . Well done! You've made everyone's life easier . . . I suppose you're happy . . . You've got what you wanted: a bestseller! . . . Did you dream of becoming a star? . . . Well bravo – job done! . . . With all those royalties you won't struggle to find a lawyer you can piss all over as much as you like . . . Because I've had enough of your bullshit."

End of highlights. And end of conversation.

Lucie picks up her bag and knocks angrily at the door, which opens immediately, and she disappears without looking back.

Probably better that way.

After a tirade like that, any explanation would have fallen on deaf ears.

And how do I explain myself to her, anyway? Maybe: "I'm staring at a trial that may well result in me spending the rest of my life in prison, as well as a vast sum of money in a secret account that I am increasingly unlikely to be able to transfer to my daughters because the people who want to recover it are a lot nastier and a lot more powerful than I could ever have imagined." Maybe not.

What about telling her that I'd never really thought about any of that?

Shit, I'm not some gangster . . . I'm just trying to survive!

How is Lucie going to defend me if she discovers that I freaked out and tried to do a runner with an oil company's slush fund? Plus, I'm not about to tell her the tax haven I chose (it's St Lucia, in the Caribbean); she'd bloody string me up.

If I manage to keep a small portion of this money, I'll give it to the girls the day I get sentenced. That's my only goal. I'm not going to escape a heavy punishment. I will die in here. But at least they'll have some money, provided I'm able to leave it to them. They can do whatever they please with it – I'll be dead by then anyway.

Living dead, but still dead.

Nicole hasn't visited for almost a month. With all the reports in the papers and on the T.V., she already has enough on her plate. But mainly I think it's because she's furious with me.

My own cell: protection and television only when I want it – the dream.

I switch on Euronews: *". . . 25 hedge fund managers who have each pocketed 464 million dollars a year . . ."*

I flick to L.C.I.: *". . . State welfare will allow companies to lay off more than 65,000 employees this year . . ."*

I turn it off and relax for the first time in a long while. I feel as though I've been here for years, but it's only been a few months.

Not even six, a mere sixtieth of what I might end up with.

Journalists are wily buggers. Yesterday, an inmate came up to me in the library and discreetly handed me a note, offering cash for an exclusive interview. This morning, I saw him again and asked him about it. He didn't know anything: he received a hundred euros to give me the piece of paper from another guy who doesn't have a clue about it either. This note must have cost someone a thousand euros to reach me, which means I'm hot property in the eyes of the media. Other extracts from my story have appeared in the press, but the jackpot will be an exclusive interview. My response was to wait and hear their best price. In truth, I'll agree to it whatever the price, but I don't want to do anything until I've seen Lucie again.

I call her, leave messages, plead for her forgiveness. I say that I'll explain everything to her. I ask her not to leave me, telling her it's not how it looks, and that I love her. It's all true.

As I wait for her arrival, I try to hone my reasoning. I would so love to tell her that I'm fighting for her, for both of them, that I'm no longer fighting for myself. But love is no different to blackmail.

My story is being scrutinised in the business section of *Le Monde*. The labour minister giving his two cents. *Marianne* goes for the headline: *"The desperate victims of the crisis."* I've negotiated an exclusive interview for fifteen-thousand euros, paid in advance to Nicole. They've forwarded me some questions and I'm agonising over getting the answers just right. We agreed it would be published within a week. A second coat of paint for my budding notoriety. Now that I'm set on this path, I need to push on, to stay in the news and keep hitting the headlines. As far as the public is concerned, I'm just another human-interest story. I need to become a real person, real flesh and blood, with a face, a name, a wife, children – an everyday tragedy that could have happened to any old reader. I must become universal.

I'm told I have a visitor.

Fontana.

I stay calm as I make my way along the corridors. I've been sheltered from the other inmates, which means my strategy has worked. And if it worked on the administration, then it worked on Exxyal, too.

But it's not Fontana, it's Mathilde.

Seeing her stops me in my tracks. I don't even dare sit opposite her. She smiles at me. I turn my head to avoid meeting her eye. My physical appearance must have changed a good deal, because she bursts into tears almost immediately. She takes me in her arms and holds me tight. Behind us, the guard bangs on the metal with his key. Mathilde lets go of me and we sit down. She's still so pretty, my daughter. I feel enormous fondness for her, because I've taken so much from her, done irreparable damage, and yet she's here. For me. It moves me very much. She says she couldn't have come any sooner, and is about to get tangled up in a futile explanation when I hold up a hand to show there's no need, that I understand. She seems grateful for that.

The world in reverse.

"I hear more of your news from the papers than the phone," she says, taking a stab at a joke.

Then:

"Maman sends her love."

And finally:

"Gregory too."

Mathilde is one of those people who always say what ought to be said. Sometimes it's a pain in the arse. Right now, it helps.

Their flat fell through. She says it doesn't matter at all. On top of everything she lent me, they also lost a large part of their deposit, since they failed to complete on the specified date.

"We'll need to start saving again. It's no big deal . . ."

She attempts another smile, but fails miserably.

The truth is that part of her life has clouded over since her father's downfall, but Mathilde (something to do with teaching English, no doubt) has acquired something of the British stiff upper lip: she keeps her cool while the storm rages around her. She stops crying almost immediately. She's standing firm. Mathilde's motto must be: "Dignity in all circumstances." The day after her wedding, she got rid of my name. She's one of those women who goes potty at the idea of taking her husband's. That means she's safe – her colleagues won't know that the poor bugger in the papers is her father. But I'm certain that if they found out and asked her about it, Mathilde would boldly hold her ground, admit the truth and, despite her wholehearted disapproval of my actions, say something like: "family is family". I love her the way she is. She's been amazing to me, as if she's forgotten that I vanished away her savings and punched her husband in the face. What more could you ask for?

"Lucie thinks you can get extenuating circumstances," she says.

"When did she say that?"

"Yesterday evening."

I breathe. Lucie's coming back. I have to get in touch with her somehow.

"Have I aged that much?"

"No, not a bit!"

That says it all.

Mathilde talks to me about her mother, who's sad and shaken up. She'll come back as well. Soon, apparently.

Our thirty minutes are up. We stand and hug one another.

"I think the flat's been sold. Maman will tell you about it next time she visits," she says just before leaving.

An image comes to me: our flat, stickers everywhere, dozens of nonchalant buyers walking about in silence, picking up an object here and there with a look of mild disdain . . .

The thought kills me.

35

I didn't have to wait much longer for Fontana's return.

The man never wears the same suit. He looks a bit like me in the glory days, back when I had a job, although the blue of his suit is hideous and supremely vulgar. It must have cost him a bomb, but more than anything it reeks of bad taste. He's the sort of guy who wears a pocket square in an attempt to come across as a smart, modern gentleman. His clothes are quite loose-fitting. In his line of work, he needs to feel at ease – function over fashion. When he tries them on, I bet he pretends to punch the shop assistant in the face to see whether the sleeves inhibit his movements, or maybe he checks that the trouser leg has enough slack for a big kick in the poor man's bollocks. Fontana is nothing if not a pragmatist. That's what scares me about him. My scrutiny of his suit is a way of occupying myself because the thought of looking him in the face, of meeting his cold glare, completely terrifies me.

I need some composure. I won the first round by the skin of my teeth, but now we're squaring up for the second and I need to know what cards he's holding. I would be surprised if he'd turned up empty-handed. Not his style. I'll need to be alert, stay focused. In the silence, Fontana's expression is blank.

"Well played again, Monsieur Delambre."

Subtext: Delambre, you piece of shit, just you wait. I'm going to destroy that other hand of yours.

I take a punt:

"I'm glad you liked it."

My voice betrays my anxiety. I sit further back in my chair, out of range.

"My client enjoyed it very much. So did I. Everybody enjoyed it, in fact."

I say nothing. I try to force out a smile.

"I see that you're resourceful," he continues. "There obviously wasn't any list. It took me two days to question my client. And then the I.T. specialist we enlisted to check it out lost us another good twelve hours. In the meantime, you managed to garner some interest in your case from the press, denying me any means of intervention. For now."

I make as if to stand up.

"Don't go, Monsieur Delambre. I've got this for you."

His voice remained level. He didn't think for a second that I was really going to leave. He's a skilful player. I turn around and let out a cry.

Motherfucker!

Fontana has just laid a large black-and-white photo on the table.

It's Nicole.

I feel like my legs have been chopped off.

The photograph shows Nicole in the lobby of our building. She is standing with her back to the lift. Behind her, a man wearing a black balaclava is pinning her against his body, face-on to the camera. His forearm is locked across her throat. She's trying to pull his elbow but she doesn't have the strength. Her struggle is futile. It reminds me of how Bébéta held me. Nicole's face is petrified, her eyes bulging. That's why the photograph was taken. So I can see directly that Nicole's life is in extreme danger; so I can see her frenzied look. Her lips are open: she's gasping for air, suffocating. She's on the tips of her toes, because the man holding her is much taller and pulling her off the ground. Strangely she hasn't let go off her bag, which she's holding in her outstretched hand. Nicole stares at me, full frame.

The man is Fontana. I can tell it's him despite the balaclava. He's wearing a pocket square.

"Where is she?" I yell.

"Shhhh . . ."

Fontana screws up his eyes, as if the volume of my cry had come as a tremendous inconvenience.

"She's gorgeous, Nicole. You've got good taste, Delambre."

No more Monsieur Delambre – straight Delambre, now.

Everything goes into overdrive as I grip the table without registering the pain in my fingers.

I'll kill this guy, I swear it.

"Where is she?"

"At her house. I was going to say: 'Don't worry about her.' But actually you should worry about her. That time, she got away with a fright. As did you. But next time, I'll break all ten of her fingers. With a hammer. And I'll do it personally."

He accentuates the "personally". With him, you get the impression that it won't be any ordinary hammer, and that there'll be a very deliberate technique for shattering the fingers. There's a grim determination in his voice. Then, seamlessly, before I can venture a response, he pulls out a second photo and slams it down violently on the table. Same style. Black and white. Blown up.

"As for her, I'm going to break both her arms and both her legs."

My heart lurches cruelly and my stomach turns. Mathilde. I think I recognise the place, not far from the *lycée*. The kids are walking behind the public bench where she's sitting. She's pulled the cling film to one side and is eating a salad from a see-through tub with a plastic fork. I never knew she did that. She's not smiling. Her hand is suspended in mid-air as she listens attentively, even curiously, to what the man sitting nearby is saying.

Fontana again. They're chatting – a typical conversation in the park. The scene is calm, ordinary in fact, but it is shattered as I imagine the aftermath: they stand up, take a few steps back towards the *lycée*, a car pulls up, and Mathilde is bundled into it.

Fontana, unsmiling, adopts an air of concern, as if a question is nagging at him. He's really hamming it up.

"And your lawyer, yes . . . Your other daughter . . . Does she need her arms and legs for work, or can she do it from a wheel-chair?"

I want to be sick. Don't touch a hair on their heads. Shit, let me die if that's what it takes. Let Boulon come and break every bone in my body, every one, no holds barred; but don't lay a finger on my girls.

What saves me at this moment is my physical inability to articulate a single syllable. The words stay trapped at the bottom of my throat, frozen. I try to crank my brain back into action, but all the cogs have seized up and I fail to formulate any thoughts. My entire being has been consumed by the images of my girls.

I glance to my side, seeking something new to cling on to. I clear my throat, still saying nothing. No doubt my eyes are like saucers, like a druggie after an all-nighter. All the blood has drained from me, but still I've said nothing.

"I will break all three of them. Together."

I make a conscious effort to shut down my sense of hearing. I'm aware of the words, but their meaning doesn't register. There is an urgent and overwhelming need to distance myself from these unbearable pictures, before I vomit or die. Any resistance is vanishing.

He's bluffing. I must convince myself that he's bluffing. I check. I look at him.

He's not bluffing.

"I will break every one of their moving parts, Delambre. They will be alive. Conscious. Let me assure you, what happened to you in here will be child's play compared to what I have in store for them."

He'll be enunciating their names. He'll be saying: "With Mathilde, I'm going to . . .", "With Lucie, I'm going to . . ." His threats will be drawn from deep within him. "As for your wife, I'm going to tie her . . ." His threats are an extension of himself. He's saying bad things about them. When he refers to "all three of them", the anonymity sounds absurd, as if they were just things.

I need to keep talking to myself to maintain some form of defence, because I mustn't react. The photos are laid out in front of me so that I am left to fill in the blanks. He'll still be detailing everything he's going to do to them, in minute detail. I resist him with thoughts like this. My assessment of his persuasion technique? *Could do better.* It helps me hold my tongue. I forcibly dispel any notion of Nicole, even her name. I make her disappear from my memory. *My wife.* I repeat the words in my mind, repeat them ten, twenty, thirty times, until they are nothing but a string of syllables devoid of meaning. Endless seconds pass as I exercise my willpower. It enables me to continue my silence, buying me time despite my desire to cry, to vomit. *My girls . . .* I resist. *My girls my girls my girls my girls . . .* These words are emptied of meaning too. I stare straight at Fontana without blinking. Maybe there are tears streaming down my cheeks that I don't notice, like when Nicole first visited. *Nicole Nicole Nicole Nicole Nicole Nicole.* Another word without meaning. Drain the words to drive away the images. Hold Fontana's stare. What do his eyes remind me of? Craters? I focus on his pupils, and soon it's Fontana's turn to be emptied of substance. I mustn't think about what he is. All this to stay silent for as long as possible. No, that's it, they're not craters. His pupils are like those random shapes you get on audio software, those ones . . .

Fontana buckles first.

"What do you say, Delambre?"

"I'd rather it was me."

That's the truth. I manage to avoid returning to reality completely. In my head I keep on repeating *Nicole my wife my girls Nicole my wife my girls Nicole my wife my girls Nicole my wife my girls Nicole my wife my girls.* It's kind of working.

"That may be the case," Fontana replies, "but this isn't about you. It's about them."

Clear my head. Nullify the words. Don't think about anything real. Stay in the realm of ideas – conceptualise. What words of wisdom from management theory?

Find a solution. I can't.

What else?

Bypass the obstacle. I can't.

"They are going to be in a lot of pain."

What else?

Propose an alternative. I can't.

Nicole's face comes back to the surface. I see her pretty smile, but I must chase it away. *Nicole Nicole Nicole Nicole Nicole Nicole Nicole Nicole.* It works.

There's another management technique – what was it again? That's the one: *Overcome the obstacle.* I can't.

Only one thing left for it: *Reframe the issue.* I can do that. At what cost? No time to think – I launch straight in:

"Is that all?"

Fontana frowns slightly. Good. That wins me a bit more time. *Reframe the issue:* maybe this will do the trick.

He cocks his head quizzically.

"I said, 'Is that all?' Have you finished your performance?"

Fontana's eyes widen. Lips pursed, jaw clenched. Cold, hard fury.

"Are you taking the fucking piss, Fontana?"

This might work. Fontana sits bolt upright. I go in for another dose:

"You're taking me for a prize prick, aren't you?"

Fontana smiles. He's figured out my game, but I can still sense an element of doubt, so I gather my words, my energy and all my strength, and give him both barrels.

"Even if you did . . . Can you imagine 'France's most famous unemployed person' standing in front of the press holding up photos of his crippled wife and daughters? Followed by accusations against a major oil company of kidnapping, unlawful confinement, abuse, torture . . ."

I have no idea where this came from. Reframing and a bit of quick thinking. Glory be to management! It's one messed-up discipline, but wonderfully effective all the same.

"And you're prepared to take that gamble!" Fontana says with false admiration.

I see him hesitate about showing me the photos again. Maybe he reckons I've got the upper hand. I have a couple of extra rounds, so I reload.

"Is your client prepared to take that gamble?"

"Don't make me disappear your wife's body just so there won't be a photo," he says after a moment's consideration.

Reframe again: so far the technique's worked.

"Don't try any of that bullshit, Fontana. What do you think this is, for fuck's sake, 'The Sopranos'?"

That pisses him off.

Reframe again: just the ticket.

"I'm who you need to speak to. Me and me alone. And you know it. So either deal with me, or sod off back to your client empty-handed. Your threats are starting to piss me off. Your client can't afford this sort of bullshit. So, what will it be? Me, or nothing?"

That's how success works. Like a necklace – remove the knot, and everything comes undone. Same with failure. I should know. To avert disaster, you need fiendish reserves of energy. Either that or a death wish. I seem to have a bit of both.

I have an idea. Who knows if it's good or bad, but it's the best I can do. That's what they call intuition. Fontana said I had it, and maybe he was right.

I've seized the initiative, and now it's action time.

"I'm willing to give back the money. All the money."

I said it without even realising I was thinking it. But now it's said, I realise where it came from. I want peace. I don't want money.

"I want to get out of here. To be free."

There, that's what I think. I want to go home.

Fontana looks flabbergasted. I keep the momentum going:

"I'm willing to wait a bit. A few months, but no more. If I get out within a reasonable amount of time, I'll give back all the money. Absolutely all of it."

This knocks the wind out of old Fontana.

"A reasonable amount of time ..."

He is sincere when he asks:

"And how do you intend to get out?"

Maybe my idea wasn't so bad.

I give myself four seconds to think it through.

One, Nicole.

Two, Lucie.

Three, Mathilde.

Four, me.

In any case, it's the only idea I have.

I go again:

"Your client will need to try very, very hard to get me out. But it's possible. Tell him that's all I'm asking of him, and that I'll give back the whole of the slush fund. In cash."

36

I have lied so much and so often that I'm walled in. Telling Nicole the truth now is beyond my strength. We have been robbed of any confidence in our life together, our safety, our future – everything I was so desperate to recover. How can I explain it to her?

The day after Fontana's visit, I send her a long letter through Lucie, for the sake of speed. Not entirely legal, but Lucie agrees it's vital.

I ask her to forgive me for everything she's been through. I understand her fear. I write that I'm sorry, that I love her, that everything I've done has been to protect her, that I am bound to end my days here, to die here, but that all I want is for her and the girls to be alive. I write that I've been forced to do things, but I swear that nothing will ever happen to her again, that she must keep faith. I write that if she has suffered because of me then I'm sorry, and I love her, I love her so much, and I write thousands of other words like this. Most of all, I want to reassure her. As I write the letter I am haunted by the image Fontana showed me, by Nicole's eyes drowning in fear. Each time I am overwhelmed by murderous thoughts. If I get my hands on Fontana, he'll wish it was only Bébétâ or Boulon. But first I have to reassure Nicole, tell her that it won't happen again, I swear, and that soon we'll be together again. I write the word "soon" without putting a date on it – for Nicole, "soon" might be ten or twelve years, and I don't want to add another lie to the list.

After lights out in my cell, I cry, sometimes all night. The idea of anything happening to Nicole is unimaginable. Or to Mathilde . . .

I don't know what Fontana said through his ski mask. No doubt he told her to keep her mouth shut if she wanted her husband to stay alive behind bars. Nicole must have realised that the main point of this episode was to take the photograph and for me to see it.

I know she hasn't pressed charges. Lucie would have told me. Nicole hasn't said anything; she's kept it all to herself. She hasn't written to me because all the letters have to go via the investigating magistrate. Mathilde said she was getting ready to visit me, but now I don't think she'll come.

Since then, time has gone by and nothing's happened. Days and weeks have passed and I've heard nothing from her.

She must be asking herself how I managed to get into this mess, and about what's going to happen to us.

To her. To me.

To us.

Maybe Nicole sometimes thinks it would all be easier if I was dead.

To find peace, does she dream that I'm gone? Is that her way of dealing with this thing that's killing us both?

Last night I woke up, delirious, and walked to my cell door. At first I hit it once, as hard as I could, with my injured hand. The pain was blinding and my wounds reopened immediately. But I carried on because I wanted to punish myself, I wanted to end everything. I was so alone. The pain was so intense, the worst I've ever experienced, but I carried on: right, left, right, left, harder, harder, harder. I felt like the ends of my arms were stumps. I was sweating yet still I was punching the steel door. I collapsed on my feet, like a boxer on the ropes. In my unconscious state, I carried on pounding away until my legs gave way and I fell. There was so much blood that it flowed in rivulets through my bandages. Fists on steel – a lot of damage and not much noise.

In the morning, the pain was extreme. My fingers were broken and reset, and both hands are now bandaged up again. More X-rays and no doubt another operation.

Five more weeks pass, and still no news from her.

They could have put me in solitary, in a hole, in a dungeon. Anything would have been better than this.

My point of reference is not time or meals or noise or days turning to night.

Only Nicole.

My world is defined by her love. Without her, I no longer know where I am.

37

"And it has nothing to do with you?"

The news is so momentous that Nicole has decided to come and see me again.

I see the change close up, and it's terrible. She's been washed out by this affair, ageing ten years in the space of a few months. I miss my Nicole, the one I relied on so much. I miss her horribly. I want to dispense with this new, shattered version sitting before me, and bring back *my* Nicole, my wife, my love.

"Did you get my letter?"

Nicole nods.

"Nothing else is going to happen to you, you know that?"

She doesn't answer. Instead she does something ghastly: she attempts to smile. Her way of saying, "I'm behind you"; of saying, "I have no words, but I'm behind you, I'm here, and that's all I can do." No questions. No reproaches. Nicole has given up trying to understand. A man assaulted her. She doesn't want to know who. He strangled her. She doesn't want to know why. Will he come back? She doesn't want to know. I promise her it was an accident, and she appears to believe me. What's hard for her is not that I'm lying, but that she can never believe me again. But what the hell can I do?

One thing has shifted between us, and it's what she's come to discuss. This is a game-changer. I'm bursting to say:

"Did you see? I did it! How can you not believe in me any-more?"

But Nicole is drained. The bags beneath her eyes tell of hundreds of sleepless nights, but there is a small glimmer of hope, and I can feel it too. Fucking hope.

"A colleague told me about the programme. I went home early to record it and Lucie came over to watch it with me in the evening."

She's cross, but one of her great qualities is her total inability to lie (if I was like her, I'd already be dead).

"Lucie's wondering whether you've got anything to do with it," she says.

I make a show of looking outraged, but Nicole stops me dead by lifting her hand. With Lucie, lying is an option. With Nicole, it's not even worth considering. She closes her eyes for a second before saying her piece.

"I don't know what you're planning, Alain, and I can assure you that I don't want to. But don't drag our girls into this mess! It's different with me, it doesn't count – I'm with you. Fine if you had to do what you did. But not the girls, Alain!"

As she defends her daughters, she turns into a different Nicole. Not even her love for me would get in the way of this. If only I could have placed her in front of Fontana when he threatened to dismember them. Although we might be past "not dragging our girls into this mess" – the two of them are already up to their necks in it. One of them has lost a vast amount of what little she had; the other has been instructed to get her father out of this quagmire.

"Please let me explain . . ."

All it takes is a shake of the head for me to stop.

"If it helps us, then great, but I don't want to know."

She looks down, trying to hold back her tears.

"Not our girls, Alain," she says as she pulls out a tissue.

The fact is that this might be a wonderful opportunity, and Nicole knows it.

"Do you think it's going to change anything?" she says, changing the subject.

"Did you get the money? For the interview?"

"Yes, you already asked me."

Various publishers have offered me advances of forty, fifty, sixty-five thousand euros, and good royalties, which will be paid straight into Nicole's account. Since I'm going to have to give Exxyal back all their money, this is undoubtedly all the girls will have left.

"I split your advance between Lucie and Mathilde," Nicole confirms. "It helped a lot."

I chose the most sensationalist, rabble-rousing publisher I could, the one who could make the biggest splash. The book's called: *I Just Wanted a Job . . .* with the sub-title: *Out of work, over the hill and in prison.* It's coming out just a month before the trial. Lucie objected to the title, but I insisted. The cover has an Order of Merit with my mug-shot superimposed over *Marianne.* It's going to cause a massive stir. The publicist can barely cope on her own, so she's taken on an intern (unpaid, of course – no point wasting money). Lucie will be appearing on the T.V. and radio shows on my behalf, not to mention speaking to the papers. The first print run will be a hundred and fifty thousand copies, and the publisher thinks the trial will boost sales.

"I'm trying to take you out of harm's way . . ."

"So you keep saying, Alain. You want to protect us, but all you do is make things worse. I'd rather you did nothing at all – that way we'd still be living together. But you didn't want that life anymore, and now it's too late. Now I'm completely alone, can't you see?"

She pauses. We're like uncommunicating vessels – as soon as one of us goes up, the other goes down.

"I don't need money," Nicole says. "I couldn't care less. All I want is for you to be there, with me. I don't need anything else."

Her words are a bit disjointed, but I get the overall message: she's willing to resume our impoverished life from where we left off, even if it means being poorer.

"You don't need anything, but that didn't stop you from selling our flat!" I protest.

Nicole shakes her head, as if confirming my inability to understand a thing. It really gets to me.

"So do you think it'll make a difference?" she asks, changing the subject.

"What?"

"The programme."

I shrug, but inside I'm in overdrive.

"If everything goes to plan, it should."

A long table. The media everywhere. The place was sizzling.

Behind the table, the entire wall was taken up with a banner bearing the EXXYAL EUROPE logo in enormous red lettering.

"It must be said, he's got stage presence, your C.E.O.," Nicole says with a hint of a smile.

Alexandre Dorfmann was in his element. Last time I'd seen him he was sitting on the ground with my loaded Beretta resting on his forehead, and me saying: "So, your higher-than-highness, how many exactly are you firing from Sarqueville?" or something like that. Not even a bead of sweat that day – a frozen-blooded animal. At the press conference, he was cool and calm too. When he entered the room, it was as if I still had the Beretta held to his head. It might not have looked that way, but I've got him by the bollocks, old Alexander the Great. He entered the fray like a circus performer: solid yet supple movements, rigid smile, bright face. His lapdogs were lined up behind, stretching back into the wings.

"Were they all there?" asks Nicole.

"No, they were one down."

Right from the start, I noticed that Jean-Marc Guéneau, our red-lingerie-wearing friend, was late. Maybe he'd been held up in a sex shop – who knew. Something told me he wouldn't be joining the party. I hoped I wasn't in for a nasty surprise.

The stars' entrance had been edited, but I was able to catch a glimpse of the main characters: behind Dorfmann, Paul Cousin was first in line. He was standing so straight you'd swear he was a head taller than the others. Seconds later, there they all were sitting next to each other. Like the Last Supper. Dorfmann playing Jesus Christ, revving up to beatify the world with His word. Four brown-nosers instead of twelve: not bad going in these days of austerity. At the Lord's right hand: Paul Cousin and Évelyne Camberlin. At His left: Maxime Lussay and Virginie Tràn.

Dorfmann put on his glasses. There was a swarm of journalists and reporters, but silence fell as the crackle of flashes died out.

"The whole of France has been moved, and rightly so, by the unfortunate fate of a man, stricken by unemployment, resorting to . . . violent extremes during his search for work."

His announcement was pre-prepared, but this bombastic start to proceedings was not Dorfmann's usual style. He took off his glasses, more confident in his natural brilliance than his memory. He looked out to the assembly, staring straight at the camera.

"The name of our company has become embroiled in this regrettable matter because a man, Monsieur Alain Delambre, in a moment of madness, took several of our company's executives, including myself, hostage for several hours."

His expression hardened for a split second at the memory of the ordeal. Bravo – a marvellous turn. The faint shadow that crossed Dorfmann's face for a split second conveyed a clear message: we've been to hell and back, but we're not going to make a song and dance out of it; we have the dignity and the nobility to keep our pain to ourselves. The apostles flanking him joined in this almost indiscernible display of keen emotion. One looked down, desolate at the memory of the unbearable nightmare they'd been through; another swallowed hard, visibly racked by those hours of horror and the indelible mark they'd etched on her heart. Bravo to them too! The vultures didn't miss out on any of it: flashes burst into action, seizing on this prize-winning pang of televisual suffering. Even I felt an urge to turn to my cellmates and applaud the show. But I was on my own (V.I.P.).

"They're a real bunch of smarmy gits, aren't they?" Nicole says.

"You could put it like that."

Dorfmann again:

"Whatever this jobseeker's motivations, no circumstances – I repeat, *no circumstances* – can justify physical violence."

"How are your hands?" Nicole asks.

"Up to six functioning fingers. These four, and these two. So not bad – that's over half. The others aren't healing too well. The doctor hinted that bending them might not be easy in the future."

Nicole smiles at me. My love's smile, the entire reason for my fighting and my suffering. I could die for this woman. Shit, that's what I am doing!

Or maybe not:

"However," Dorfmann continued, "we cannot be deaf to the cries of the suffering. As business leaders, we must fight every day to win the economic struggle that would guarantee their return to work. We understand their frustration. And the truth is, we share it."

I would have loved to be watching the show in a café in Sarqueville. It must have been like a World Cup match. They'll have that little soundbite playing on loop.

"Monsieur Delambre's terrible misdemeanour perhaps epitomises the tragedy faced by many unemployed people. That is why, on my initiative, Exxyal Europe has decided to drop all charges against him."

A huge commotion followed, with photographers greedily snapping the table of execs.

"My colleagues," he continued, with a proprietorial sweep of the hand, which set off a Mexican wave of earnest eye-closing, "have stood by me in this decision, and for that I thank them. Each of them, individually, had pressed charges. All of them have been withdrawn. Monsieur Delambre will face court action for what he did, but the State prosecution alone will be responsible for ensuring that justice is served."

The executives on either side of God the Father remained deadpan, fully aware of their momentous role. Dorfmann had just unveiled a new stained-glass panel in the history of capitalism: *The Lord shows Pity to the Unemployed and the Needy.*

That was when I truly fathomed the value Dorfmann placed on his ten million There must have been plenty of chatter backstage at Exxyal, because he'd just painted on another layer, and not just any colour: a fine, virginal, almost Christ-like white. The white of innocence.

"Of course, far be it from either Exxyal or its staff to sway the scales of justice, which must be served with total impartiality. Our show of compassion is, nonetheless, a plea for lenience. A plea for clemency."

There was a general hubbub around the room. Everyone knows that C.E.O.s are capable of superiority – just look at their bonuses – but this magnanimity . . . honestly, it brings a tear to the eye.

"Lucie thinks their dropping the charges might have a big impact on the verdict," Nicole says.

She said the same to me. I think it's far from enough, but I hold my tongue. We'll see. The trial will take place in three or four months, record time apparently. It's not every day that France's most famous unemployed person goes up to the high court.

Back on screen, Dorfmann cranked it up:

"Having said that . . ."

Silence almost fell. Dorfmann hammered each syllable home, asserting His word.

"Having said that . . . this move will have no bearing on jurisprudence."

That's a tricky word for the mere mortals of T.F.1.

Simplify: return to the universal principles of communication.

"Our gesture is an exception. Anyone tempted to follow the example of Monsieur Delambre . . ." – cue rapturous applause in the cafés of Sarqueville – ". . . should know that our Group will stand firm in its absolute condemnation of brutality, and unreservedly support the prosecution of anyone who commits violent acts against any assets or personnel belonging to the Group."

"No one seems to have picked up on that," Nicole says, "but it was weird, no?"

She sees that I'm not following her, so explains:

"Dorfmann spoke about the 'assets or personnel belonging to the Group,'" says Nicole. "That's pretty serious."

No, still not with her.

"The 'assets', fine, but the 'personnel', Alain! They don't 'belong' to their company!"

Without thinking, I say:

"That didn't shock me. At the end of the day, didn't I do what I did to 'belong' to a company again?"

Nicole is appalled, but she lets it rest.

She supports me, no matter what. She'll support me to the very end. But our worlds are expanding in opposite directions.

"Here," she says.

She rummages in her bag and brings out some photographs.

"I'm moving in a fortnight. Gregory's being very good to me – he's coming with a couple of friends to do the removals."

I am only half-listening because my attention is on the photographs. Shots from various angles, ambient lighting . . . Nicole's gone to a lot of effort to make the place look nice, but it's no use. It's dingy. She's talking about the move, about the lovely neighbours, about taking a few days off, but I'm looking at the shots and I'm devastated. She tells me which floor it's on, but the number doesn't stick. Maybe the twelfth? I'm treated to several zoomed-out photos of Paris. When you're dealing with estate agents, panoramic shots are rarely a promising sign. I don't even bother with the bird's-eye views.

"We can eat in the kitchen . . ." Nicole says.

We can puke in there, too. The patterned parquet is a real '70s throwback: a dull, right-angled affair. Just by looking at the photographs you can hear the voices echoing around the empty rooms and, come nightfall, the sound of the neighbours yelling at each other through the hollow partition walls. Lounge. Corridor. Bedroom. Another bedroom. Everything I hate. How much is a shithole like this worth? Did she really trade in our flat for this, when we were so close to paying off the mortgage?

"Close to paying it off? With what payments? I'm not sure if you noticed, Alain, but we've got a few cash flow issues!"

I sense that it's better not to test her. Nicole has reached a level of exasperation that is close to breaking point. She opens her mouth and I close my eyes in readiness for the tirade, but she goes for the underhand option instead.

"It's not like I'm the only one who's decided to move house," she says, motioning towards the decor around us.

That was below the belt. I chuck the photographs onto the table and she gathers them into her bag. Then she looks at me:

"I don't give a damn about the flat. I would have been happy anywhere so long as I was with you. All I wanted was to be with you. So without you, it's there or somewhere else . . . At least we'll be in less debt."

This new place perfectly matches my notion of where a prisoner's wife should live.

There's too much to say, so I say nothing. Save it. Keep my strength for the trial, my best shot at being allowed to come home to her soon, even if it's in that dump.

38

Everyone knows that there are good days and bad days. And you definitely want the day you go before the high court to be a good day. In fact, I'm going to need two of those days, as that's how long the trial is expected to last.

Lucie is buzzing. No more talk of Sainte-Rose, who downed tools after my previous antics. Curiously, as irritating as I found the presence of this phantom by Lucie's side (especially when I found out how exorbitantly high his fees were), seeing her reduced to making all these decisions by herself does panic me a little. What she said sixteen months ago about the need to be defended by a proper professional starts making perfect sense. I feel for her – her anxiety is overwhelming. The press have highlighted the fact that she's my daughter, and numerous photos of her have been printed alongside weepy headlines. I know she hates this, but she shouldn't.

My worry has increased in the run-up to the trial, but when she told me her line of defence, I once again found myself thinking I'd made the right choice. Broadly speaking, there are two potential strategies: political or psychological. Lucie is convinced the assistant public prosecutor will opt for the former, so she's gone for the latter.

Everyone is on standby.

Alexandre Dorfmann's press conference had been unanimously hailed a success. His magnificent gesture was all the more appreciated since neither he nor a single one of his executives had agreed to any follow-up interviews. This extreme modesty seemed to confirm – not that any confirmation was needed – that his move contained no ulterior motives whatsoever, and that it was rooted in nothing but the purest sense of humanity. A few of the rags seemed sceptical, suggesting that there might have been some underlying, suspicious reason lurking behind his actions. But thankfully the majority of them fell in line with the broadcast media: in this tense period tarnished by labour disputes, with an almost permanent atmosphere of confrontation between business heads and employees, Exxyal's benevolent decision represents a new chapter in social relations. After two centuries of relentless class war, the torch of peace now shines bright on a new *entente cordiale*, marking a historic instance of reconciliation between leaders, workers and employees.

In the meantime, Exxyal have made me confirm that I will indeed be paying back all their money.

The second promising sign before the trial was the U-turn from Pharmaceutical Logistics. Lucie's initial belief was that my former employer's position had been morally compromised by my heroic, man-of-the-people status, and that they were afraid of defeat at the tribunal, but we recently found out the real reason: their key witness, Romain, quit overnight and is not even replying to urgent emails from head office. Lucie looked into it. Romain has gone back to his home province, back to farming the land. Gleaming new tractors, vast irrigation projects, the works. It seems the young man is pushing ahead with some ambitious investments.

Despite these good omens, Lucie still has her concerns. Trial by jury can, apparently, be somewhat unpredictable.

The day before the start of the trial, the radio and T.V. stations summarise the charges against me and rebroadcast the archive footage. I beg Lucie to be kind with her predictions: best-case scenario, she's hoping for eight years, four of which will be mandatory.

I do the sums in my head and start panicking. Four years of mandatory prison means another thirty months inside! If I wasn't already sitting down, I would collapse. Even if I manage to stay in the V.I.P. section, I'm so exhausted that . . .

". . . I'll die!"

Lucie rests her hand on mine.

"You're not going to die, Papa. You're going to be patient. But I'm warning you, even that would be an absolute miracle."

I hold back my tears.

Last night, I didn't sleep a wink. Thirty months in here! Almost three more years . . . When I get out, I'll be an old man. And I will have given all the money back to Exxyal. I'll be old and poor. The thought is completely shattering, and makes me feel so alone.

All this in mind, I enter the courtroom with my shoulders sagging and a washed-out complexion. I am a shadow of a man. It's not exactly what I had in mind, but it seems to make a decent impression.

The clutch of jurors has been picked at random from the kind of people I used to rub shoulders with on the *métro* back when I was employed. Men and women of all ages. But in the context of the high court, I find these familiar faces infinitely more sinister. Even though they've taken their juror's oath (". . . I do solemnly, sincerely and truly declare and affirm that I will well and truly try the issues joined between the parties and a true verdict give according to the evidence …"), I'm on edge. These people are like me – I'm sure they're perfectly sensible.

I spot my little crew nearby.

Close family first: Nicole, more beautiful than ever, sending me discreet, confidence-boosting looks; Mathilde, on her own because her husband hadn't managed to get away.

A bit further along there's Charles. He must have borrowed a suit from a better-heeled but much larger neighbour. He's floating in the clothes, which look as though they're being inflated by an air duct. Knowing from experience that he's not allowed to booze in the courtroom, he must have pre-loaded his units. I saw him walking in earlier, determined but slightly wobbly. When he raised a hand at me to make his salute, he veered off-balance, forcing him to grip the back of a chair. Expressive as ever, Charles. He views the proceedings from some inner place, utterly engrossed. At every phase of the hearings, his face seems loaded with comments. Charles is almost a barometer for the entire event. He makes frequent sideways glances at me, like a mechanic looking up from under the bonnet to assure his client that, for the moment, everything's alright.

After the close family, the more distant relatives. Fontana, grave and earnest, calmly polishing his nails without looking at me once. His two colleagues are here too: the young woman with the cold eyes, whose first name, Yasmine, was cited in the court documents; and the Arab who conducted the interrogations, Kader. They are on the list of witnesses cited by the public prosecutor. But first and foremost, they're here just for me. I ought to feel flattered.

Then there are the journos and the radio and T.V. lot. And my representative from the publisher, who'll be somewhere in the room licking his lips at the thought of how many sales this trial is going to rack up.

And Lucie, who I haven't seen wearing her gown for ages. She has a good number of young colleagues in the room who, like me, must be shocked by how much weight she's lost this past year.

As the first day draws to a close, I simply don't understand why Lucie is predicting eight years. If the reporter summing up the courtroom action is anything to go by, the verdict will be nothing but lenient and the entire world is on my side. Except, of course, the assistant public prosecutor. A real shitbag, that guy. Bitter. He takes every opportunity to display his contempt for me.

It's perfectly clear from the statement made by the psychiatric expert: my physical state at the time of the events was marked by a temporary disorder that "completely eliminated [my] judgement and control over [my] actions". The assistant public prosecutor grills him, brandishing article 122-1 of the *Code pénal* and seeking to emphasise that I cannot possibly be considered to have diminished responsibility on psychological grounds. All this wrangling goes over my head. Lucie contests his opinion. She has worked hard on this aspect of the case, which she sees as vital to the trial. The exchange between her and the assistant public prosecutor gets heated, and the judge has to call the court to order. In the evening, the reporter concludes soberly: "Will the jury deem Monsieur Delambre to be responsible for his actions, as the assistant public prosecutor strongly maintains? Or, as his lawyer insists, will they see him as a man whose judgement was severely impaired by depression? We'll know tomorrow evening at the end of the deliberations."

The assistant public prosecutor, for his part, glorifies in the detail. He describes the prisoners' anxiety as though he had been there himself. To hear his version, this hostage-taking rivals Fort Alamo. He calls to the stand the R.A.I.D. commandant who arrested me. Lucie makes few interventions. She's relying on the witness testimonies.

Enter Alexandre Dorfmann, lord of all he surveys. Tribute to whom tribute is due. His testimony has been hotly anticipated ever since that overblown press conference he gave.

I look over at Fontana, who is watching and listening to his boss with an almost religious devotion.

A few days before, I said to him:

"I'm warning you, I want my ten mill's worth! No way your client's getting away with the legal minimum, you hear me? For three mill, I'm a lost soul. For five, I'm a brave man. For ten, I'm a bloody saint! That's the way I see it, so go and tell that to your

Lord on high. No way he's playing the C.E.O. up there – this time, he's going to have to do some bloody work. For ten big ones and an honourable gesture from me to calm down his board of directors, he'd better pull his bloody finger out."

Dorfmann turns out to be a total natural.

Not even in her wildest dreams did Lucie expect such a testimony.

Yes, of course, the hostage-taking was "an ordeal", but fundamentally the person before him was "no murderer, just a man who'd lost his way". Dorfmann looks pensive as he runs through his memory. "No, I never felt threatened. The fact is, he wasn't at all sure what he wanted." In answer to a question about physical violence, Dorfmann says, "No, none whatsoever." The public prosecutor presses him. I urge him on in my head: *go on, your excellency, one more kind word.* Dorfmann scrapes the barrel: "When he was firing, we could all see that he was aiming at the windows and not at anyone in particular. It was more like an act of . . . deterrence. The man seemed broken, exhausted."

The assistant public prosecutor goes on the offensive. He brings to mind Dorfmann's initial statements from a few minutes after the R.A.I.D. operation, statements that appear "very damning for Delambre", and then from the press conference, which were "astonishing almost to the point of suspicion", in which Delambre was absolved of all wrongdoing.

"It's hard to keep up, Monsieur Dorfmann."

He's going to have to do better than that to throw Alexander the Great.

He brushes aside this criticism with three clear arguments, emphasising each salient point by turn with a wag of the finger at the assistant public prosecutor, a look over at the jury, and a prodigal hand gesture in my direction. A flawless performance. The fruit of thirty years of sitting on supervisory boards. By the end, no-one has understood a word of what he's said, but everyone agrees that he is right. Everything seems clearer; logic perfectly restored. The assembly congregates reverently around the evidence Dorfmann puts before us. A business leader in full swing is as beautiful as an archbishop in his cathedral.

Lucie looks at me with pure elation.

My words to Fontana had been:

"I want everyone to be on their game! It's a team game, and for ten million I want real unity, real team spirit, got it? Dorfmann picks the gap and then the pack follows behind in a nice, tight formation. No weak links! Tell them to remember the management tips they give their underlings – that ought to help."

It does help.

Évelyne Camberlin steps up. A doyenne; dignity personified.

"Yes, I won't deny that I was scared, but I soon realised that nothing was going to happen to us. What really frightened me was that he might do something clumsy; a blunder of some sort."

As soon as the assistant public prosecutor intervenes, the audience starts jeering at him as if he were a pantomime villain. He asks Évelyne Camberlin to describe her "terror".

"I was afraid, but I wasn't terrified."

"Oh, but of course! A man waves a gun in your face and you don't find that terrifying? You must be exceptionally cool under pressure," he adds with a derisory tone.

Évelyne Camberlin glares at him before smiling and saying:

"Weapons have little effect on me. I spent my entire childhood in a barracks – my father was a lieutenant colonel."

The audience is in raptures. I look at the jurors. A few smiles, but hardly all-out hysterics.

The assistant public prosecutor takes a sly turn.

"You dropped your charges entirely of your own volition, is that correct?"

"What you're really asking," she says, "is whether I did so under pressure from my employer. What would be the point?"

Deep down, this is the question on everyone's lips. It's at moments like this that we can tell whether the big man has got his case sewn up. With ten million on the table, I hope he has.

Before the assistant public prosecutor can respond, Madame Camberlin cracks on:

"Perhaps you're suggesting that my employers might stand to gain from projecting a generous image."

You're fired, Camberlin! If it were up to me, I would kick her out immediately for making that kind of insinuation. Where did she learn her public-speaking? I'm livid. If she doesn't pull this one back, I'm making Dorfmann promise that her head will be the first to roll when the redundancy plan gets under way at Sarqueville. She must have realised her error, because she backtracks:

"Do you really think Exxyal needs to boost its image in the eyes of the media by appearing charitable?"

O.K., that's a bit better. But I need you to hammer this into the jurors' heads.

"If so, why not ask whether I've been given a special bonus to testify before you? Or whether I'm being blackmailed with the threat of dismissal? Are these questions too tedious for you?"

There's a general hubbub, and the judge calls the court to order. The jury seems perplexed, and I panic that my plan's about to come apart at the seams.

"In that case," the assistant public prosecutor says after a pause, "if you and Monsieur Delambre are in such close communion, why did you press charges the day after the event?"

"Because the police asked me to. They recommended it, and at the time it seemed logical," Madame Camberlin replies.

Much more like it. Dorfmann's instructions were clear after all. There's a sense that all these people's futures are in the dock, too. That makes me happy – it makes me feel less alone.

Maxime Lussay falls in line with his colleague. His approach is less polished, a bit more rustic. He speaks in straightforward but effective terms, answering with a simple "yes" or "no". Low profile. Perfect.

Virginie Tràn, on the other hand, causes quite a stir. She's wearing a pale-yellow dress and a silk scarf. She is made up like it's her wedding day, and she strides to the witness stand like a catwalk model. I can tell how badly she wants to please her boss. I reckon she's still in bed with the competition. If I were her, I'd be treading very carefully.

She goes for the categorical approach.

"Monsieur Delambre made no demands. I struggle to believe that his actions were premeditated. If so, surely he would have asked for something?"

Objection from the public prosecutor, and she gets a ticking off from both the assistant public prosecutor and the judge.

"We are not asking for your personal views on Monsieur Delambre's motivations. Stick to the facts."

She takes this onslaught as a chance to go all coquettish, lowering her eyes and blushing with embarrassment, like a little girl caught with her hand in the sweetie jar. This paragon of innocence would have made the most hardened soul burst into tears.

Up last is His Majesty Paul Cousin. He's the only one who takes a good look at me, square in the eye, as he walks to the stand. He's even taller than I remember. The audience are going to love him.

Me to Fontana:

"That tall bastard of yours is the key to everything. It's thanks to him that I'm behind bars, so you tell him that I want some serious tact, otherwise I'll make sure he's back on bloody unemployment benefit until he retires."

Solemn and austere, Cousin seems aware of his big-man status. Calm and collected, he's an example to all.

With every question from the judge, with each cross-examination from the assistant public prosecutor, Paul Cousin makes a slight turn towards me. Before relaying his position, The Upstanding One observes The Lost One, then responds with a few sparse sentences. We barely know each other, he and I, but I feel like we're old friends.

He answers the judge by confirming that he is currently posted in Normandy. With a heavy heart, he announces that there'd been a vast restructuring programme: a difficult operation, "from a human perspective". I hope he doesn't overdo that phrase, because it has a bizarre ring when he says it. He explains that Sarqueville is at the heart of the group's economic difficulties. In other words, he knows full well that times are tough. When they start quizzing him about his attitude during the hostage-taking, we get a recap of the events: his opposition, his confrontation, his courageous dash for the exit . . .

"In order to stop you, Monsieur Delambre attempted to shoot you!"

A murmur of admiration goes round the room. Cousin swats it aside irritably.

"Monsieur Delambre didn't shoot me, that's all that matters. Perhaps he attempted to, but I cannot testify to that, since I never turned to see what he was doing."

The audience interprets this as modesty.

"Everyone else seemed to see it!"

"So ask everyone else – don't ask me."

Another murmur, and the judge calls Cousin to order.

"The overriding impression we get from your different, yet remarkably unanimous, testimonies is that this hostage-taking was something of a picnic in the park. But if Monsieur Delambre really didn't represent any danger, why did it take so long for you to intervene?"

Paul Cousin shifts his whole body and stares right at him:

"In any situation, sir, there is a time for watching, a time for understanding, and a time for action."

Magnificent, Cousin.

The audience is mesmerised. Hats off.

I'd said to Fontana:

"What about old Jean-Marc Guéneau – he's not going to pull a fast one on us? If he tries anything, I'll have him back in his panties and sobbing before the jury!"

The man's a shadow of his former self.

I remember how he used to be all smartly dressed and swaggering. Now he's like a ghost. He confirms his identity and status: an out-of-work professional.

That's the nice, official way of saying "unemployed prick". Exxyal fired him two months after the event. He's clearly had a rough time of it, his employers would have said, but we simply cannot maintain our confidence in a finance manager who goes around with women's lingerie on under his suit. Despite being sacked, Guéneau has agreed to testify, and he says exactly what's necessary. Because everyone knows it's a small world, and even if Exxyal is no longer his employer, the company still has a major say if he ever wants a job in the sector again.

I inspect him more closely.

Fourteen months out of work, and he looks like he's still firmly in the rut. Guéneau reminds me of myself after a year and a half of unemployment. He carries himself like he still believes. He's clinging on. I picture him in six months' time revising (downwards) his expected salary by 40%, and then in nine months negotiating some temp work, and in two years accepting a low-level position to cover half the cost of his bills. In five years he'll get kicked in the arse by the first Turkish supervisor willing to stoop low enough to bother. At one point in his statement, I thought the sleeve of his suit might rip. The audience would have found that hilarious.

I also said to Fontana:

"As for that wanker Lacoste, make sure you keep him on a short leash. If he struggles to get the hang of it, you have my full permission to snap every single one of his fingers. I know from first-hand experience how much that helps clarify matters."

Fontana's face did something that no-one except his mother could call a smile.

Lacoste's testimony is delivered with great humanity. His firm has gone into receivership – nothing to do with the present scandal, of course, but just another casualty of the economic crash. The very same crisis to which Monsieur Delambre fell victim, along with so many others. He does well, Lacoste. I hope that Rivet girl has given him his just deserts.

Lucie is looking at me more and more often.

Soon the assistant public prosecutor will be summing up on behalf of the enemy forces. Lucie has prepared for war, and all the combatants appear eager to sign the armistice. She questions the witnesses with a light touch. She realises that the odds were in our favour, but that we mustn't get ahead of ourselves.

The day before, Nicole had expressed her amazement:

"It's quite remarkable. Your father's going to the high court for a hostage-taking, but no-one seems fazed by the fact that a big company can arrange precisely the same thing to assess its staff. With complete impunity. If they hadn't organised the role play, there wouldn't have been a hostage-taking, right?"

"I know, Maman," Lucie replied, "but what can we do? Not even the employees seemed to bat an eyelid . . ."

This argument has obviously played on her mind. She was even considering cross-examining the witnesses to put the matter in the spotlight, to push the point about the company's cruelty – to make Exxyal responsible for my actions. But aside from the fact that I'm on trial, not them, it's not even necessary anymore. At one point, Lucie looks towards me, concerned about the proceedings. I make a little two-handed gesture at her to show my surprise. I try to implore her as much as I can, but Lucie, seeming more and more dazed, has already turned back to attend to the litany of witnesses.

"As for you, Fontana," I said in the lead-up, "you're going to do what you do best: play the good little soldier. No doubt you're getting paid for results?"

Fontana didn't flinch, which meant I was bang on: he's on commission. The more money Exxyal recover, the more he pockets.

"I know you'd love nothing better than to crush me like a piece of shit, but you're going to be disciplined. You're going to go the extra distance for me. And I'll make it easier for you. For every syllable that's not perfectly on song, I'll take away one of those big ones that Dorfmann's hoping to get back. I'll let you explain that to him when he notices the shortfall and comes looking for an explanation."

You don't have to be a mind-reader to guess that at that moment, if I didn't have such a strong advantage over him, he would have had no qualms about sticking my feet in a concrete block and dropping me into the canal Saint-Martin with an oxygen bottle and six hours of free time. What's going to happen when all this is over and I'm poor again? I hope he's not the sort to hold a grudge and get all personal about it.

In any case, for now, he's obedient.

He plays along with the general "not-dangerous" analysis. Lucie makes him run through his credentials to lend weight to his opinion. David Fontana, a man who has rubbed shoulders with warriors, soldiers and worse, can assure the court that Delambre, Alain is a little lamb. His wound? Just a scratch. Any grievances on his part? Nothing of the sort.

Perhaps I laid it on too thick. We need to get the testimonies over and done with – all this unanimity is becoming a nuisance.

At the start of the afternoon, it's time for the defence's closing statement.

Lucie is glorious. Her voice is steady and compelling as she summarises the arguments, carefully negotiating the witnesses' statements to avoid patronising the jury. She addresses each juror in turn, both the men and the women, and does what she does best: explaining that my story could have happened to any one of them. And she does it well. She highlights her client's challenging living conditions, the decline of his self-esteem, the humiliation; then the brutal, incomprehensible action, then the turmoil and the inability to escape after cornering himself. Her client was alone and desperate.

She now needs to defuse the bombshell that is my book.

Yes, Monsieur Delambre wrote a book, Lucie explains. Not, as has been too often said, to achieve any sort of fame, but because he needed support. He needed to share his ordeal with others. And that's precisely what happened. Thousands, tens of thousands of others just like him saw their own plight reflected in his, identifying with his misfortune and humiliation. And they forgave his actions. Actions which, let us not forget, were of no consequence whatsoever.

Her client's extenuating circumstances are no different from the circumstances endured by anyone in a time of crisis.

It's really not bad at all.

If I weren't so afraid of the nasty public prosecutor, who's shaking his head throughout – at times scandalised, at others deeply dubious – I'd be saying that her prediction looked likely. No jury could ever acquit me. I came to the assessment with a loaded weapon: premeditation, pure and simple. You can't expect a thirty-year sentence to be lowered to under eight or ten years. Yet Lucie leaves no stone uncovered. And if anyone can reduce my sentence, it's her, my daughter. Nicole looks at her with admiration. Mathilde wills her on, giving her confidence.

Lucie was right: the assistant public prosecutor's case is exemplary.

It rests on three pitilessly simple arguments.

One: Alain Delambre, three days before coming to the Exxyal assessment, had sourced, found and purchased a pistol, which he had then loaded with live bullets. He evidently had aggressive, possibly murderous, intentions.

Two: Alain Delambre exposed his story to the media in order to sway his trial; to influence the jury by manipulating and intimidating them. The hostage-taker has turned master-blackmailer.

Three: Alain Delambre is setting a dangerous precedent. If his sentence does not serve as an example, tomorrow every unemployed person will feel entitled to take up arms. At a time when dismissed workers are resorting more and more often to brutality, arson, threats, looting, extortion and kidnapping, can the jury really rank a hostage-taking as an acceptable, legitimate form of negotiation?

In his view, this question answers itself.

We need an example. He continues addressing the jury:

"Today you are the last bastion against a new form of violence. Be aware of your duty. Realise that to afford mitigating circumstances when real bullets are involved, is to prefer civil war to social dialogue."

We need a firm indictment. Fifteen years?

He calls for thirty. The maximum sentence.

When he sits back down, the crowd is left stunned.

Not least me.

Lucie is shell-shocked. Nicole holds her breath.

Charles, for the first time in his life, looks sober.

Even Fontana lowers his head. Given how long I'm going to spend in jail, he won't be seeing his loot any time soon.

As per protocol, the judge passes the floor back to Lucie for the final word. Inevitably it's the result of so many months of intense work and sleepless nights, but she chokes. She tries to speak, but the words don't come. She clears her throat and utters a few inaudible phrases.

The judge seems perturbed:

"We didn't hear you, maître . . ."

A heavy, stormy atmosphere has fallen on the room.

Lucie turns to me, tears in her eyes. I look at her and say:

"It's over."

She gathers her strength and turns to the jury. But it's beyond her – nothing comes out. The entire room holds its breath.

I'm right. It is over.

Lucie, deathly pale, raises her hand to the judge to signify that she has nothing to add; nothing she is able to add.

The jury is invited to deliberate.

Late that evening, to everyone's surprise, they still haven't reached a unanimous verdict. Deliberations are to continue tomorrow.

In the coach back to prison, I can't stop running through the possible scenarios. If they haven't reached a decision, it's because there are some sticking points. The trial went as well as it possibly could, but the verdict is set to go against me. If they were convinced by the prosecution, some will no doubt see themselves as upholders of justice and appeal for an exemplary sentence.

That night in prison is like being on death row, long enough to die twenty times over. My life flashes before me. All that for this.

I don't sleep a wink. Thirty years is unthinkable. Twenty years is impossible. Even ten years . . . there's no way.

An unbearable night. At one point I thought I was going to cave completely, but no, my anger returned, perfectly intact. A terrible fury, like in the good old days: death wishes about the injustice of it all.

The following day, I return to the courtroom white as a sheet. I've made a decision.

I closely examine the police officer in charge of transferring me. The doppelganger of the one guarding me in the dock. I scrutinise the lock system on the holster of his weapon. As far as

I can make out, there's a large push-button that releases the tongue, leaving the gun to be lifted out unhindered. I rack my brains to recall Kaminski's information from before . . . SIG Sauer S.P.2022: no manual safety, but a slide catch lever.

I think I'll know how to use it.

I'll have to be very quick.

Once I'm in the dock, I see my opportunity: barge him powerfully, send him off-balance, and pin him with my shoulder. Then use my hand with the good fingers.

Lucie hasn't slept either. Nicole's not much better. Mathilde too.

Charles is distraught. His anxiety has contorted his face into a dramatic mask. He tilts his head as he looks at me, as though deeply affected by my fate. I feel a terrible urge to say goodbye to Charles.

Fontana is prowling around the back of the room, as watchful and supple as a sphinx.

Suddenly Lucie leans towards me and says:

"Sorry. For yesterday . . . I just couldn't speak anymore . . . I'm sorry."

Her shattered voice rings in my ear. I squeeze her hand and kiss her fingers. She feels all my tension, says kind words that I don't listen to.

The policeman guarding me is considerably taller and chunkier than the one yesterday. Square-jawed. It's not going to be easy, but it's doable.

I stand a little further back in the dock. I need good, efficient leverage from my legs.

I can secure his weapon in under five seconds.

39

The jury returns. It's 11 a.m.

Solemn silence. The judge begins. Words pour out. Questions echo. One juror stands and answers.

No. Yes. No.

Premeditation. Yes.

Extenuating circumstances. Yes.

Verdict: Alain Delambre is sentenced to five years, of which he will serve eighteen months.

Shock.

I've already been remanded in custody for sixteen months.

With special remissions, I'm free.

My emotions overwhelm me.

The room erupts in applause. The judge demands silence, but brings the session to a close.

Lucie hurls herself into my arms, screaming as the photographers flock around us.

I start crying. Nicole and Mathilde join us immediately; we become four sets of hugging arms, squeezing each other and choking on our tears.

I wipe my eyes. I could hug the entire world.

There's a ruckus of some sort at the back of the room. Some shouting, but I can't make out the words.

Standing a few metres away, Charles lifts his left hand and makes his humble, complicit salute.

A little further away, Fontana, flanked by his two minions, gives me his first proper smile, albeit with those predator's lips. He even stretches to a thumbs up.

Genuine admiration.

The only person hanging his head a little is my publisher: a good, chunky sentence would have really boosted sales.

The policemen pull me backwards. I can't figure out why – everything is so unexpected.

"Just formalities, Papa, it's nothing," Lucie assures me.

I have to go back to prison to be formally released from custody and collect my things.

Lucie hugs me tightly again. Mathilde holds both my hands. Nicole has coiled up against my back, her arms around my waist and her cheek on my shoulder.

The policemen are still yanking at me. Not violently – just respecting the rules and evacuating the room.

The girls and I say silly things to each other, like "I love you". I hold Lucie's face in my hands, trying to find the words. Lucie plants an enormous smacker on my lips. She says: "Papa."

This is the last word.

It's time for our hands to unlock, our fingers to part. Except Nicole, who continues to cling on to me.

"That's enough, madame," says one of the officers.

"It's over," Nicole says to me, kissing me passionately on the lips.

She extricates herself from me, crying and laughing all at the same time.

I would do anything to leave with her now, right now. A quick getaway with Nicole, the girls, my life – everything.

Mathilde says: "See you tonight." Lucie nods as if to say: of course, she'll be there too. Tonight, all of us together.

Time to leave. More hand gestures, promising each other a thousand things.

From the other side of the room, Fontana smiles at me with a barely perceptible nod of the head.

His message is clear: "See you very soon."

40

I come to my senses in the coach on the way back to prison. The news has spread like wildfire among the inmates. I hear tin trays banging on iron bars. Congratulations. A few whoops and cheers. Returning here knowing I'm a free man is almost a pleasant experience.

Officer Morisset is on duty, and he pays me a visit to offer his congratulations. We wish each other good luck.

"And don't forget, officer: outline your argument *in* your introduction, not after."

He smiles at me and we shake hands.

I walk into my cell for the last time, piss in the latrine for the last time. Everything's for the last time.

Sixteen months in jail.

What will I have to show for it all?

I try to fast-forward to tomorrow. My girls. I start crying again, but they're good tears. My fingers feel better, even though a couple of them, the left index and the middle right, don't bend like before.

I get back my civilian clothes. They're fairly worn out – last used during the hostage-taking. For my official discharge through the custody office, lots of things need signing, and I'm handed endless papers that I shove in my pocket. A painfully slow process; lots of waiting. I'm sitting on a bench.

A creeping bitterness overwhelms me as I tot up the damage on my wonky fingers. I have:

aged ten years in here.

ruined Mathilde.

extorted Lucie.

drained Nicole.

estranged my son-in-law.

sold the flat.

spent the proceeds from my book on the trial.

postponed my retirement indefinitely.

wound up in a depressing one-bed.

still not found a job.

I'm back to square one.

It's been a story of abject failure, and it's unbearable.

All I wanted for tonight was my freedom, but now that I have it, I see that it's not enough.

I have to give back the money now; what little I've won will end up in the hands of those institutional crooks.

But have I lost everything? I can't let this happen to me.

There's just one last question.

Is there still a way for me to keep my hard-earned cash: yes or bloody no?

I think hard, turning all the options over in my head. Only one solution presents itself.

Sarqueville.

Let's pay Paul Cousin a visit.

41

The doors open and close. There's a positive feel to the dreary thud, yet I'm scared. I've come out alive and in one piece, with the exception of a few fingers. I don't want to make one more mistake.

And when I step through the prison door, I'm still not sure whether I'm going to attempt one last play.

As ever, I'm going to let circumstances decide for me.

The street is divided into a perfect triangle.

There's me with my back to the prison gate, empty-handed and wearing my last remaining suit.

To my left, on the other side of the road, there's Charles. Good old Charles. Confronted with the dual challenge of staying both upright and stationary, he is leaning against a wall. As soon as I get out, he lifts his left hand as a sign of victory. He must have come by bus which, if true, is nothing short of miraculous.

There to my right, on the far pavement, is David Fontana, who gets out of an enormous 4x4 to intercept me. Full of beans, Fontana, with that same dynamic stride.

And no-one else.

Just the three of us.

I look left and right to find Nicole. The girls are meant to be joining us later for dinner, but Nicole . . . where is she?

On seeing Fontana heading my way so purposefully, my gut instinct is to look for help. I take a backward step.

Charles has kicked into gear too. Fontana turns and points a finger at him. Clearly intimidated, Charles stops dead in the middle of the street.

Fontana's in front of me, a metre away. He is radiating a negative aura. I know that if he pretends to smile, it gets even worse: he exudes ferociousness.

He pretends to smile.

"My client has kept his side of the deal. Now it's your turn."

He rummages in his pocket.

"Here are your keys. The keys to your flat."

My internal alarm is triggered.

"Where's my wife?"

"As you've never been to the place before," he adds, ignoring my question, "I've made a note of the address. And here's the number for the keypad."

He holds out a piece of paper, which I grab. His steely eyes don't blink.

"You have one hour, Delambre. One hour to make the transfer into my client's account."

He nods towards the piece of paper.

"The bank details are at the top."

"But . . ."

"I can assure you that your wife is eager to have you home."

I try to support myself, but behind me is just empty space.

"Where is she?"

"She's safe, don't panic. At least she'll be safe for the next hour. After that, I'm no longer answerable for anything."

He gives me no time to respond. His mobile is already in his hand. The blood drains from me. Fontana listens, then holds it out to me.

"Nicole?"

I pronounce her name as if I'd just come home and couldn't figure out where she was.

"Alain . . ."

She pronounces my name as if she were on the brink of drowning but trying to remain calm.

Her voice pierces me and runs right down my spine.

Fontana snatches the phone out of my hand.

"One hour," he says.

"It's not possible."

He already looked set to leave, so I blurted this out with as much conviction as I could manage. Fontana glares at me. I take a deep breath. Crucial to speak slowly, to make my sentences flow.

Another golden rule of management: *trust in your skillset.*

"The money's stored in various accounts, all of them offshore. What with the different time zones and stock exchange trading hours . . ."

I egg myself on: *Believe in yourself! You're an international finance expert; he's just an arsehole! You know what you're talking about! He's got no fucking idea! Keep hammering it home!*

". . . the time needed to verify sales, redeem shares, process payments, approve passwords . . . It's just not possible. I'll need at least two hours. More like three, in fact."

Fontana didn't see this one coming. He thinks about it, looking for a shred of doubt in my eyes, a bead of sweat on my forehead, or an unusual dilation of the pupil. Then he looks at his watch.

"You've got until 6.30 p.m."

"What guarantee do I have . . . ?"

Fontana wheels around furiously.

"None."

He doesn't pick up on my distress. I, on the other hand, have just noticed a crucial development: for Fontana, this is no longer simply about sealing a deal; I have become an object of personal hatred. Despite all his experience, I've caught him off-guard several times. For him, this is now a matter of honour.

In a few seconds, the street is deserted. Charles, who'd managed to make it as far as the street lamp, resumes his journey along the pavement unaided.

I rest my hand on his shoulder.

Charles is all I have left.

We hug each other. It's weird, but he reeks of kirsch. It's been ten years since I smelt that.

"I get the feeling you're in deep shit," Charles says.

"It's my wife, Nicole . . ."

I have no way of explaining why I hesitate. I should already be sprinting to the nearest computer, getting online, fetching the lucre, filling up the bucket and dumping it in Exxyal's coffers. I'm holding the keys to our new apartment. There's a little label on a green, plastic thing, like an estate agent's set. I read the address. Jesus wept, it's on avenue de Flandre. There's nothing but dreary low-rises and tower blocks out there. I could have guessed as much from the photos. This settles it for me.

"Your wife not there?"

Whenever I've thought about this money, I've pictured maybe twenty, a hundred, a thousand times the sort of immaculate apartment Nicole and I would be able to afford. The girls too.

"Don't worry sure as anything she'll be there waiting."

In this place, I imagine Nicole laying out the same knackered kitchenware. In the sitting room, the carpet will be as frayed as her cardigan. Fuck. After all we've been through, we can't just let it all go. Rouen's two hours away. It's doable. They can't do anything to her. They won't touch her. But first I have to call her.

"Have you got your mobile?"

It takes Charles a bit of time to grasp what I'm on about.

"Your mobile . . ."

Charles twigs. He goes in search of his telephone – this could take all day.

"Here, let me."

I sink my hand into the pocket he was heading for, grab the phone and punch in Nicole's number. I picture her with her mobile. The girls have teased her about it for years. It's an ancient thing that she's never wanted to part with. A horrendous orange job, virtually first generation, that weighs a tonne and barely fits in her hand. There can't be another one like it anywhere in the world. She's always telling us to leave her old gizmo alone – it's hers and it works just fine. When it dies, how will she be able to pay for a new one?

A woman's voice. It must be Yasmine, the young Arab woman from the hostage-taking.

"You calling your wife?" Charles asks.

"Put my wife on!" I scream.

The girl weighs it up, then says: "Wait there."

Then it's Nicole.

"Have they hurt you?"

That's my first question. Because in my head, they've already done awful things. I feel a tingle in each of my knuckles, even the ones that don't work anymore.

"No," Nicole says.

I barely recognise her voice. It's completely hollow. Her fear is palpable.

"I don't want them to hurt you. You mustn't be afraid, Nicole. You have nothing to be afraid of."

"They say they want the money . . . What money, Alain?"

She's crying.

"Did you take their money?"

Too complicated to answer that.

"I'll give them everything they want, Nicole, I promise you. Promise me they haven't touched you!"

Nicole can't speak through her tears. She utters syllables that I can't make out. I try to keep her on the line.

"Do you know where you are? Nicole, tell me if you know where you are?"

"No . . ."

Her voice is like a little girl's.

"Are you in pain, Nicole?"

"No . . ."

I've only heard her cry like this once before. It was six years ago, when she lost her father. She collapsed on the kitchen floor in tears, screaming endless words, in a horrendous state. She had the same sobbing, high-pitched voice.

"That's enough," says the woman.

The line goes dead. I'm rooted to the pavement. The silence is brutally abrupt.

"That your wife?" Charles asks, slow on the uptake as ever. "You in the shit then?"

He's a sweet man, Charles. I've been paying him no attention, but he's still there, waiting patiently, bathed in his *eau de kirsch*. He's worried for me.

"I need a car, Charles. Now. Right now."

Charles whistles. Yup, that really is a thinker. I keep going:

"Listen, I don't have time to explain . . ."

He stops me with a direct, almost precise gesture, not the kind I would usually associate with him.

"Don't mess around with me!" I say.

A short silence, then:

"Right," he says.

He pulls a few crinkled notes out of his pocket, unfolds them and starts counting.

"Cabs are over there," he says, jerking his head somewhere behind him.

I don't need to bother counting – I know how much the custody office lot gave me. I say:

"I've got twenty euros."

"And I . . ." says Charles, counting shakily.

It takes him a crazy amount of time.

". . . I have twenty too!" he yells suddenly. "Snap!"

It takes a moment for him to come back to earth after this giddying revelation.

"It's not quite enough for a full tank, but it'll have to do."

42

The taxi hardly hung about. I'm buzzing, adrenaline coursing through my veins as fast as a galloping horse. It takes me less than ten minutes to jack up Charles' Renault 25, kick away the blocks and get it back on its tyres. Charles is swaying back and forth, always a few steps behind. Everything's going hellishly fast for him. So fast, in fact, that while he's still filling up at the Centre Leclerc on the corner at 3.45 p.m., we're actually zooming past Porte Maillot. Five minutes later and we're joining the *autoroute*, where the traffic is fine. The car's steering is pulling hard to the side, and the fact that half my fingers are in a mush doesn't help the matter. I compare my watch with the clock on the dashboard.

"Aha, look no further," Charles says, waving his gargantuan watch, "this puppy doesn't lose a minute in three months!"

A quick bit of arithmetic tells me I have just over two hours left. I call directory enquiries and request the Exxyal refinery in Sarqueville. "I'm putting you through," the voice says. I ask for Paul Cousin. I get pinged from one secretary to another. I ask for Paul Cousin again.

Not there.

I slam on the brakes.

Charles, his bottle of kirsch clenched between his thighs, looks round as quickly as he can, peering through the back window to check whether we're about to be crunched by a lorry.

"How can he not be there?"

"He's not here yet," says the girl.

"But he'll be in today?"

The girl checks her calendar.

"He'll be in, but it's a bit of a tricky day . . ."

I hang up. For me, he'll be in. Meetings, appointments, whatever – he'll be there. I chase away the thought of Nicole, the sound of her voice. I don't know where she is, but nothing will happen to her before 6.30 p.m. By which time I'll have sorted out the problem.

Fuck you, Fontana.

I clench my jaw. If I could, I'd clench the steering wheel too, destroying my joints that are already in pieces.

Charles watches the traffic race past. He puts his bottle of kirsch back in its spot under the seat. The enormous chrome bars that serve as bumpers come a third of the way up his windscreen and stick out into the other lane a bit. I've no idea what the police will say if they stop us. I don't even have my licence on me.

In theory, Charles' home is a six-cylinder, 2.5-litre turbo V6. In theory. In reality, it flat-lines at 90 km.p.h. and shudders like a Boeing 747 preparing for take-off, with noise levels to match. We can barely hear each other. I stick firmly to the fast lane.

"You can give her some more, you know!" Charles says. "She's not shy!"

I don't want to upset him by telling him that my foot's down as far as it'll go. He'd be so disappointed. We surrender to the sound of the engine. The car stinks of kirsch.

About an hour in, I tap the dial with my finger. The gauge is going down so fast I can scarcely believe my eyes.

"Yup," says Charles, "she's a thirsty girl!"

You're telling me. She's sucking it down at ten kilometres per litre, no problem. It should get us there, but only just. I do everything I can to bat Nicole from my thoughts. The further I get from Paris, the closer I feel to her, to saving her.

Fucking hell, I will do this.

I hold the wheel tight because the steering's wildly, danger-ously off-kilter.

"Sore is it?" Charles asks, pointing at my bandages.

"No, that's not . . ."

Charles nods in agreement. He thinks he knows what I mean. It suddenly strikes me that since his first wave outside the prison gate, I have taken his mobile, his twenty euros and his car, subjecting him to this hazardous journey without saying or explaining anything to him. Charles hasn't asked me a single question. I turn to him. As he watches the landscape flash past, his face enthrals me.

Charles is a beautiful man. There's no other word.

He has a beautiful soul.

"Let me explain . . ."

Charles doesn't look away from the landscape, but just lifts his hand as though to say tell me what you want, when you want, if you want. Don't fret.

A beautiful, big soul.

So I start explaining.

In doing so, I replay everything. Nicole. The last few years and months. I relive the pathetic hope of landing a job at my age and I see Nicole's face again as she leans against the door of my office, holding the letter and saying: "My love, this is unbelievable!" The tests, the interview with Lacoste, all my idiotic preparation.

"Ah well, holy shit!" Charles says admiringly. He is deep in thought, his eyes fixed on the passing *autoroute*.

I talk about my stubbornness and Nicole's anger. Mathilde's money and my fist in her husband's face. The hostage-taking. It all comes out.

"Ah well, holy shit!"

By the time he's digested all the information, we've made another twenty-eight kilometres.

"This Fontana," he says, "is he that squat guy with metally eyes?"

Charles had been struck by him at the trial, too.

"Always on the lookout, that guy! And he had some back-up as well. Tough bastard that one. What did you say his name was again?"

"Fontana."

Charles mulls over the name for a long while. He murmurs "Fontana", chewing on each syllable.

The dial continues its breakneck descent. You'd think there was a leak in the fuel tank.

"She's going at less than ten kilometres per litre!"

Charles looks sceptical.

"I'd say more like fifteen . . ." he says at last.

Perhaps Renault 25 actually means litres . . . At this rate, we won't have enough. He offers me the bottle but thinks better of it.

"No that's true – you're driving."

However hard I try to concentrate on other things, I am assailed by the thought of Nicole and her tears over the phone. I'm confident that they haven't hurt her. They must have grabbed her at the foot of the building. Adrenaline pumps through my veins faster and faster, surging from head to toe. I picture Nicole sitting tied to a chair. No, that's crazy – if there are still hours to go, she'll still be free to move. What use would it be to tie her up? No. They're just minding her. What sort of place? Nicole. I think I might be sick. I concentrate on the road ahead. Paul Cousin. Sarqueville. All my thoughts must stay focused on that. If I win this round, I win the whole thing. Nicole will be back, back with me.

I lied to them: transferring their money would have taken half an hour. By now, it could be back in Exxyal's account.

Nicole could be free.

Instead, I'm getting as far away from her as this old banger will allow.

Have I completely lost my mind?

"Mustn't cry, my man . . ." Charles says.

I hadn't even noticed. I wipe away my tears with the back of my sleeve. This suit . . . Nicole.

Criquebeuf: almost a hundred and twelve kilometres to go. The fuel gauge is sputtering like a candle.

"There's no way she's even doing twenty, Charles. Come on, it's got to be less!"

"Could be . . ."

He leans towards the dial.

"Oh yeah, look at that! Well then, we'll need to have a think about that . . ."

A sign indicates it's about six kilometres to the next service station.

It's 5.00 p.m.

We've only got four euros and a bit of shrapnel left.

A few minutes later, the Renault 25 starts juddering. Charles makes a face. I feel ready to cry again and start smacking the steering wheel like a maniac.

"We'll find something," Charles assures me.

Will we now. The car bunny hops more and more severely, so I pull into the slow lane and ease off the accelerator to save the last few seconds. The engine stalls, but I manage to use our momentum to carry us onto the exit for the service station. We can put in four euros of petrol. The car doesn't so much stop as collapse. It dies. Silence descends on the cockpit. Despondence. I look at the time. I have no idea what to do. Even if I were to change my mind and make the transfer straight away, how would I do it? Where would I go?

I'm not entirely sure where we even are. Charles frowns.

"Hold on!" he yells, pointing at the *autoroute* behind. "Back there! I saw it: Rouen, twenty-three kilometres!"

Another forty clicks to Sarqueville, and the car has drunk its last drop.

Nicole.

Think.

I can't thread two thoughts together. My brain stopped functioning with the image of Nicole and the sound of her voice on the telephone. I didn't even notice Charles open the passenger door. He's embarked on a roundabout route towards the service station.

Think.

Thumb a lift. Find another vehicle. There's no other choice. I drag myself out of the car and run to catch up with Charles. He's already in discussion with an enormous blond-haired man with a red face and a grubby cap. Charles motions towards me as I approach them.

"This is him, my pal . . ."

The guy looks at me. He looks at Charles. We must seem a funny pair.

"I'm going the other side of Rouen," he says.

"Sarqueville?" I ask.

"Not far from there."

"You can take my pal then?" Charles says, rubbing his hands.

These words reveal where dear Charles' strength lies. No-one can resist him. His sincerity is so disarming, his generosity overwhelming.

"No problem," the guy says.

"Well, no time to lose," Charles says, still rubbing his hands.

The man is shuffling impatiently. Charles and I shake hands, and he senses my embarrassment.

"Don't worry!" he says.

I rummage in my pockets and give him the four euros.

"Bah what about you?"

Without waiting for an answer, he gives me back three.

"Share like brothers." He chuckles.

The driver says:

"Look, gents, sorry but . . ."

I hug Charles. He barely touches me. He takes off his massive green fluorescent watch and hands it to me. I strap it to my wrist and squeeze his shoulder. He looks to one side and nods to indicate that the driver's waiting.

As I watch him disappear in the wing mirror, he gives his salute.

It's a huge articulated lorry. He's transporting stationery, a heavy load. We're hardly going to be blasting down the *autoroute*. Is this turning into a suicide mission?

Nicole.

Throughout the journey, the guy respects my silence. I play back the image of Nicole over and over. At times, it's like she's already dead and I'm remembering her. I dispel this idea as forcefully as I can and try to focus on something else. A few headlines. *"This year's unemployment forecasts of 639,000 are set to be exceeded, according to the Ministry of Labour."* Good of them to be so honest.

When the lorry drops me at the Sarqueville exit, it's 5.30 p.m. One hour to go.

I have to call. I go into a telephone box on the roadside that stinks of cigarettes and put in two coins.

Fontana picks up.

"I want to speak to my wife."

"Have you done what you were supposed to?"

It's like he's here, standing in front of me. My heart's pounding at a hundred thousand beats per minute.

"Everything's under way. I want to speak to my wife!"

My eyes fall on the plastic-covered sheet with all the international dialling codes and user instructions, and immediately I realise my error.

"Where are you calling from?"

It doubles: two hundred thousand b.p.m.

"From an online connection, why?"

Silence. Then:

"I'm handing you over."

"Alain, where are you?"

The anxiety in her voice sums up her distress. She starts crying.

"Don't cry, Nicole, I'm coming to get you."

"When?"

What am I supposed to reply to that . . .

"It'll be over soon, I promise."

But my tone is too harsh for her. I shouldn't have called. She starts screaming:

"Where are you, Alain, where the fuck are you! Where are you? WHERE ARE YOU?"

The last bit gets lost in her sobbing. She breaks down, overcome by her tears. I feel desolate.

"I'm coming, my love, I'll be there soon."

I say that, but I'm light years away from her.

Fontana comes back:

"My client still hasn't received anything. What stage are you at exactly?"

I feel feverish. The screen in front of me is flashing. I put in another coin. My credit's being guzzled as quickly as the fuel in the Renault 25. The cost of living is crazy now. I've had enough.

"I've already explained: nothing can be done in under three hours."

I hang up. He's going to run a search on the number that came up. In five minutes he'll know I'm near Rouen. Will he make the link? Definitely. Will he realise the significance? I don't think so.

5.35 p.m.

I sprint towards the *péage*. I make for the right-hand side of the first car. It's a woman. I huddle down and knock on the window. Alarmed, she gathers her change and drives off like a shot.

"What are you doing?" asks the girl in the booth.

Twenty-five, at a guess. Big girl.

"I ran out of petrol," I say, pointing back down the *autoroute*.

She makes an ambiguous sound.

Two more cars turn me down. *Where are you?* The words are still ringing in my ears. I sense the girl's irritation increasing as I hassle the drivers. Can hardly blame her . . .

A van. A big, dog-like face. A setter, perhaps. The man's about forty. He leans across and opens the door. I glance at my watch.

Where are you?

"In a hurry?"

"Yes, yes I am."

"Typical. Always happens when you're in a hurry . . ."

I don't listen to the rest. I say: "Sarqueville . . . The refinery . . . Eight kilometres."

We arrive in the town.

"I'll drop you off," offers the setter.

The town's deserted. No-one in the streets. Shops closed and banners everywhere: "No to the closure!", "*Vive* Sarqueville!", "Yes to Sarqueville! No to Sarkoville!"

No wonder Paul Cousin's not in the office – his work is already done.

"The town's dead. Everyone's getting ready for the march tomorrow."

It's really not my day. Where will Cousin be? I remember the secretary's hesitation on the phone.

"When is it?"

"The march? On the radio they said four o'clock," the guy answers as he drops me at the barrier. "They're aiming to be outside the refinery in time for the seven o'clock news on France 3."

"Thank you," I say.

The refinery is a monstrosity, all cylinders, overhead tubes, giant ducts and pipes of every size. Never-ending smokestacks tower into the sky. Red and green lights flash away on the sides of vats. The whole thing takes your breath away. It's like the site is dormant. Operations on hold. Banners beat in the breeze. Same slogans as in town, but here, engulfed in the vastness of the factory, they seem pitiful. Everything is dominated by the pipework. The defiant words spray-painted on the flags are a rallying cry for a struggle that seems over before it's even begun.

Paul Cousin's done a fine job: all the baying, the blustering, the howls of indignation are happening down the road, out of sight. At the refinery, there's not a single burning tyre, no barricades or vehicles blocking the way, no picket lines of protesters stoking empty oil drums to grill their sausages. Not even a leaflet littering the ground.

I hesitate for a split second before walking past the barrier as confidently as possible. I don't get away with it.

"Excuse me!"

I turn to the guard.

Alain? Where are you?

It's true: what the fuck am I doing here? I walk up to the booth, go around the side and climb two steps. The guard scrutinises my suit, which by now has certainly seen better days.

"Sorry. I have a meeting with Monsieur Cousin."

"And you are . . .?" he says, picking up his telephone.

"Alain Delambre."

If Cousin hears my name he might think twice, but he'll definitely see me. I look at Charles' watch. So does the guard. Between my tattered suit and fluorescent timepiece, I seem an unlikely candidate for a meeting with the boss. Time passes at an alarming rate. I pace about next to the booth, trying to look relaxed.

"His secretary says that you don't have an appointment. I'm sorry."

"That must be a mistake."

The way the guard spreads his arms and looks at me leaves no room for doubt – I'm dealing with a stubborn bastard. The sort who really believes in his remit. The worst sort. If I keep pestering him, it's only going one way.

Normally speaking, a man in my position would look surprised, take out his mobile and call his contact at the refinery to clarify matters. The guard eyes me closely. I reckon he thinks I'm a tramp. He's begging me to try and jump the barrier. I turn, take a couple of steps, pretend to dig around in my pocket and take out an imaginary phone. I look up at the sky as though I'm deep in thought, all the while getting further and further away. The refinery is served by a single, S-shaped tarmac strip. Over on the *autoroute* the traffic is getting thicker and thicker, but here there's no-one. Still engrossed in my pretend conversation, I end up in a spot where the guard can't see me anymore. If there were any vehicles passing by I'd be able to hop aboard, but there's zero movement on this side of the refinery. It's gone 5.45 p.m. Barely forty-five minutes left. Whatever happens, it's too late. Even if I wanted to reverse everything, I can't.

Alain?

Nicole's somewhere over there with the killers. She's crying. They're going to hurt her. Will they snap her fingers too?

Can't find Paul Cousin.

No mobile and not a centime on me.

No car.

I'm alone. The wind picks up. It's about to rain.

I have absolutely no idea what to do.

Alain?

Where are you?

43

What's the point in coming all the way to Sarqueville only to wander aimlessly around the streets? It's not like I'm going to bump into Paul Cousin in town, visiting the cemetery before the battle commences. I stay put, shifting from one foot to the other.

The *autoroute* runs all the way down one side of the refinery. The traffic's mounting up. Ahead of tomorrow's march, police vehicles are starting to pile into the area, followed by coachloads of C.R.S. riot police. They're all converging on the town in preparation for the protests. On my side, the refinery side, everything's dead calm. It starts drizzling a little after 6.00 p.m.

A few minutes later, it's chucking it down.

I'm in no-man's-land. I have to speak to Nicole. No, to Fontana. I have to come up with a reason to push back the deadline.

I can't. Nothing.

The rain gets even harder. I flip up my jacket collar and walk towards the refinery once more, racking my brains as I go. I draw on every last weapon from my arsenal of management-speak. Hypothesis after hypothesis, what-if after what-if, but nothing works. I attempt to run through the list of possibilities, but still nothing comes.

My brain is refusing to function. I'm back in front of the booth, pummelled by the rain. I look like an unemployed man fresh out of prison. I'm Jean Valjean.

The guard looks at me through the water running down his window. He doesn't even flinch. I go up on my tiptoes and knock on the glass. Still no movement. He's just standing there. This can't be happening ... I tap again. He makes up his mind and opens the door. Not a word. I hadn't noticed before, but he's about my age. More or less my height. He's got a tummy on him, a belt propping it up from underneath. Apart from that and his moustache, we look more or less alike. Give or take. The rain is dripping down the collar of my drenched jacket and pouring down my face. I have to screw up my eyes to make out the guard, who's still standing in the open door, looking at me without moving.

"Listen ..."

The rain, my saturated suit, my stance, my bandaged hand tugging at my tieless collar, my humiliation ... everything about me screams rock bottom. He cocks his head, a motion I am unable to decipher.

He's a guard. About sixty. Same age as me.

Alain?

I've got less than half an hour left. I don't know what else I can do to rescue the situation. All I know is it involves getting past him. He's the only living being between me and my life.

The last one.

Where are you?

"Listen ..." I repeat. "I really must make a call. It's very urgent."

I've just thought of something. Dead battery. My mobile's bust. He can't hear me over the sound of the rain hammering on his booth. He moves closer to the door, leans his head out slightly and stoops down to me. A drop of water on his neck startles him. He recoils and angrily brings a hand to his collar. He looks at me again, before saying:

"Get the fuck out of here! Now!"

Those are his words as he slams the door violently. What really

347

riled him up were those drops of water on his neck. That's what tipped him over the edge.

So no help, no telephone, no nothing. Nicole might suffer, I might die, the refinery might fire everyone, the town might become a wasteland, the civilised world might disappear. But he – he has shut his door. Must be one of the few who kept his job.

It's over. In a few minutes, Fontana will walk up to Nicole and fix his steely eyes on hers. I'm at a loss. I'm a hundred and fifty kilometres from her, and she's going to suffer horribly.

The guard pretends to peer into the distance through his rain-spattered window, like the captain of a cargo ship. I reach a conclusion with absolute certainty: this man represents everything I abhor; he is my hatred in human form.

The only sensible course of action is to kill him.

I stretch my neck muscles, climb the two steps and open the door. The guy takes a backwards step as I pile into him.

This man is the Enemy: killing him will save us all.

My fist makes contact at the precise moment that the image of Nicole arrives. She's sitting in a chair, tied up, a large piece of duct tape over her mouth. Someone's holding her hand, preparing to break her fingers, and the guard falls back and cracks his head on the desk, his chair rolling towards the door. Fontana looks Nicole in the eye and says: "You do know that you can't count on your husband," and suddenly snaps back all her fingers. Nicole screams, a bestial, primordial cry, the same sound I make when the guard knees me in the bollocks. Nicole and I scream together. We're being tortured together. We're twisting in pain together. We're going to die together, I've known it from the start. From the start. Death. I stagger back two paces towards the door and the guard's back on his feet. Nicole has fainted. *Alain? Where are you?* Fontana slaps her cheek and says: "Wake up, time for the other hand," and the guard hits me, I'm not sure what with, but it knocks me into the swivel chair, which tips over and sends me flying out of the booth, completely off-balance as I bounce down the steps, rolling backwards, skidding down the slick concrete. Nicole can't bear to look at her hands, the pain's too much, and I'm floundering, battered by the rain. My head cracks into the ground first, and Nicole is in so much pain she can't even scream, nothing comes from her throat and her eyes are bulging out, mesmerised by the agony – *Alain? Where are you?* – and my head bounces once, twice as I close my eyes and everything stops and I clutch my skull, feeling nothing.

I'm a body without a soul, from the start I've had no soul.

My hand covers my eyes and I try to figure out what position I'm in, try to turn over but I can't – I might die here – car fumes hit my sinuses, and through squinting eyes I make out the edge of a chrome exhaust pipe, big tyres, silver rims, then shoes, perfectly polished shoes, and a man is standing over me, and I rub my eyes as the figure towers above me, his legs firmly set, and I notice how very tall he is.

How thin he is.

It takes me two more seconds to recognise him.

Paul Cousin.

44

It's really bucketing now, the rain coursing down the windscreen and drowning the scenery in a milky blur. The daylight is fading. I think of the demonstrators on the far side of the *autoroute* who are preparing for tomorrow. They must be keeping a close eye on the grey sky. It looks leaden for another generation at least. Paul Cousin can rest easy: even the elements are working in his favour. It's like a sign from heaven.

St Cousin is at the wheel. He doesn't bother with the wipers. Instead his severe, puritanical eyes are trained on my suit as it drips on the floor of his car. My whole body is shaking. I should be with Nicole. Nicole is with Fontana, and I'm here, lost. The back of my head's bleeding. I'm struggling to breathe – must have cracked some ribs. Nicole's right . . . I do screw up everything. I've taken off my jacket and I'm clutching the rolled-up sleeve against the top of my skull. Cousin's not hiding his disgust.

He managed to calm the guard.

We're in his parking space at the refinery. Swanky car. Cousin has both hands on the wheel. He is projecting a patient demeanour, but the underlying message is clear: don't abuse the situation.

"Any chance of turning that off?" I ask.

The air conditioning is freezing. I'm chilled to the bone. It's arctic, very much Cousin's style. I picture him rubbing his torso with snow. His Reverend Dimmesdale side.

Luxury dashboard for a luxury car.

"Company wheels?"

Cousin doesn't move. Of course it's a company car. It's only the second time I've seen him close-up: the size of his head is simply astonishing. It gives me the creeps. All this is giving me time to focus. I compose myself, determined not to rush headlong into the fray. Only twenty minutes to go. The Patron Saint of Lost Causes has let me get away by the skin of my teeth. I can't make the same mistake I did with the guard and blow my last chance. I take a deep breath. Nicole's fear is at the forefront of my mind.

I can't miss this last chance.

Cousin's patience is wearing thin.

"It's not like I don't have better things to be doing!" he snaps at last.

If that were really true, we wouldn't be here in this stationary car, the rain hammering down, on the day the whole region is rallying against the redundancy plan he's enforcing, in the shadow of a substantial police presence. It doesn't add up.

I keep quiet because I can tell Paul Cousin is on edge. Despite all my instincts to get moving, and fast, I know that would be the best way to ruin everything.

The last time Cousin saw me was yesterday, in the dock. He testified in my favour on the orders of his boss. And now, twenty-four hours later, he finds me – coming apart at the seams in more ways than one – smacking the guard in the face at his factory, which happens to be on strike. It doesn't bode well at all. If anything, I'm here to make demands. Yet St Paul seems intrigued. Ever since I saw him enter the courtroom, I could tell he was furious with me, because he knew full well that he'd been screwed over. Only he doesn't know to what extent, and that's what intrigues him – he's itching to know. The fact is, he's the one who should be making demands. He did me a favour. He contributed to my freedom. Somehow I've become his boss' protégé, the man he's gone to extreme lengths to help. But Cousin doesn't know what demands to make. Seeing me here, destitute, has flipped his world on its head. My patience pays off. Cousin can't resist:

"During the hostage-taking," he says, "you let me go on purpose, didn't you?"

"Let's say I wasn't opposed to the idea."

"You could have shot me."

"That wasn't in my interests."

"Because you needed someone to escape and warn the police. Didn't matter who. Me or any of the others."

"Yes, but I hoped it would be you."

I inspect my jacket sleeve: I'm still bleeding, so I press it hard against the top of my head again. This dithering annoys Cousin, since it forces him to wait. I will myself to take my time, which is no mean feat because I can't help glaring at the clock on the dashboard every other second. *Nicole.* The minutes drag. I continue distractedly:

"I was so pleased when you became the hero of the day in your boss' eyes. It was just what you needed to be welcomed back into the company fold after slogging it out free of charge for all those years. I was glad you were the first to stand up and be counted. You were the one I wanted. You were my favourite. Call it solidarity for the unemployed."

Cousin turns all that over in his enormous head.

"What did you take from Exxyal?"

"How do you know about that?"

"Come on!"

His nose is out of joint, old Cousin. He continues:

"Alexandre Dorfmann organises a press conference to announce loud and clear that Exxyal is dropping all charges, and demands his execs testify in your favour at the trial . . . It's not hard to tell that you've got him cornered. So I'll ask you again: what did you take?"

The moment of truth. I've got fifteen minutes left. I close my eyes. I look at Nicole. All my courage lies with her. I ask the question calmly:

"How pissed off will Dorfmann be when he finds out the two of us are in agreement?"

"Agreement over what? Agreement over nothing!"

Cousin's outraged, shouting.

"Yes, agreement over nothing . . . But only me and you need to know that. If I tell him that we've agreed to screw him over, who's he going to believe? You or me?"

Cousin concentrates hard. I set out my argument:

"The way I see it, he's going to let you handle things at Sarqueville because it's a shitty business. Both hands deep in the shit. C.E.O.s don't tend to be too keen on that. Then afterwards, when you've fired everyone, your head will be the next to roll. And this time, you won't be bailed out by a courageous unemployed person who's no longer eligible for jobseeker's allowance."

His fury seems to fill his entire head, which is saying something.

"And what exactly are we agreeing on?"

I wheel out the big guns.

"I ran off with Dorfmann's slush fund. My plan is to tell him that we've gone halves on it."

You might expect him to be scandalised, but not a bit of it. Paul Cousin thinks about it. He's a manager. He assesses the situation, runs through the various strategies, analyses his objectives. In my mind, he could buy himself some time by considering how fucked he is. I try to jog him:

"You're pretty fucked, my friend."

I jog him because I'm in a chronic state of urgency. I hope Fontana hasn't stuck a clock in front of Nicole. He's capable of it. He's capable of counting down the minutes, the seconds. I go for a second volley.

"I'm giving you three minutes."

"I doubt that."

He needs to reframe the issue. Eight minutes to go. Nicole.

"How much did you take?" he asks.

"Tut tut tut."

Nice try, but I'm not going to fall for that.

"What do you want?"

Fine application of the reality principle.

"Some dirt on Exxyal. Something really dirty. I want to blow Dorfmann out of the sky. Give me what I want and I'll make it worth your while. A seven-figure bribe, a disgraceful back-hander, a deal with a terrorist state, a nasty payoff . . . I don't care."

"And how would I know about any of that?"

"Because you've been here for twenty years. You've spent more than fifteen at the top. And you're the kind of person who laps up the shady stuff. Why else would you be here in Sarqueville? I'm not asking for the whole file – just a few highlights will do. Nothing more. You have two minutes."

Make or break.

"How can you guarantee me confidentiality?"

"It has to be something from the company system, that's all. I hacked into Exxyal's servers. I could feasibly have snatched anything from in there. I'm not asking for a top secret document . . . it doesn't even need to be confidential. All I want is some key information – I'll take care of the rest."

"I see."

Sly dog, Cousin.

"Three million."

Even slyer than I thought.

Nothing if not pragmatic. It took him just a few seconds to analyse the situation in front of him and weigh up the pros and cons before deciding to up the ante. Three million euros. I've no idea how he came up with that number. He knows I ran off with the kitty. He's made an educated guess. In his mind, what percentage does that represent? I'll try another round. Got to wrap this up.

"Two," I say.

"Three."

"Two and a half."

"Three."

"O.K., three million and thirty thousand."

Cousin looks surprised, but my face is deadpan.

"Deal," he says.

"Give me a name!"

"Pascal Lombard."

Holy shit. A former interior minister. I'm blown away. The guy's face comes to me clearly. Prime example of a dodgy politician: no shortage of talent; murky past; relentlessly cynical; a few past misdemeanours that investigators were never quite able to untangle; hounded for fifteen years but still holding forth noisily at the Assemblée, crapping all over public morality. Re-elected time and time again. Two or three sons in business or politics. Classic.

"What about him?"

"Insider trading. 1998. The time of the merger with Union Path Corp. Textbook stuff: when he heard the news from Dorfmann, he bought up a whole stack of shares from one of his sons, and three months later, when the merger was announced, he sold them all on."

"Profit?"

"Ninety-six million francs."

I dial Nicole's number on the car phone. Fontana picks up after the second ring.

"Let me speak to my wife."

"I hope you've got some good news for me."

"Oh, I do. Some excellent news!"

"I'm listening."

"Pascal Lombard. Union Path. 1998. Ninety-six million."

Silence. I give it time to sink in. You don't need to be a senior-ranking spook to realise that this involves something fishy. Pascal Lombard's name is infamous. He's a political Pandora's box. Fontana's silence confirms I'm right. All the same, he gives it a go:

"Don't play with me, Delambre."

I think I can hear a sound from behind him. I can't help blurting out:

"I want my wife! Let me speak to her!"

My voice fills the car. Paul Cousin looks at me, finding me increasingly dazed.

"Sorry, Delambre," Fontana says, "but my client hasn't received anything, and you've missed your deadline."

"What's that sound behind you? What is it?"

He doesn't like failure, Fontana. And right now, things might be bad for me, but they're bad for him too. That's what I'm banking on. His client has enlisted his services, and right now everything's going pear-shaped.

"Call your client," I say. "Speak to Alexandre Dorfmann in person and simply tell him this from me: 'Pascal Lombard. Union Path. 1998.'"

I gather my strength and wait a few seconds.

Ready:

"Just say that, and all your problems are over, Fontana. Because that'll put his mind to rest immediately."

Aim:

"But if you choose not to call him, he's going to be very, very, very angry with you."

Fire:

"And if that happens, think hard about how powerful Dorfmann is: my problems will pale compared to yours."

Silence.

Good sign. I breathe. Well handled.

"How do I call you back?"

"I'll call you, but first let me speak to my wife."

Fontana hesitates. He really doesn't like having his hand forced like this.

"I said let me speak to my wife!"

"Hello."

It's Nicole. No more fear. We're beyond fear. Her voice is so weary it sounds lifeless.

"Alain? Where are you?"

"I'm here, my love, I'm with you. It's all over."

My voice catches a little as I try to reassure her, to give her some grounds for hope.

"Why are they keeping me?" Nicole asks.

"They're going to let you go, I promise. Have they hurt you?"

"When will they let me go?"

Her voice is thin and shaky, tense and bruised.

"Have they hurt you?"

Nicole doesn't answer. She asks me question after question with a mix of anguish and despondency. Her mind is stuck on one point:

"What do they want? Where are you?"

No time to reply because the phone changes hands.

"Call me back in ten minutes," Fontana says.

He hangs up. My stomach lurches so violently that I retch from the nausea. All the while, Cousin's been drumming his fingers on the wheel.

"I've got a lot of work to do, Monsieur Delambre. Perhaps it's time to formalise our deal, wouldn't you say?"

Indeed, time for formalities. He suggests we agree on the practical aspects of our transaction without delay. Cousin is shafting his boss in the same methodical manner he serves him. A true professional.

As for me, I'm badly shaken up by Nicole's words.

"Just one thing to finish with . . ." Cousin says.

"Yes, what?" I say, still in a daze.

"Why the thirty thousand?"

"Three million into your account."

I pat the dashboard.

"Plus your car. It's coming with me."

45

"I'm sorry, but I haven't received any instructions along those lines."

"Fuck you, Fontana!"

I'm screaming. Back on the *autoroute* to Paris and I'm doing well over a hundred, my palm flat against the horn. The car in front is dawdling and refusing to budge, so I honk even harder.

"Things have changed, you piece of shit!"

Even if I wanted to I'd struggle to remember the terror Fontana inspired in me not long ago. I know I'll win, I can feel it all the way to the tips of my fingers, but more than anything in the world I want Nicole.

I keep going:

"I'm the one giving the orders now, you hear me, dickhead?"

The dickhead stays quiet. The mere mention of the names Pascal Lombard and Union Path made Alexandre Dorfmann instruct him to suspend the operation until he has met me in person. He's expecting me at his office in less than two hours. Even if I allow myself the luxury of being forty minutes late, I reckon he'll rejig his diary to see me. I've turned the speakerphone up to full volume, and I carry on shouting as I weave in and out of the traffic, a hundred and twenty on the dial:

"And I can even tell you how this is going to end up, you bull-dog. In one hour, you're going to release my wife and go running back to your kennel. And let me assure you, if there's so much as a hair missing from her head, your antics in Sudan will feel like the fucking *Rescuers!*"

Words fail me for a moment.

"So listen to these instructions, you prick, and follow them. I want three photos of my wife immediately. The first of her face, the second of her hands, and lastly I want one full-length. All of her. Do it on your mobile. And on each one I want today's date and time. Send them to . . ."

I scrabble around for the number in the telephone. I take one hand off the wheel and lean towards the screen, pressing one button, then another: "how does this bastard thing work?" A deafening horn blares out and I look up immediately. The car has pitched dangerously into the left-hand lane and is heading at full pelt towards a Dutch H.G.V. that is honking its foghorn as loud as it'll go. I barely have time to register the situation, flinging the wheel round to the left to avoid the car I'm bearing down on at the speed of light. It doesn't even occur to me to brake. The dial says I'm going at a hundred and thirteen.

I yell out the car phone number to Fontana.

"I'm giving you five minutes! Don't make me call back, or I swear, every last cent I extort from your boss will go towards ripping off your bollocks!"

I continue slaloming across the four lanes. I have to calm down. No big deal if I'm flashed by a camera, but getting myself stopped by the police is not a good move. I stick to the fast lane and ease off the accelerator. Ninety-three – that's reasonable. Every ten seconds, I glare at the screen. I'm desperate to see the photos of Nicole. I picture Fontana rushing to get me what I want. There are a few minutes to go.

To try and relax, I look around the inside of Cousin's car. It's a smart one. A real gem of French engineering, which seems pretty damn cynical when you consider his job is to close down industrial sites. I fiddle with the controls and find a radio station. I end up on France Info. ". . . *last year John Arnold, a 33-year-old trader, earned between 2 and 2.5 billion dollars. Then came . . .*" I switch it off. The planet never stops spinning in the same direction and at the same speed.

I make sure the call waiting option is activated and dial Charles' number. One ring, two, three, four.

"Hello!"

Good old Charles. Sure, his voice doesn't exude freshness, but the tone is there, buoyant and big-hearted.

"Hi, Charles!"

"Whoa it's you damn yeah I was expecting you where are you calling from?"

All that in the same stride. Charles is delighted. He's relieved, thrilled that the effort he put in to answering the phone has paid off.

"I'm on the *autoroute* to Paris."

The information swirls around the remaining brain cells bobbing up and down in his kirsch-soaked head. I don't wait for the next question before explaining everything: Cousin, Fontana, Dorfmann.

"Ah but damn!" Charles says over and over once I've finished my account.

He is flabbergasted by my performance. I keep on the lookout for Fontana's call – the time seems to be dragging horrendously. I ask Charles where he is.

"Like you, on the *autoroute*."

Good god, Charles is behind the wheel!

"Massive stroke of luck," he continues. "I call my pal and guess what his brother-in-law has a little place two shakes from the service station where we broke down and he filled me up didn't I tell you it was lucky?"

"Charles . . . are you driving?"

"Weeell doing my best."

It knocks the breath out of me.

"I'm being sensible you know," Charles assures me. "I'm staying in the slow lane and not going above forty."

The safest way to get pranged from behind and stopped by the police.

"Hold on . . . how far along the *autoroute* are you?"

"That I cannot really tell you because the signs are all written so small you see."

I can imagine. But just as I start answering, I make out his scarlet car with its immense chrome bars in the distance, hogging the right-hand lane, with a thick cloud of white smoke stretching behind him like the train of a wedding dress. I slow down slightly, and once I'm alongside him, I honk my horn. He seems so small, as though he's been compacted, his eyes barely higher than the steering wheel.

It takes him a couple of seconds to take stock of the situation.

"It's you! Ah well damn!" he screams when he recognises me.

He's giddy with joy. He gives me his little salute, beaming from ear to ear.

"I can't hang around, Charles, they're expecting me."

"Don't fret yourself about me," he answers.

There are so many things I'd like to say to him. I owe him so much. I owe him an enormous amount. If everything works out O.K., I'm going to change Charles' life. I'm going to give him a house with a cellar full of kirsch. There are so many things I want to say to him.

I put my foot down and start racing again. In a few seconds, the white cloud and the red body of his car are just blurs in my rear-view mirror.

"Everything should be alright from now on, Charles."

"Ah well good," he says, "a doddle."

A "doddle" . . . he must be the only person left in the world who uses words like that. I round things off:

"I'm meeting Dorfmann . . . just dropping in to nail his balls to his desk, then I'll pick up Nicole. After that it's finished."

Charles is over the moon, thrilled.

"I couldn't be happier for you my friend. You deserve it!"

Hearing that from Charles sends me over the edge. To be so genuinely happy for someone else . . . I'd never be capable of that level of selflessness.

"You already shafted that other prick whatshisname again Montana?"

"Fontana."

"That's the one!" Charles shouts.

And he's off again on another round of jubilant celebrations.

My victory is certain. The meeting called by Dorfmann is in itself an order to fall back, a thinly veiled request for an armistice. I will get Nicole released and meet her at the flat. We'll take home the compensation we've earned, the fair price for all our misfortunes. Our miserable existence will come to an end. I want Charles to be with us. Nicole will love him.

"Ah well no," says Charles, "after all this you have to stay with your sweetheart you don't need me there like a lemon!"

I insist.

"I want you to be there, Charles. It's important to me."

"You sure?"

I fumble in my pocket, unfold the piece of paper Fontana gave me and read him the address.

"Wait," says Charles.

Then:

"Say it again?"

I read it again and Charles lets out a shriek.

"Ah you have to say that's strange I lived in that neighbourhood when I was a boy no even younger than that when I was a nipper."

That'll help.

"Listen wait," Charles continues, "I've got to make a note of the number of the street because I'm not sure I'll remember it."

I picture him lurching spectacularly from left to right then pouncing towards the glove compartment.

"No!" I shout.

In his state, if he doesn't remain completely focused on his driving, it's going to end in disaster.

"Don't sweat, Charles, I'll send you a text message."

"As you wish."

"O.K. let's do it that way. Shall we say half eight? I've got to go now. Promise? I'm counting on you, alright."

The first photograph is of her hands, and I'm completely fixated by it. No doubt this is because mine still hurt so much, and because driving for the first time in months has made me aware that they will never work like before, that some of my fingers won't bend until I die, or even after I die. I recognise her wedding ring. The sight of her two hands, open and exposed as though waiting for the hammer, leaves a horrible impression. The second photo is marked with the right day and the right time, but it's of the wrong Nicole. My Nicole from before, from always, has been replaced by a woman in her fifties with greying hair and drawn features, and she's standing facing the camera with a combination of fear and defeat. Nicole looks ravaged by this ordeal. In the space of a few hours, she's become an old woman. It tears at my heart. She looks like one of those pictures of hostages you see on the television in Lebanon, Colombia or Chad, her eyes inexpressive, blank with anxiety. In the third image, her left cheekbone is marked by a cut, around which a violet bruise has spread. From a fist, or maybe a baton.

Did Nicole fight back?

Did she try to escape?

I bite down on my lip until it bleeds. Tears prick my eyes.

I smack the wheel, screaming. Because that Nicole, the one in the picture, is my doing.

I mustn't let the guilt overwhelm me. I have to pull myself together. No giving up now. Must stay focused for the home straight. I sniff and wipe my eyes. Quite the opposite – seeing her like that on the screen must renew my strength. I will fight to the very end. I feel happy in the knowledge that what I'm bringing her will reconcile everything: it will heal all the wounds, erase all the scars. I'm coming home to her, with all the riches to secure our life and our future. I'm coming home with the solution to each and every one of our problems.

All I want now is for the time to pass quickly, for her to be freed, to come home; to hold her in my arms.

I must call her. The tone barely rings before Fontana answers with a clear, firm, definitive "No". I'm about to unleash more insults but he's faster than me.

"You're not getting anything else until I've received instructions from my client."

He hangs up straight away. The fine thread between Nicole and me has been broken. Everything is in my hands. I must free her, save her, right now.

I step down on the accelerator again.

46

La Défense.

I look up. At the summit of the gleaming glass skyscraper, a fiery gold sign bearing Exxyal Europe's name and logo spins on its axis. You can imagine it turning into a deity when night falls, transfiguring into a tremendous, shining beacon that lights up the world.

Paul Cousin's car is equipped with a device that can open the car park gate remotely. It's past 7.30 p.m., but on the second level, which is reserved for company executives, most of the spaces are still full. Space no. 198 lights up automatically as my car enters and the aluminium bollard sinks into the ground. I park and walk quickly towards the lift. Cameras follow my every move. They are everywhere, making it hard to concentrate. I'm unsure about my destination, so I push the button that shoots me to the top floor of the building. This is where the gods have resided since the dawn of time.

Stylish, luxurious lift, postmodern design, with uplighting and a smart carpet. I look like a ragdoll in my rumpled, horribly out-of-date suit. As the floors file by, a creeping anxiety comes over me.

This is how battles are lost.

Management theory says: avoid irrational behaviours and choose to deal in what is real and measurable.

I take a deep breath, but it doesn't help. Alexandre Dorfmann – big French business leader, pillar of European industry – is about to greet me. Confronting one so powerful is getting the better of me. I run through the facts, and one doubt still lingers: why does he want to meet me?

He doesn't stand to gain anything from it.

All he needed was to relay his instructions anonymously. Proposing to meet me seems an imprudent move on his part. I feel certain he doesn't know the details of Nicole's kidnapping – he pays Fontana handsomely enough to be exempt from knowing details, making sure he is safe from any allegation of wrongdoing.

So why does he feel the need to step into the ring himself?

There must be something I haven't considered. The cards have been stacked without me noticing. I'm convinced he's going to squash me beneath his thumb. He's going to skin me alive. Such an easy victory against a man like this is simply not possible. It never happens. I'm climbing the scaffold. When the elevator door opens, I'm already half defeated. There's a veil before my eyes, and printed on it is Nicole's beleaguered face. I too am drained as I step out of the lift.

Up here, the secretaries are all men. Young and highly qualified. They're called advisers or associates. One of them flashes me a corporate smile. Very professional. The sort of guy who's never happier than when he's at some smug media event with all his pals. He's been briefed: "Monsieur le Président" will see me.

A quilted, carpeted, padded antechamber. I stay on my feet. I know the rules of the waiting game – long simmer over a low heat. My breathing is steady, but my heart must be racing at a hundred and twenty beats per minute. Clearly I don't know the rules, because there's no wait at all: thirty seconds later, the door opens, and the young associate makes himself scarce.

I am summoned.

The first thing that strikes me is the unbelievable beauty of the city glittering through the enormous floor-to-ceiling windows. God has a wonderful view over the world. One of the many perks of the job. Alexandre Dorfmann is engrossed in some paperwork, but he pulls himself away from his desk. Despite the interruption, he removes his glasses in a dignified manner. His face transforms as he directs a smile at me that's as thin as a blade.

"Ah, Monsieur Delambre!"

The voice alone is an instrument of domination. Immaculately honed, down to the smallest intonation. Dorfmann takes a few paces towards me, shakes me warmly by the hand, all the while holding my elbow with his left one, before drawing me to a corner of the room covered with bookcases, a small library that screams: "I am a business leader, yes, but above all I am a humanist."

I sit down. Dorfmann takes his place next to me. Casual.

My feelings at this point are indescribable. This man has an astonishing aura. Some people are like that: electrifying. They emit waves.

Dorfmann radiates power in the same way Fontana radiates danger. He personifies the instinct for mastery.

If I were an animal, I'd start growling.

I try to remember him on the day of the hostage-taking, sitting mute on the ground. But neither he nor I are the same men as then. Here we are back in the real world. The social order has corrected itself. I might be wrong, but I think the real reason we're here face-to-face today is to explore just that: what I put him through.

"Do you play golf, Monsieur Delambre?"

"Er . . . no."

They say prison ages you, but surely not so much that I look like a bloody golfer now?

"That's a shame. I had a metaphor in mind that summarises our situation nicely."

Dorfmann waves his arm as though swatting a fly away.

"No matter," he says, before adopting an air of regret and spreading his arms in apology:

"Monsieur Delambre, I don't have much time . . ."

He smiles at me. An outside observer would swear that he felt a deep fondness for me; that I was a dear old friend with whom he'd love to talk at length if the circumstances permitted.

"I'm rather pressed myself," I say.

He nods then pauses, looking me up and down for a long time in perfect silence: observing me, detailing me, studying me without the slightest embarrassment. Finally he fastens his dispassionate eyes on mine. He keeps them there for a long while, and it unsettles me right down to my belly. This moment feels like a distillation of every fear I have endured throughout my professional life. Dorfmann is an expert in the intimidation department: he must have terrorised, tortured and frightened an incalculable number of colleagues, secretaries and advisers, filling them with enough panic to want to defenestrate themselves. His entire bearing is an assertion of one simple, clear truth: he has got where he is because he's killed the competition.

"Good . . ." he says at last.

The reason for my presence before him finally dawns on me.

From a technical perspective, it's impossible to justify. In practical terms, everything advises against it. But he wanted to make absolutely sure. From the start, this conflict has involved two men who have virtually never seen one another, with the exception of a few minutes when I had a Beretta pressed against his temple. It's not Dorfmann's style to conclude business in this manner.

In any professional contest, there has to come a moment of truth.

Dorfmann couldn't let me go without satisfying the burning need to see me in the flesh, to assess whether or not his power really has been put in check.

And, by extension, to see whether I represent any threat to him. He's measuring any potential risk.

"We could have settled this over the telephone," he says.

Evaluating the harmfulness of my intentions towards him.

"But I wanted to congratulate you personally."

Deciding whether or not I'm waging all-out war, a challenge he'd have no qualms in accepting.

"You have handled this affair masterfully."

Or maybe he's figuring out whether he can take my word. Simply put: can a pair of bastards like us trust each other?

I don't move a muscle. I hold his stare. The only thing Dorfmann trusts is his intuition. This may well be the key to his success: the certainty that he will never be outmanoeuvred by another man.

"We should have given you the job," he says at last, almost to himself.

He laughs at this notion, all on his own, as if I wasn't there.

Then he returns to earth, like someone reluctantly coming round from a waking dream. He shakes himself, then smiles to indicate a change of tack:

"So, Monsieur Delambre, what are you going to do now with all this money? Invest it? Start your own business? Launch yourself into a new career?"

This is the final test in the conclusive assessment he's just made of me. It's like he's handing me an invisible cheque for thirteen million euros but holding it tight between his fingers, forcing me to pull harder and harder. For now, he's refusing to relent.

"I want rest and relaxation. I just want a well-deserved retirement."

I'm clearly offering him a truce.

"Goodness, don't we all!" he assures me, as though he too only ever dreamed of the good life.

On the balance of this, after a final second's reflection, he releases the invisible cheque.

This is what baffles me more than anything: the sum is of no importance whatsoever. It'll simply be written off.

In Alexandre Dorfmann's world, the sum is not what makes him tick. The sum is not what he's fought for.

The idea that I've extorted him of a slush fund evaporates. I'm just a minnow leaving with a handful of change.

47

The car is as comfortable as it gets, but it's still taking unbearably long. 8.05 p.m. It's the tail-end of people leaving the office. Most employees are heading back to their cars, apart from the execs, who are staring at another two or three hours' work, best-case scenario. Even though I've been given the definitive green light, I don't let myself think it's over, that I've won, that I've nabbed the pot once and for all. My eyes are glued to the car phone. Nothing's happening. Nothing. I reason with myself: for now, there's nothing to worry about. I run through the numbers again, extending the margins of safety and rounding everything up: it all depends how fast Dorfmann relays his instructions. I look at the clock on the dashboard again: 8.10 p.m.

I keep myself occupied, sending Charles a text with the address for the apartment. Quick glance at the dashboard: still nothing. I'm tempted to look at the photos of Nicole again, but I resist. They'll scare me, and I have to believe that it's futile to fear that everything is over. It's counter-productive. I'm a few minutes away from the most important moment of my life. If everything goes well, this will be a great day for making amends.

8.12 p.m.

I can't bear it any longer. I dial Nicole's mobile number. One ring, two, then a "hello" at the third: it's her, straight through to her.

"Nicole? Where are you?"

I shout this. It takes her several seconds to answer. I'm not sure why. It's as if she doesn't recognise my voice. Maybe my screaming has sent her into a panic.

"In a taxi," she says eventually. "What about you, where are you?"

"Are you by yourself in the taxi?"

Why is she taking so long to answer my questions?

"Yes, they . . . they let me go."

"Are you sure?"

What a stupid question.

"They told me I could go home."

There it is. I breathe. It's over.

Victory. I've won.

An irrepressible wave of joy washes over me.

My chest opens, and I feel an urge to shout out, to howl.

Victory.

Move over job-centre Delambre, here comes wealth-tax Delambre. Without the tax. I could cry. In fact I'm already crying, gripping the wheel with all my strength.

Then I smack it furiously.

Victory, victory, victory.

"Alain . . ." Nicole says.

I shriek with joy.

Fucking hell, I managed to stuff the lot of them. I can't help gloating.

I can spend 50,000 euros a month for the rest of my life. I'm going to buy three apartments. One for each of my girls. The whole thing's unbelievable.

"Alain . . ." Nicole repeats.

"We won, my love! Where are you, tell me, where are you?"

I realise that Nicole is crying. Very softly. I hadn't noticed straight away but now that I'm listening more closely, I can hear her little sobs, which are causing me so much pain. It's normal, a normal after-effect of fear. She needs reassurance.

"It's finished, my love, I promise you it's finished. You've got nothing to fear anymore. Nothing else can happen to you. I need to explain . . ."

"Alain . . ." she says again, unable to go any further.

She repeats my name on a continuous loop. There are so many things to explain to her, but that will take time. First, I must reassure her.

"What about you, Alain . . ." Nicole asks. "Where were you?"

She's not asking me where I am right now, but where I was when she needed me. I understand, but she doesn't know the full extent of the problem. I'll need to explain to her that I never left her, that all the time she was so afraid I was scoring a definitive victory over our miserable existence. For both of us. In the time we've been speaking, I've started the engine, left the Exxyal car park and am heading for the fast lane back into Paris.

"Right now, I'm in La Défense."

Nicole is taken aback.

"But . . . what are you doing in La Défense?"

"Nothing, I'm coming home. I'll explain everything. You've got nothing to fear. That's the most important thing, right?"

"I'm scared, Alain . . ."

We're having a lot of trouble understanding each other. She's going to need to get over all this, forget everything she's been through. We'll have to work on it together. I join the Périphérique.

"There's no reason to be scared, my love."

I'm repeating myself, but what else can I do?

"We'll be together again in no time."

I'm going as fast as possible so I can hold her in my arms.

"Do you know what we're going to do?"

I must encourage her.

"We're going to start from scratch, a brand-new life, that's what we're going to do. I've got some big news for you, my darling. Some really big news! You can't begin to imagine . . ."

But for now, telling her all this isn't making any difference. She's still crying. I can't do anything while she's in this state.

"I'm going to be . . ."

I want to say "at the house", but I can't bring myself to use that word for the place I'm meeting her. Physically impossible. I try to find the words. Nicole's still going round in circles ("Alain, Alain . . .") and it's unsettling me. It's making me nervous.

"I'll be there in half an hour, O.K.?"

Nicole takes this in.

"Yes," she says eventually, sniffing noisily. "O.K."

Silence on the line. She hung up before me.

Five minutes later, I've reached Porte de Clignancourt. I call back. It's ringing. Once, twice, three times. Voicemail. I redial. Porte de la Villette. Voicemail again. I feel waves of dread. I don't even dare think the name Fontana, but he's there in front of me, all around me, everywhere. I tap the steering wheel nervously. I've won and I refuse to be scared now. I try Nicole's number again. She finally picks up.

"Why didn't you answer? Where were you?"

"What?"

Her voice is vacant, mechanical.

"I was in the lift," Nicole says at last.

"Are you . . . Have you arrived? Are you back, have you shut the door?"

"Yes."

She lets out an immense sigh.

"Yes, I've shut the door."

I picture her taking off her shoes like she always does, the tips of her toes pushing against the heel. Her sigh is one of pure relief. For me too.

"I'll be there in fifteen minutes, my love, O.K.?"

"O.K.," Nicole says.

This time it's me who hangs up. I punch the address into the G.P.S. and come off the Périphérique. By some miracle, I'm at avenue de Flandre just a few minutes later. But my heartache isn't over yet – the roads are jam-packed with parked cars. I turn off in search for a space. Is there a public car park around here? I look up at the tower blocks. Hideous. I smile. This flat that Nicole bought, I'm going to give it to Emmaus. I take a right, then a left, then go back on myself, scanning the vehicles parked along the street. I go further, then come back, mapping out concentric circles that start to make me prodigiously angry. Crawling along, I look closely at the cars lining the right- and left-hand pavements.

Suddenly my heart skips a beat and my stomach churns.

No, it can't be possible. I saw it wrong.

I swallow hard.

But something tells me that yes, it is possible.

My reflexes were good – instead of stopping, I carried on driving. I must be absolutely sure. My hands are shaking because this time, if I'm right, it's a catastrophe. I'll be dangling in mid-air without a safety net. I take a right, then another, then a third and find myself back on the same street, going faster now, keeping my head firmly upright like a man absorbed in his commute or lost in thought. As I drive past I can clearly see a woman sitting behind the wheel of a black 4×4: Yasmine. She's wearing an earpiece.

It's her, no doubt about it.

She's waiting.

No – she's on the lookout.

If she's there, parked on a street thirty metres from where Nicole lives, then it means Fontana's there too.

They're on the lookout for me. They're on the lookout for us. Nicole and me.

I carry on driving, turning at random. I need some time to figure out what's going on.

Dorfmann gave his instructions. Fontana obeyed. His assignment is over.

It's not a hard one to deduce: his contract with his former employer is over, so Fontana has decided to go it alone. Nothing like thirteen big ones for an incentive. It's enough to see out your days, no trouble whatsoever.

And that doesn't even factor in his personal hatred for me. I've tripped him up time and again, and now the bell's rung for last orders. He's only got one boss now: himself. No strings attached. The man is capable of anything.

Fontana is using Nicole as bait, but it's me he wants. He wants to make me spit out my bank details one hammer blow at a time. To make me pay in every sense of the word.

I think he'll attempt to take both of us. He'll make Nicole scream until I give him everything, everything, everything.

And afterwards he'll kill her.

He'll kill me too, no doubt reserving some special fate for me. Fontana wants to settle a personal difference with me.

I have absolutely no idea what to do, turning and swerving from one street to the next, making sure at every cost that I don't get too close to the surveillance vehicle again. Fontana must have positioned himself somewhere he can apprehend me as soon as I arrive. I've managed to avoid his eye so far because he didn't imagine I would arrive by car. They're probably expecting me to come in a taxi or on foot, who knows.

If Fontana lays a finger on us . . . I can already picture Nicole tied up in a chair. This isn't possible. I'm at a total loss, and I also don't know the area. I unfold the piece of paper with the address. Nicole is on the eighth floor.

My thoughts are confused, all over the place. Is there a car park? I must not be seen. But what can I do?

I can only see one way out. The worst option, but it's the only one: go in guns blazing (albeit unarmed), then flee. It's not ideal, but I don't see any other option. This trap has made my brain shut down.

I reach out for the car phone but my hand's trembling so much I drop it. I recover it with difficulty and clamp it against my chest. A space is free in front of the entrance to a building; I park up for a moment and leave the engine running. I have to call Nicole. I dial her number.

"Nicole, you have to leave," I say as soon as she picks up.

"What? Why?"

She's lost.

"Listen, I can't explain. You have to leave right now. This is what you're going to do . . ."

"But why? What's happening? Alain! You're not telling me anything, I can't take this anymore . . ."

She realises my panic and understands that the situation is serious; sensing the danger ahead, her voice fails her and gives way to violent sobbing. The terror of the last few hours returns intact.

"No, no," she says again and again. I have to get her moving. I come out with it:

"They are here."

No point saying who. Nicole sees Fontana's face again, Yasmine's too, and a fresh wave of fear grips her.

"You promised me this was over, Alain," she sobs. "*I'm fed up with your crap, I can't take any more of it.*"

She's leaving me with no choice. I need to scare her even more to get her moving.

"If you stay there, Nicole, they'll come and find you. You have to leave. Now. I'm downstairs."

"Where are you?" she screams. "Why aren't you coming?"

"Because that's what they want! It's me they want!"

"Fucking hell, who are 'they'?"

She's howling in sheer terror.

"I'm going to lead you through this, Nicole. Listen carefully.

Go downstairs, turn right, and that's rue Kloeckner. Take the right-hand pavement. That's all you have to do, Nicole, nothing else, I swear, I'll take care of the rest."

"No Alain, I'm sorry. I can't anymore. I'm calling the police. I can't take this, I can't."

"DON'T DO ANYTHING! YOU HEAR ME? DON'T DO ANYTHING EXCEPT WHAT I TOLD YOU!"

Silence. I keep going. I have to make her.

"I don't want to die either, Nicole! So do what I say, nothing else! Come downstairs, turn right, and do it now, for fuck's sake!"

I hang up. I'm so scared for us both. Deep down, I know my plan is rubbish, but I've thought hard and it's the best I can do. Nothing else for it. I wait for three minutes, four . . . how long can it take to make up your mind and come downstairs? Then I start the engine. No-one's expecting to find me in this car. Not even Nicole.

Act fast.

All guns blazing.

I speed down rue Kloeckner and from a distance see Nicole's outline on the right-hand pavement; I drive up behind her and see how laboured her walk is, so stiff, and as I come level with her she makes out the sound of an engine, quietly and to her left, but she doesn't turn to look; she's expecting the worst at any split second, and her stride is still rigid, like she's walking to the gallows. I stay alert for the right moment, see there's nothing in front, nothing behind, then accelerate, overshoot her by three metres, brake hard, pile out of the car, leap onto the pavement and grab her by the arm; she lets out a yelp as she recognises me but before she can do anything else, I open the passenger door, bundle her into the car, run round the other side and get back behind the wheel. The whole thing takes no more than seven or eight seconds. Still nothing in front or behind, I rev the engine softly as Nicole stares at me, then at the car, then back at me, everything seeming intensely strange to her, and it's hard to know whether she's less scared now that she's in this silent car, sliding along like a wave, with me at the wheel; but she closes her eyes as I gingerly take the first right, still nothing in front or behind, and I shut my eyes too for a moment and when I open them, I recognise the catlike figure of Fontana thirty metres ahead, sprinting along the pavement and then disappearing; I speed up without thinking, overtaking the point in the street he dived into, the point from where the tip of a black 4×4 as high as a bus is emerging; I trigger the central locking, startling Nicole, and I put my foot down and the car surges forward, and Nicole lets out a shriek as she's pinned against her seat by the acceleration; Fontana's car turns behind us and I veer left, already speeding, clipping the back of a stationary car as I pass, my car lurching, forcing another cry from Nicole who grabs her safety belt and fastens it with a sharp click. In this neighbourhood the traffic's not so bad: everything converges on two large boulevards that thrust into the centre of Paris or retreat to the suburbs. I cross the next intersection without even slowing down and a red Renault 25 with enormous chrome bumpers stops abruptly to let me past. Charles is back in the frame.

I'd forgotten all about Charles.

He sees us tear past at top speed and barely has time to raise his hand before we are well beyond him, a black 4×4 seconds behind us in pursuit. I know it'll take Charles a bit of time to figure it out, but he'll get there eventually, and anyway I don't have time to think about it because I'm on the boulevard, in the right-hand lane, where stationary cars are banked up in a traffic jam; if I stop now, Fontana will rush us, shoot out the windows, tear open the doors and I'll be helpless. All he needs is for us to stop for just long enough to pounce and he'll take care of the rest, lodging a bullet straight into Nicole's head to paralyse me, before punching me about and stuffing me into Yasmine's 4×4 . . .

We come up behind the final car in the queue and I've got no idea what to do; Nicole clamps both hands on the dashboard as she sees the line of stopped cars bearing down on us, and I ram the steering wheel roughly to the left, accelerate and head back up the left lane in the wrong direction, horn full blast and lights full beam. Fontana does something I never saw coming: he sets off a flashing police light, stretches an arm out of the window and sticks it on the roof – a ballsy move that says a lot about his determination – and now anyone who sees us will think it's a chase and won't move to let me through. We're being hunted down and the whole city will turn against us. I've no idea how (we must have taken symmetrical routes) but again Charles' car is haring down on us, and I swing right to avoid it and then left to straighten up, flinging Nicole against the door; her feet are buried beneath her seat and her head's tucked down, hands crossed behind her neck, like she's trying to protect herself from the roof caving in; as soon as she hears the police siren she turns to the rear-view mirror, her eyes bright with hope, but the second she realises it's a trap, she resumes her foetal position and starts moaning.

As he whips past us, Charles is wide-eyed and looking right at me, then at the car pursuing us.

I'm not thinking anymore, I'm just a bundle of reflexes, pinballing between horror and joy, invincibility and mortality, and violently I turn full lock to the left up a street, then left and right again, without any idea which direction I'm going; the moment an obstacle appears I turn again, one street, two, three, skimming cars here and there, avoiding pedestrians and bicycles, and scraping a bus down the left-hand side as it pulls away from its stop. Fontana is still behind us, however close or far, and I don't know which way to go before suddenly, strangely, we're on a one-way street running alongside the Périphérique.

It's walled in on both sides by parked cars.

Long and straight as an arrow.

One-way, single lane.

We can barely see to the end.

I put my foot down, and in the mirror I see Fontana. My driving's not quick enough, the hands he destroyed not strong enough. Fontana retrieves the flashing light and pulls it inside and shuts off the siren, the 4×4 sticking to a constant speed fifty metres behind us because there's no escape.

I don't manage to keep in a straight line, drifting constantly and hitting the cars on my side as well as Nicole's.

At the end, a few hundred metres away, there's a red light where the street hits a wide boulevard that's thick with moving vehicles. Another wall. I accelerate even faster towards this desperate impasse.

I know it's over. Nicole knows it too.

The boulevard we're heading towards is a fast lane; stopping there with Fontana behind us would be like getting out of a car on a Formula 1 track; blasting our way through the traffic like taking on a T.G.V.

Nicole pushes back in her chair, bracing herself for the merciless obstacle ahead.

The rear window explodes. Fontana's shooting at us. Saving himself some time for when it comes to the collision. It feels as if the inside of the car is being ripped apart and the wind is rushing through the shattered glass. Nicole shrinks into her seat.

And now for the final scene.

Here's how the story ends.

Right here, in the space of a few seconds.

In the space of a few hundred metres.

In this immensely long, straight street that we're driving down at almost ninety kilometres an hour, chased by a black, metallic beast with its headlights glaring.

The image haunts me still, all these months later.

It will never go away.

For many years to come I'll see it over and over, dream about it, enquire about its mysterious, tragic meaning.

Nicole has looked up again and is hypnotised by our rapid advance towards the wall of cars barring our way.

And the two of us, both mesmerised, witness before us the sudden eruption of a red car equipped with a vast, gleaming bumper and spewing out a great plume of white smoke. It has just turned in to the far end of the road and is driving directly towards us, the wrong way. Two hundred metres apart, our cars are bearing down on each other at full speed.

I start braking lightly, at a loss about what to do next.

Death is hovering over us.

Charles, on the other hand, is accelerating. When his car is barely more than a hundred metres away, I can make out his face between the chrome bars of his front bumper.

The final message.

Charles puts on his indicator.

The left one.

There's nowhere for him to turn, and I realise that's not the message. It's not about which direction Charles wants to take. He's showing me the direction to take. It's a message: *turn right*.

I speed up and desperately scan the uninterrupted line of cars parked to my right. Charles is less than sixty metres away now. His face is growing, starting to fill up the screen. We're tearing towards each other faster and faster, drawn together into the eye of the hurricane.

Suddenly I see the exit.

It's a dead-end. It opens out on our right a few dozen metres ahead. I yell over at Nicole. She grabs her seatbelt and thrusts her legs far out in front, pushing back against the footwell. I slam on the brakes and thrash the wheel round. The car skids, striking an obstacle at the back that I don't see before bouncing roughly into the little alley and smashing straight into a van. The airbags burst open, flattening us against our seats. The car comes to a halt.

Now we've made way, Charles and Fontana's cars are left face-to-face in the dead-straight road.

They smash into each other like meteorites.

When he sees Charles' bright-red banger in his headlights, Fontana tries his best to stop, but of course it's too late.

The two cars pile into each other at a combined speed of over a hundred and seventy kilometres an hour.

I can still see Charles' final gesture in slow motion.

In the moment his car comes in line with us, I see it, clear as anything. He's sitting very low behind the wheel, his head turned towards me, smiling.

Charles' wonderful smile, brotherly and generous. The same as ever. *Don't you fret about me.*

He looks me in the eye as he goes past, and lifts his arm towards me: his little salute.

The next second, the crash is hideous.

The two vehicles smash into each other at full speed, then fall on top of each other tangled, crushed, fused.

The body parts that don't disintegrate in the collision are shredded by the metal carnage, and flames overwhelm them.

Now it's over.

EPILOGUE

Dinner at Mathilde's. I buzz and wait on the landing. I've brought flowers and I'm wearing a smart suit, a raw-silk pinstripe number. And my enormous diving watch with its fluorescent green strap, which never leaves my wrist, much to everyone's astonishment. As always, it's Gregory who opens the door, while Mathilde, tucked away in the kitchen, calls out excitedly: "Oh Papa, you're here already?" My son-in-law's handshake is so firm that I can feel the challenge, the macho gauntlet being thrown down. But I never fight back. Those days are over.

Mathilde emerges when I enter the sitting room, always saying the same thing as she fixes her hair: "Oh my god, I must look dreadful. Papa, help yourself to whisky, I'll be back in a second."

She then disappears into the bathroom for a good half hour, leaving Gregory and me to exchange various pleasantries, sticking to the safe, uncomplicated ground that experience has shown us.

Gregory has gained in self-confidence since taking office in the brand-new apartment I bought them, a large five-room pad in the heart of Paris. The way he handles the decanter, the haughty postures he adopts . . . you'd be forgiven for thinking that his fortunate circumstances are due to his own considerable merits, his undeniably superior qualities. The two of us are like boxers: we owe our success to being smacked in the face. I never say anything. I hold my tongue. I smile. I tell myself it's fine, that I'm just waiting for my daughter. Eventually she'll arrive, each time wearing a brand-new dress that she twirls on entry.

"What do you think?" she asks, as though I'm her husband.

I try to mix up my compliments. I really ought to start a list of adjectives for future evenings, because these monthly visits (always the second Thursday) will make my dwindling linguistic resources dry up before long.

I always feel unprepared. Sometimes I say "Marvellous!", but that seems too old-fashioned, or maybe "Holy smoke!" – that sort of thing.

Charles' words, I suppose.

From the window you can make out the spires of Notre-Dame. I sip the whisky that Mathilde buys specially for me. My own bottle at my daughter's house. In spite of this, please don't assume I'm becoming an alcoholic. Quite the opposite – I'm doing everything I can to stay in shape. Nicole is very appreciative of my attempts at self-maintenance. My discipline. I've joined a gym near her place. It's pretty far, I'm not sure why I chose that one, but that's how it is.

We sit down for dinner. Mathilde has the presence of mind to give me a quick update on Lucie, because she knows I'm keen to hear her news. It's my only link with her since the end of all that.

With Lucie, it finished in the flat on avenue de Flandre. I hadn't been expecting anyone, but the doorbell rang, and when I opened, Lucie was there.

"Oh, it's you," I said.

"I was in the area and decided to drop by," she replied.

And she came in. It wasn't hard to see she was lying. She hadn't been in the area – she'd come specially. Her face said it all. Anyway, she got to the point immediately. She's not as polite as the others, so no attempt to keep up appearances.

"I've got some questions for you, now," she said.

No talk of sitting down, going for dinner or any of that. Her "now" resounded heavily, so heavily, and I looked down expecting the first barrage, knowing how difficult it was going to be.

"But," she continued, "I'm going to start with the main one: do you really take me for a complete fucking idiot?"

Terrible start.

The whole thing had finished barely two weeks earlier.

The day before her visit, I'd written cheques for everyone. Big cheques. Mathilde looked at hers and took it for what it was: an unimaginable Christmas present, bang in the middle of the year. It was like she'd won the lottery.

In reality, these were fake cheques. Just to mark the occasion. I explained to them that their millions of euros were stashed in offshore accounts and that using such sums would require various precautions regarding the tax authorities. We'd need to get creative with our accounting. Nothing major, but just be patient, I had it all under control.

Nicole laid hers on the table carefully. She'd already known about this for several days. I'd explained it to her straight away. With Nicole it was different, it wasn't like with the girls. She put her cheque in front of her as you might place a napkin on the table at the end of a meal. She said nothing. There was no point in her repeating herself. Quite simply, she didn't want to ruin it for the girls.

Lucie looked at her present, and it was obvious that it had plunged her into a state of deep reflection. She stammered "thank you" a few times, listening to my enthusiastic explanations in a manner that was both attentive and absent-minded, like she was hearing a different speech in parallel.

That evening, I told my two girls that whatever happened, their futures were assured. They could use what I'd given them to buy themselves an apartment (or two or three) and do whatever they wanted to feel safe. This was a gift from their father. I was paying everyone back.

I'd split it three ways. I was paying everyone back a hundred times over. I even thought my gesture might earn me a bit of respect.

It did, but only in part. Mathilde was in raptures; Gregory asked endless questions about the practicalities. I said as much as I could without giving away the essentials, all the while feeling like it wasn't going at all as I'd planned, nothing like I had dreamed.

And the following day Lucie was back, asking: "Do you really take me for a complete fucking idiot?" It was non-stop because, as it always is with Lucie, she provided the question along with the answer to the question. Because she hadn't stopped thinking from the first second she saw her enormous cheque, from the moment it had dawned on her.

"You manipulated me in the most contemptible way possible," she said.

She spoke without anger, her voice level. That was what scared me the most.

"You hid the truth from me throughout because you thought that, in my naivety, I would defend you better if I thought you were innocent."

That hit the nail on the head. I'd had a thousand opportunities to explain what I'd really done, but I thought it would have undermined her defence. And I had my reasons. If I had given her the full picture, I would be in prison right now for a very, very long time.

Until the very last second, I never thought I'd be certain to hold on to the money.

Could I have reasonably told them about it, raising their hopes about a life finally free of need, only to pull the carpet out from under their feet if I didn't manage to see my plan through?

I tried to make her appreciate all this, but she cut me dead:

"You wanted me to come across as genuine. You made a spectacle of our relationship. You did everything in your power to make the press think that this was about a poor victim of unemployment being defended by his well-meaning, generous daughter. You got exactly what you wanted when I choked up in front of the jury. Maybe that final moment was what exonerated you the next day. That single second was the culmination of months and months of lies, of making me believe the same as everyone else. You wanted me to defend you because you wanted someone hard-working and credulous, someone clumsily honest. And to achieve that, you needed me to be a silly little girl. I was the only person in the world who could play the dummy so perfectly. I was a shoo-in. Your best stab at being let off was to have a muppet at your side. What you did was disgraceful."

Exaggerating as ever.

But that's in her nature, it's how she is – she can't resist taking it a bit further.

Lucie is always mixing up cause and effect. I need her to realise that there was never any strategy. At no stage did I think she needed to be a dummy to be effective. She was an incredible lawyer. I couldn't have asked for a better one. All that happened was I realised – too late in the day to tell her the truth – that even her *faux pas* would work in my favour. That's it.

Things are not at all the same when seen from her angle and from mine.

I needed to say all this, but Lucie didn't give me a chance. Not another word. An argument would have reassured me. I would have taken insults, but this . . .

Lucie looked at me.

And she left.

It kills me when I think back to it. I stayed there for a while, frozen in the middle of the room. She left the door ajar. I went as far as the landing and heard the little click the lift makes when it reaches the ground floor. I returned to the flat, battered with exhaustion and feeling totally demoralised.

On the doormat there was a scrunched-up piece of paper that I picked up and unfolded. It was Lucie's cheque.

I can't stop thinking about that, and it breaks my heart.

Gregory is still talking as we sit at the table, regaling me with the latest drama at work, from which, of course, he emerges the hero. Mathilde stares at him, transfixed. He's her big man. It makes me want to kill myself, but I weigh in with a "No?" or a "Nice one!", not listening to a bloody word.

Lucie hasn't called me once for almost a year.

All I have left are these monthly conversations with Gregory.

I'm finding life pretty tough.

So I drift off and think of Charles.

Of Nicole.

I picture us a year ago. God it was miserable.

After Charles died, when everything was over, we stayed together for two days in that gloomy flat on avenue de Flandre. We stayed by each other's side, lying on our backs for nights at a time, simply holding hands like a pair of petrified snow angels.

And on the third day, Nicole said she was leaving. She told me that she loved me, but that she just couldn't go on. She couldn't – something was broken.

Finally, my epic ego trip had come to an end. We had to go through all that for this simple realisation to dawn on me.

"I need to live, Alain, and that's not good enough for you," she said.

She and Lucie stood in exactly the same place when they left me. Lucie chucked away her rolled-up cheque as she left; Nicole gave me one of those smiles that I never come away from unscathed. I'd just said to her:

"But Nicole, it's all over and we're rich! Nothing can happen to us anymore. Nothing can stop us from being everything we've ever dreamed of!"

Apparently I had some nerve saying that.

Nicole simply touched my cheek and shook her head, as though she were thinking: "Poor thing."

After a bit, she said:

"My poor love . . ."

And she left, perfectly calmly.

In this respect, Lucie reminded me of her mother a great deal.

I'm not sure, but maybe this is why I decided to stay living at avenue de Flandre, despite being capable of buying myself a stunningly expensive place.

I filled the ordinary flat with ordinary furniture, like a show house straight out of an Ikea catalogue.

And to be honest, I don't actually mind it that much.

Nicole moved into a place in Ivry, I'll never understand why. It was impossible to persuade her to let me buy her a beautiful apartment like Mathilde's. Absolutely impossible to discuss it with her. It was a no, and that was that. She didn't even let me buy her the place in Ivry. She pays the rent herself out of her salary.

We have dinner from time to time. At the start, I'd take her out to one of the grand Parisian restaurants. I was aiming to sweep her off her feet again, trying to look all handsome in my first ever tailored suit. But it didn't take long to realise she wasn't impressed. She'd eat in virtual silence then head home on the *métro*, not even agreeing to a taxi.

Now, we don't see each other so often. Before I suggested endless outings to the opera, the theatre; I tried to give her books on art, weekends away, things like that. I told myself that I had to win her back, that it would take time and no little sleight of hand, but that bit by bit we would find our way back to each other, that she'd realise how wonderful our new life could be. That's not how it went. She said yes to one or two things, but after a while she stopped. To begin with, I called her all the time; then one day she told me I was doing it too often.

"I love you, Alain. I'm always glad to hear you're doing well. But that's all I need to know. I don't need anything more."

At the start, without her, time went slowly.

I felt like a moron in my sparse apartment with my made-to-measure suits.

I've become a sad man.

Nothing disastrous, but I don't get the enjoyment from life that I'd hoped for. Without Nicole, nothing has any real meaning.

Without her, nothing has any meaning at all.

The other day, something came back to me that Charles had said in those bizarre sentences of his: "If you want to kill a man start by giving him what he seeks the most. More often than not that's enough."

I miss Charles an awful lot.

I've put the rest of the money in accounts opened under the girls' names. I don't pay much attention to it. I know it's there. It's what I won. That's all I need to know.

The first few months were terribly long, being alone like that.

But then I started a new job a few weeks ago, a volunteer position: a "senior consultant" at a small charity that helps young entrepreneurs.

The fact is I can't help it: I can't not work.

Vézénobres, August 2009

ACKNOWLEDGEMENTS

My first thought is for Pascaline, of course. For her patience and her tireless re-readings. For her presence.

Afterwards, thank you as ever to all the following:

Samuel, for his constant advice and mending (at times up on the high wire), which have proved unfailing and valuable companions. My thanks to him for understanding so well that meaning must prevail over precision . . . He is not answerable for any of the lingering errors;

Gerald, for his helpful remarks at a time when the text needed them;

Joëlle de Cubber, for being so responsive to my requests for medical advice;

Eric Prungnaud, whose reading and observations were of great comfort at just the right moment;

Cathy, my affectionate sponsor;

Gérard Guez, for being so welcoming and kind;

and to Charles Nemes, who came up with the title for this book over a meal (a relatively dry one, by the way).

A huge thank you, of course, to the whole team at Calmann-Lévy, my French publishers.

Finally, readers may well have picked up on references to Alain, Bergson, Céline, Derrida, Guilloux, Hawthorne, Kant, Mailer, Marías, Onfray, Proust, Sartre, Scott Fitzgerald and others.

Each one of these references can be considered a homage.

PIERRE LEMAITRE was born in Paris in 1951. He worked for many years as a teacher of literature before becoming a novelist. For *Alex*, he was awarded the C.W.A. International Dagger, alongside Fred Vargas, and was sole winner for *Camille* and *The Great Swindle*. In 2013, *The Great Swindle* also won the Prix Goncourt, France's leading literary award.

SAM GORDON is a translator from French and Spanish. His previous translations include works by Karim Miské, Sophie Hénaff, Timothée de Fombelle and Annelise Heurtier.